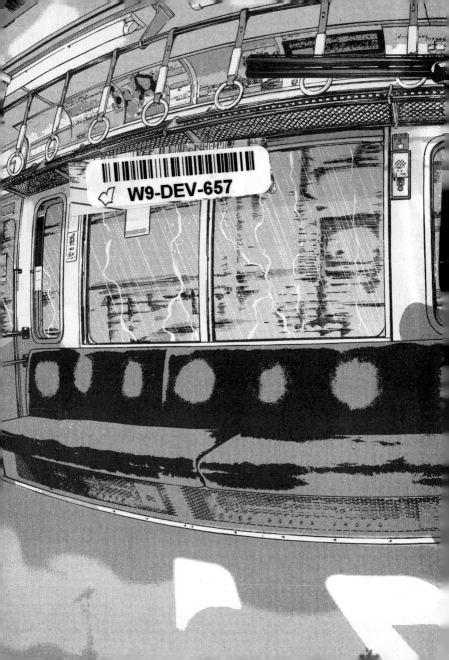

OMNIBUS 2

I AM A HERO

KENGO HANAZAWA
花沢健吾

This Dark Horse Manga omnibus
presents *I Am a Hero* chapters
23 to 46, first collected in Japan
as *I Am a Hero* Volumes 3 and 4.

Translation
KUMAR SIVASUBRAMANIAN

English adaptation
PHILIP R. SIMON

Lettering
STEVE DUTRO

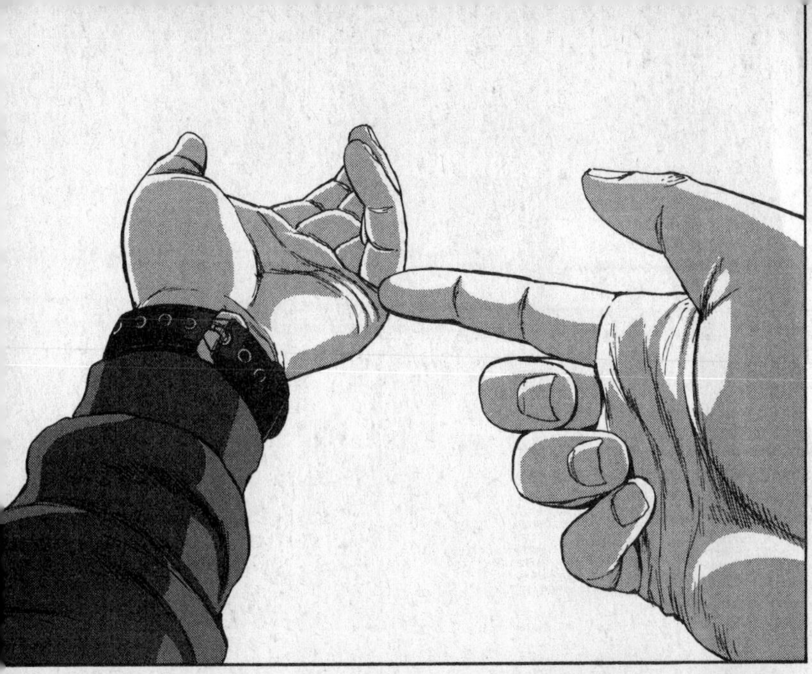

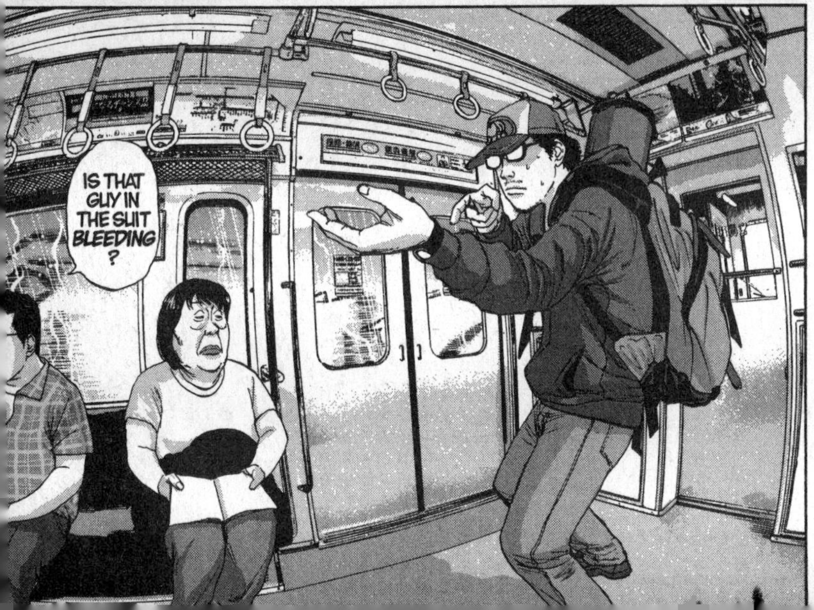
IS THAT GUY IN THE SUIT BLEEDING ?

...

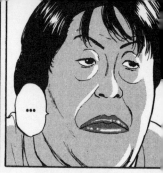

...

SNAP

SNAP

SNAP

SNAP

FWOO! DANGEROUS! VERY DANGEROUS! THE ACT OF TAKING A GUN OUT IN PUBLIC IS A VIOLATION OF THE FIREARM AND SWORD CONTROL LAWS.

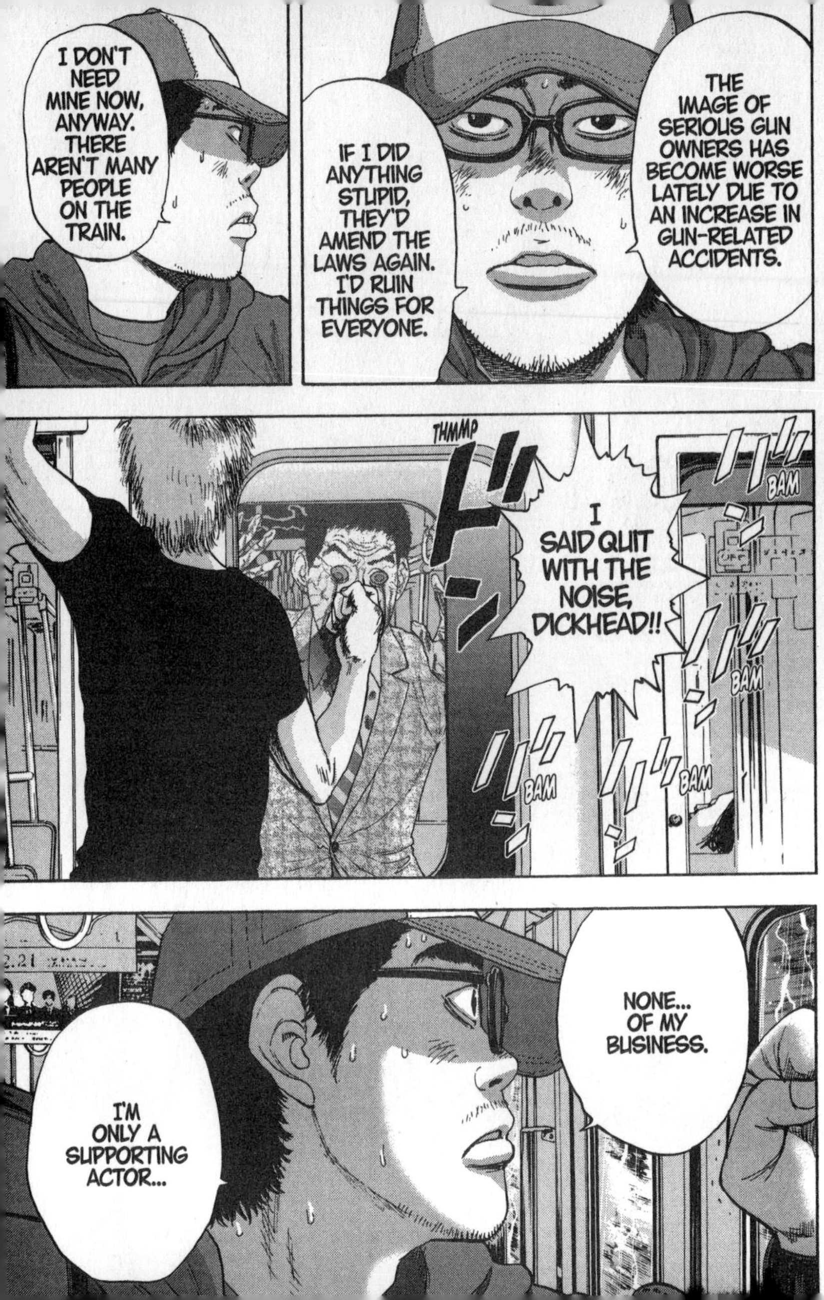
THE IMAGE OF SERIOUS GUN OWNERS HAS BECOME WORSE LATELY DUE TO AN INCREASE IN GUN-RELATED ACCIDENTS.
IF I DID ANYTHING STUPID, THEY'D AMEND THE LAWS AGAIN. I'D RUIN THINGS FOR EVERYONE.
I DON'T NEED MINE NOW, ANYWAY. THERE AREN'T MANY PEOPLE ON THE TRAIN.
THMMP
BAM
I SAID QUIT WITH THE NOISE, DICKHEAD!!
BAM
BAM
BAM
NONE... OF MY BUSINESS.
I'M ONLY A SUPPORTING ACTOR...

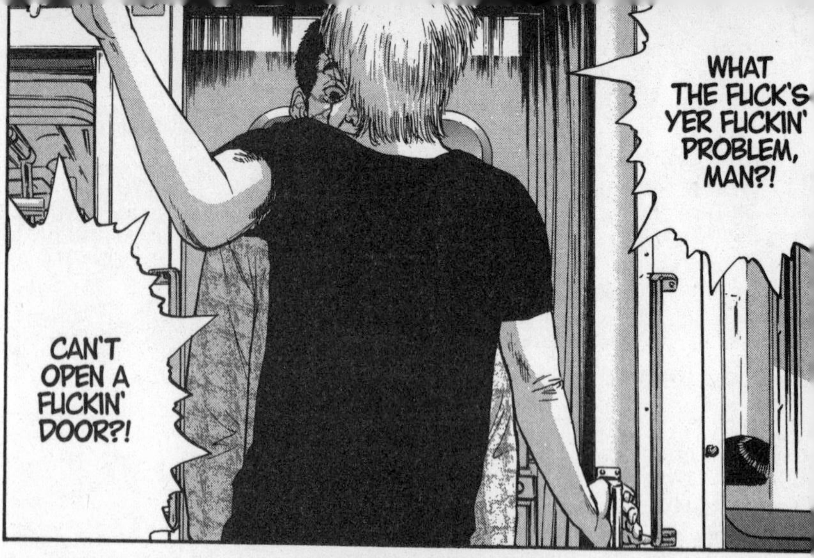
WHAT THE FUCK'S YER FUCKIN' PROBLEM, MAN?!
CAN'T OPEN A FUCKIN' DOOR?!

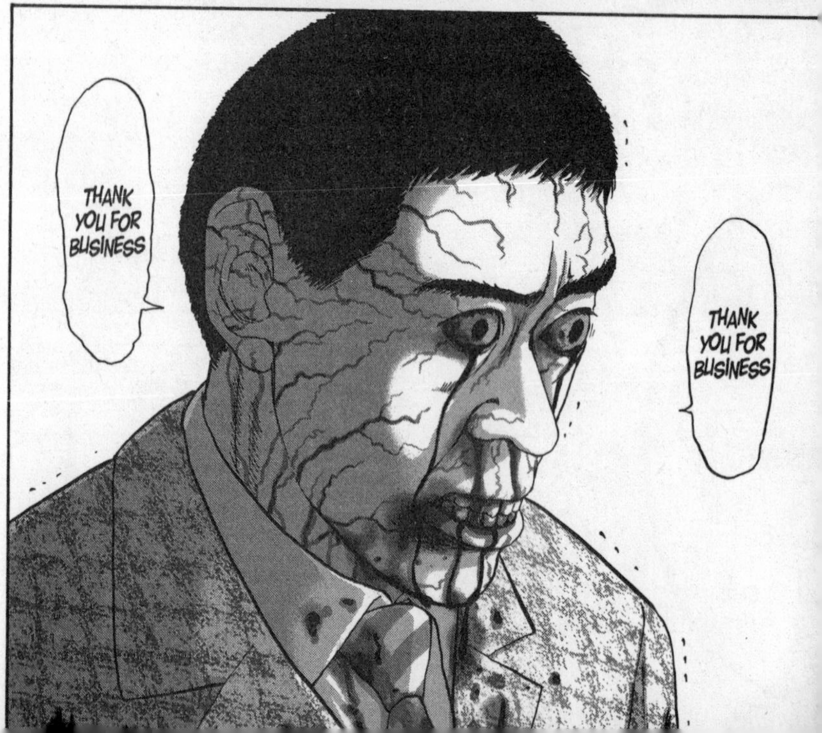
THANK YOU FOR BUSINESS
THANK YOU FOR BUSINESS

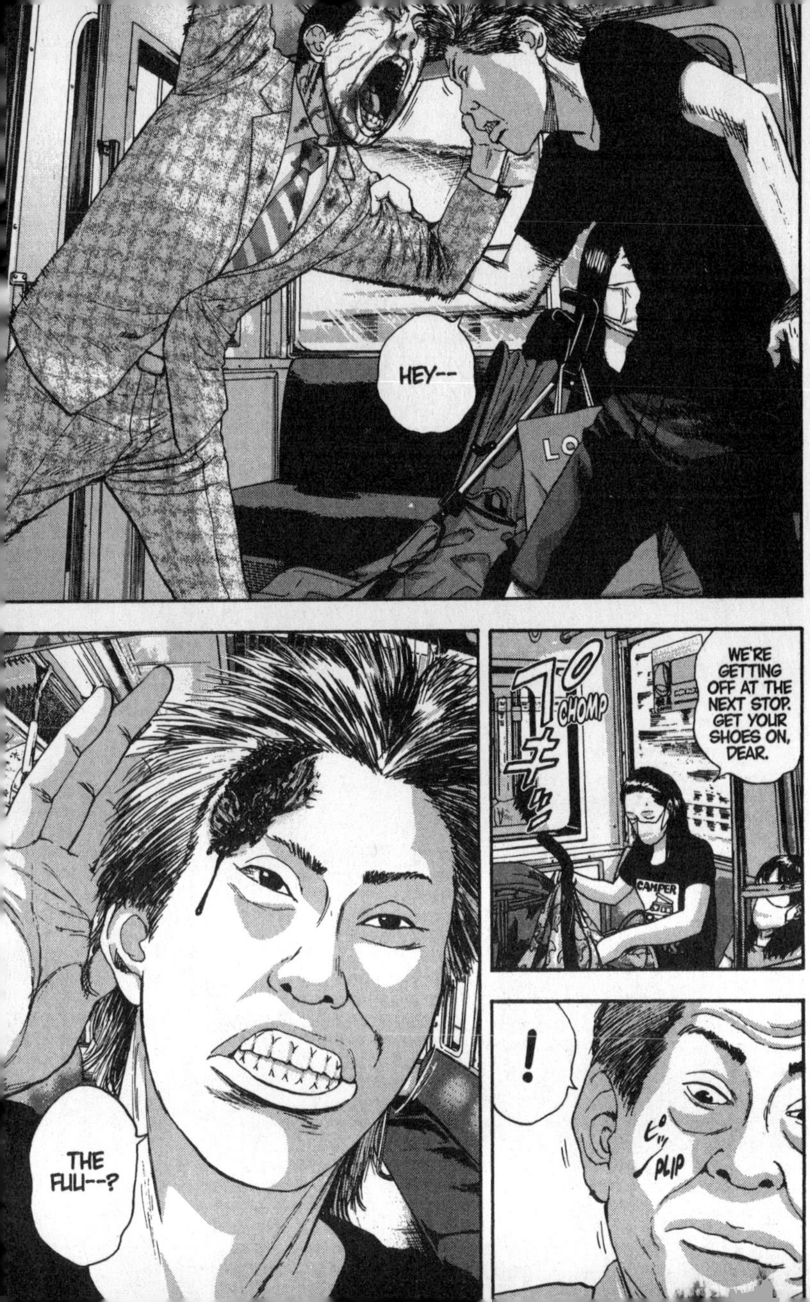
HEY--
CHOMP
WE'RE GETTING OFF AT THE NEXT STOP. GET YOUR SHOES ON, DEAR.
!
PLIP
THE FUU--?

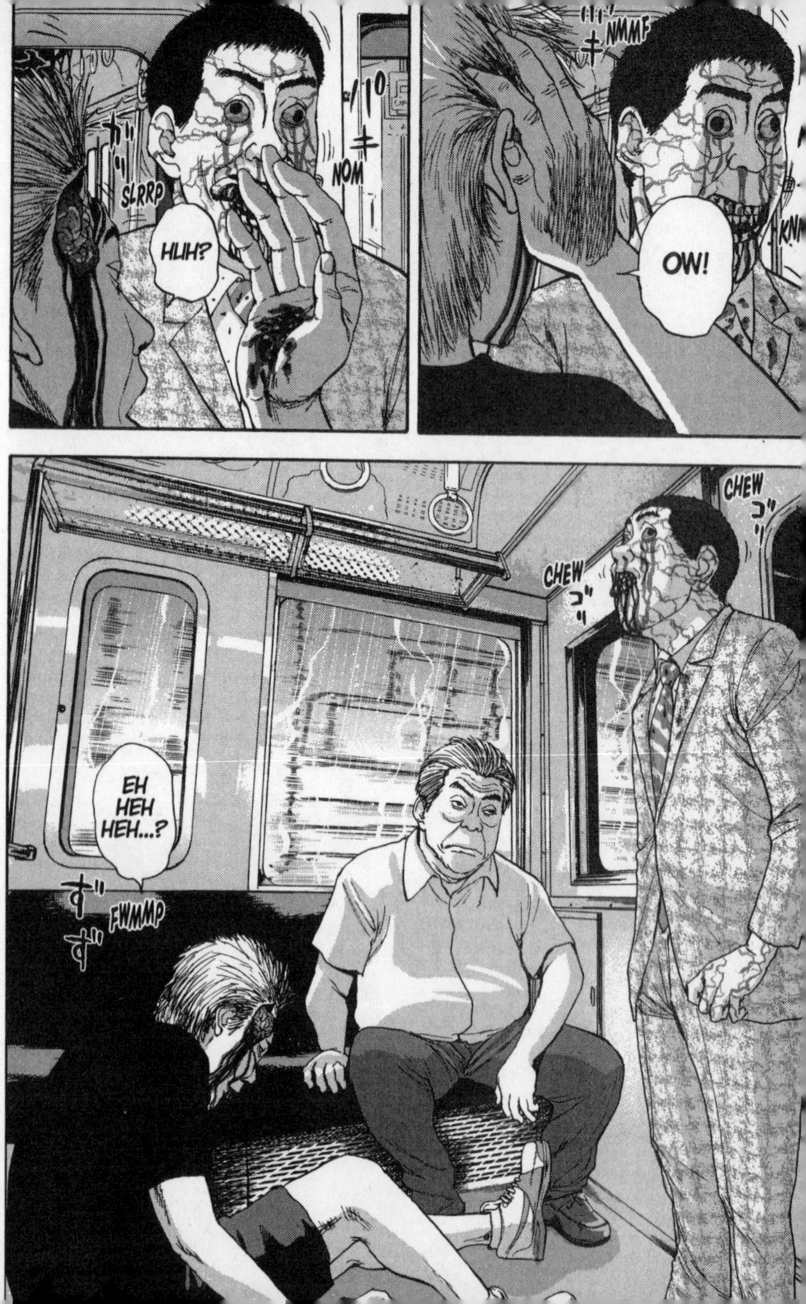
NMMF
OW!
NOM
HUH?
SLRRP
CHEW
CHEW
EH HEH HEH...?
FWMMP

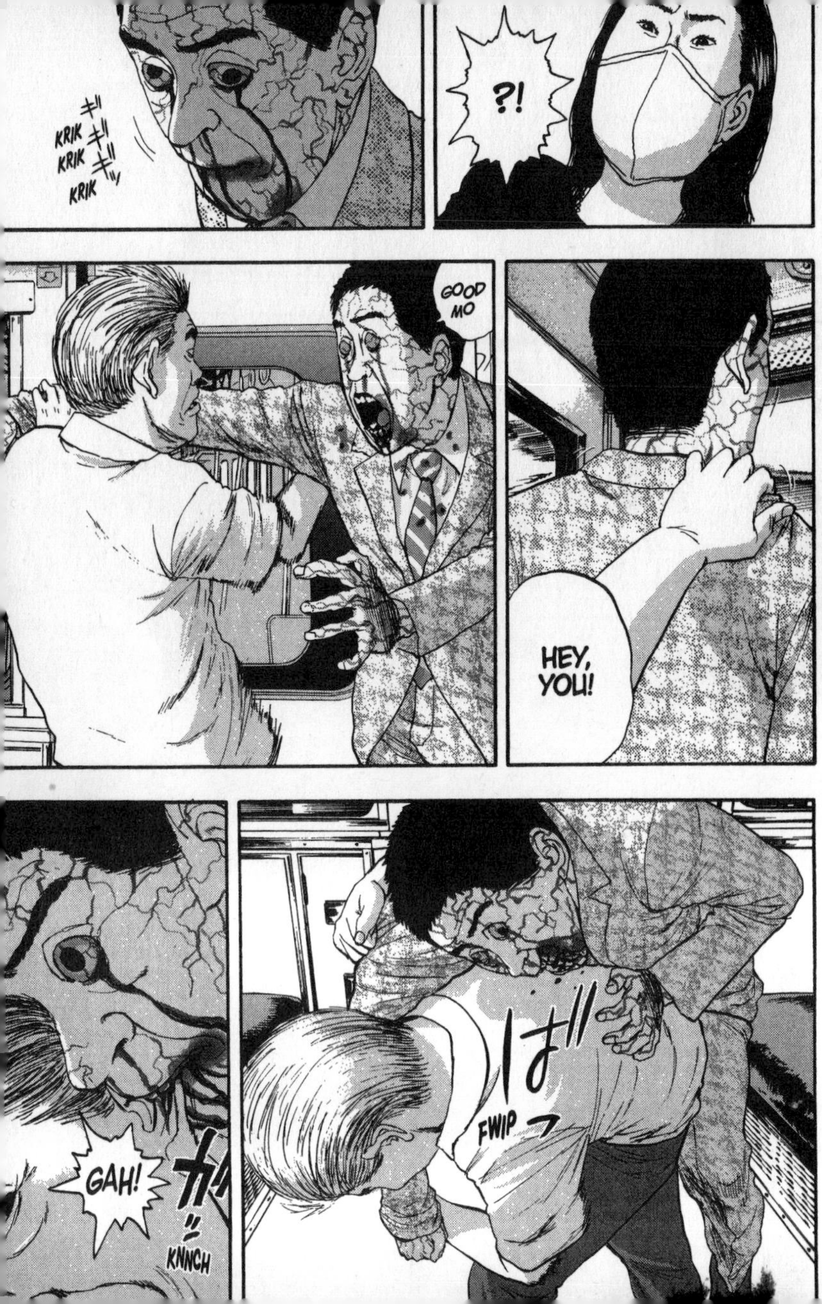
?!
KRIK KRIK KRIK
HEY, YOU!
GOOD MO
FWIP
GAH!
KNNCH

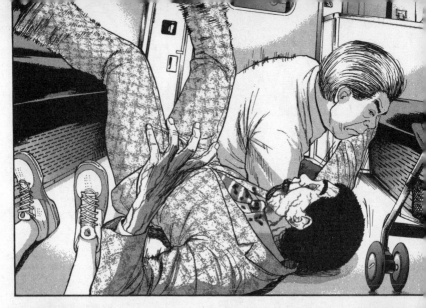

HEY!!

SOMEONE HELP ME!!

WHOA! CALM DOWN, SIR!!

HURRY! HELP ME! ANYBODY!!

WHMMP

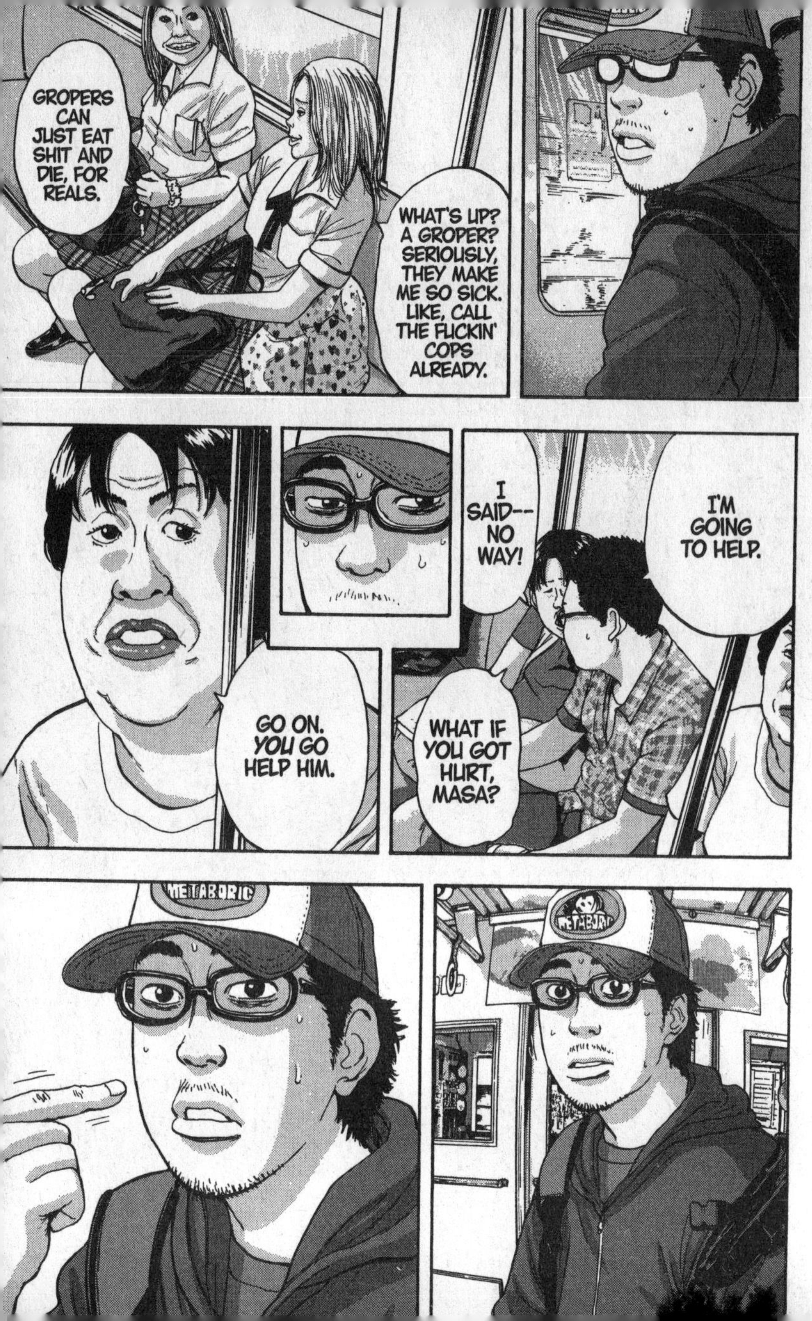
WHAT'S UP? A GROPER? SERIOUSLY, THEY MAKE ME SO SICK. LIKE, CALL THE FUCKIN' COPS ALREADY.
GROPERS CAN JUST EAT SHIT AND DIE, FOR REALS.
I'M GOING TO HELP.
I SAID-- NO WAY!
WHAT IF YOU GOT HURT, MASA?
GO ON. YOU GO HELP HIM.
METABORIC
METABORIC

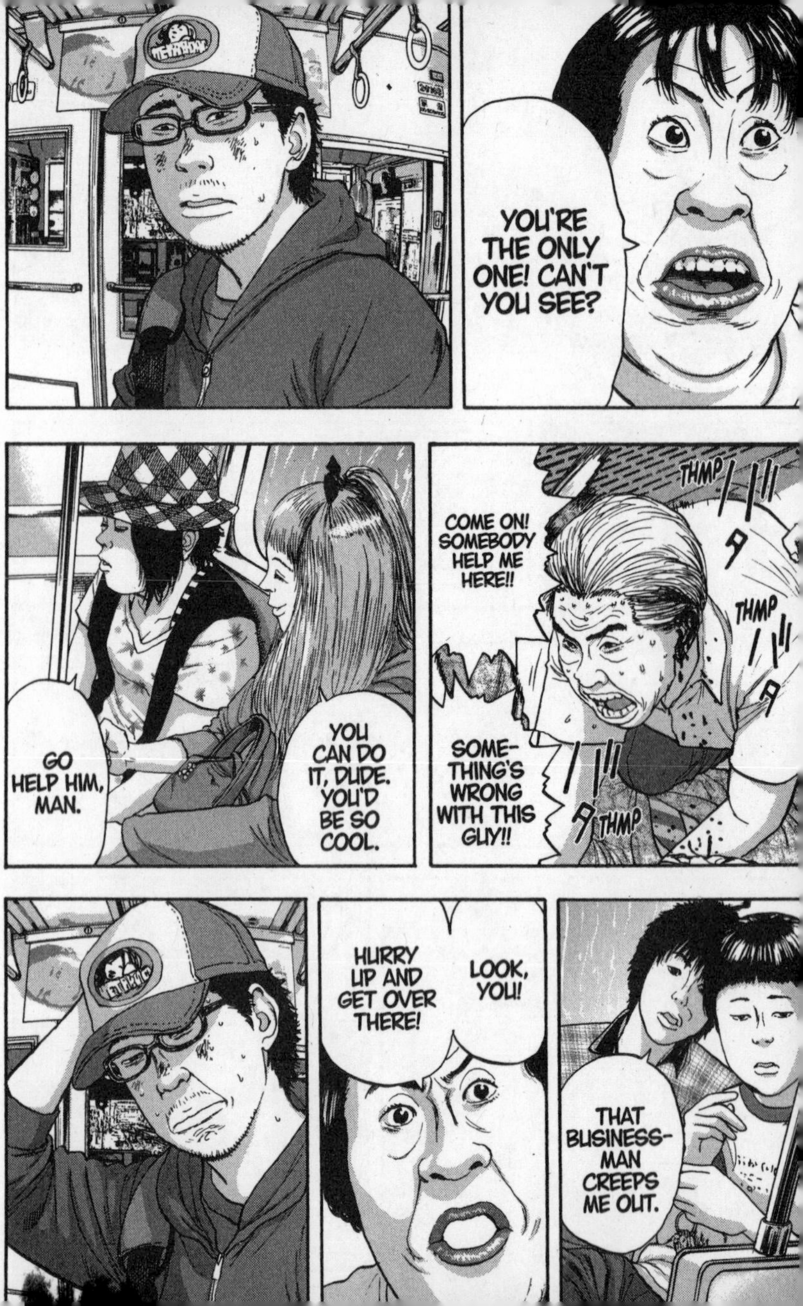
YOU'RE THE ONLY ONE! CAN'T YOU SEE?
THMP
COME ON! SOMEBODY HELP ME HERE!!
THMP
SOME-THING'S WRONG WITH THIS GUY!!
THMP
YOU CAN DO IT, DUDE. YOU'D BE SO COOL.
GO HELP HIM, MAN.
THAT BUSINESS-MAN CREEPS ME OUT.
LOOK, YOU!
HURRY UP AND GET OVER THERE!

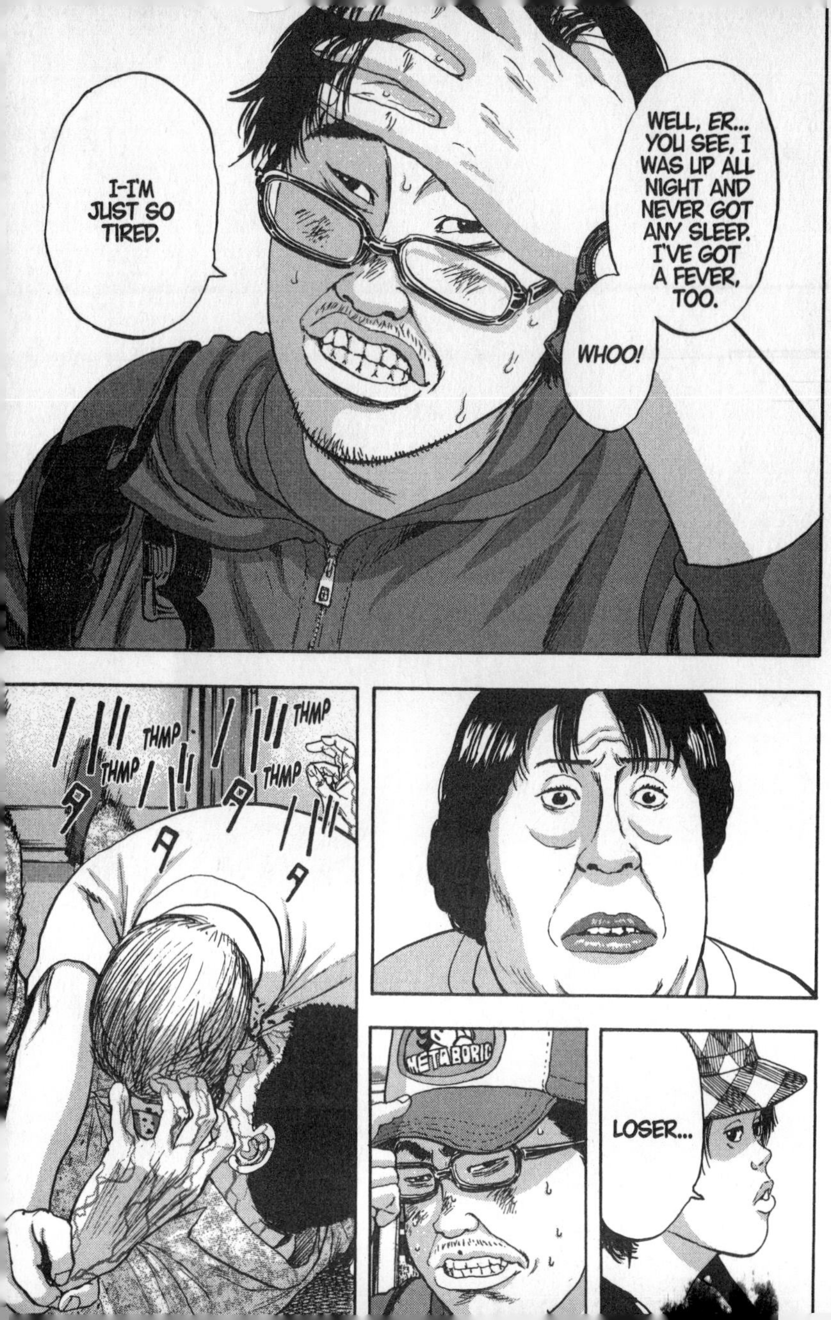
WELL, ER... YOU SEE, I WAS UP ALL NIGHT AND NEVER GOT ANY SLEEP. I'VE GOT A FEVER, TOO.
WHOO!
I-I'M JUST SO TIRED.
THMP
THMP
THMP
THMP
LOSER...
METABORIC

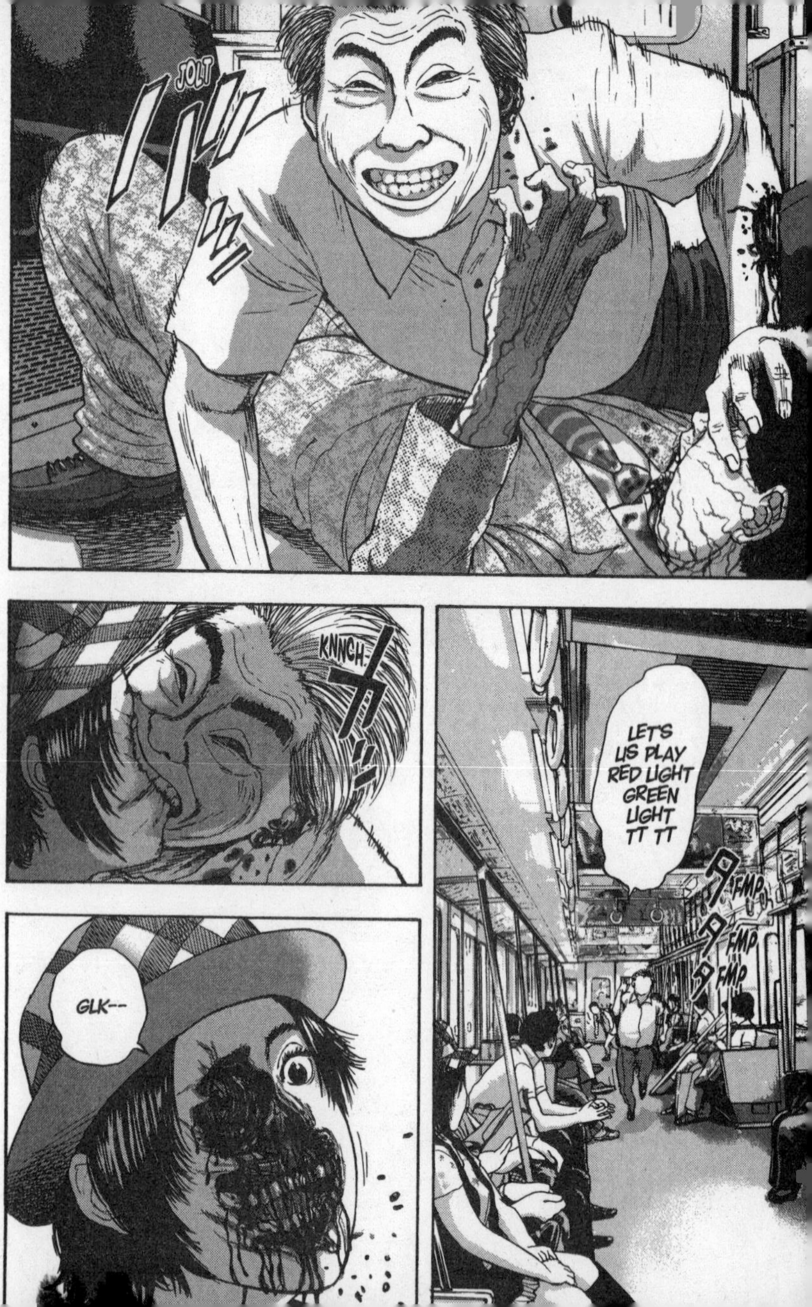
JOLT
LET'S US PLAY RED LIGHT GREEN LIGHT TT TT
FMP
FMP
FMP
KNNCH
GLK--

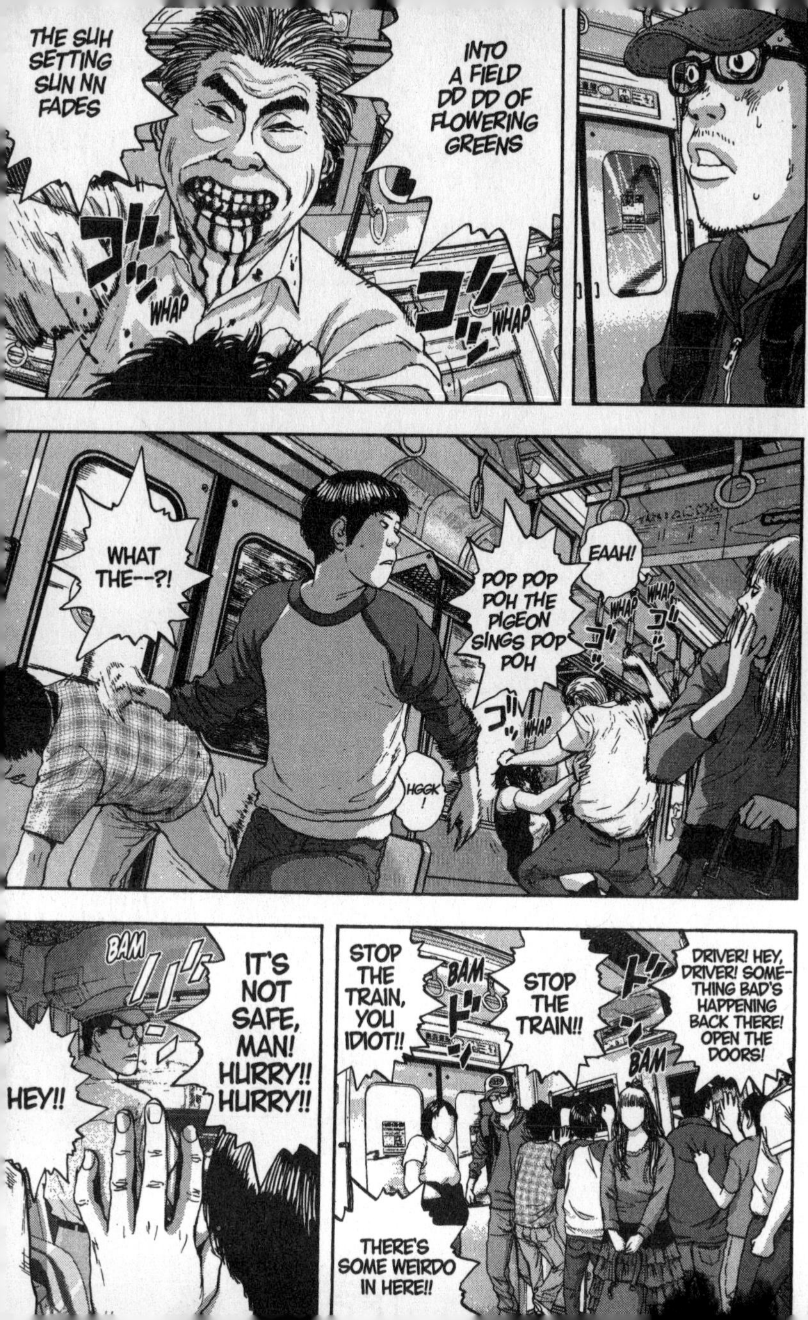
THE SUH SETTING SUN NN FADES
INTO A FIELD DD DD OF FLOWERING GREENS
WHAP
WHAP
EAAH!
WHAP
WHAP
POP POP POH THE PIGEON SINGS POP POH
WHAT THE--?!
WHAP
HGGK!
DRIVER! HEY, DRIVER! SOME-THING BAD'S HAPPENING BACK THERE! OPEN THE DOORS!
BAM
STOP THE TRAIN!!
BAM
STOP THE TRAIN, YOU IDIOT!!
THERE'S SOME WEIRDO IN HERE!!
IT'S NOT SAFE, MAN! HURRY!! HURRY!!
BAM
HEY!!

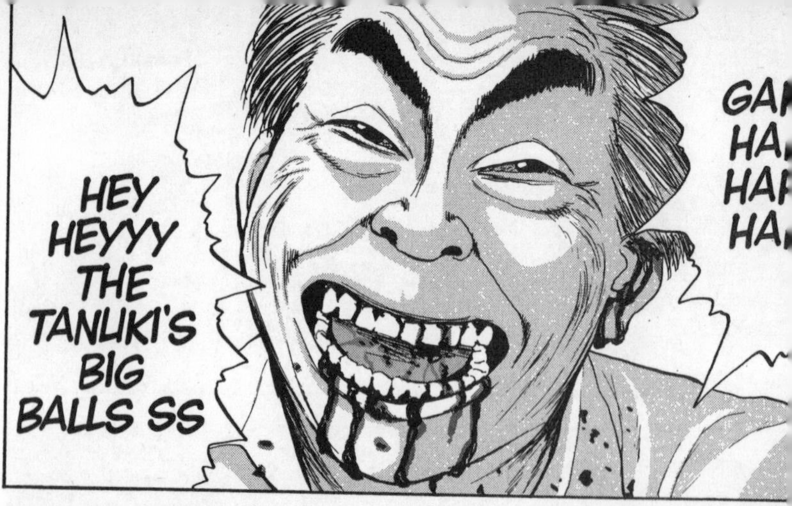
GA
HA,
HA
HA
HEY HEYYY THE TANUKI'S BIG BALLS SS

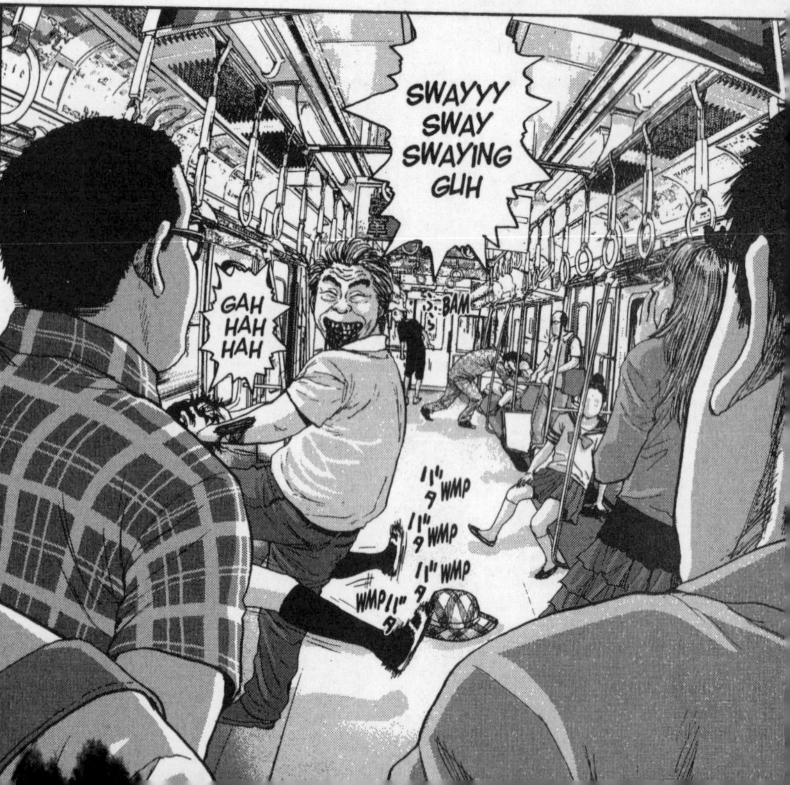
SWAYYY SWAY SWAYING GUH
BAM
GAH HAH HAH
バタ WMP
バタ WMP
バタ WMP
WMP バタ

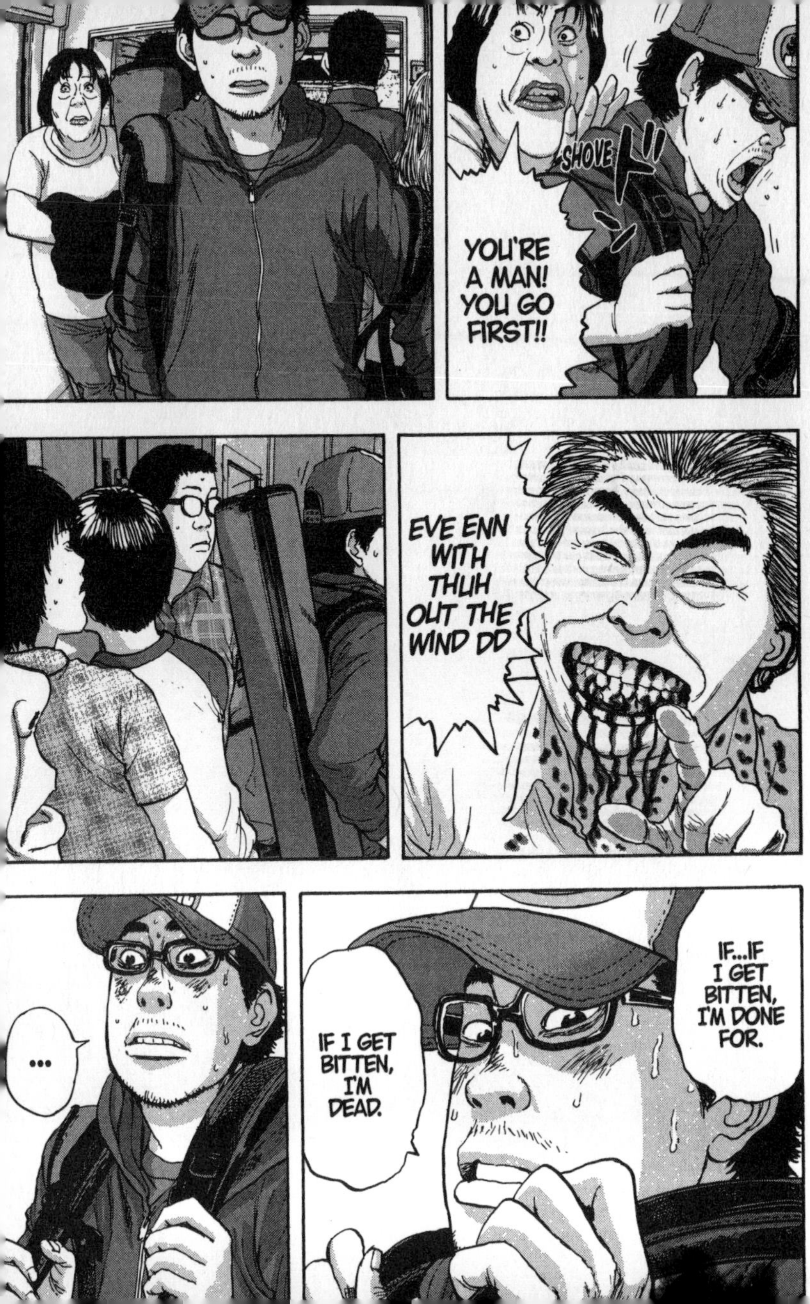
SHOVE
YOU'RE A MAN! YOU GO FIRST!!
EVE ENN WITH THUH OUT THE WIND DD
IF...IF I GET BITTEN, I'M DONE FOR.
IF I GET BITTEN, I'M DEAD.
...

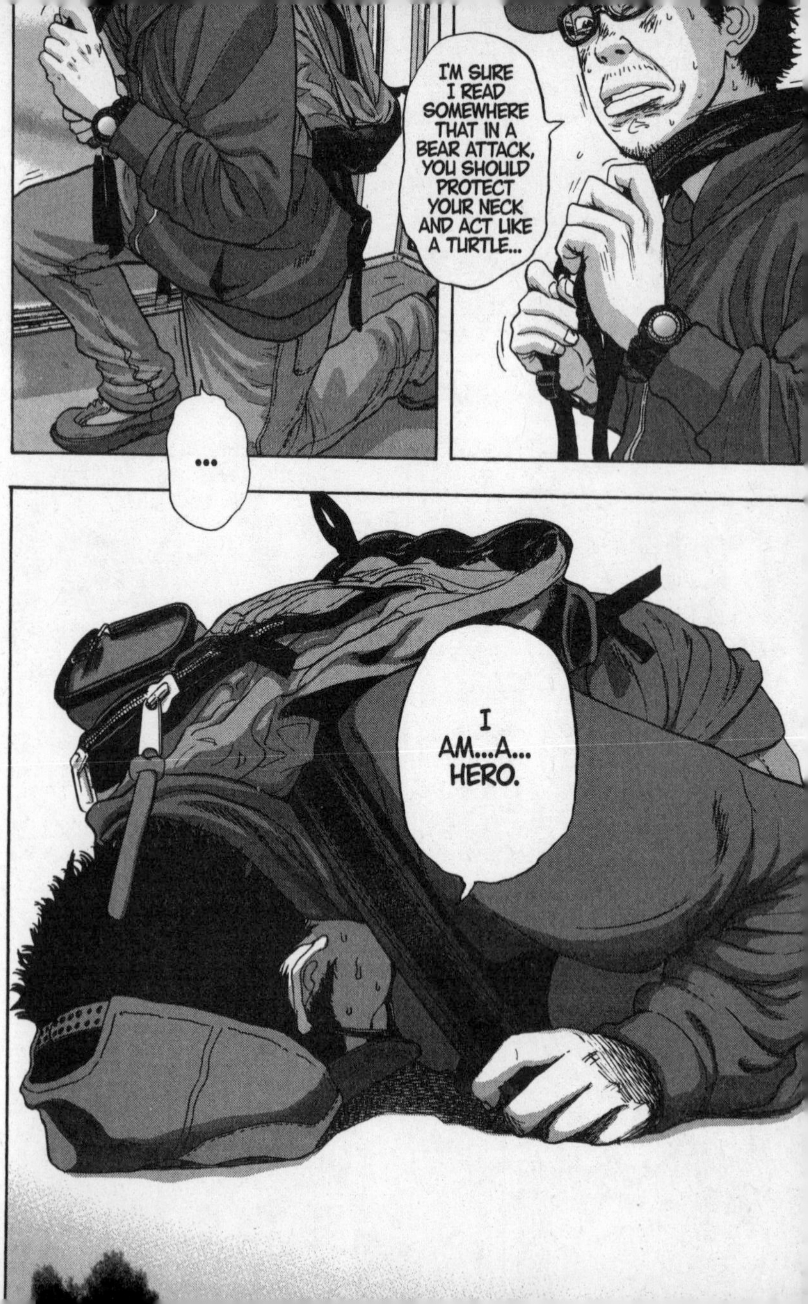
I'M SURE I READ SOMEWHERE THAT IN A BEAR ATTACK, YOU SHOULD PROTECT YOUR NECK AND ACT LIKE A TURTLE...
...
I AM...A... HERO.

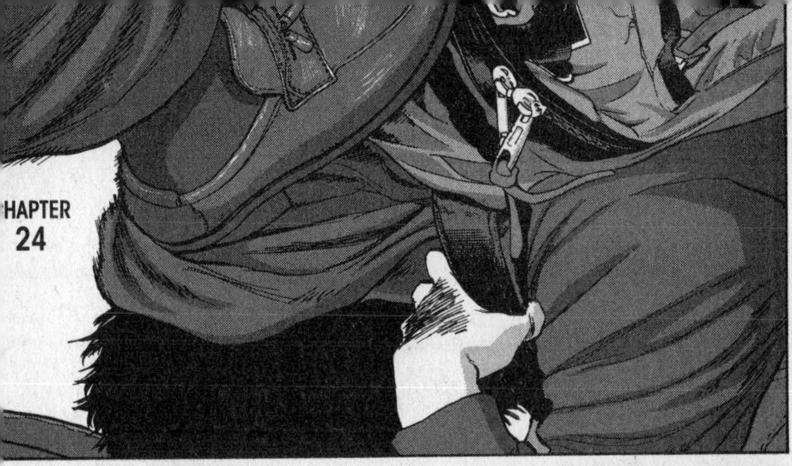
CHAPTER
24
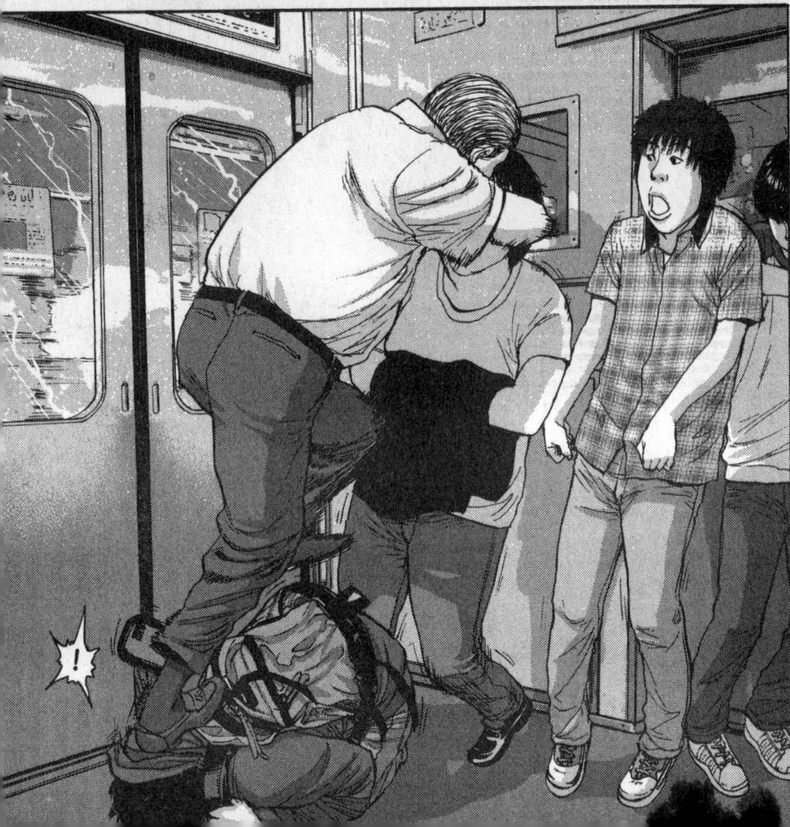
!

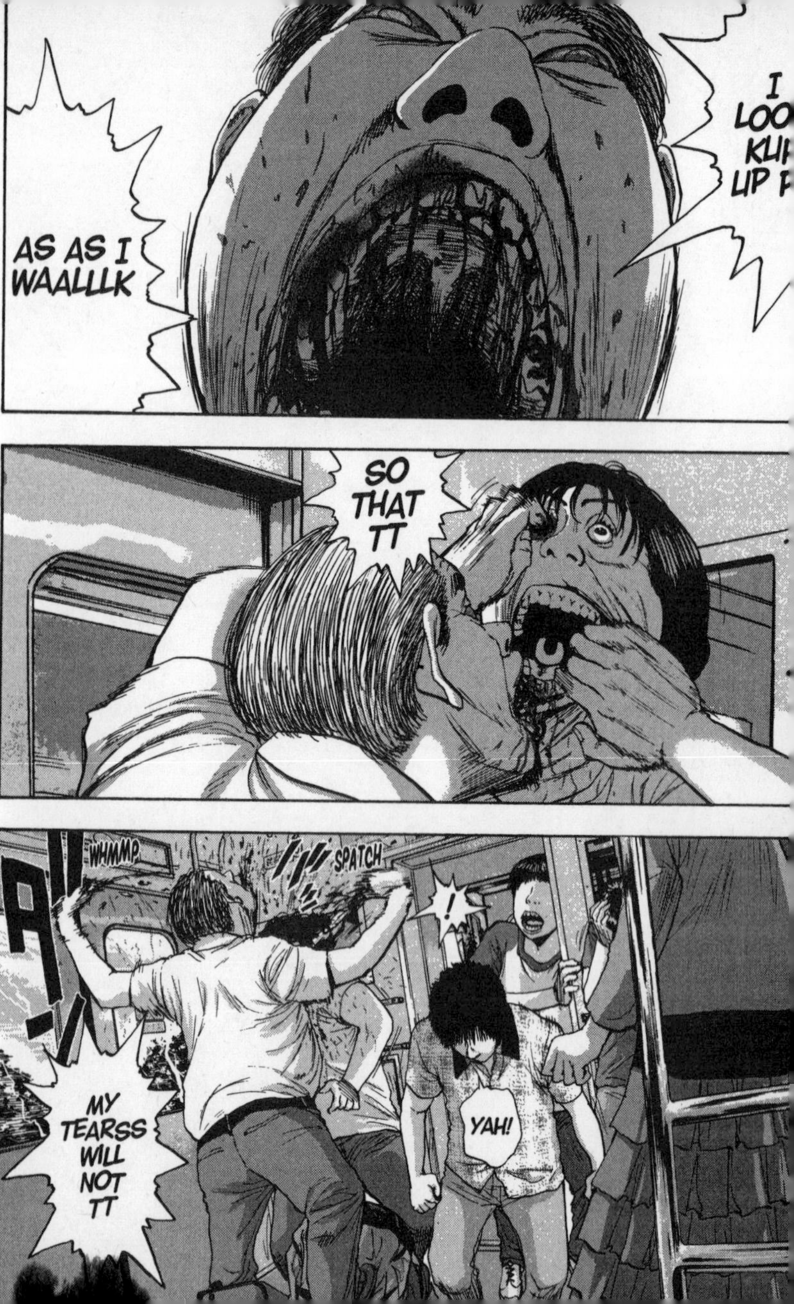
I LOO KU UP
AS AS I WAALLLK
SO THAT TT
!
SPATCH
WHMMP
YAH!
MY TEARSS WILL NOT TT

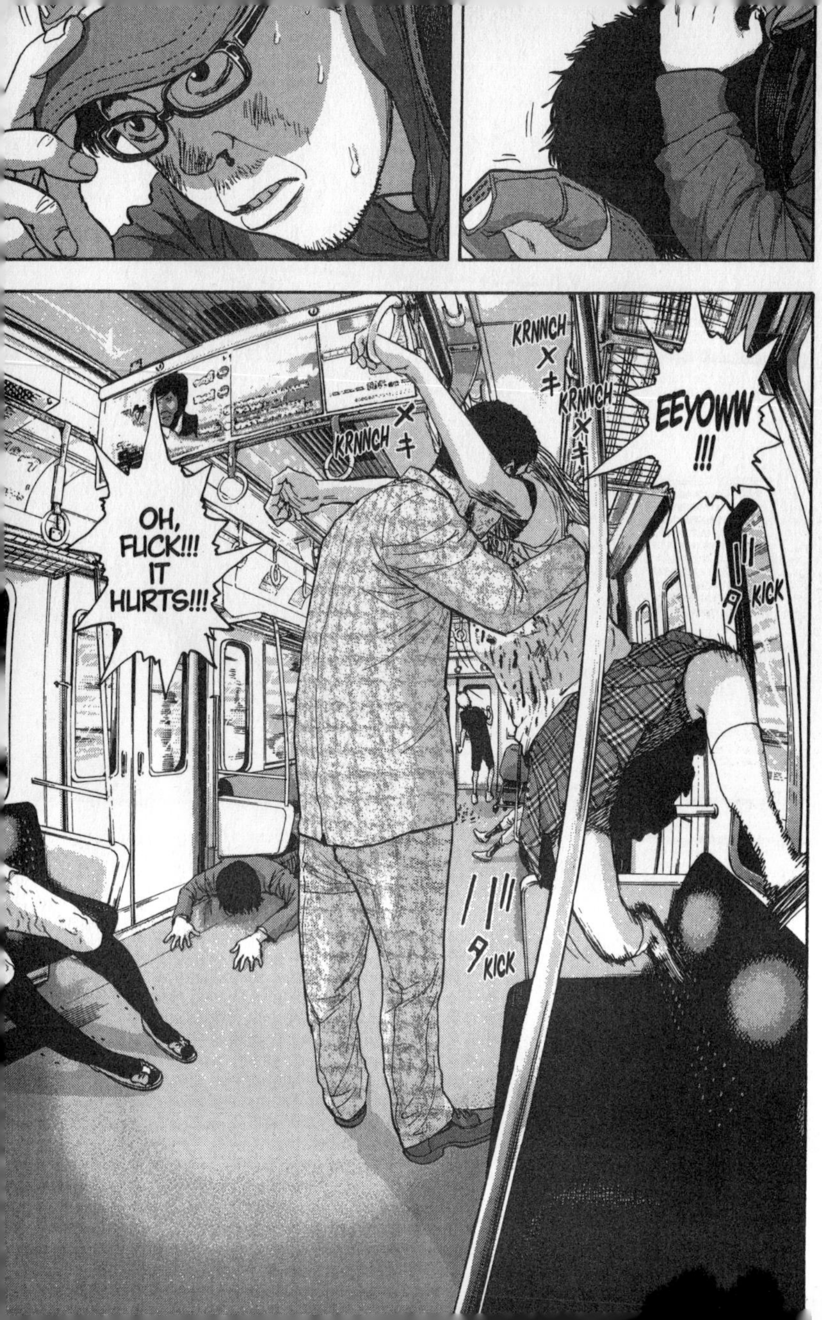
EEYOWW !!!
KRNNCH
KRNNCH
KRNNCH
KICK
KICK
OH, FUCK!!! IT HURTS!!!

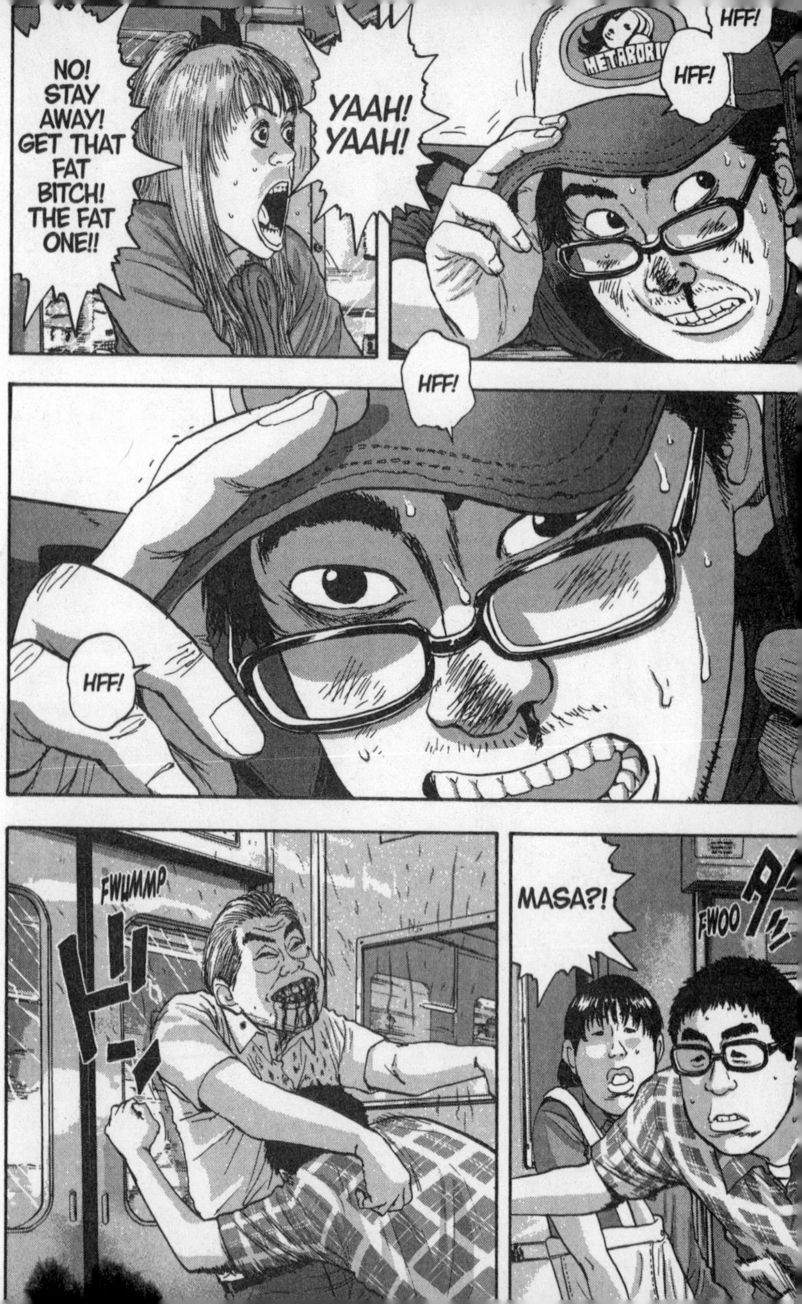
HFF!
HFF!
YAAH! YAAH!
NO! STAY AWAY! GET THAT FAT BITCH! THE FAT ONE!!
HFF!
HFF!
MASA?!
FWOO
FWUMMP

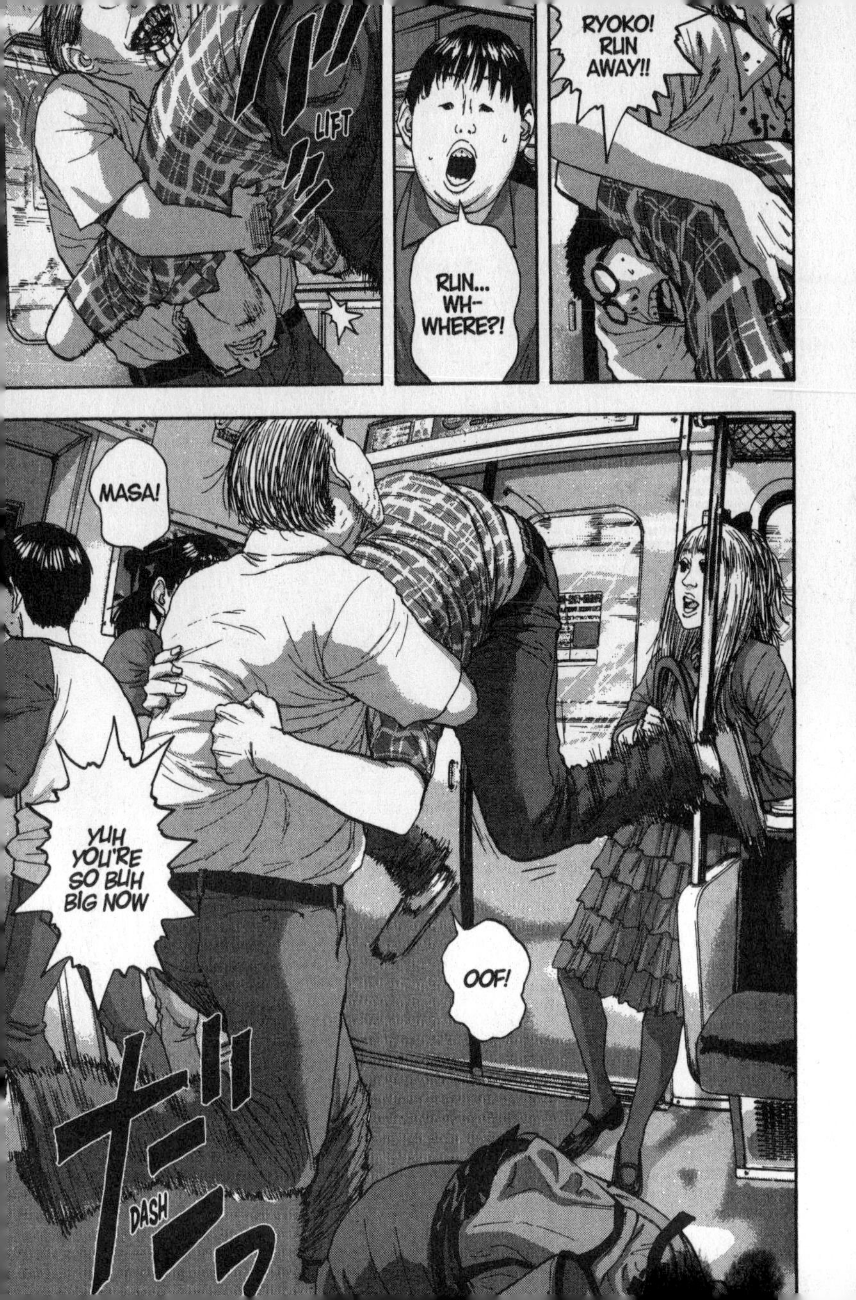
RYOKO! RUN AWAY!!
RUN... WH- WHERE?!
LIFT
MASA!
OOF!
YUH YOU'RE SO BUH BIG NOW
DASH

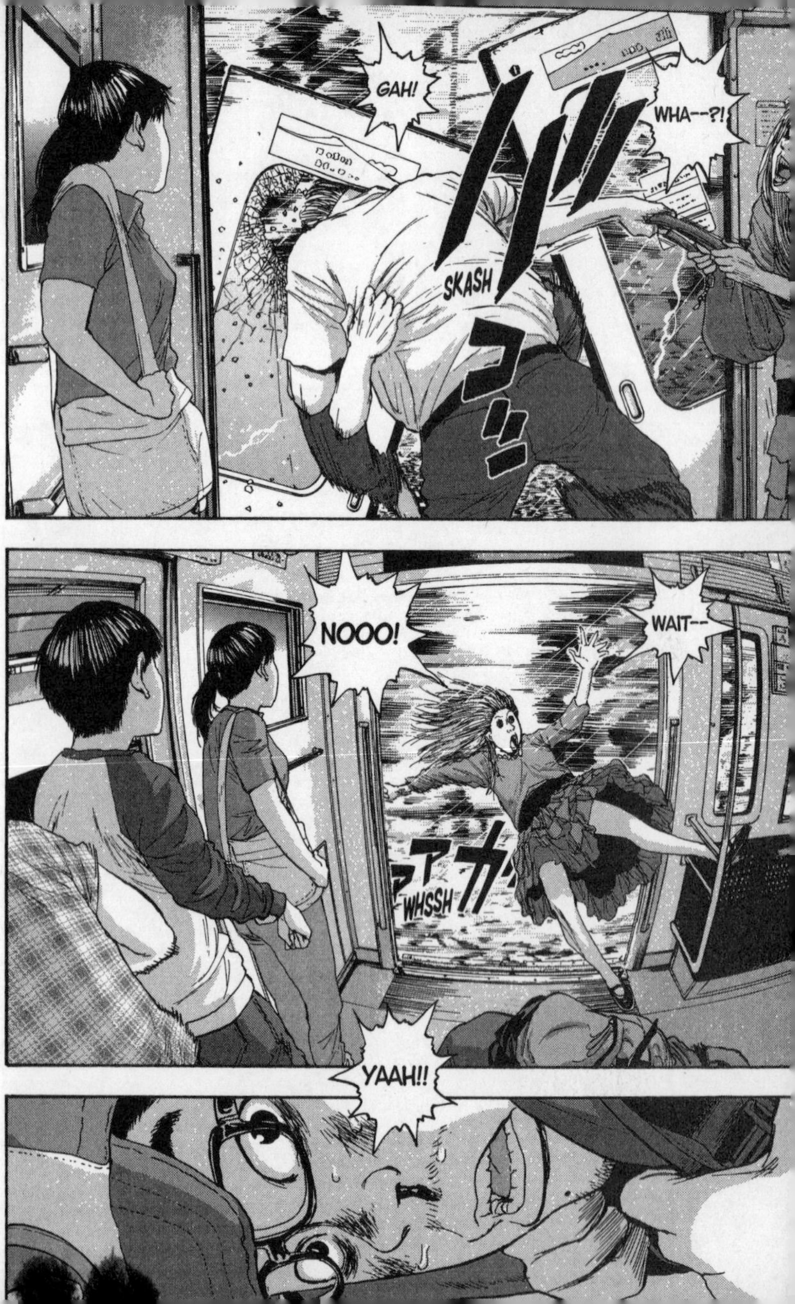
WHA--?!
GAH!
SKASH
WAIT--
NOOO!
WHSSH
YAAH!!

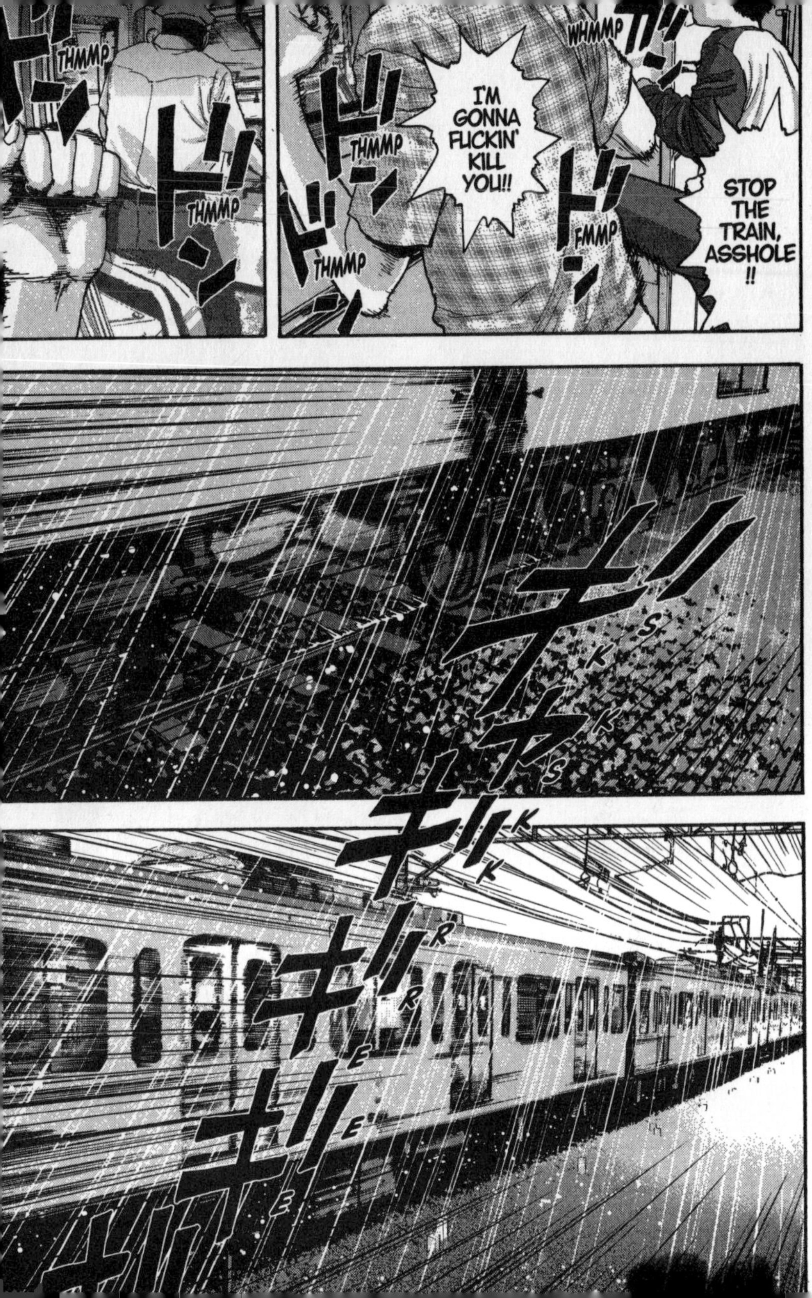
WHMMP
STOP THE TRAIN, ASSHOLE!!
I'M GONNA FUCKIN' KILL YOU!!
THMMP
FMMP
THMMP
THMMP
THMMP
SKKS
KKRREEE

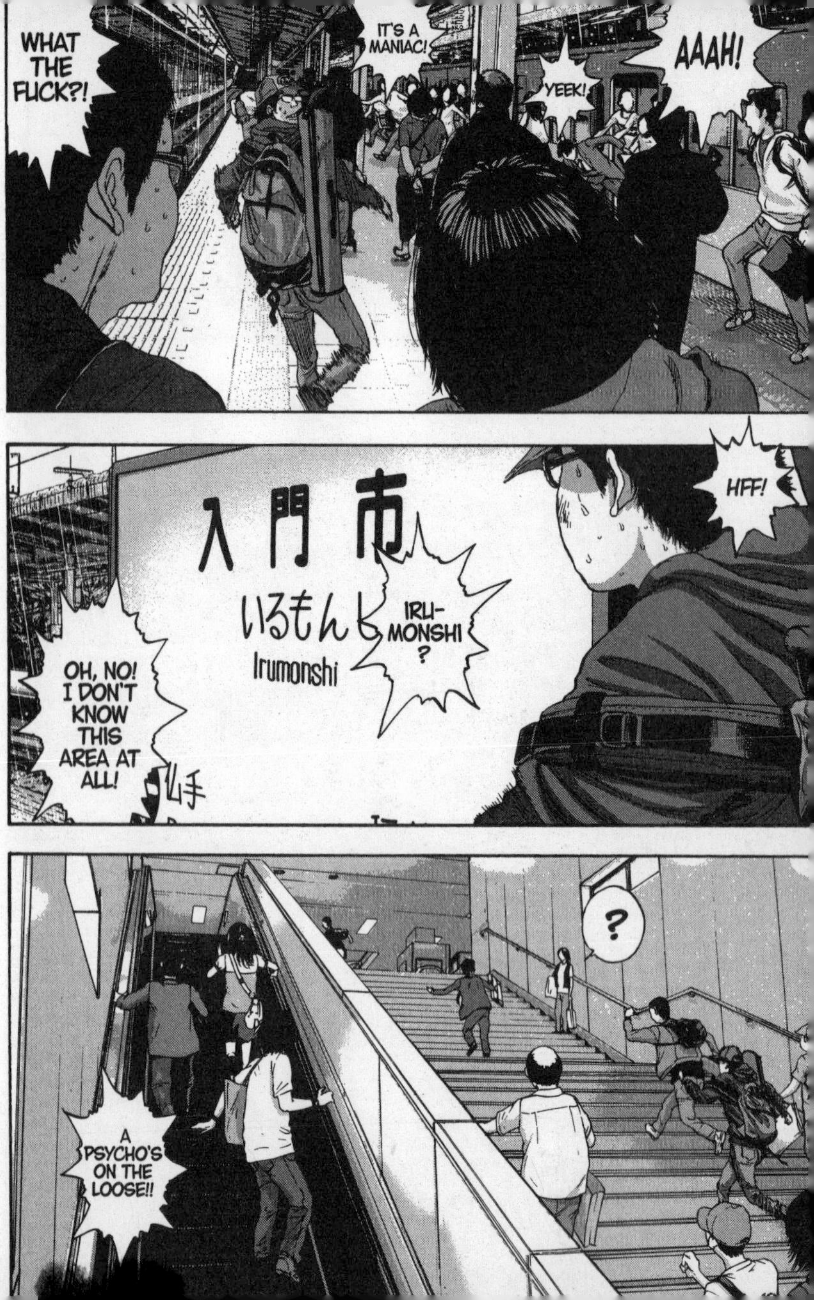
AAAH!
YEEK!
IT'S A MANIAC!
WHAT THE FUCK?!
HFF!
入門市
いるもんし
Irumonshi
IRU-MONSHI?
OH, NO! I DON'T KNOW THIS AREA AT ALL!
?
A PSYCHO'S ON THE LOOSE!!

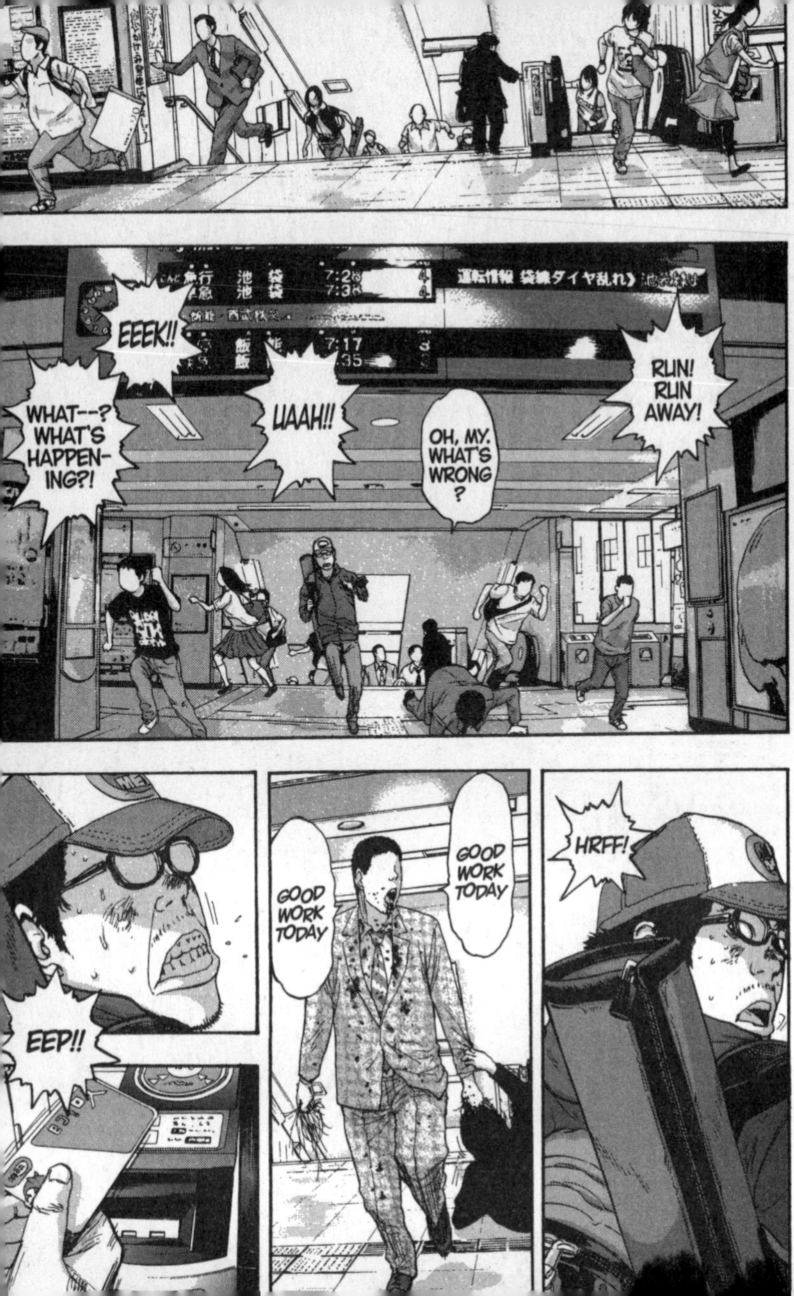
RUN! RUN AWAY!
OH, MY. WHAT'S WRONG?
UAAH!!
EEEK!!
WHAT--? WHAT'S HAPPENING?!
HRFF!
GOOD WORK TODAY
GOOD WORK TODAY
EEP!!

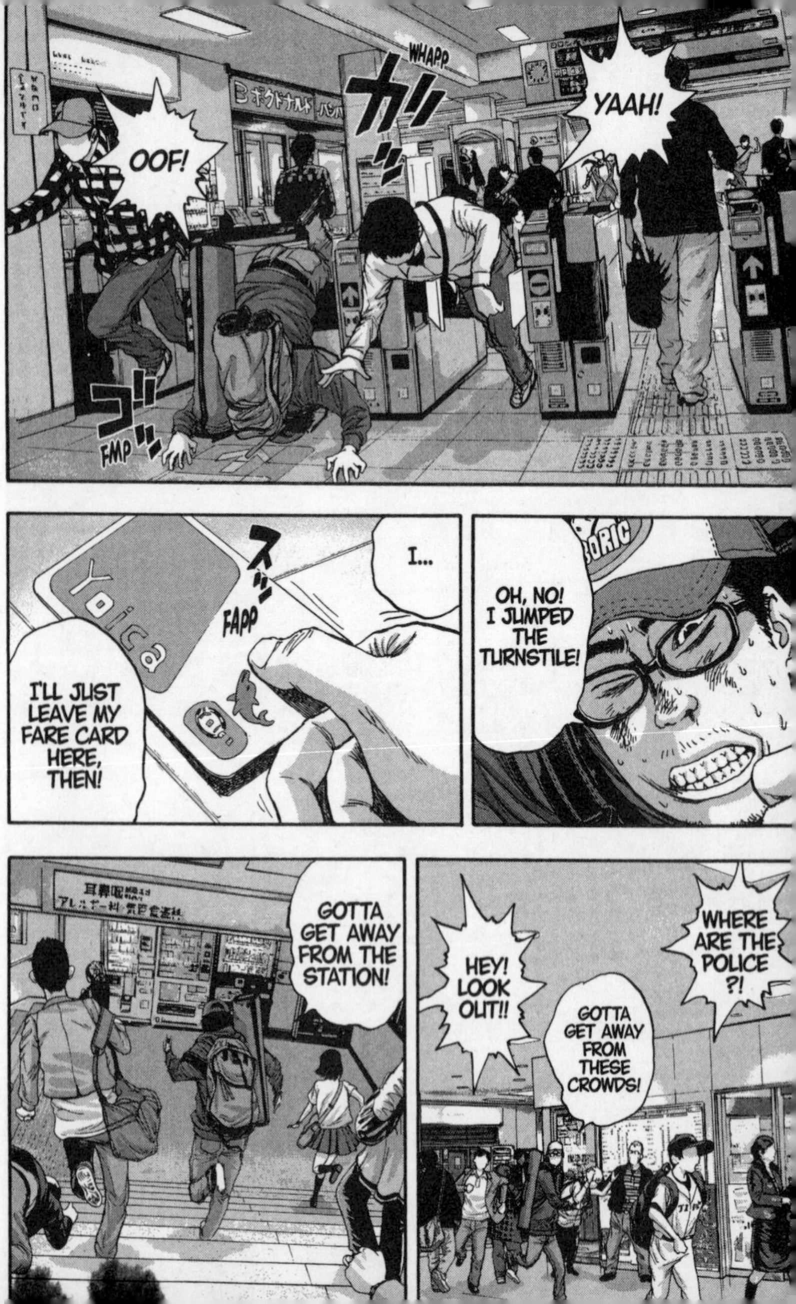
YAAH!
WHAPP
OOF!
FMP
OH, NO! I JUMPED THE TURNSTILE!
I...
FAPP
I'LL JUST LEAVE MY FARE CARD HERE, THEN!
WHERE ARE THE POLICE?!
HEY! LOOK OUT!!
GOTTA GET AWAY FROM THESE CROWDS!
GOTTA GET AWAY FROM THE STATION!

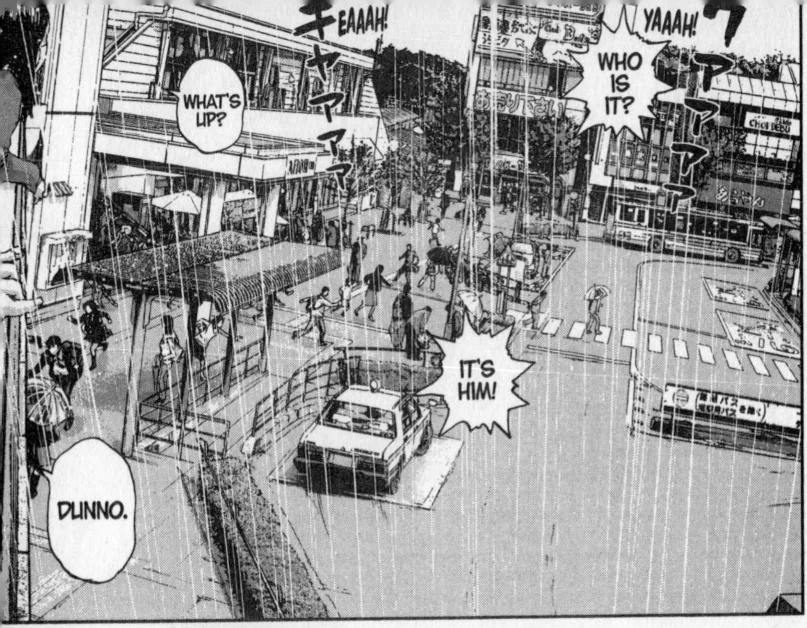
YAAAH!
WHO IS IT?
EAAAH!
WHAT'S UP?
IT'S HIM!
DUNNO.

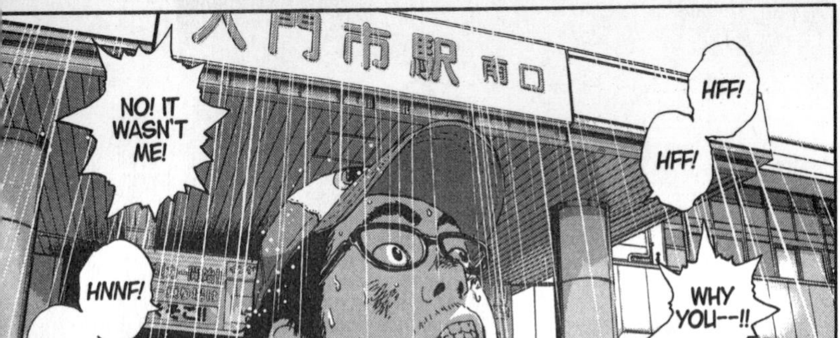
入門市駅 南口
HFF!
HFF!
NO! IT WASN'T ME!
WHY YOU--!!
HNNF!
HAHH!

SIGN: IRUMONSHI STATION SOUTH ENTRANCE

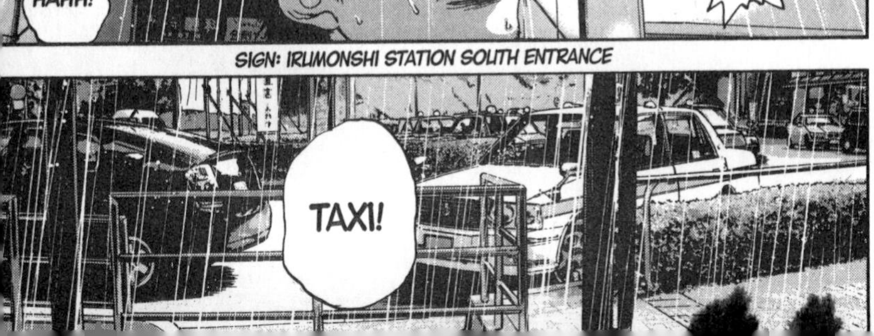
TAXI!

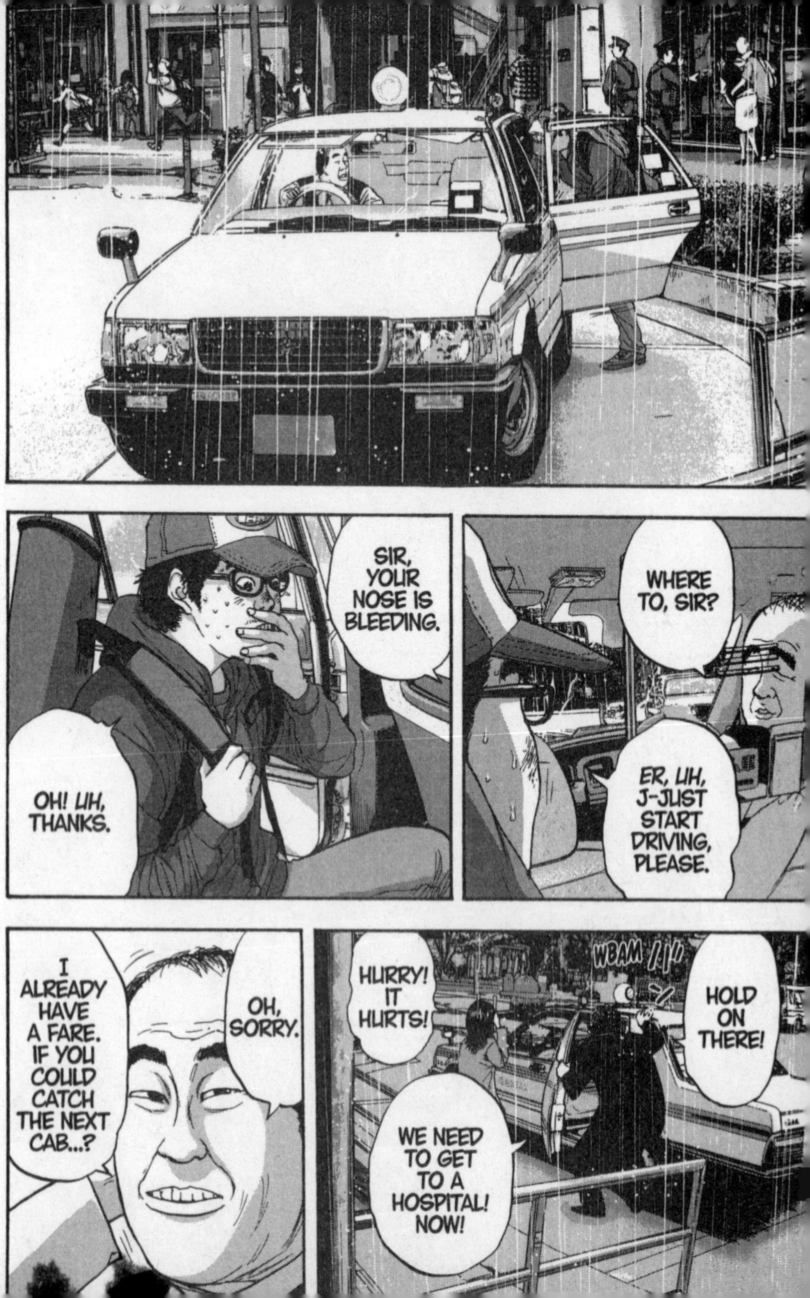
WHERE TO, SIR?
ER, UH, J-JUST START DRIVING, PLEASE.
SIR, YOUR NOSE IS BLEEDING.
OH! UH, THANKS.
WBAM
HOLD ON THERE!
HURRY! IT HURTS!
WE NEED TO GET TO A HOSPITAL! NOW!
OH, SORRY.
I ALREADY HAVE A FARE. IF YOU COULD CATCH THE NEXT CAB...?

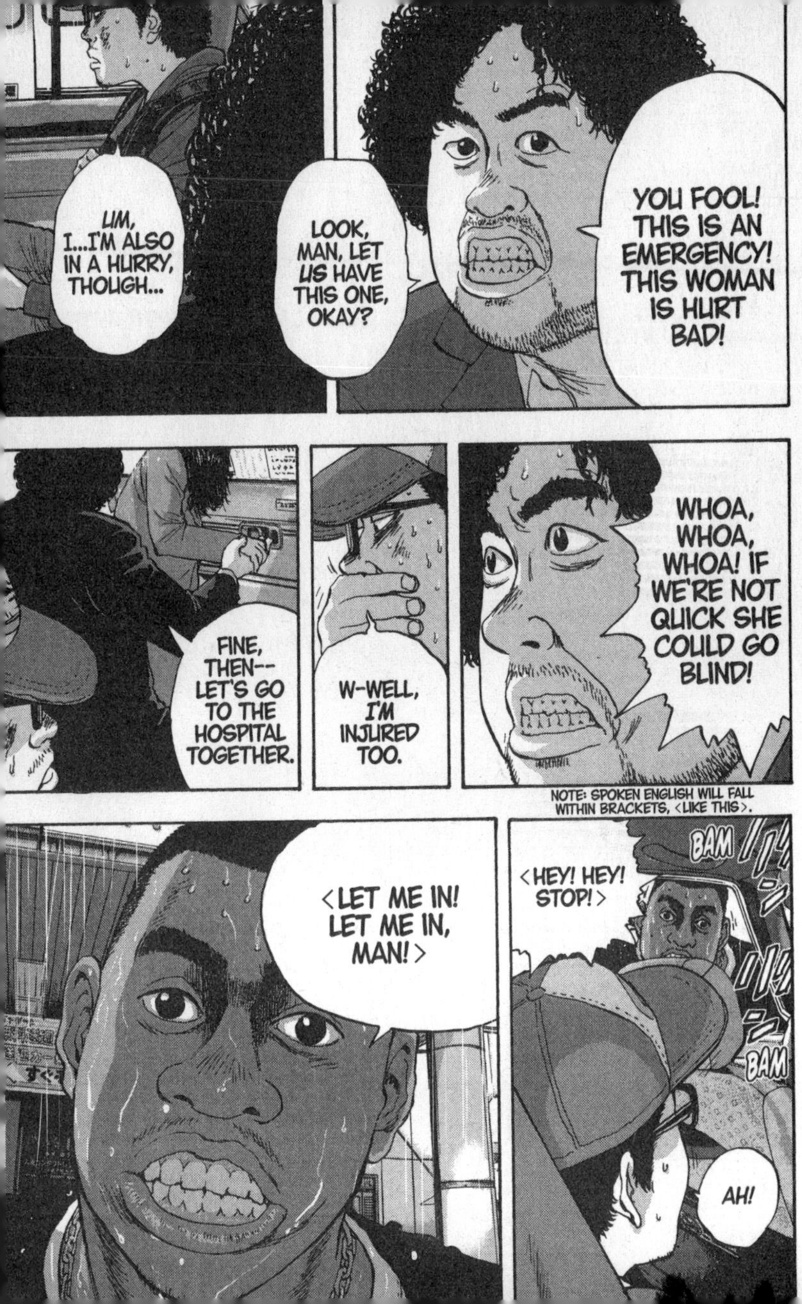
YOU FOOL! THIS IS AN EMERGENCY! THIS WOMAN IS HURT BAD!
LOOK, MAN, LET US HAVE THIS ONE, OKAY?
UM, I...I'M ALSO IN A HURRY, THOUGH...
WHOA, WHOA, WHOA! IF WE'RE NOT QUICK SHE COULD GO BLIND!
W-WELL, I'M INJURED TOO.
FINE, THEN-- LET'S GO TO THE HOSPITAL TOGETHER.
NOTE: SPOKEN ENGLISH WILL FALL WITHIN BRACKETS, <LIKE THIS>.
BAM
<HEY! HEY! STOP!>
BAM
AH!
<LET ME IN! LET ME IN, MAN!>

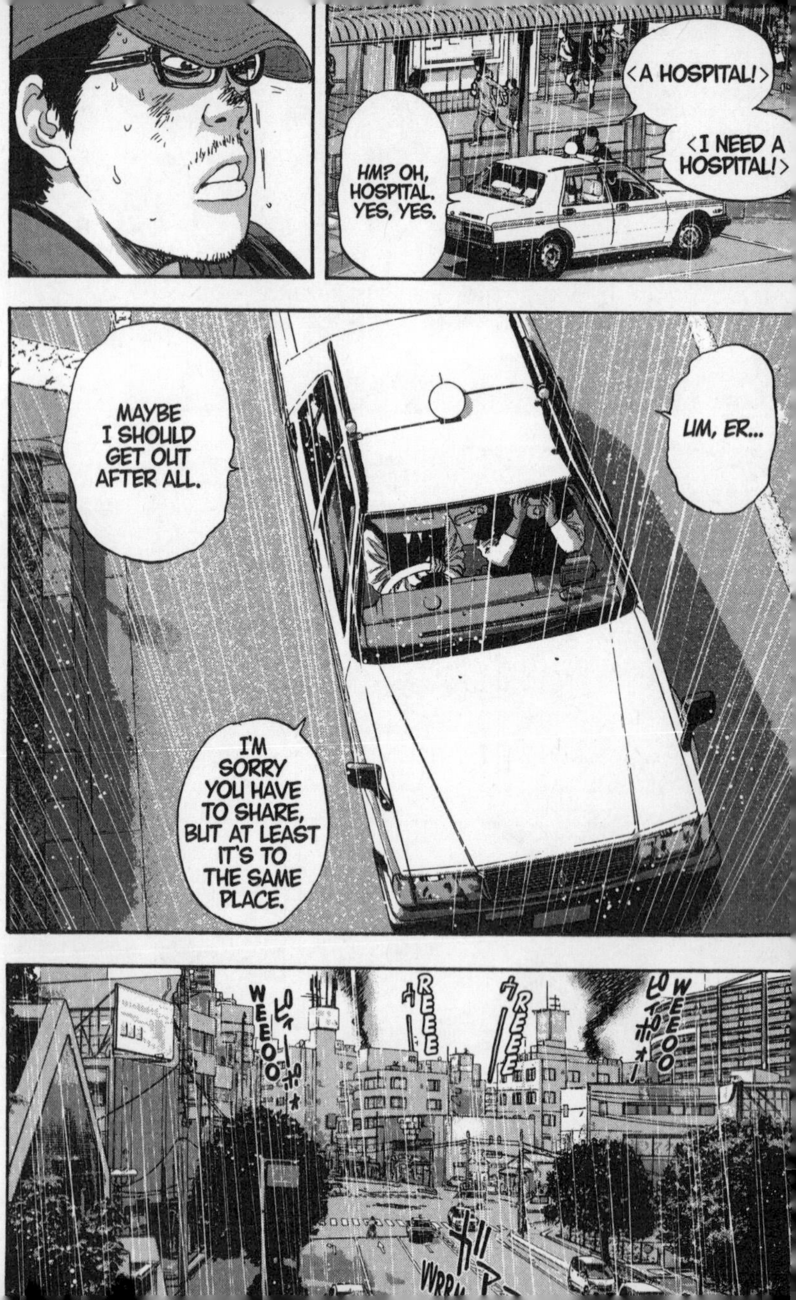
<A HOSPITAL!>
<I NEED A HOSPITAL!>
HM? OH, HOSPITAL. YES, YES.
UM, ER...
MAYBE I SHOULD GET OUT AFTER ALL.
I'M SORRY YOU HAVE TO SHARE, BUT AT LEAST IT'S TO THE SAME PLACE.
WEEOO
REEE
REEE
WEEOO

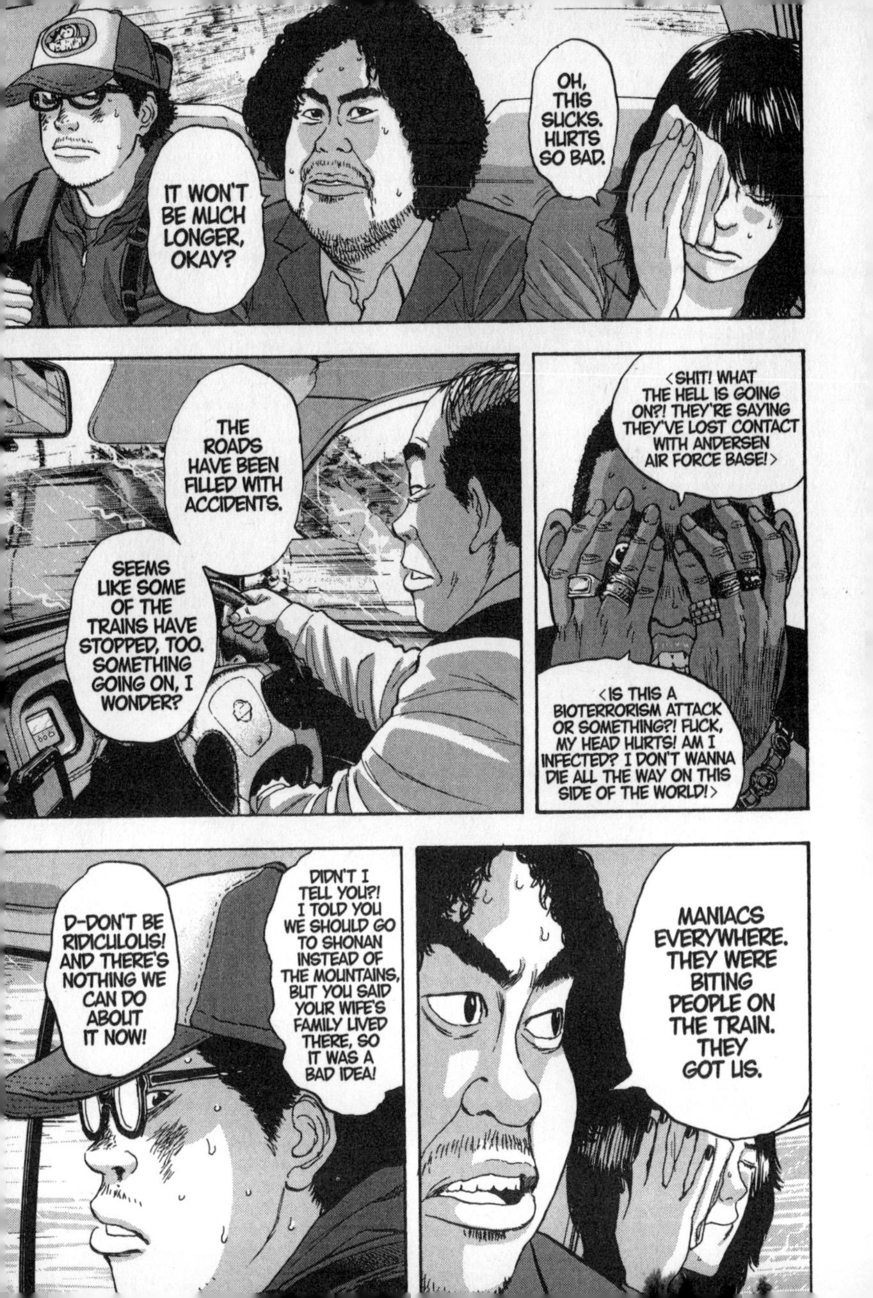
OH, THIS SUCKS. HURTS SO BAD.
IT WON'T BE MUCH LONGER, OKAY?
<SHIT! WHAT THE HELL IS GOING ON?! THEY'RE SAYING THEY'VE LOST CONTACT WITH ANDERSEN AIR FORCE BASE!>
<IS THIS A BIOTERRORISM ATTACK OR SOMETHING?! FUCK, MY HEAD HURTS! AM I INFECTED? I DON'T WANNA DIE ALL THE WAY ON THIS SIDE OF THE WORLD!>
THE ROADS HAVE BEEN FILLED WITH ACCIDENTS.
SEEMS LIKE SOME OF THE TRAINS HAVE STOPPED, TOO. SOMETHING GOING ON, I WONDER?
MANIACS EVERYWHERE. THEY WERE BITING PEOPLE ON THE TRAIN. THEY GOT US.
DIDN'T I TELL YOU?! I TOLD YOU WE SHOULD GO TO SHONAN INSTEAD OF THE MOUNTAINS, BUT YOU SAID YOUR WIFE'S FAMILY LIVED THERE, SO IT WAS A BAD IDEA!
D-DON'T BE RIDICULOUS! AND THERE'S NOTHING WE CAN DO ABOUT IT NOW!

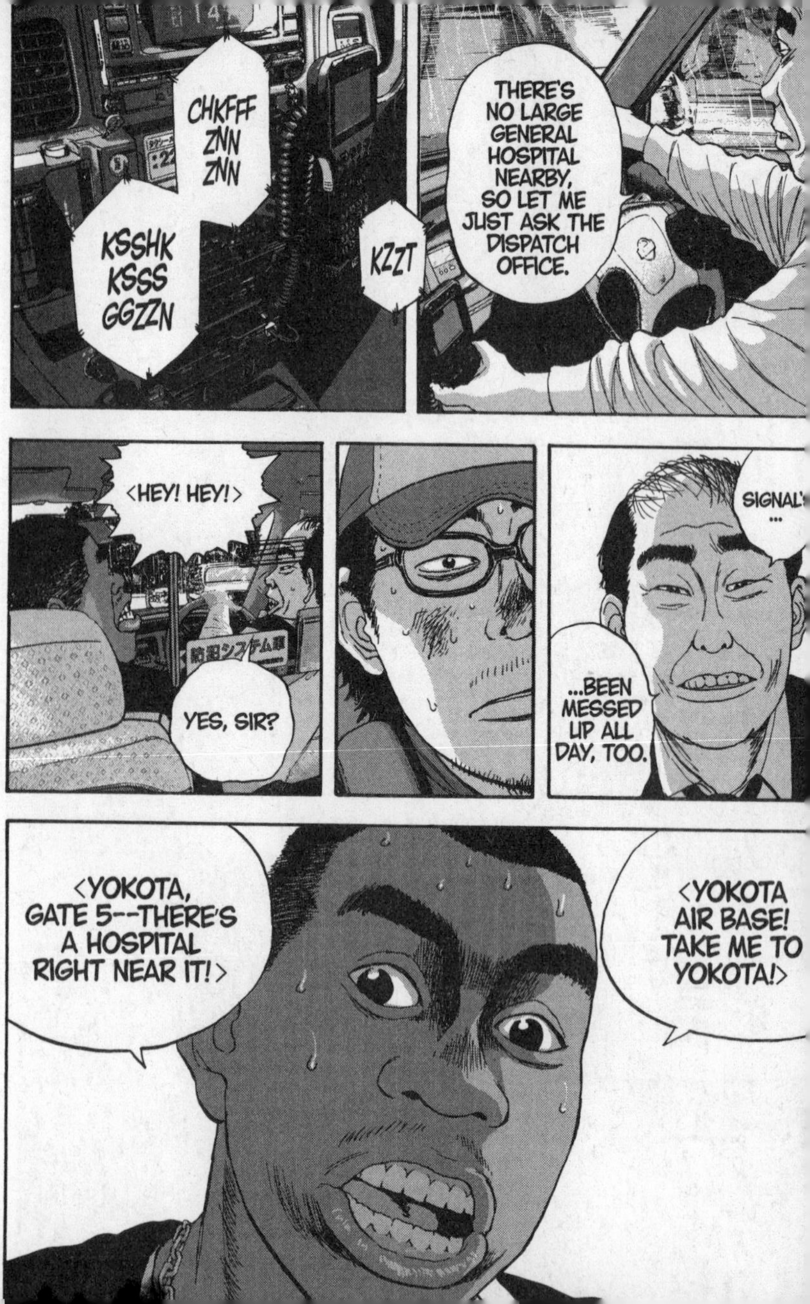
THERE'S NO LARGE GENERAL HOSPITAL NEARBY, SO LET ME JUST ASK THE DISPATCH OFFICE.
CHKFFF ZNN ZNN
KSSHK KSSS GGZZN
KZZT
SIGNAL'S ...
...BEEN MESSED UP ALL DAY, TOO.
<HEY! HEY!>
YES, SIR?
<YOKOTA AIR BASE! TAKE ME TO YOKOTA!>
<YOKOTA, GATE 5--THERE'S A HOSPITAL RIGHT NEAR IT!>

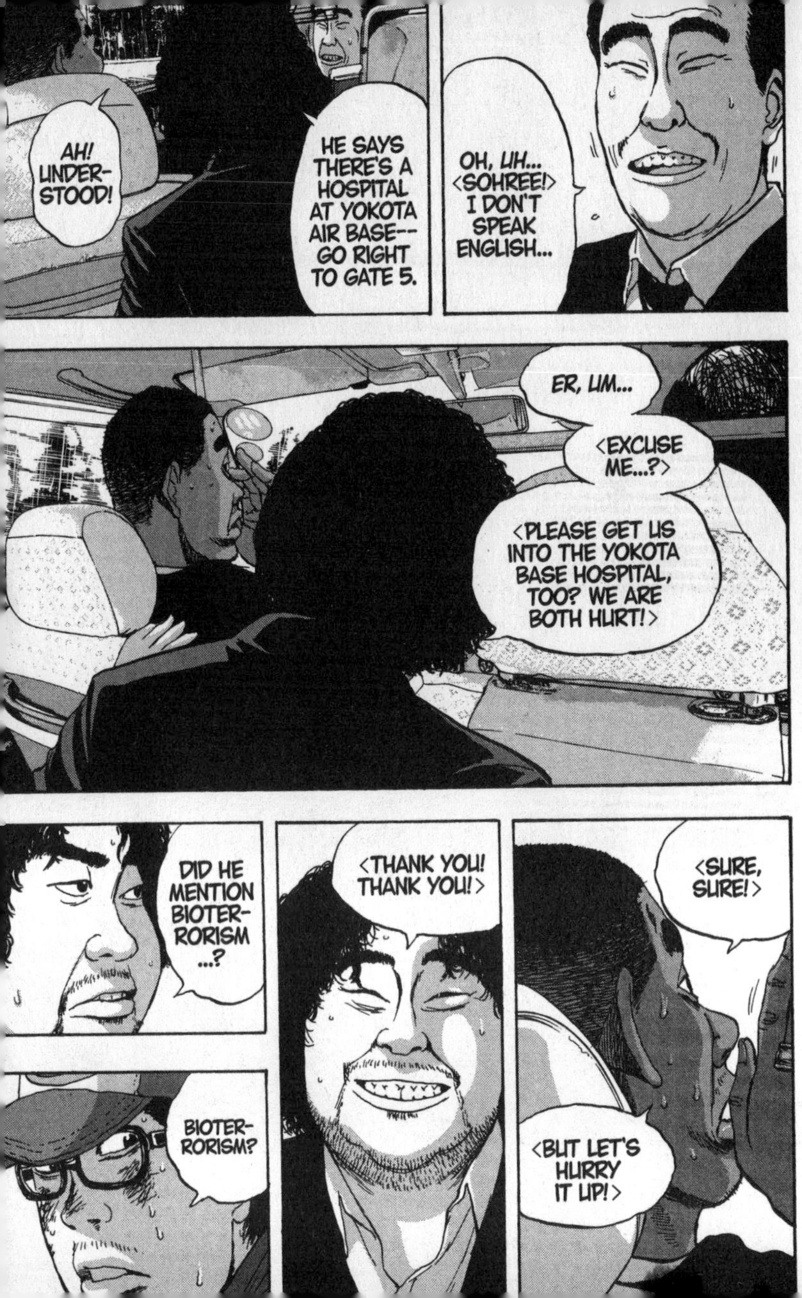
OH, UH... <SOHREE!> I DON'T SPEAK ENGLISH...
HE SAYS THERE'S A HOSPITAL AT YOKOTA AIR BASE-- GO RIGHT TO GATE 5.
AH! UNDER-STOOD!
ER, UM...
<EXCUSE ME...?>
<PLEASE GET US INTO THE YOKOTA BASE HOSPITAL, TOO? WE ARE BOTH HURT!>
<SURE, SURE!>
<BUT LET'S HURRY IT UP!>
<THANK YOU! THANK YOU!>
DID HE MENTION BIOTER-RORISM ...?
BIOTER-RORISM?

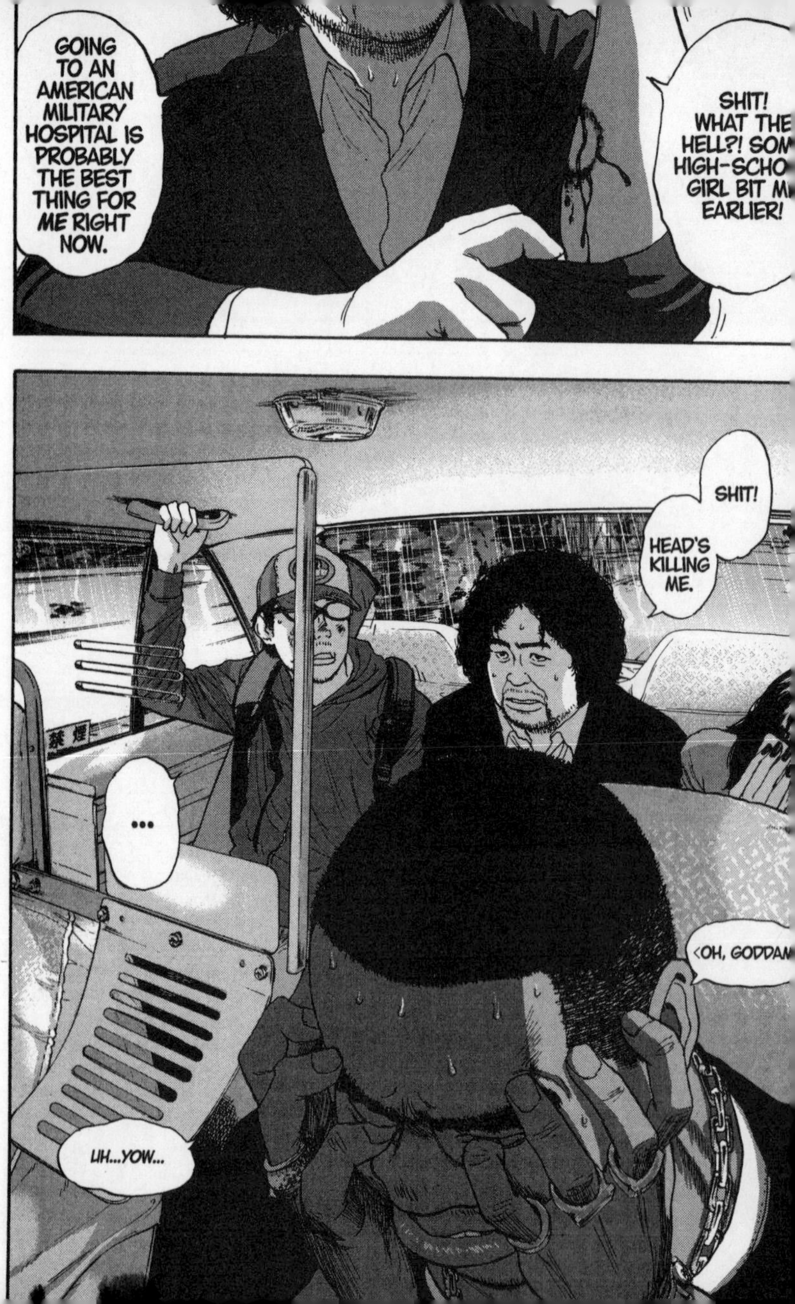
SHIT! WHAT THE HELL?! SOM HIGH-SCHO GIRL BIT M EARLIER!
GOING TO AN AMERICAN MILITARY HOSPITAL IS PROBABLY THE BEST THING FOR ME RIGHT NOW.
SHIT!
HEAD'S KILLING ME.
<OH, GODDAM
...
UH...YOW...

CHAPTER 25

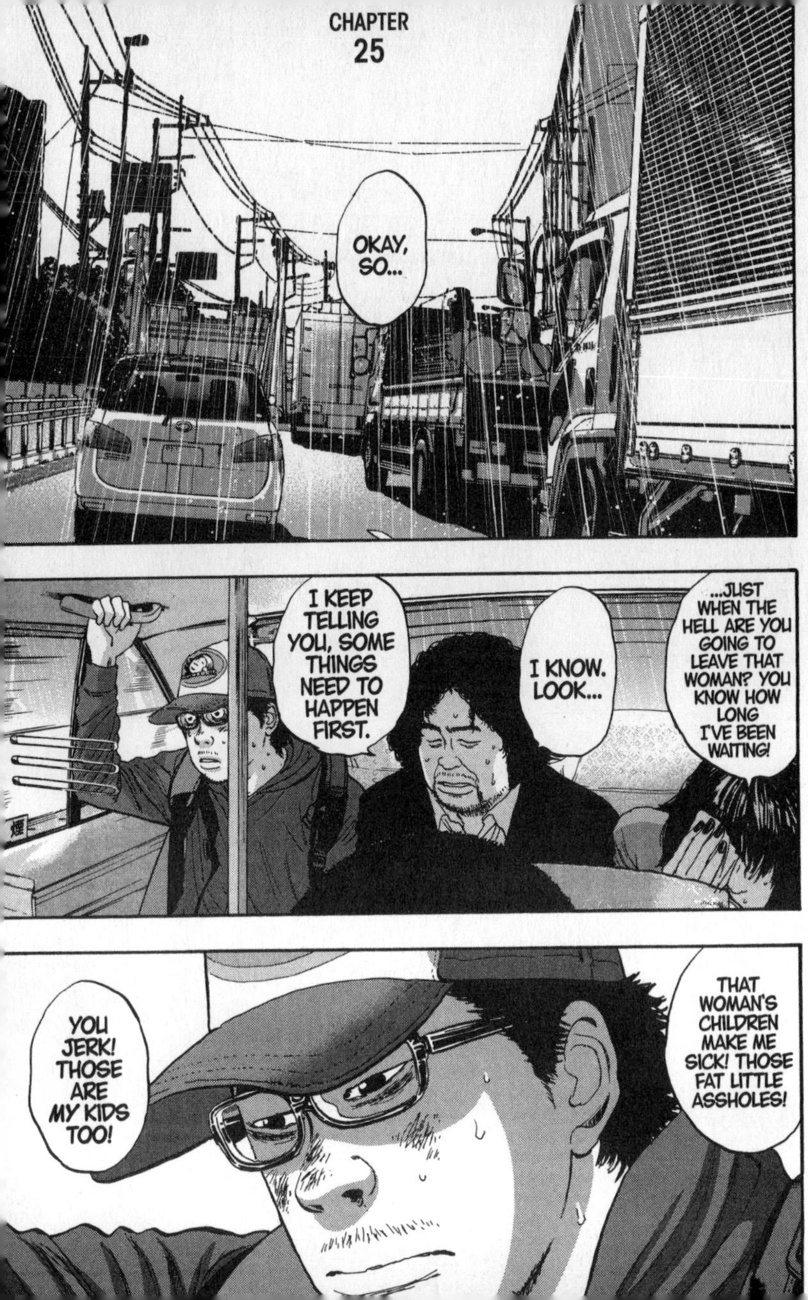
OKAY, SO...
...JUST WHEN THE HELL ARE YOU GOING TO LEAVE THAT WOMAN? YOU KNOW HOW LONG I'VE BEEN WAITING!
I KNOW. LOOK...
I KEEP TELLING YOU, SOME THINGS NEED TO HAPPEN FIRST.
THAT WOMAN'S CHILDREN MAKE ME SICK! THOSE FAT LITTLE ASSHOLES!
YOU JERK! THOSE ARE MY KIDS TOO!

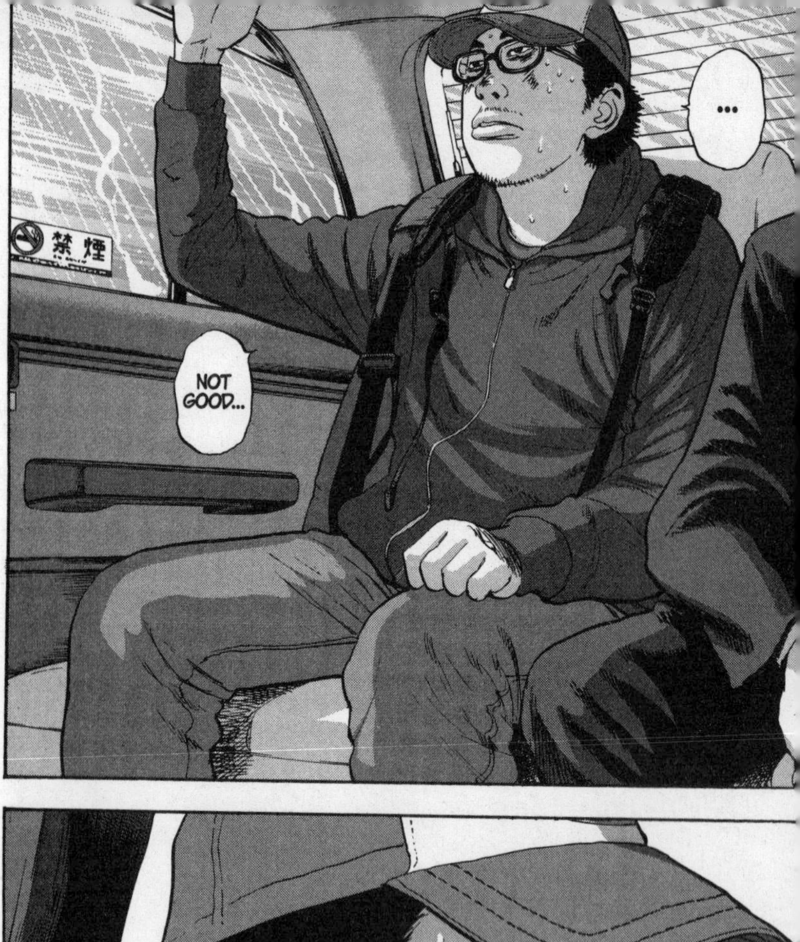
...
禁煙
NOT GOOD...
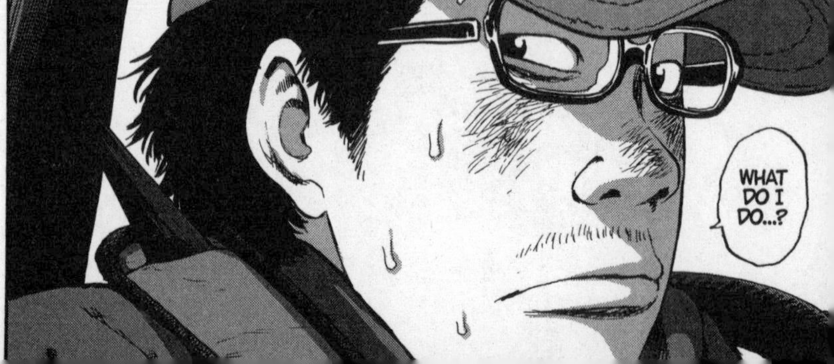
WHAT DO I DO...?

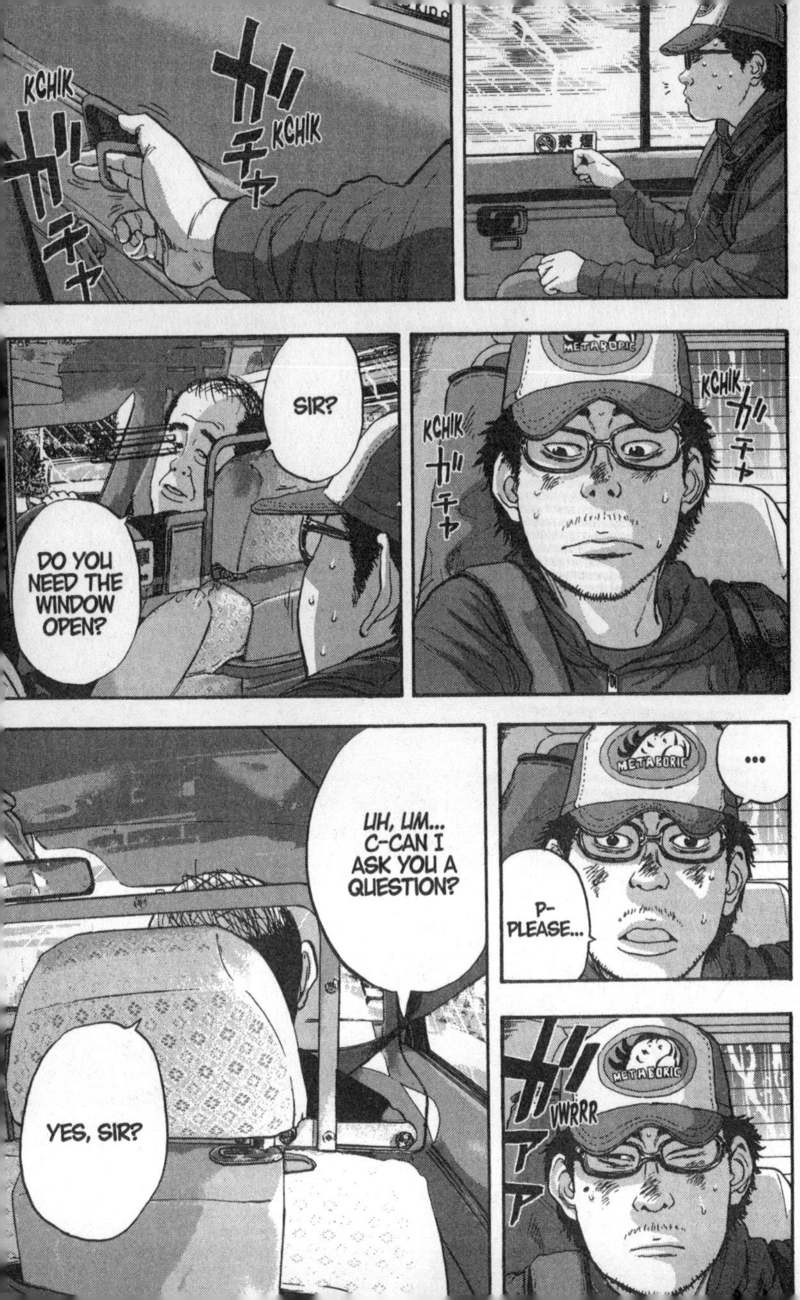
禁煙
KCHIK
KCHIK
ガチャ
ガチャ
KCHIK
ガチャ
KCHIK
ガチャ
SIR?
DO YOU NEED THE WINDOW OPEN?
...
P-PLEASE...
VWRRR
ガァ
UH, UM... C-CAN I ASK YOU A QUESTION?
YES, SIR?

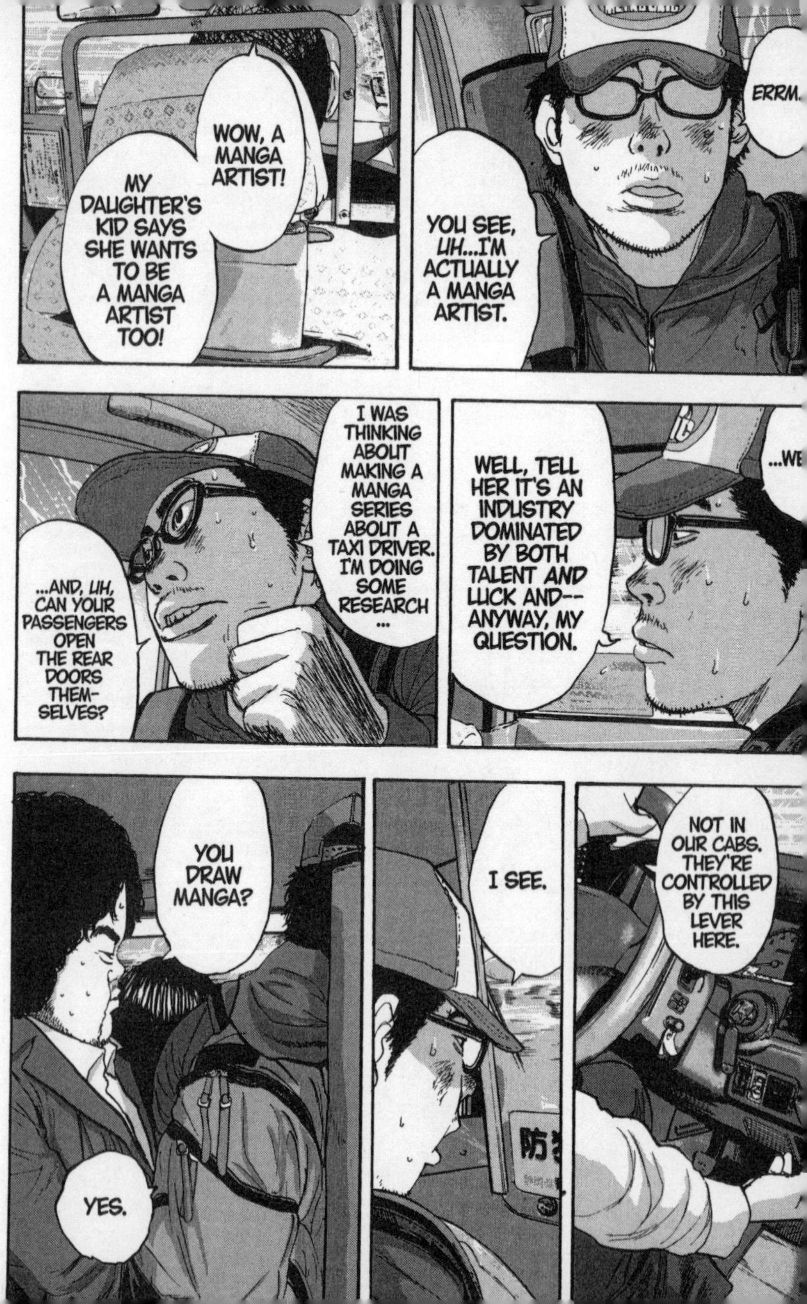
ERRM.
YOU SEE, UH...I'M ACTUALLY A MANGA ARTIST.
WOW, A MANGA ARTIST!
MY DAUGHTER'S KID SAYS SHE WANTS TO BE A MANGA ARTIST TOO!
...WE
WELL, TELL HER IT'S AN INDUSTRY DOMINATED BY BOTH TALENT AND LUCK AND-- ANYWAY, MY QUESTION.
I WAS THINKING ABOUT MAKING A MANGA SERIES ABOUT A TAXI DRIVER. I'M DOING SOME RESEARCH ...
...AND, UH, CAN YOUR PASSENGERS OPEN THE REAR DOORS THEM-SELVES?
NOT IN OUR CABS. THEY'RE CONTROLLED BY THIS LEVER HERE.
I SEE.
YOU DRAW MANGA?
YES.

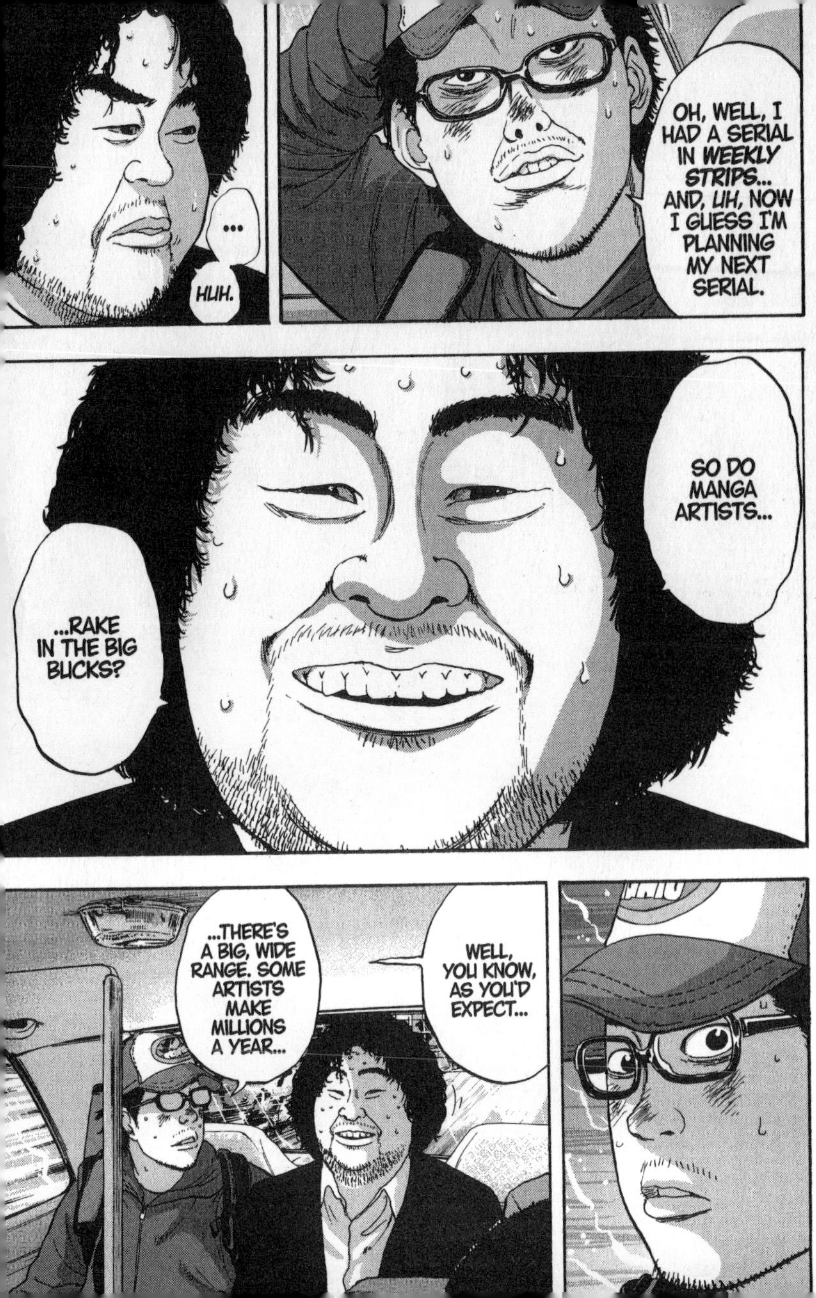
OH, WELL, I HAD A SERIAL IN *WEEKLY STRIPS*... AND, UH, NOW I GUESS I'M PLANNING MY NEXT SERIAL.
...
HUH.
SO DO MANGA ARTISTS...
...RAKE IN THE BIG BUCKS?
WELL, YOU KNOW, AS YOU'D EXPECT...
...THERE'S A BIG, WIDE RANGE. SOME ARTISTS MAKE MILLIONS A YEAR...

IT REALLY AMAZES ME. PEOPLE COMPLAIN ABOUT INEQUALITY IN THE WORK FORCE, AND THIS INDUSTRY'S SO BAD... AND HAS BEEN FOR AGES...

...AND OTHERS, LIKE ME, ARE DROWNING IN DEBT.

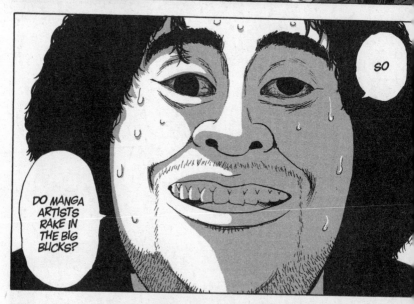

SO

DO MANGA ARTISTS RAKE IN THE BIG BUCKS?

•••

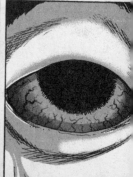

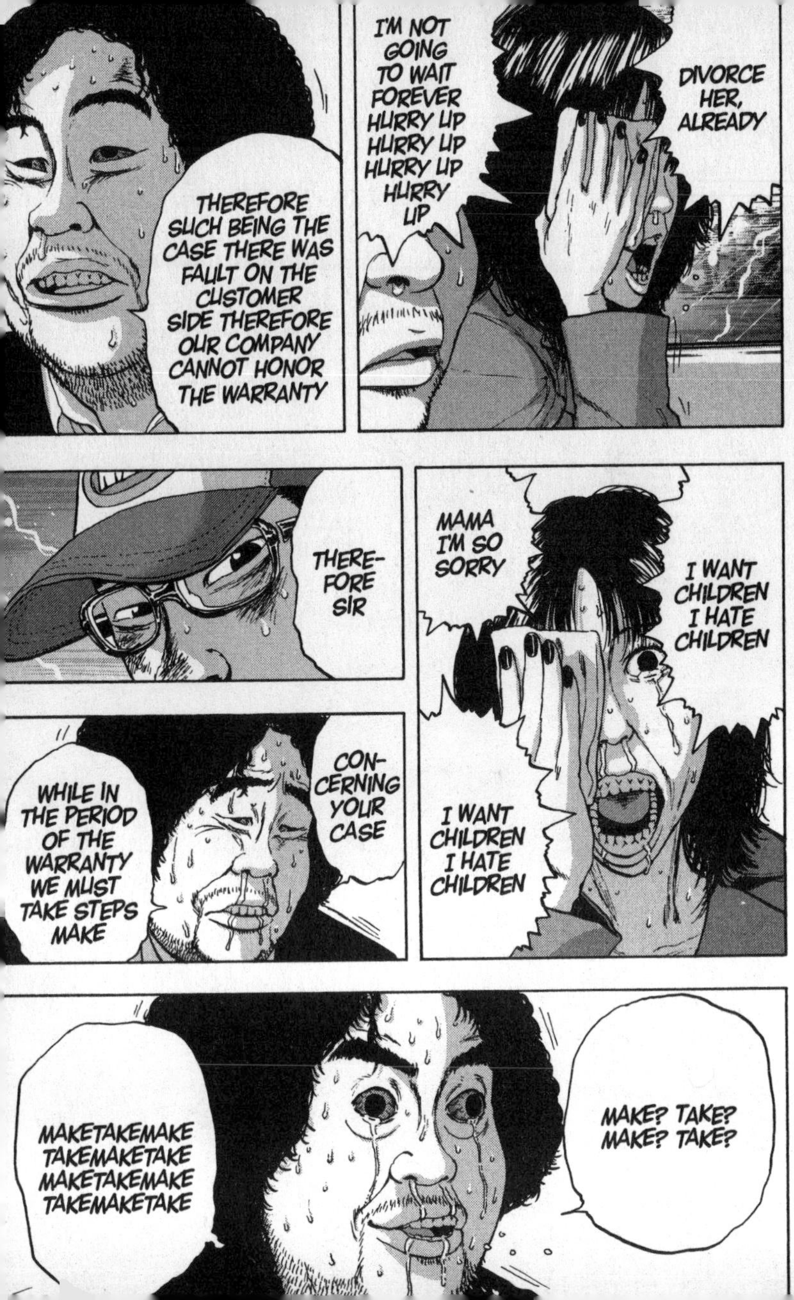
DIVORCE HER, ALREADY
I'M NOT GOING TO WAIT FOREVER HURRY UP HURRY UP HURRY UP HURRY UP
THEREFORE SUCH BEING THE CASE THERE WAS FAULT ON THE CUSTOMER SIDE THEREFORE OUR COMPANY CANNOT HONOR THE WARRANTY
MAMA I'M SO SORRY
I WANT CHILDREN I HATE CHILDREN
I WANT CHILDREN I HATE CHILDREN
THERE-FORE SIR
CON-CERNING YOUR CASE
WHILE IN THE PERIOD OF THE WARRANTY WE MUST TAKE STEPS MAKE
MAKE? TAKE? MAKE? TAKE?
MAKETAKEMAKE TAKEMAKETAKE MAKETAKEMAKE TAKEMAKETAKE

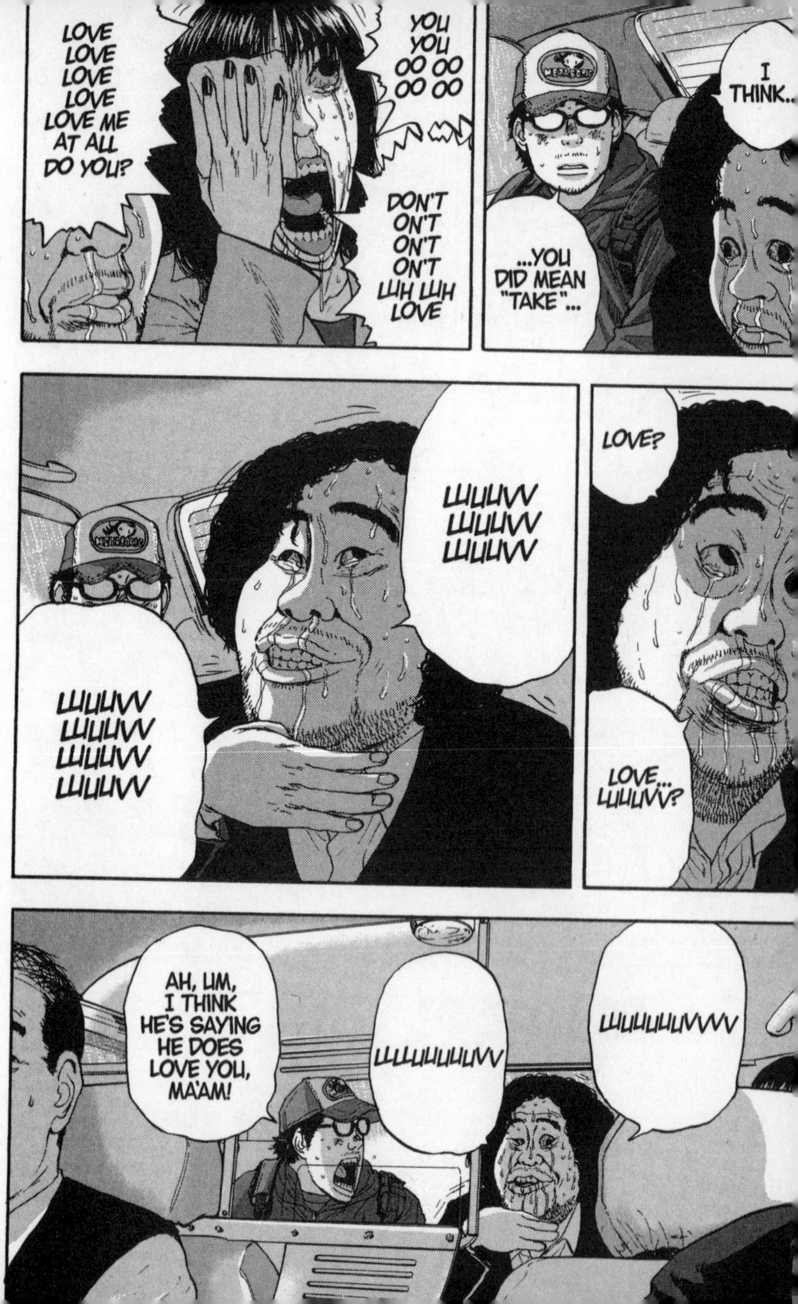

I THINK...
...YOU DID MEAN "TAKE"...
YOU YOU OO OO OO OO
LOVE LOVE LOVE LOVE LOVE ME AT ALL DO YOU?
DON'T ON'T ON'T ON'T LUH LUH LOVE
LOVE?
LOVE... LUUUVV?
LUUUVV LUUUVV LUUUVV
LUUUVV LUUUVV LUUUVV LUUUVV
LUUUUUUVVVV
LLUUUUUUVV
AH, UM, I THINK HE'S SAYING HE DOES LOVE YOU, MA'AM!

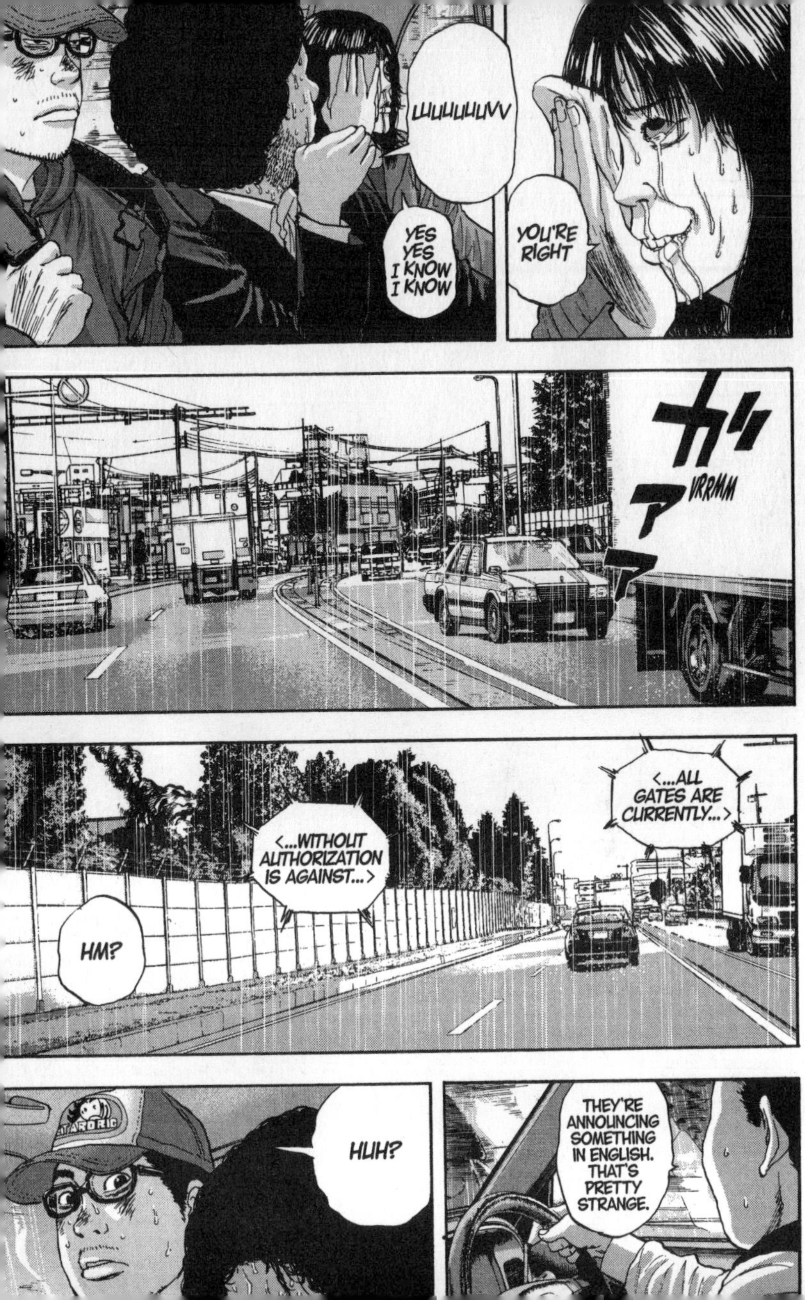
YOU'RE RIGHT
LUUUUUUVV
YES YES I KNOW I KNOW
カッ
VRRMM
ア
ア
<...ALL GATES ARE CURRENTLY...>
<...WITHOUT AUTHORIZATION IS AGAINST...>
HM?
THEY'RE ANNOUNCING SOMETHING IN ENGLISH. THAT'S PRETTY STRANGE.
HUH?

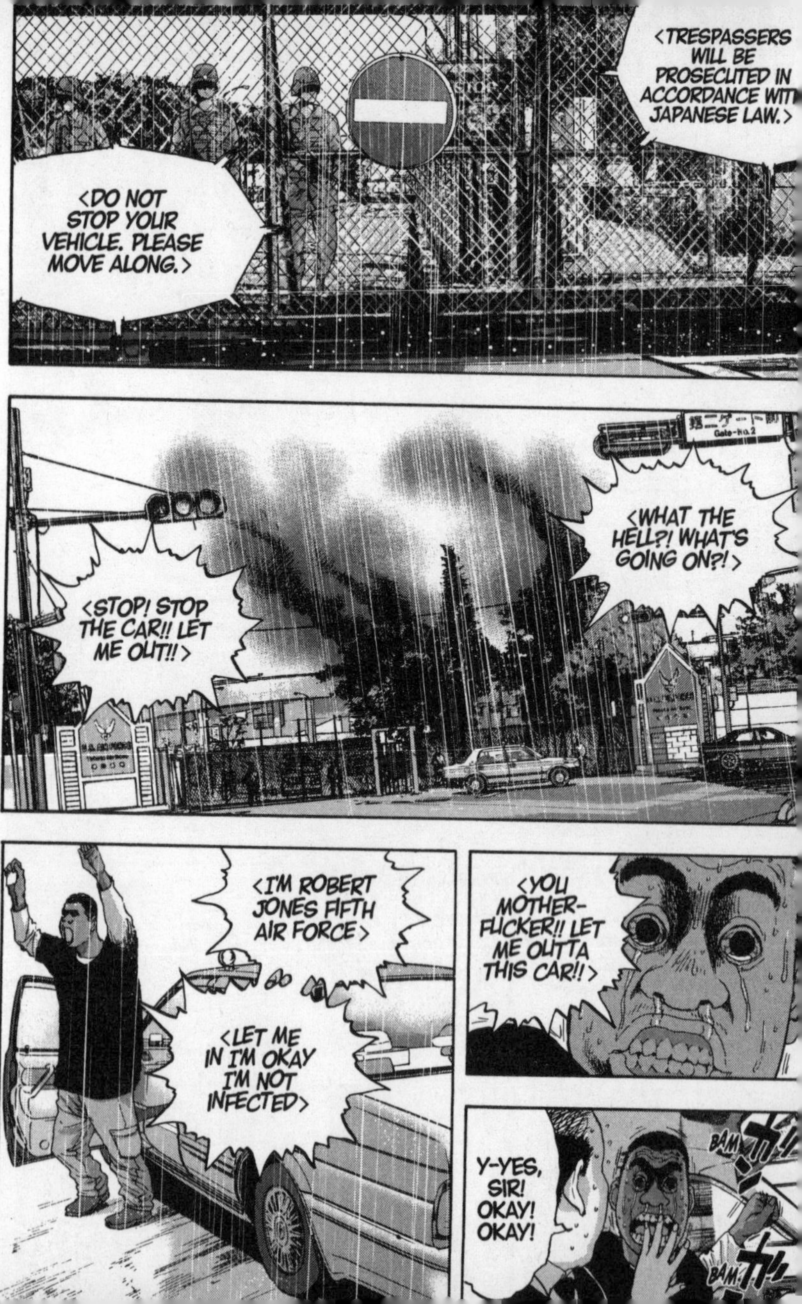
<TRESPASSERS WILL BE PROSECUTED IN ACCORDANCE WITH JAPANESE LAW.>
<DO NOT STOP YOUR VEHICLE. PLEASE MOVE ALONG.>
<WHAT THE HELL?! WHAT'S GOING ON?!>
<STOP! STOP THE CAR!! LET ME OUT!!>
<YOU MOTHER-FUCKER!! LET ME OUTTA THIS CAR!!>
BAM
Y-YES, SIR! OKAY! OKAY!
BAM
<I'M ROBERT JONES FIFTH AIR FORCE>
<LET ME IN I'M OKAY I'M NOT INFECTED>

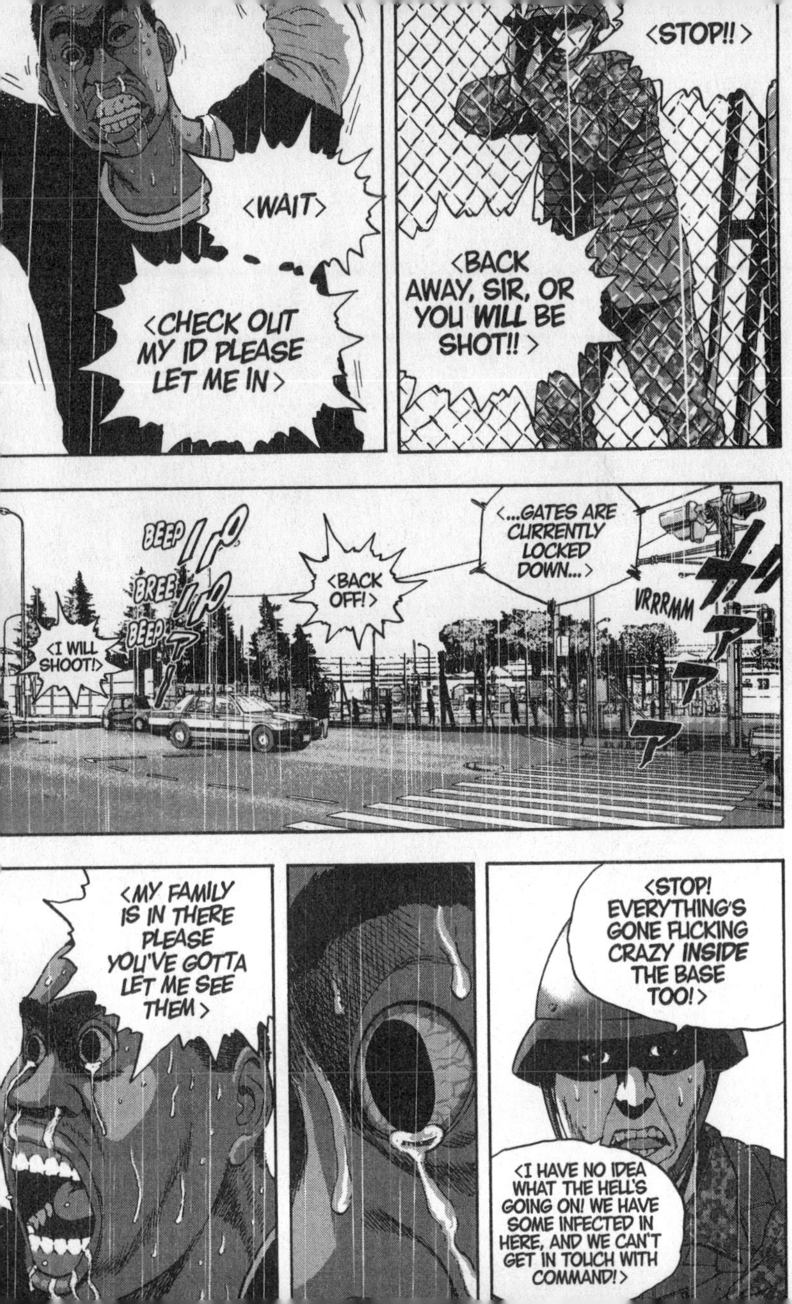
<STOP!!>
<BACK AWAY, SIR, OR YOU WILL BE SHOT!!>
<WAIT>
<CHECK OUT MY ID PLEASE LET ME IN>
<...GATES ARE CURRENTLY LOCKED DOWN...>
VRRRMM
<BACK OFF!>
BEEP
BREE
BEEP
<I WILL SHOOT!>
<STOP! EVERYTHING'S GONE FUCKING CRAZY INSIDE THE BASE TOO!>
<I HAVE NO IDEA WHAT THE HELL'S GOING ON! WE HAVE SOME INFECTED IN HERE, AND WE CAN'T GET IN TOUCH WITH COMMAND!>
<MY FAMILY IS IN THERE PLEASE YOU'VE GOTTA LET ME SEE THEM>

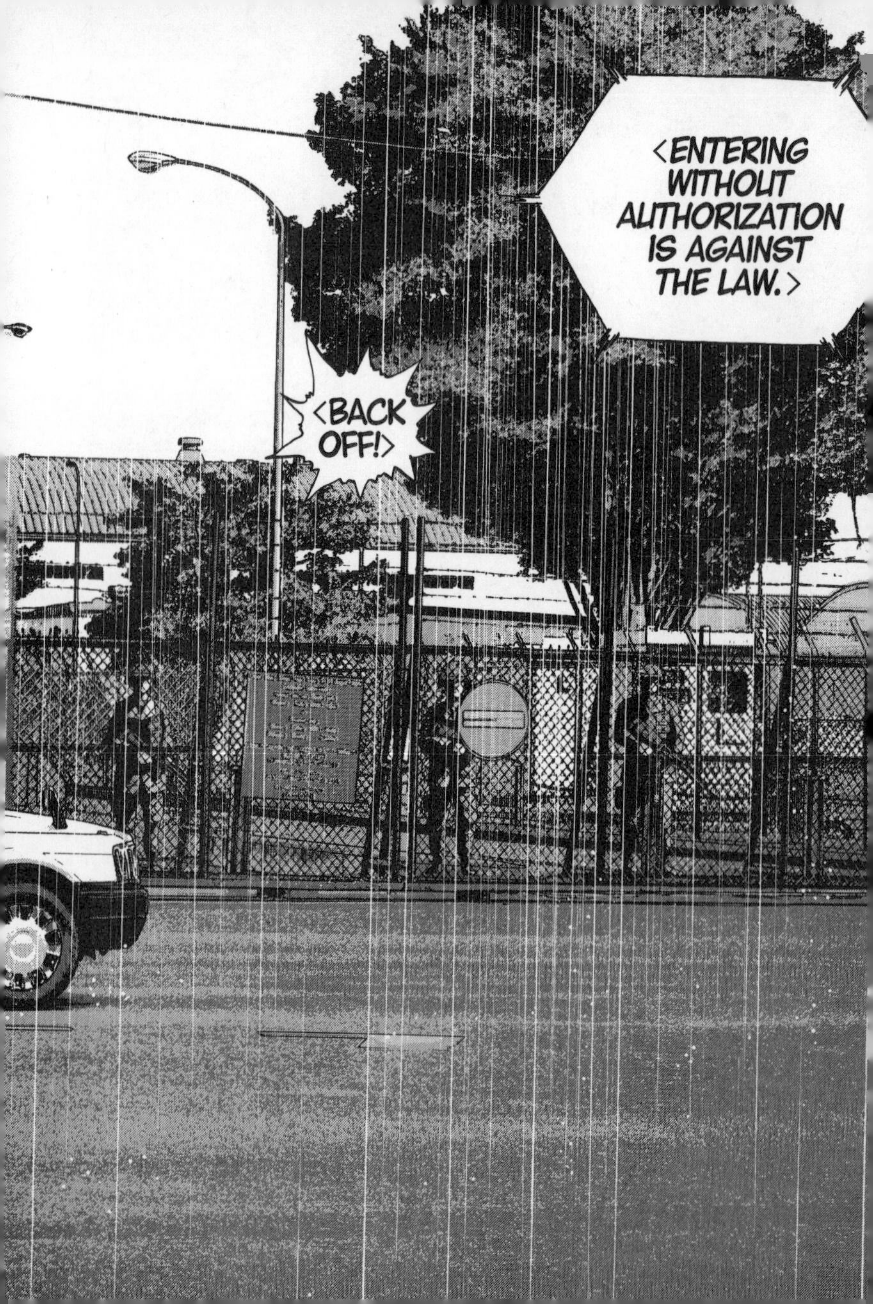
<ENTERING WITHOUT AUTHORIZATION IS AGAINST THE LAW.>
<BACK OFF!>

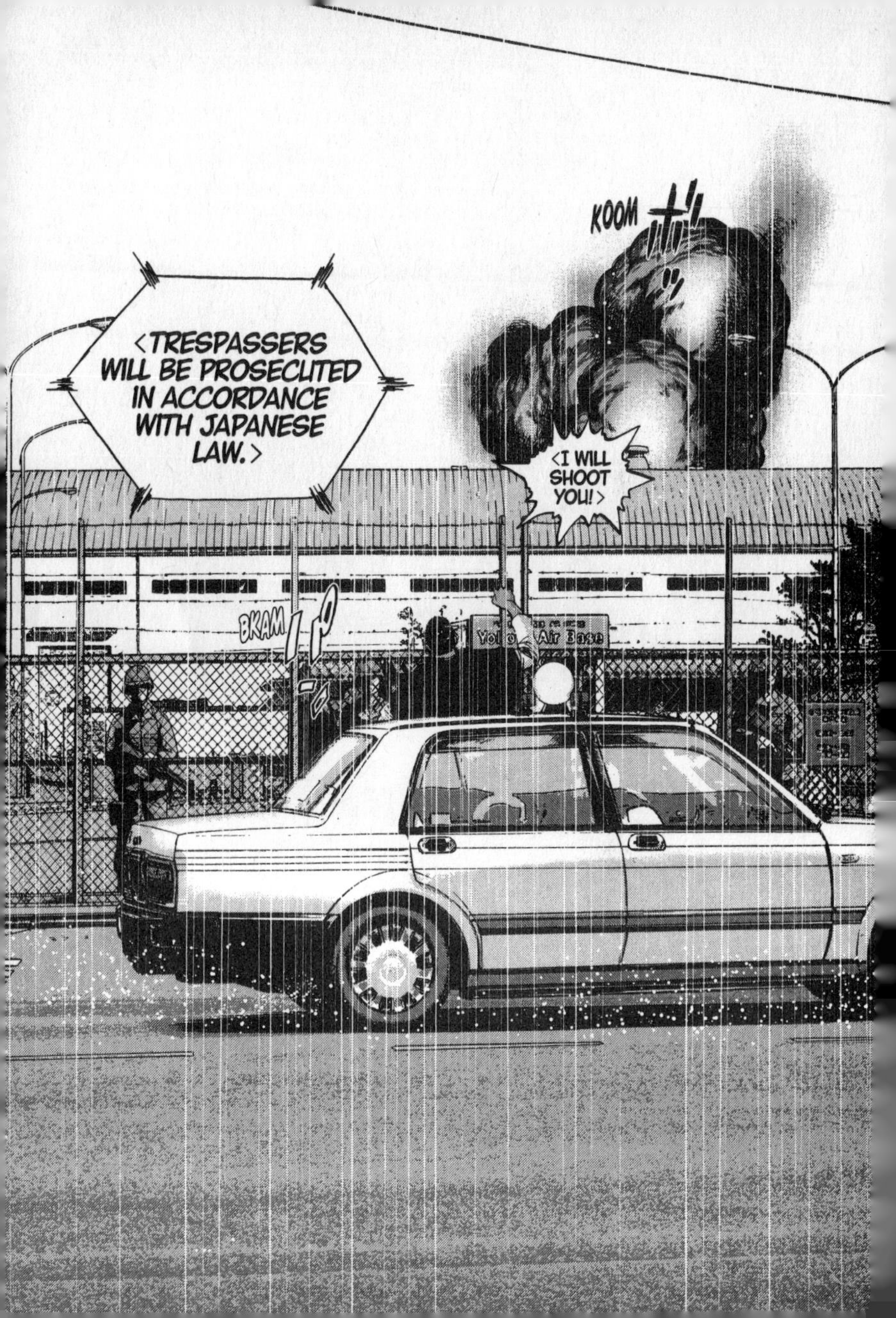
KOOM
<TRESPASSERS WILL BE PROSECUTED IN ACCORDANCE WITH JAPANESE LAW.>
<I WILL SHOOT YOU!>
BKAM

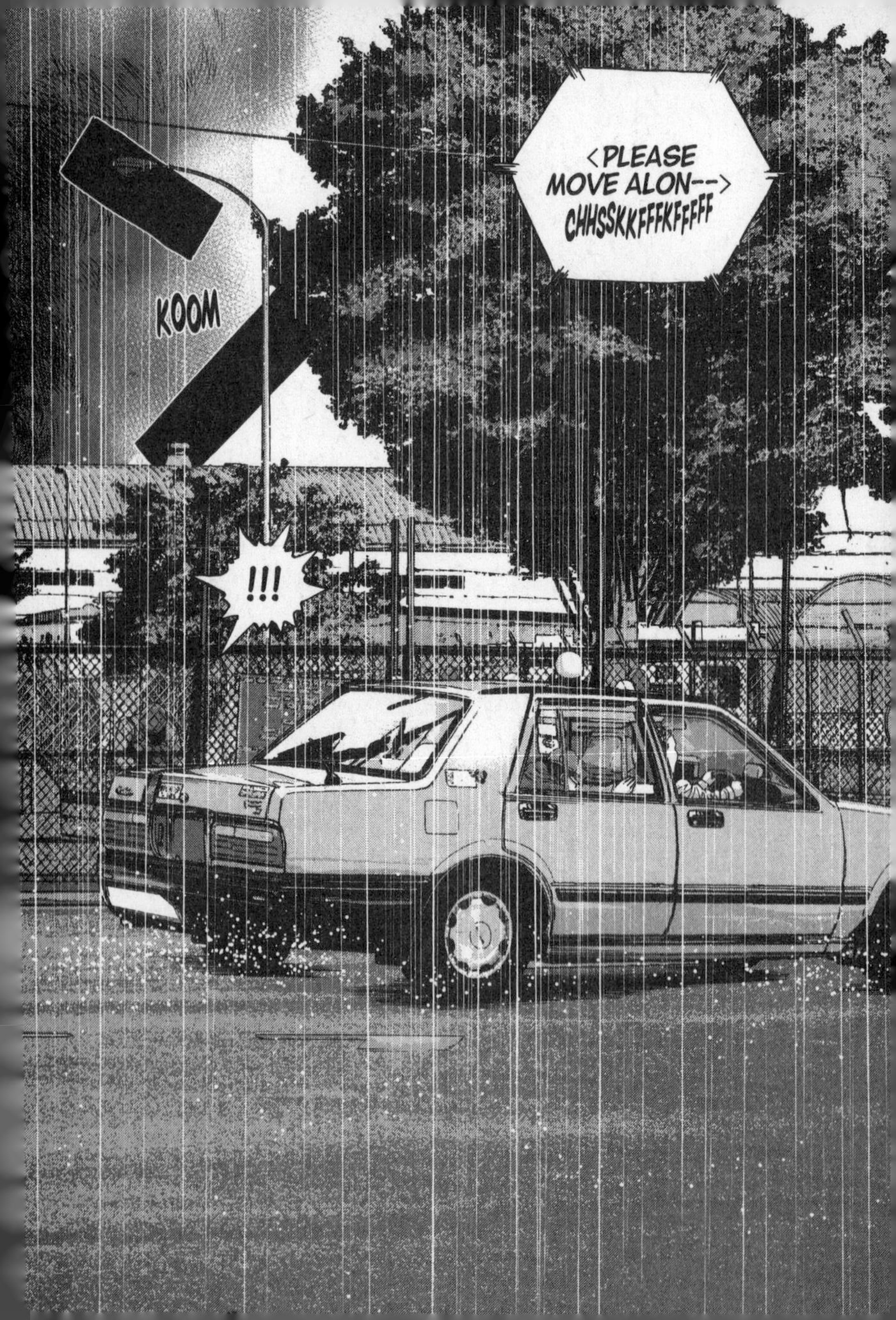
<PLEASE MOVE ALON--> CHHSSKKFFFKFFFFF
KOOM
!!!

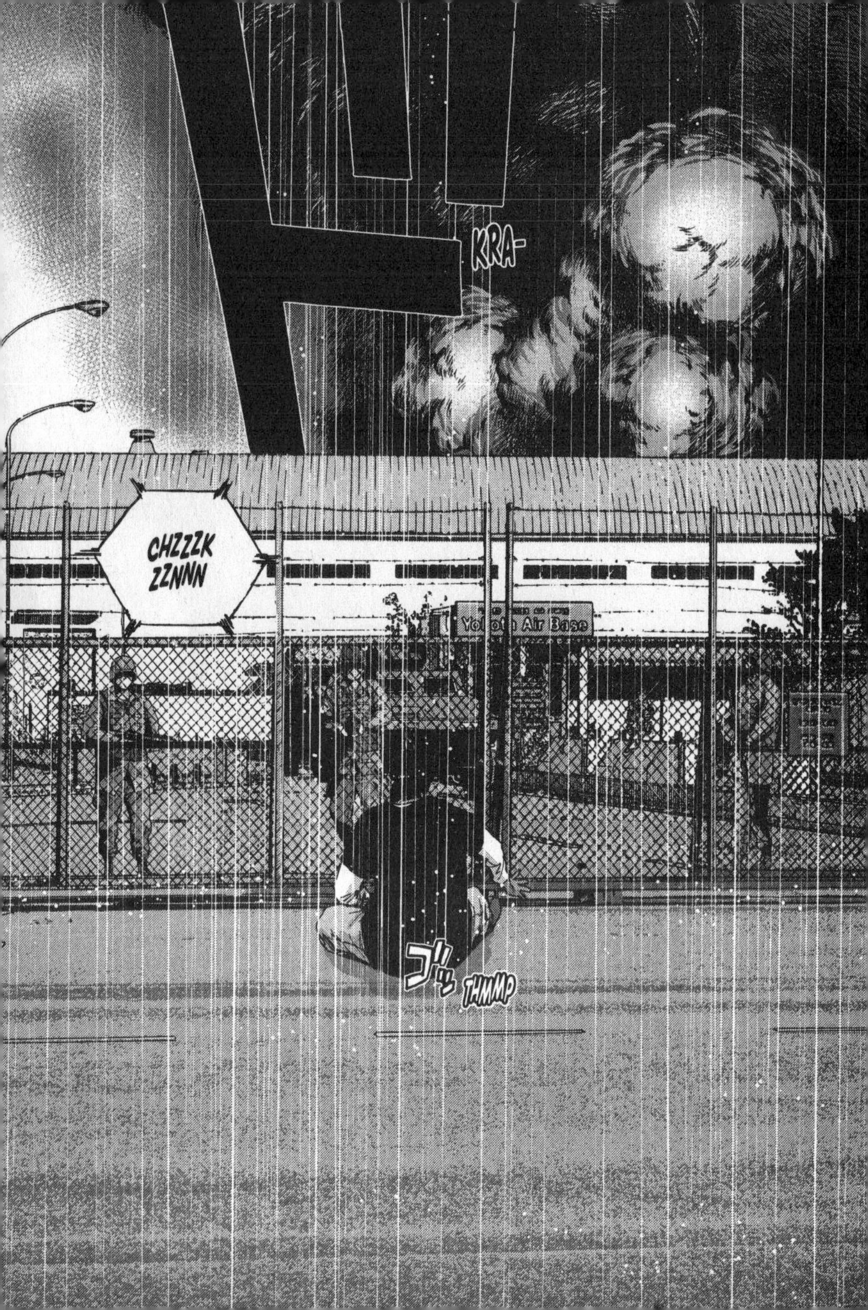
KRA-
CHZZZK ZZNNN
ゴッ
THMMP

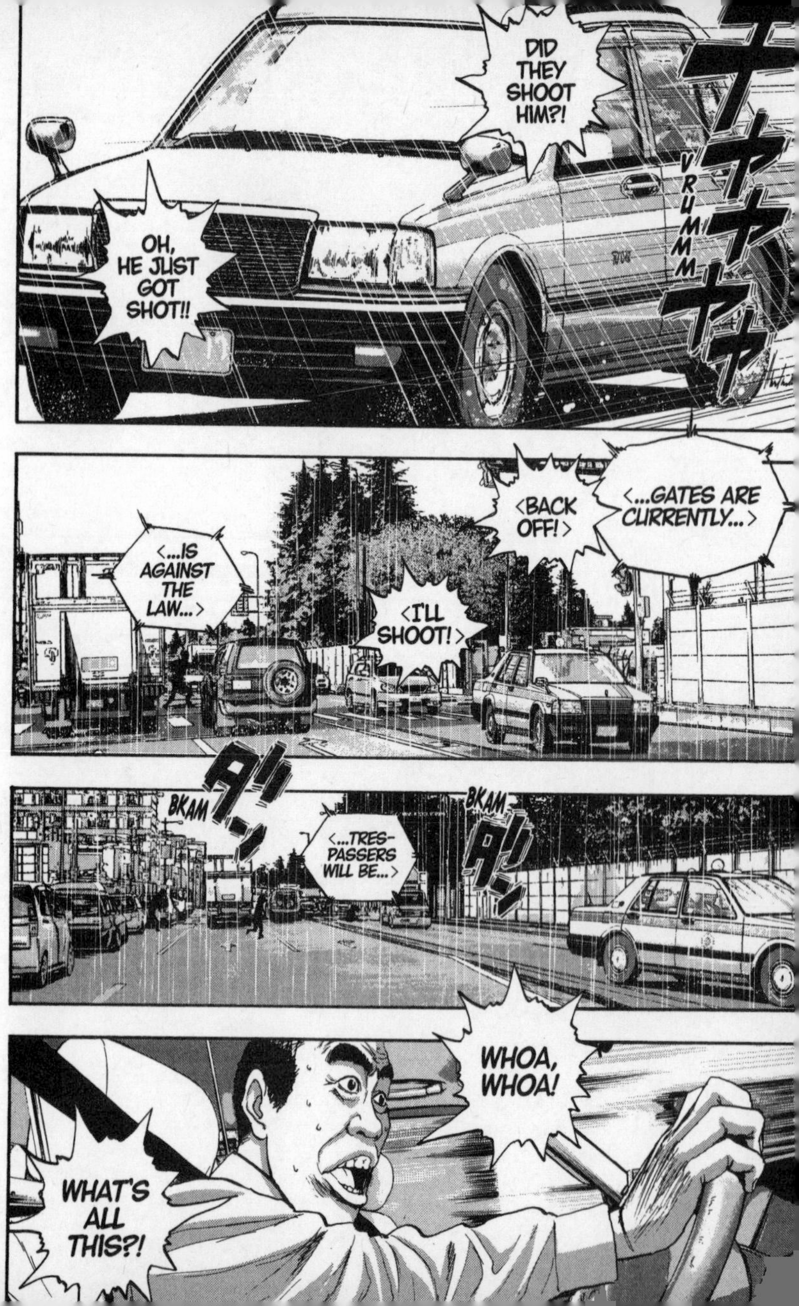
VRUMMM
DID THEY SHOOT HIM?!
OH, HE JUST GOT SHOT!!
<...GATES ARE CURRENTLY...>
<BACK OFF!>
<I'LL SHOOT!>
<...IS AGAINST THE LAW...>
BKAM
<...TRES-PASSERS WILL BE...>
BKAM
WHOA, WHOA!
WHAT'S ALL THIS?!

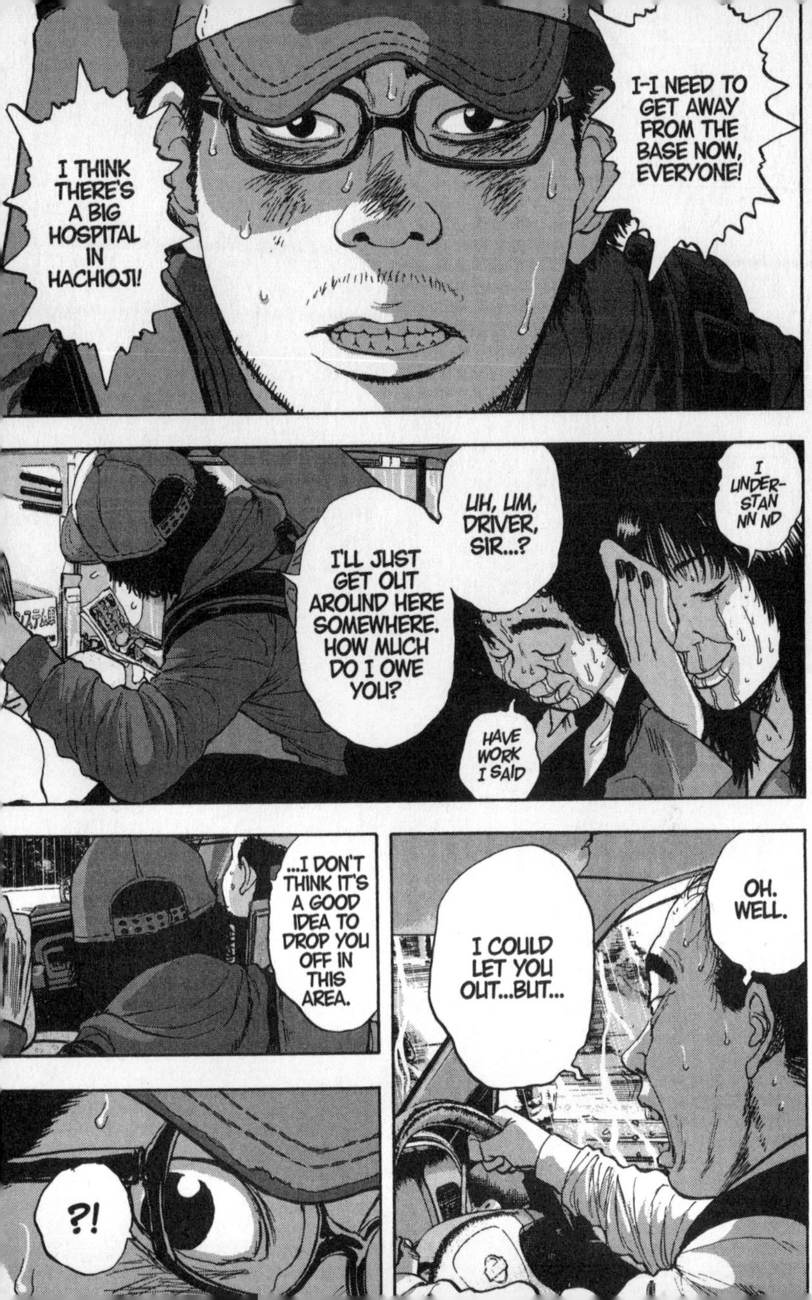
I-I NEED TO GET AWAY FROM THE BASE NOW, EVERYONE!
I THINK THERE'S A BIG HOSPITAL IN HACHIOJI!
I UNDER-STANN NN ND
HAVE WORK I SAID
UH, UM, DRIVER, SIR...?
I'LL JUST GET OUT AROUND HERE SOMEWHERE. HOW MUCH DO I OWE YOU?
OH. WELL.
I COULD LET YOU OUT...BUT...
...I DON'T THINK IT'S A GOOD IDEA TO DROP YOU OFF IN THIS AREA.
?!

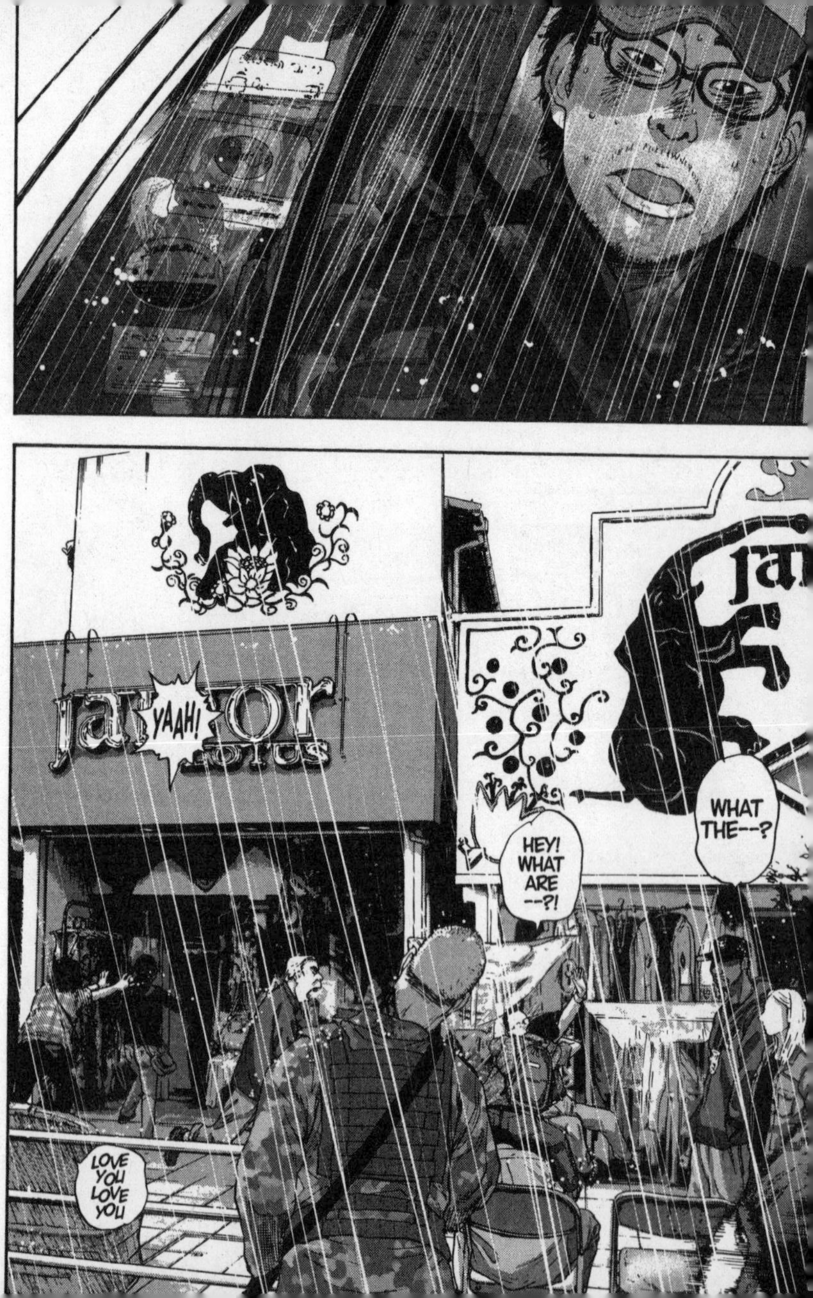
WHAT THE--?
HEY! WHAT ARE --?!
YAAH!
LOVE YOU LOVE YOU

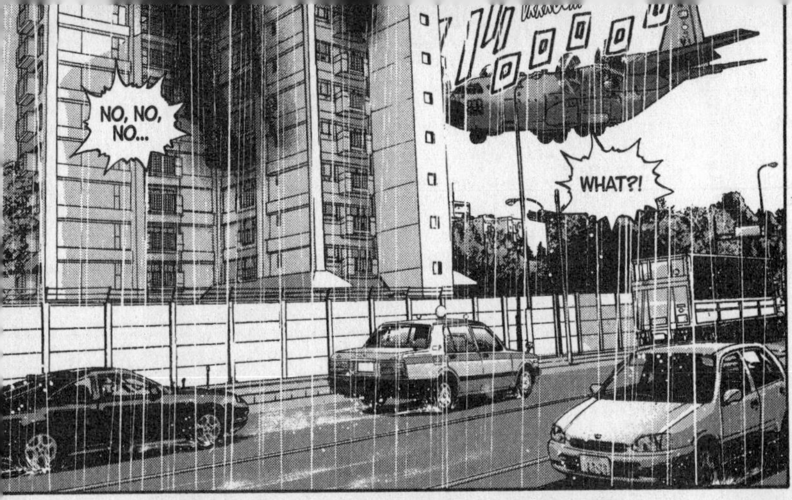
WHAT?!
NO, NO, NO...

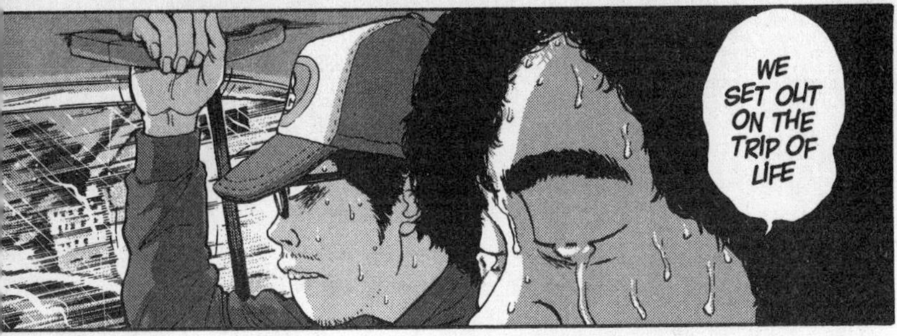
WE SET OUT ON THE TRIP OF LIFE

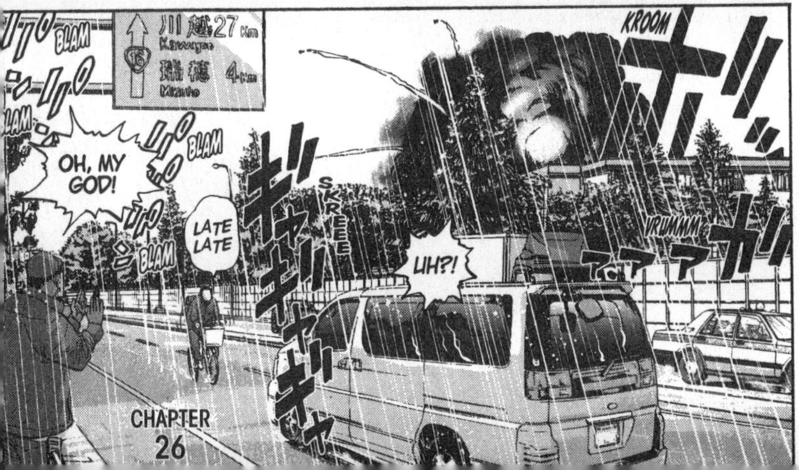
KROOM
VRUMMM
UH?!
SKREEE
LATE LATE
BLAM
OH, MY GOD!
BLAM
BLAM
BLAM
川越 27 Km
16
瑞穂 4 Km
CHAPTER 26

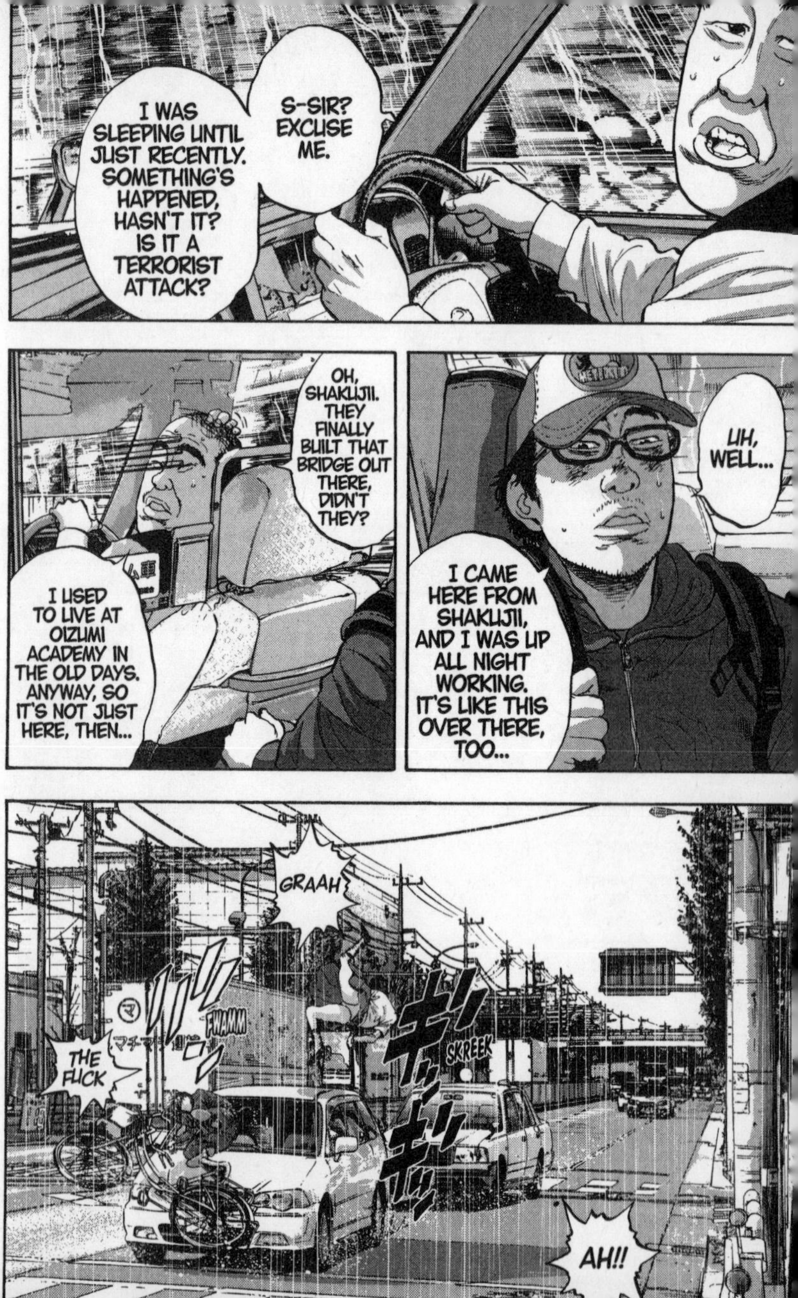
S-SIR? EXCUSE ME.
I WAS SLEEPING UNTIL JUST RECENTLY. SOMETHING'S HAPPENED, HASN'T IT? IS IT A TERRORIST ATTACK?
UH, WELL...
I CAME HERE FROM SHAKUJII, AND I WAS UP ALL NIGHT WORKING. IT'S LIKE THIS OVER THERE, TOO...
OH, SHAKUJII. THEY FINALLY BUILT THAT BRIDGE OUT THERE, DIDN'T THEY?
I USED TO LIVE AT OIZUMI ACADEMY IN THE OLD DAYS. ANYWAY, SO IT'S NOT JUST HERE, THEN...
GRAAH
SKREEK
FWAMM
THE FUCK
AH!!

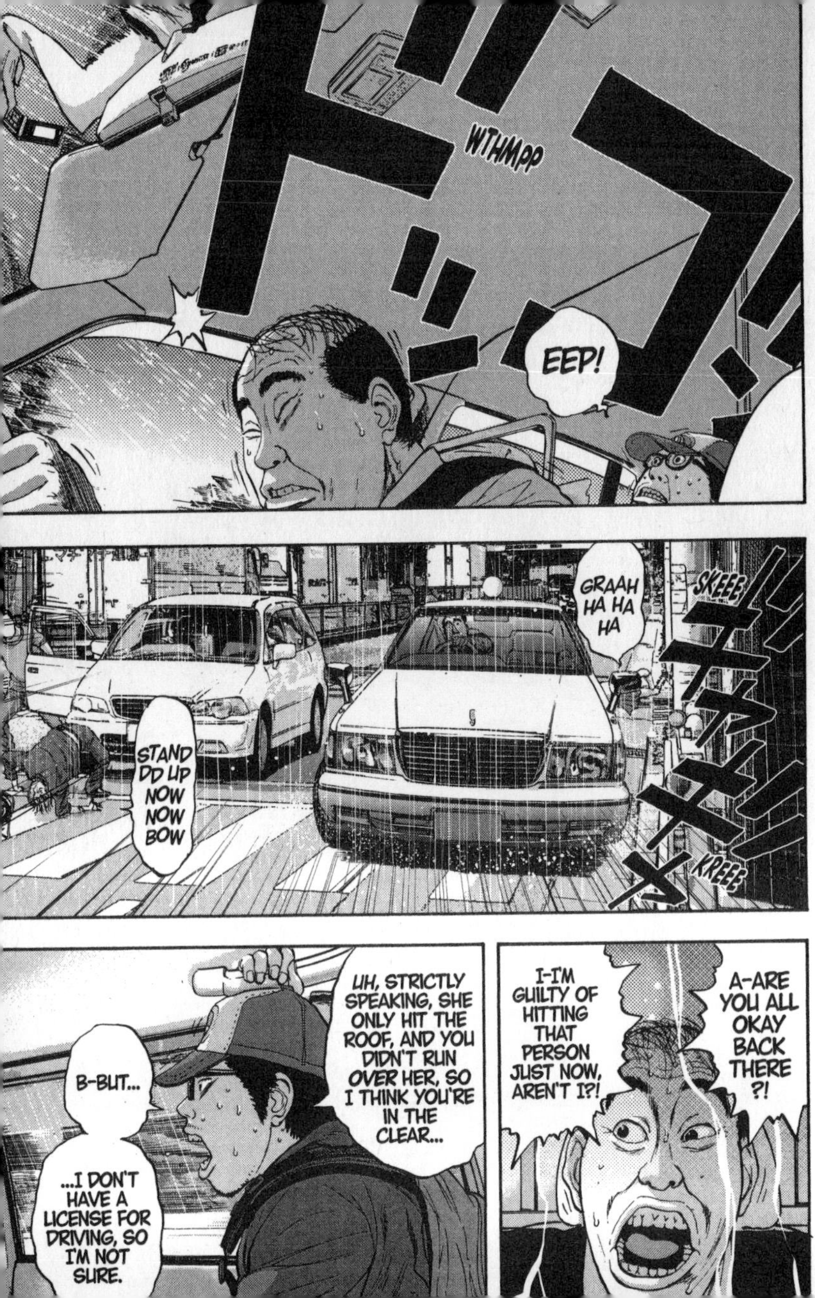
WTHMPP
EEP!
SKEEE
GRAAH HA HA HA
STAND DD UP NOW NOW BOW
KREEE
A-ARE YOU ALL OKAY BACK THERE?!
I-I'M GUILTY OF HITTING THAT PERSON JUST NOW, AREN'T I?!
UH, STRICTLY SPEAKING, SHE ONLY HIT THE ROOF, AND YOU DIDN'T RUN OVER HER, SO I THINK YOU'RE IN THE CLEAR...
B-BUT...
...I DON'T HAVE A LICENSE FOR DRIVING, SO I'M NOT SURE.

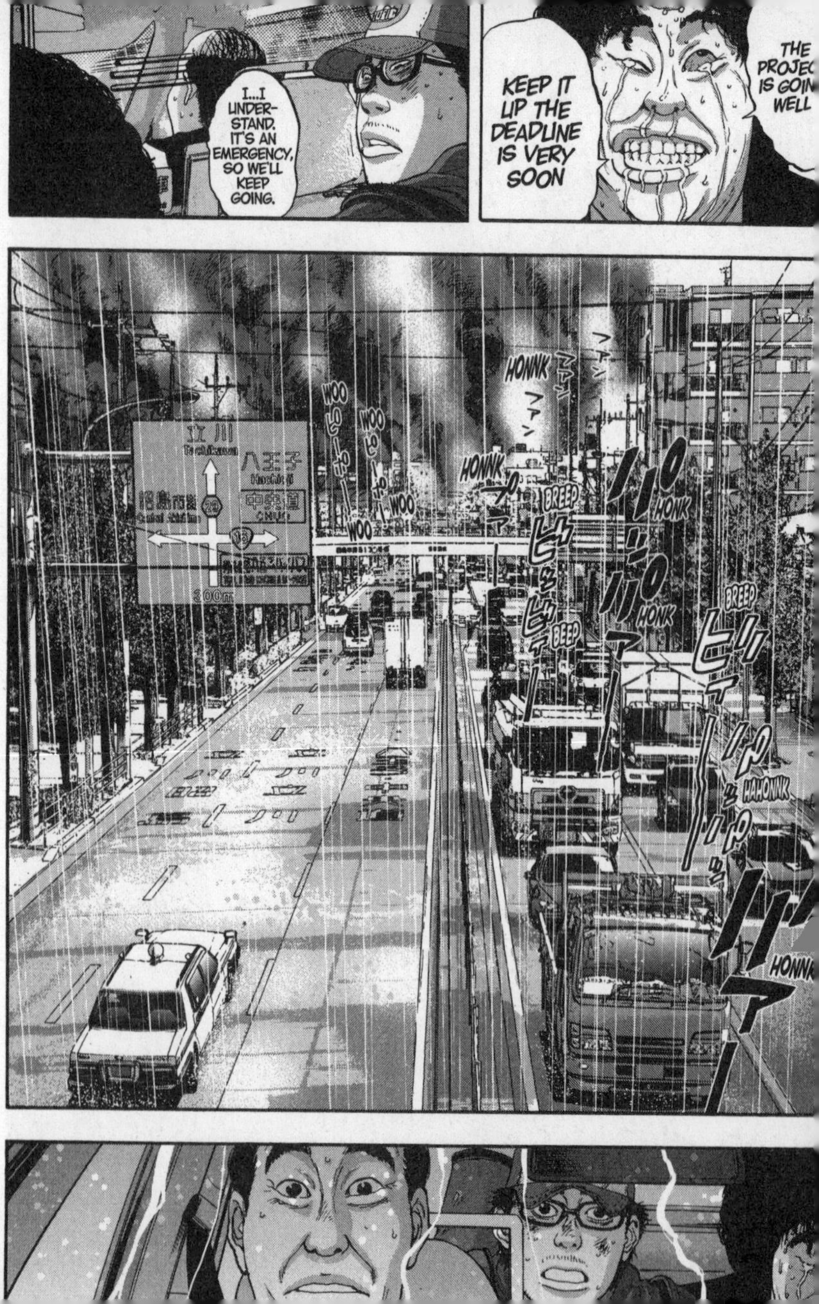
THE PROJEC IS GOIN WELL
KEEP IT UP THE DEADLINE IS VERY SOON
I...I UNDER-STAND. IT'S AN EMERGENCY, SO WE'LL KEEP GOING.
HONNK
ファン ファン
WOO
WOO
WOO
WOO
HONNK
BREEP
BEEP
HONK
HONK
BREEP
HAHONNK
HONNK
立川
八王子
中央道
300m

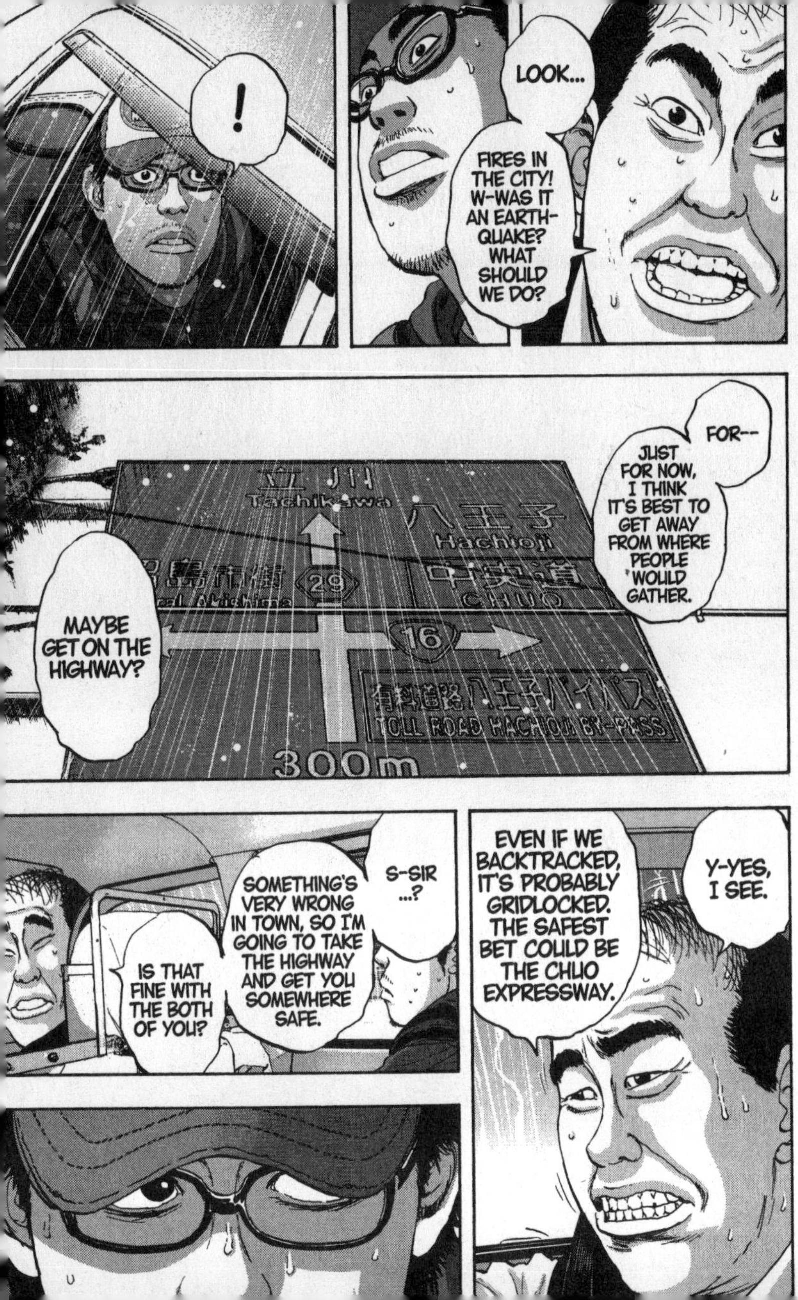
LOOK...
FIRES IN THE CITY! W-WAS IT AN EARTHQUAKE? WHAT SHOULD WE DO?
!
FOR--
JUST FOR NOW, I THINK IT'S BEST TO GET AWAY FROM WHERE PEOPLE WOULD GATHER.
立川
Tachikawa
八王子
Hachioji
中央道
CHUO
29
16
有料道路八王子バイパス
TOLL ROAD HACHIOJI BY-PASS
300m
MAYBE GET ON THE HIGHWAY?
Y-YES, I SEE.
EVEN IF WE BACKTRACKED, IT'S PROBABLY GRIDLOCKED. THE SAFEST BET COULD BE THE CHUO EXPRESSWAY.
S-SIR ...?
SOMETHING'S VERY WRONG IN TOWN, SO I'M GOING TO TAKE THE HIGHWAY AND GET YOU SOMEWHERE SAFE.
IS THAT FINE WITH THE BOTH OF YOU?

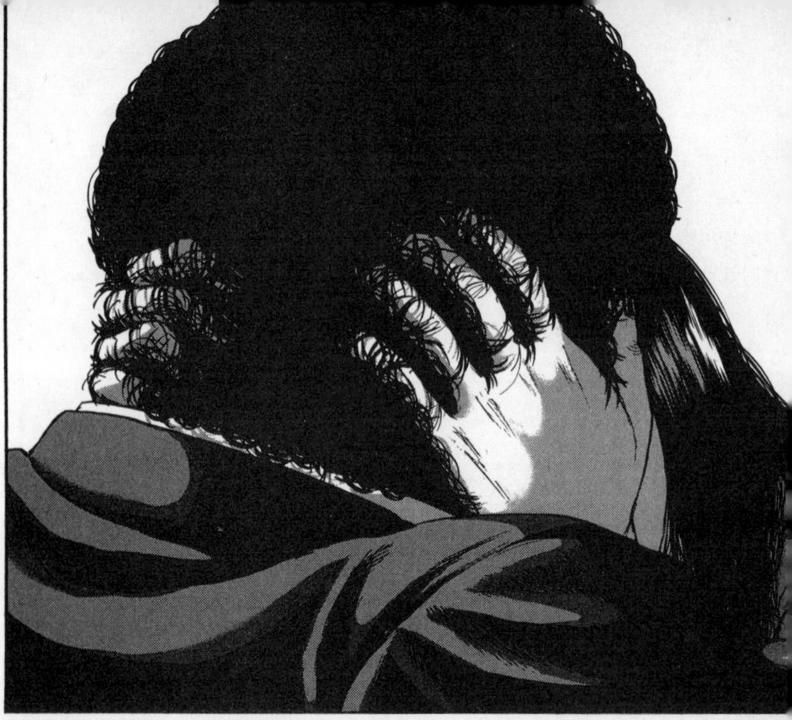

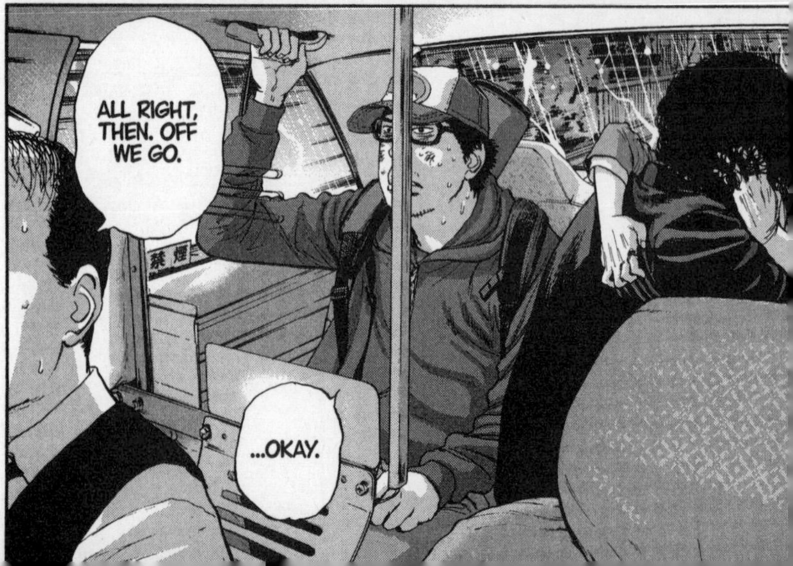
ALL RIGHT, THEN. OFF WE GO.
禁煙
...OKAY.

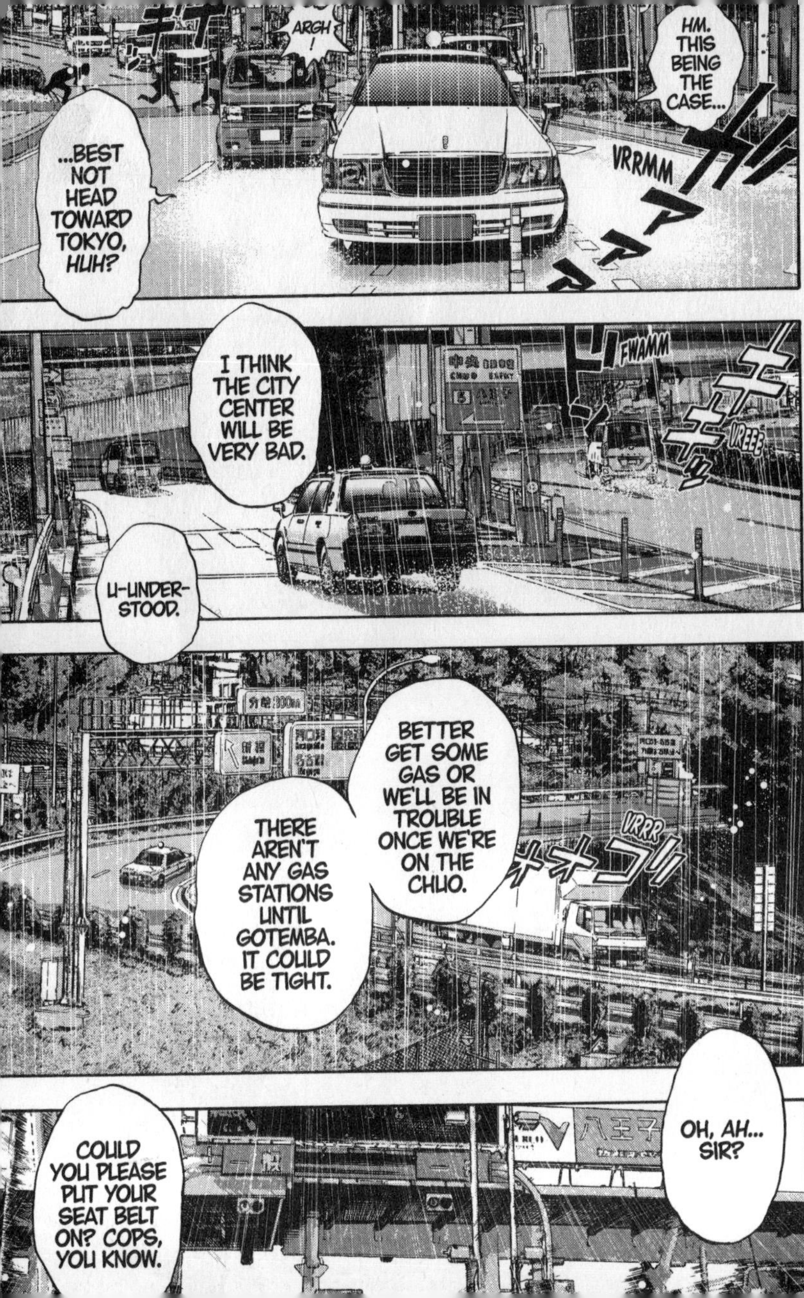
HM. THIS BEING THE CASE...
VRRMM
ARGH!
...BEST NOT HEAD TOWARD TOKYO, HUH?
FWAMM
VREEE
I THINK THE CITY CENTER WILL BE VERY BAD.
U-UNDERSTOOD.
BETTER GET SOME GAS OR WE'LL BE IN TROUBLE ONCE WE'RE ON THE CHUO.
VRRR
THERE AREN'T ANY GAS STATIONS UNTIL GOTEMBA. IT COULD BE TIGHT.
OH, AH... SIR?
COULD YOU PLEASE PUT YOUR SEAT BELT ON? COPS, YOU KNOW.

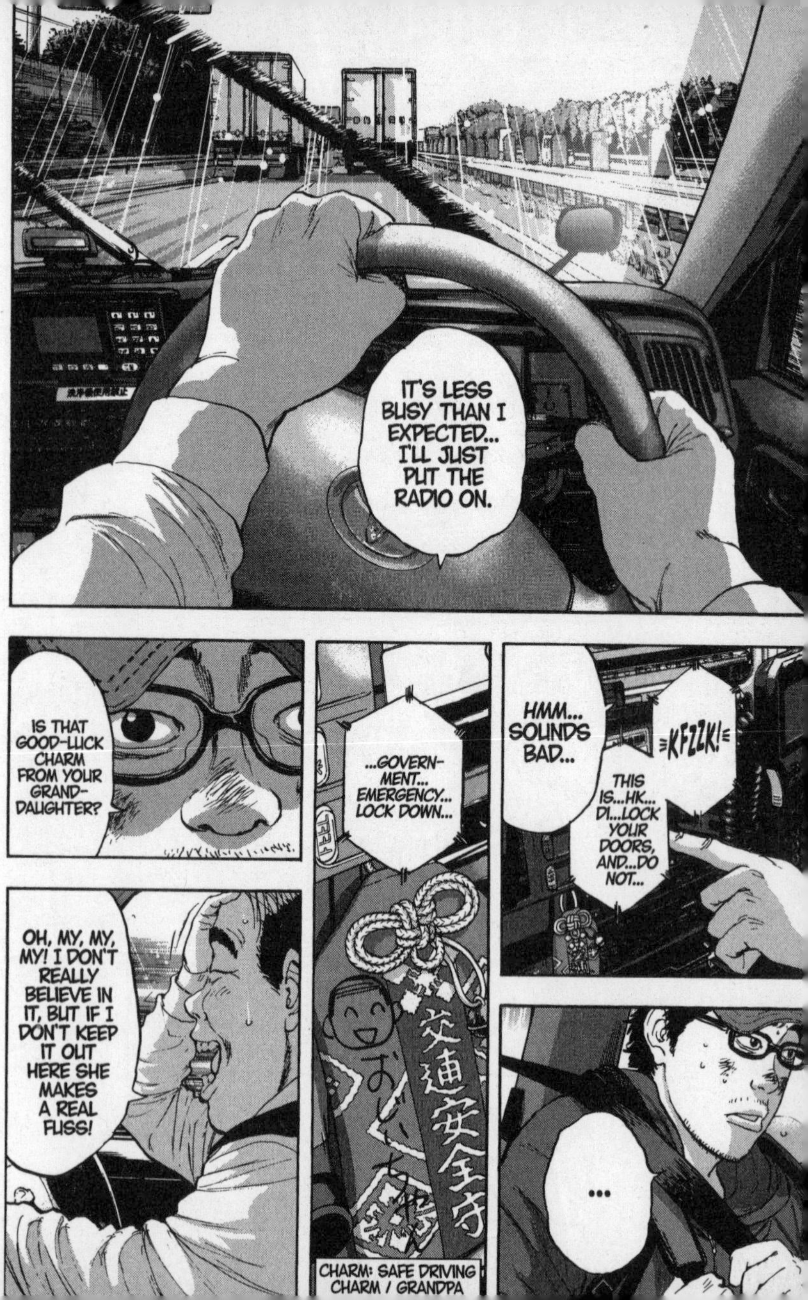
IT'S LESS BUSY THAN I EXPECTED... I'LL JUST PUT THE RADIO ON.
=KFZZK!=
HMM... SOUNDS BAD...
THIS IS...HK... DI...LOCK YOUR DOORS, AND...DO NOT...
...
...GOVERN-MENT... EMERGENCY... LOCK DOWN...
交通安全守
CHARM: SAFE DRIVING CHARM / GRANDPA
IS THAT GOOD-LUCK CHARM FROM YOUR GRAND-DAUGHTER?
OH, MY, MY, MY! I DON'T REALLY BELIEVE IN IT, BUT IF I DON'T KEEP IT OUT HERE SHE MAKES A REAL FUSS!

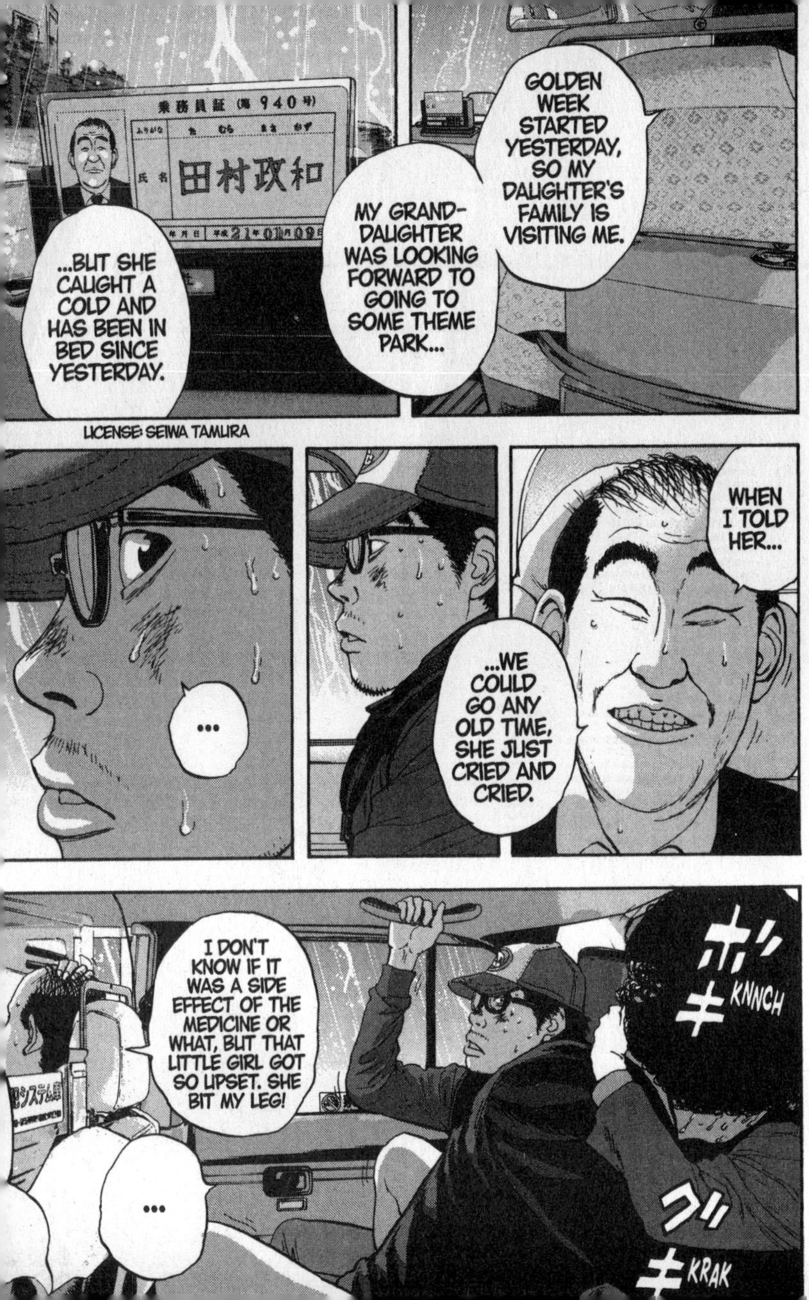
GOLDEN WEEK STARTED YESTERDAY, SO MY DAUGHTER'S FAMILY IS VISITING ME.
MY GRAND-DAUGHTER WAS LOOKING FORWARD TO GOING TO SOME THEME PARK...
乗務員証
氏名 田村政和
...BUT SHE CAUGHT A COLD AND HAS BEEN IN BED SINCE YESTERDAY.
LICENSE: SEIWA TAMURA
WHEN I TOLD HER...
...WE COULD GO ANY OLD TIME, SHE JUST CRIED AND CRIED.
...
ボキ KNNCH
ゴキ KRAK
I DON'T KNOW IF IT WAS A SIDE EFFECT OF THE MEDICINE OR WHAT, BUT THAT LITTLE GIRL GOT SO UPSET. SHE BIT MY LEG!
...

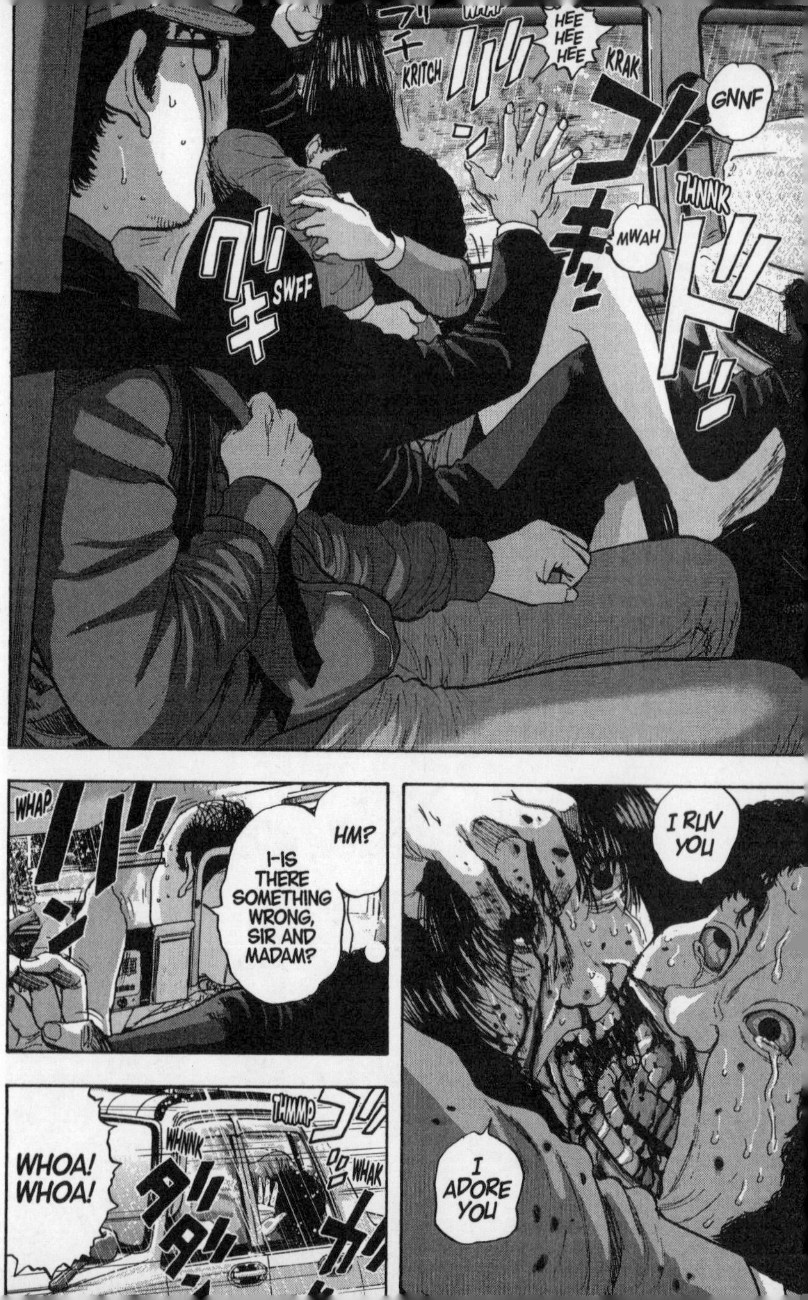
GNNF
KRAK
HEE HEE HEE
KRITCH
THNNK
MWAH
SWFF
I RUV YOU
I ADORE YOU
HM?
I-IS THERE SOMETHING WRONG, SIR AND MADAM?
WHAP
THMMP
WHAK
WHNNK
WHOA! WHOA!

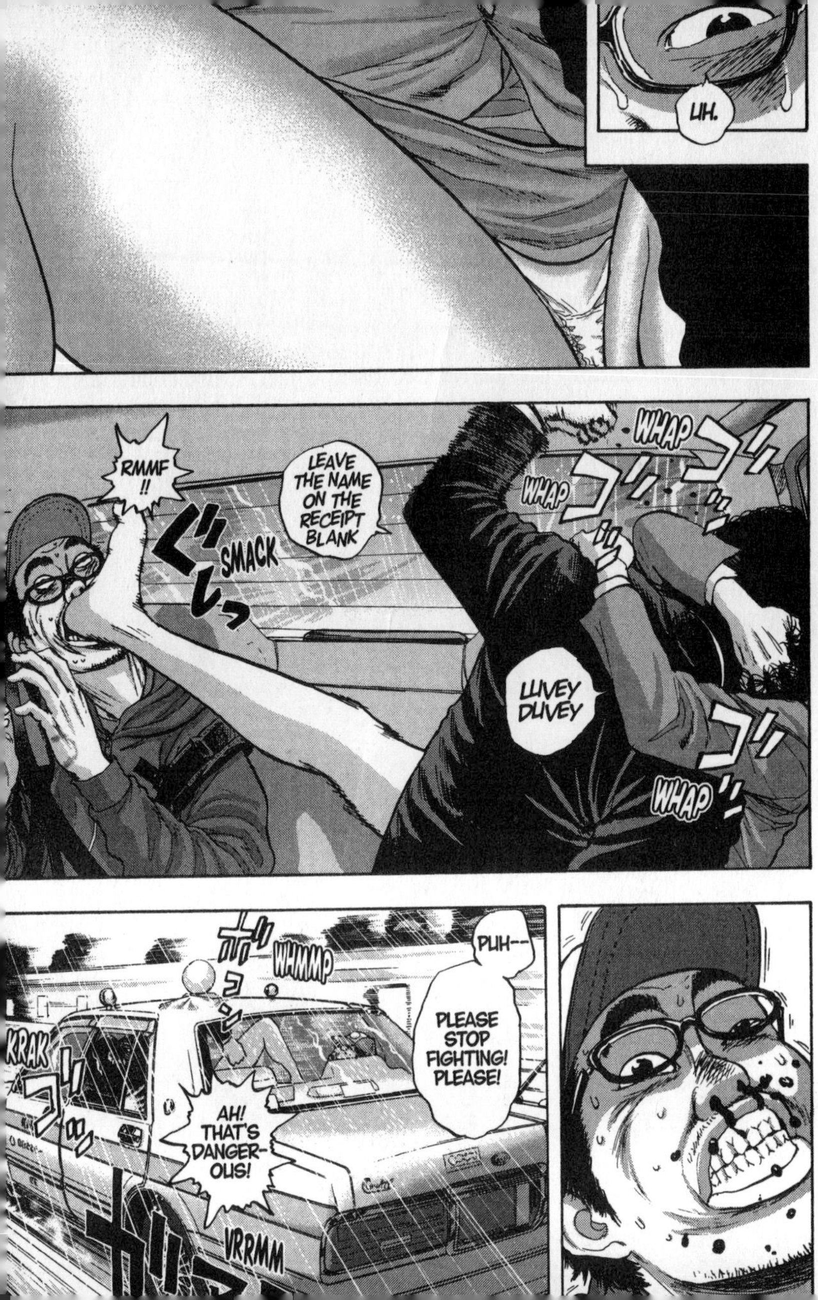
UH.
WHAP
WHAP
LEAVE THE NAME ON THE RECEIPT BLANK
RMMF !!
SMACK
LUVEY DUVEY
WHAP
PUH--
PLEASE STOP FIGHTING! PLEASE!
WHMMP
AH! THAT'S DANGER-OUS!
KRAK
VRRMM

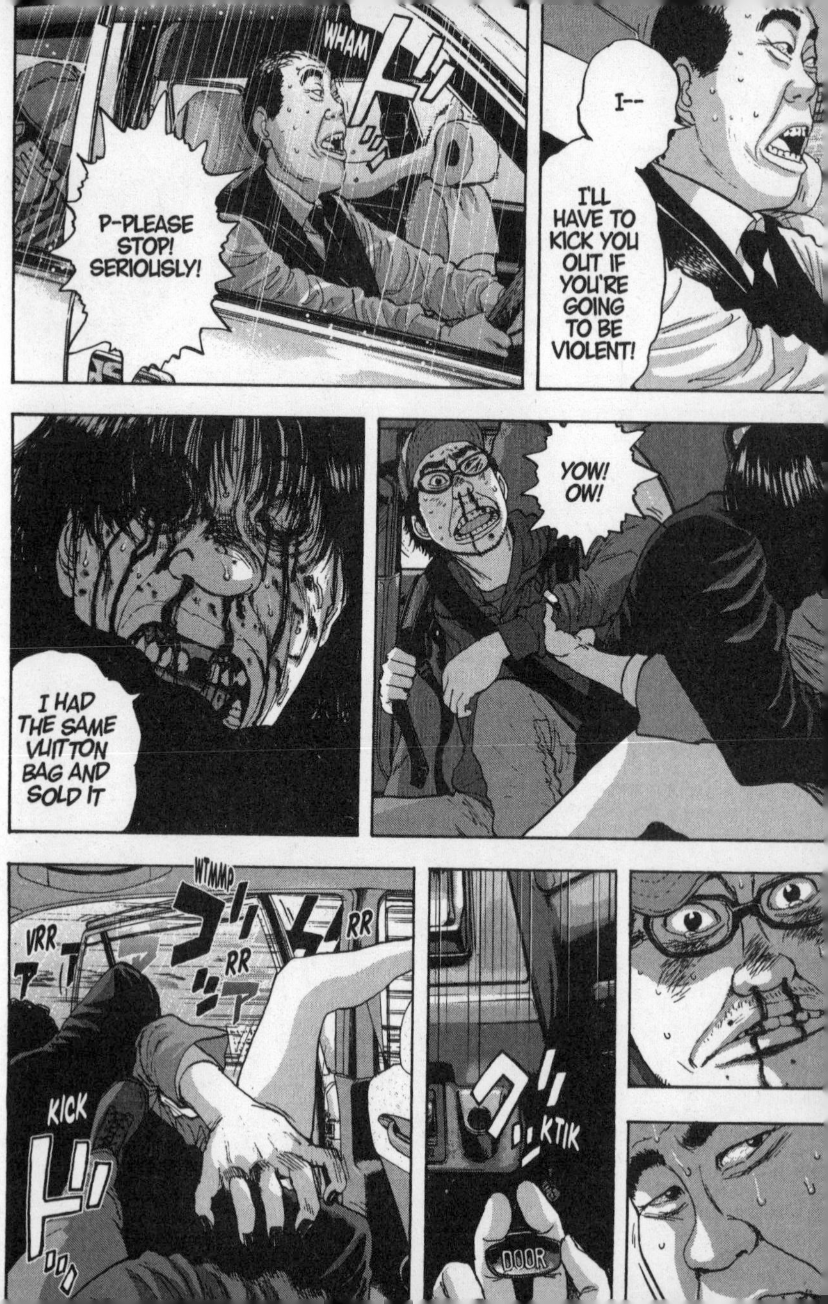
I--
I'LL HAVE TO KICK YOU OUT IF YOU'RE GOING TO BE VIOLENT!
WHAM
P-PLEASE STOP! SERIOUSLY!
YOW! OW!
I HAD THE SAME VUITTON BAG AND SOLD IT
KTIK
DOOR
WTMMP
RR
RR
VRR
KICK

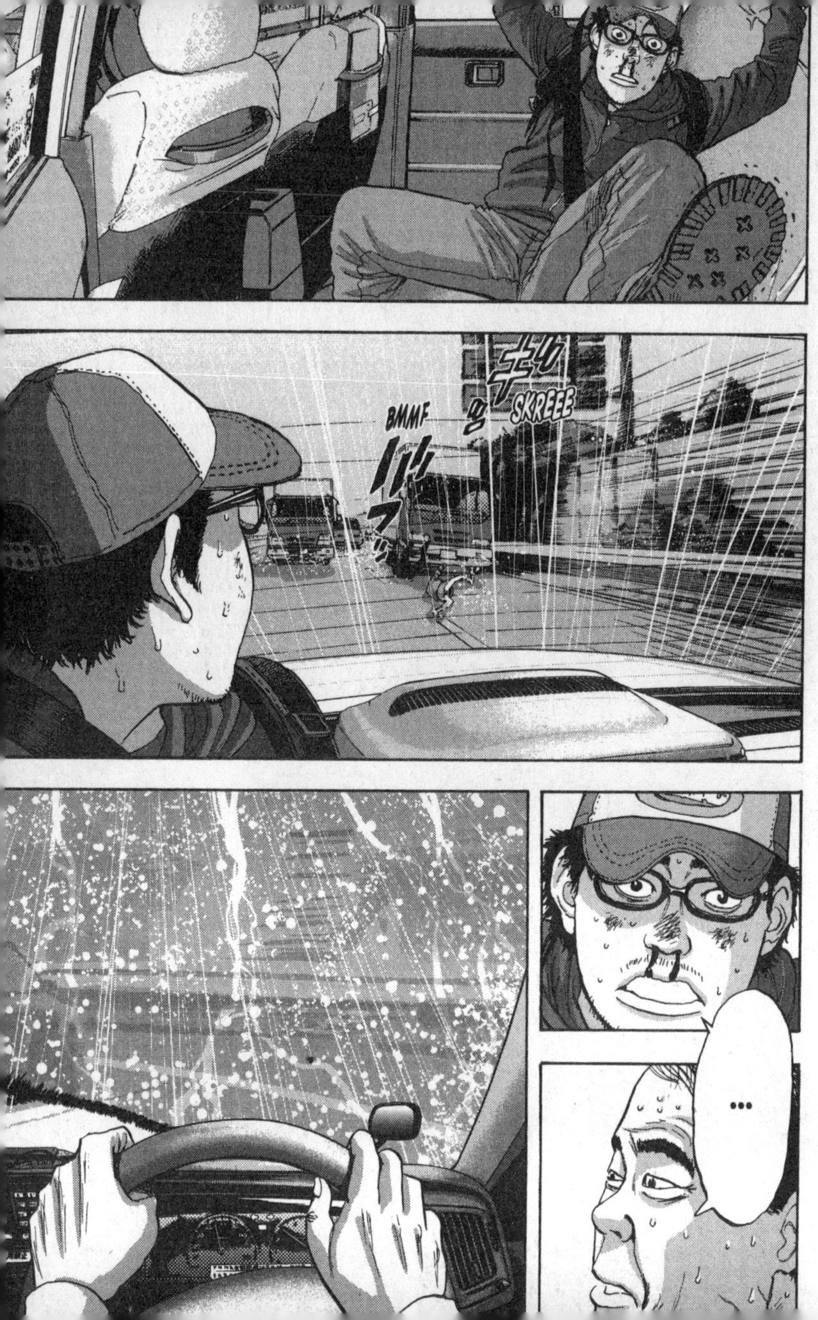
SKREEE
BMMF
...

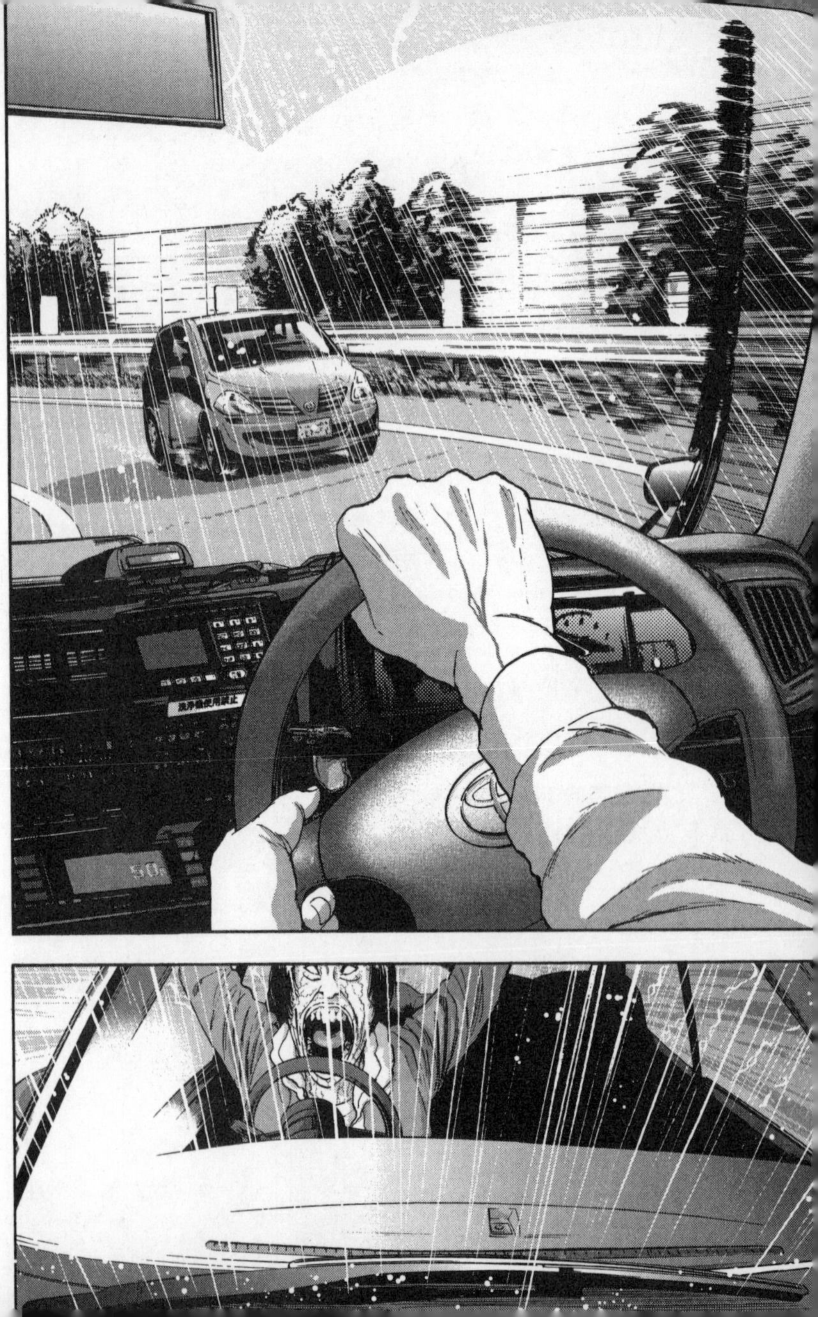
洗浄機使用禁止

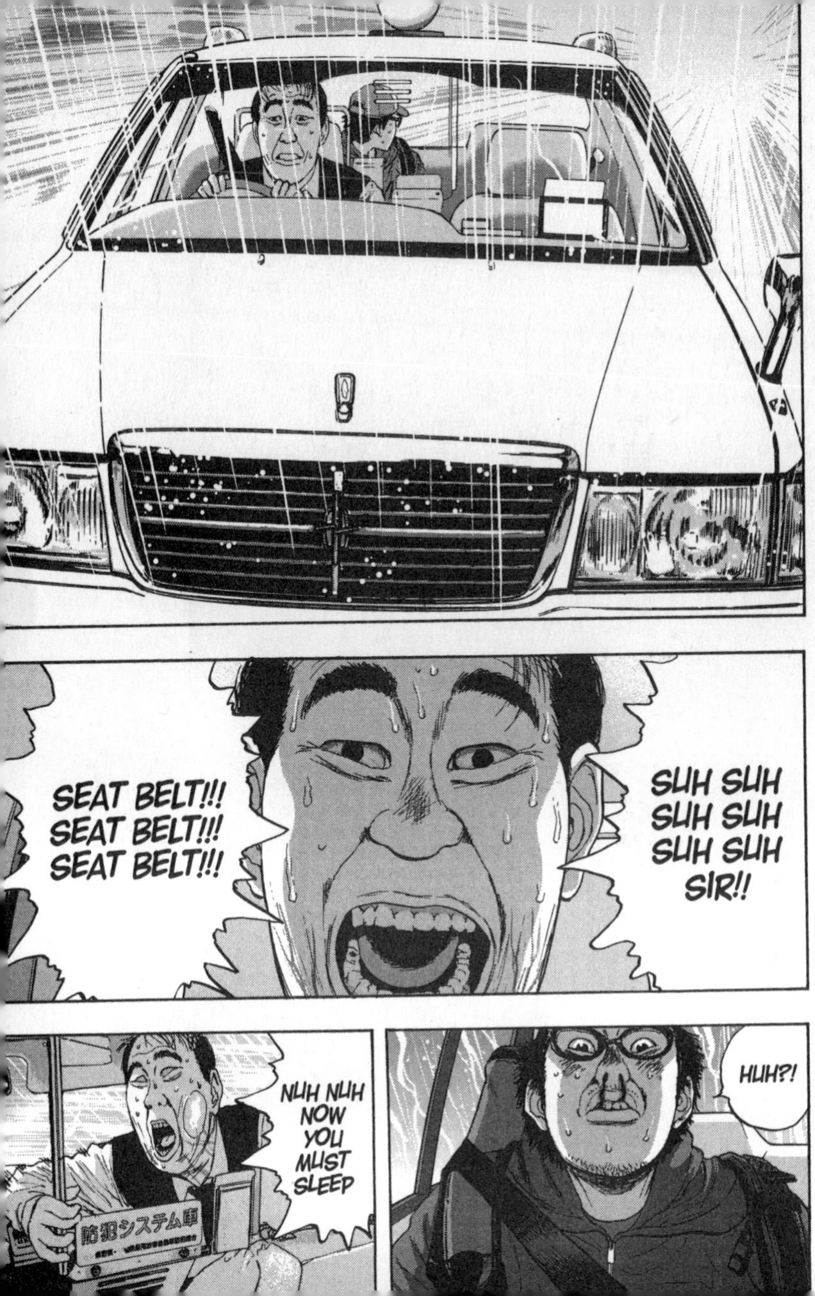
SUH SUH SUH SUH SUH SUH SIR!!
SEAT BELT!!! SEAT BELT!!! SEAT BELT!!!
HUH?!
NUH NUH NOW YOU MUST SLEEP
防犯システム車

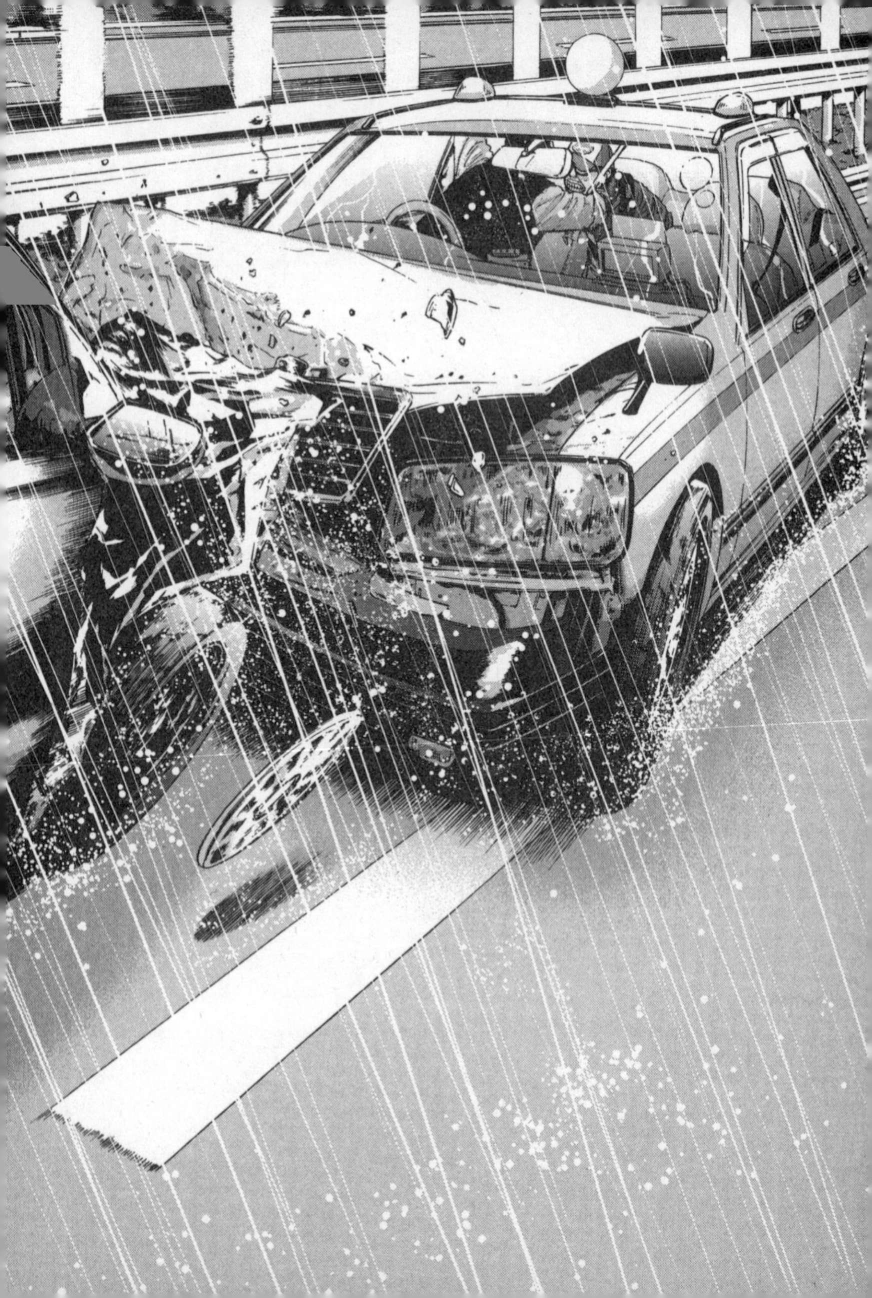

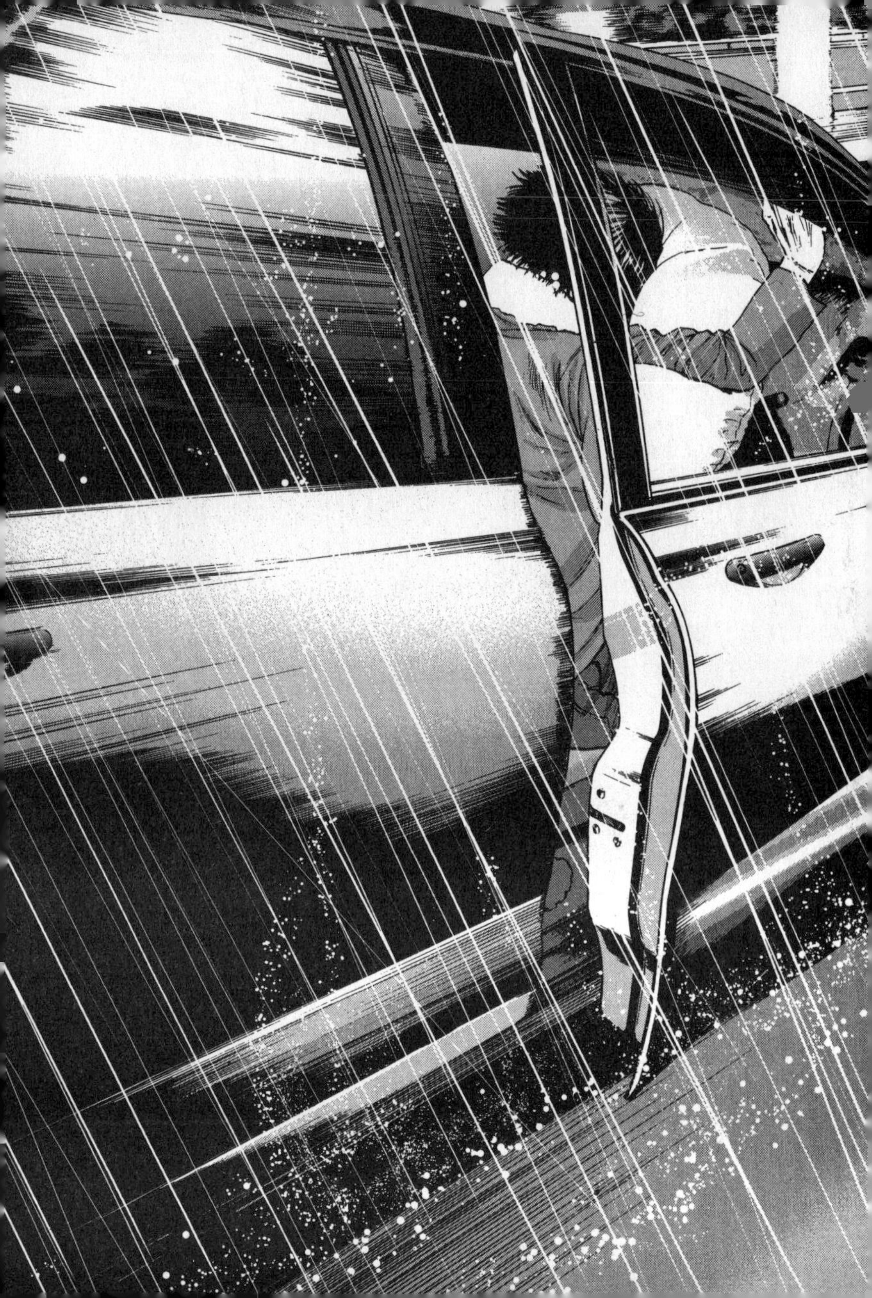

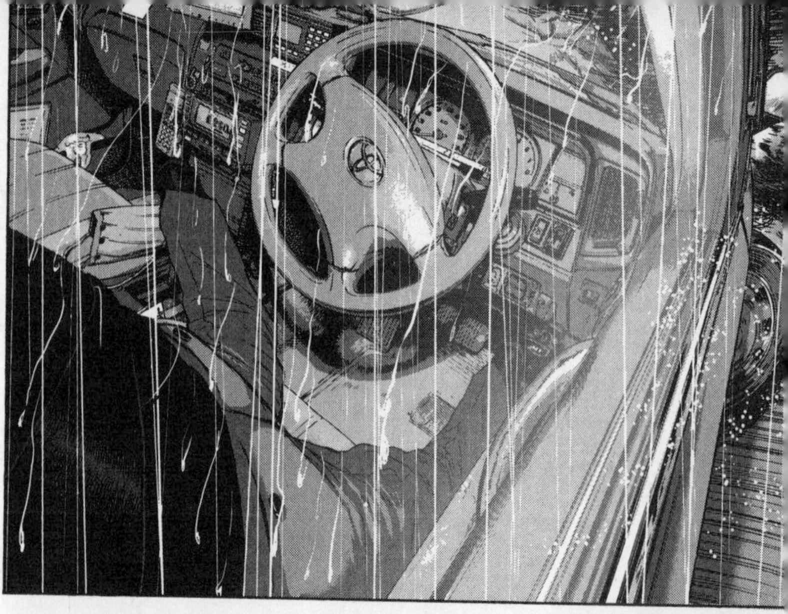
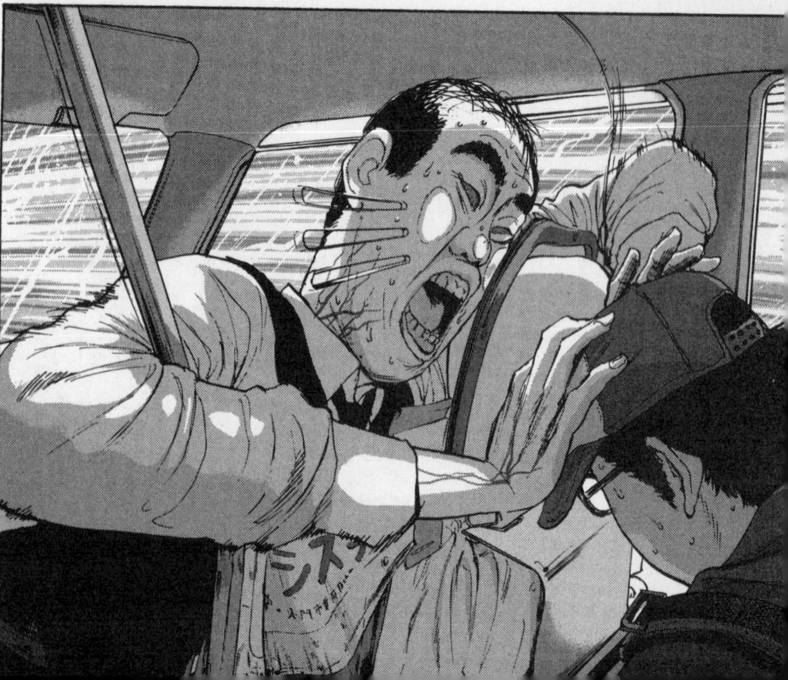

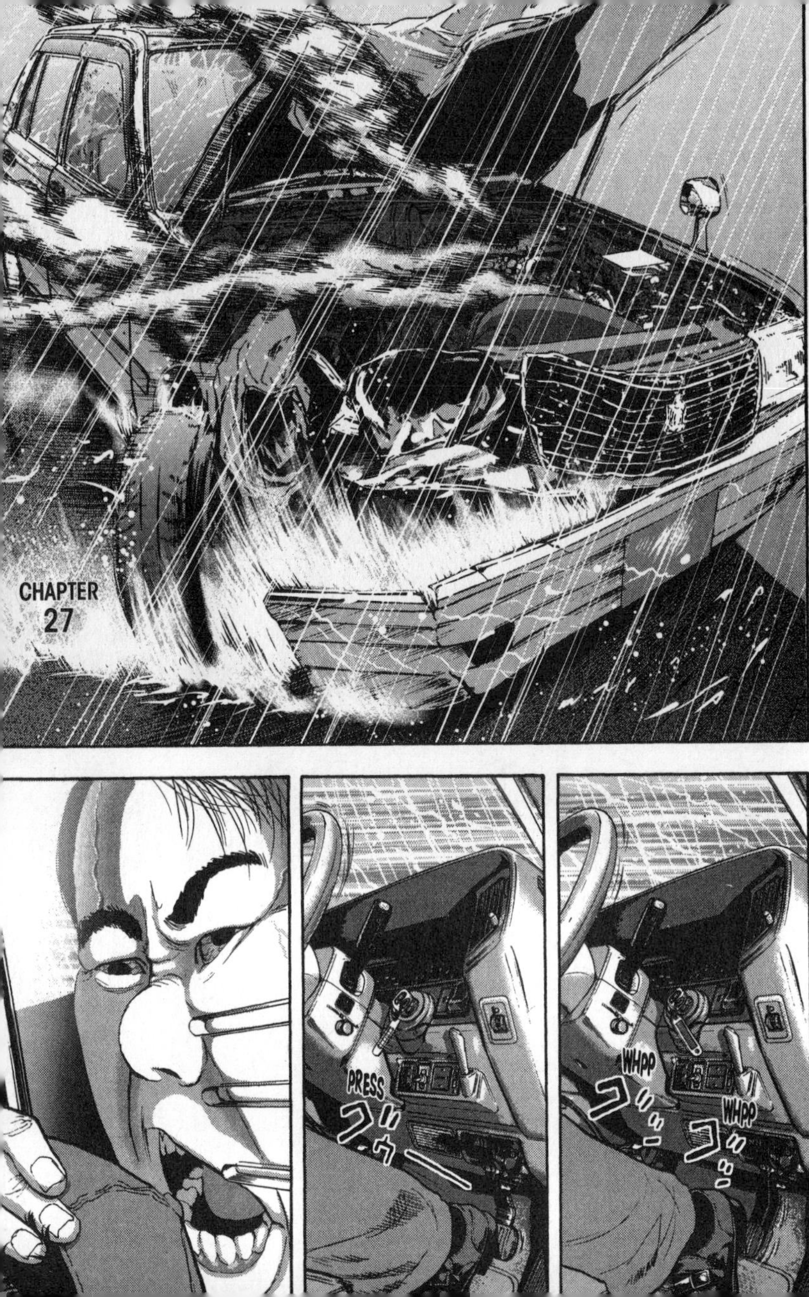
CHAPTER
27
WHPP
WHPP
PRESS

I AM
A HERO

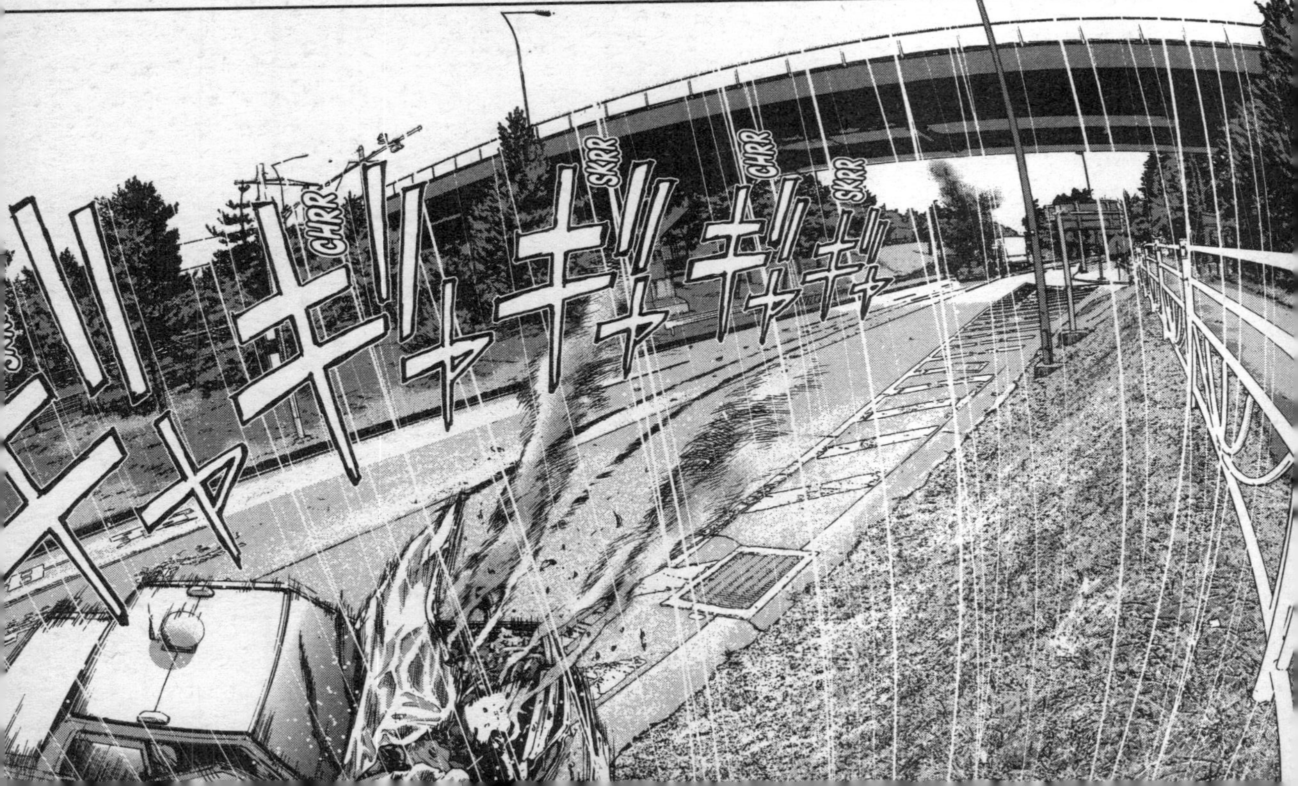
CHRR
SKRR
CHRR
SKRR

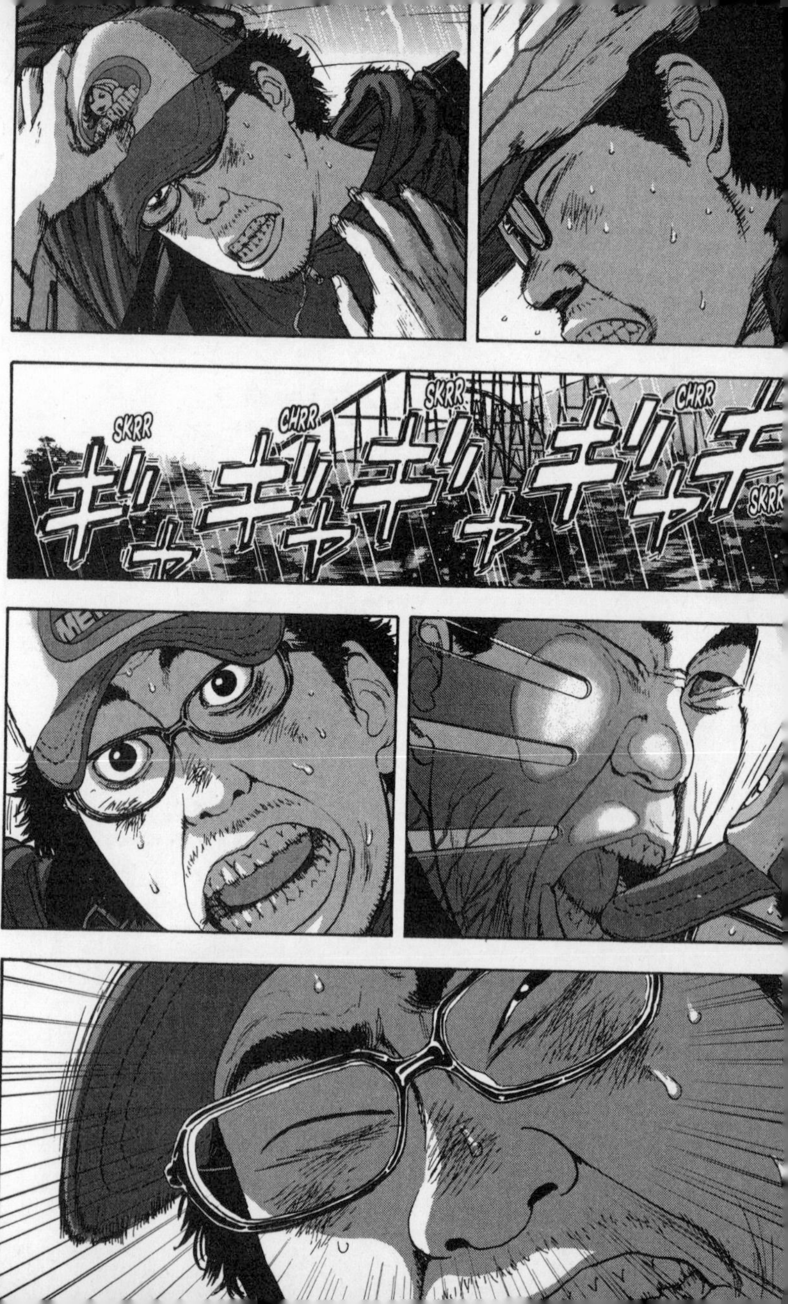
SKRR
CHRR
SKRR
CHRR
SKRR

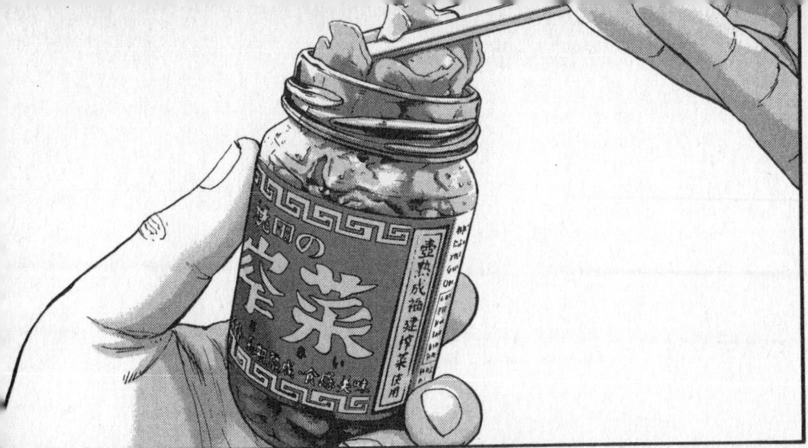

LABEL: MOMOTA BRAND / PICKLED VEGETABLES

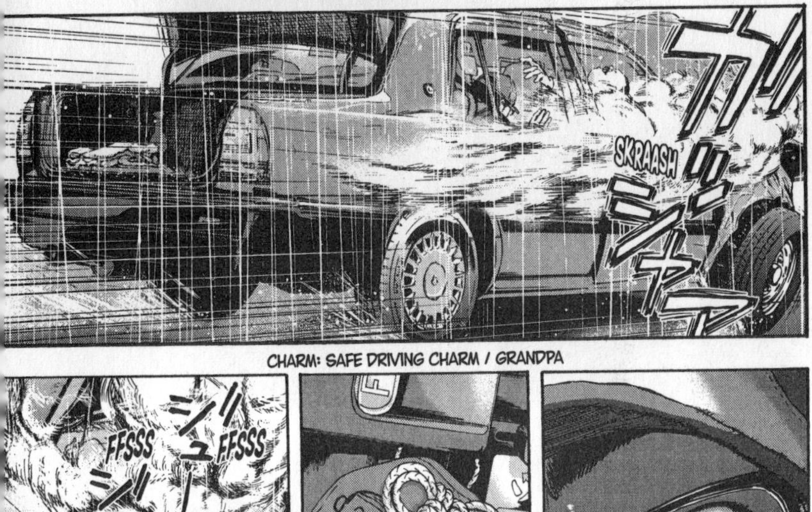
SKRAASH

CHARM: SAFE DRIVING CHARM / GRANDPA

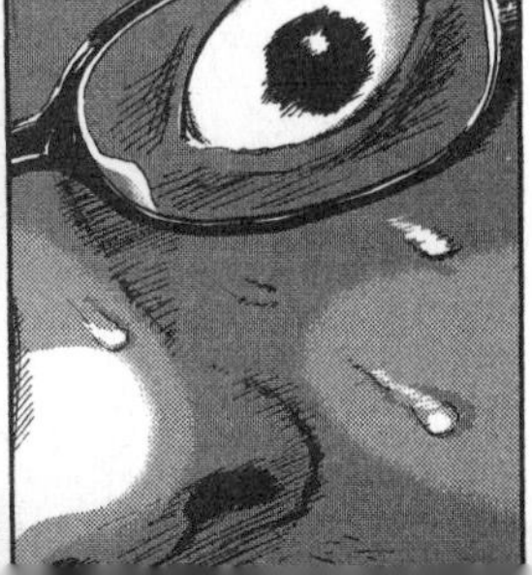

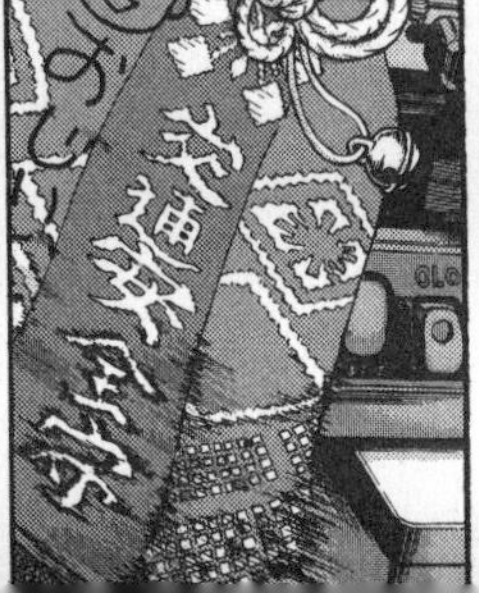

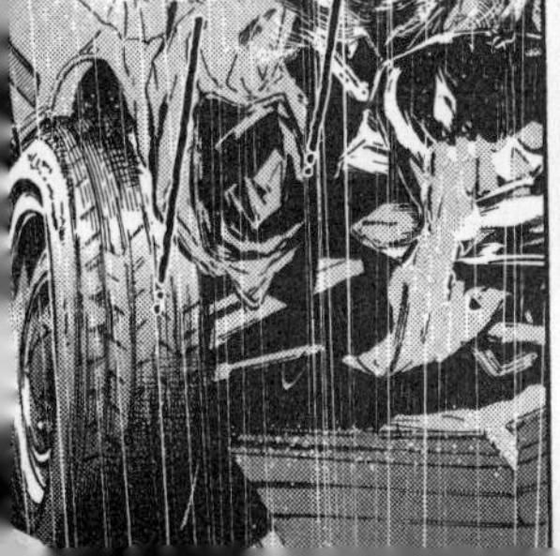
FFSSS
FFSSS

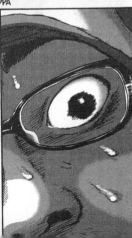

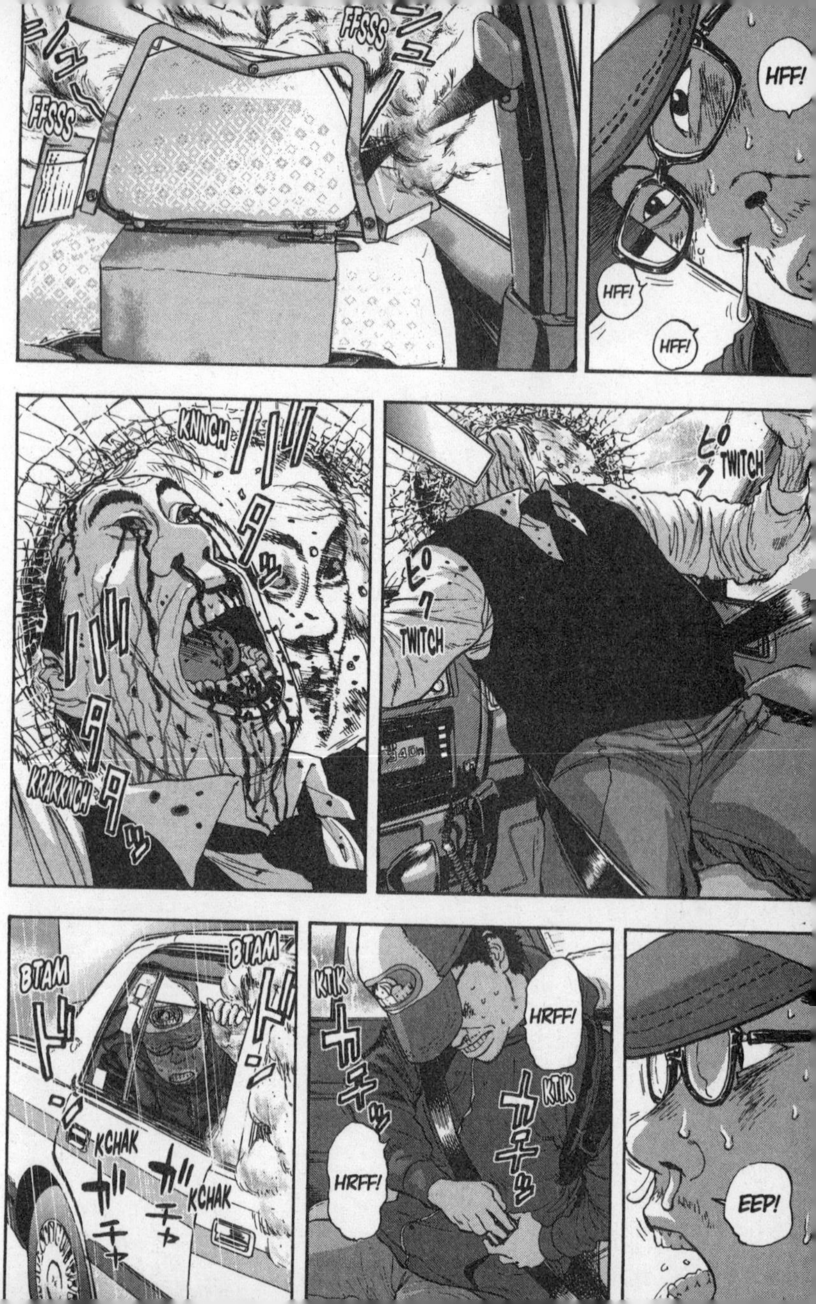
HFF!
HFF!
HFF!
FFSSS
FFSSS
TWITCH
TWITCH
KNNCH
KRAKKNCH
EEP!
KTIK
HRFF!
KTIK
HRFF!
BTAM
BTAM
KCHAK
KCHAK

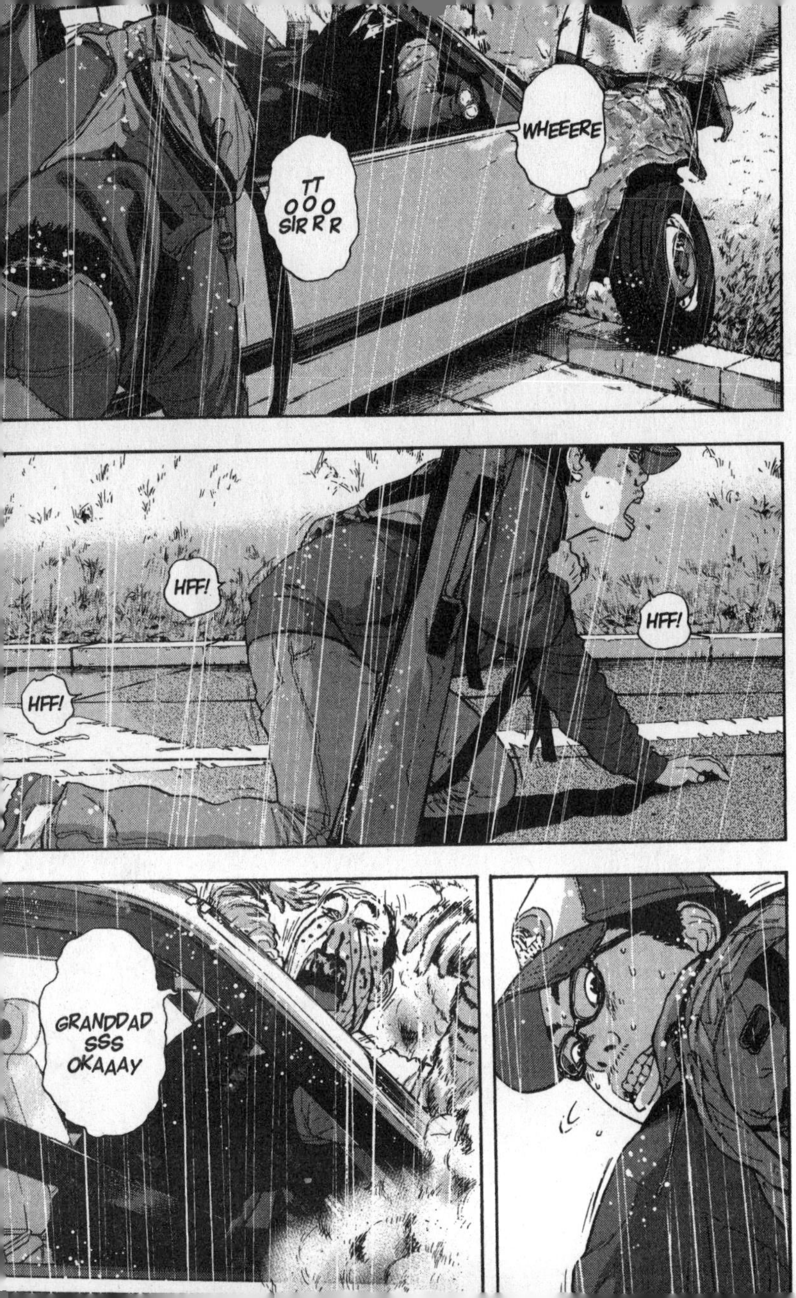
WHEEERE
TT OOO SIRRR
HFF!
HFF!
HFF!
GRANDDAD SSS OKAAAY

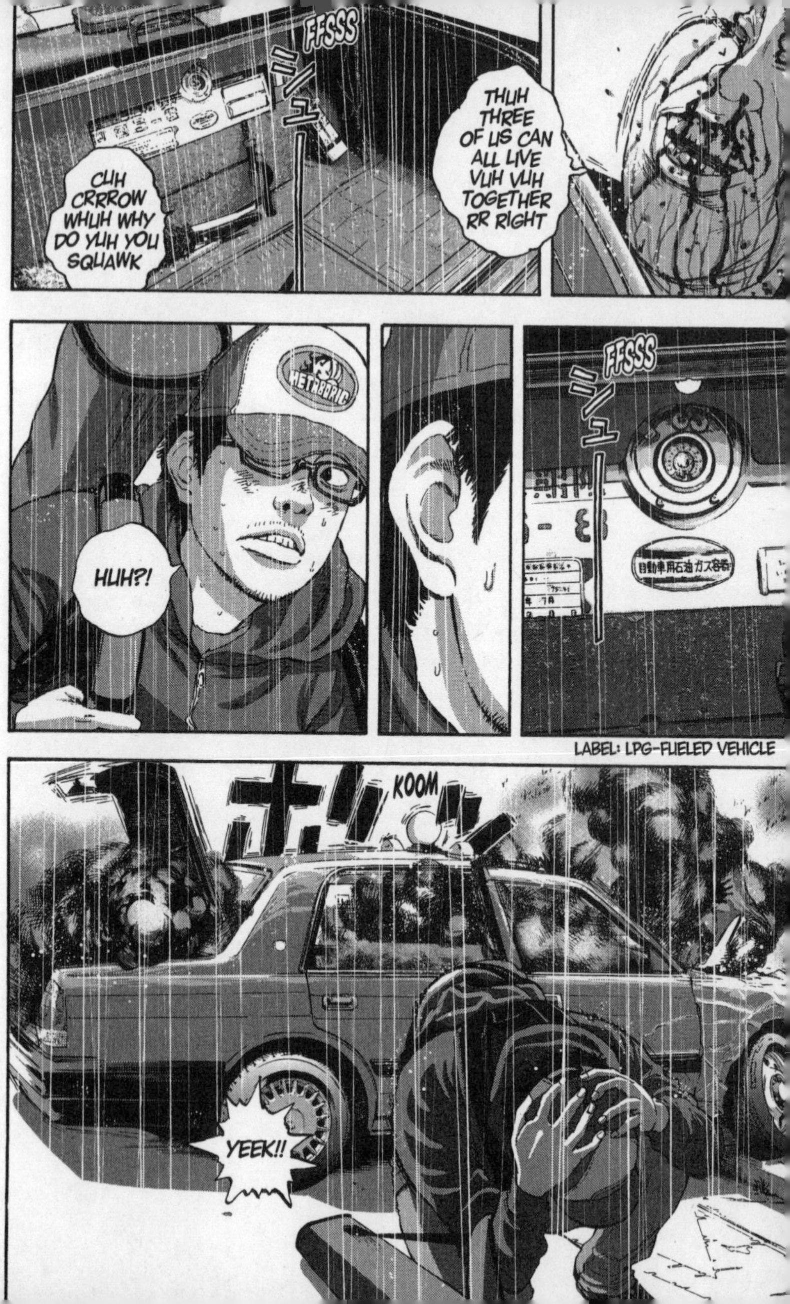
FFSSS
シュー
THUH THREE OF US CAN ALL LIVE VUH VUH TOGETHER RR RIGHT
CUH CRRROW WHUH WHY DO YUH YOU SQUAWK
FFSSS
シュー
自動車用石油ガス容器
HETNORIC
HUH?!
LABEL: LPG-FUELED VEHICLE
KOOM
YEEK!!

SUH
RR

IS NUH
NINETEEN
THOUSANNND
YEN NN

YOURRR
FF FARE

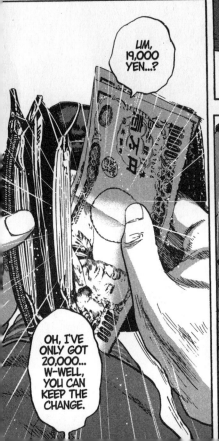

UM,
19,000
YEN...?

OH, I'VE
ONLY GOT
20,000...
W-WELL,
YOU CAN
KEEP THE
CHANGE.

AH!

Y-YES...

YES, OF
COURSE.

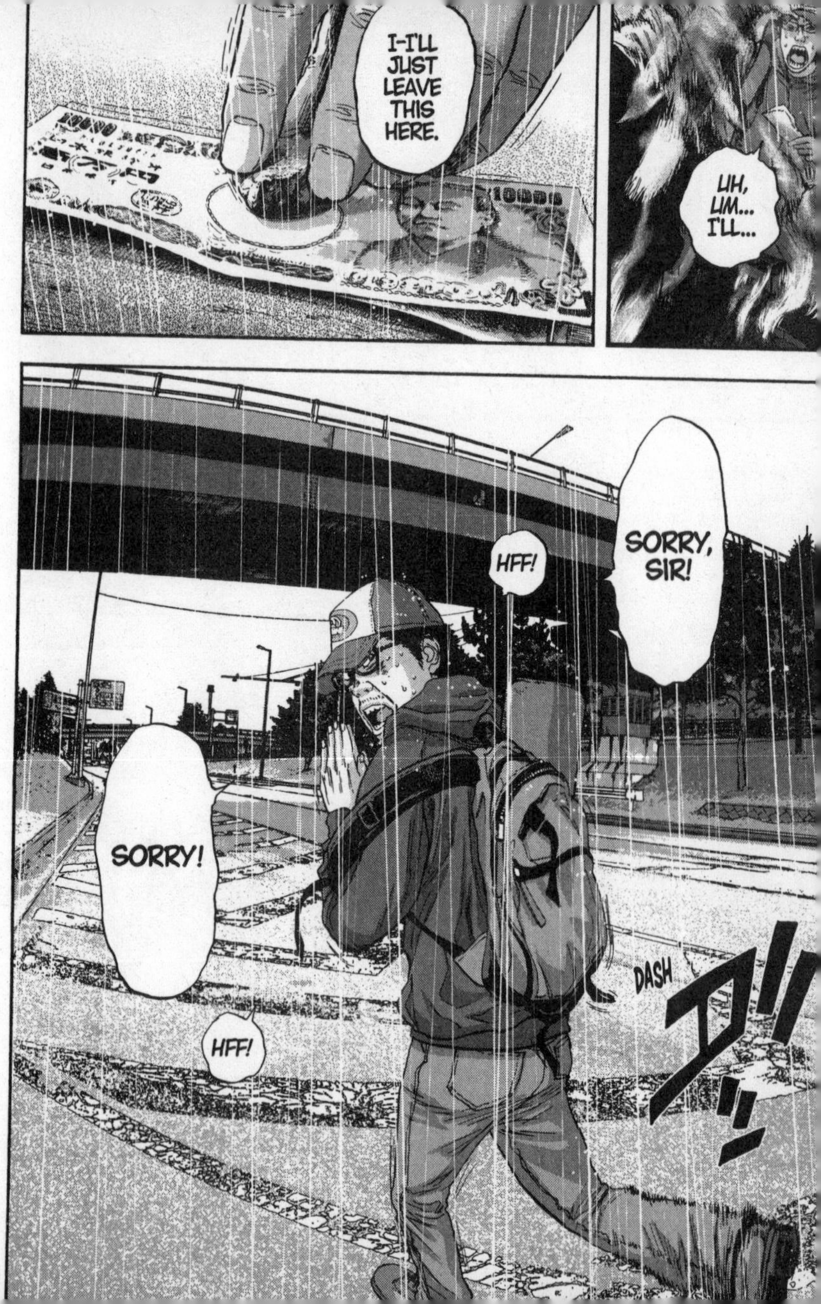
UH, UM... I'LL...
I-I'LL JUST LEAVE THIS HERE.
SORRY, SIR!
HFF!
SORRY!
DASH
HFF!

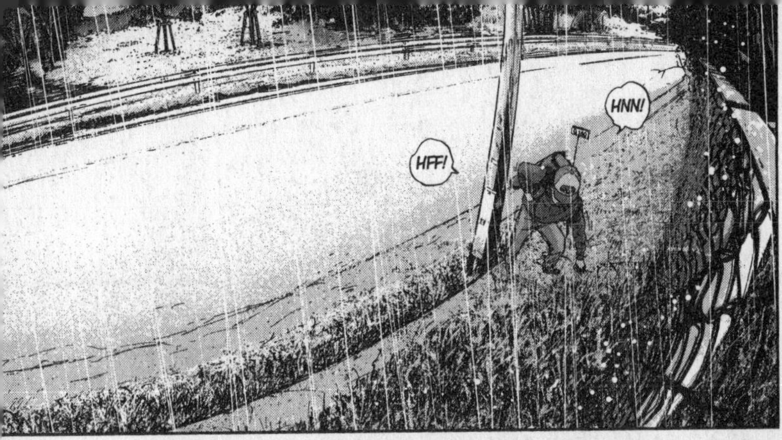
HNN!
HFF!
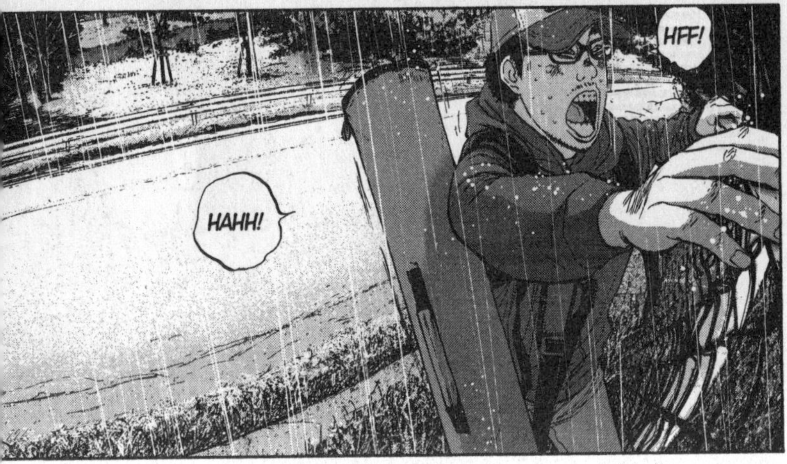
HFF!
HAHH!
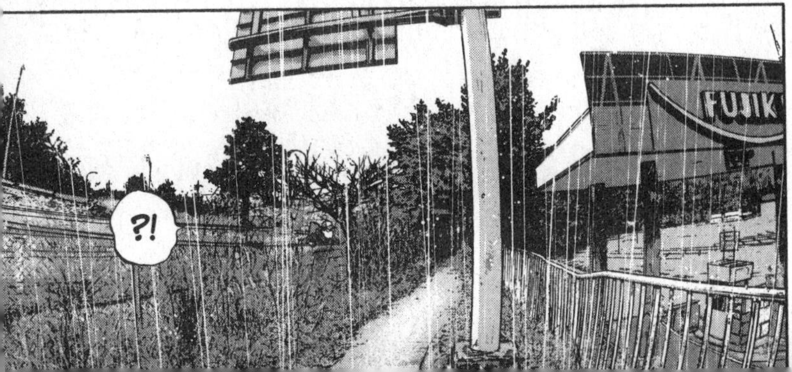
FUJIK
?!

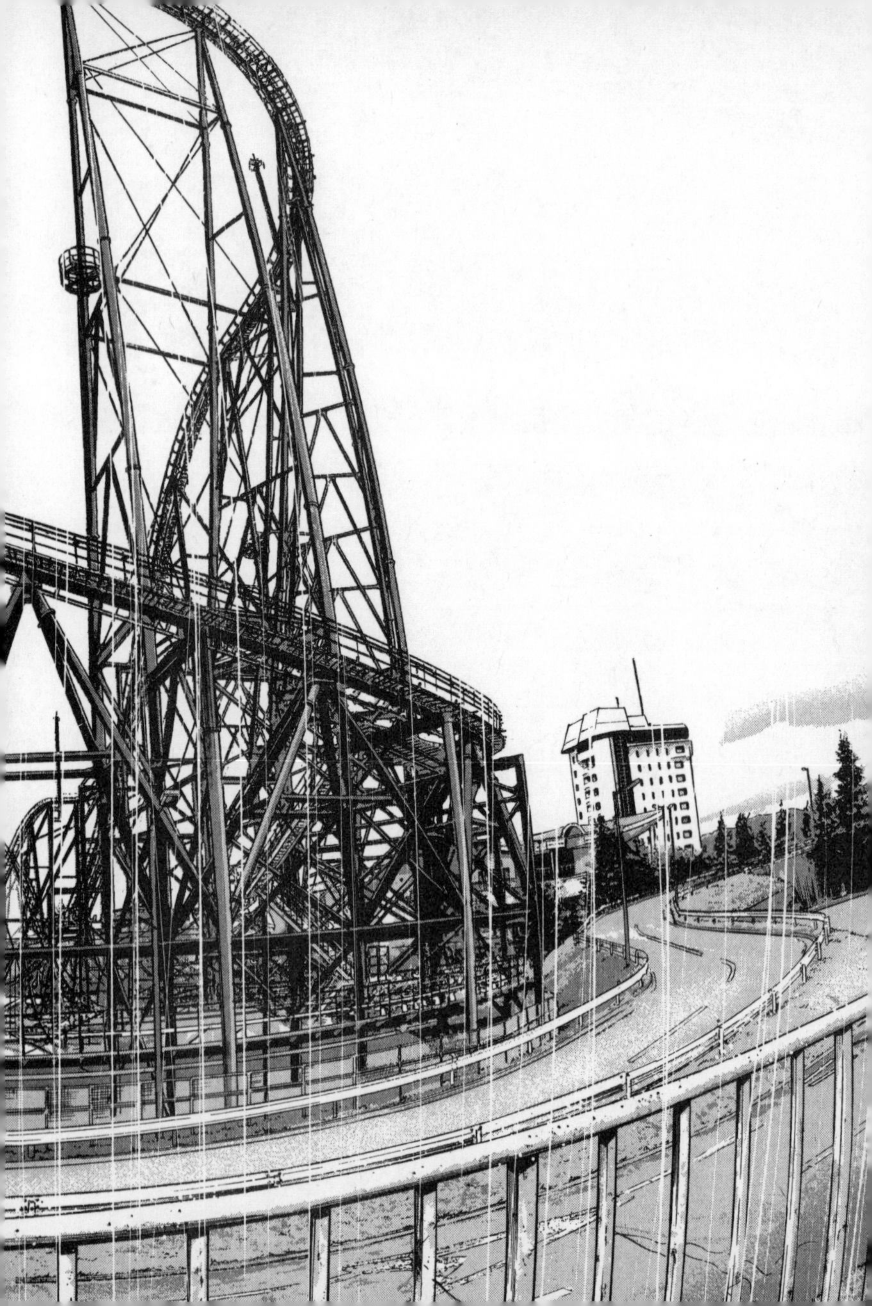

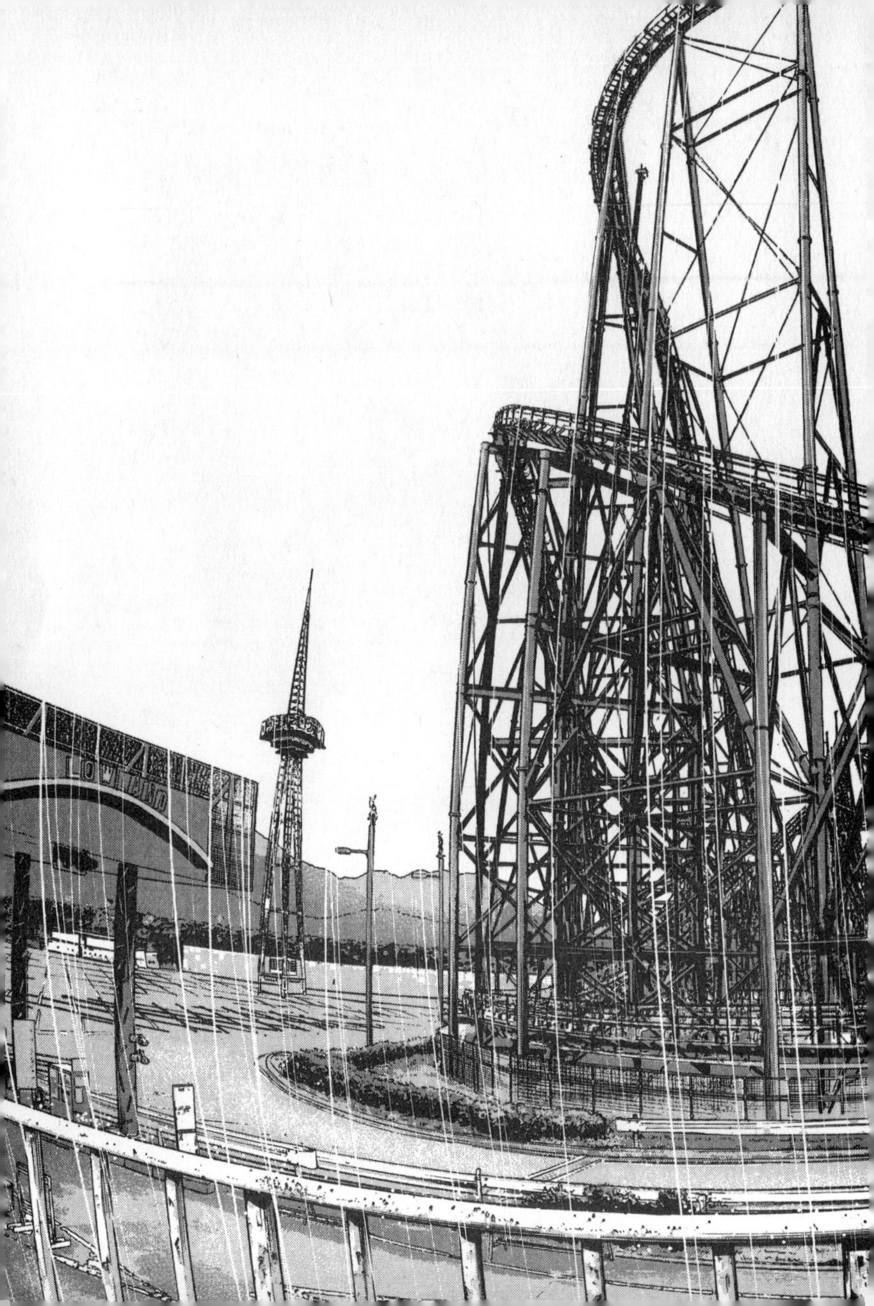

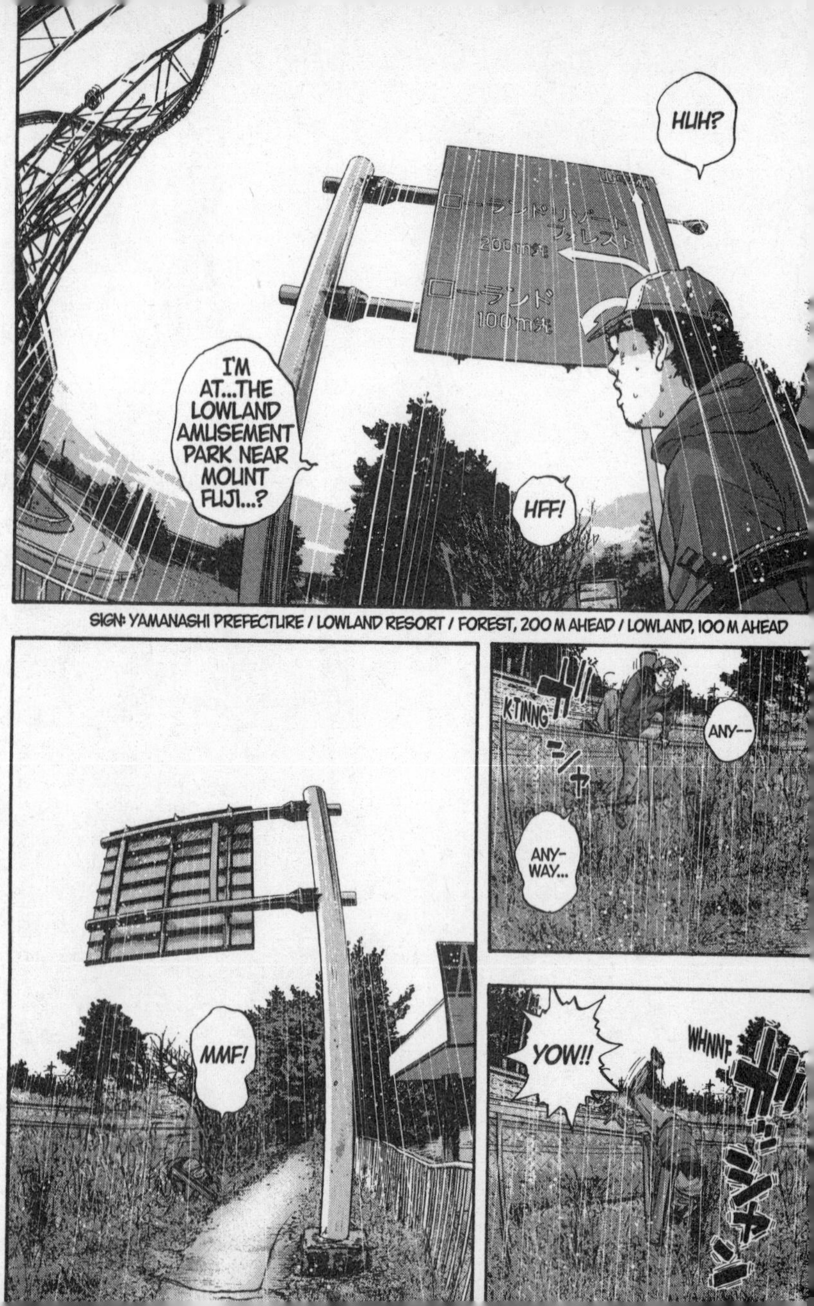
HUH?
I'M AT...THE LOWLAND AMUSEMENT PARK NEAR MOUNT FUJI...?
HFF!
SIGN: YAMANASHI PREFECTURE / LOWLAND RESORT / FOREST, 200 M AHEAD / LOWLAND, 100 M AHEAD
ANY--
KTINNG
ANY-WAY...
WHNNF
YOW!!
MMF!

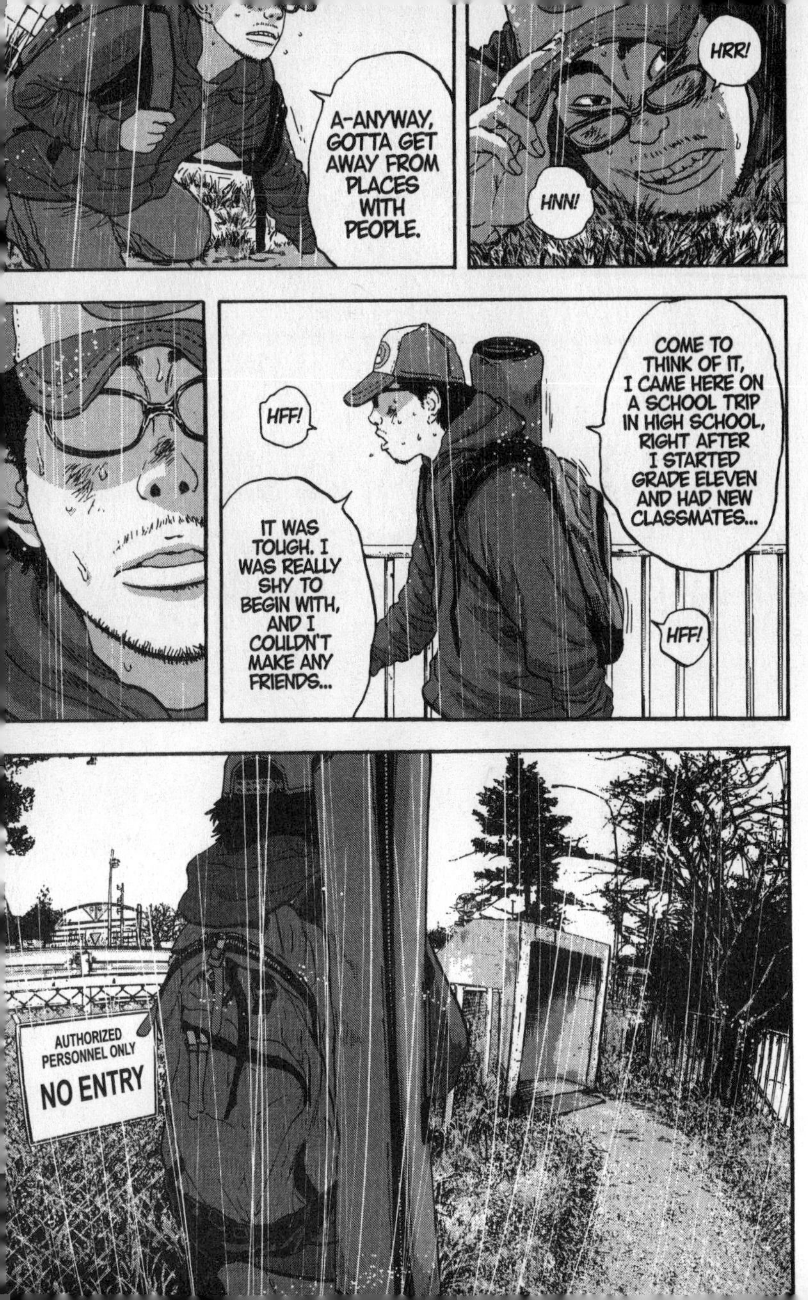
HRR!
HNN!
A-ANYWAY, GOTTA GET AWAY FROM PLACES WITH PEOPLE.
COME TO THINK OF IT, I CAME HERE ON A SCHOOL TRIP IN HIGH SCHOOL, RIGHT AFTER I STARTED GRADE ELEVEN AND HAD NEW CLASSMATES...
HFF!
IT WAS TOUGH. I WAS REALLY SHY TO BEGIN WITH, AND I COULDN'T MAKE ANY FRIENDS...
HFF!
AUTHORIZED PERSONNEL ONLY
NO ENTRY

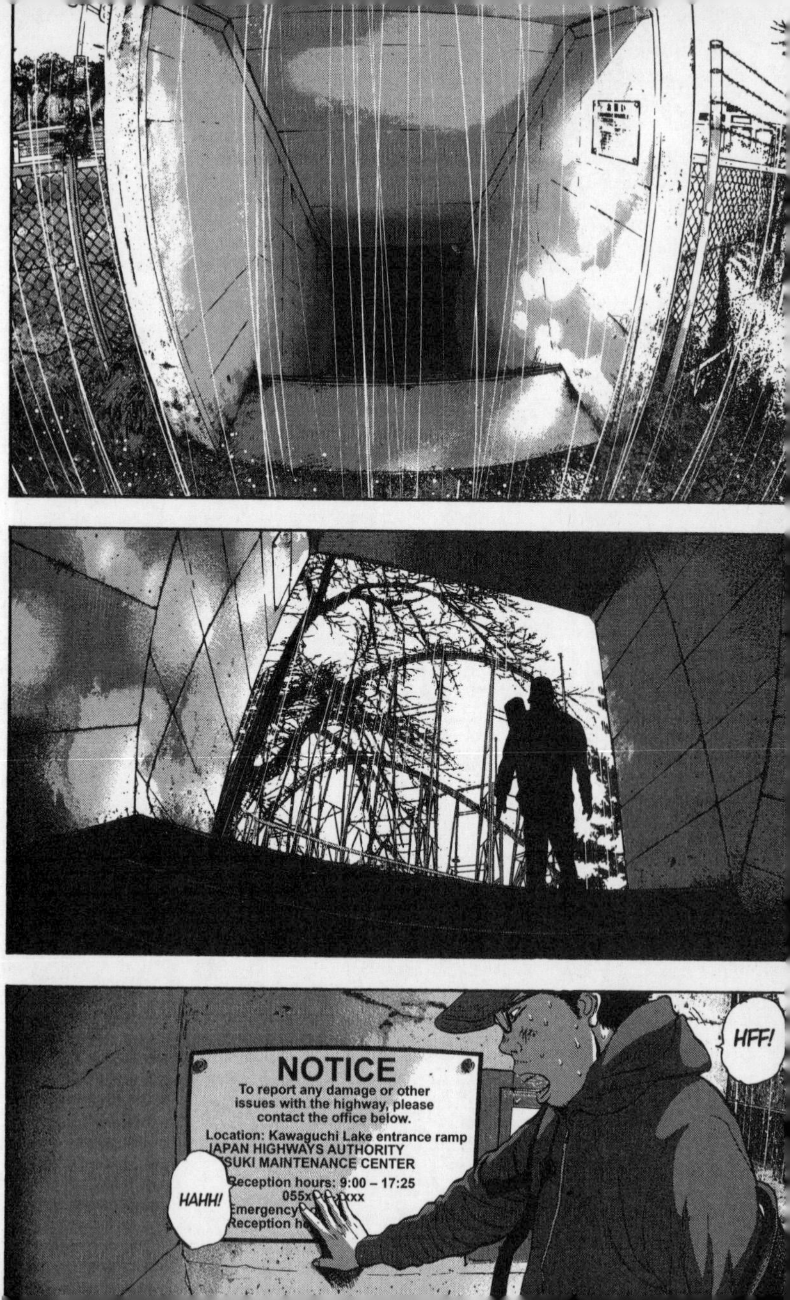
HFF!
NOTICE
To report any damage or other issues with the highway, please contact the office below.
Location: Kawaguchi Lake entrance ramp
JAPAN HIGHWAYS AUTHORITY
SUKI MAINTENANCE CENTER
eception hours: 9:00 – 17:25
055x
Emergency
Reception h
HAHH!

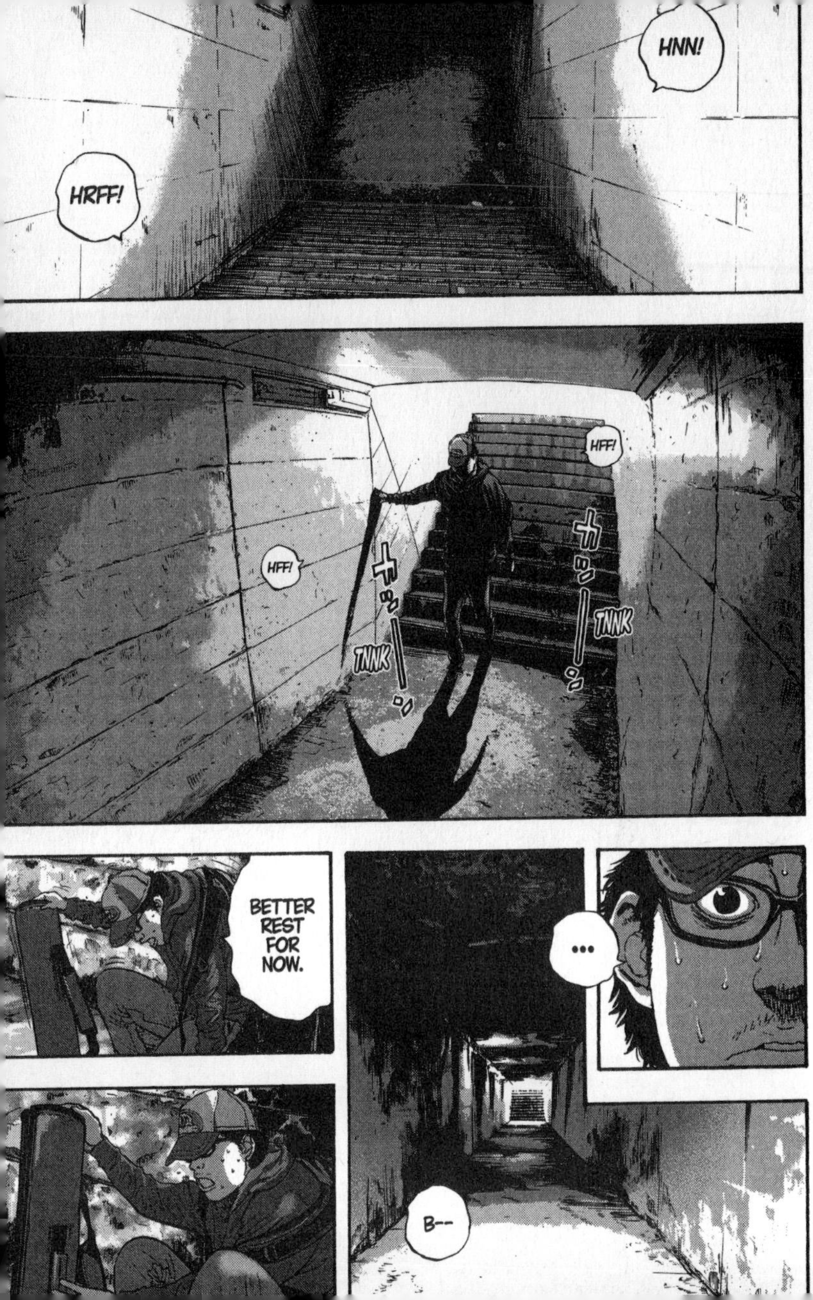
HNN!
HRFF!
HFF!
TNNK
HFF!
TNNK
...
B--
BETTER REST FOR NOW.

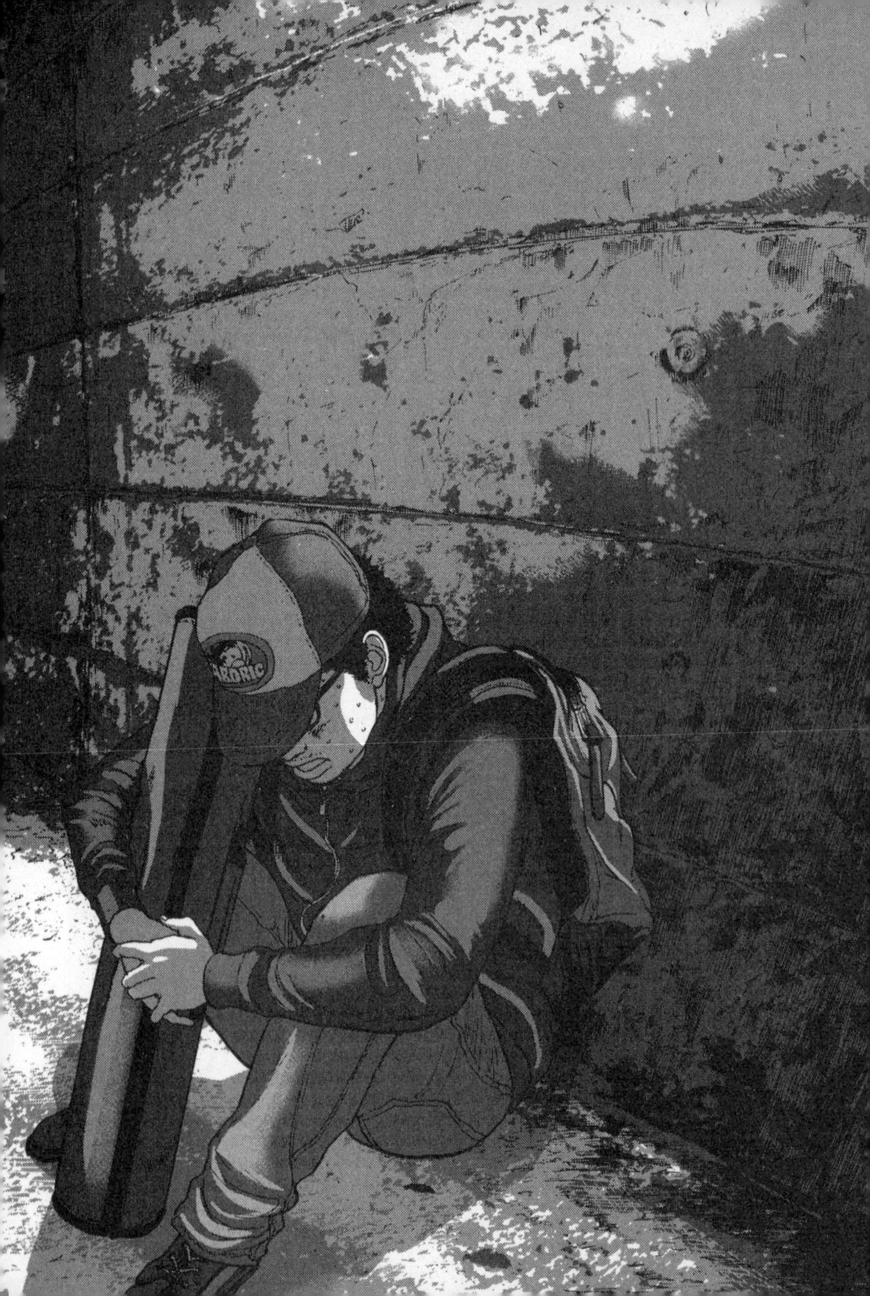

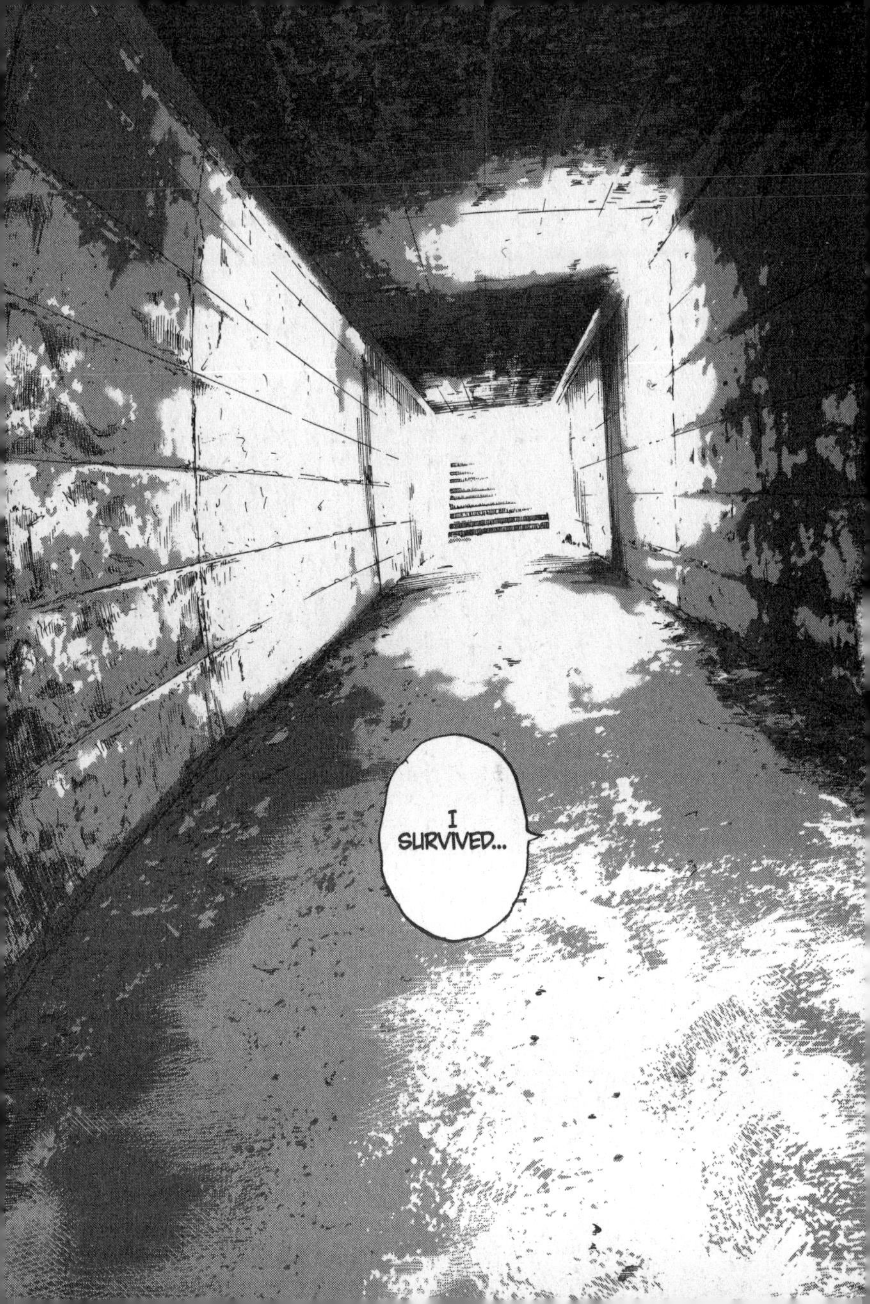
I SURVIVED...

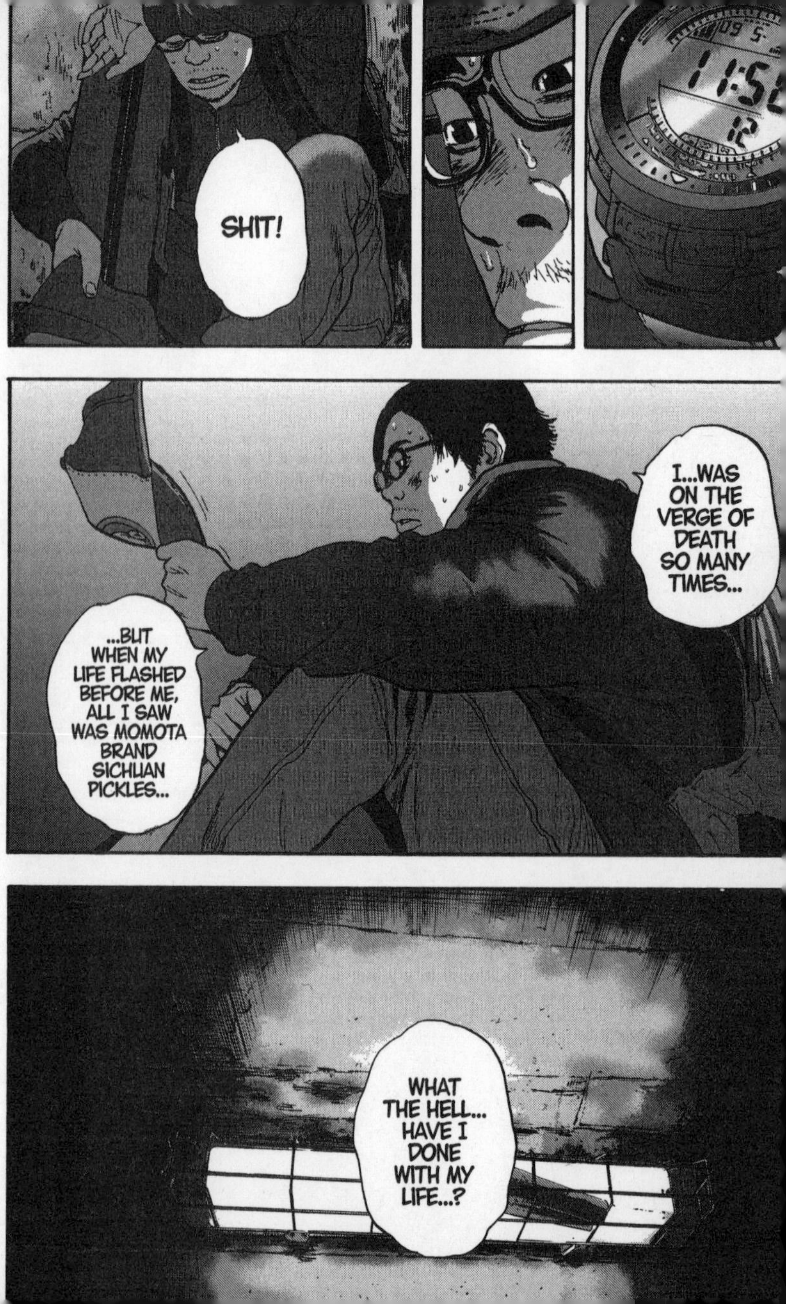
SHIT!
I...WAS ON THE VERGE OF DEATH SO MANY TIMES...
...BUT WHEN MY LIFE FLASHED BEFORE ME, ALL I SAW WAS MOMOTA BRAND SICHUAN PICKLES...
WHAT THE HELL... HAVE I DONE WITH MY LIFE...?

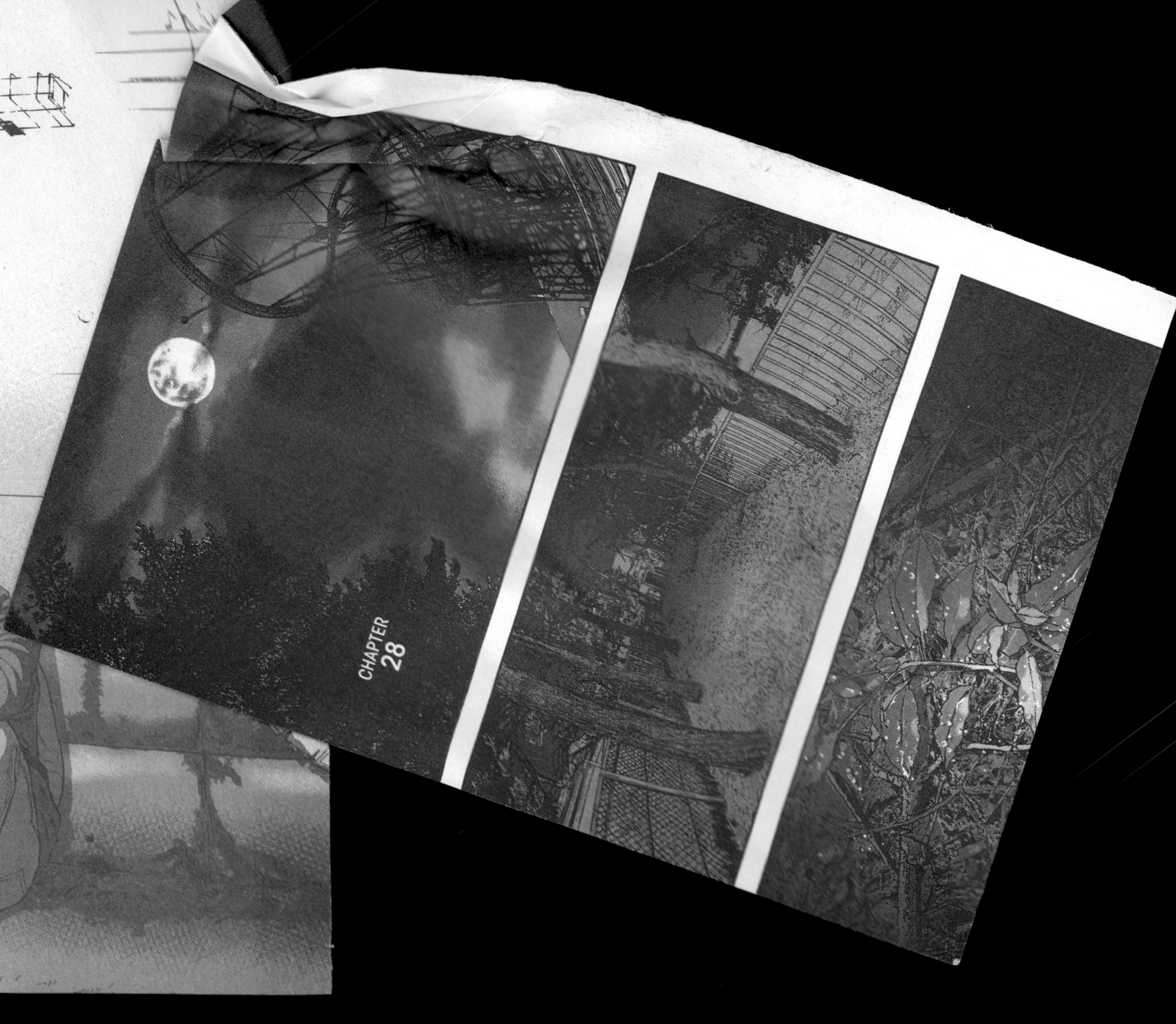
CHAPTER
28

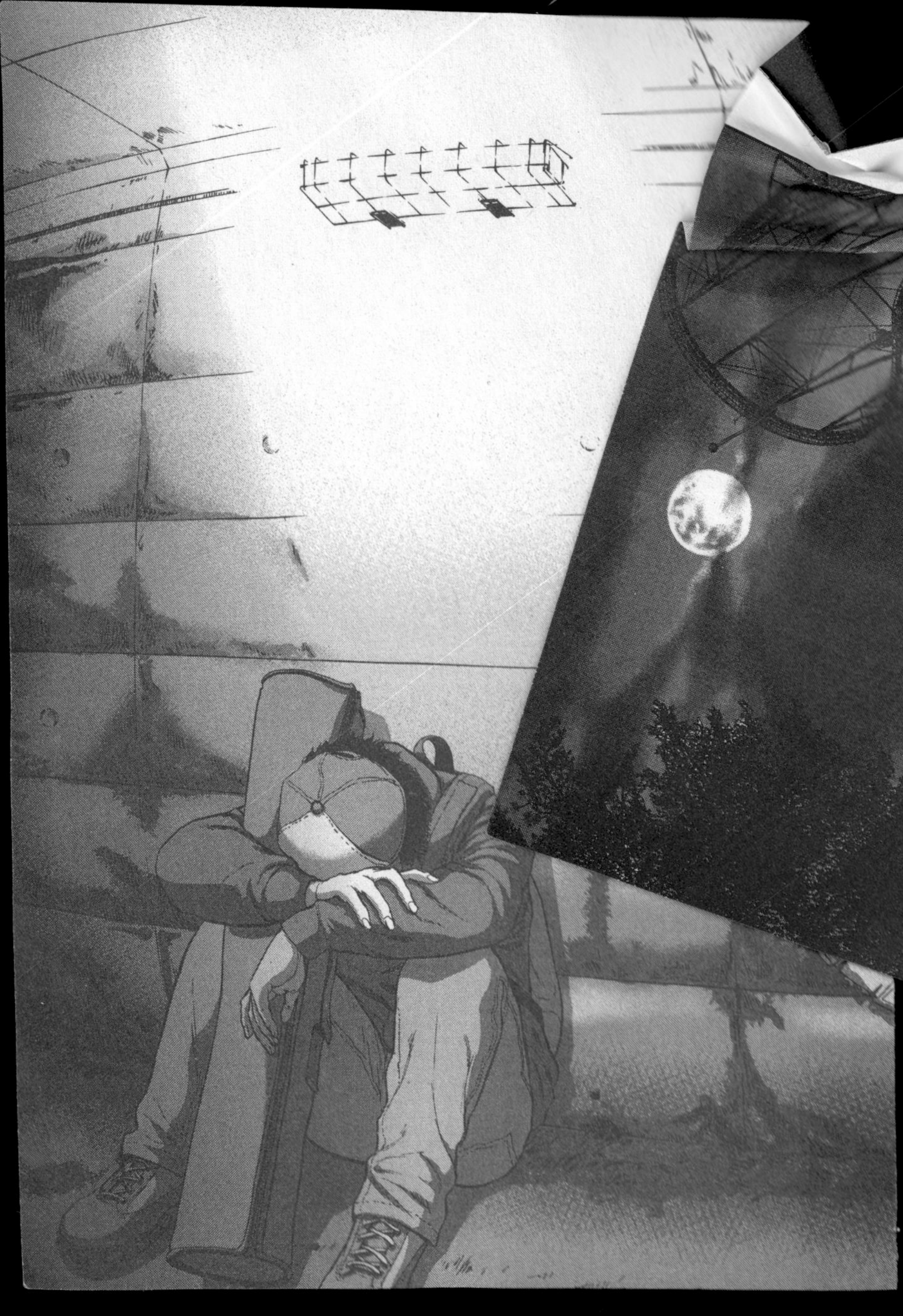

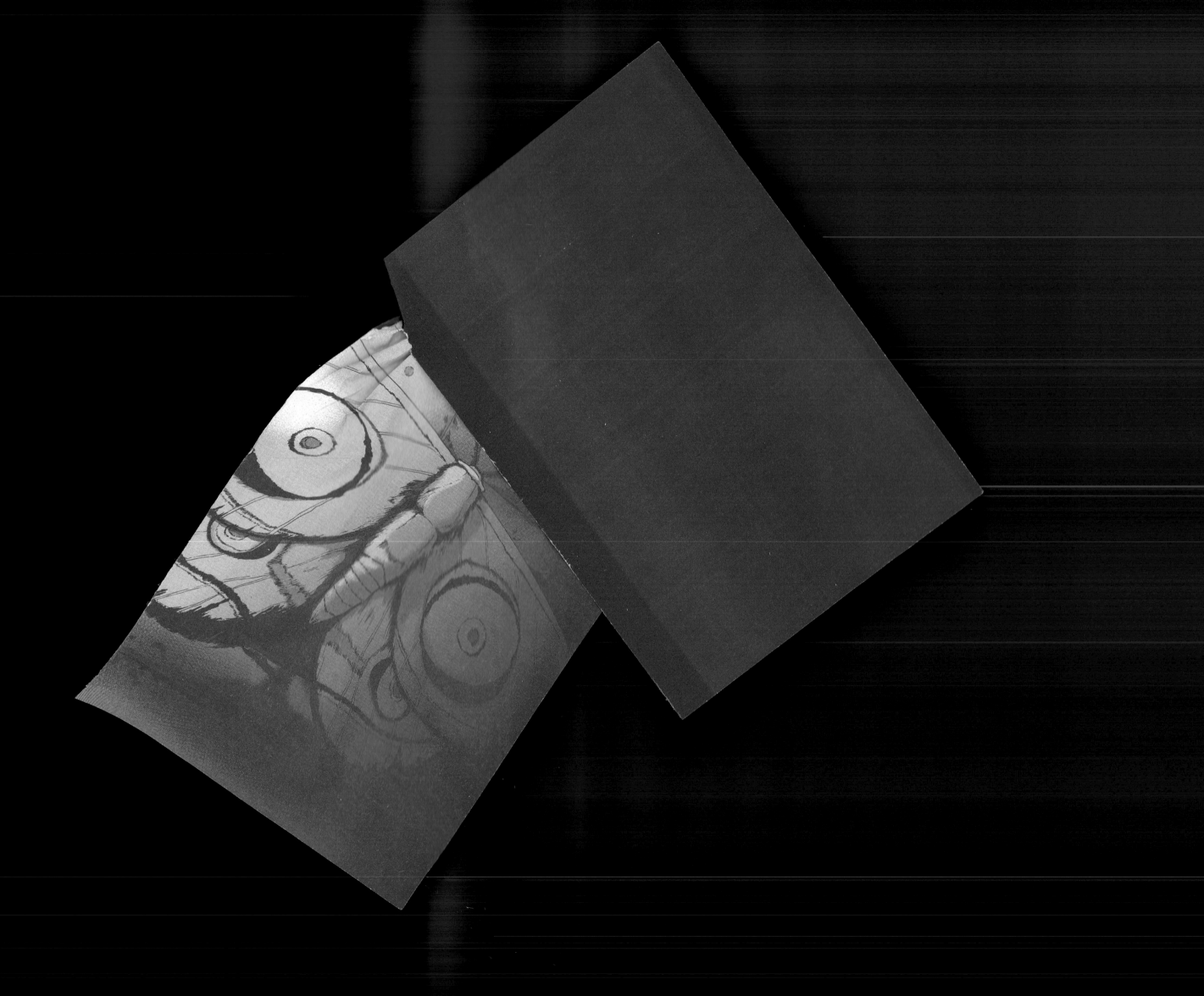

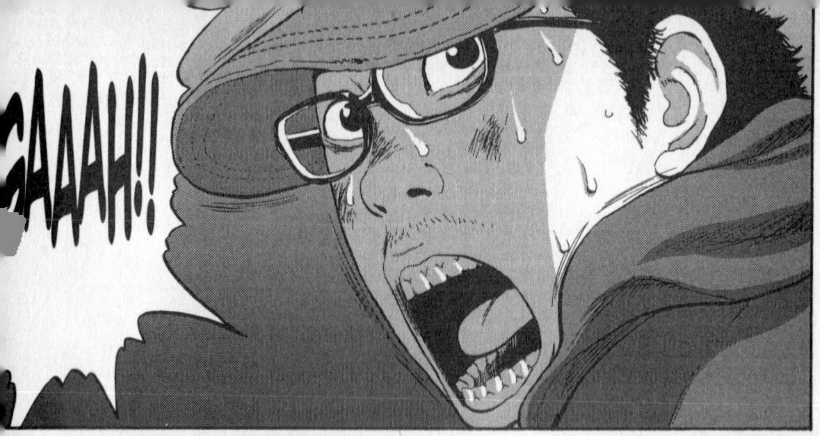
GAAAH!!
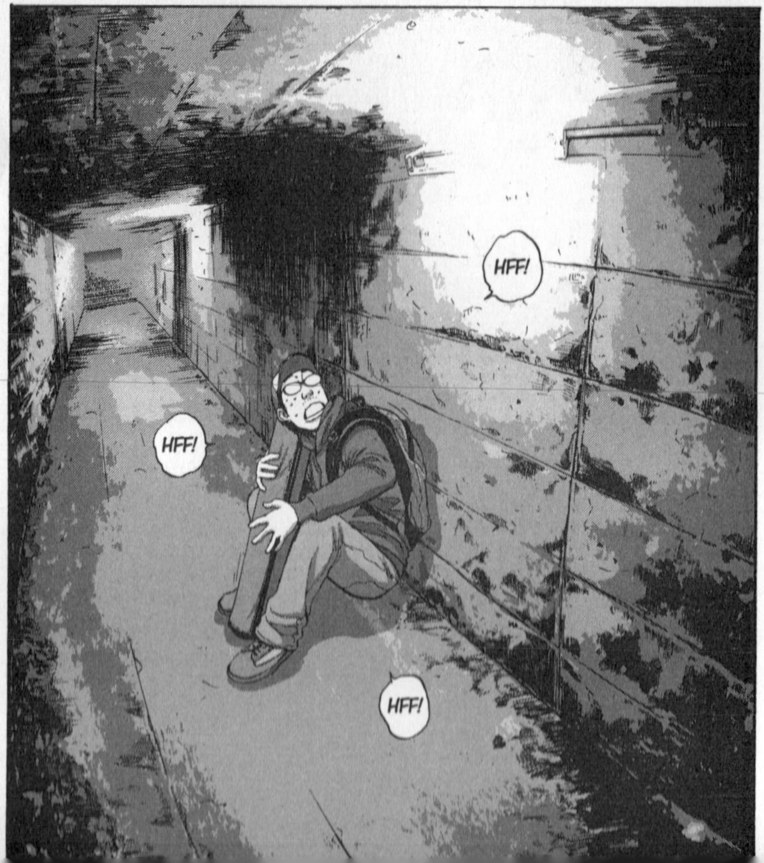
HFF!
HFF!
HFF!

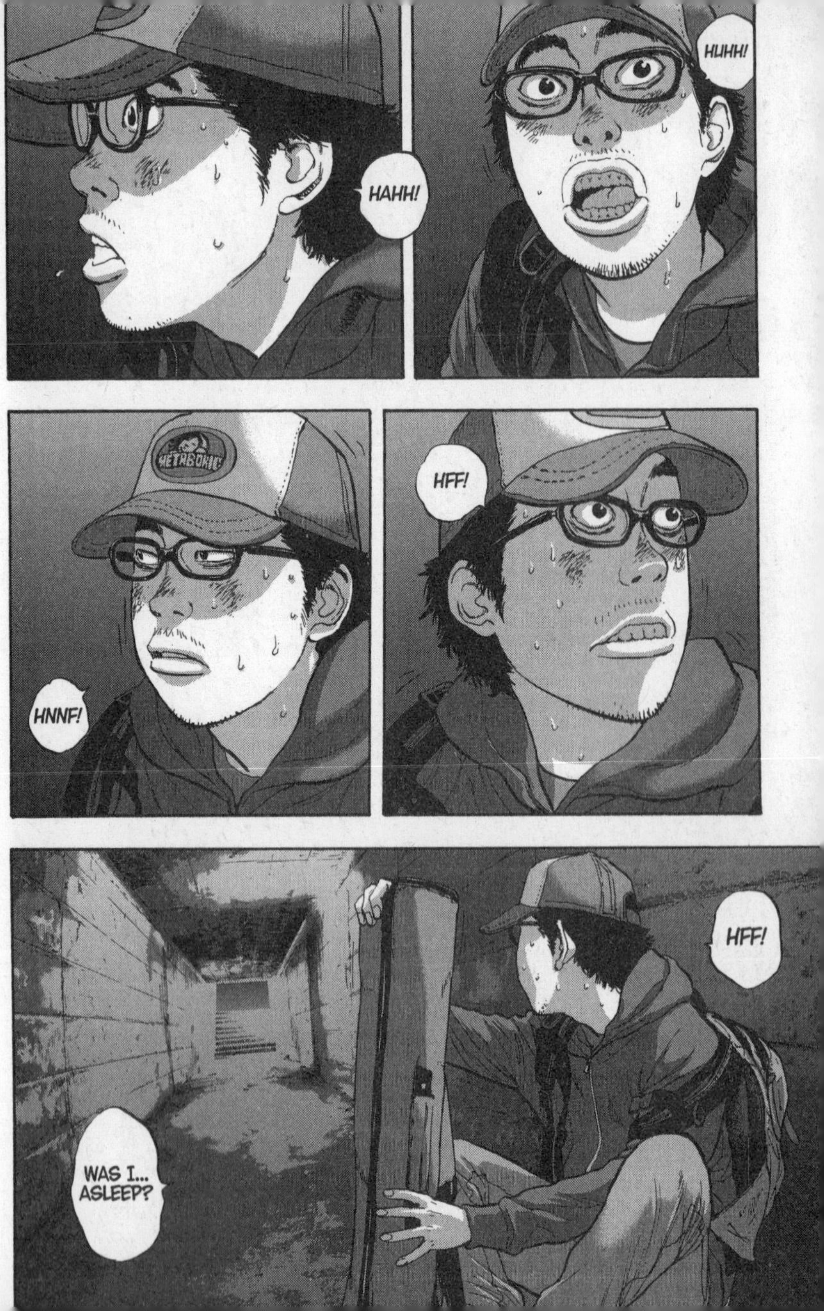
HUHH!
HAHH!
HFF!
HNNF!
HFF!
WAS I... ASLEEP?

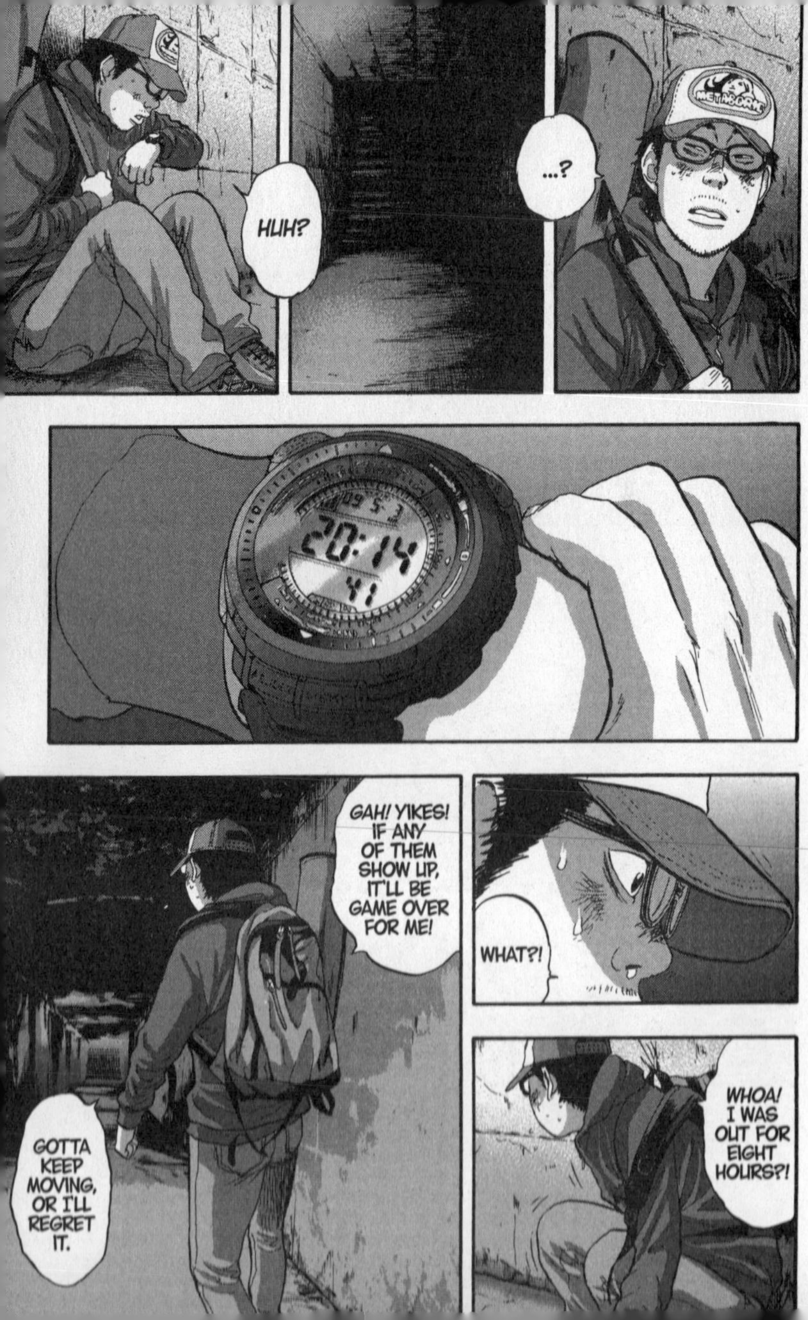
...?
HUH?
WHAT?!
WHOA! I WAS OUT FOR EIGHT HOURS?!
GAH! YIKES! IF ANY OF THEM SHOW UP, IT'LL BE GAME OVER FOR ME!
GOTTA KEEP MOVING, OR I'LL REGRET IT.

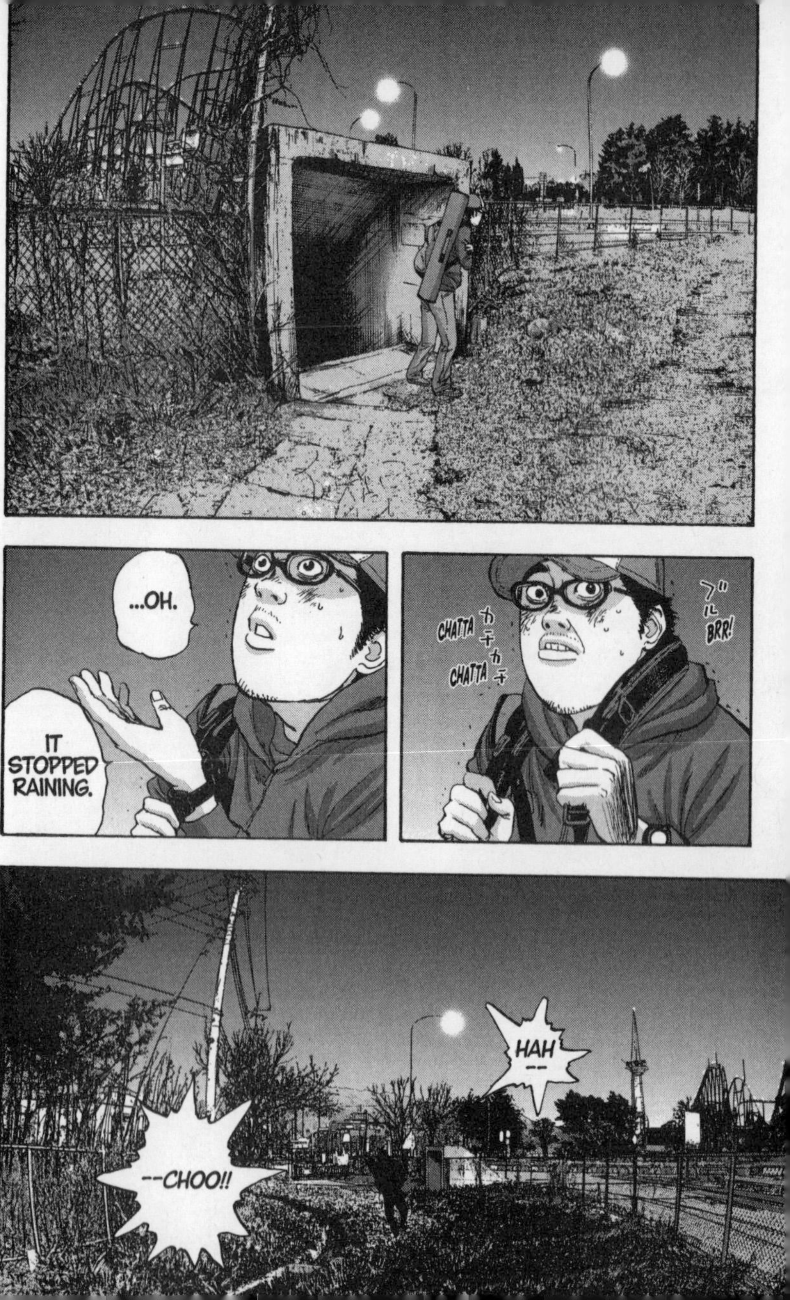
ブル BRR!
カチ CHATTA
カチ CHATTA
...OH.
IT STOPPED RAINING.
HAH --
--CHOO!!

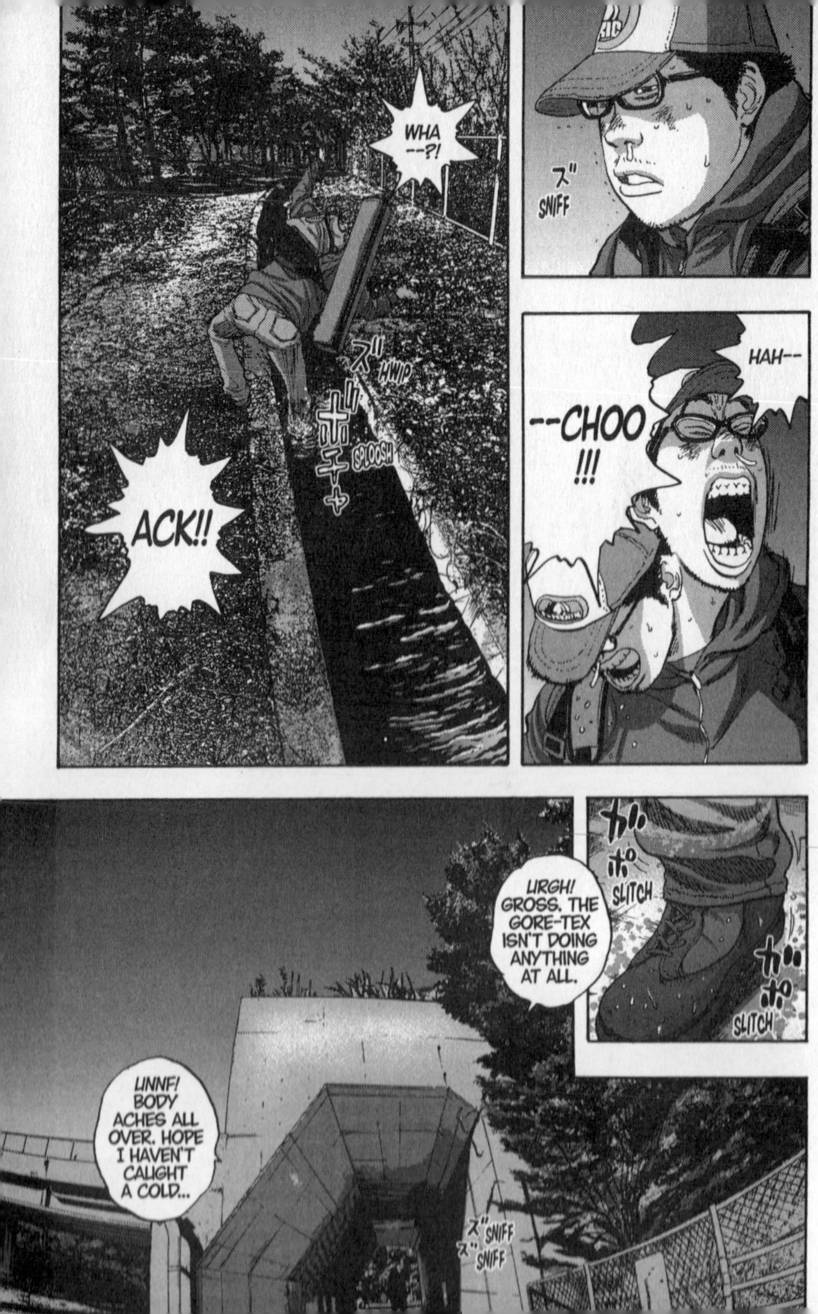
SNIFF
HAH--
--CHOO !!!
WHA --?!
HWIP
SPLOSH
ACK!!
SLITCH
URGH! GROSS. THE GORE-TEX ISN'T DOING ANYTHING AT ALL.
SLITCH
UNNF! BODY ACHES ALL OVER. HOPE I HAVEN'T CAUGHT A COLD...
SNIFF
SNIFF

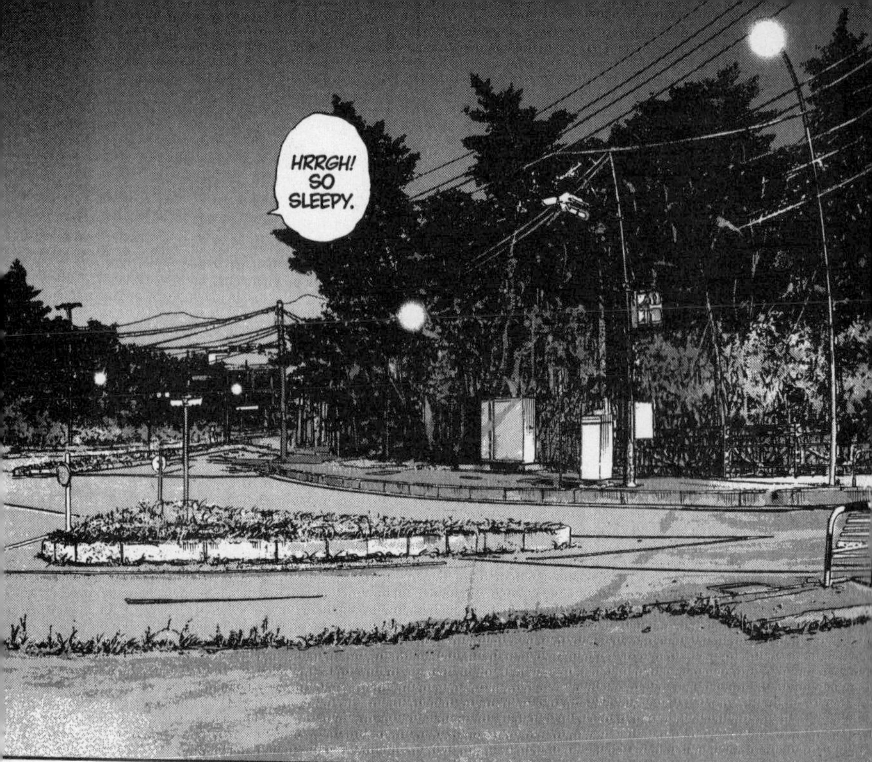
HRRGH! SO SLEEPY.

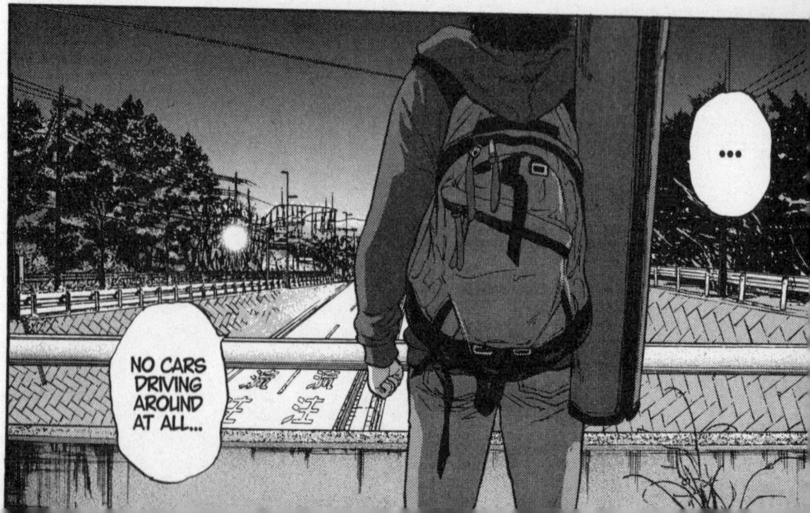
...
NO CARS DRIVING AROUND AT ALL...

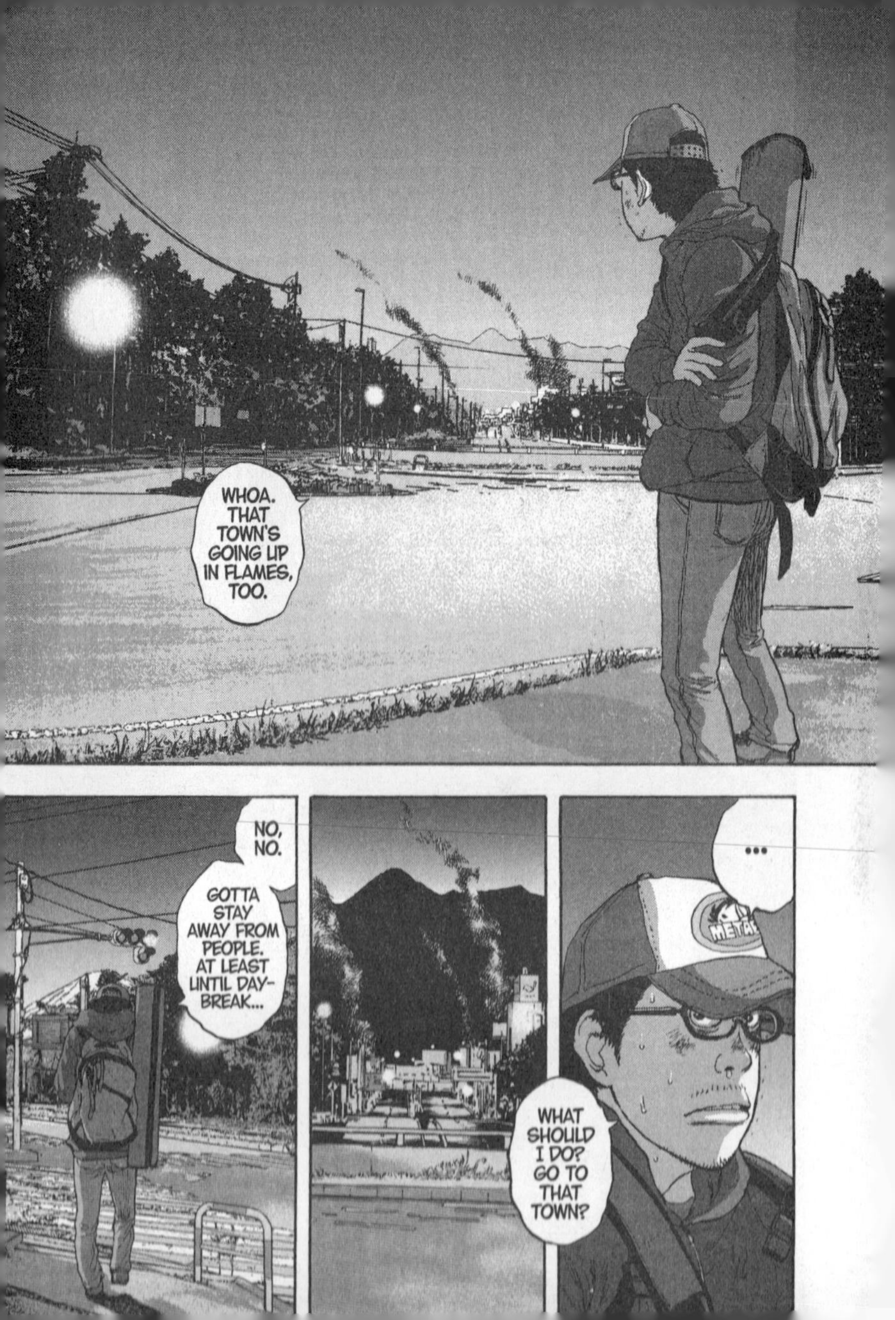
WHOA. THAT TOWN'S GOING UP IN FLAMES, TOO.
...
WHAT SHOULD I DO? GO TO THAT TOWN?
NO, NO.
GOTTA STAY AWAY FROM PEOPLE. AT LEAST UNTIL DAY-BREAK...

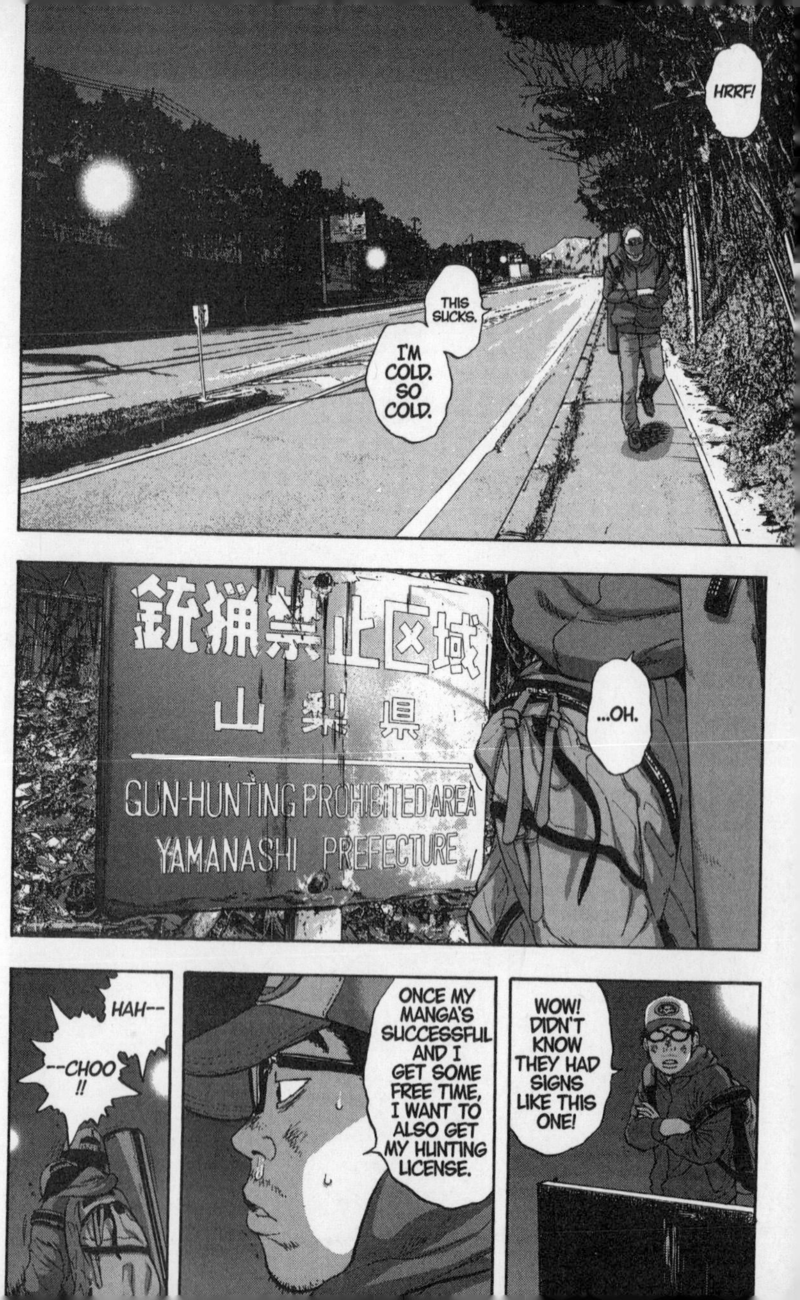
HRRF!
THIS SUCKS.
I'M COLD. SO COLD.
銃猟禁止区域
山梨県
GUN-HUNTING PROHIBITED AREA
YAMANASHI PREFECTURE
...OH.
WOW! DIDN'T KNOW THEY HAD SIGNS LIKE THIS ONE!
ONCE MY MANGA'S SUCCESSFUL AND I GET SOME FREE TIME, I WANT TO ALSO GET MY HUNTING LICENSE.
HAH--
--CHOO!!

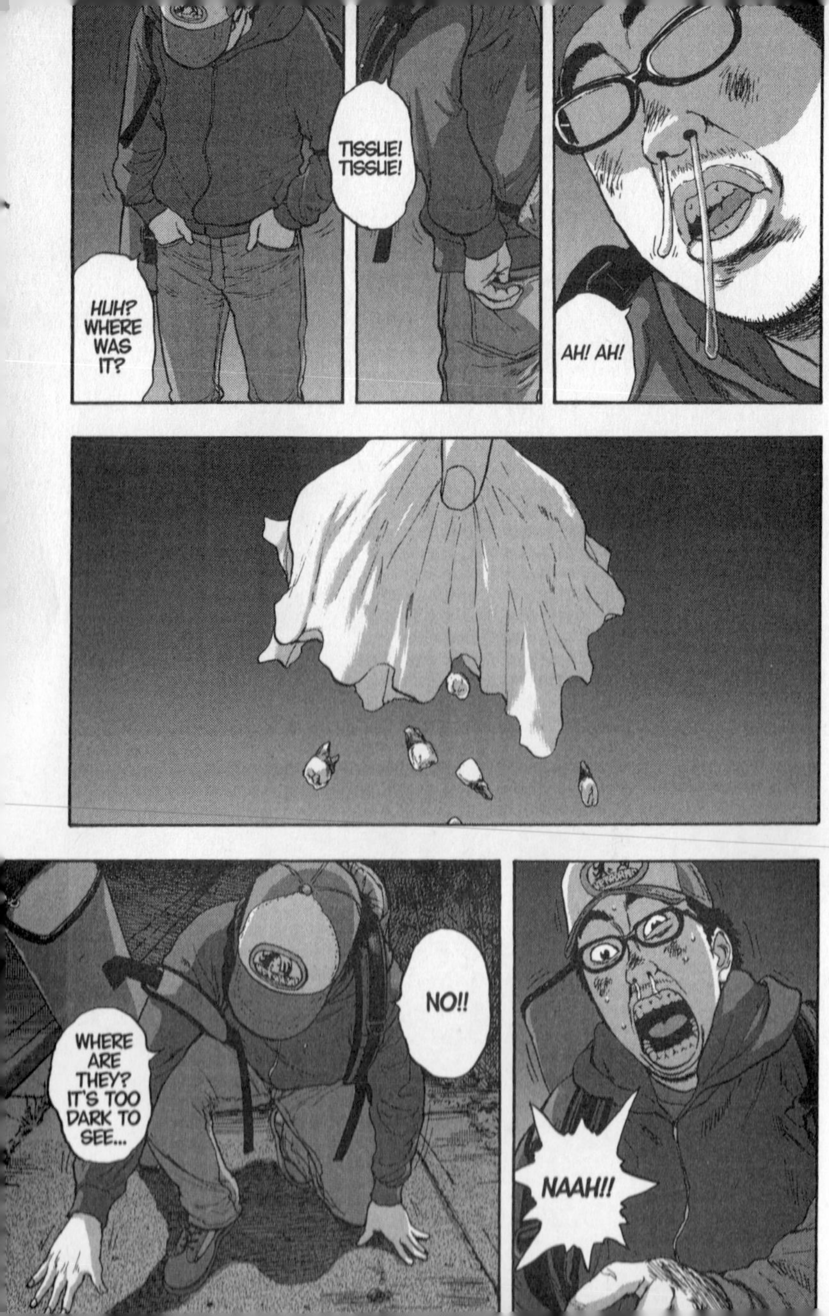
AH! AH!
TISSUE! TISSUE!
HUH? WHERE WAS IT?
NAAH!!
NO!!
WHERE ARE THEY? IT'S TOO DARK TO SEE...

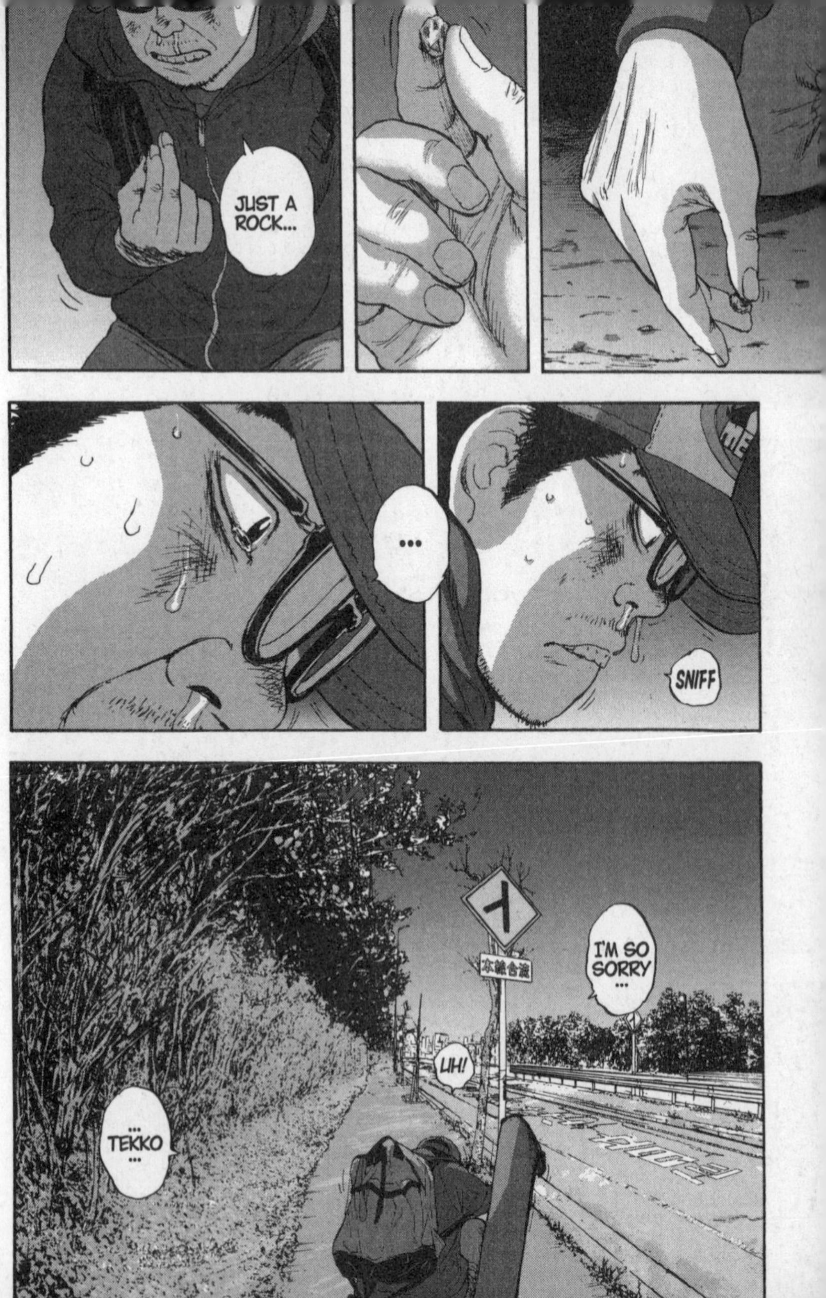
JUST A ROCK...
...
SNIFF
I'M SO SORRY...
UH!
...TEKKO...

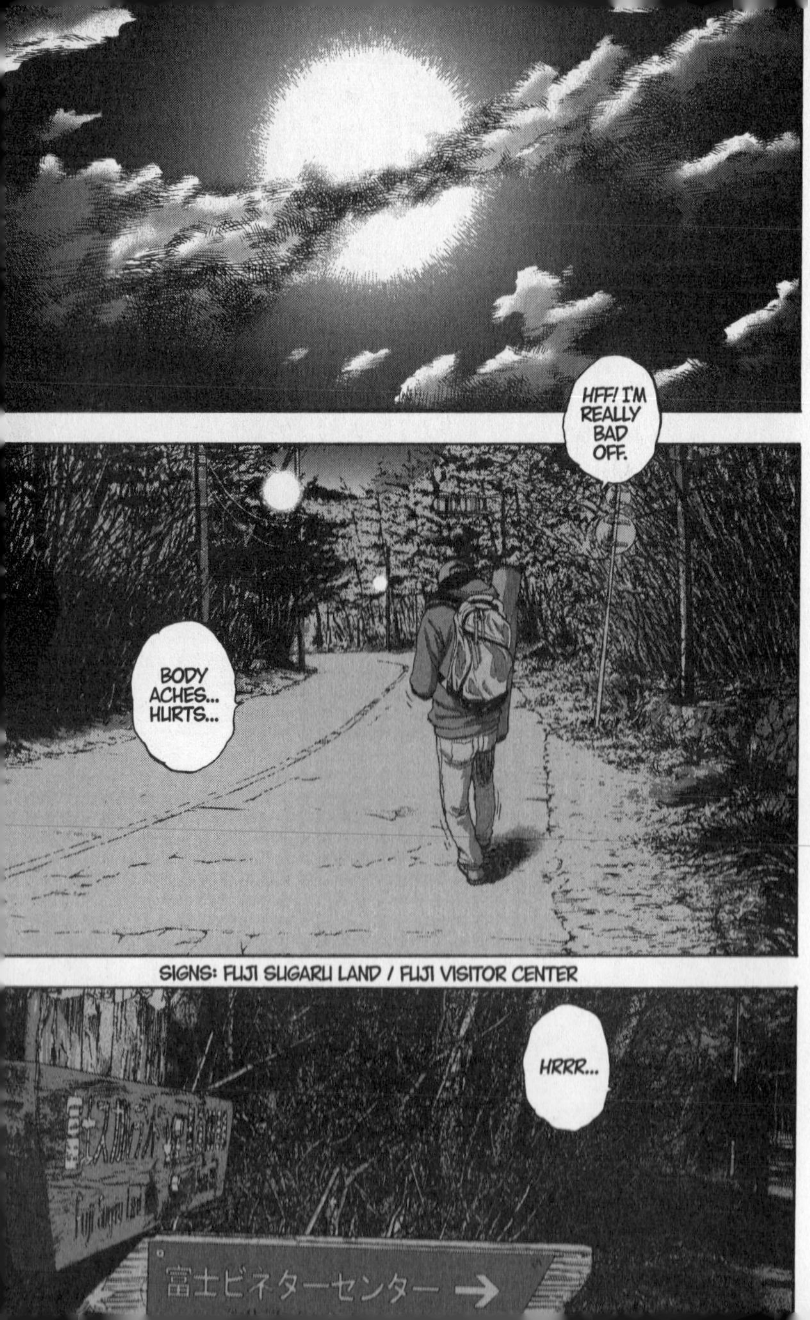
HFF! I'M REALLY BAD OFF.
BODY ACHES... HURTS...
SIGNS: FUJI SUGARU LAND / FUJI VISITOR CENTER
HRRR...
富士ビネターセンター

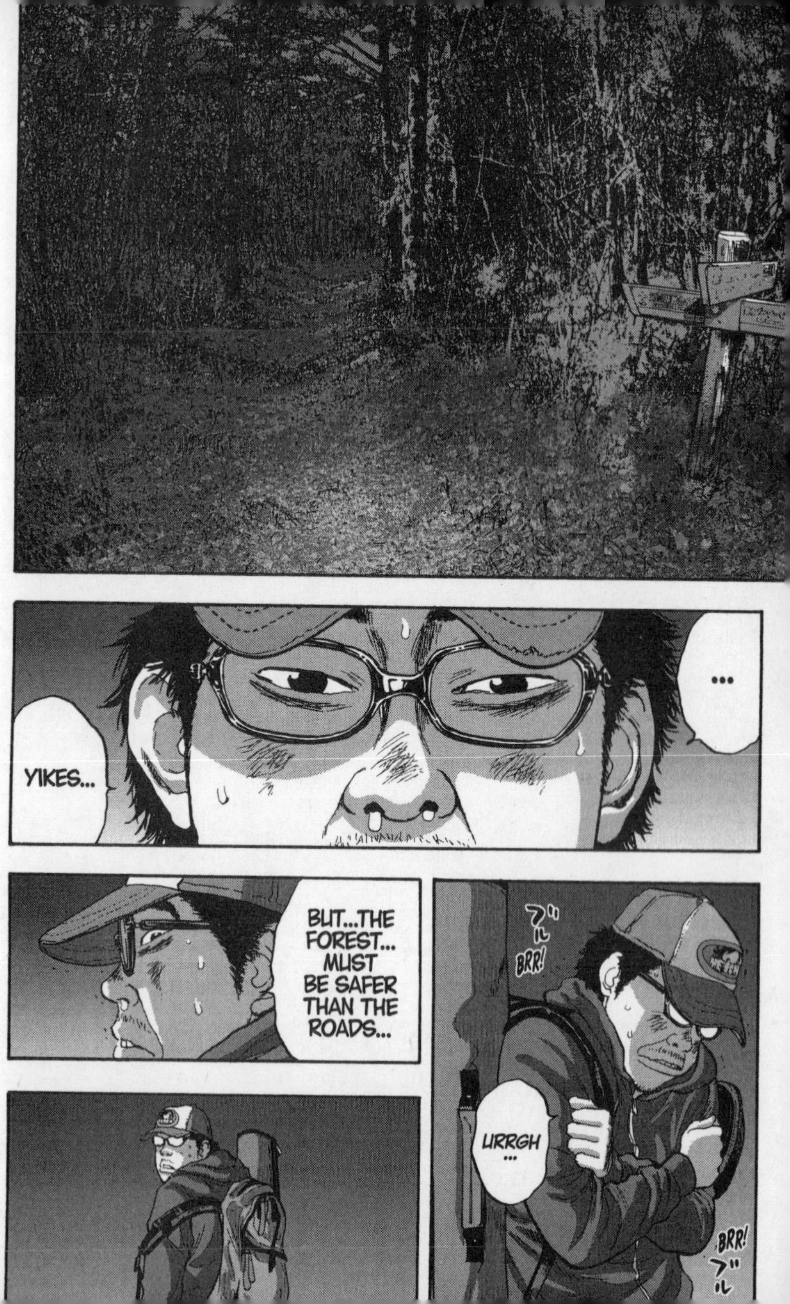
...
YIKES...
ブル
BRR!
URRGH...
BRR!
ブル
BUT...THE FOREST... MUST BE SAFER THAN THE ROADS...

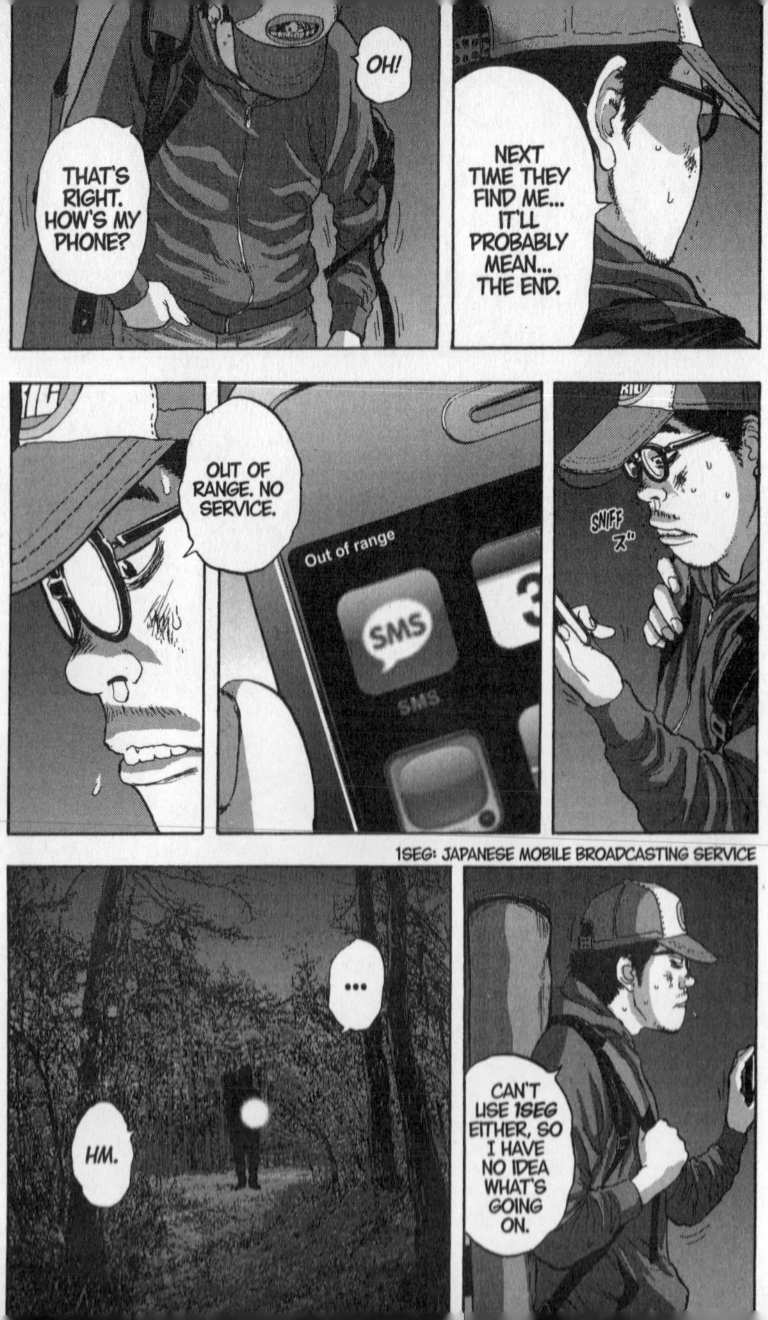
NEXT TIME THEY FIND ME... IT'LL PROBABLY MEAN... THE END.
OH!
THAT'S RIGHT. HOW'S MY PHONE?
SNIFF
ズ
Out of range
SMS
SMS
OUT OF RANGE. NO SERVICE.
CAN'T USE 1SEG EITHER, SO I HAVE NO IDEA WHAT'S GOING ON.
1SEG: JAPANESE MOBILE BROADCASTING SERVICE
...
HM.

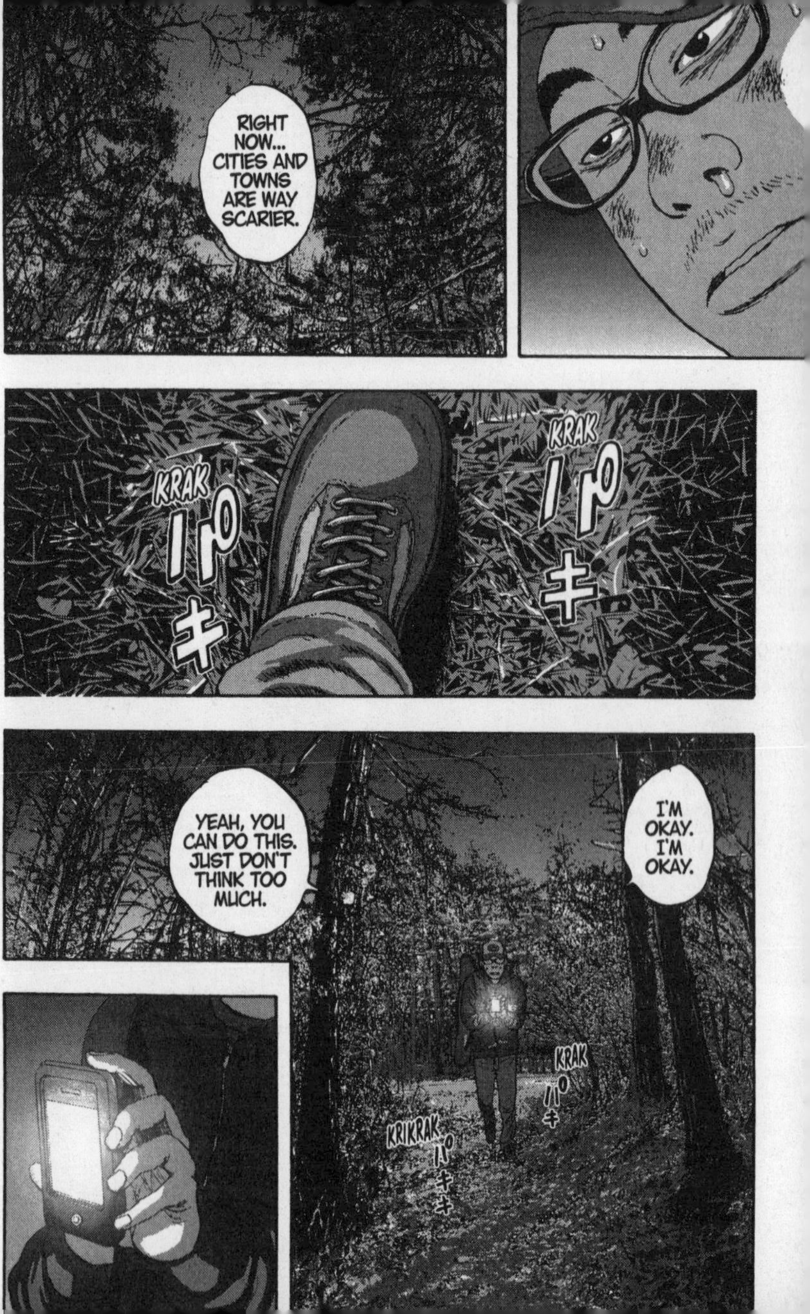
RIGHT NOW... CITIES AND TOWNS ARE WAY SCARIER.
KRAK
パキッ
KRAK
パキ
I'M OKAY. I'M OKAY.
YEAH, YOU CAN DO THIS. JUST DON'T THINK TOO MUCH.
KRAK
パキ
KRIKRAK
パキキ

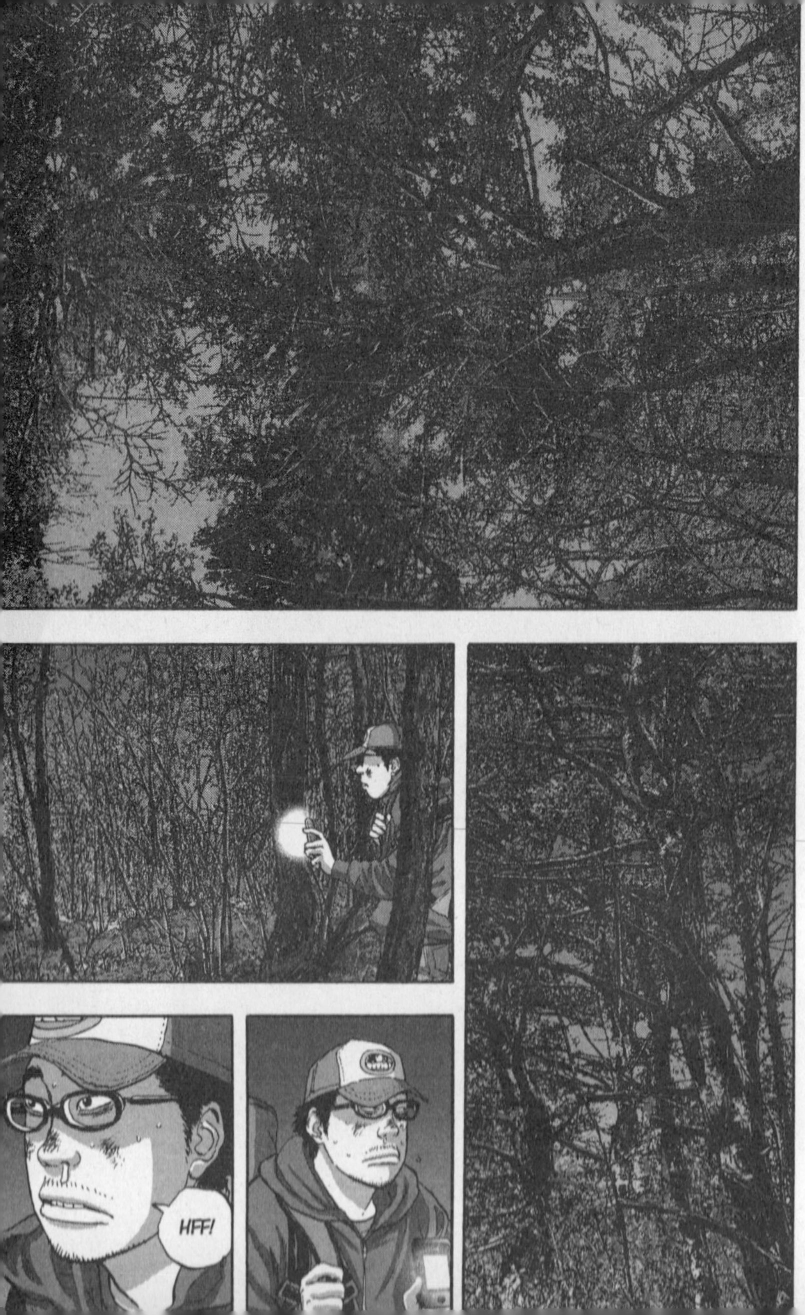
HFF!

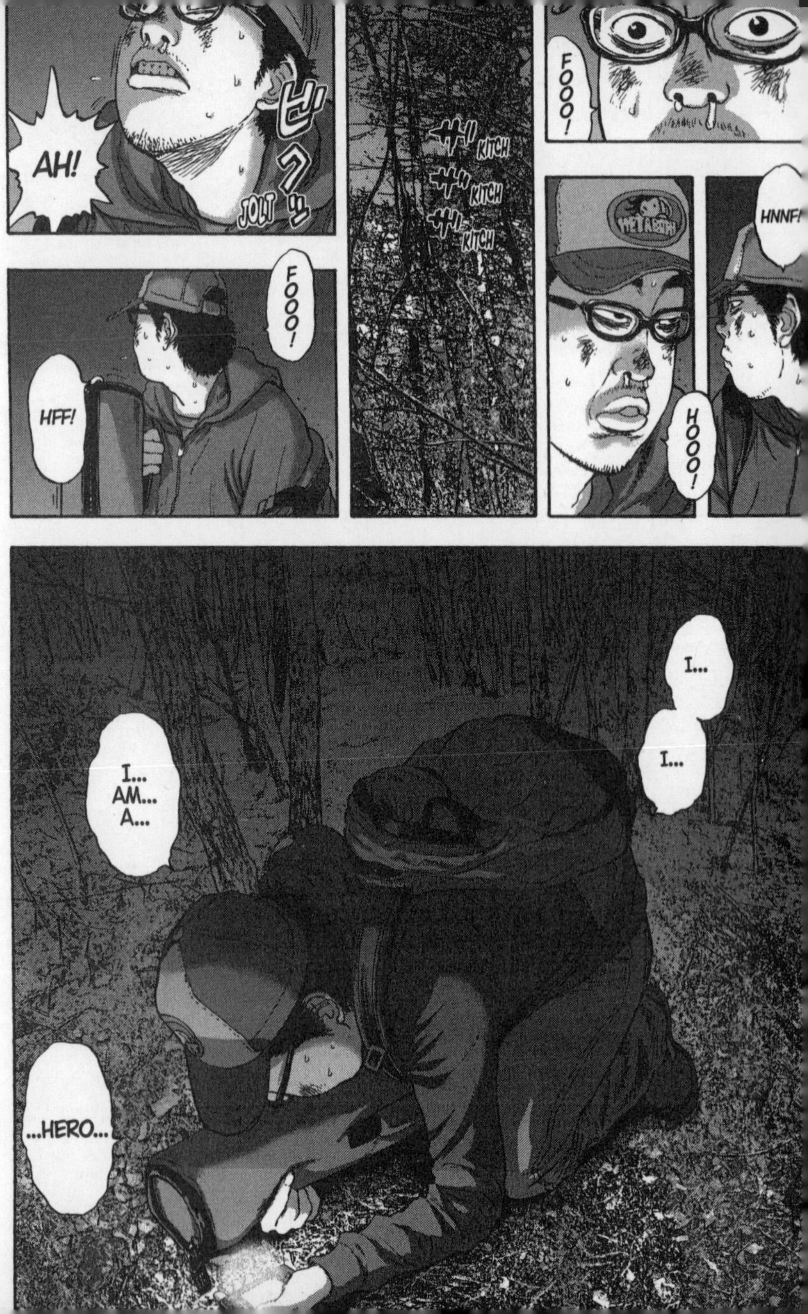
FOOO!
HNNF!
HOOO!
KITCH
KITCH
KITCH
AH!
JOLT
FOOO!
HFF!
I...
I...
I... AM... A...
...HERO...

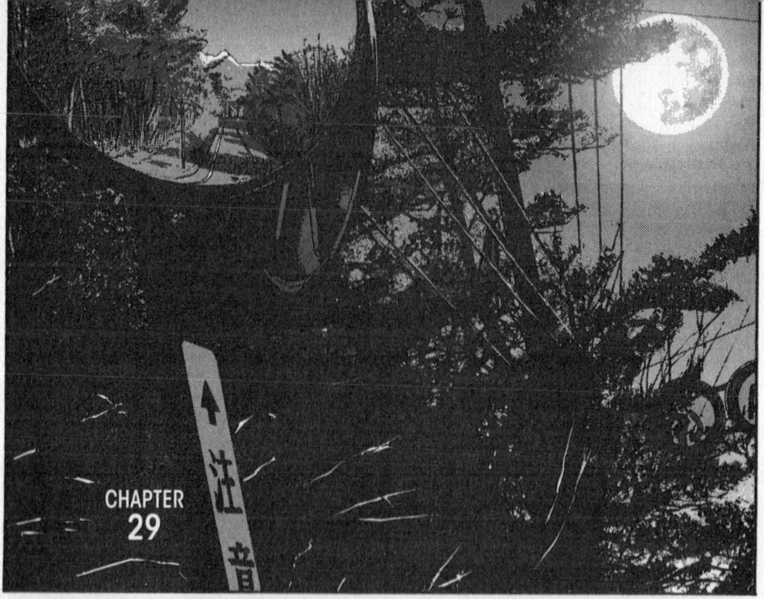
CHAPTER
29

SIGN: CAUTION

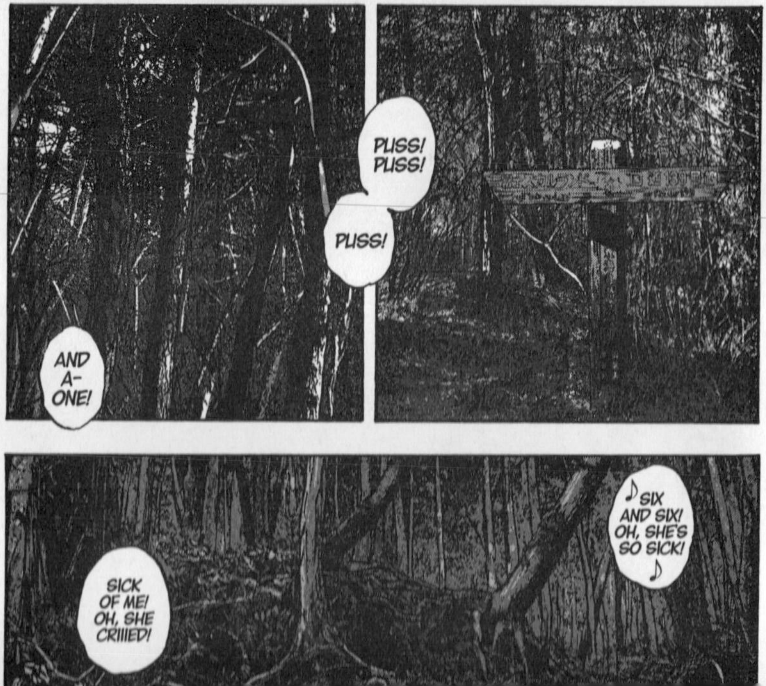
PUSS! PUSS!
PUSS!
AND A-ONE!
♪SIX AND SIX! OH, SHE'S SO SICK!♪
SICK OF ME! OH, SHE CRIIIED!

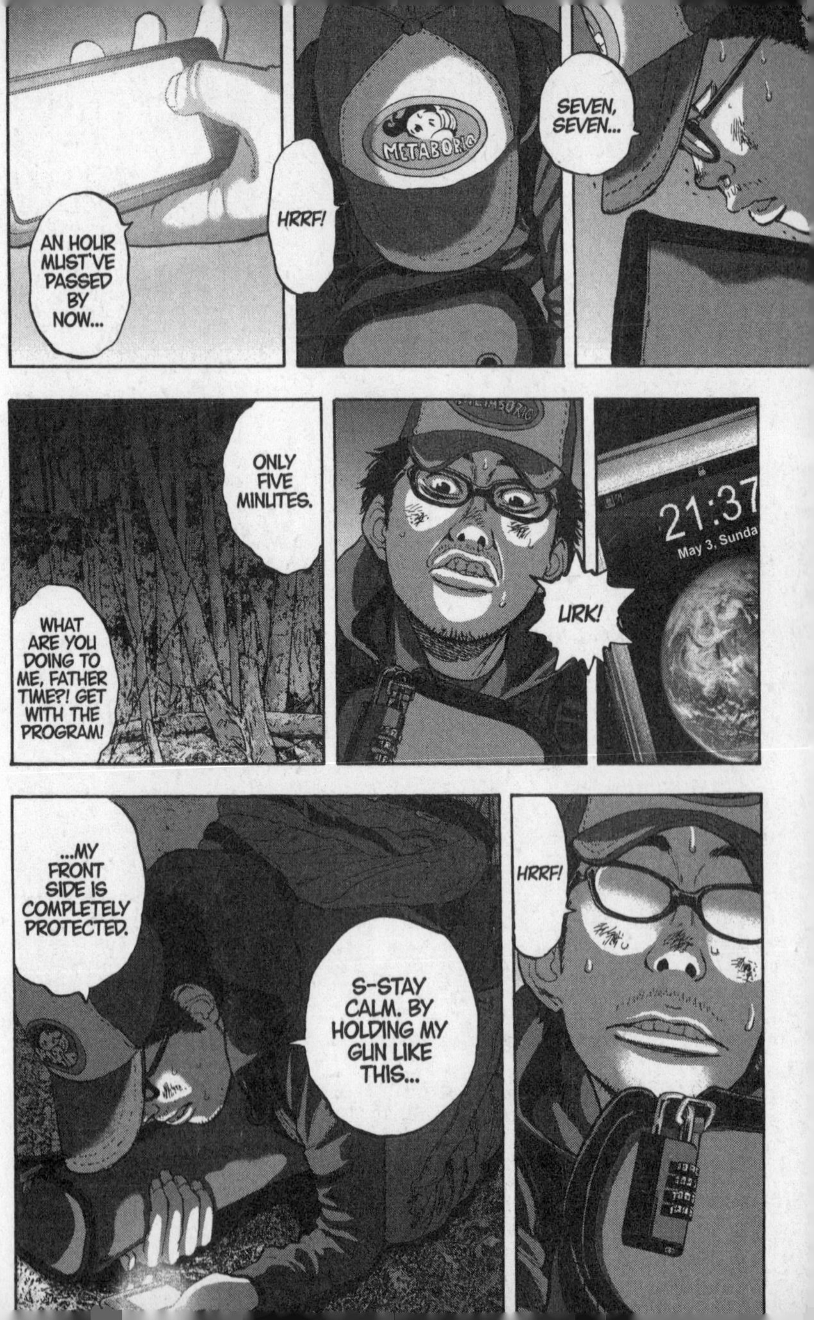
SEVEN, SEVEN...
METABORIC
HRRF!
AN HOUR MUST'VE PASSED BY NOW...
21:37
May 3, Sunda
URK!
ONLY FIVE MINUTES.
WHAT ARE YOU DOING TO ME, FATHER TIME?! GET WITH THE PROGRAM!
HRRF!
S-STAY CALM. BY HOLDING MY GUN LIKE THIS...
...MY FRONT SIDE IS COMPLETELY PROTECTED.

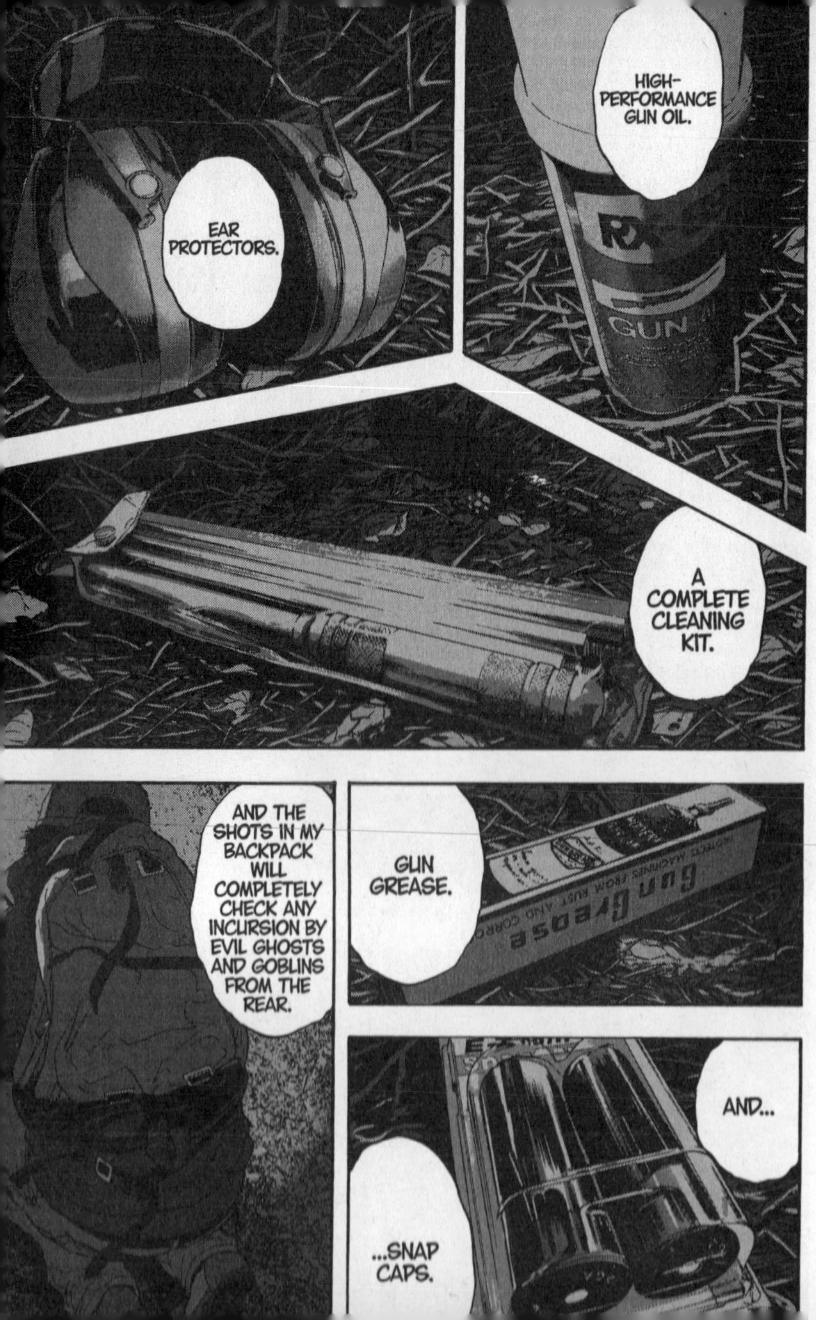
HIGH-PERFORMANCE GUN OIL.
GUN
EAR PROTECTORS.
A COMPLETE CLEANING KIT.
GUN GREASE.
Gun Grease
AND...
...SNAP CAPS.
AND THE SHOTS IN MY BACKPACK WILL COMPLETELY CHECK ANY INCURSION BY EVIL GHOSTS AND GOBLINS FROM THE REAR.

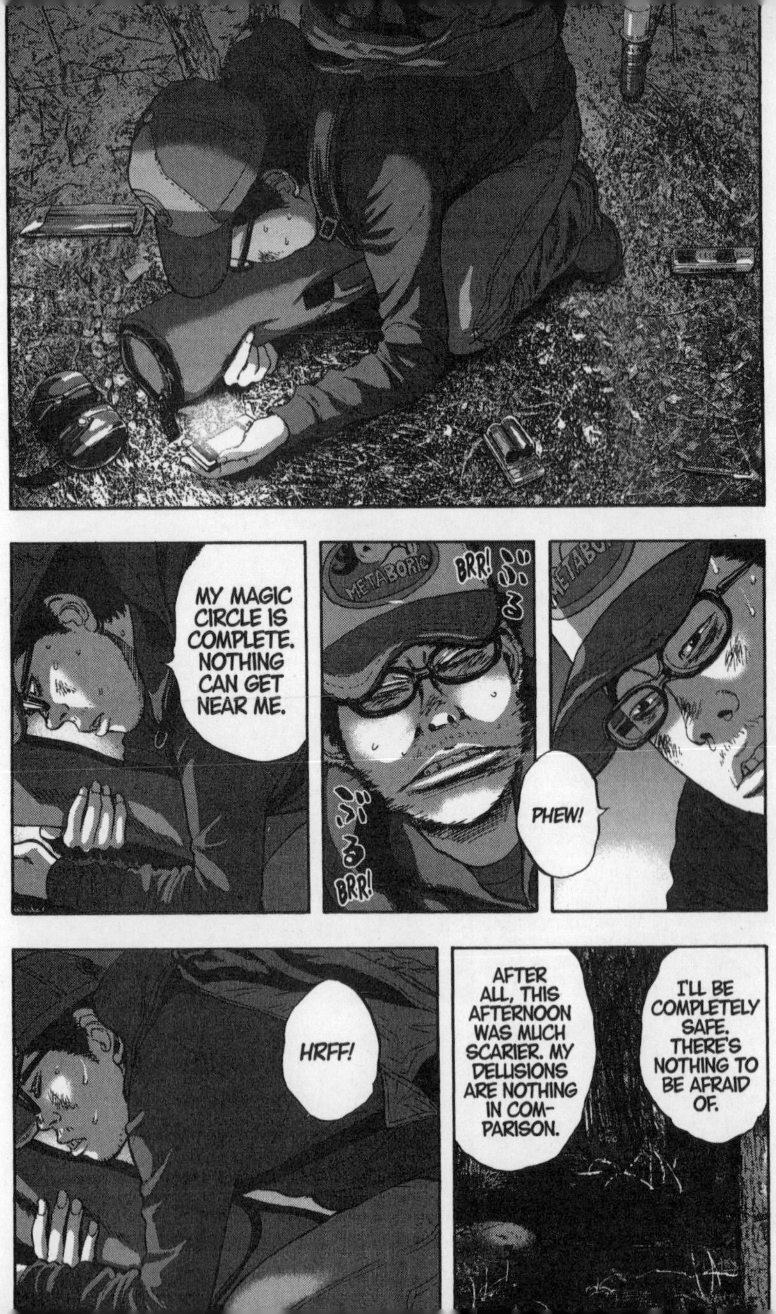
PHEW!
ぶる
BRR!
ぶる
BRR!
MY MAGIC CIRCLE IS COMPLETE. NOTHING CAN GET NEAR ME.
I'LL BE COMPLETELY SAFE. THERE'S NOTHING TO BE AFRAID OF.
AFTER ALL, THIS AFTERNOON WAS MUCH SCARIER. MY DELUSIONS ARE NOTHING IN COM-PARISON.
HRFF!

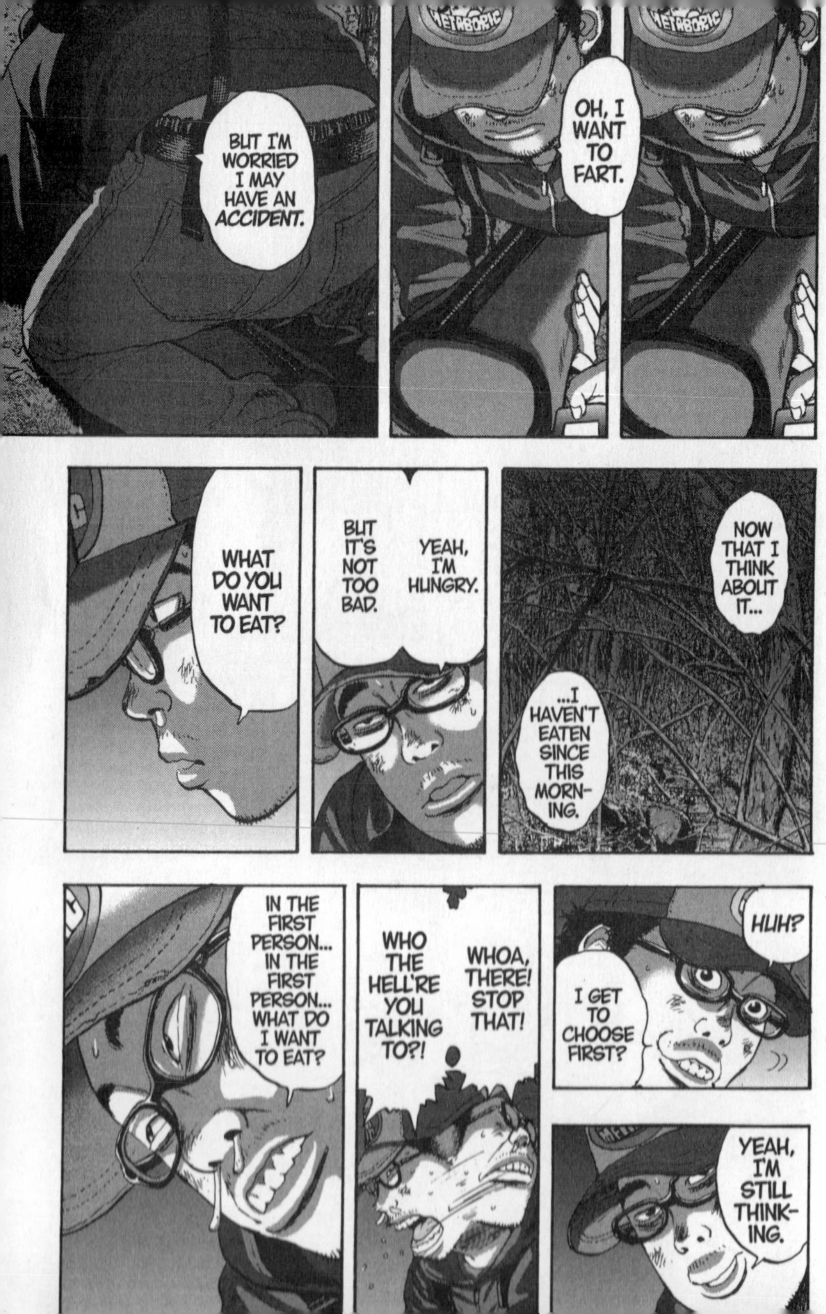
OH, I WANT TO FART.
BUT I'M WORRIED I MAY HAVE AN ACCIDENT.
NOW THAT I THINK ABOUT IT...
...I HAVEN'T EATEN SINCE THIS MORNING.
YEAH, I'M HUNGRY.
BUT IT'S NOT TOO BAD.
WHAT DO YOU WANT TO EAT?
HUH?
I GET TO CHOOSE FIRST?
YEAH, I'M STILL THINKING.
WHOA, THERE! STOP THAT!
WHO THE HELL'RE YOU TALKING TO?!
IN THE FIRST PERSON... IN THE FIRST PERSON... WHAT DO I WANT TO EAT?

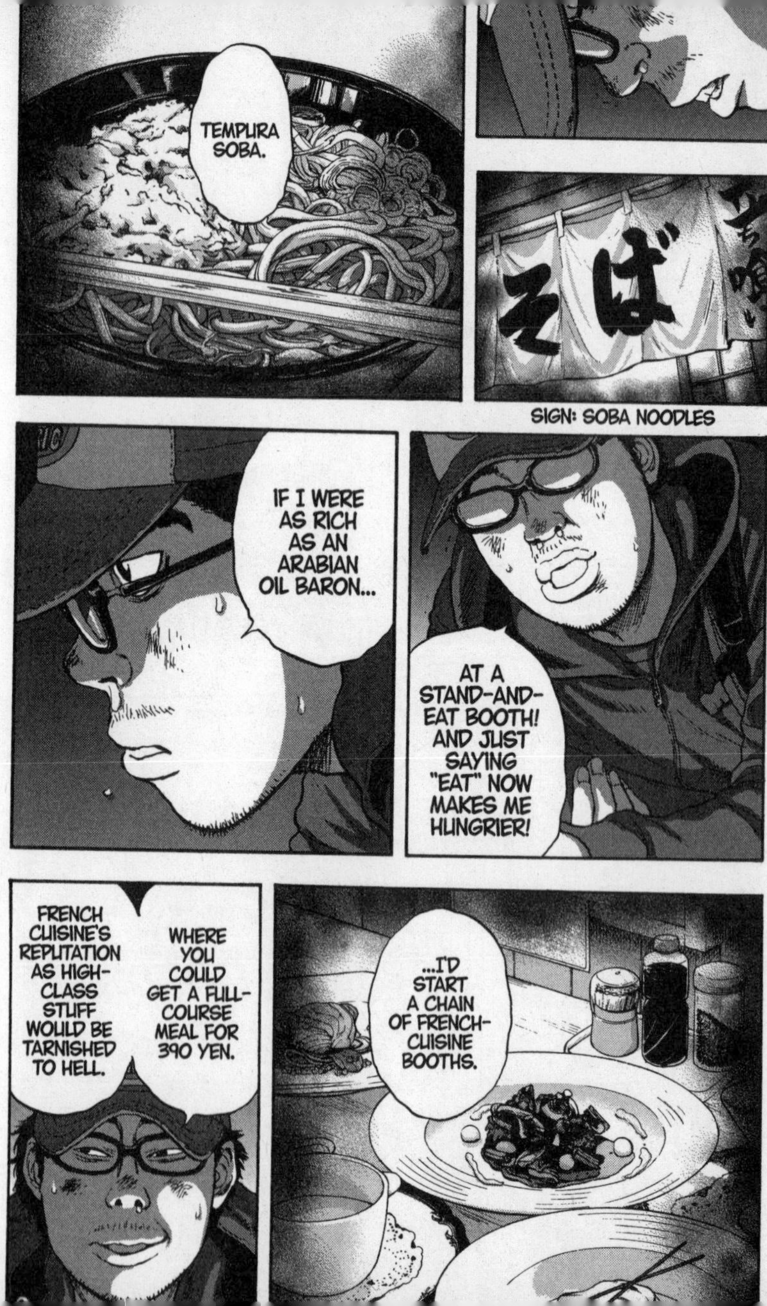
そば
SIGN: SOBA NOODLES
TEMPURA SOBA.
AT A STAND-AND-EAT BOOTH! AND JUST SAYING "EAT" NOW MAKES ME HUNGRIER!
IF I WERE AS RICH AS AN ARABIAN OIL BARON...
...I'D START A CHAIN OF FRENCH-CUISINE BOOTHS.
WHERE YOU COULD GET A FULL-COURSE MEAL FOR 390 YEN.
FRENCH CUISINE'S REPUTATION AS HIGH-CLASS STUFF WOULD BE TARNISHED TO HELL.

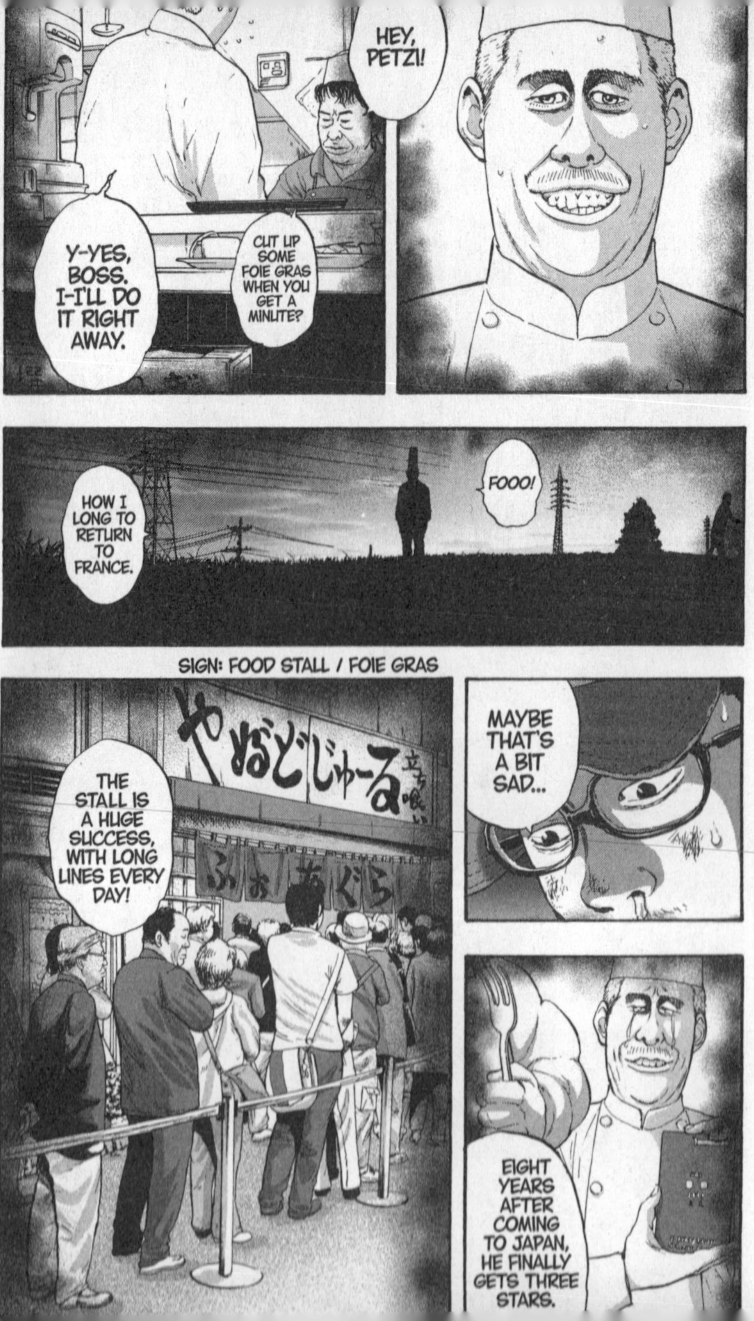
HEY, PETZI!
CUT UP SOME FOIE GRAS WHEN YOU GET A MINUTE?
Y-YES, BOSS. I-I'LL DO IT RIGHT AWAY.
FOOO!
HOW I LONG TO RETURN TO FRANCE.
MAYBE THAT'S A BIT SAD...
EIGHT YEARS AFTER COMING TO JAPAN, HE FINALLY GETS THREE STARS.
SIGN: FOOD STALL / FOIE GRAS
THE STALL IS A HUGE SUCCESS, WITH LONG LINES EVERY DAY!

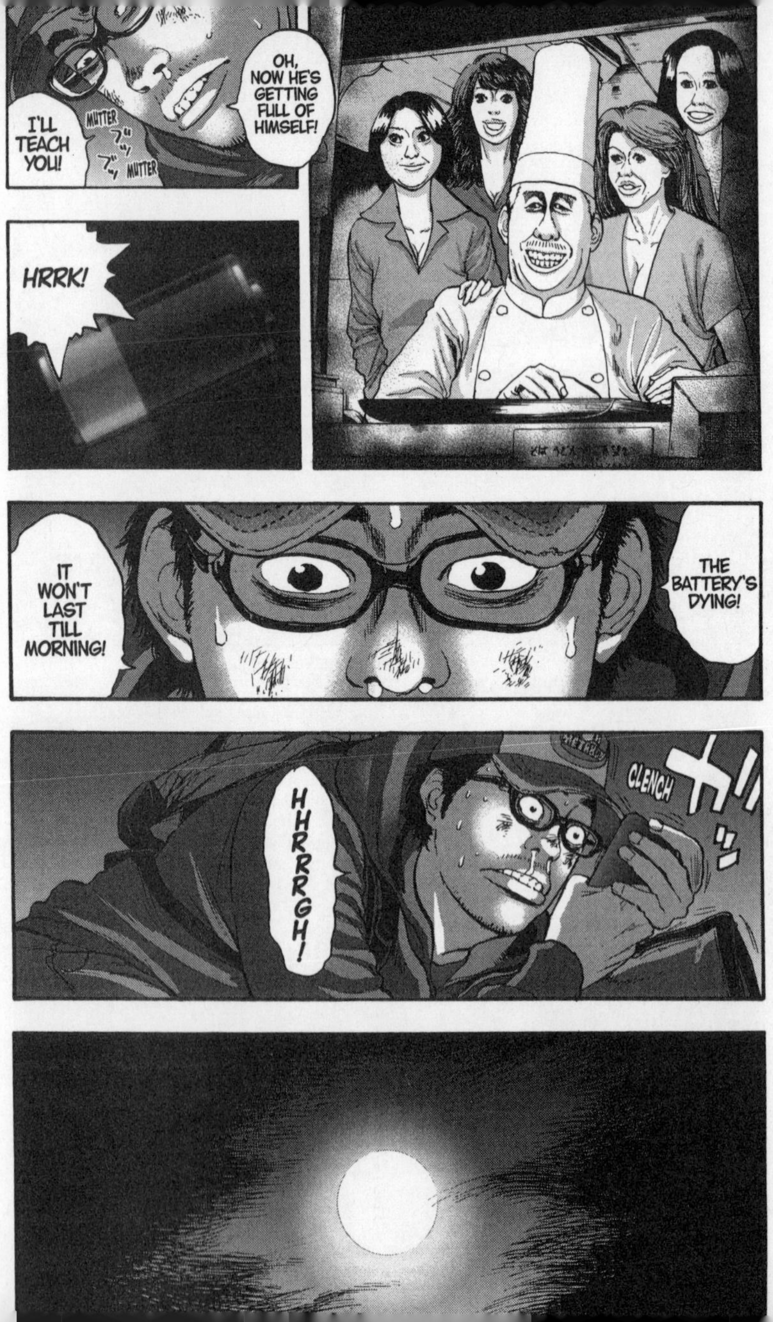
OH, NOW HE'S GETTING FULL OF HIMSELF!
I'LL TEACH YOU!
MUTTER ブツ
ブツ MUTTER
HRRK!
THE BATTERY'S DYING!
IT WON'T LAST TILL MORNING!
CLENCH ガッ
HHRRRGH!

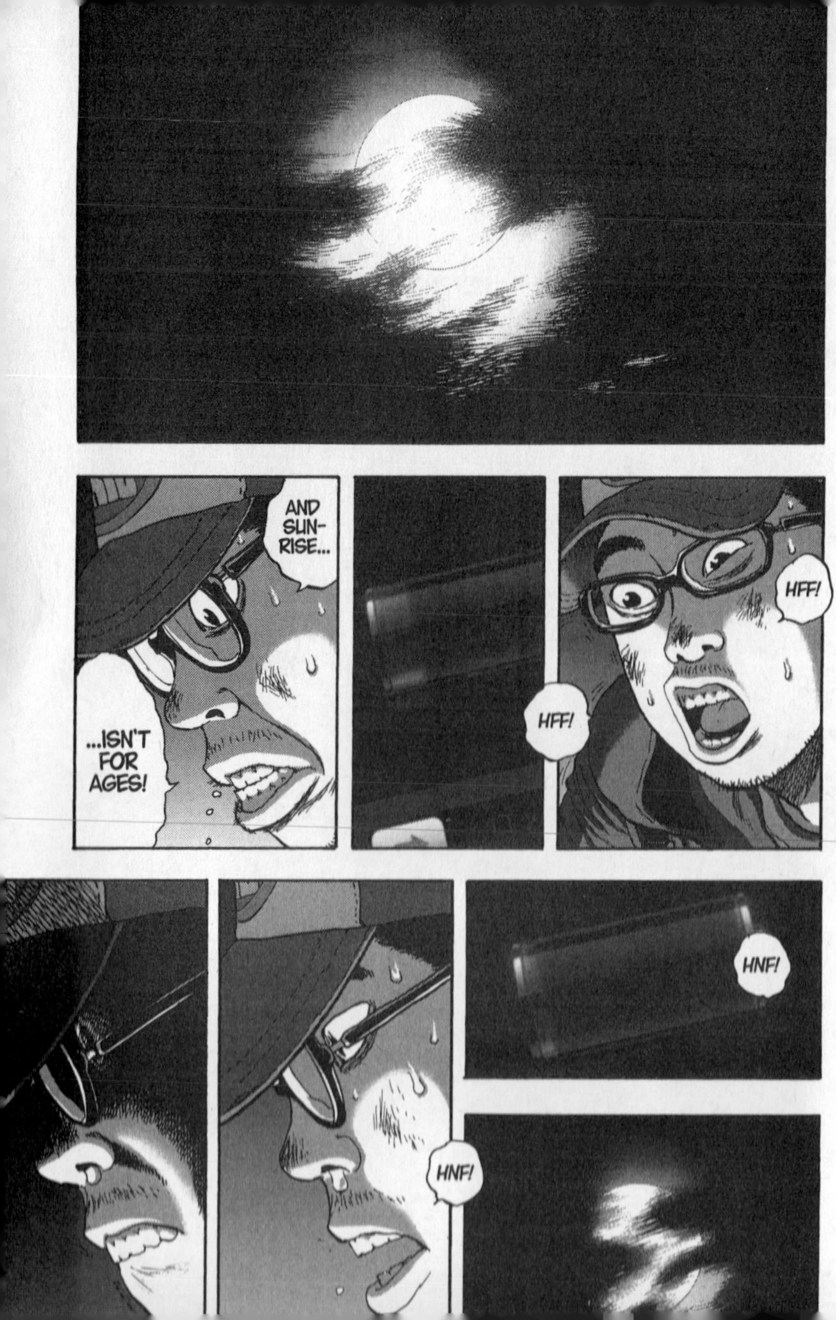
HFF!
HFF!
AND SUN-RISE...
...ISN'T FOR AGES!
HNF!
HNF!

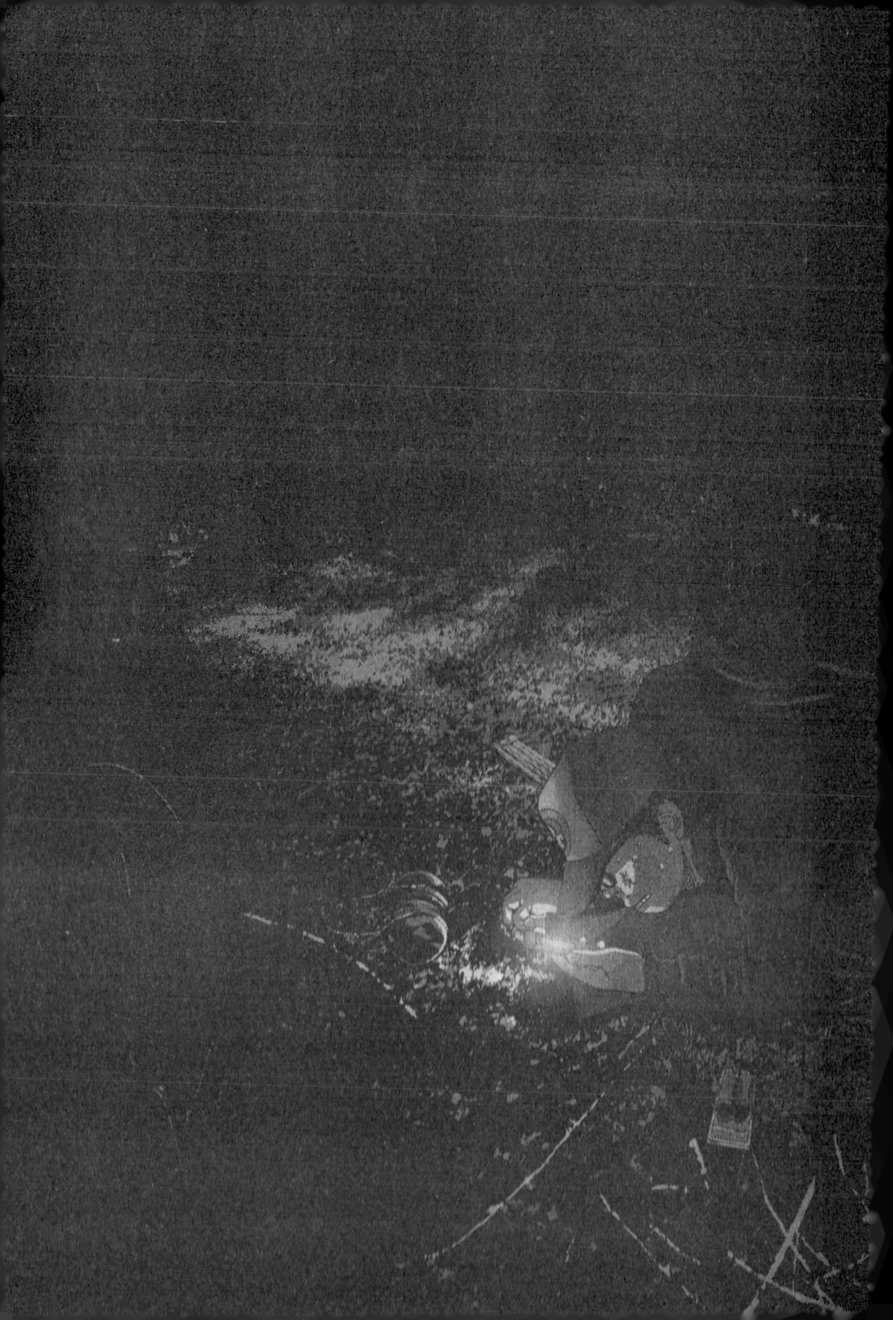

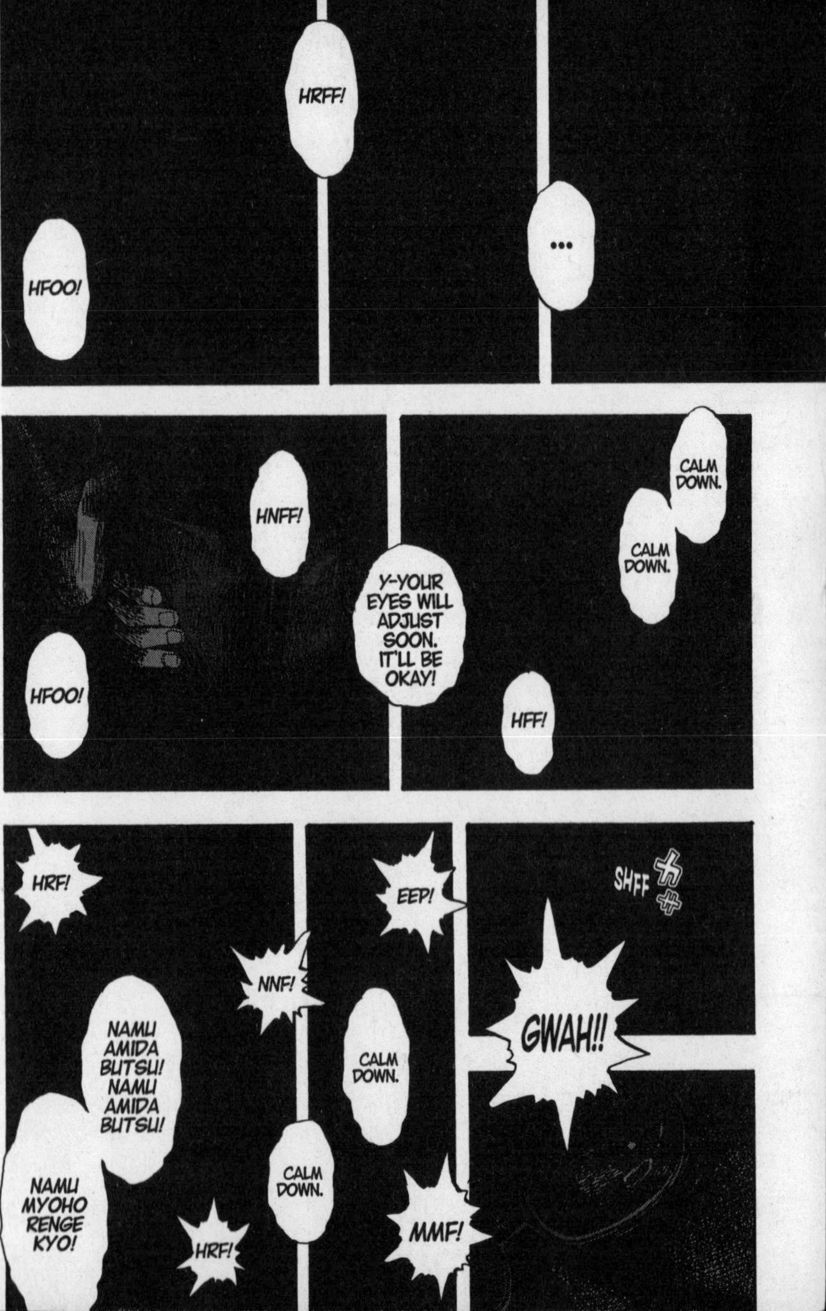
...
HRFF!
HFOO!
CALM DOWN.
CALM DOWN.
Y-YOUR EYES WILL ADJUST SOON. IT'LL BE OKAY!
HFF!
HNFF!
HFOO!
SHFF
GWAH!!
EEP!
CALM DOWN.
CALM DOWN.
MMF!
HRF!
NNF!
NAMU AMIDA BUTSU! NAMU AMIDA BUTSU!
NAMU MYOHO RENGE KYO!
HRF!

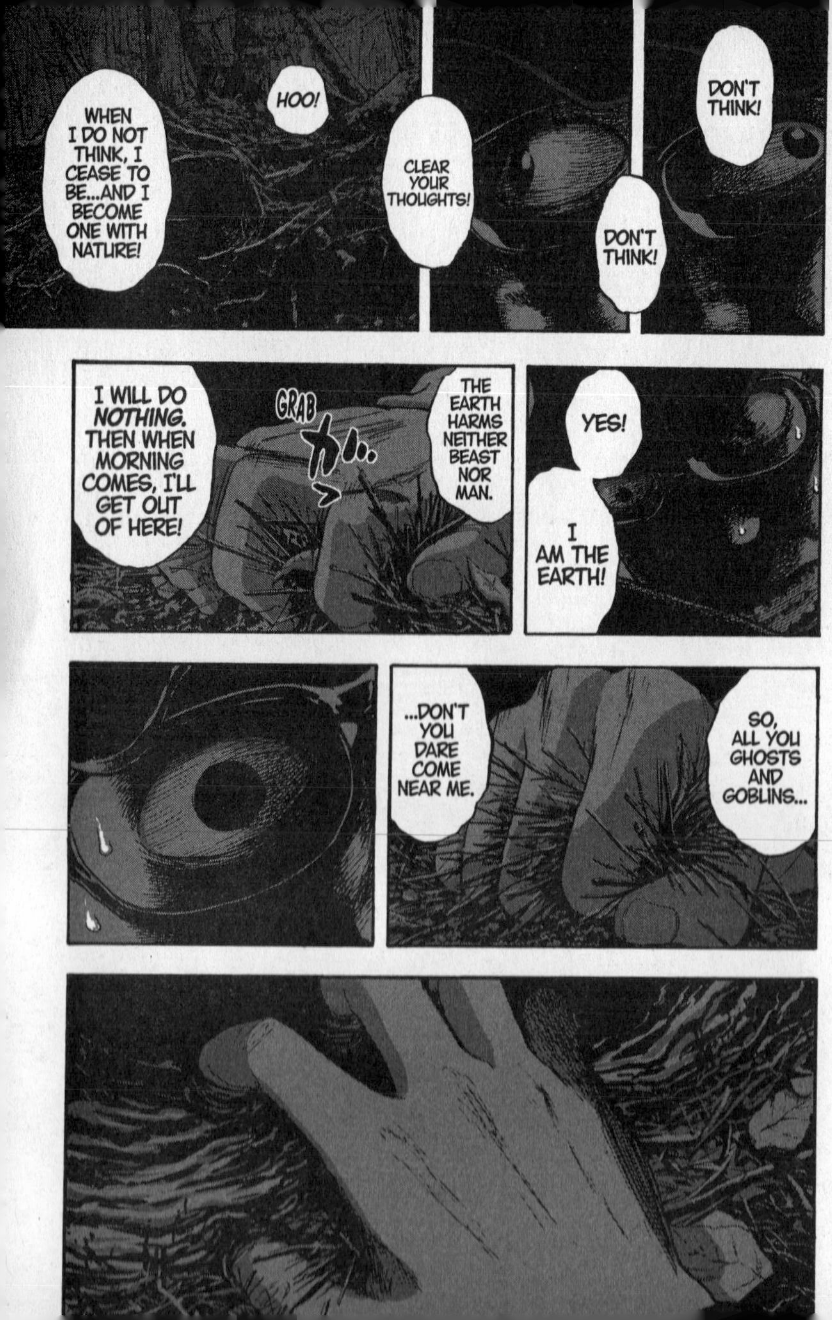
DON'T THINK!
DON'T THINK!
CLEAR YOUR THOUGHTS!
HOO!
WHEN I DO NOT THINK, I CEASE TO BE...AND I BECOME ONE WITH NATURE!
YES!
I AM THE EARTH!
THE EARTH HARMS NEITHER BEAST NOR MAN.
GRAB
I WILL DO *NOTHING.* THEN WHEN MORNING COMES, I'LL GET OUT OF HERE!
SO, ALL YOU GHOSTS AND GOBLINS...
...DON'T YOU DARE COME NEAR ME.

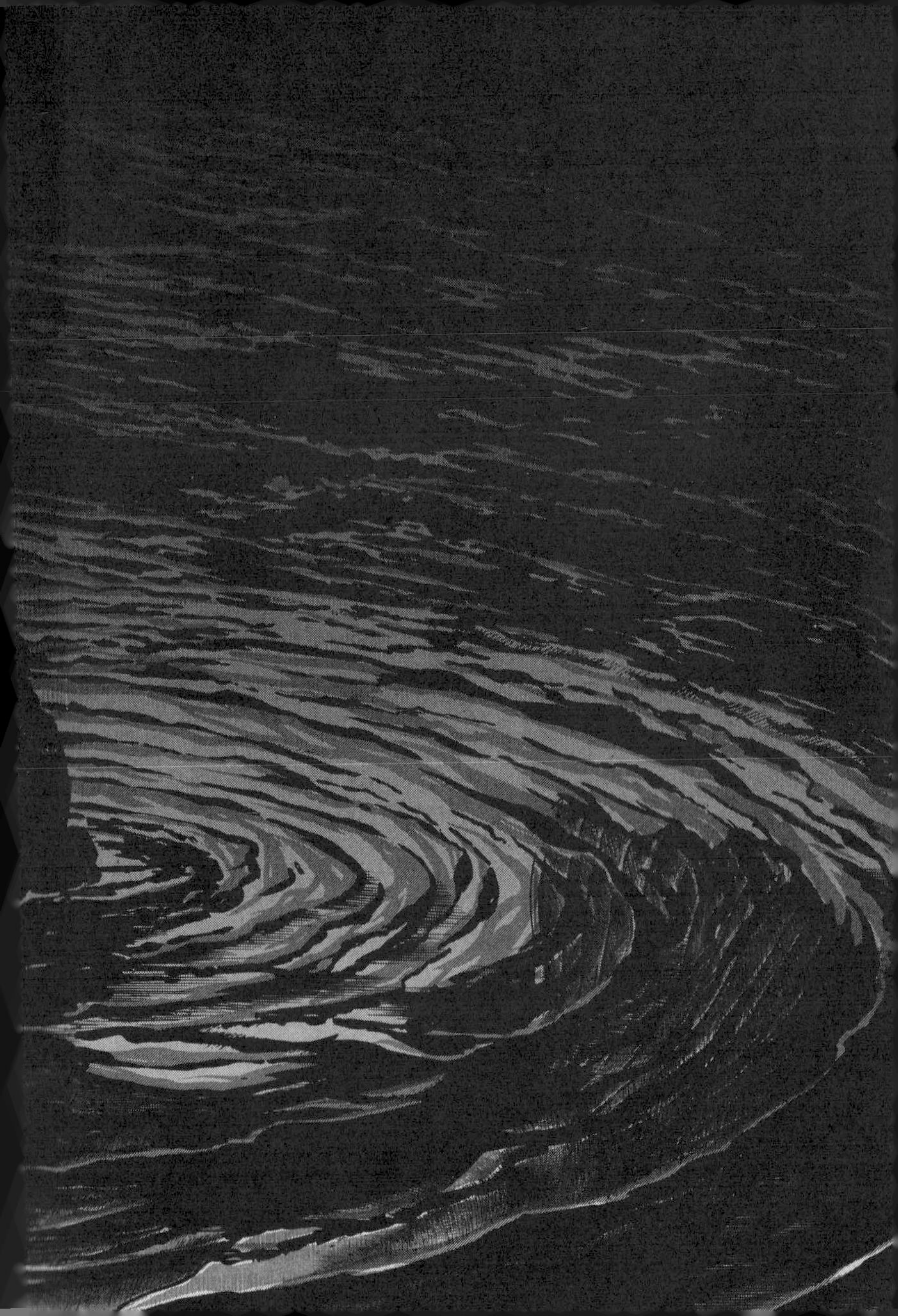

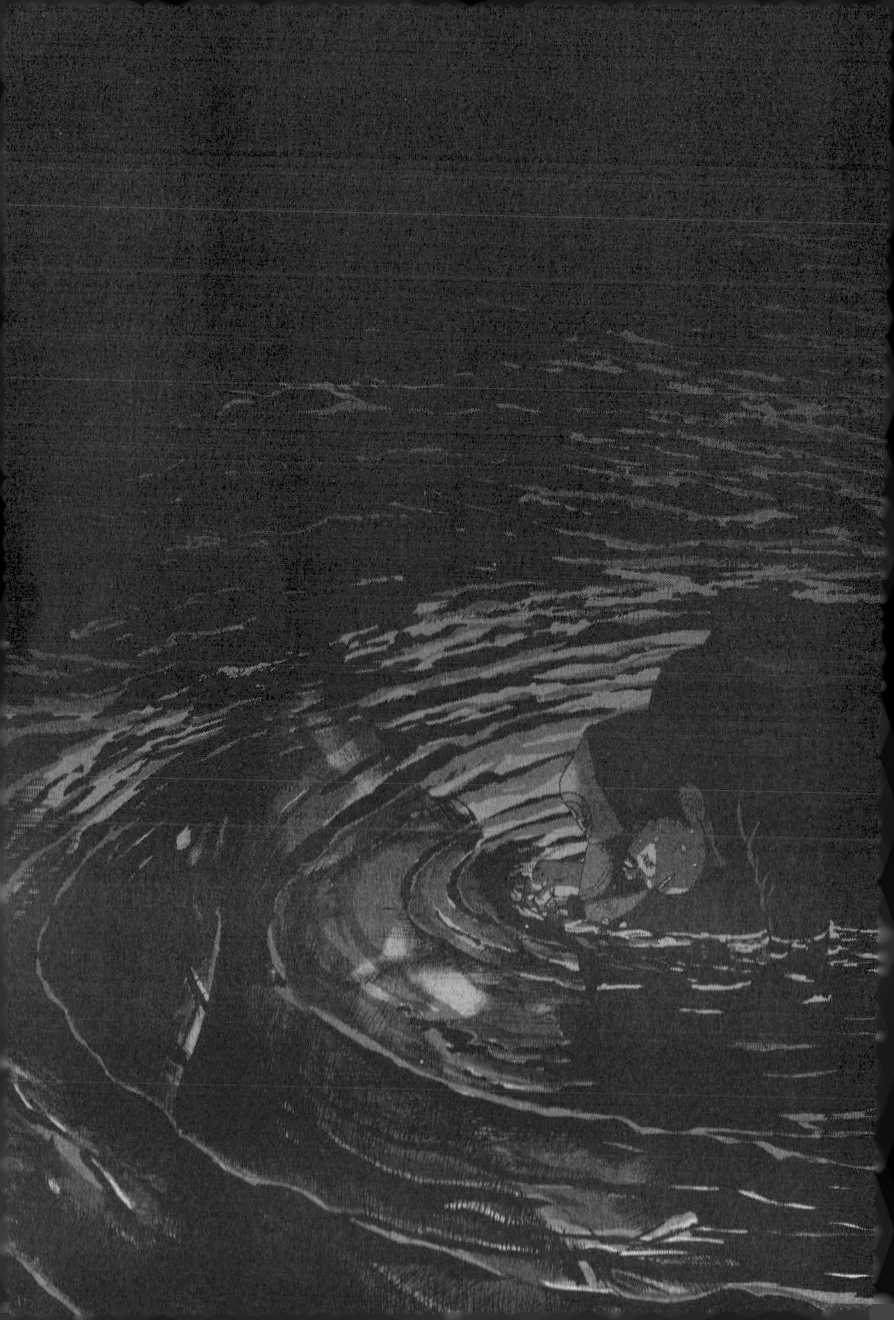

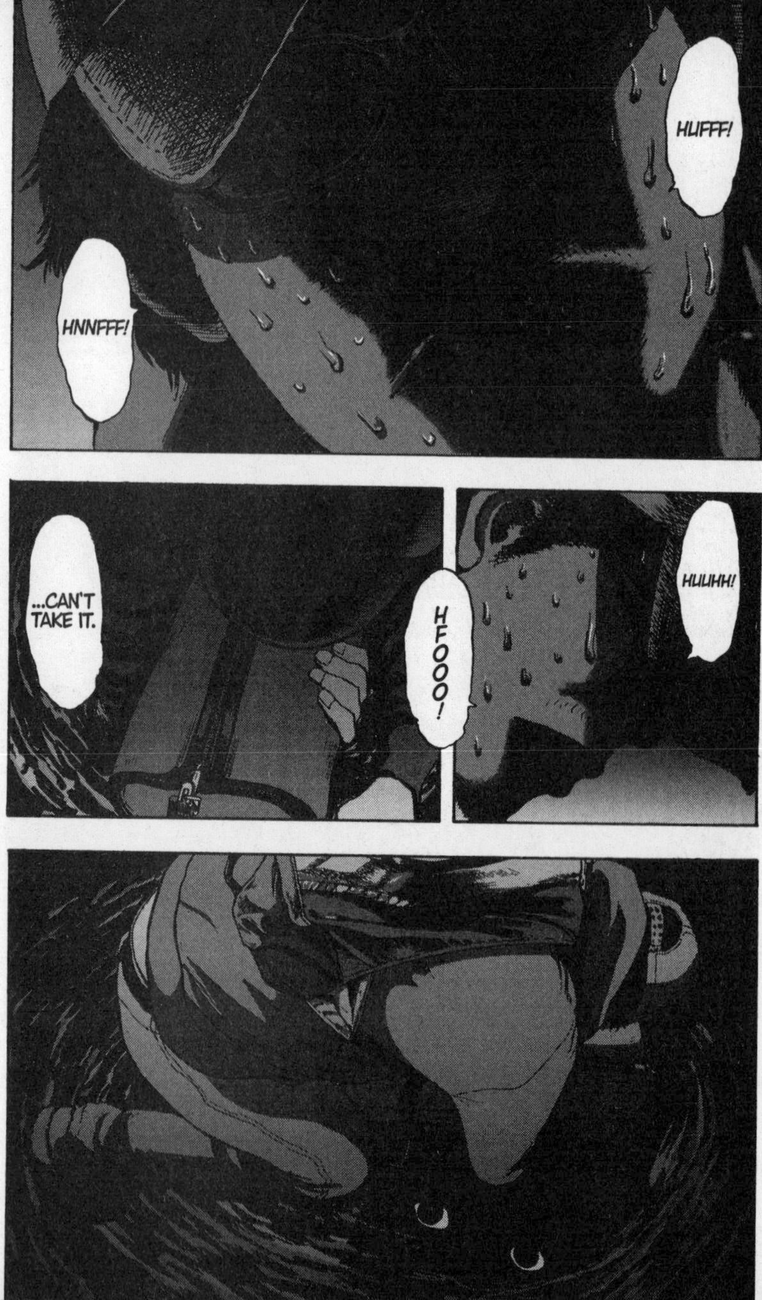
HUFFF!
HNNFFF!
HUUHH!
HFOOO!
...CAN'T TAKE IT.

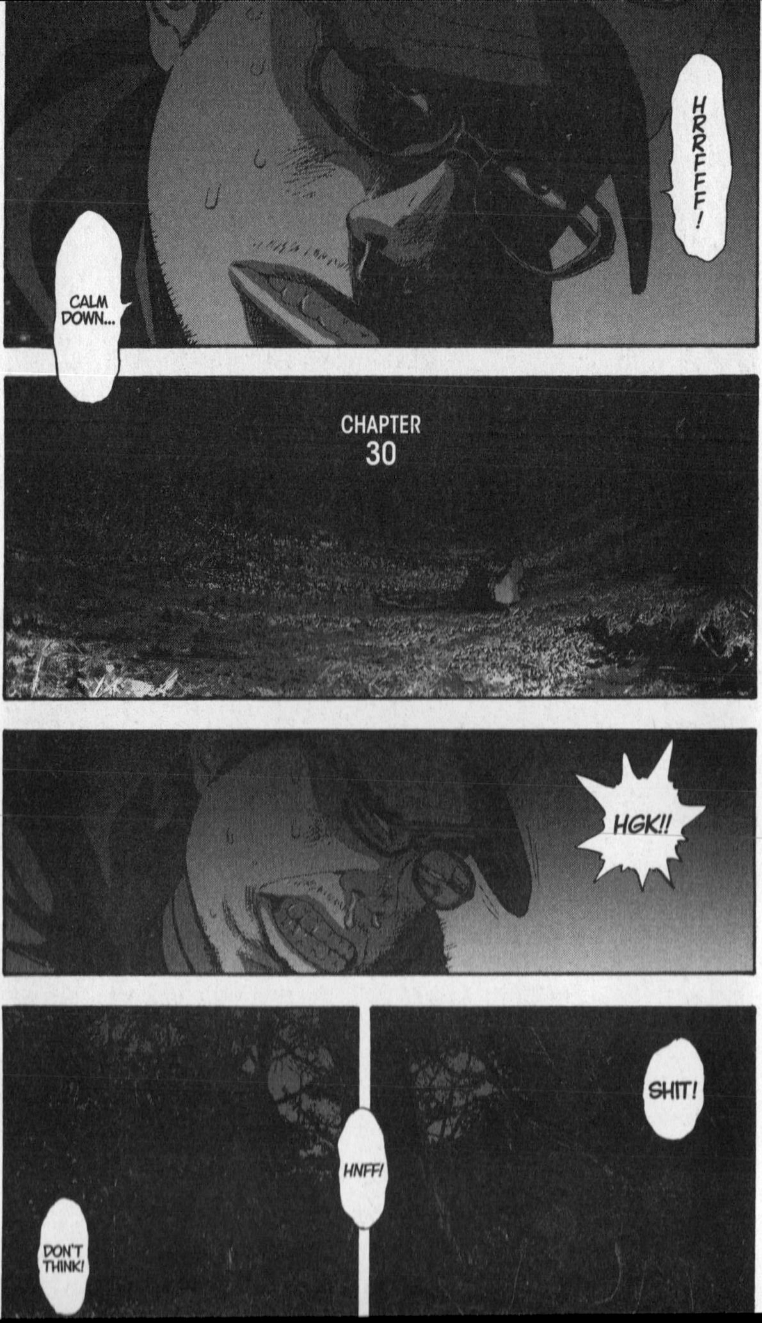
HRRFFF!
CALM DOWN...
CHAPTER 30
HGK!!
SHIT!
HNFF!
DON'T THINK!

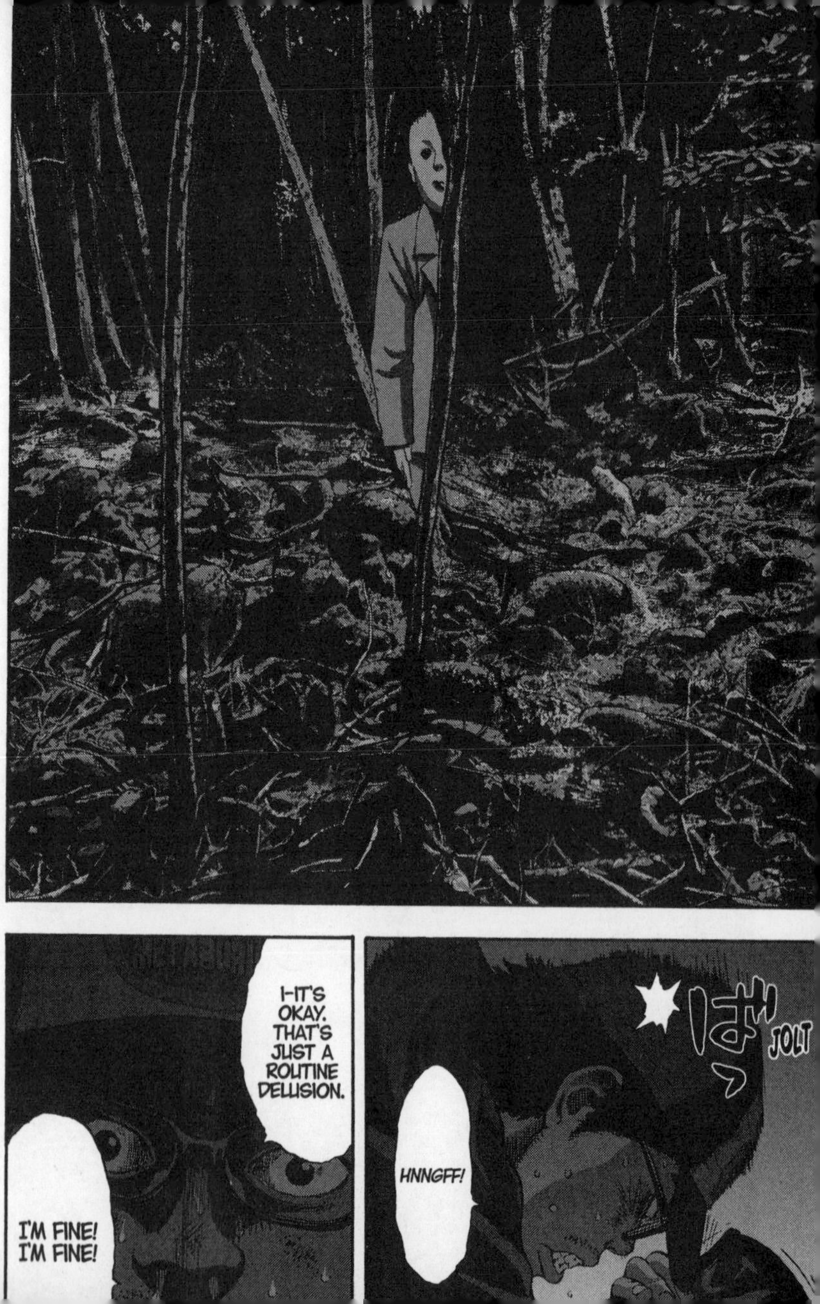
ぱっ
JOLT
HNNGFF!
I-IT'S OKAY. THAT'S JUST A ROUTINE DELUSION.
I'M FINE! I'M FINE!

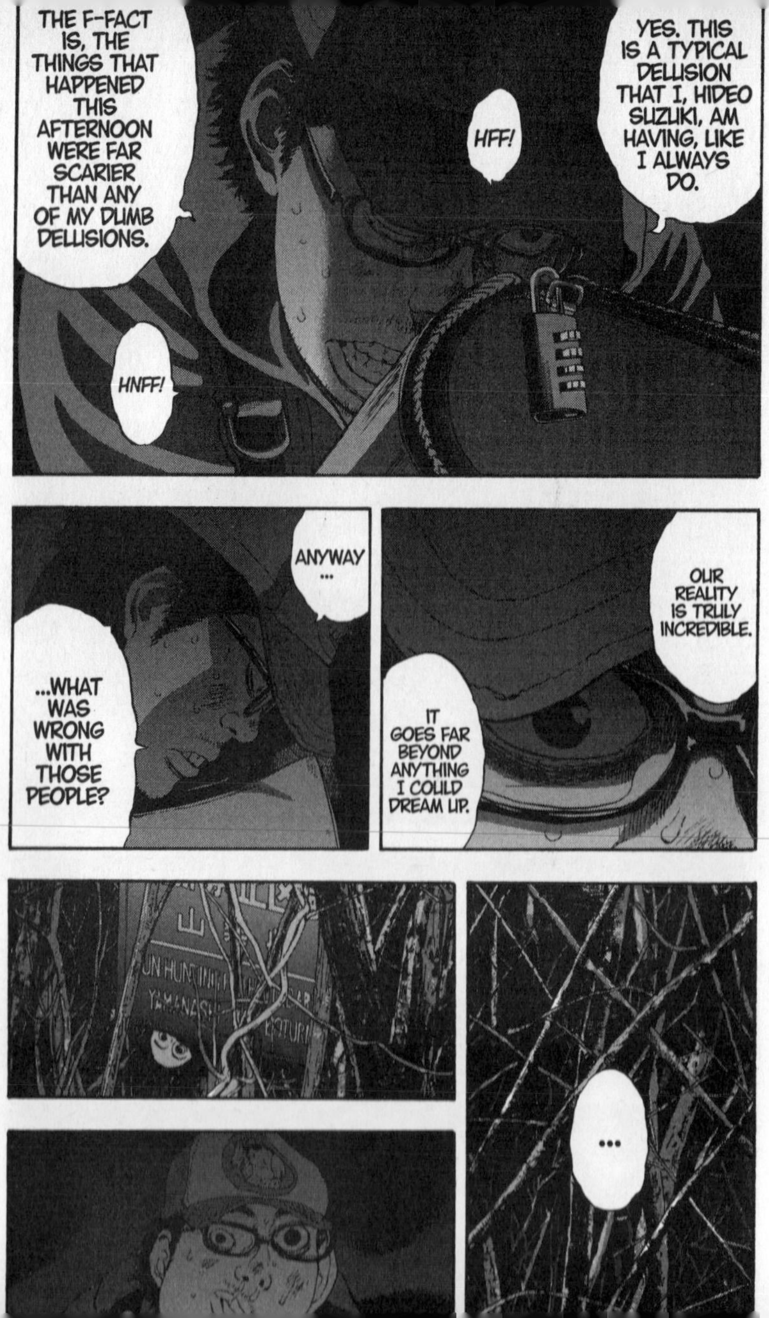
YES. THIS IS A TYPICAL DELLUSION THAT I, HIDEO SUZUKI, AM HAVING, LIKE I ALWAYS DO.
HFF!
THE F-FACT IS, THE THINGS THAT HAPPENED THIS AFTERNOON WERE FAR SCARIER THAN ANY OF MY DUMB DELLUSIONS.
HNFF!
OUR REALITY IS TRULY INCREDIBLE.
IT GOES FAR BEYOND ANYTHING I COULD DREAM UP.
ANYWAY ...
...WHAT WAS WRONG WITH THOSE PEOPLE?
...

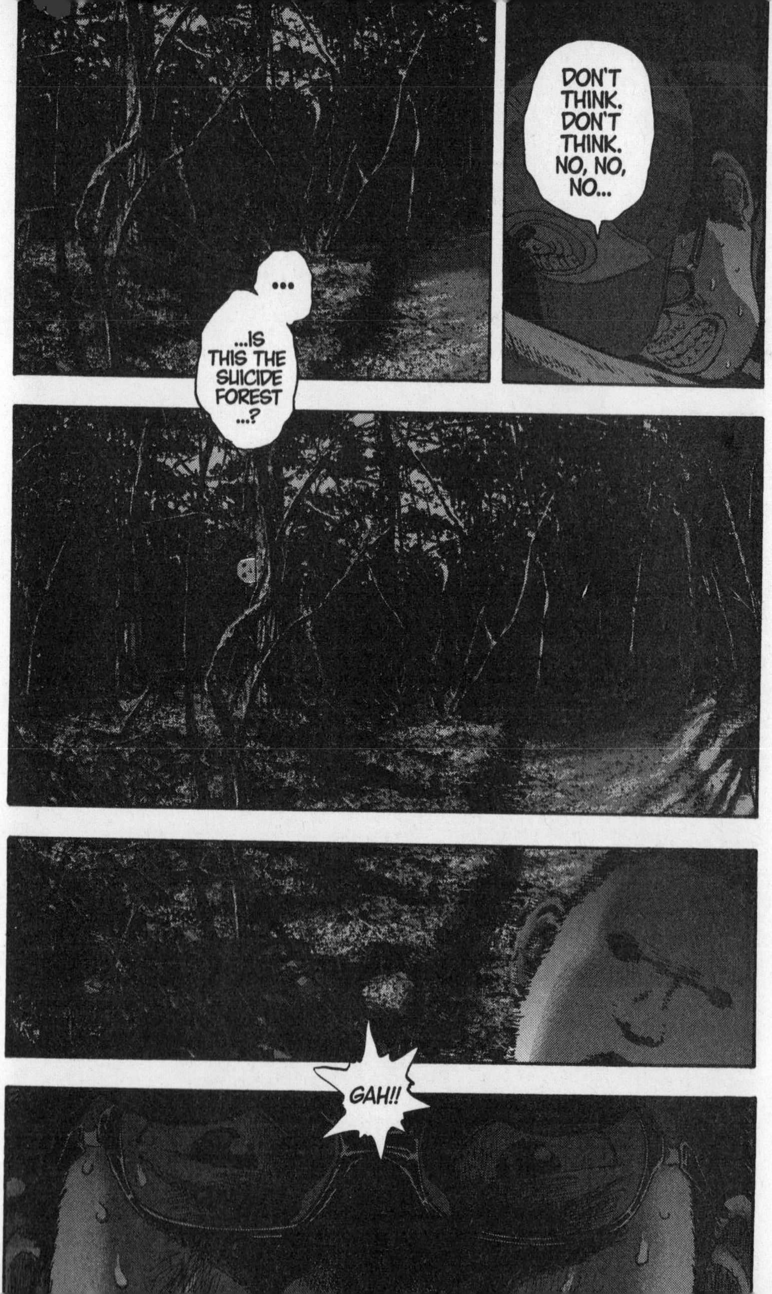
DON'T THINK. DON'T THINK. NO, NO, NO...
...
...IS THIS THE SUICIDE FOREST ...?
GAH!!

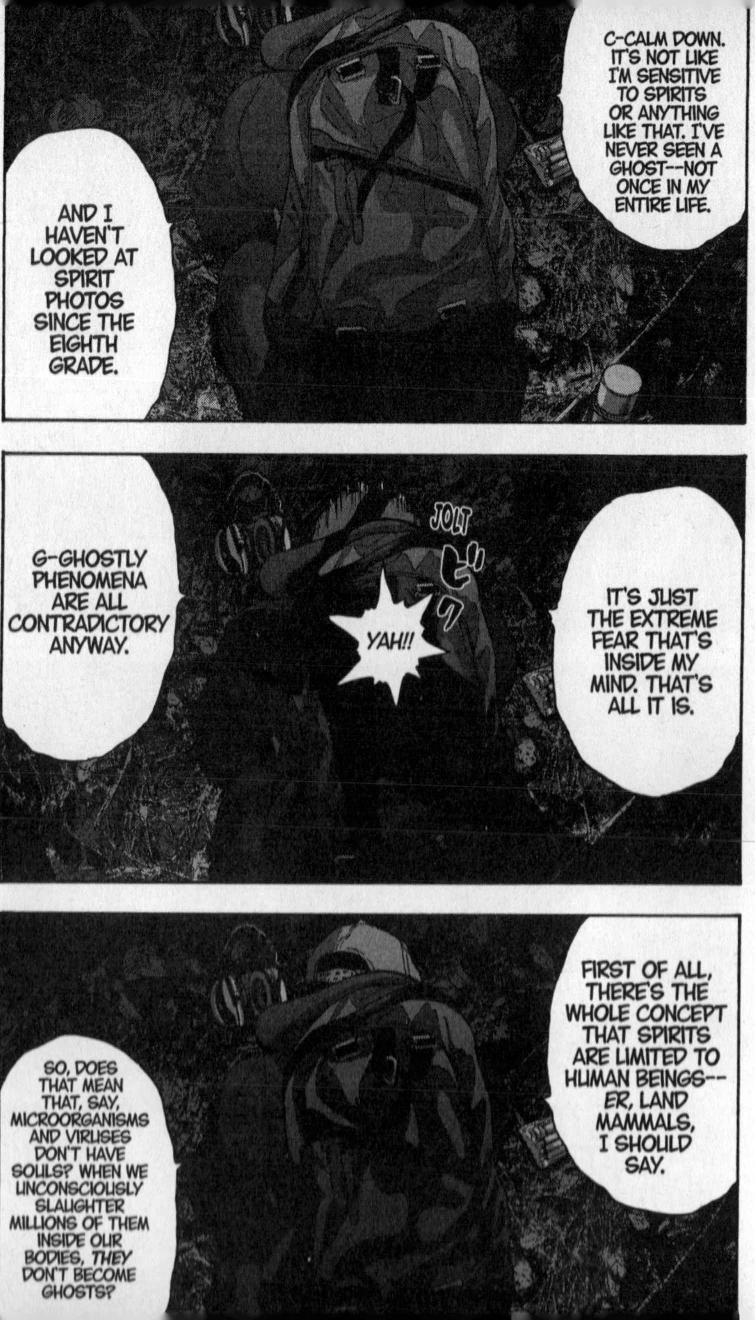
C-CALM DOWN. IT'S NOT LIKE I'M SENSITIVE TO SPIRITS OR ANYTHING LIKE THAT. I'VE NEVER SEEN A GHOST--NOT ONCE IN MY ENTIRE LIFE.
AND I HAVEN'T LOOKED AT SPIRIT PHOTOS SINCE THE EIGHTH GRADE.
IT'S JUST THE EXTREME FEAR THAT'S INSIDE MY MIND. THAT'S ALL IT IS.
JOLT
YAH!!
G-GHOSTLY PHENOMENA ARE ALL CONTRADICTORY ANYWAY.
FIRST OF ALL, THERE'S THE WHOLE CONCEPT THAT SPIRITS ARE LIMITED TO HUMAN BEINGS-- ER, LAND MAMMALS, I SHOULD SAY.
SO, DOES THAT MEAN THAT, SAY, MICROORGANISMS AND VIRUSES DON'T HAVE SOULS? WHEN WE UNCONSCIOUSLY SLAUGHTER MILLIONS OF THEM INSIDE OUR BODIES, *THEY* DON'T BECOME GHOSTS?

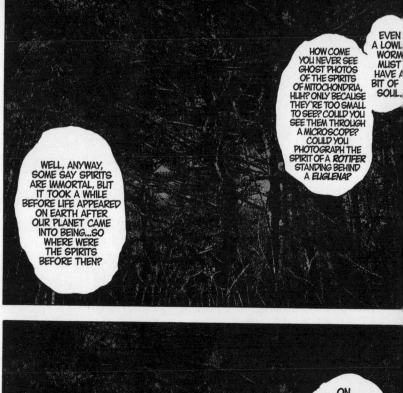

EVEN A LOWLY WORM MUST HAVE A BIT OF SOUL.

HOW COME YOU NEVER SEE GHOST PHOTOS OF THE SPIRITS OF MITOCHONDRIA, HUH? ONLY BECAUSE THEY'RE TOO SMALL TO SEE? COULD YOU SEE THEM THROUGH A MICROSCOPE? COULD YOU PHOTOGRAPH THE SPIRIT OF A *ROTIFER* STANDING BEHIND A *EUGLENA*?

WELL, ANYWAY, SOME SAY SPIRITS ARE IMMORTAL, BUT IT TOOK A WHILE BEFORE LIFE APPEARED ON EARTH AFTER OUR PLANET CAME INTO BEING...SO WHERE WERE THE SPIRITS BEFORE THEN?

ON THE OTHER HAND, IF A METEOR HIT EARTH RIGHT NOW AND WIPED OUT ALL LIFE, WHERE WOULD ALL THE SOULS GO? HEAVEN? HELL? NO, THANKS, MAN!

HRM...

IF YOU DIE SUDDENLY, YOU SUPPOSEDLY BECOME A LOCALLY BOUND SPIRIT, AND YOUR GHOST GOES AROUND HAUNTING PEOPLE-- BUT EVENTUALLY THERE'D BE NOBODY ON EARTH! WHO WOULD YOU VENT YOUR RESENT- MENT ON?

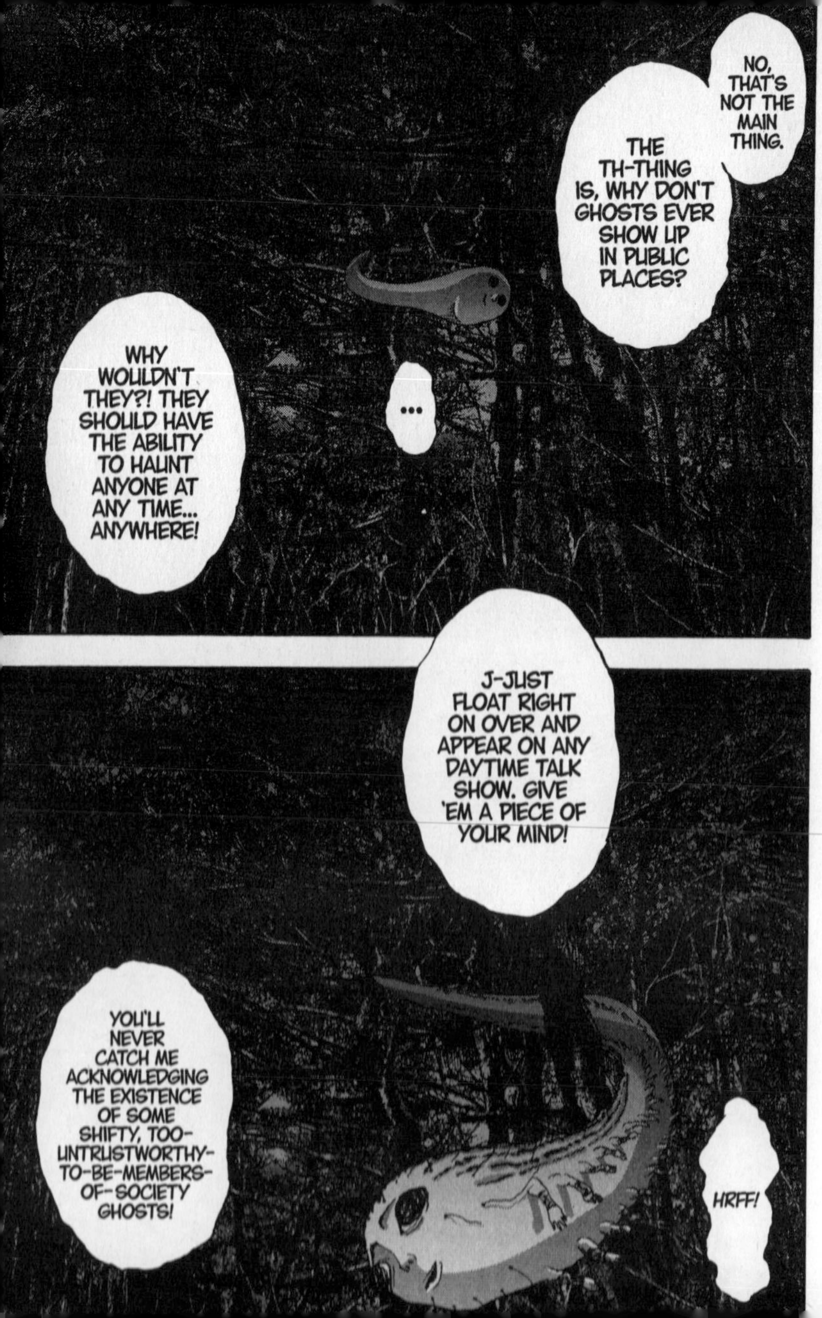
NO, THAT'S NOT THE MAIN THING.
THE TH-THING IS, WHY DON'T GHOSTS EVER SHOW UP IN PUBLIC PLACES?
...
WHY WOULDN'T THEY?! THEY SHOULD HAVE THE ABILITY TO HAUNT ANYONE AT ANY TIME... ANYWHERE!
J-JUST FLOAT RIGHT ON OVER AND APPEAR ON ANY DAYTIME TALK SHOW. GIVE 'EM A PIECE OF YOUR MIND!
YOU'LL NEVER CATCH ME ACKNOWLEDGING THE EXISTENCE OF SOME SHIFTY, TOO-UNTRUSTWORTHY-TO-BE-MEMBERS-OF-SOCIETY GHOSTS!
HRFF!

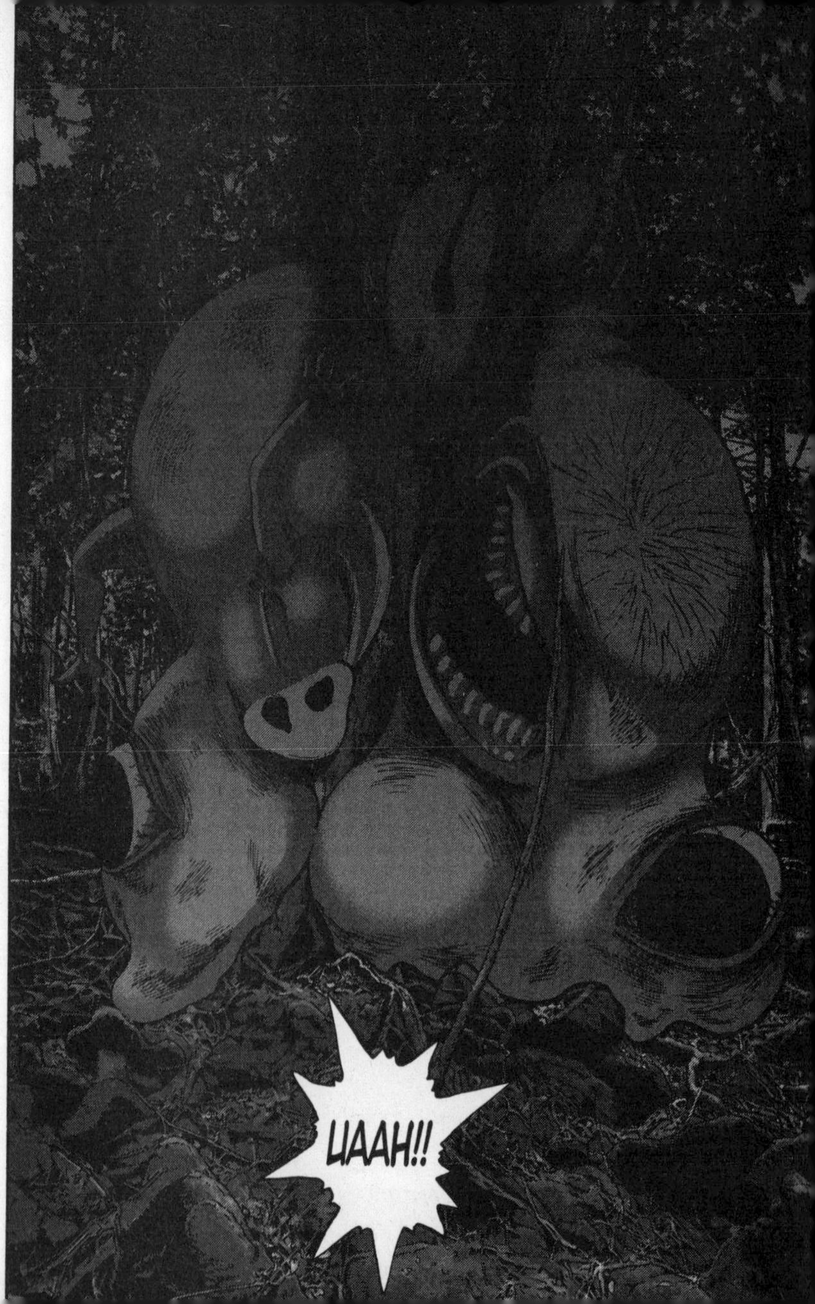
UAAH!!

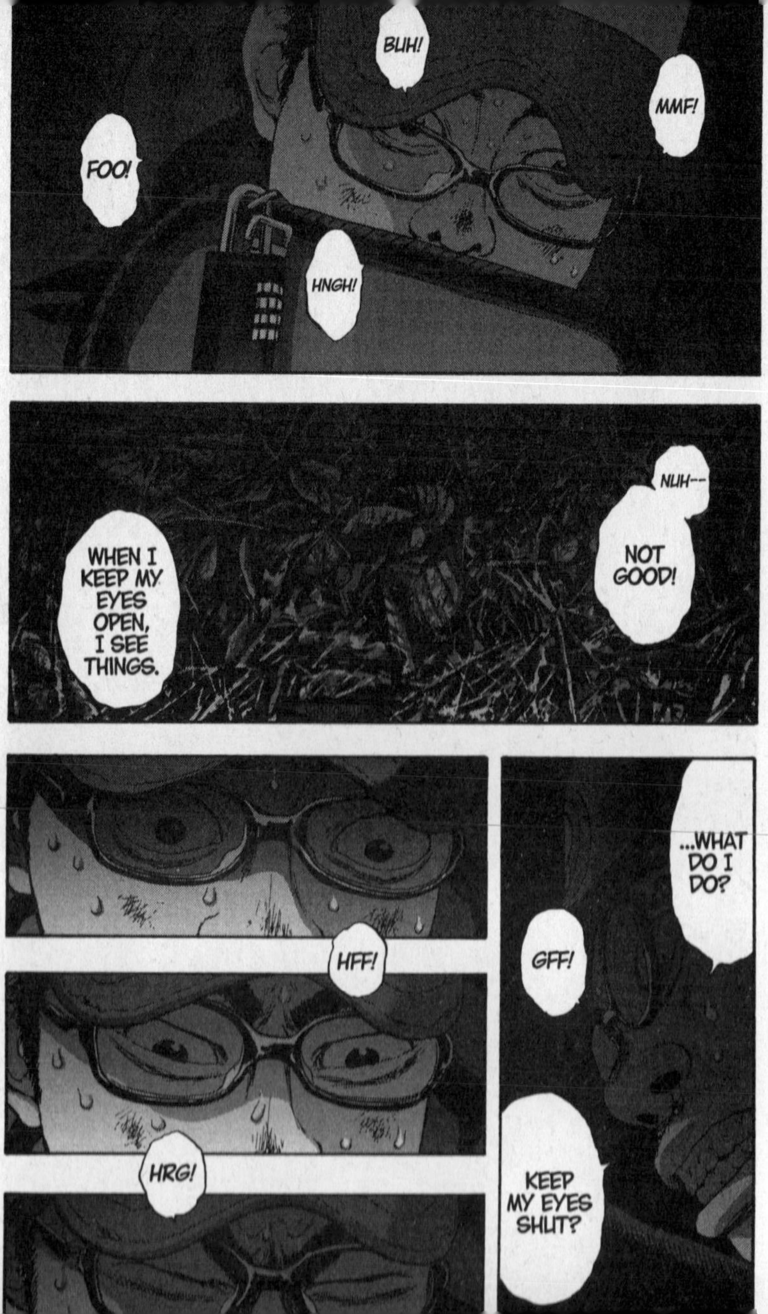
BUH!
MMF!
FOO!
HNGH!
NUH--
NOT GOOD!
WHEN I KEEP MY EYES OPEN, I SEE THINGS.
...WHAT DO I DO?
GFF!
KEEP MY EYES SHUT?
HFF!
HRG!

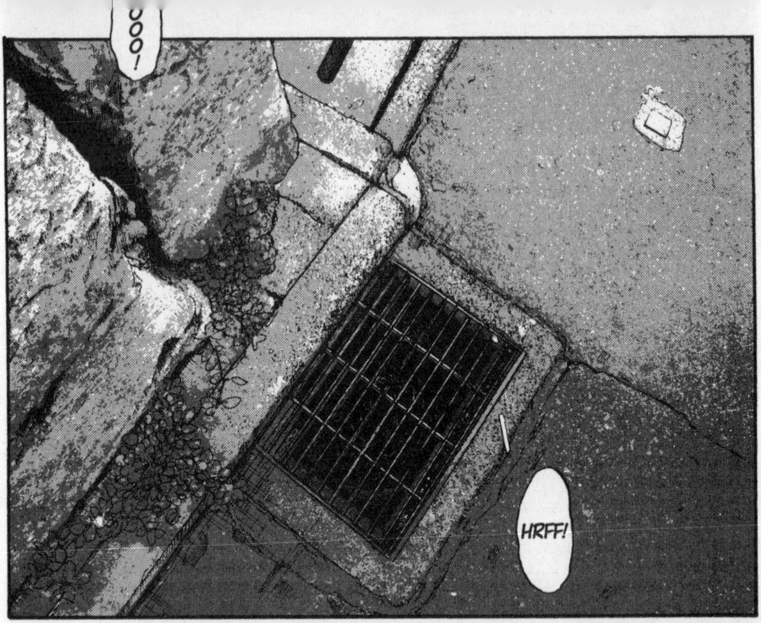
OOO!
HRFF!
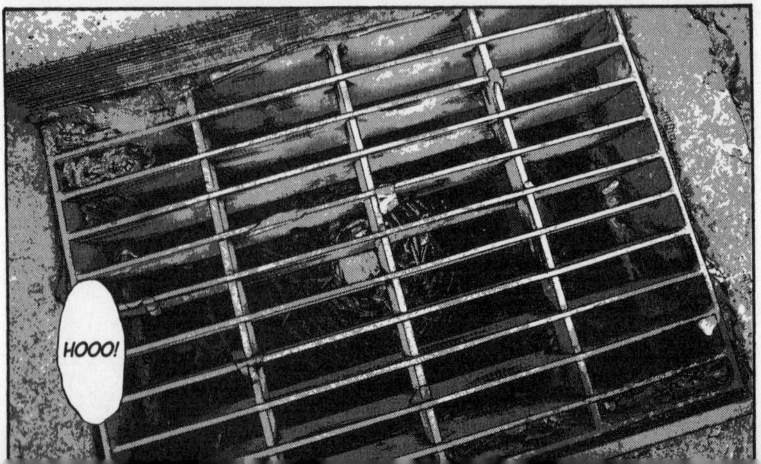
HOOO!

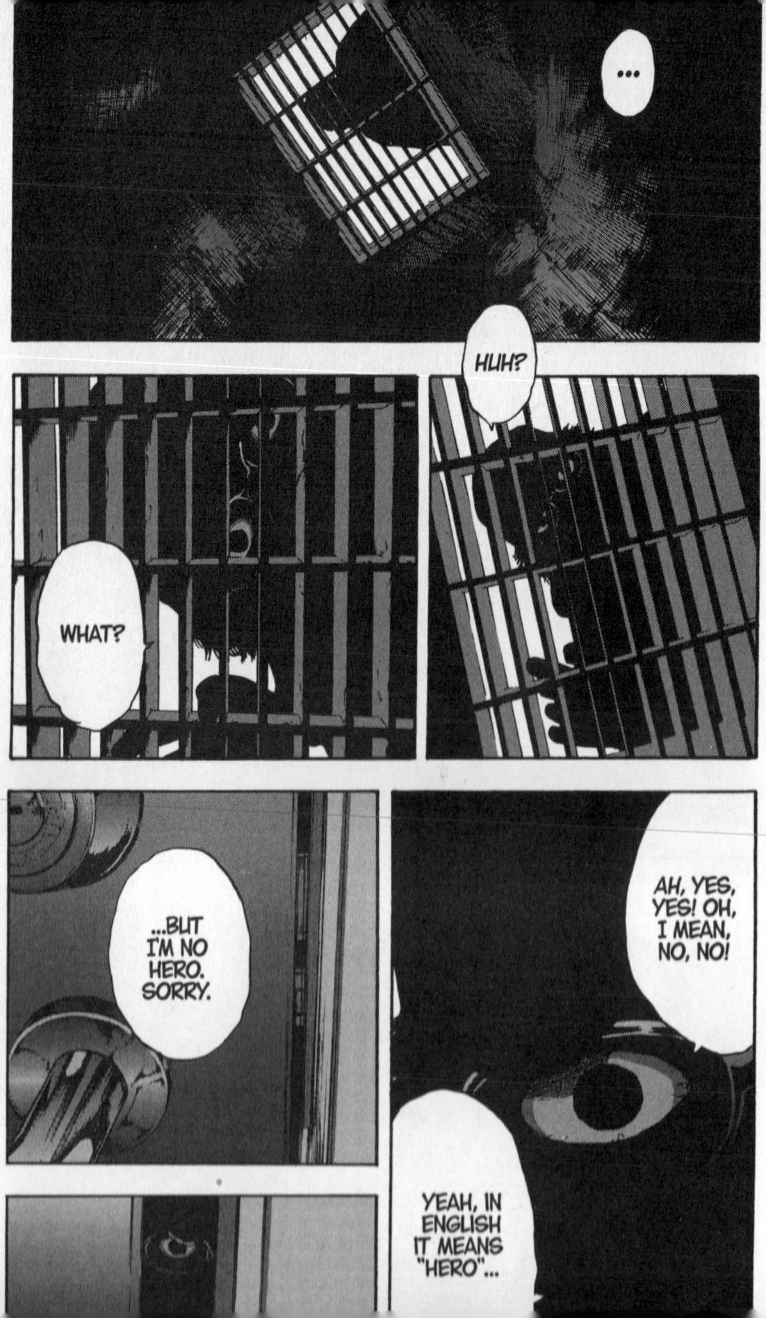
...
HUH?
WHAT?
AH, YES, YES! OH, I MEAN, NO, NO!
YEAH, IN ENGLISH IT MEANS "HERO"...
...BUT I'M NO HERO. SORRY.

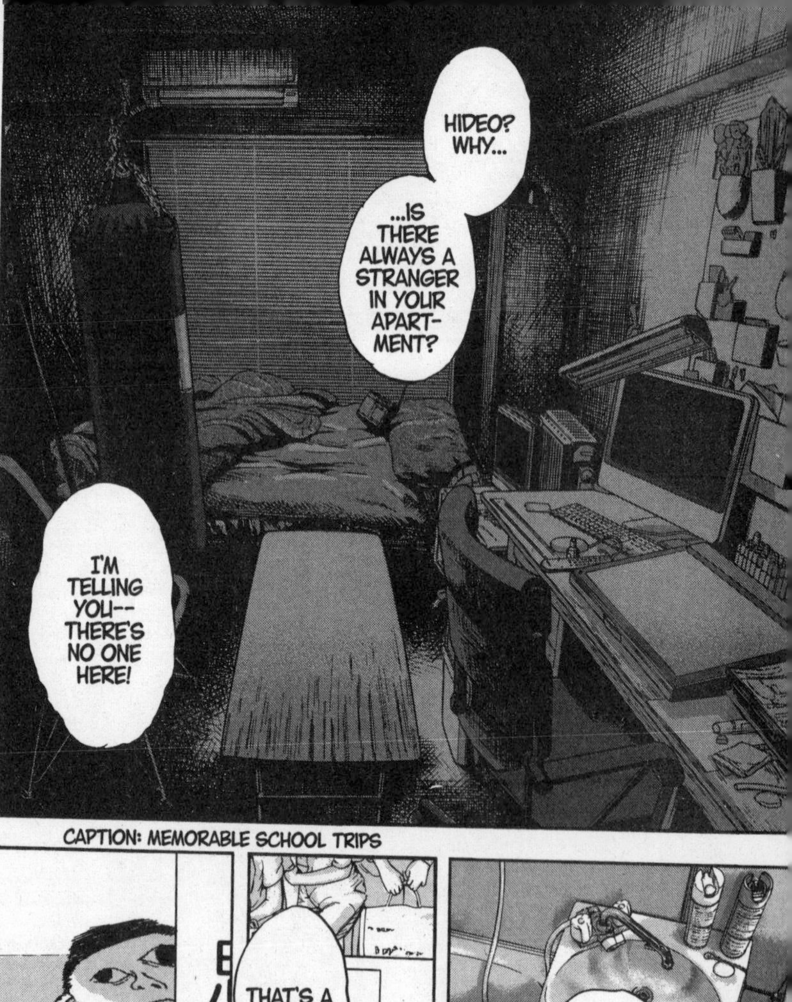
HIDEO? WHY...
...IS THERE ALWAYS A STRANGER IN YOUR APART-MENT?
I'M TELLING YOU-- THERE'S NO ONE HERE!

CAPTION: MEMORABLE SCHOOL TRIPS

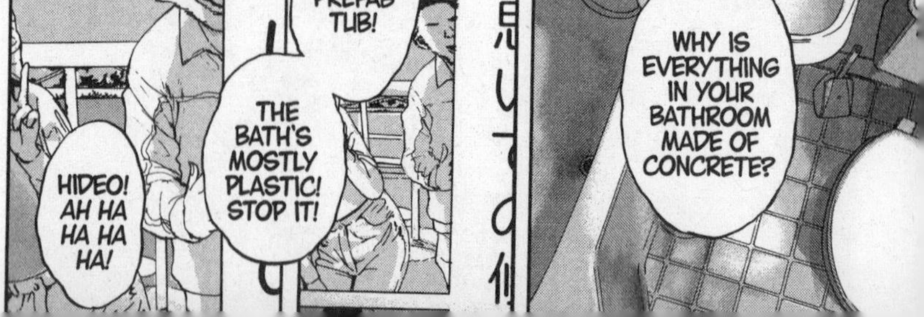
WHY IS EVERYTHING IN YOUR BATHROOM MADE OF CONCRETE?
THAT'S A PREFAB TUB!
THE BATH'S MOSTLY PLASTIC! STOP IT!
HIDEO! AH HA HA HA HA!

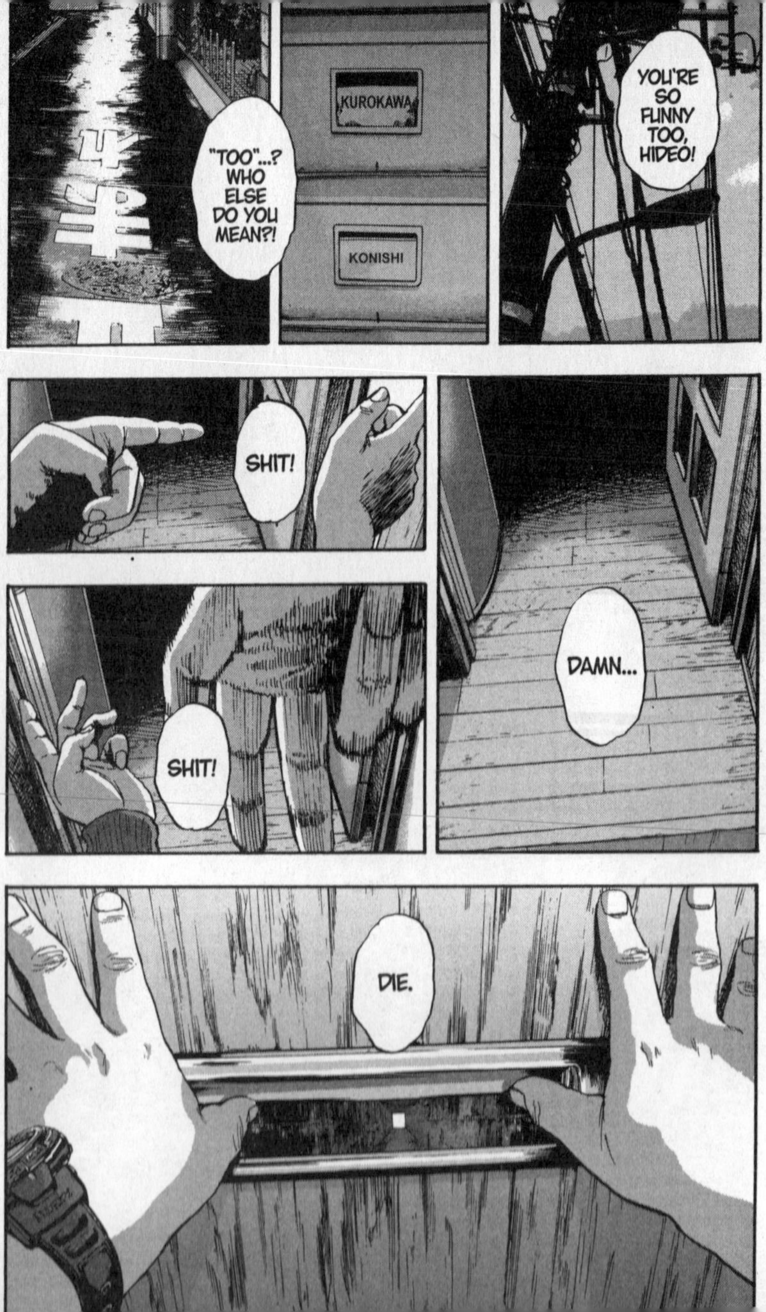
YOU'RE SO FUNNY TOO, HIDEO!
KUROKAWA
"TOO"...? WHO ELSE DO YOU MEAN?!
KONISHI
DAMN...
SHIT!
SHIT!
DIE.

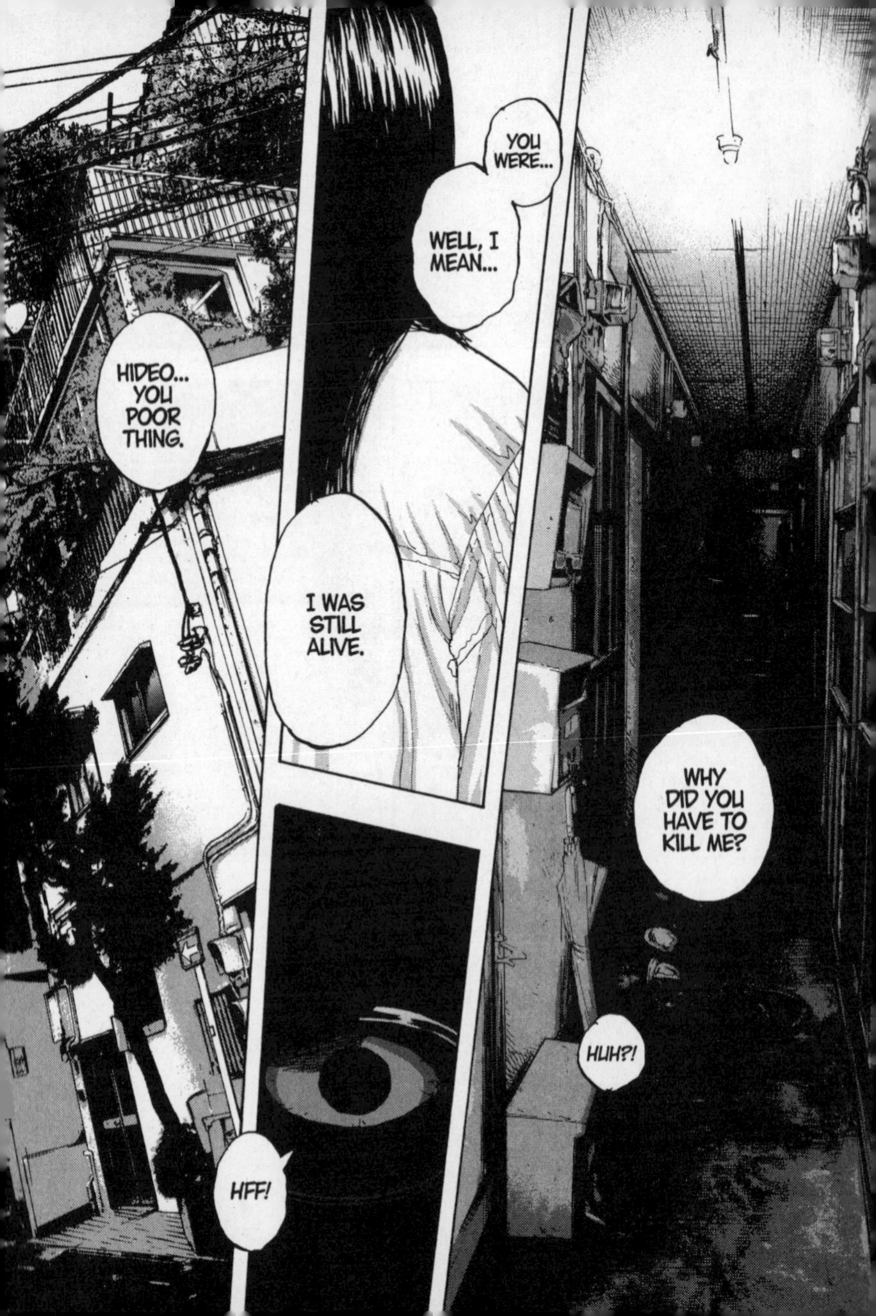
YOU WERE...
WELL, I MEAN...
HIDEO... YOU POOR THING.
I WAS STILL ALIVE.
WHY DID YOU HAVE TO KILL ME?
HUH?!
HFF!

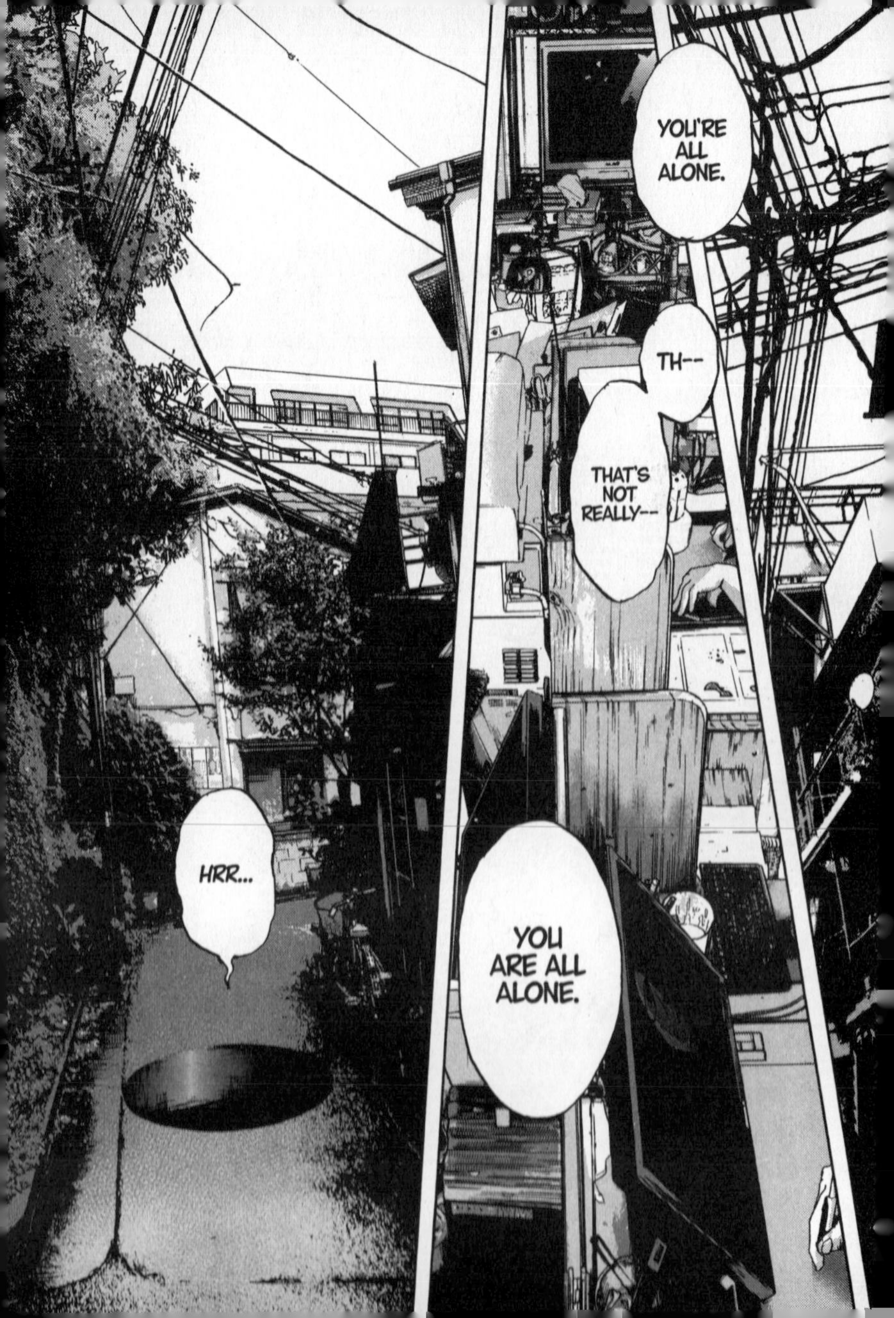
YOU'RE ALL ALONE.
TH--
THAT'S NOT REALLY--
YOU ARE ALL ALONE.
HRR...

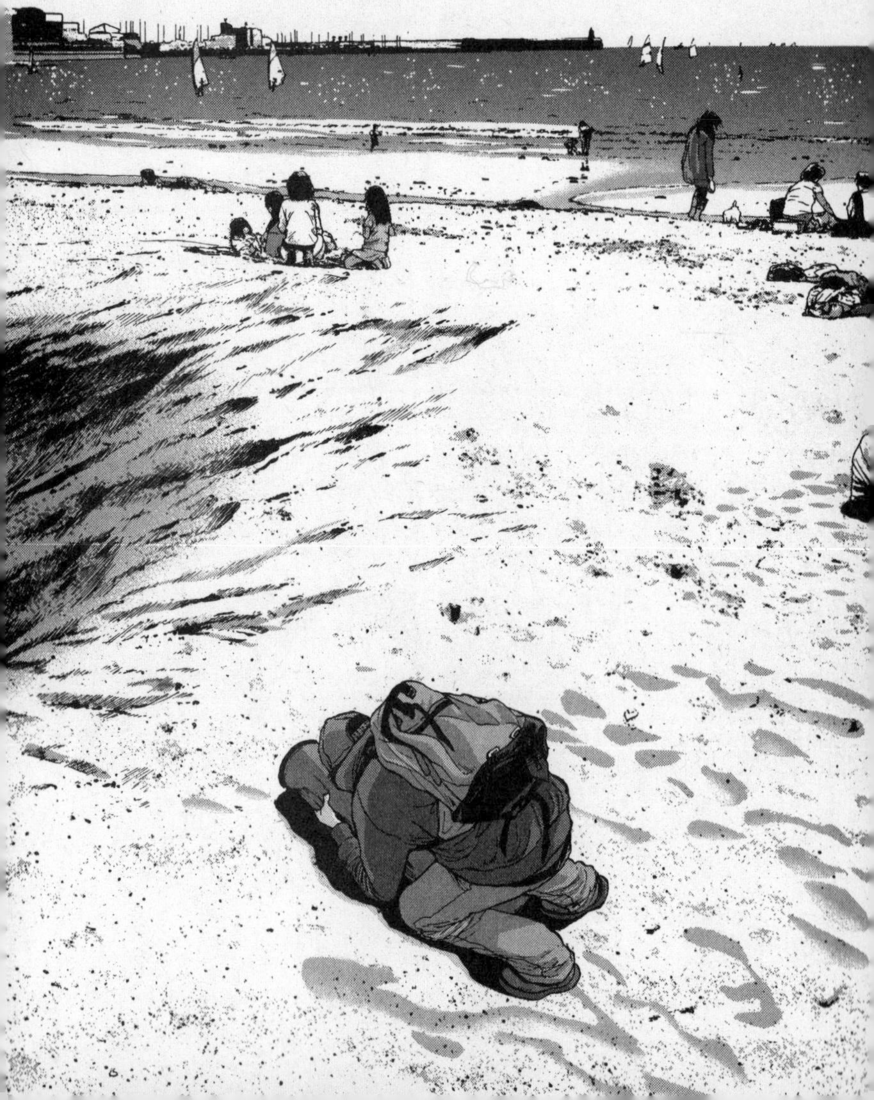

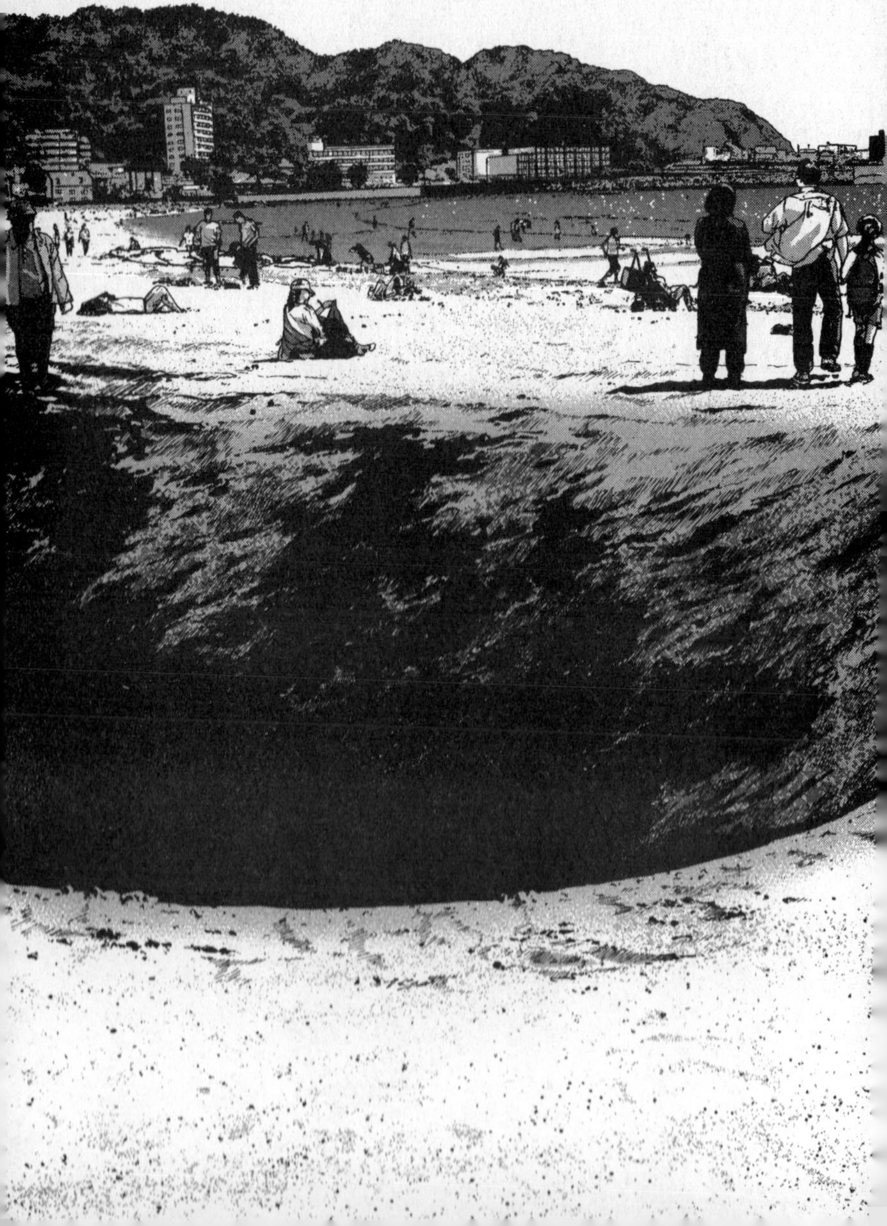

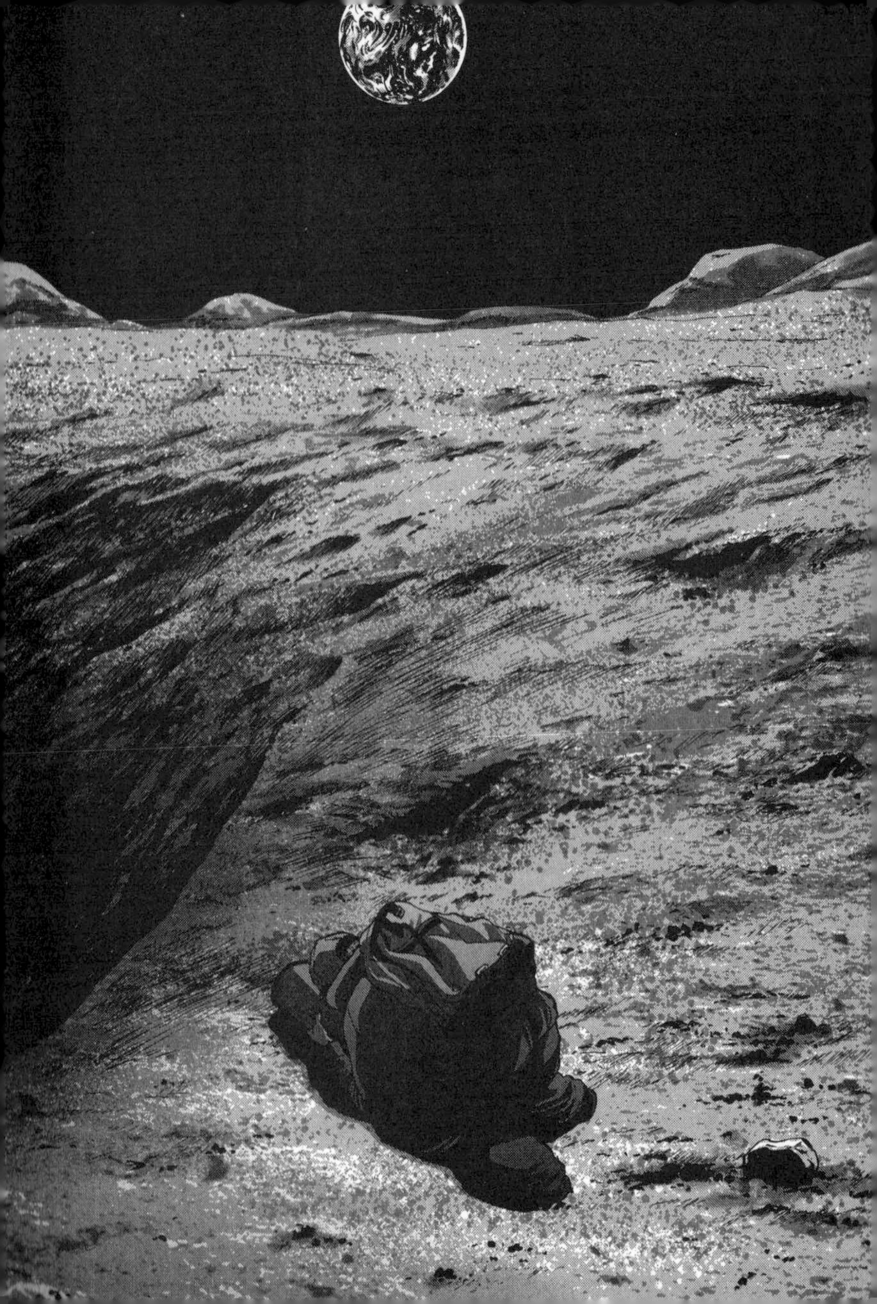

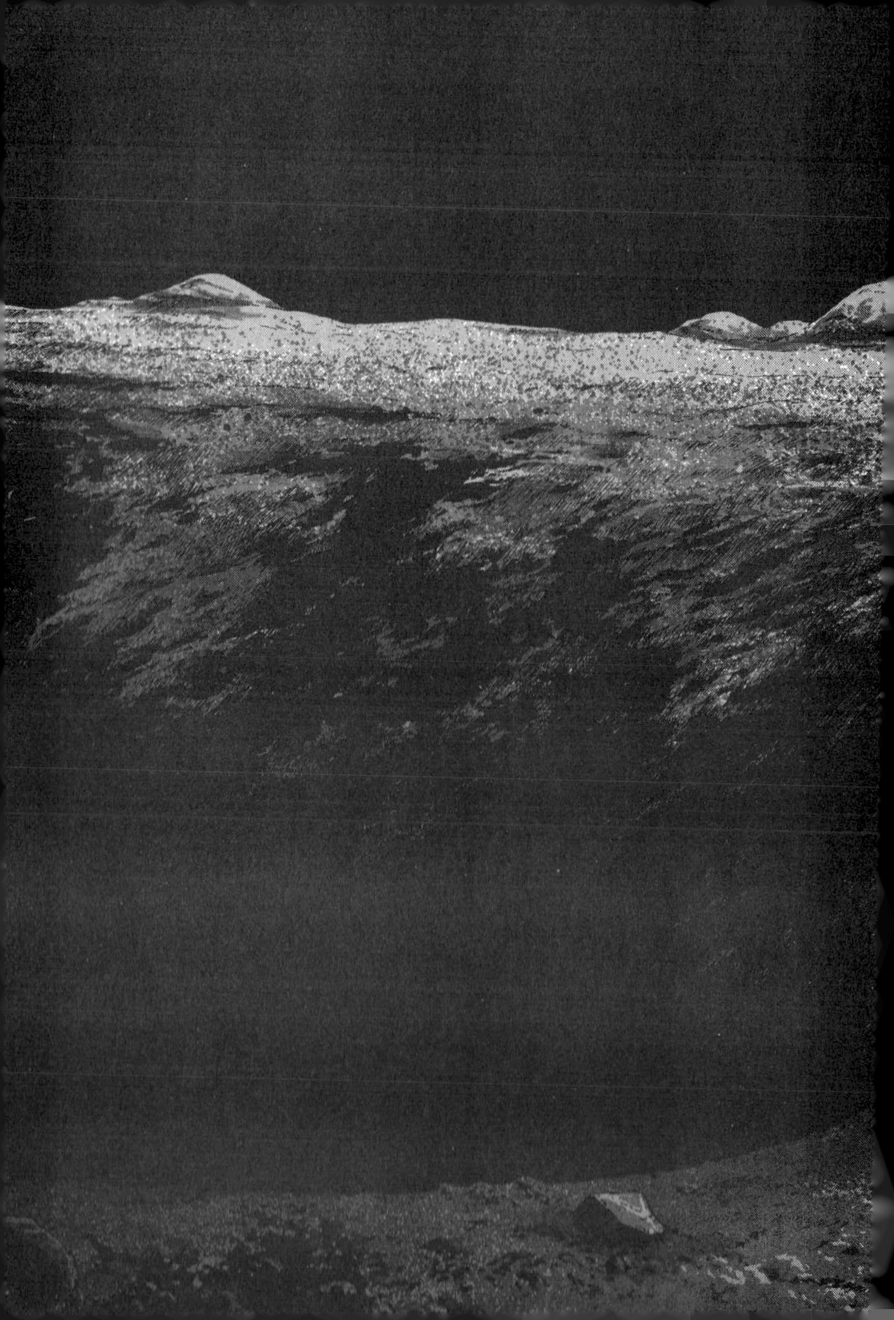

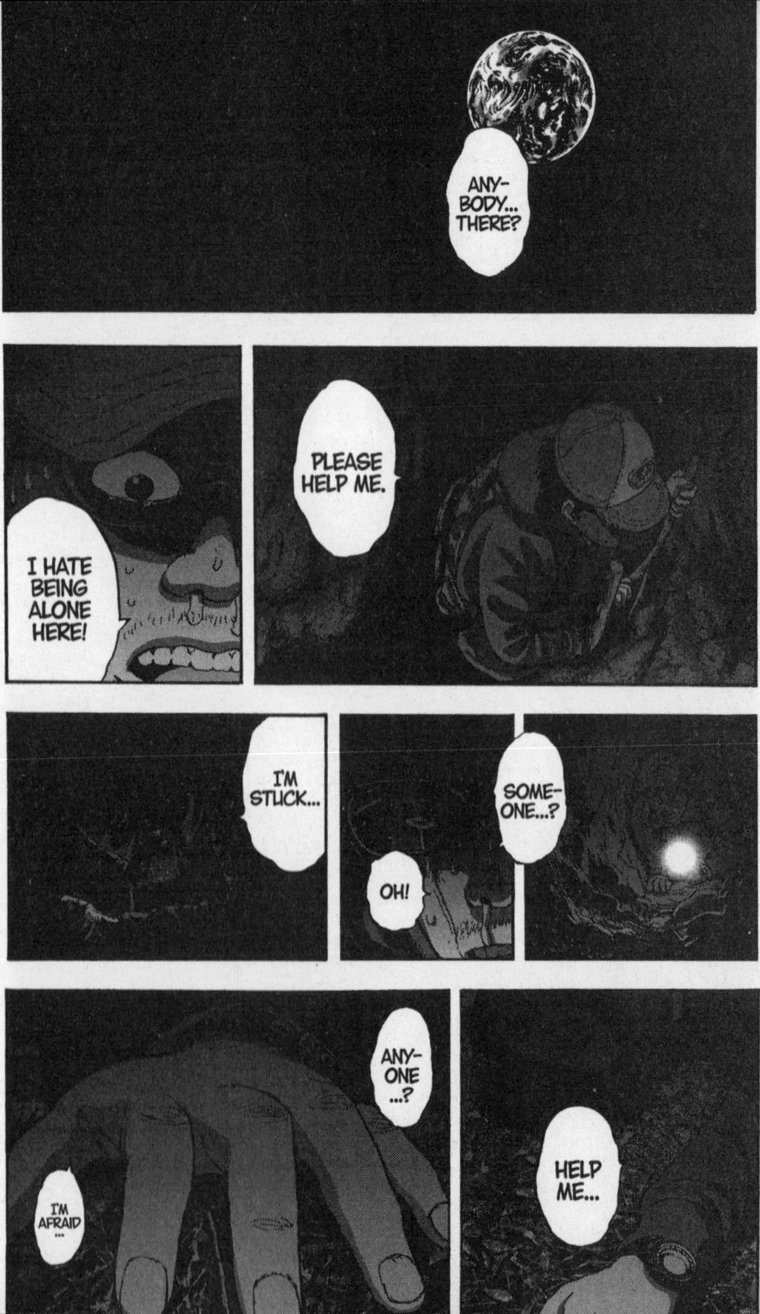
ANY-BODY... THERE?
PLEASE HELP ME.
I HATE BEING ALONE HERE!
SOME-ONE...?
OH!
I'M STUCK...
HELP ME...
ANY-ONE ...?
I'M AFRAID ...

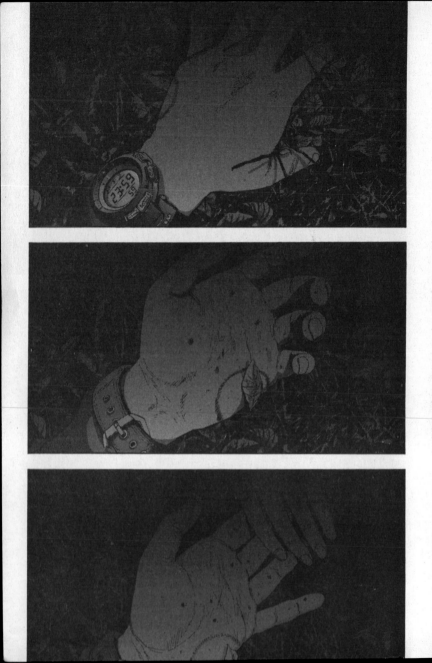

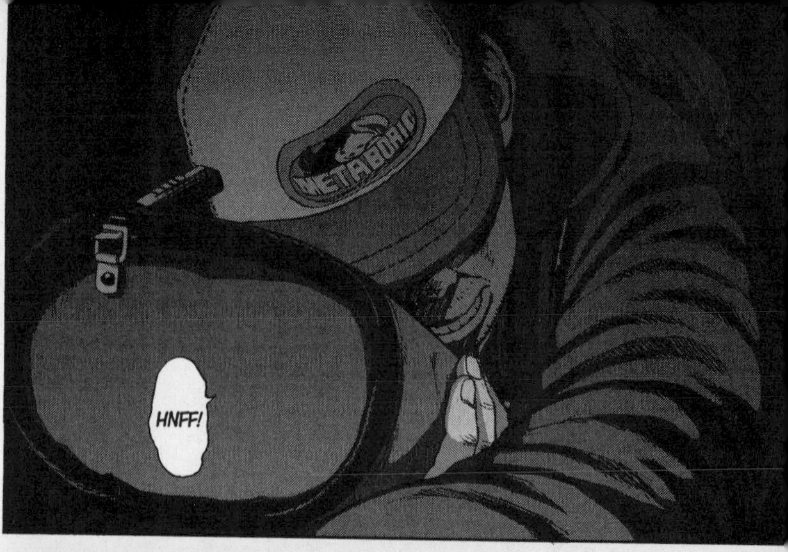
METABORIC
HNFF!
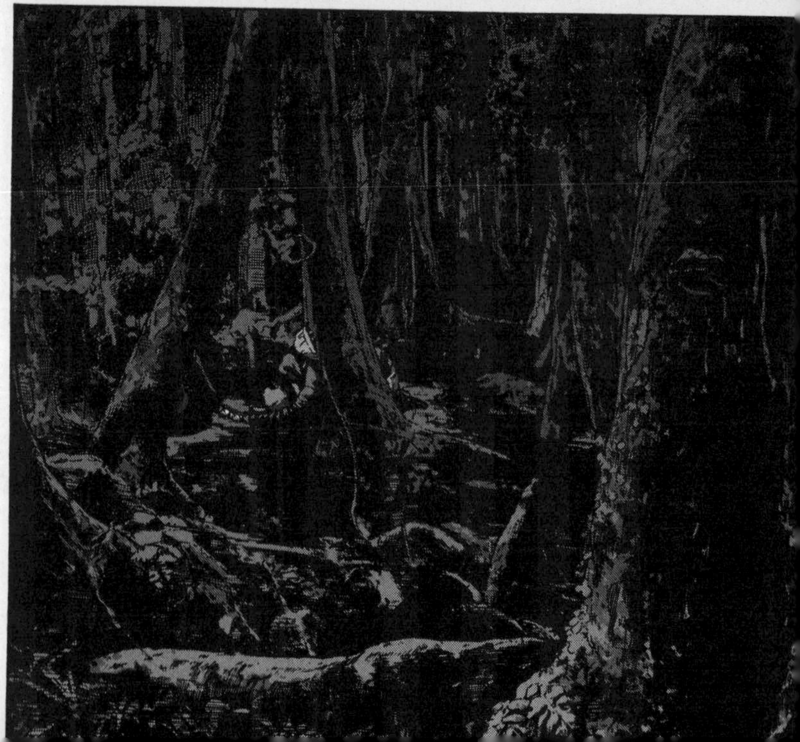

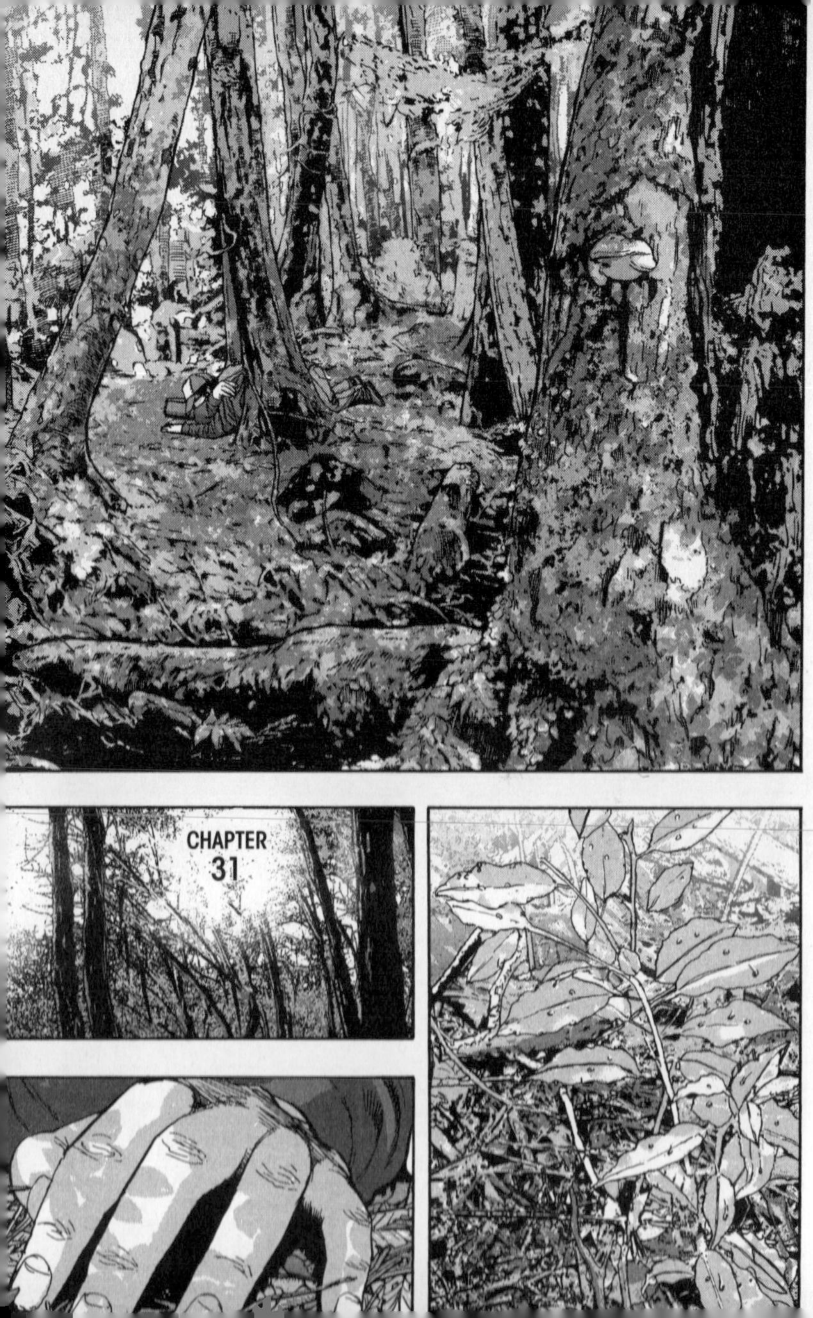
CHAPTER
31

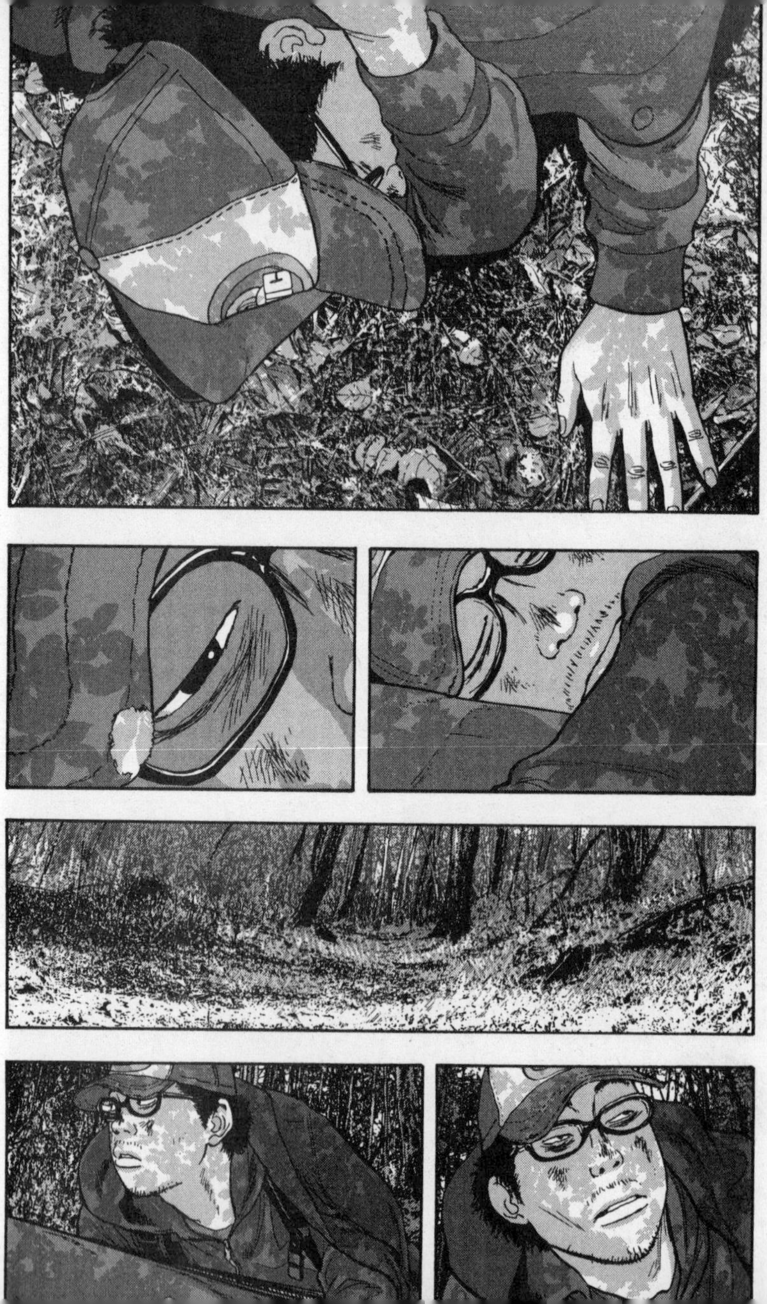

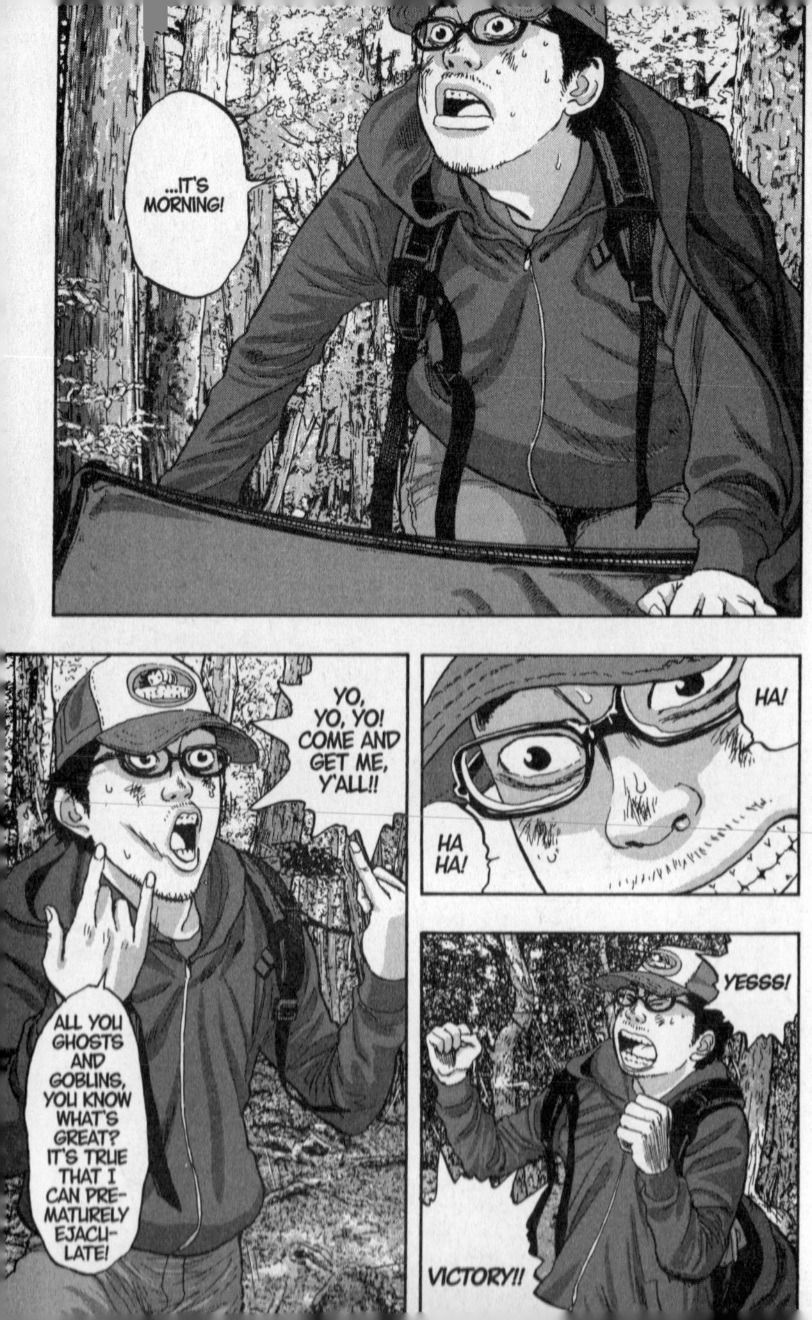
...IT'S MORNING!
HA!
HA HA!
YESSS!
VICTORY!!
YO, YO, YO! COME AND GET ME, Y'ALL!!
ALL YOU GHOSTS AND GOBLINS, YOU KNOW WHAT'S GREAT? IT'S TRUE THAT I CAN PRE-MATURELY EJACU-LATE!

GRAB

SWISHA

SWISHA

SHWIK! WIKKA!

WIKKI SHWAA!

WIKKI SHWAA!

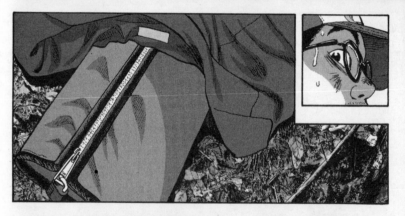

...WHAT?

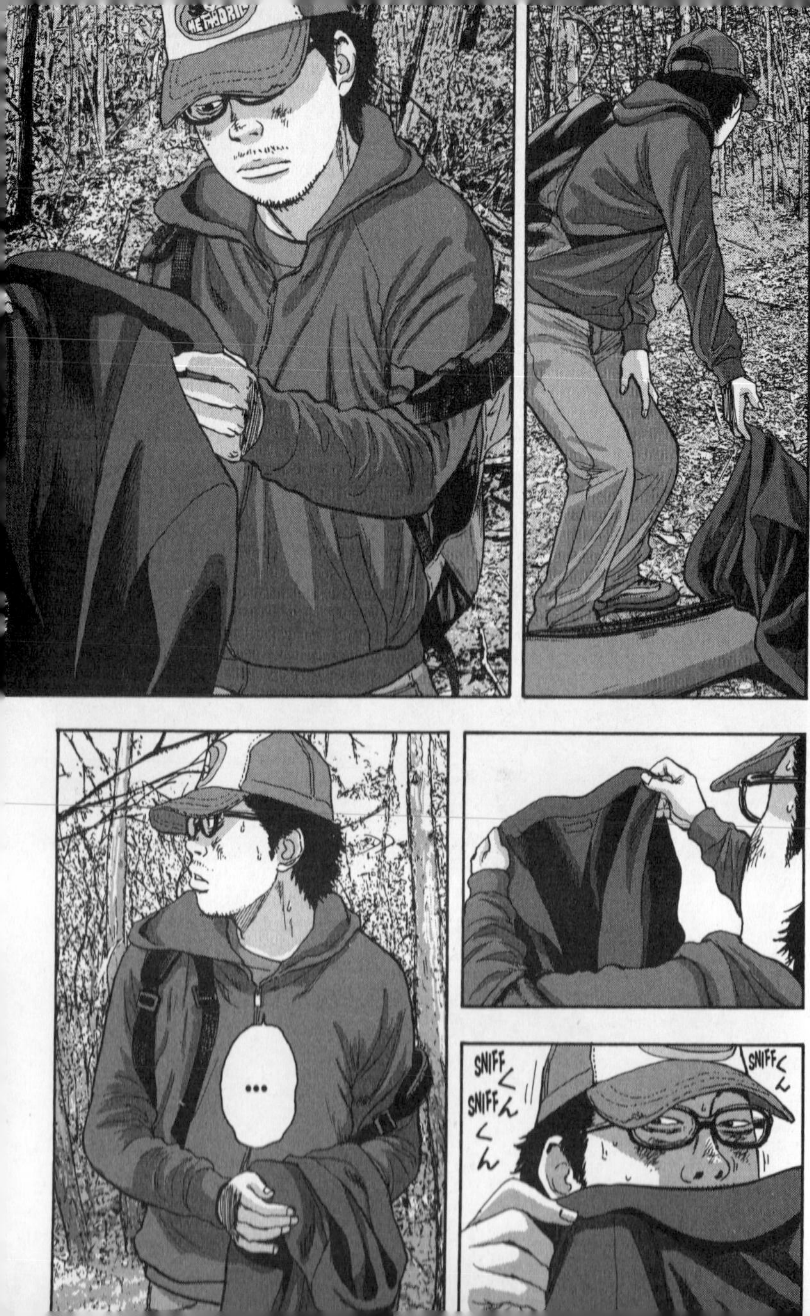
SNIFF くん
SNIFF くん
SNIFF くん くん
...

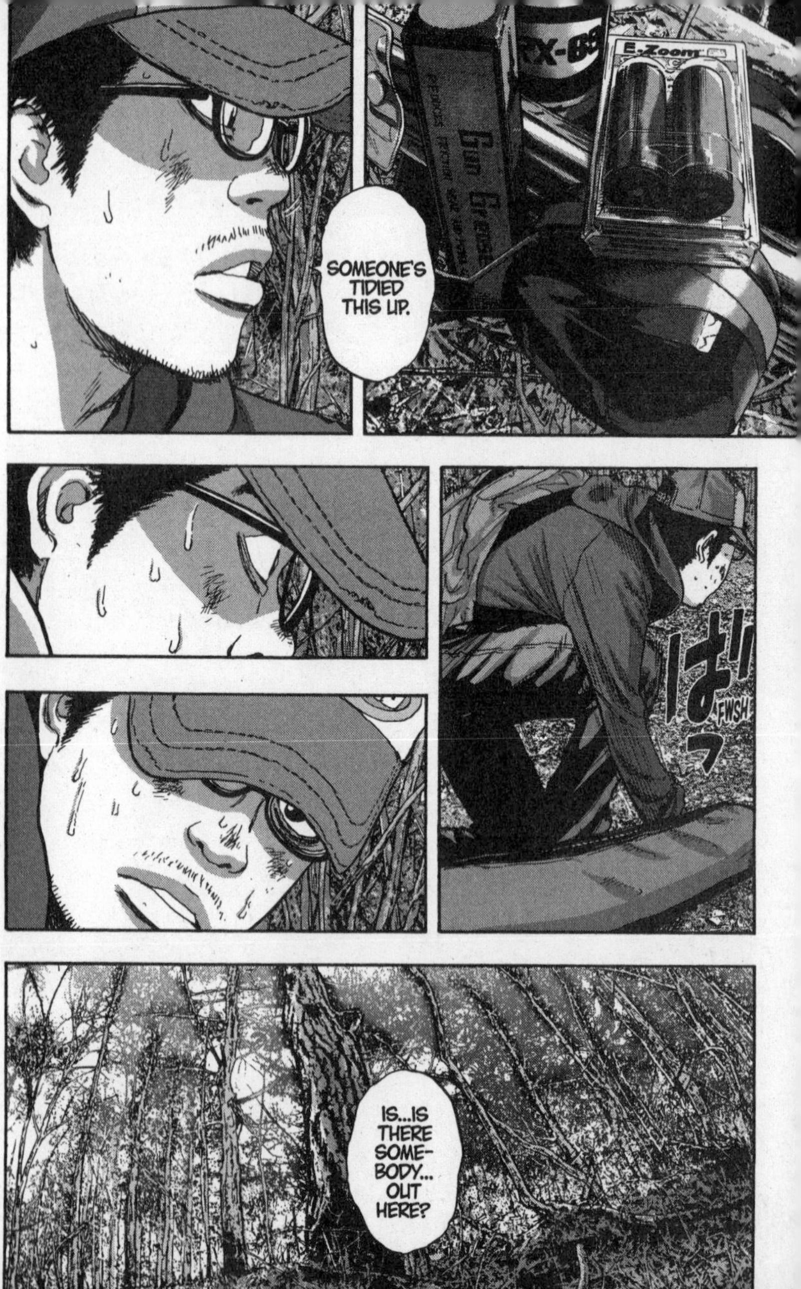
SOMEONE'S TIDIED THIS UP.
はっ
FWSH
IS...IS THERE SOME-BODY... OUT HERE?

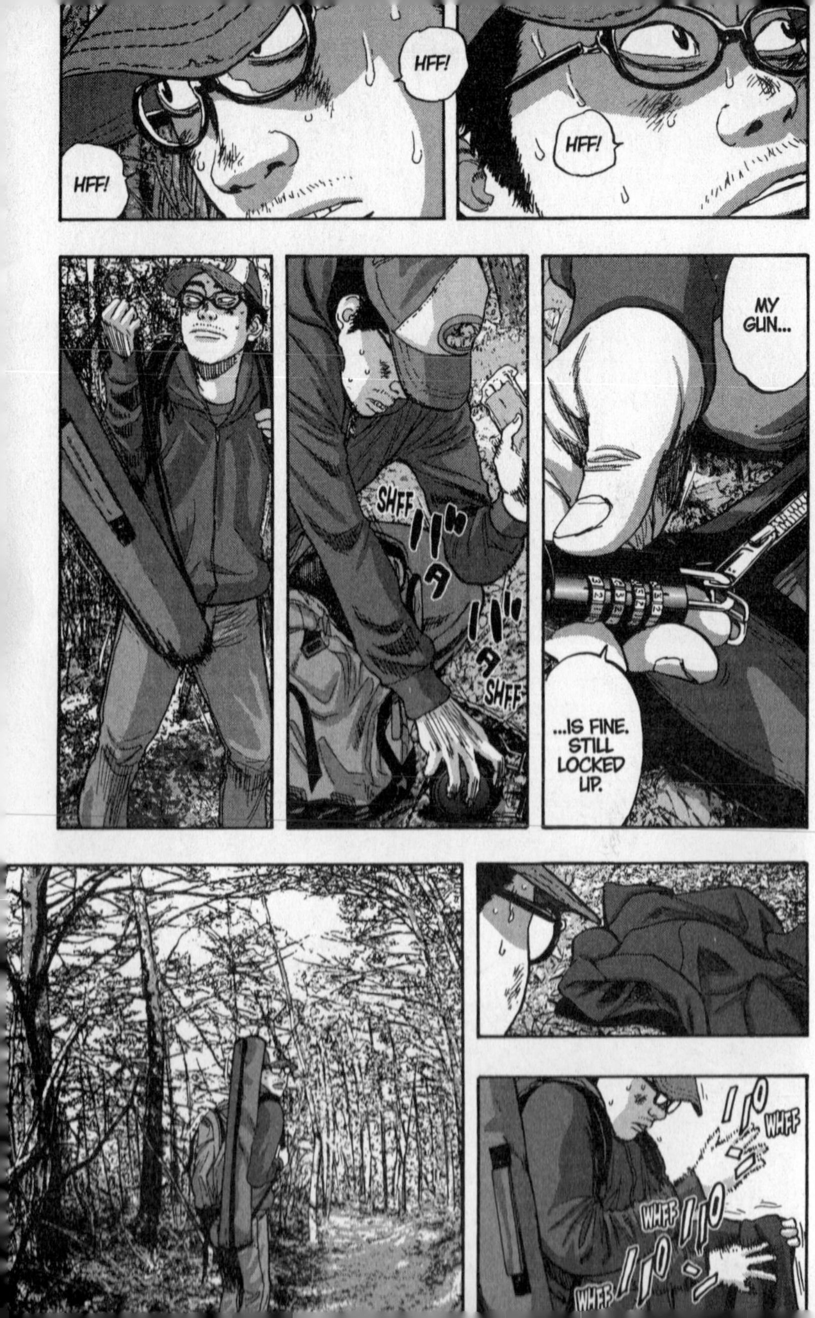
HFF!
HFF!
HFF!
MY GUN...
...IS FINE. STILL LOCKED UP.
SHFF
SHFF
WHFF
WHFF
WHFF

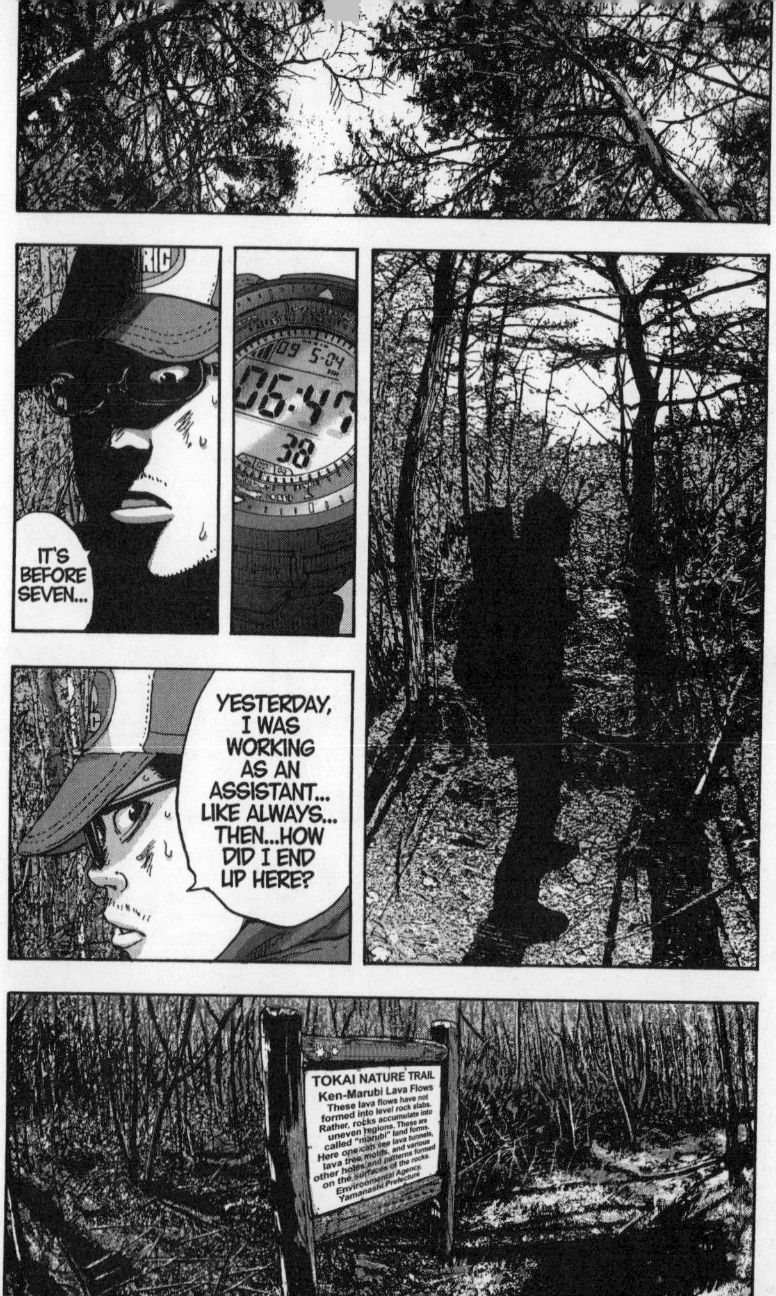
IT'S BEFORE SEVEN...
YESTERDAY, I WAS WORKING AS AN ASSISTANT... LIKE ALWAYS... THEN...HOW DID I END UP HERE?
TOKAI NATURE TRAIL
Ken-Marubi Lava Flows
These lava flows have not formed into level rock slabs. Rather, rocks accumulate into uneven regions. These are called "marubi" land forms. Here one can see lava tunnels, lava tree molds, and various other holes and patterns formed on the surfaces of the rocks.
Environmental Agency, Yamanashi Prefecture

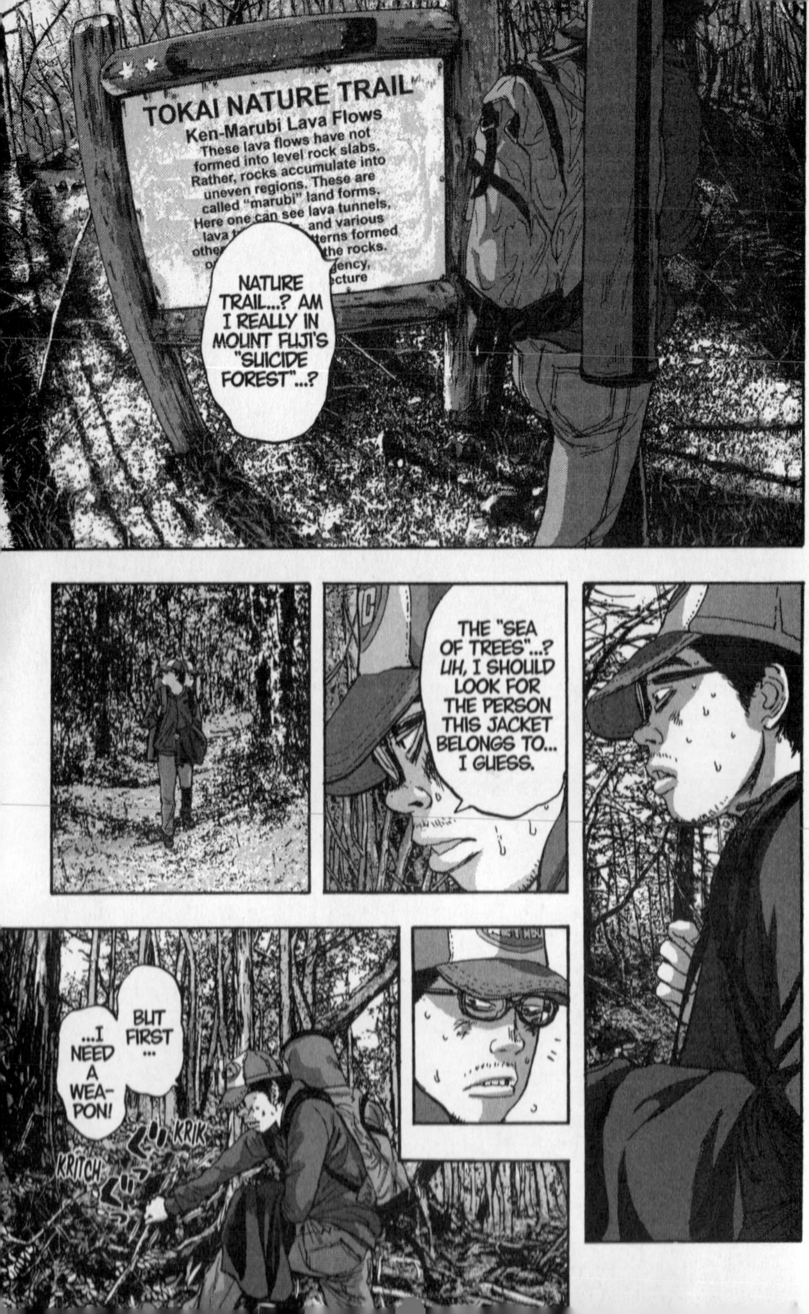
TOKAI NATURE TRAIL
Ken-Marubi Lava Flows
These lava flows have not formed into level rock slabs. Rather, rocks accumulate into uneven regions. These are called "marubi" land forms. Here one can see lava tunnels,
NATURE TRAIL...? AM I REALLY IN MOUNT FUJI'S "SUICIDE FOREST"...?
THE "SEA OF TREES"...? UH, I SHOULD LOOK FOR THE PERSON THIS JACKET BELONGS TO... I GUESS.
BUT FIRST...
...I NEED A WEAPON!
KRIK
KRITCH

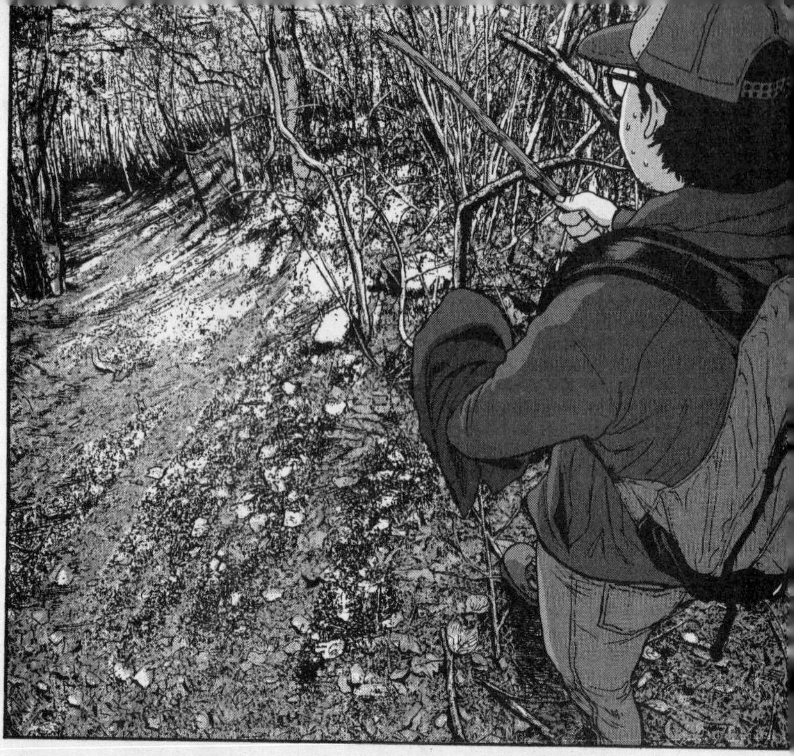

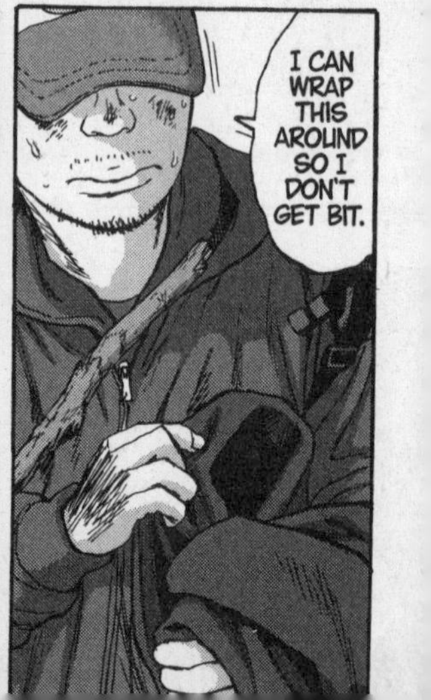
I CAN WRAP THIS AROUND SO I DON'T GET BIT.

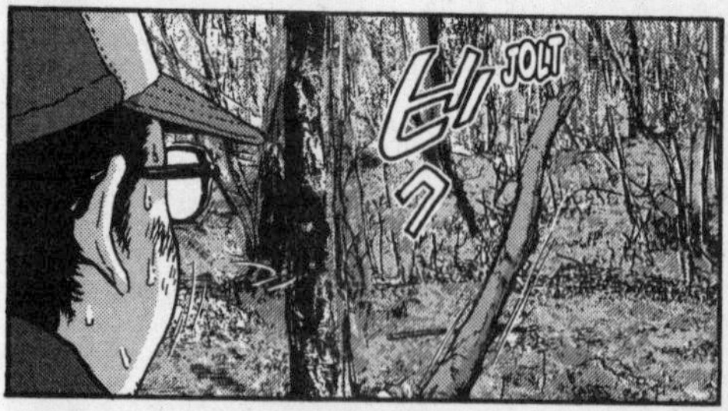
JOLT

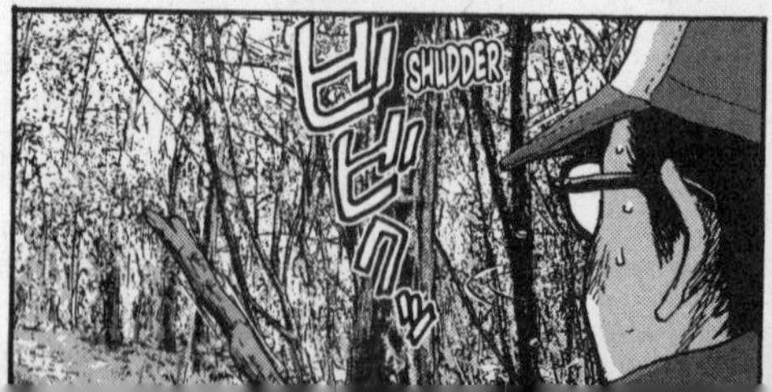
SHUDDER

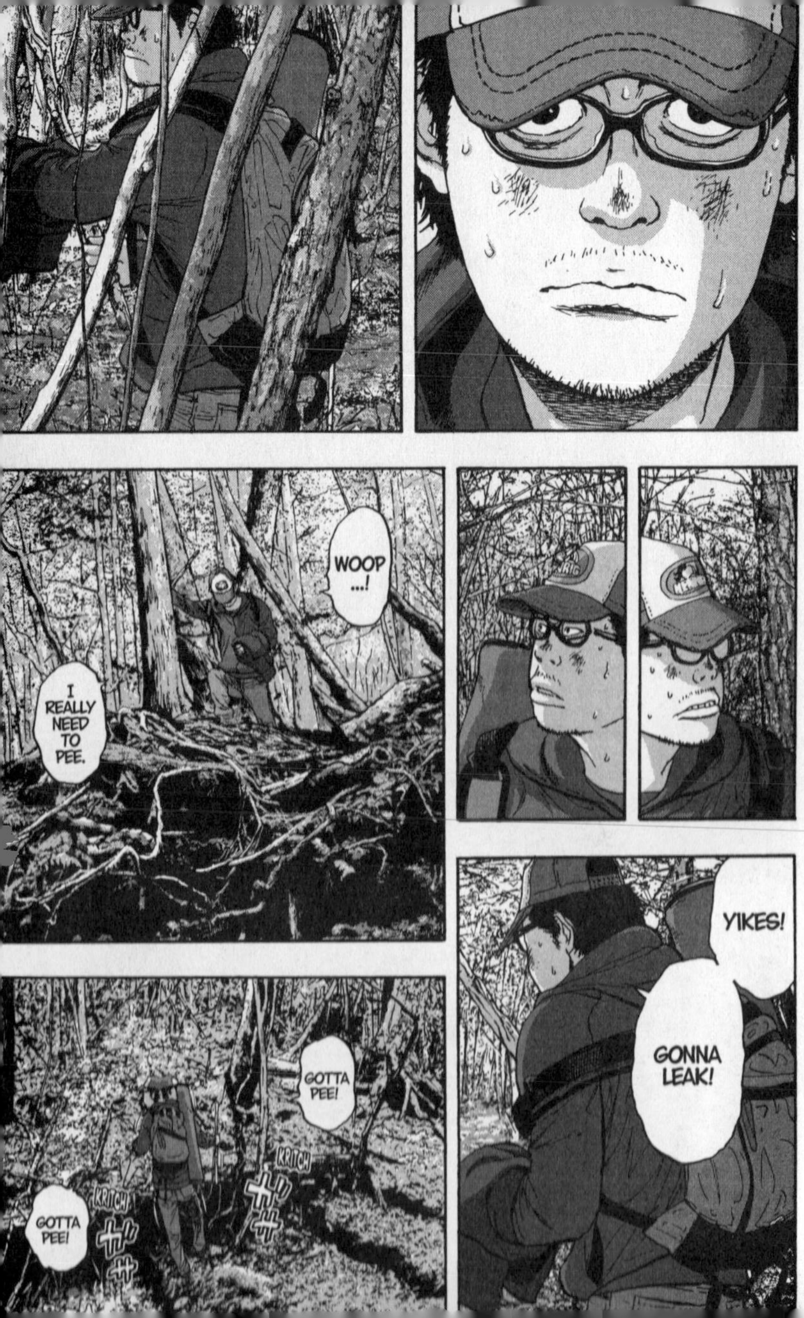
WOOP ...!
I REALLY NEED TO PEE.
YIKES!
GONNA LEAK!
GOTTA PEE!
KRITCH
KRITCH
GOTTA PEE!

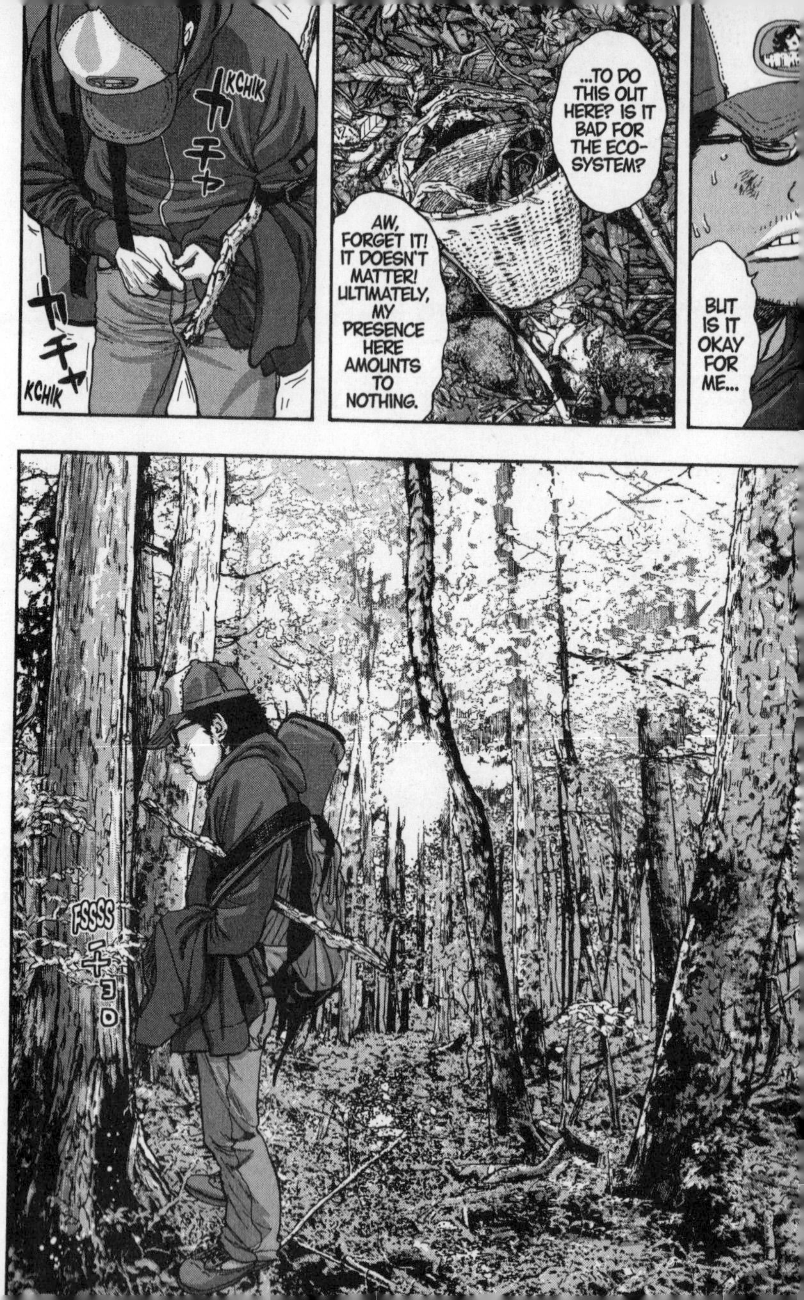
BUT IS IT OKAY FOR ME...
...TO DO THIS OUT HERE? IS IT BAD FOR THE ECO-SYSTEM?
AW, FORGET IT! IT DOESN'T MATTER! ULTIMATELY, MY PRESENCE HERE AMOUNTS TO NOTHING.
KCHIK
カチャ
KCHIK
カチャ
FSSSS
チョロ

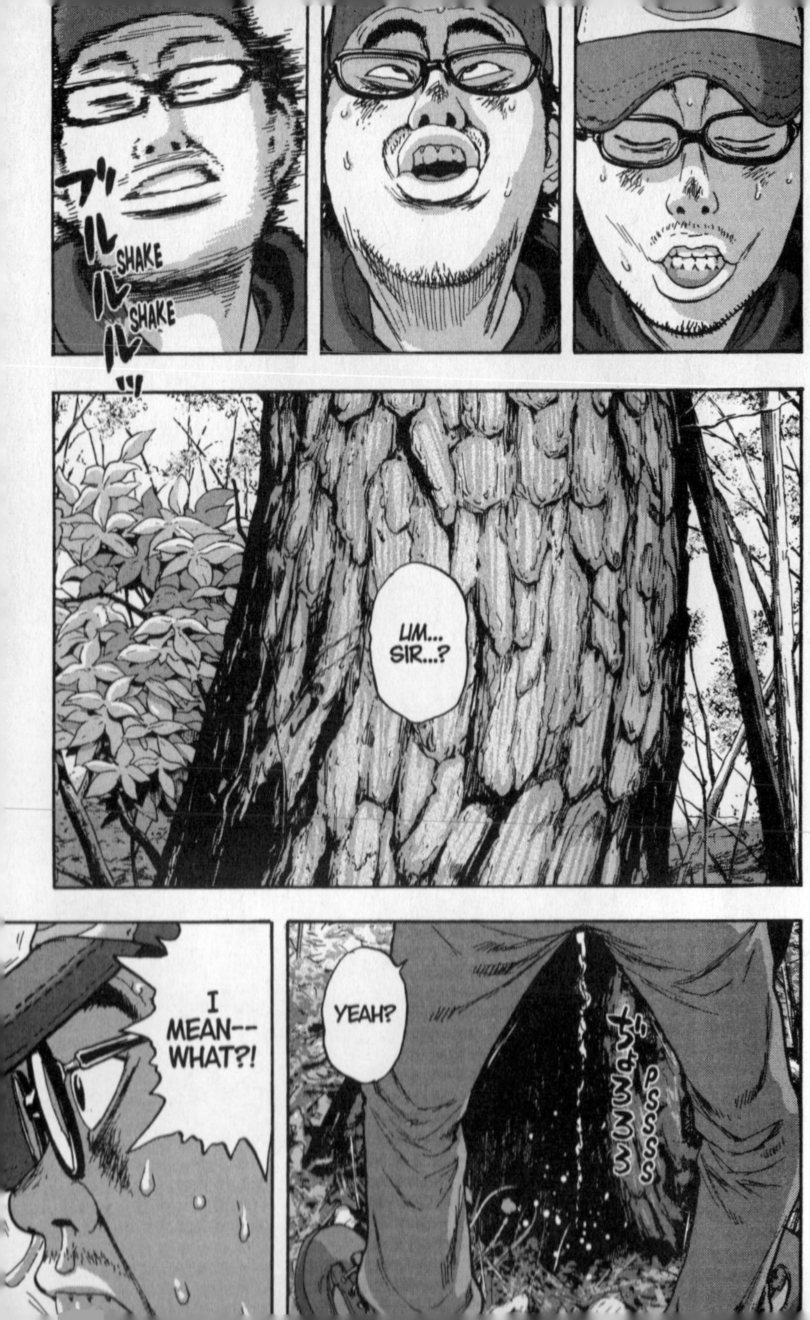

ブルルルッ
SHAKE
SHAKE
UM... SIR...?
YEAH?
ぢょろろろ
PSSSSS
I MEAN-- WHAT?!

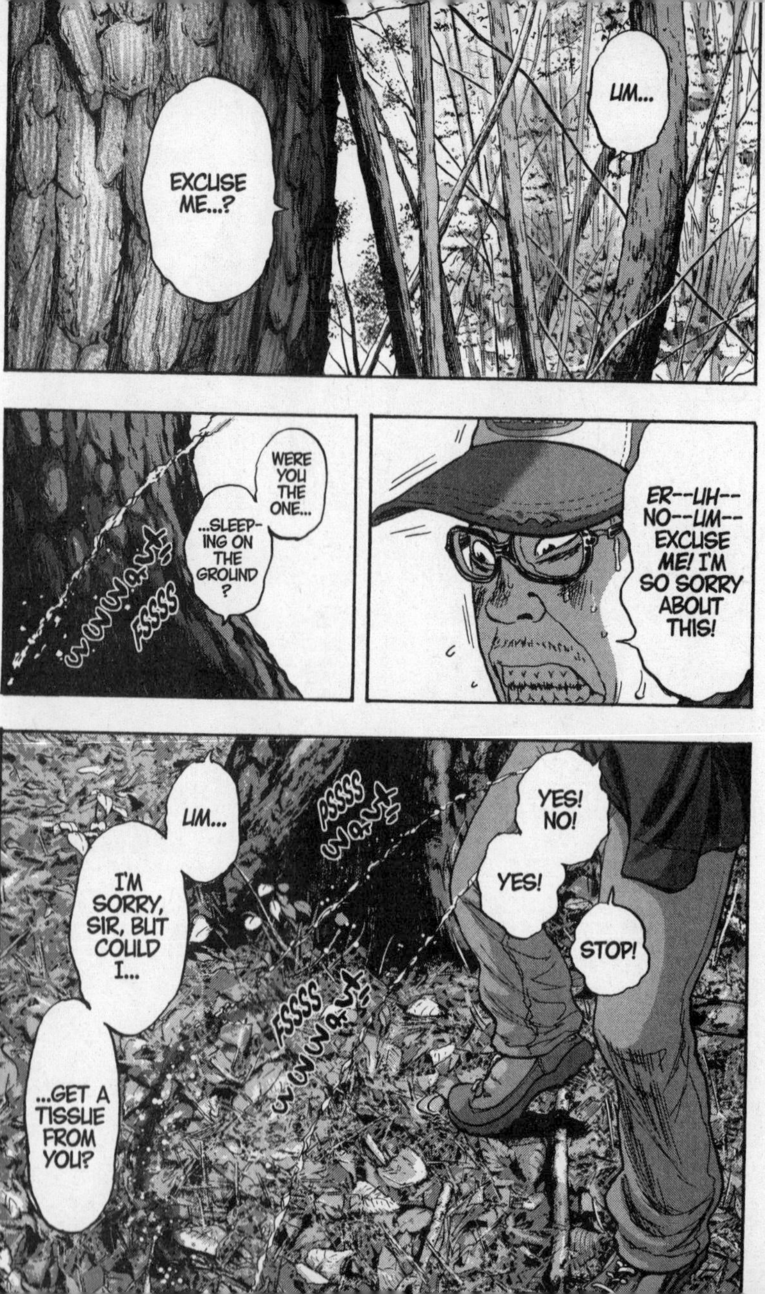
UM...
EXCUSE ME...?
ER--UH-- NO--UM-- EXCUSE ME! I'M SO SORRY ABOUT THIS!
WERE YOU THE ONE...
...SLEEPING ON THE GROUND?
FSSSS
YES! NO!
YES!
STOP!
PSSSS
UM...
I'M SORRY, SIR, BUT COULD I...
...GET A TISSUE FROM YOU?
FSSSS

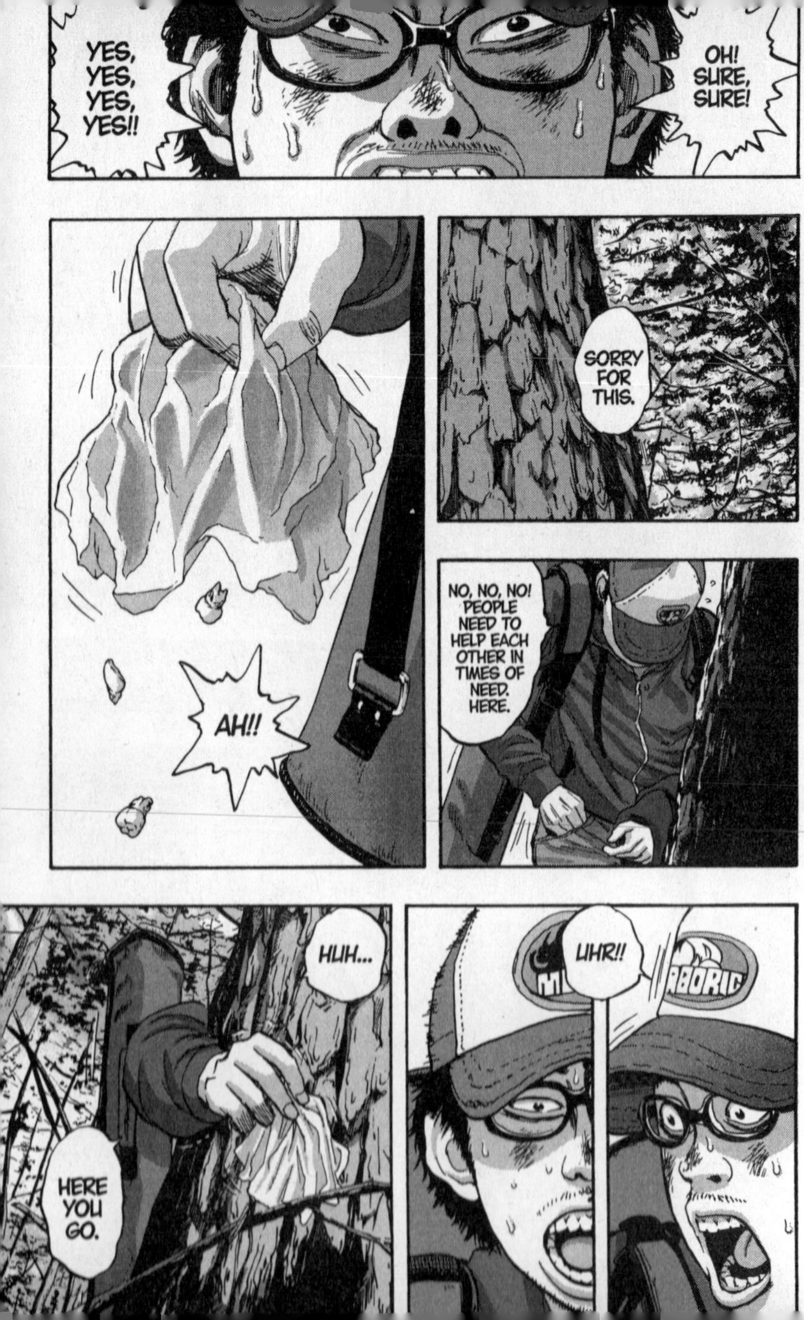
OH! SURE, SURE!
YES, YES, YES, YES!!
SORRY FOR THIS.
NO, NO, NO! PEOPLE NEED TO HELP EACH OTHER IN TIMES OF NEED. HERE.
AH!!
UHR!!
HUH...
HERE YOU GO.

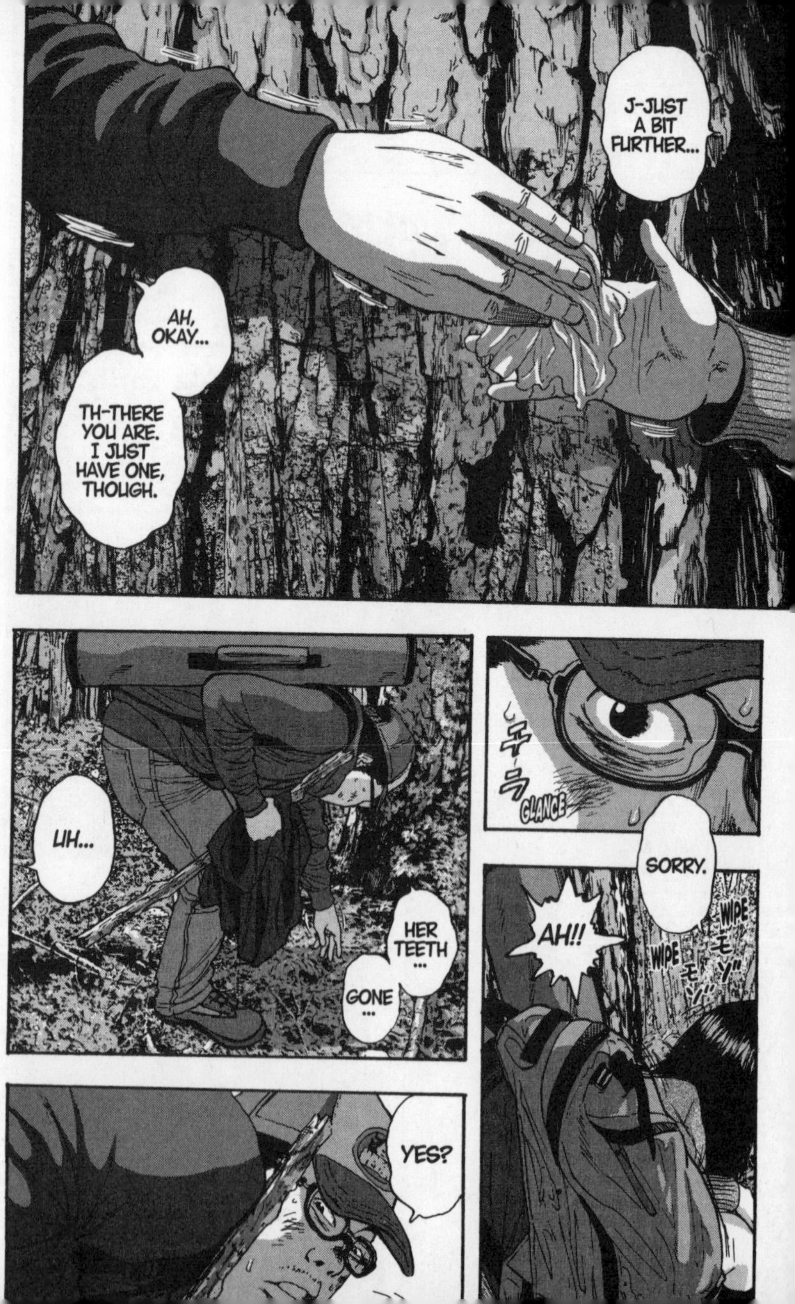

J-JUST A BIT FURTHER...
AH, OKAY...
TH-THERE YOU ARE. I JUST HAVE ONE, THOUGH.
GLANCE
SORRY.
AH!!
WIPE
WIPE
UH...
HER TEETH ...
GONE ...
YES?

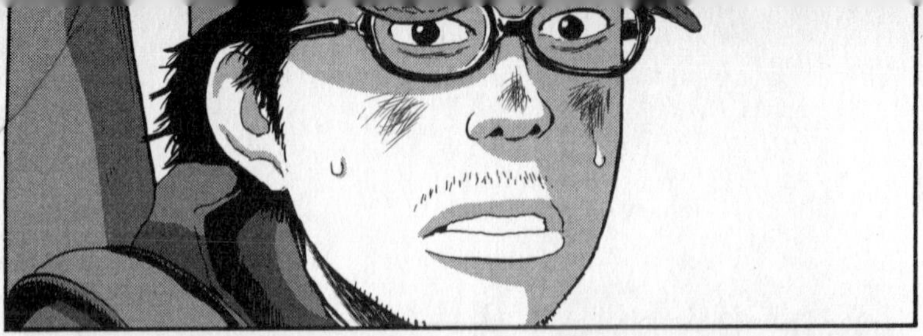
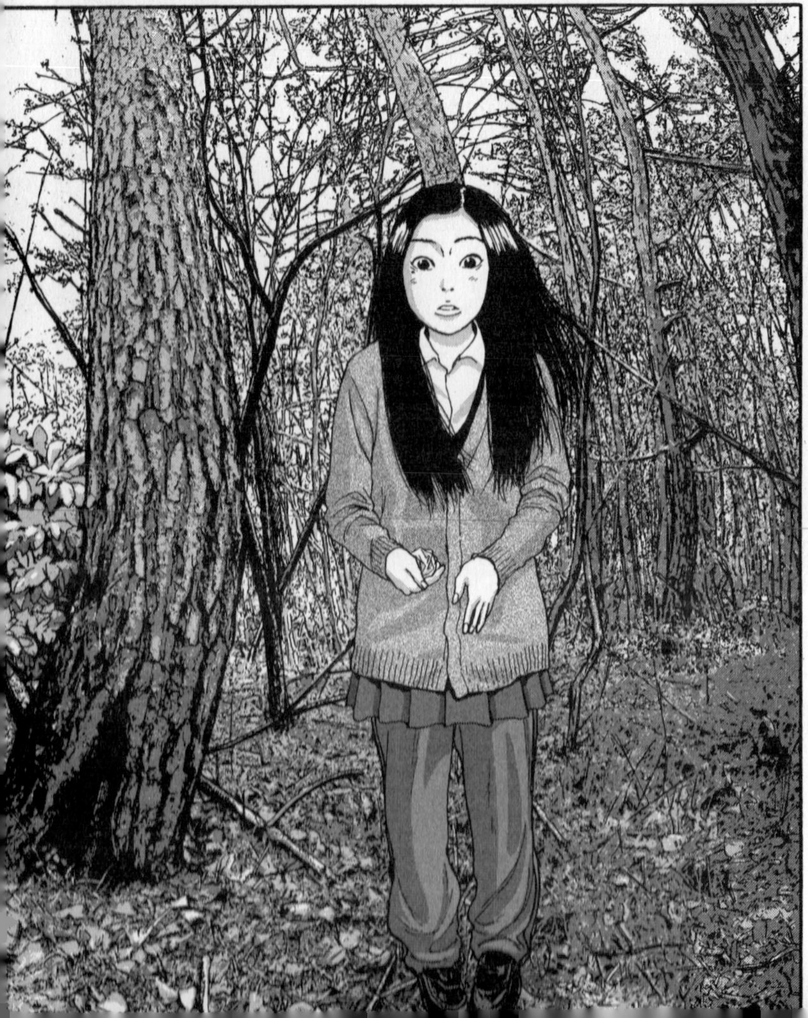

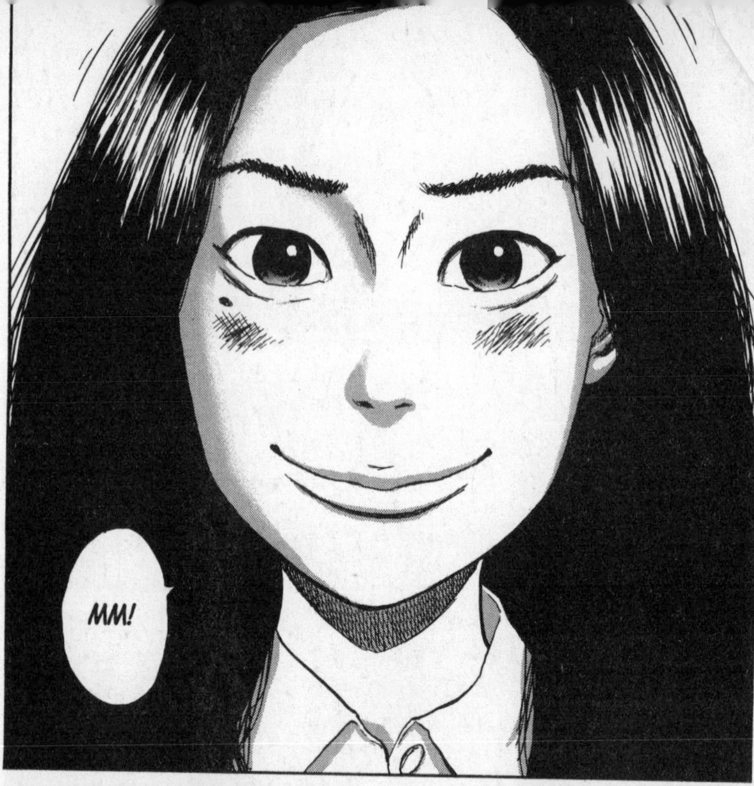
MM!

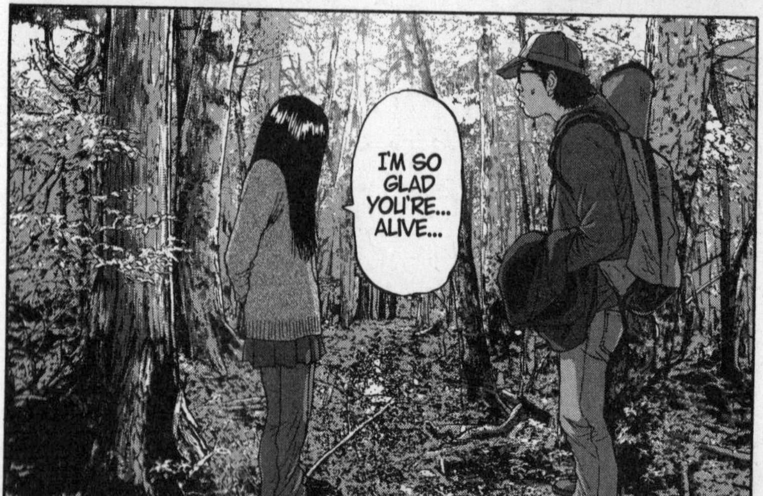
I'M SO GLAD YOU'RE... ALIVE...

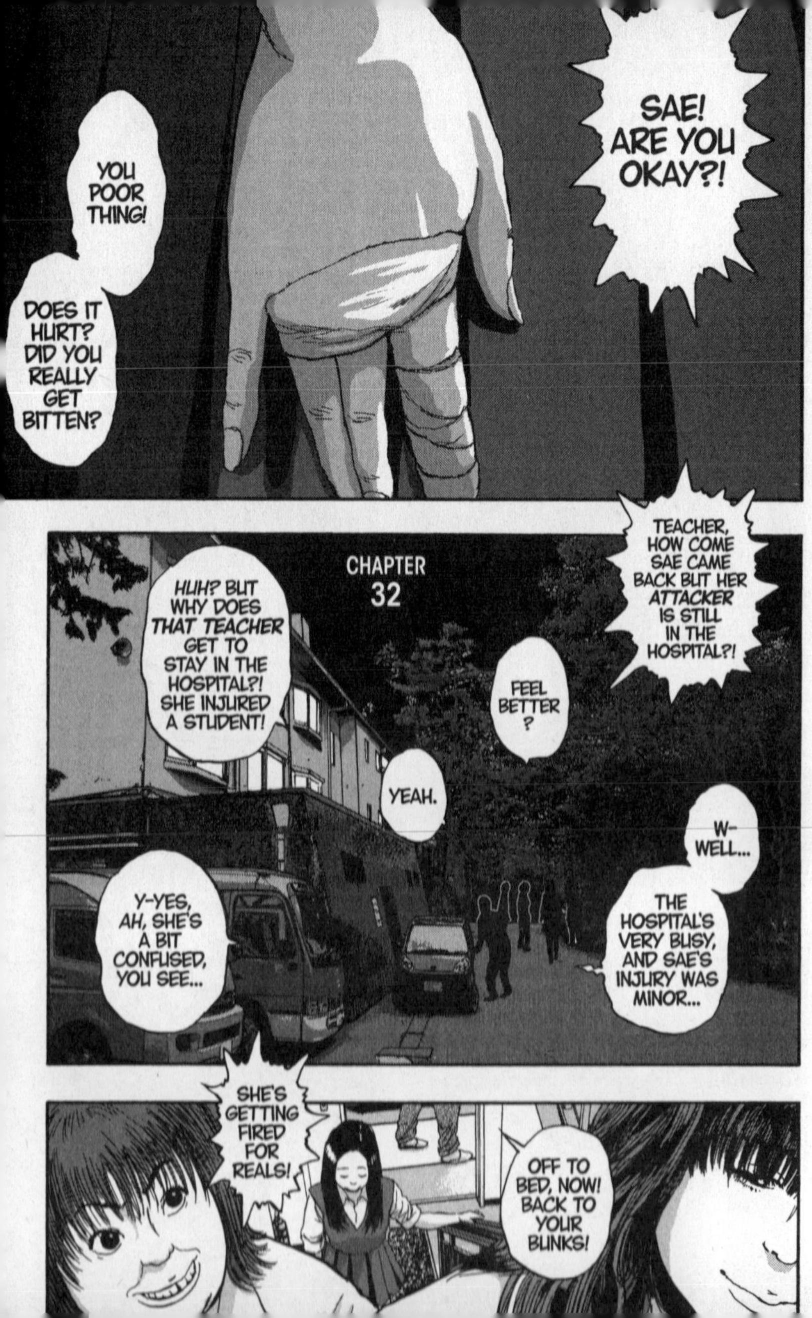
SAE! ARE YOU OKAY?!
YOU POOR THING!
DOES IT HURT? DID YOU REALLY GET BITTEN?
TEACHER, HOW COME SAE CAME BACK BUT HER ATTACKER IS STILL IN THE HOSPITAL?!
CHAPTER 32
HUH? BUT WHY DOES THAT TEACHER GET TO STAY IN THE HOSPITAL?! SHE INJURED A STUDENT!
FEEL BETTER?
YEAH.
W-WELL...
THE HOSPITAL'S VERY BUSY, AND SAE'S INJURY WAS MINOR...
Y-YES, AH, SHE'S A BIT CONFUSED, YOU SEE...
OFF TO BED, NOW! BACK TO YOUR BUNKS!
SHE'S GETTING FIRED FOR REALS!

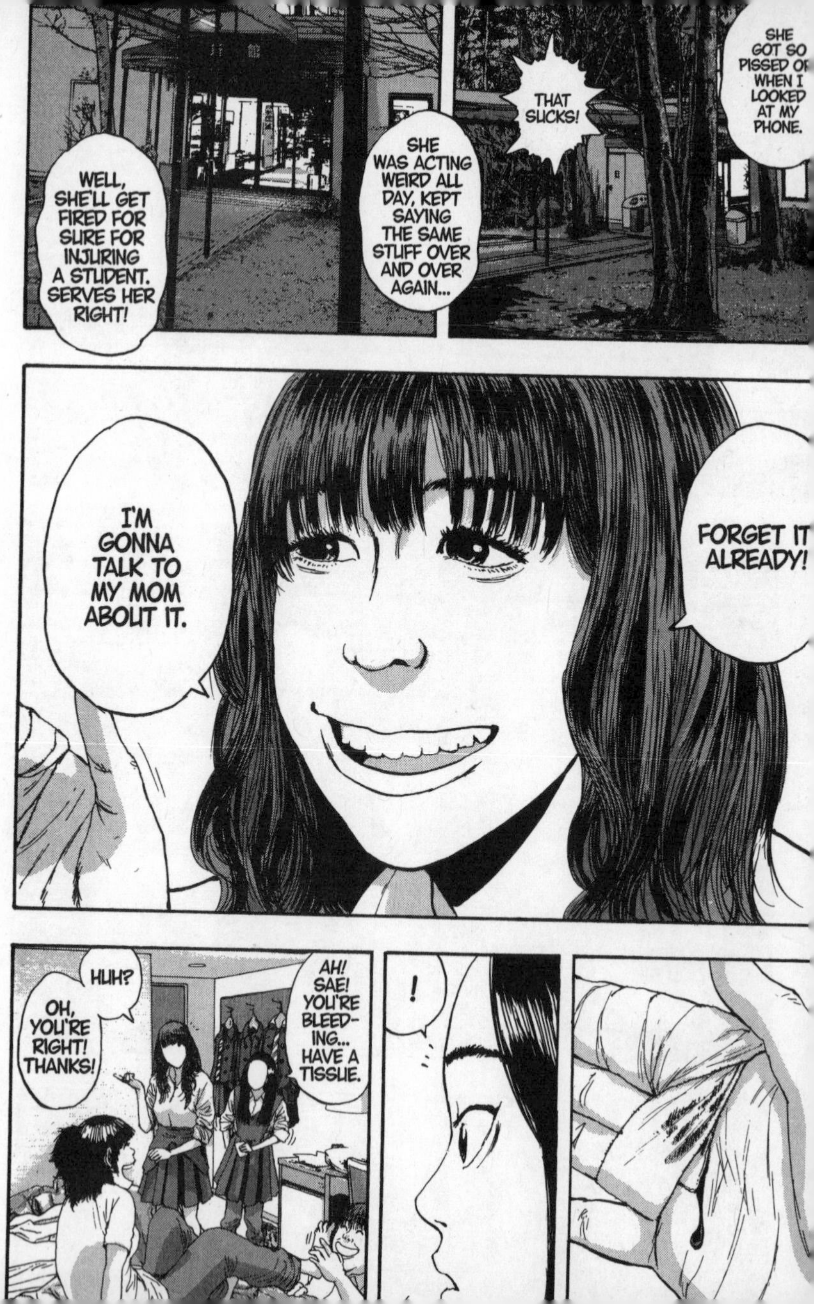
SHE GOT SO PISSED OF WHEN I LOOKED AT MY PHONE.
THAT SUCKS!
SHE WAS ACTING WEIRD ALL DAY, KEPT SAYING THE SAME STUFF OVER AND OVER AGAIN...
WELL, SHE'LL GET FIRED FOR SURE FOR INJURING A STUDENT. SERVES HER RIGHT!
FORGET IT ALREADY!
I'M GONNA TALK TO MY MOM ABOUT IT.
!
AH! SAE! YOU'RE BLEED-ING... HAVE A TISSUE.
HUH?
OH, YOU'RE RIGHT! THANKS!

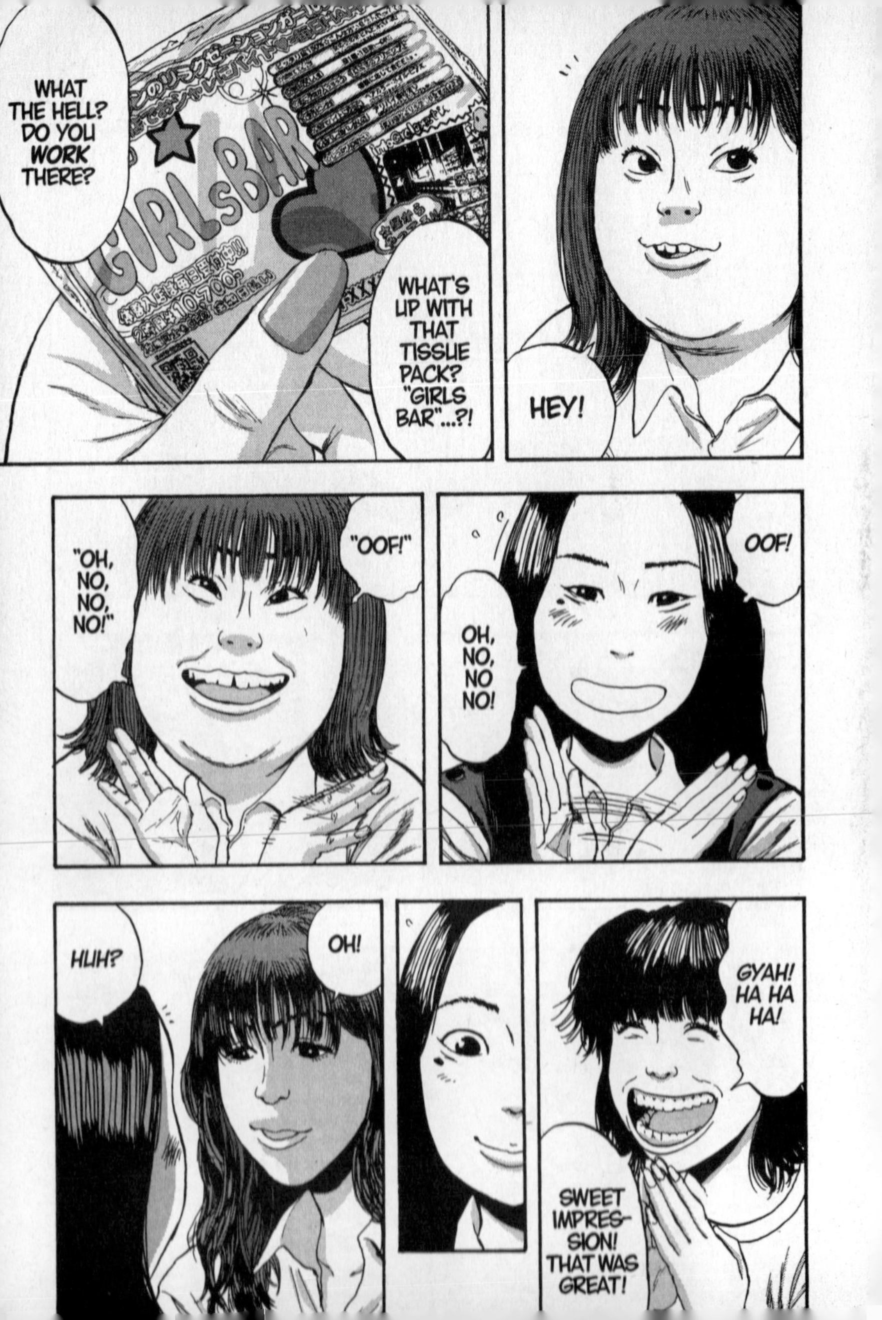
HEY!
WHAT'S UP WITH THAT TISSUE PACK? "GIRLS BAR"...?!
WHAT THE HELL? DO YOU WORK THERE?
GIRLsBAR
OOF!
OH, NO, NO NO NO!
"OOF!"
"OH, NO, NO, NO!"
GYAH! HA HA HA!
SWEET IMPRESSION! THAT WAS GREAT!
OH!
HUH?

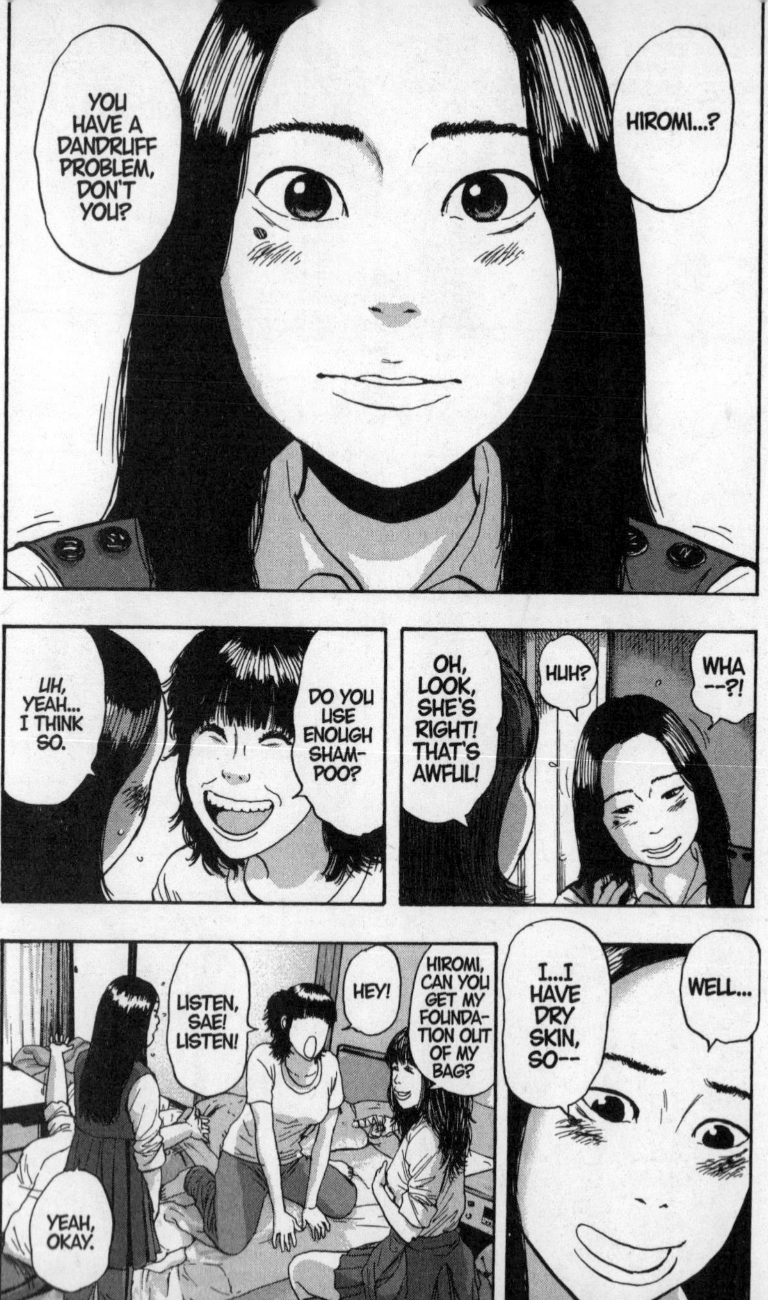
HIROMI...?
YOU HAVE A DANDRUFF PROBLEM, DON'T YOU?
WHA--?!
HUH?
OH, LOOK, SHE'S RIGHT! THAT'S AWFUL!
DO YOU USE ENOUGH SHAM-POO?
UH, YEAH... I THINK SO.
WELL...
I...I HAVE DRY SKIN, SO--
HIROMI, CAN YOU GET MY FOUNDA-TION OUT OF MY BAG?
HEY!
LISTEN, SAE! LISTEN!
YEAH, OKAY.

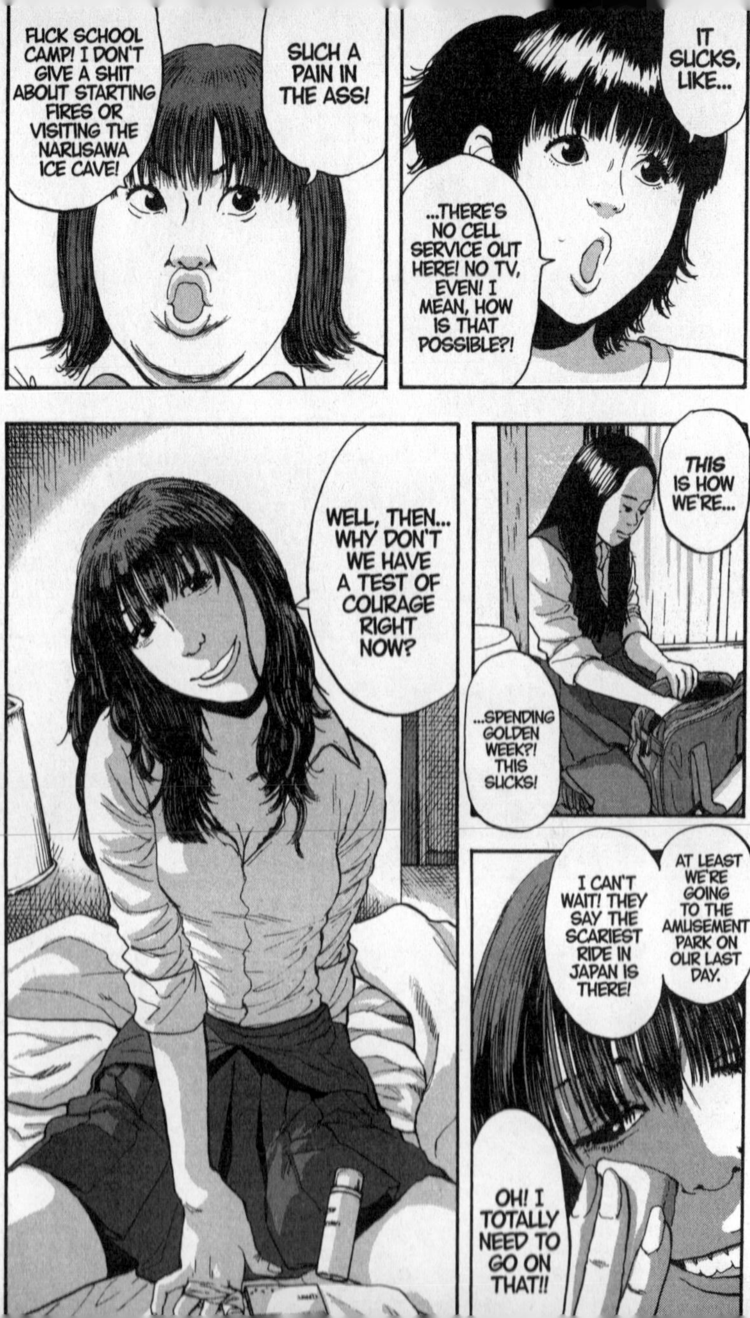
IT SUCKS, LIKE...
...THERE'S NO CELL SERVICE OUT HERE! NO TV, EVEN! I MEAN, HOW IS THAT POSSIBLE?!
SUCH A PAIN IN THE ASS!
FUCK SCHOOL CAMP! I DON'T GIVE A SHIT ABOUT STARTING FIRES OR VISITING THE NARUSAWA ICE CAVE!
THIS IS HOW WE'RE...
...SPENDING GOLDEN WEEK?! THIS SUCKS!
AT LEAST WE'RE GOING TO THE AMUSEMENT PARK ON OUR LAST DAY.
I CAN'T WAIT! THEY SAY THE SCARIEST RIDE IN JAPAN IS THERE!
OH! I TOTALLY NEED TO GO ON THAT!!
WELL, THEN... WHY DON'T WE HAVE A TEST OF COURAGE RIGHT NOW?

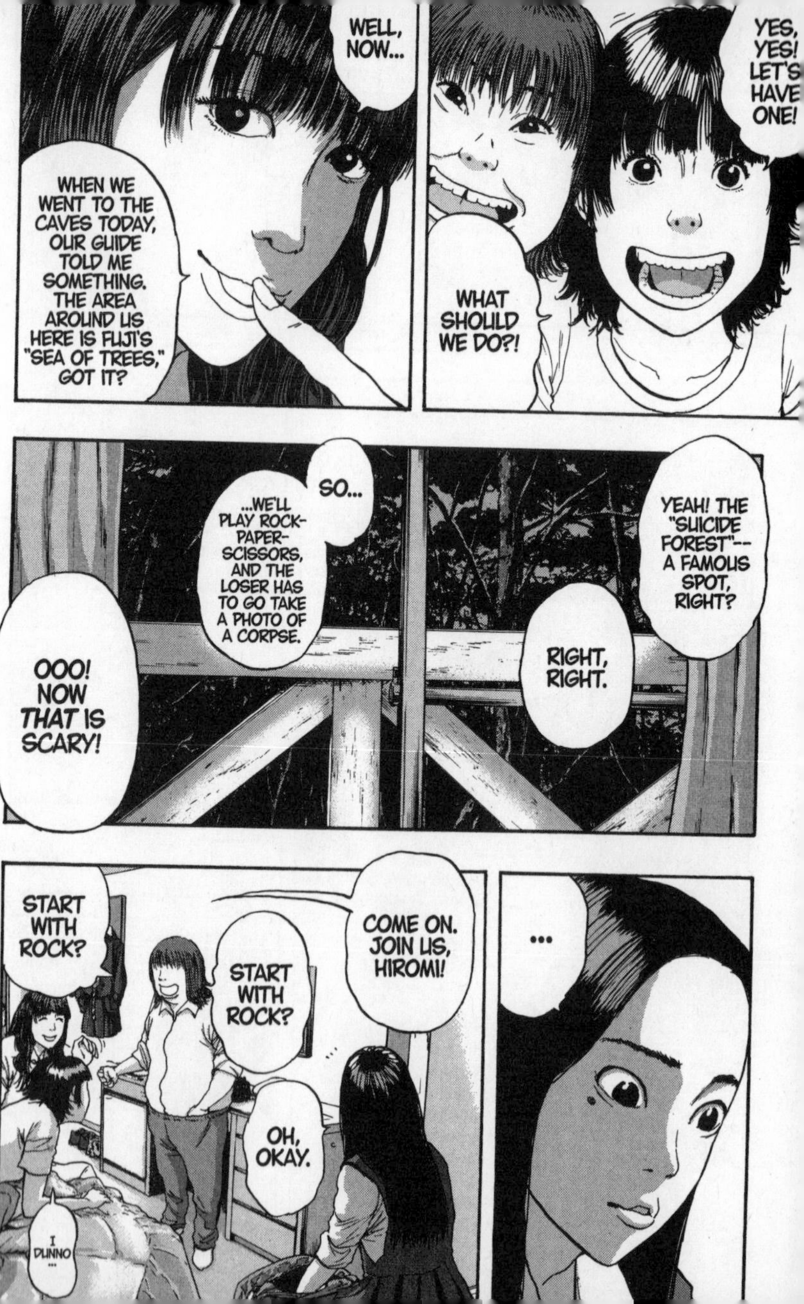
YES, YES! LET'S HAVE ONE!
WHAT SHOULD WE DO?!
WELL, NOW...
WHEN WE WENT TO THE CAVES TODAY, OUR GUIDE TOLD ME SOMETHING. THE AREA AROUND US HERE IS FUJI'S "SEA OF TREES," GOT IT?
YEAH! THE "SUICIDE FOREST"-- A FAMOUS SPOT, RIGHT?
RIGHT, RIGHT.
SO...
...WE'LL PLAY ROCK-PAPER-SCISSORS, AND THE LOSER HAS TO GO TAKE A PHOTO OF A CORPSE.
OOO! NOW *THAT* IS SCARY!
...
COME ON. JOIN US, HIROMI!
START WITH ROCK?
START WITH ROCK?
...
OH, OKAY.
I DUNNO ...

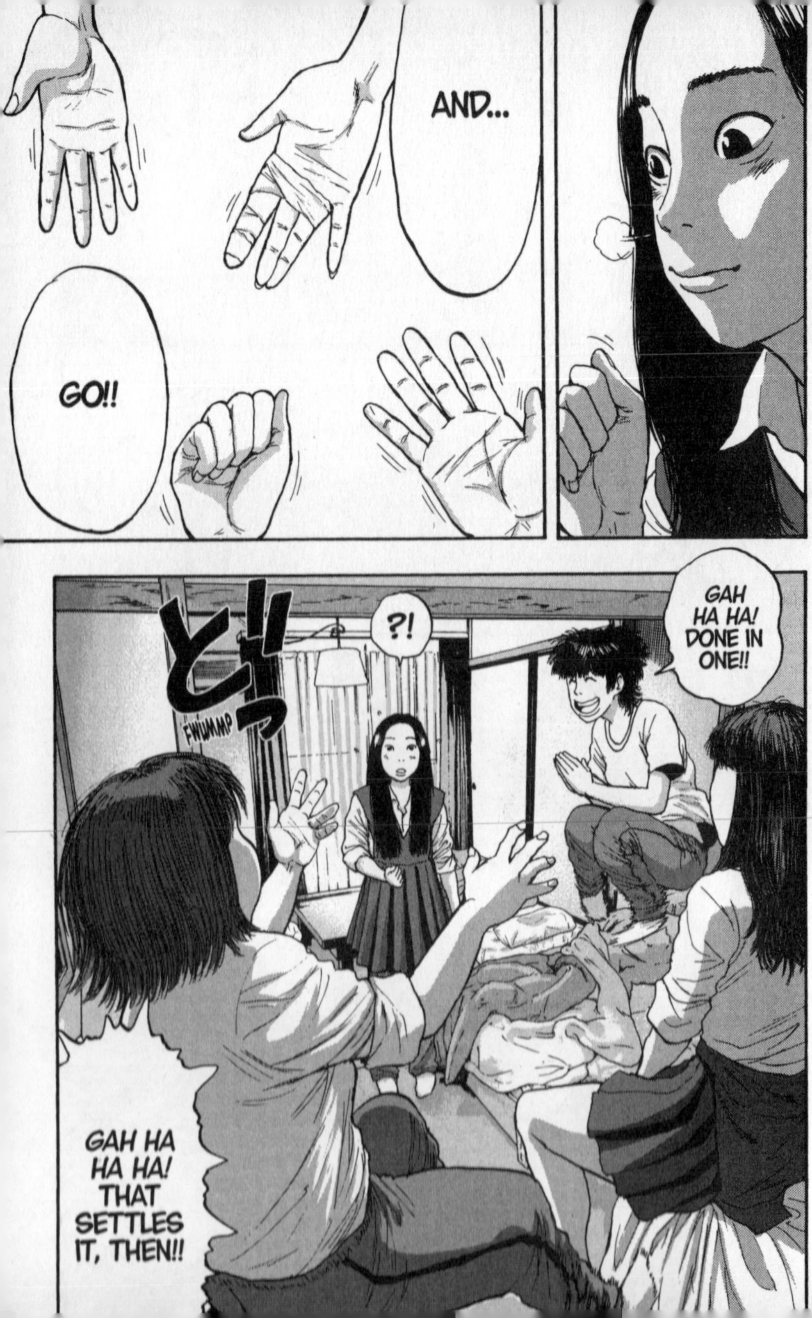
AND...
GO!!
GAH HA HA! DONE IN ONE!!
?!
どっ
FWUMMP
GAH HA HA HA! THAT SETTLES IT, THEN!!

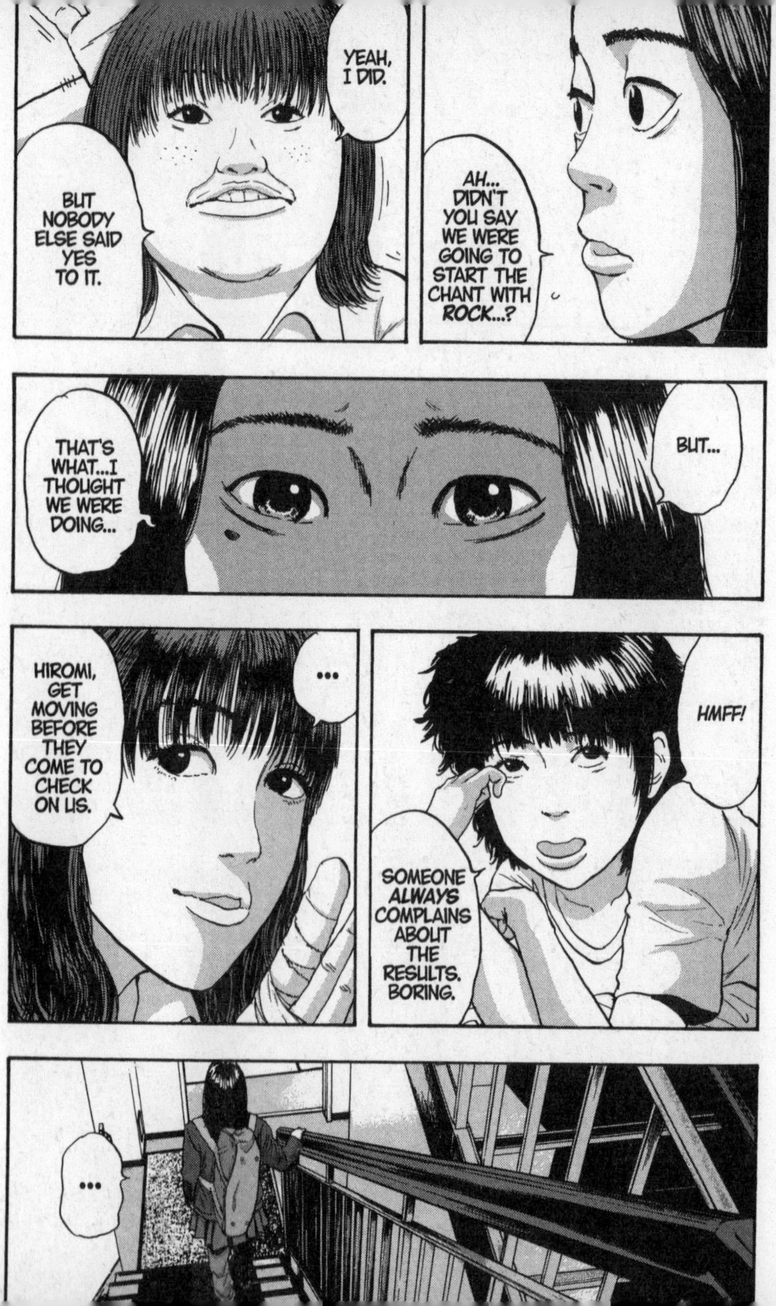
AH... DIDN'T YOU SAY WE WERE GOING TO START THE CHANT WITH ROCK...?
YEAH, I DID.
BUT NOBODY ELSE SAID YES TO IT.
BUT...
THAT'S WHAT...I THOUGHT WE WERE DOING...
HMFF!
SOMEONE ALWAYS COMPLAINS ABOUT THE RESULTS. BORING.
...
HIROMI, GET MOVING BEFORE THEY COME TO CHECK ON US.
...

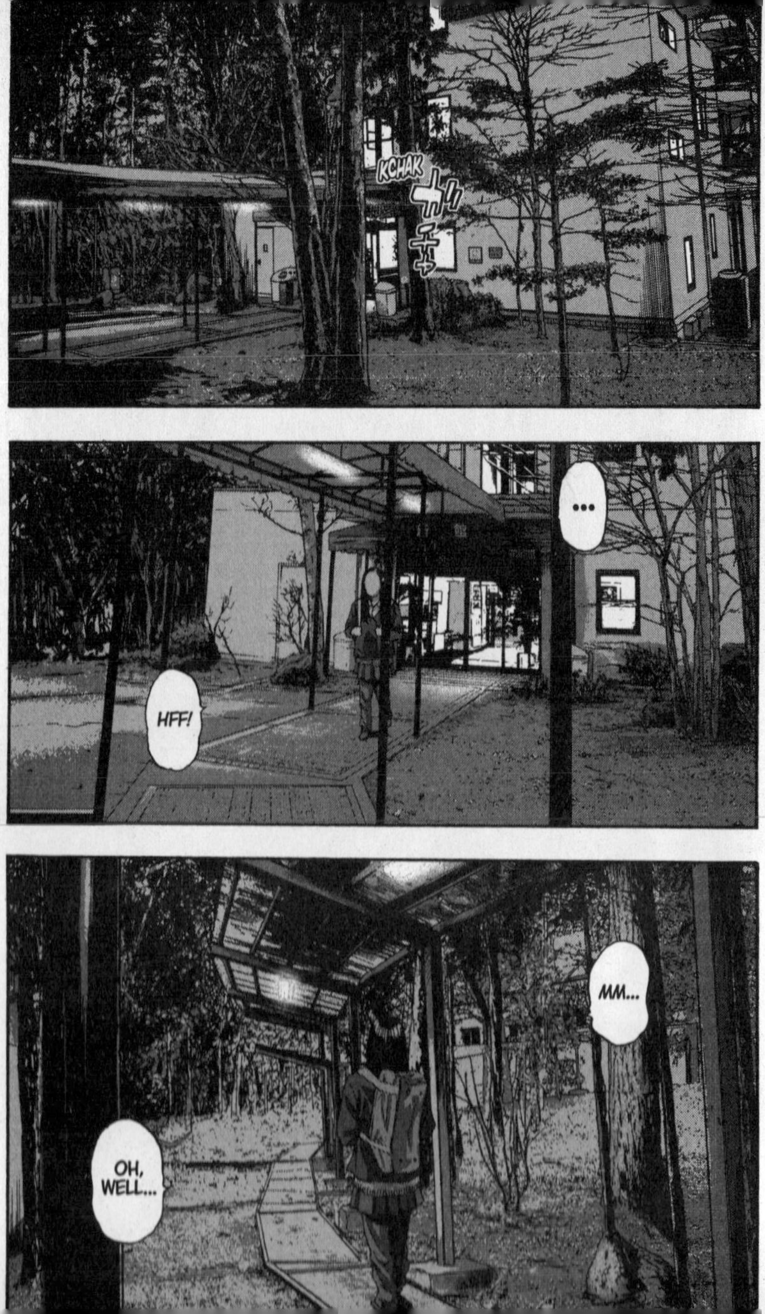
KCHAK
...
HFF!
MM...
OH, WELL...

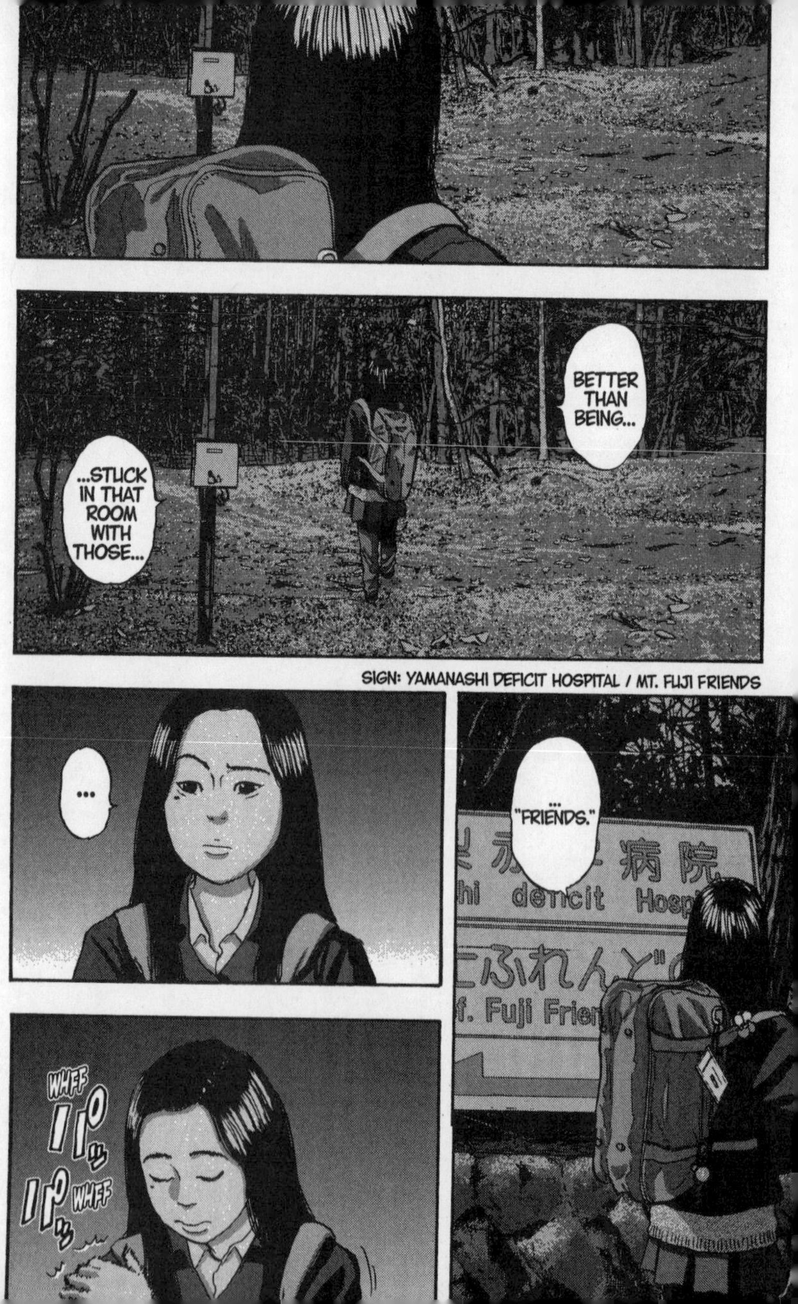
BETTER THAN BEING...
...STUCK IN THAT ROOM WITH THOSE...
SIGN: YAMANASHI DEFICIT HOSPITAL / MT. FUJI FRIENDS
... "FRIENDS."
hi deficit Hosp
f. Fuji Frien
...
WHFF
WHFF

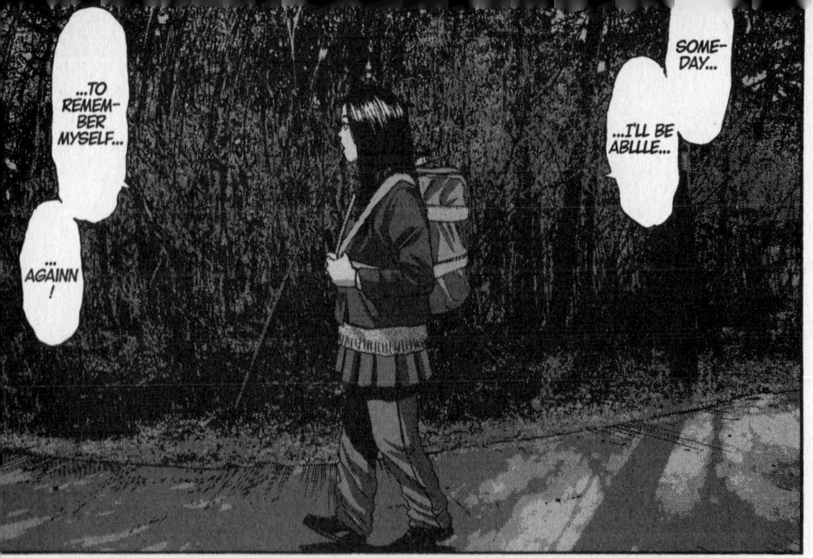
SOME-DAY...
...I'LL BE ABLLLE...
...TO REMEMBER MYSELF...
... AGAINN!

PHONE: NO SERVICE

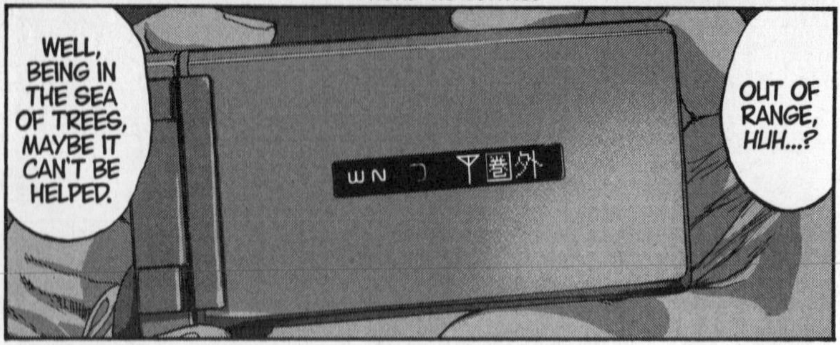
OUT OF RANGE, HUH...?
WELL, BEING IN THE SEA OF TREES, MAYBE IT CAN'T BE HELPED.

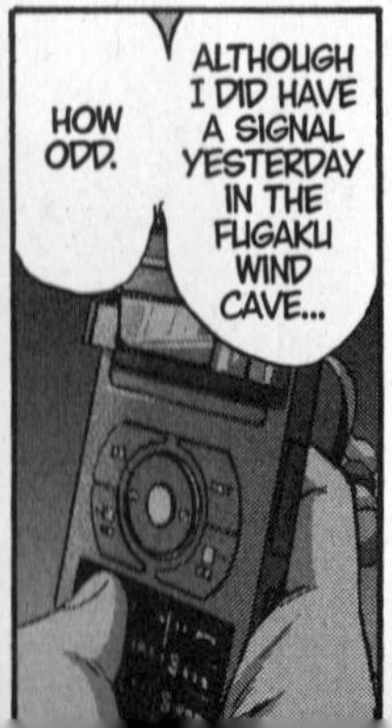
ALTHOUGH I DID HAVE A SIGNAL YESTERDAY IN THE FUGAKU WIND CAVE...
HOW ODD.

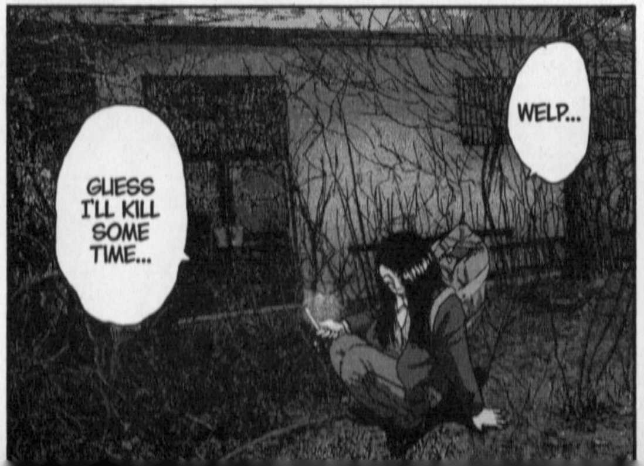
WELP...
GUESS I'LL KILL SOME TIME...

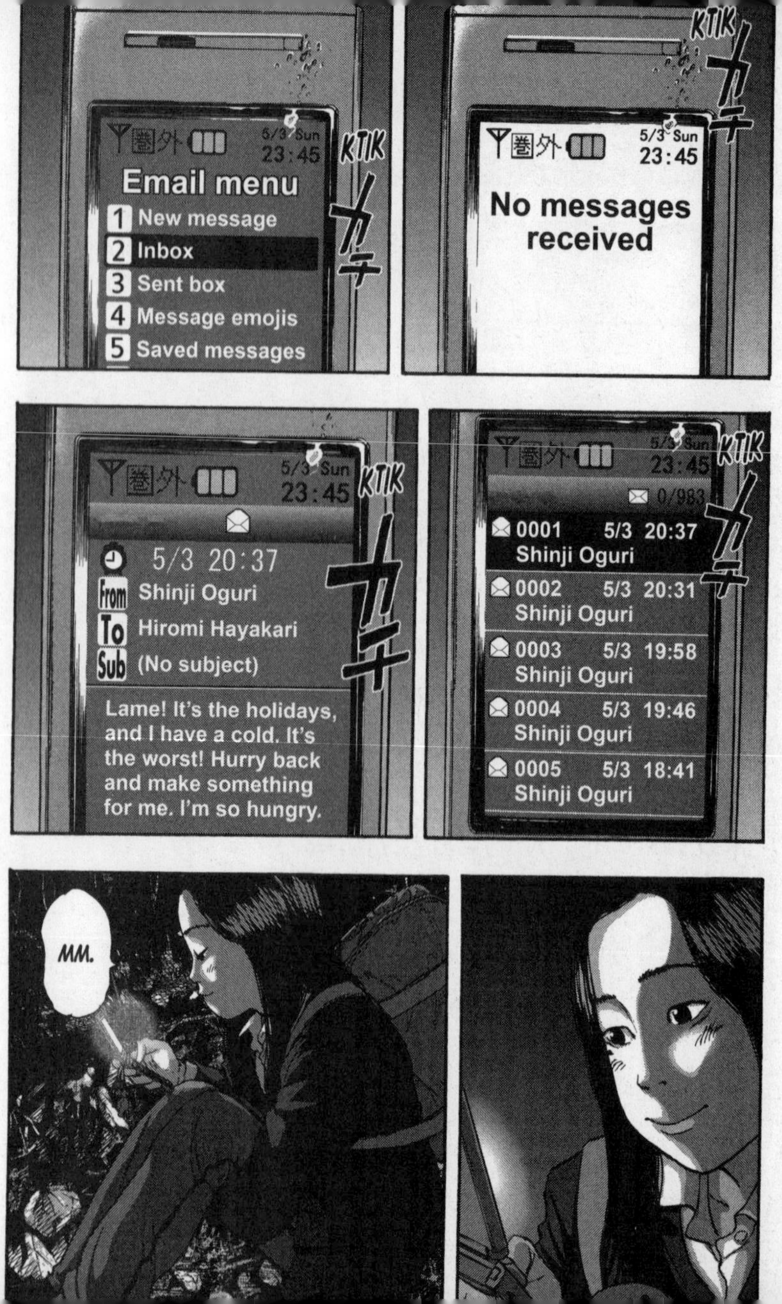

KTIK
カチ
5/3 Sun
23:45
No messages received
KTIK
カチ
5/3 Sun
23:45
Email menu
1 New message
2 Inbox
3 Sent box
4 Message emojis
5 Saved messages
KTIK
カチ
5/3 Sun
23:45
0/983
0001 5/3 20:37
Shinji Oguri
0002 5/3 20:31
Shinji Oguri
0003 5/3 19:58
Shinji Oguri
0004 5/3 19:46
Shinji Oguri
0005 5/3 18:41
Shinji Oguri
KTIK
カチ
5/3 Sun
23:45
5/3 20:37
From Shinji Oguri
To Hiromi Hayakari
Sub (No subject)
Lame! It's the holidays, and I have a cold. It's the worst! Hurry back and make something for me. I'm so hungry.
MM.

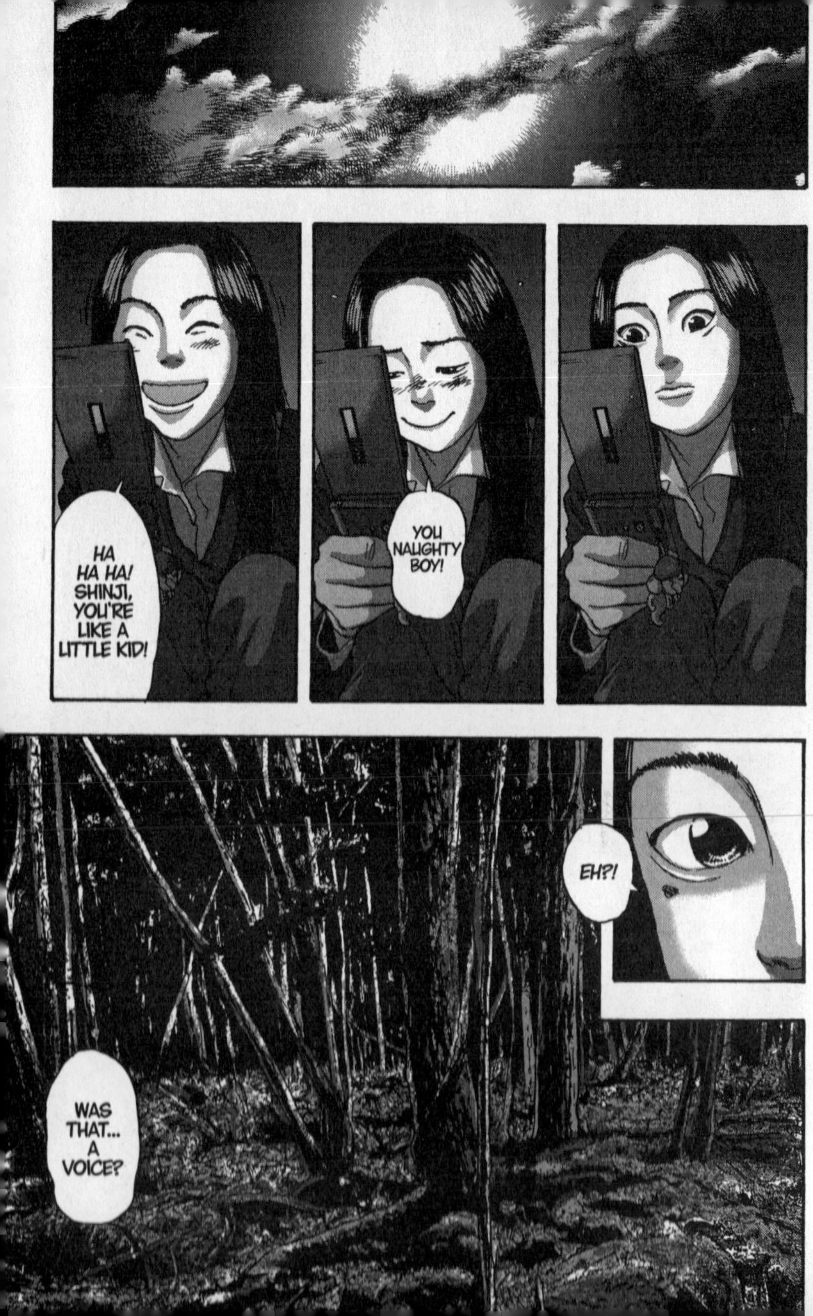
YOU NAUGHTY BOY!
HA HA HA! SHINJI, YOU'RE LIKE A LITTLE KID!
EH?!
WAS THAT... A VOICE?

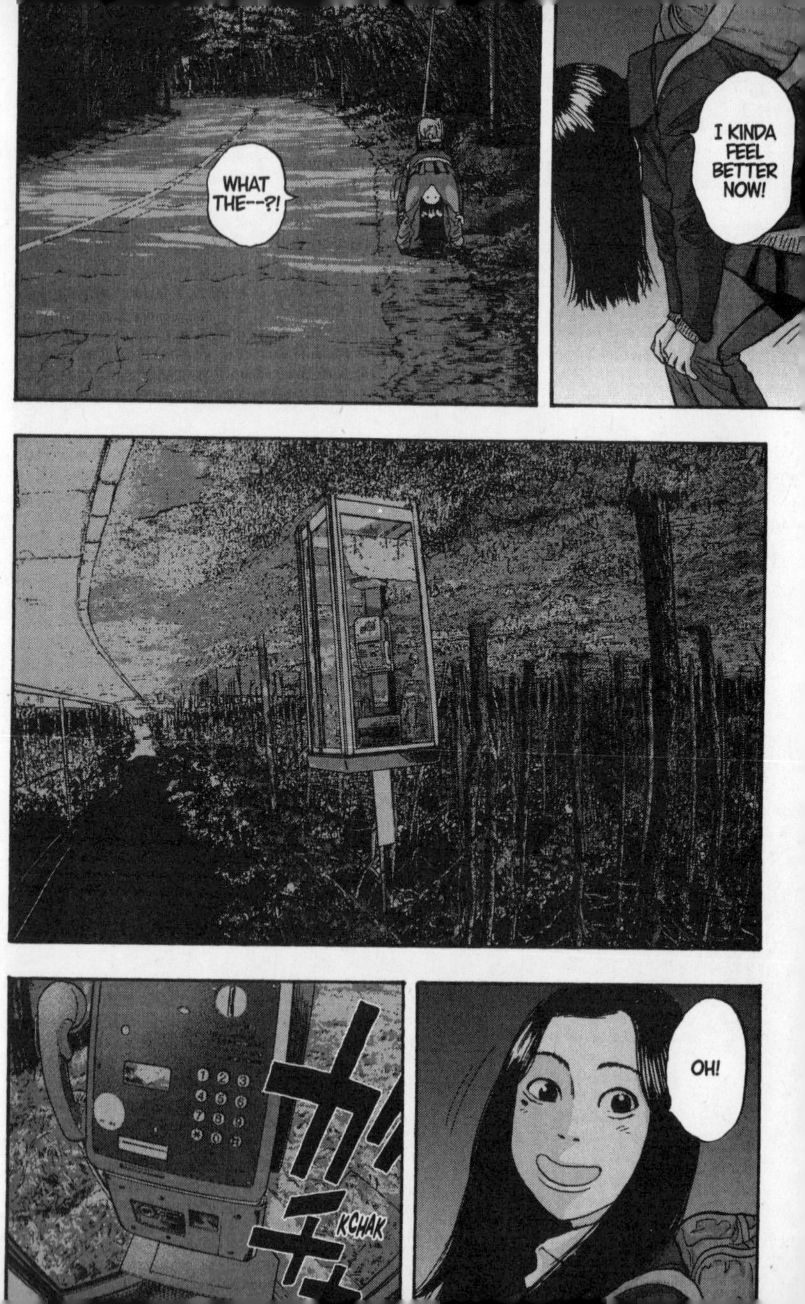
I KINDA FEEL BETTER NOW!
WHAT THE--?!
OH!
KCHAK

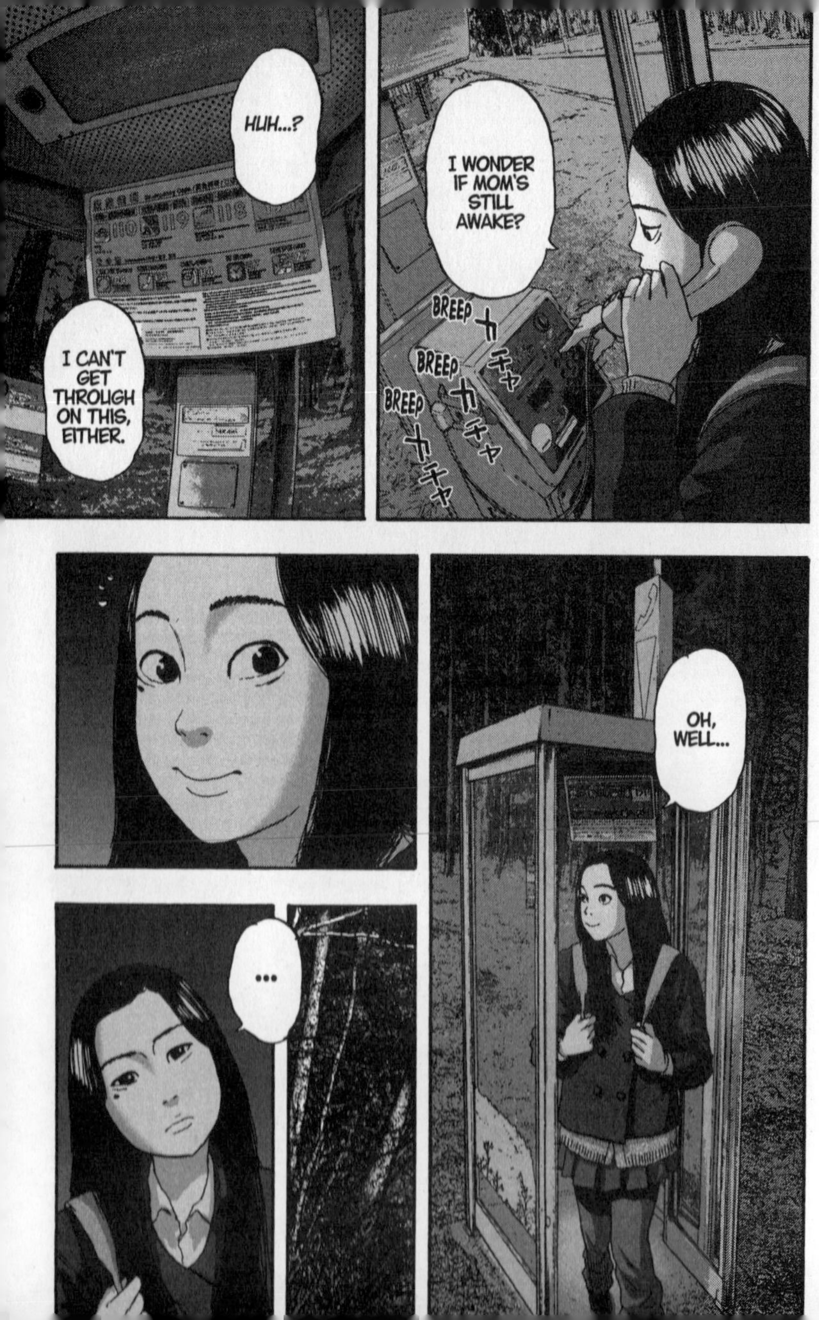
I WONDER IF MOM'S STILL AWAKE?
BREEP
カチャ
BREEP
カチャ
BREEP
カチャ
HUH...?
I CAN'T GET THROUGH ON THIS, EITHER.
OH, WELL...
...

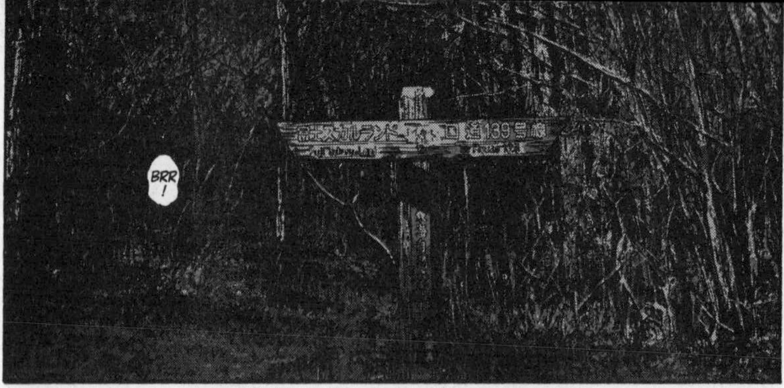
BRR!

SIGN: FUJI SUGARU LAND / ROUTE 139

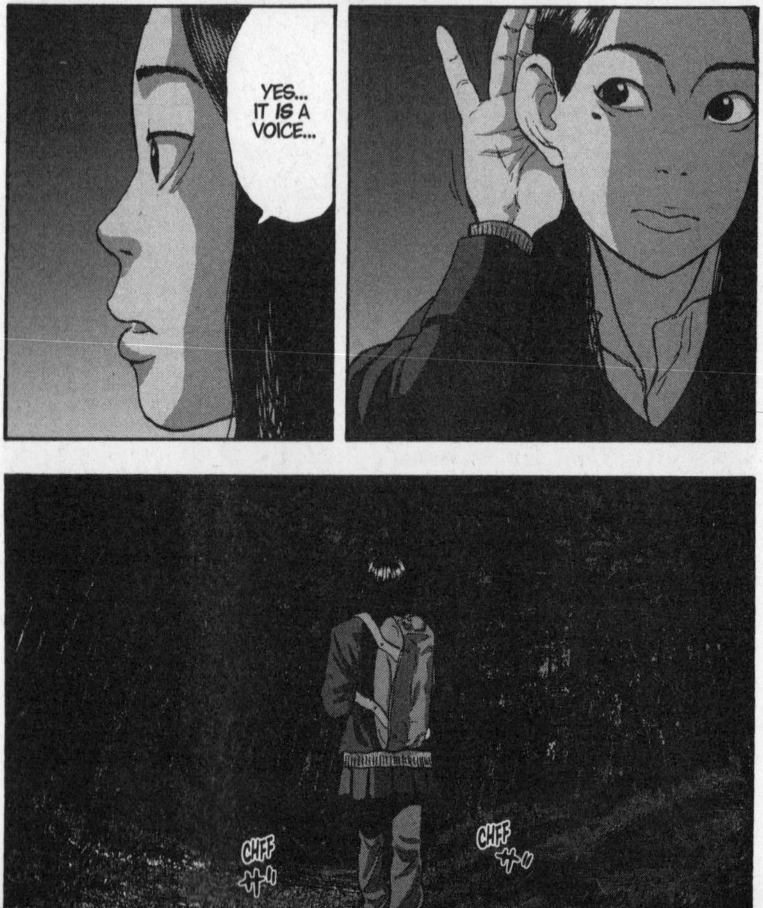
YES... IT IS A VOICE...
CHFF
CHFF

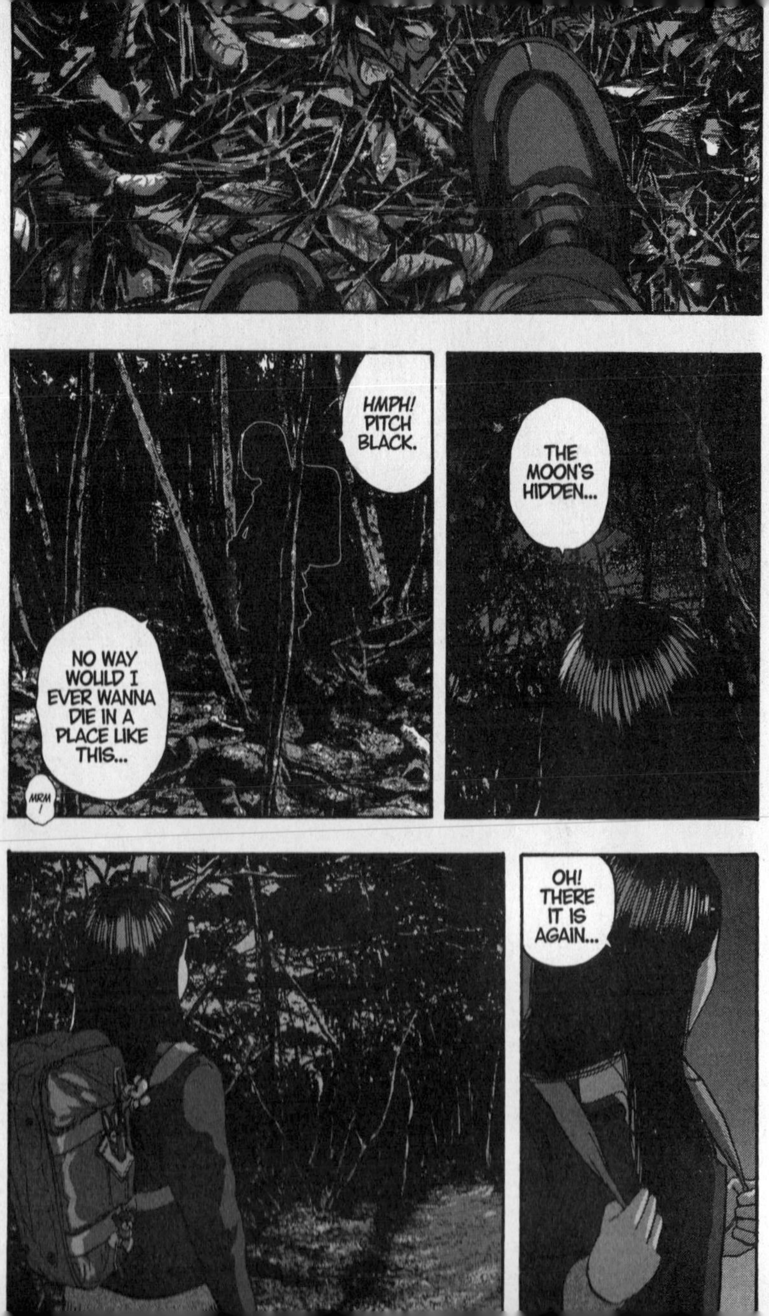
THE MOON'S HIDDEN...
HMPH! PITCH BLACK.
NO WAY WOULD I EVER WANNA DIE IN A PLACE LIKE THIS...
MRM!
OH! THERE IT IS AGAIN...

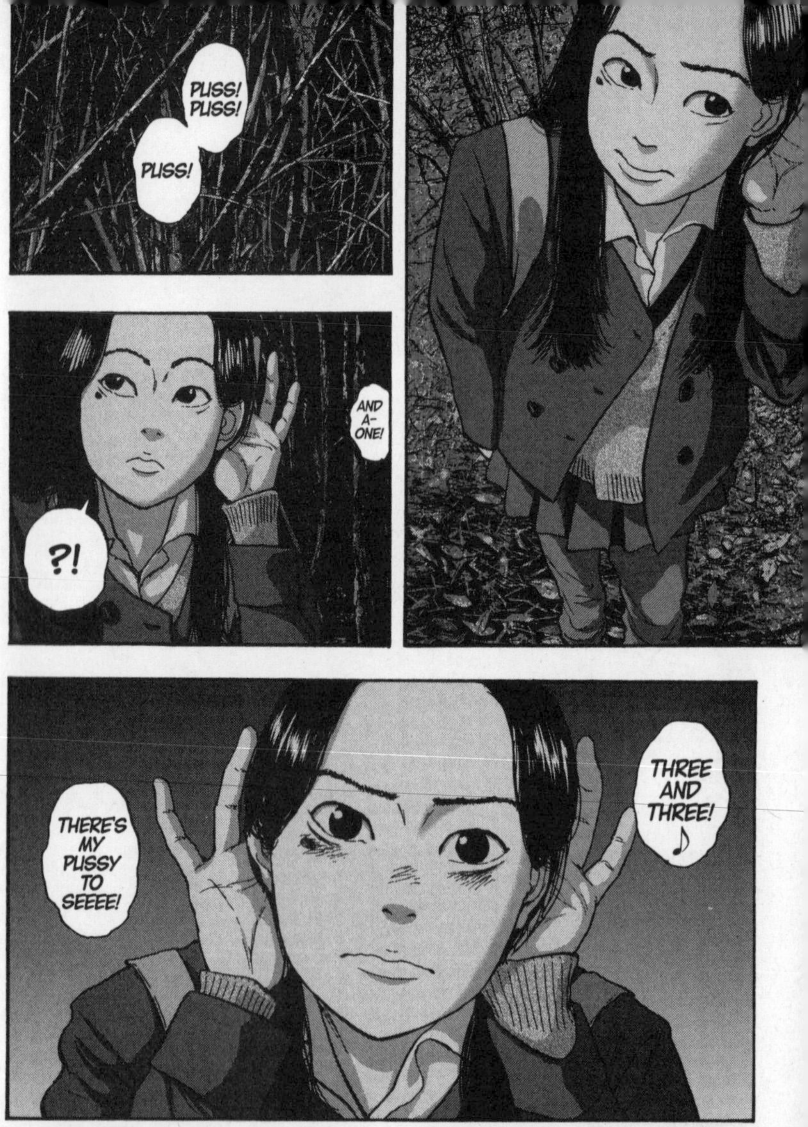
PUSS! PUSS!
PUSS!
AND A-ONE!
?!
THREE AND THREE! ♪
THERE'S MY PUSSY TO SEEEE!

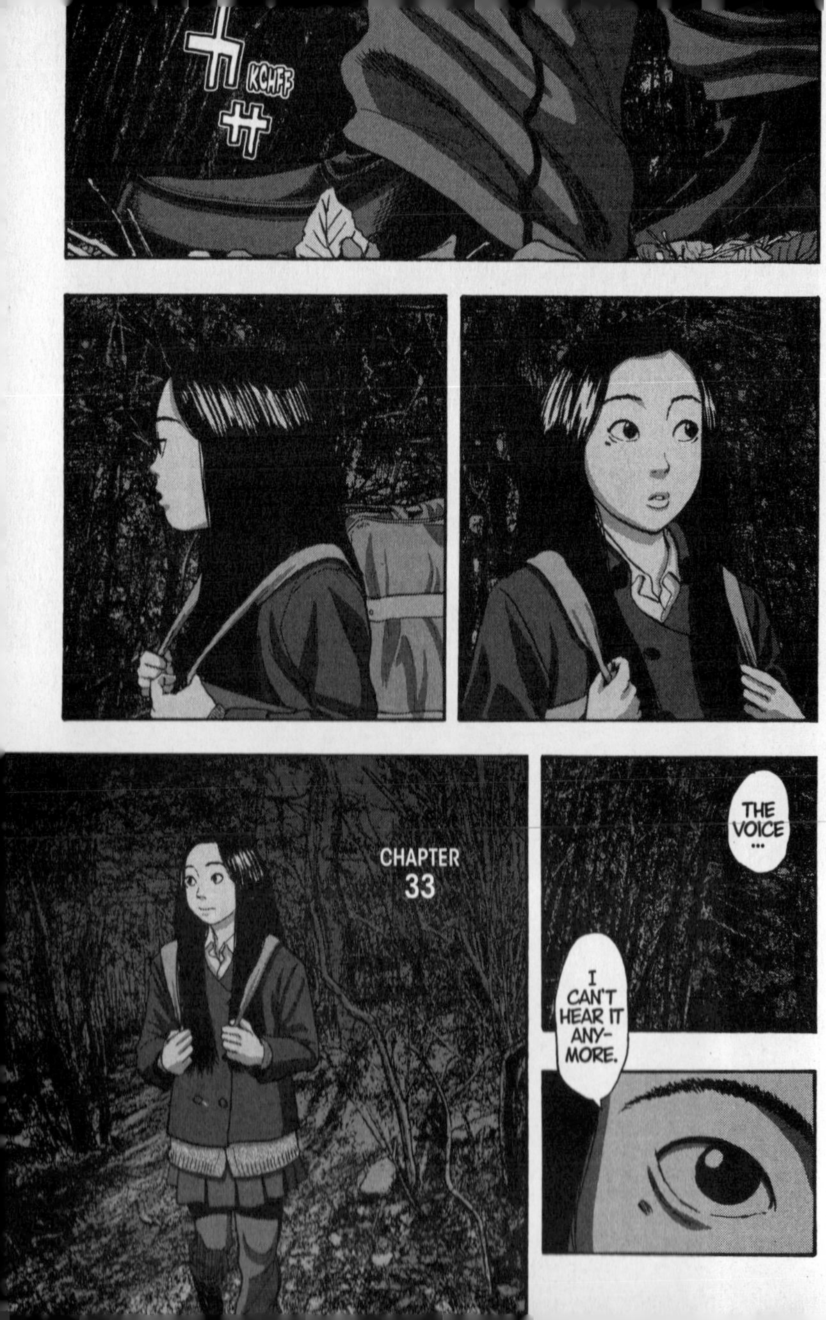
KCHFF
CHAPTER 33
THE VOICE...
I CAN'T HEAR IT ANY-MORE.

WSHH
WSHH
WSHH
RUSTLE
RUSTLE
RUSTLE
KNNCH
KRIK
CHFF
KITCH

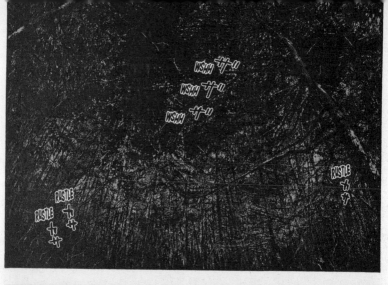

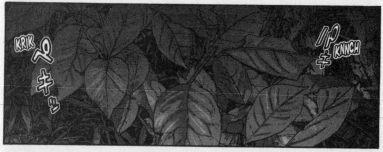

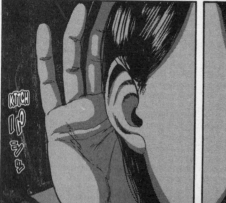

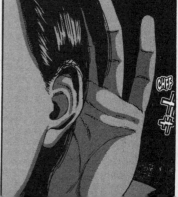

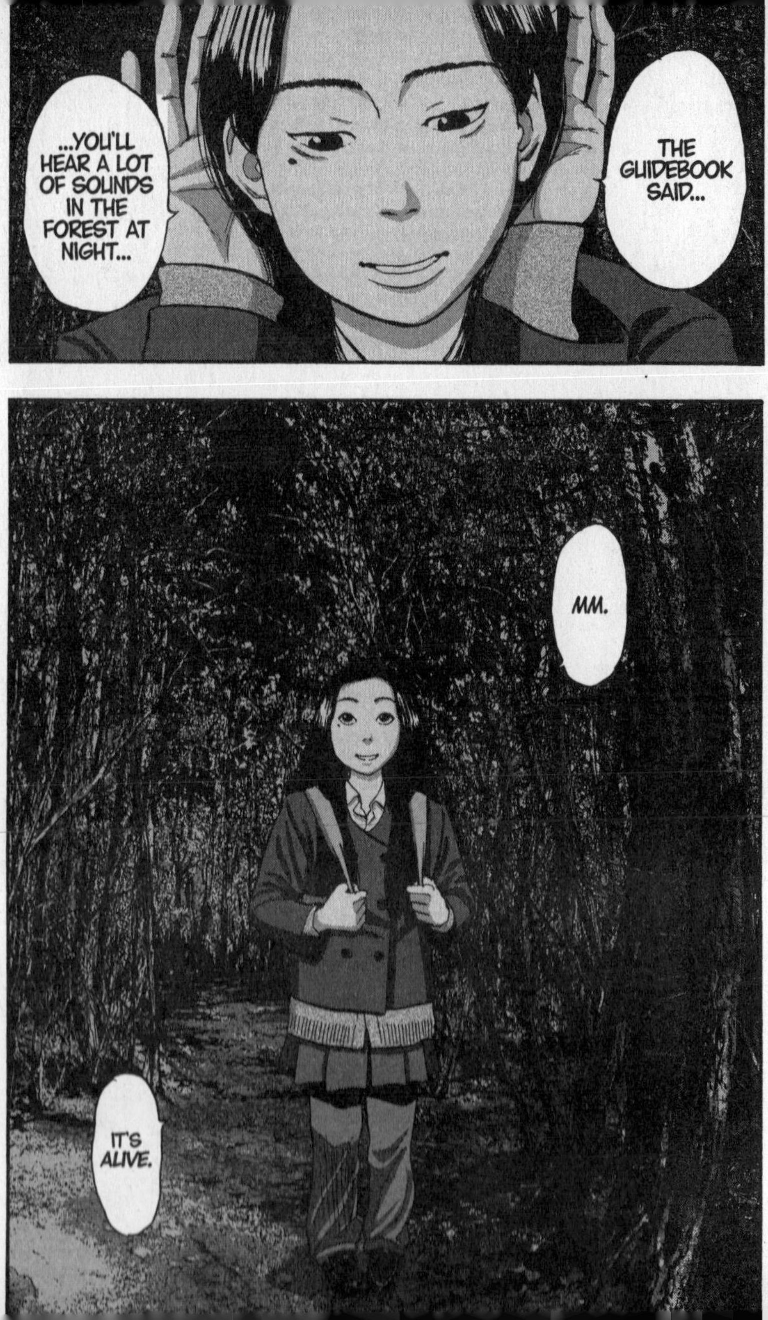
THE GUIDEBOOK SAID...
...YOU'LL HEAR A LOT OF SOUNDS IN THE FOREST AT NIGHT...
MM.
IT'S ALIVE.

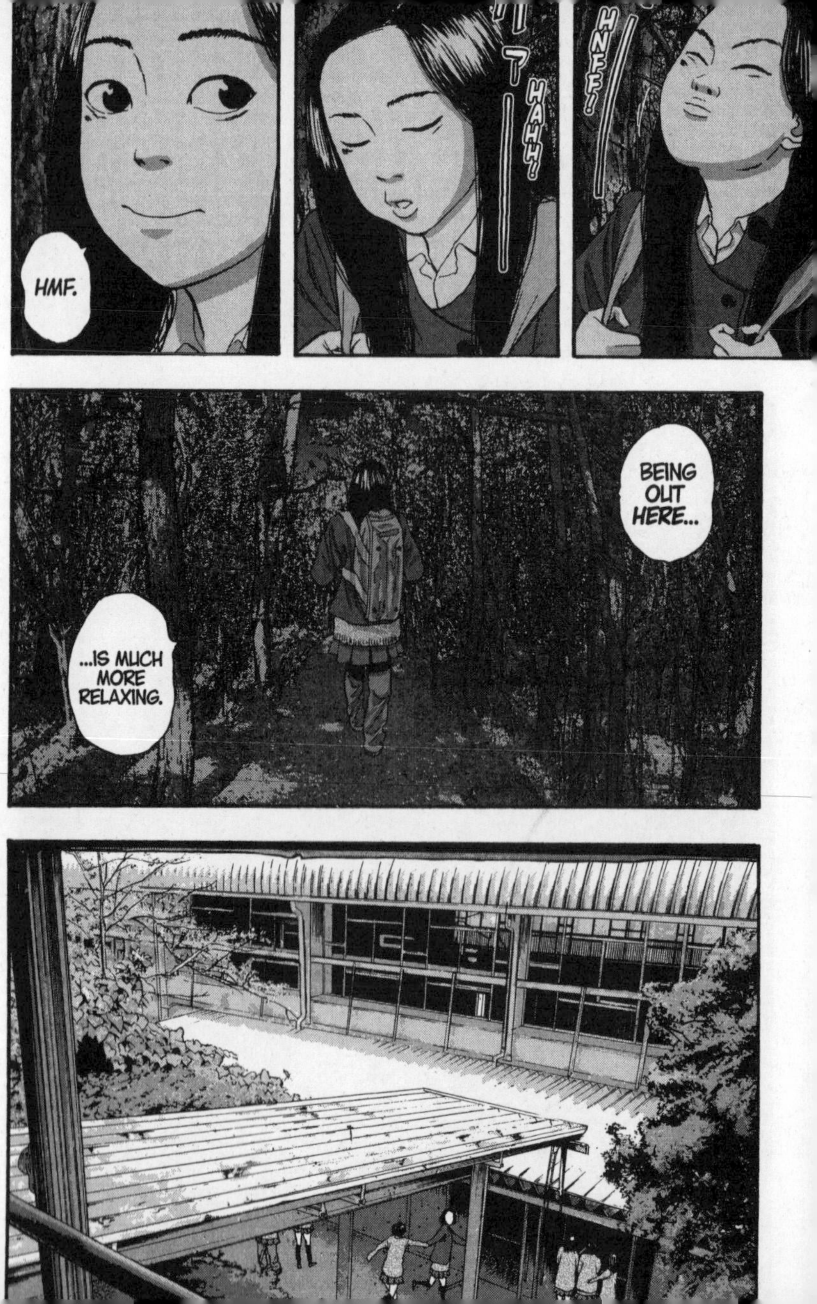
HNFF!
HAHH!
HMF.
BEING OUT HERE...
...IS MUCH MORE RELAXING.

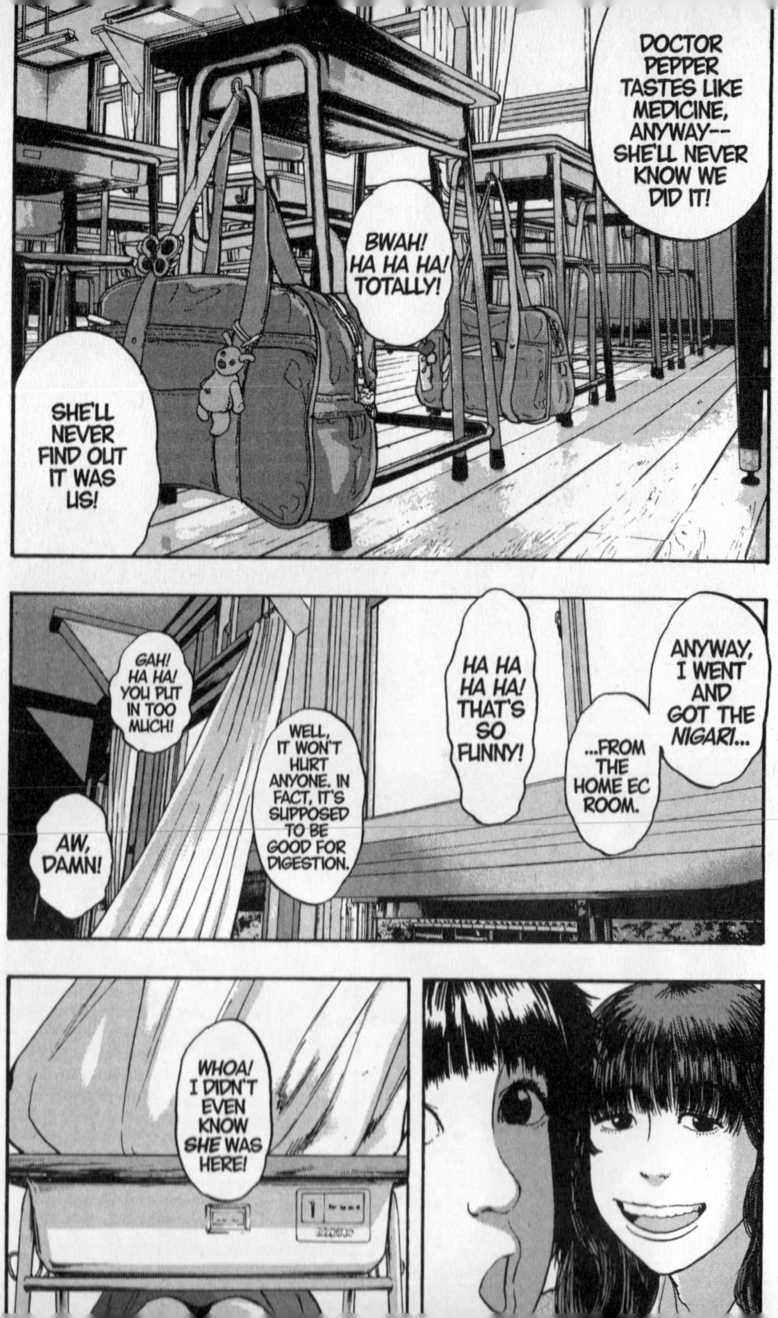
DOCTOR PEPPER TASTES LIKE MEDICINE, ANYWAY-- SHE'LL NEVER KNOW WE DID IT!
BWAH! HA HA HA! TOTALLY!
SHE'LL NEVER FIND OUT IT WAS US!
ANYWAY, I WENT AND GOT THE *NIGARI*...
...FROM THE HOME EC ROOM.
HA HA HA HA! THAT'S SO FUNNY!
WELL, IT WON'T HURT ANYONE. IN FACT, IT'S SUPPOSED TO BE GOOD FOR DIGESTION.
GAH! HA HA! YOU PUT IN TOO MUCH!
AW, DAMN!
WHOA! I DIDN'T EVEN KNOW SHE WAS HERE!

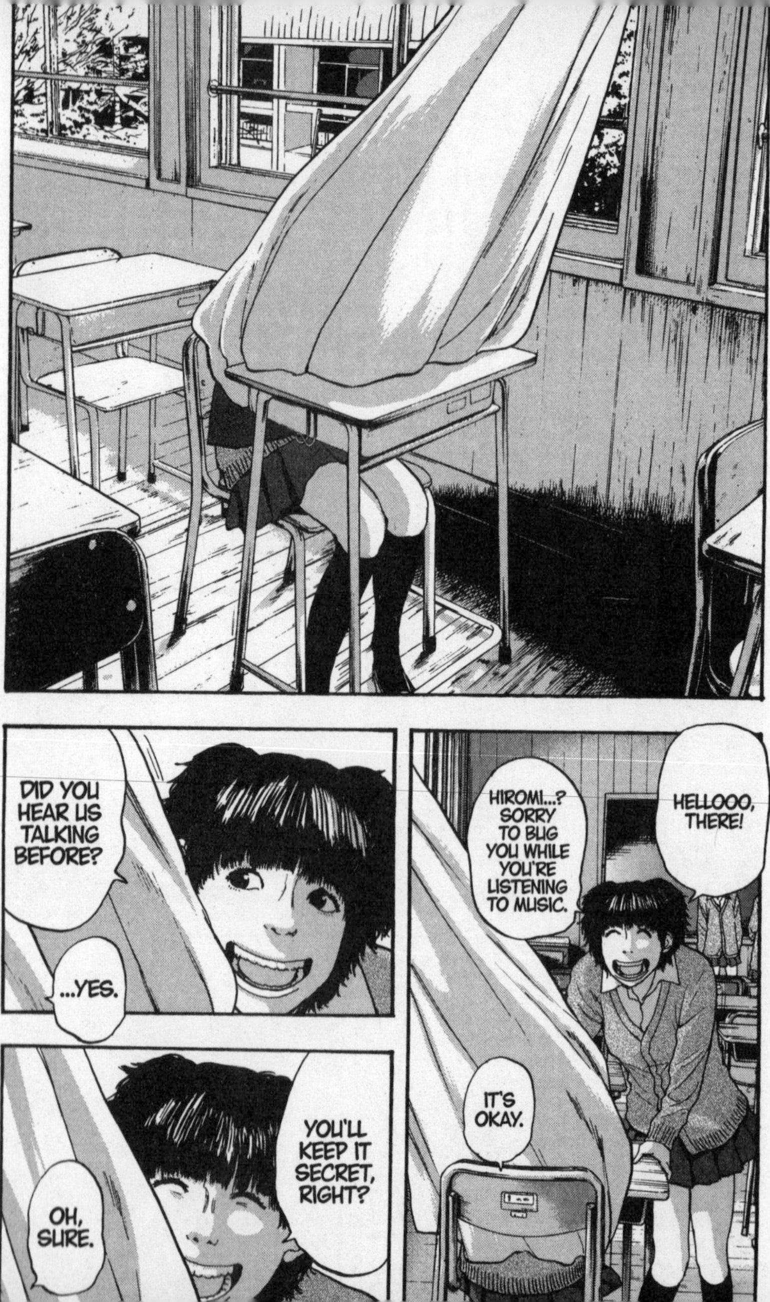
HELLOOO, THERE!
HIROMI...? SORRY TO BUG YOU WHILE YOU'RE LISTENING TO MUSIC.
IT'S OKAY.
DID YOU HEAR US TALKING BEFORE?
...YES.
YOU'LL KEEP IT SECRET, RIGHT?
OH, SURE.

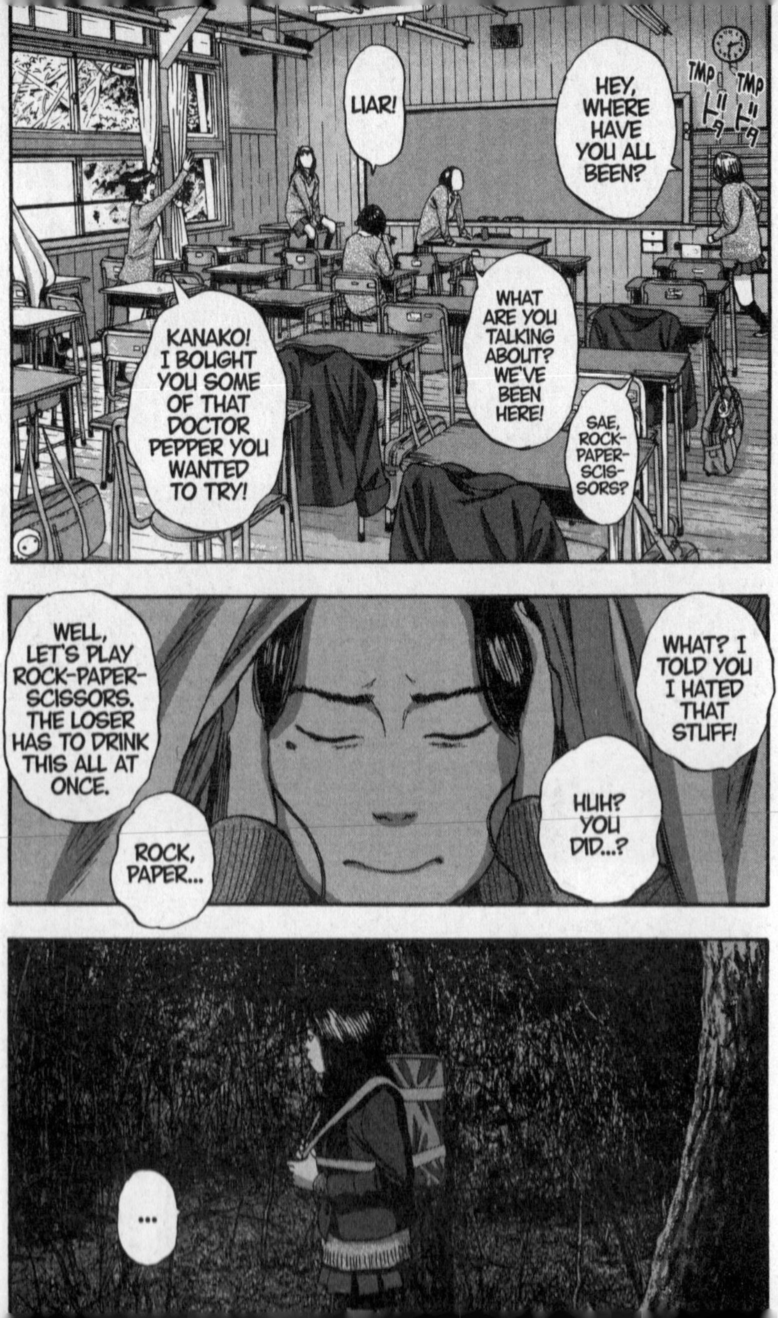
TMP TMP
HEY, WHERE HAVE YOU ALL BEEN?
LIAR!
WHAT ARE YOU TALKING ABOUT? WE'VE BEEN HERE!
SAE, ROCK-PAPER-SCISSORS?
KANAKO! I BOUGHT YOU SOME OF THAT DOCTOR PEPPER YOU WANTED TO TRY!
WHAT? I TOLD YOU I HATED THAT STUFF!
HUH? YOU DID...?
WELL, LET'S PLAY ROCK-PAPER-SCISSORS. THE LOSER HAS TO DRINK THIS ALL AT ONCE.
ROCK, PAPER...
...

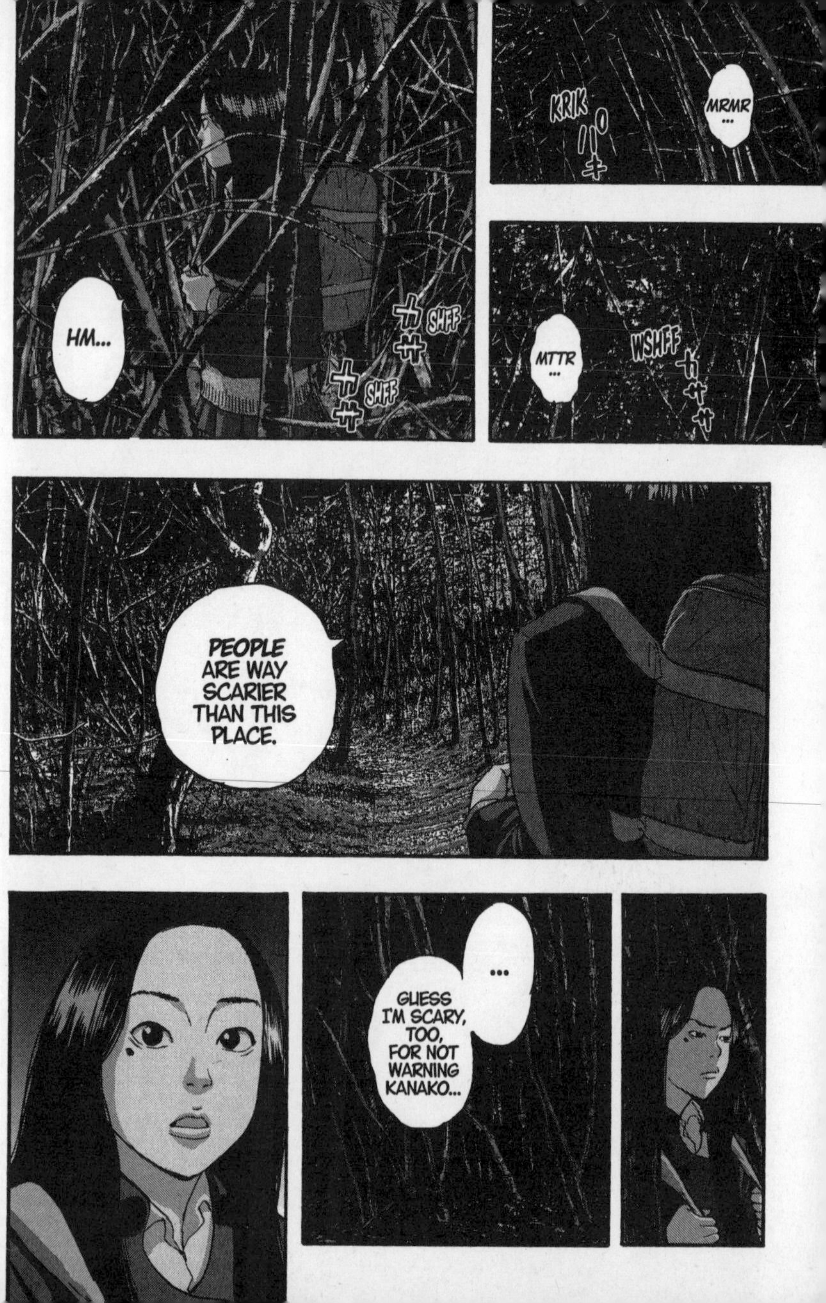
MRMR...
KRIK
WSHFF
MTTR...
SHFF
HM...
SHFF
PEOPLE ARE WAY SCARIER THAN THIS PLACE.
...
GUESS I'M SCARY, TOO, FOR NOT WARNING KANAKO...

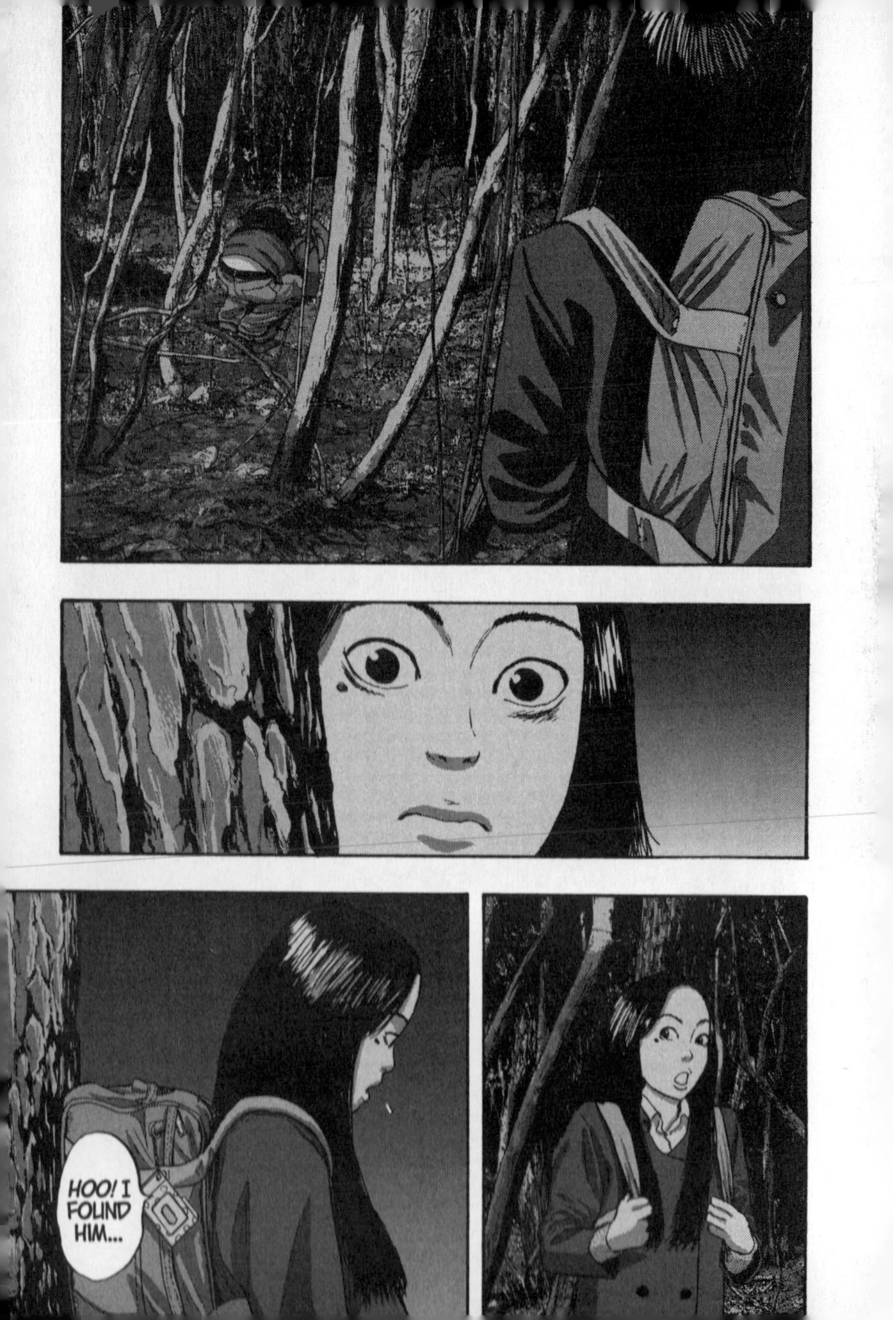
HOO! I FOUND HIM...

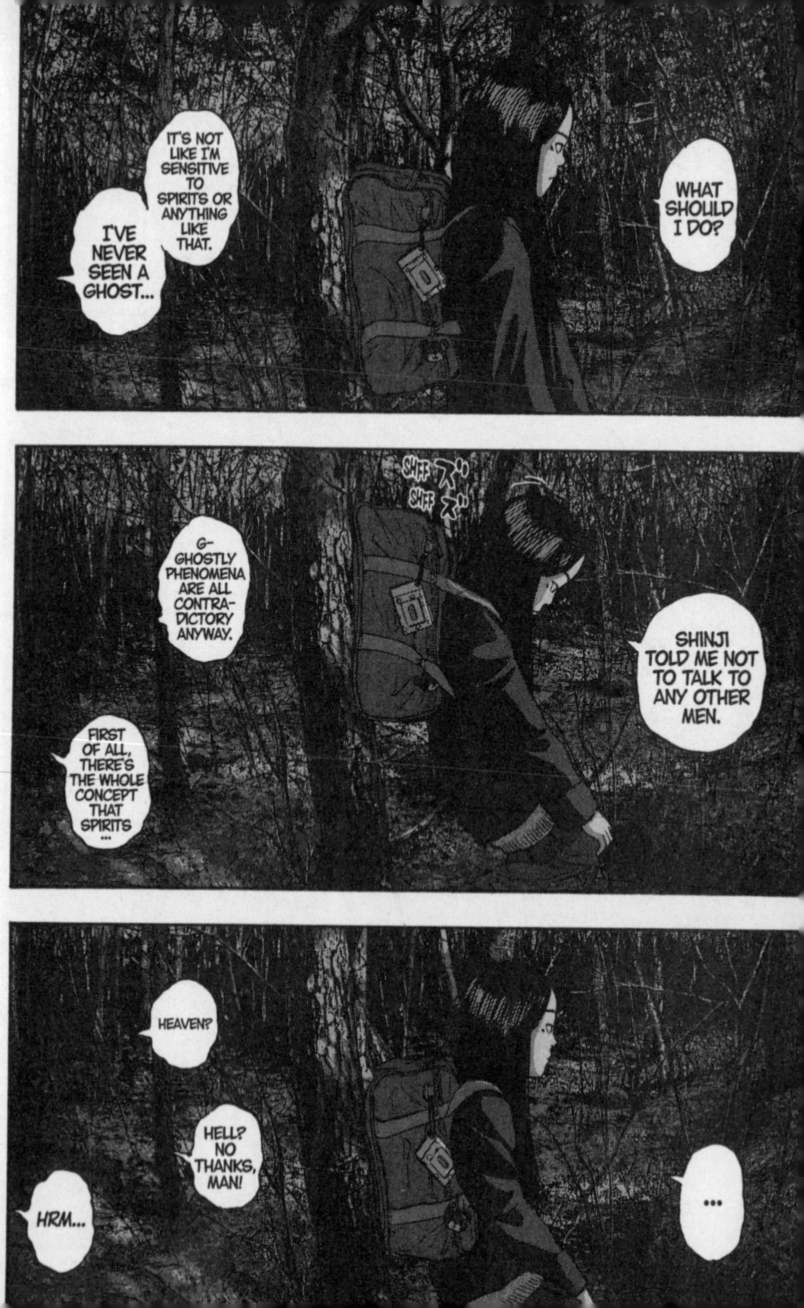
WHAT SHOULD I DO?
IT'S NOT LIKE I'M SENSITIVE TO SPIRITS OR ANYTHING LIKE THAT.
I'VE NEVER SEEN A GHOST...
SHFF ズッ
SHFF ズ
SHINJI TOLD ME NOT TO TALK TO ANY OTHER MEN.
G-GHOSTLY PHENOMENA ARE ALL CONTRA-DICTORY ANYWAY.
FIRST OF ALL, THERE'S THE WHOLE CONCEPT THAT SPIRITS ...
...
HEAVEN?
HELL? NO THANKS, MAN!
HRM...

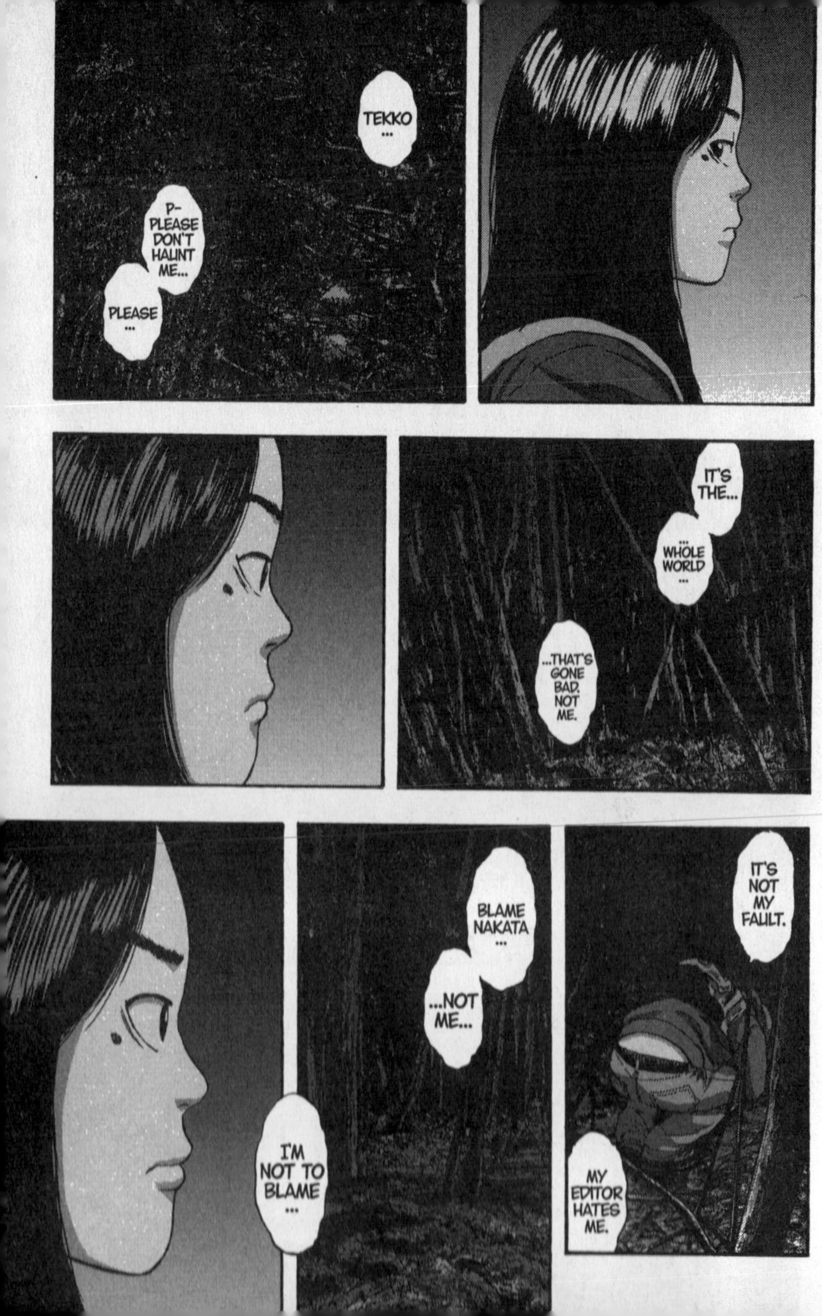
TEKKO...
P-PLEASE DON'T HAUNT ME...
PLEASE...
IT'S THE...
...WHOLE WORLD...
...THAT'S GONE BAD, NOT ME.
IT'S NOT MY FAULT.
MY EDITOR HATES ME.
BLAME NAKATA...
...NOT ME...
I'M NOT TO BLAME...

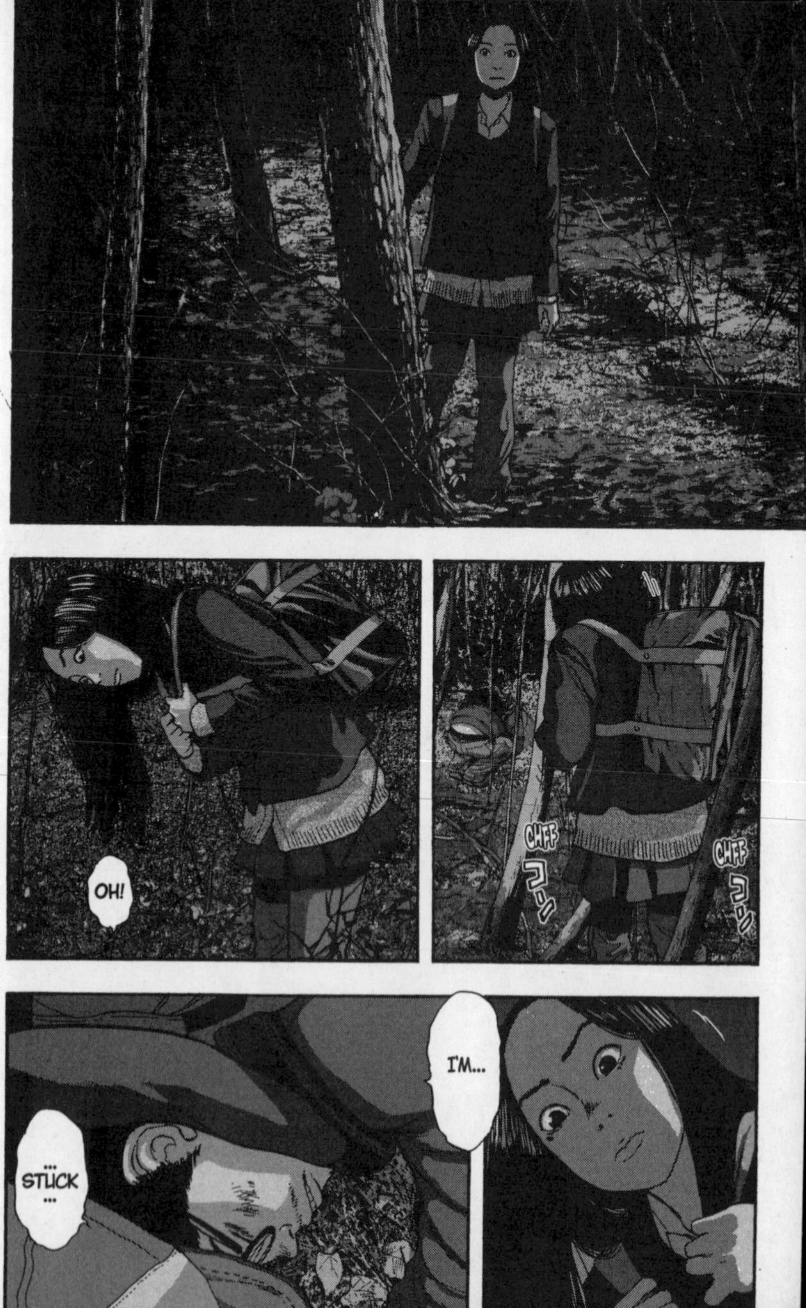
CHFF
CHFF
OH!
I'M...
... STÜCK ...

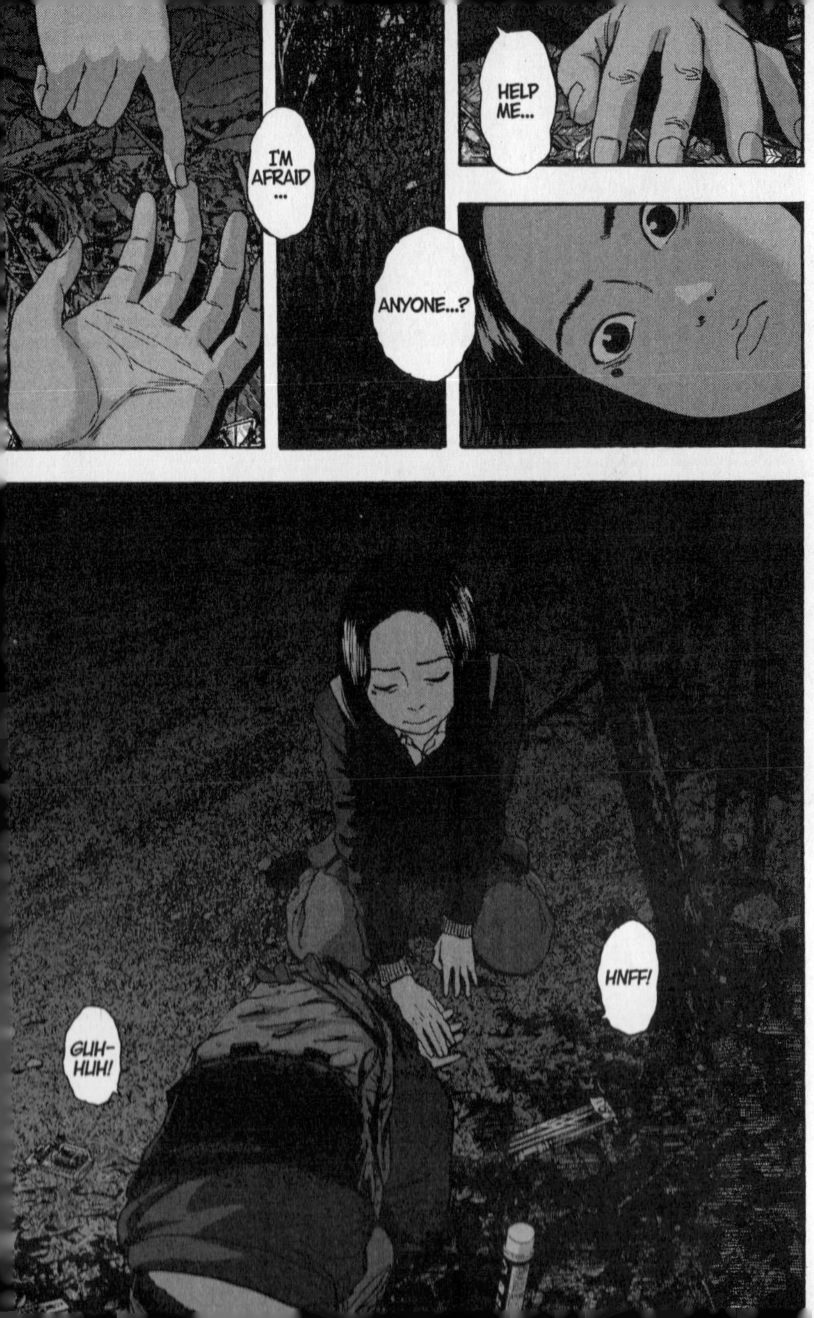
HELP ME...
ANYONE...?
I'M AFRAID ...
HNFF!
GUH-HUH!

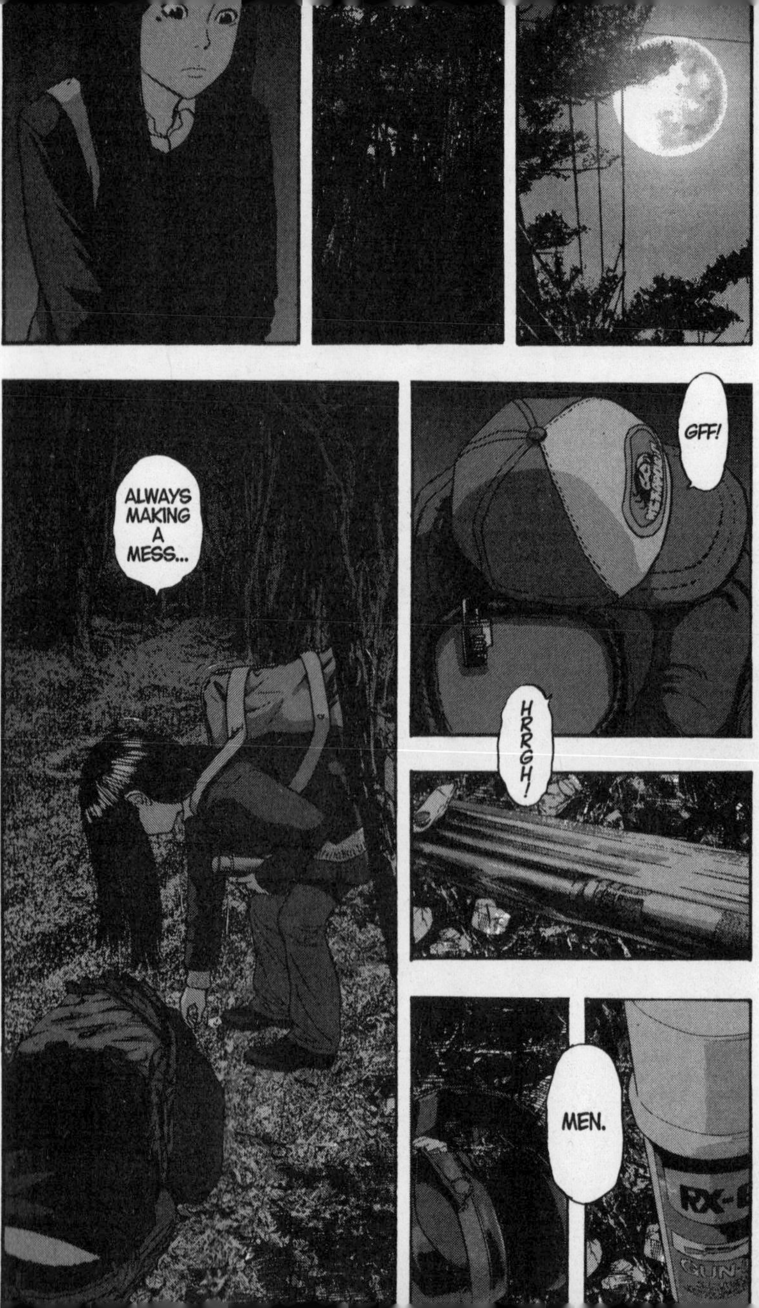
GFF!
HRRGH!
MEN.
ALWAYS MAKING A MESS...

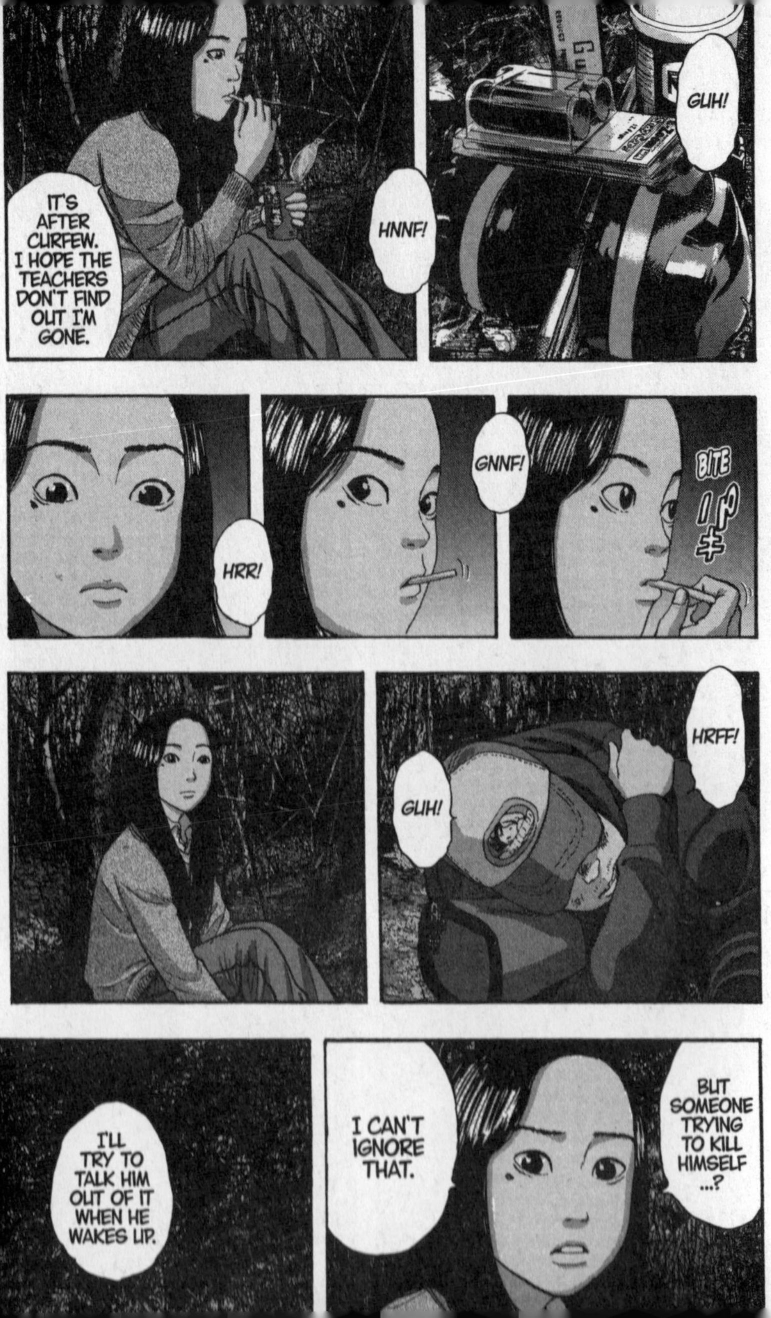
GUH!
HNNF!
IT'S AFTER CURFEW. I HOPE THE TEACHERS DON'T FIND OUT I'M GONE.
BITE
GNNF!
HRR!
HRFF!
GUH!
BUT SOMEONE TRYING TO KILL HIMSELF ...?
I CAN'T IGNORE THAT.
I'LL TRY TO TALK HIM OUT OF IT WHEN HE WAKES UP.

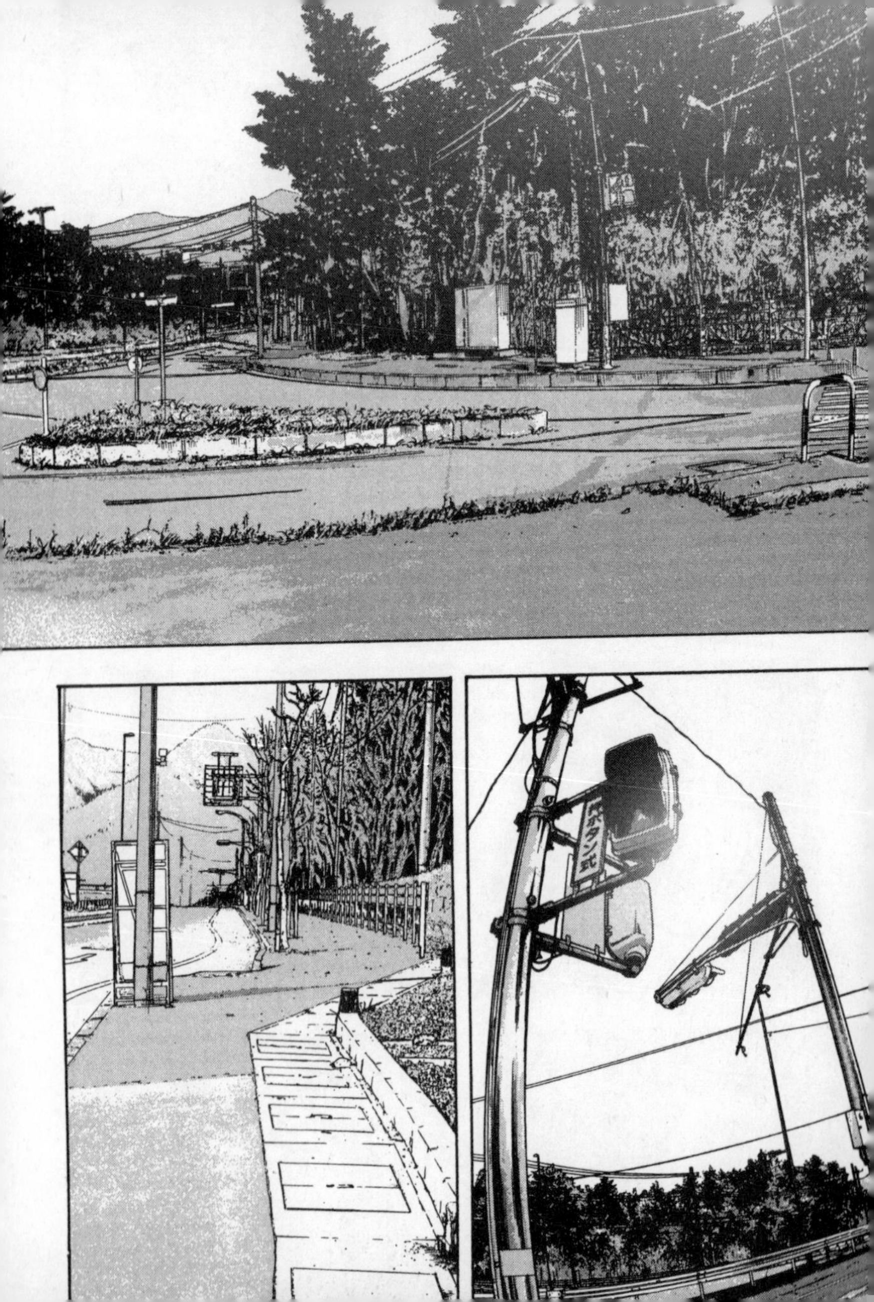
ボタン式

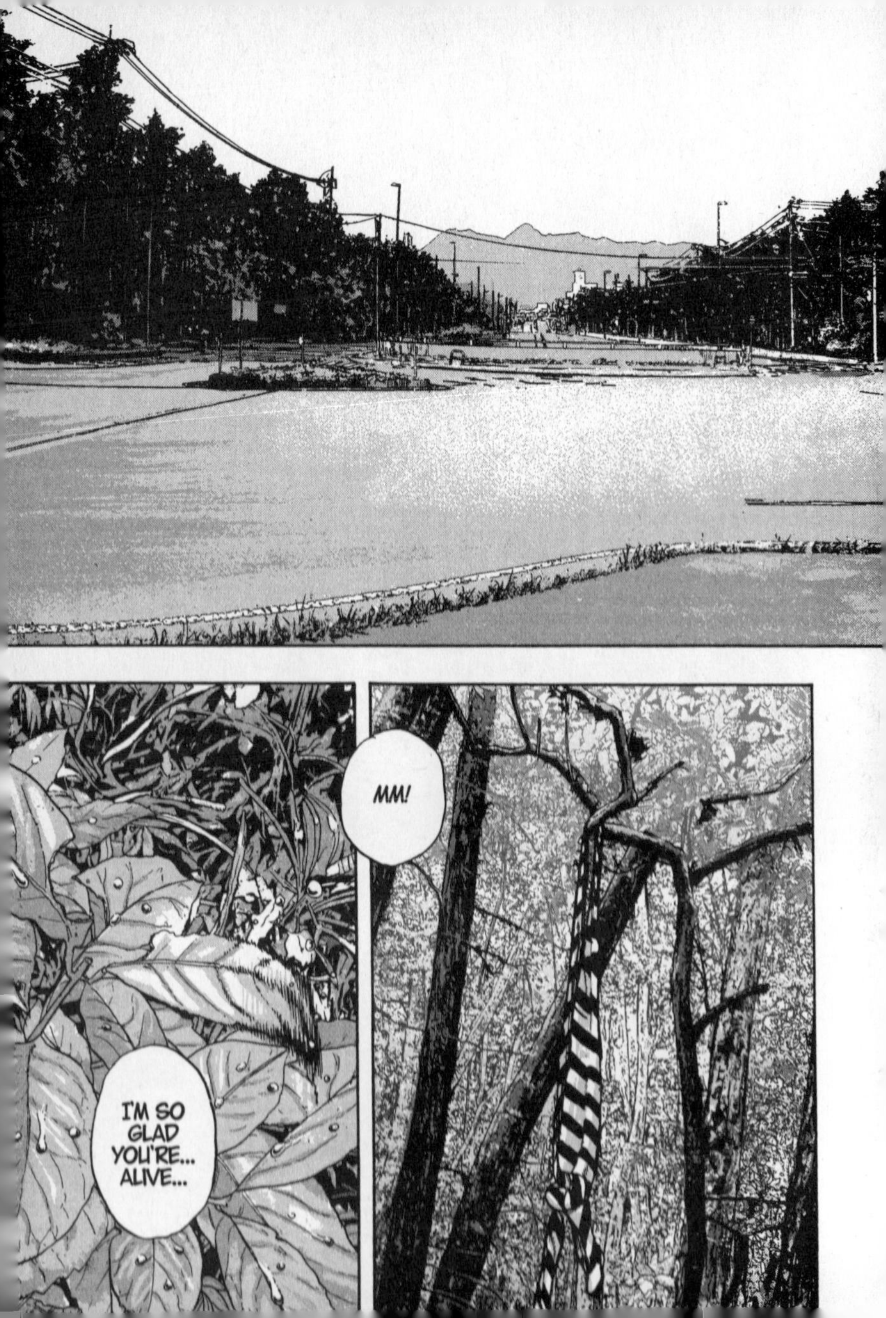
MM!
I'M SO GLAD YOU'RE... ALIVE...

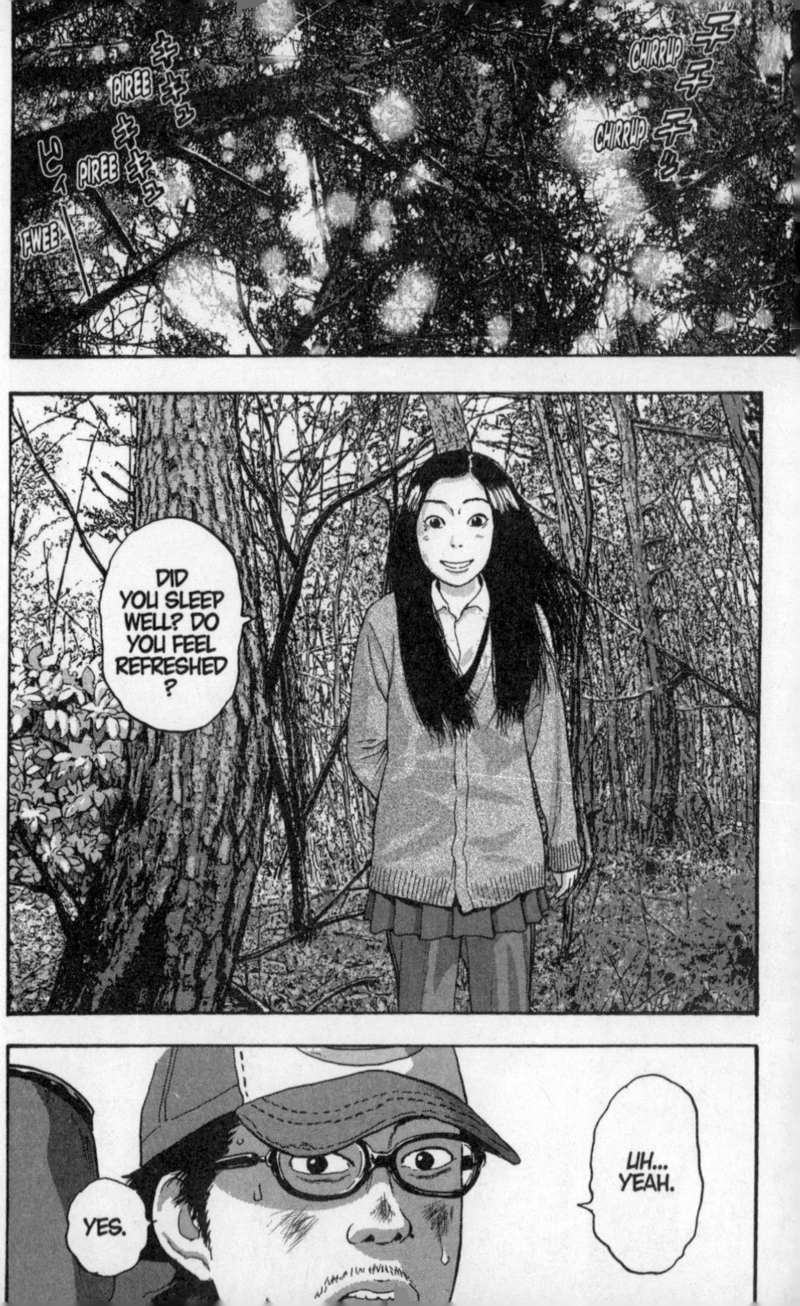
CHIRRUP
CHIRRUP
PIREEB
PIREEB
FWEE
DID YOU SLEEP WELL? DO YOU FEEL REFRESHED?
UH... YEAH.
YES.

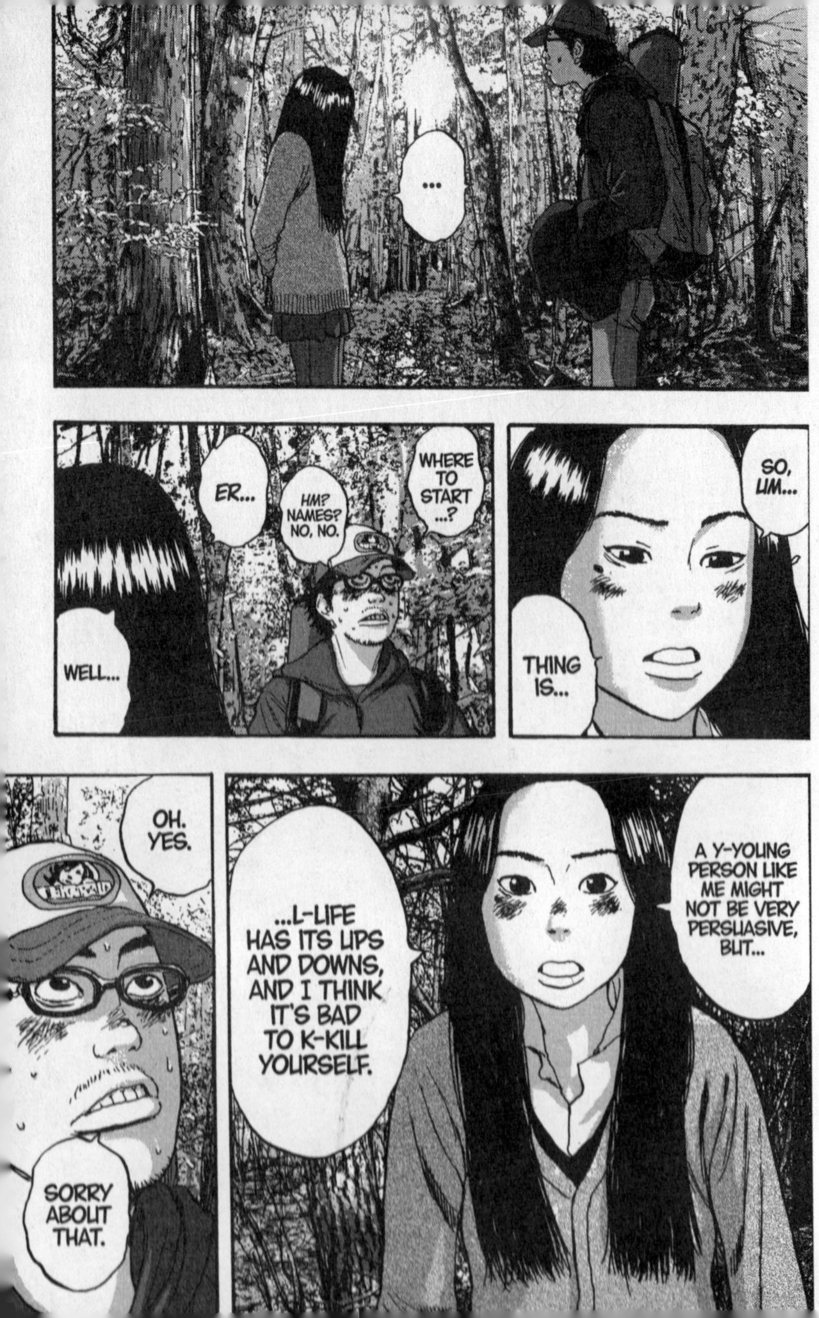
...
SO, UM...
THING IS...
WHERE TO START ...?
HM? NAMES? NO, NO.
ER...
WELL...
A Y-YOUNG PERSON LIKE ME MIGHT NOT BE VERY PERSUASIVE, BUT...
...L-LIFE HAS ITS UPS AND DOWNS, AND I THINK IT'S BAD TO K-KILL YOURSELF.
OH. YES.
SORRY ABOUT THAT.

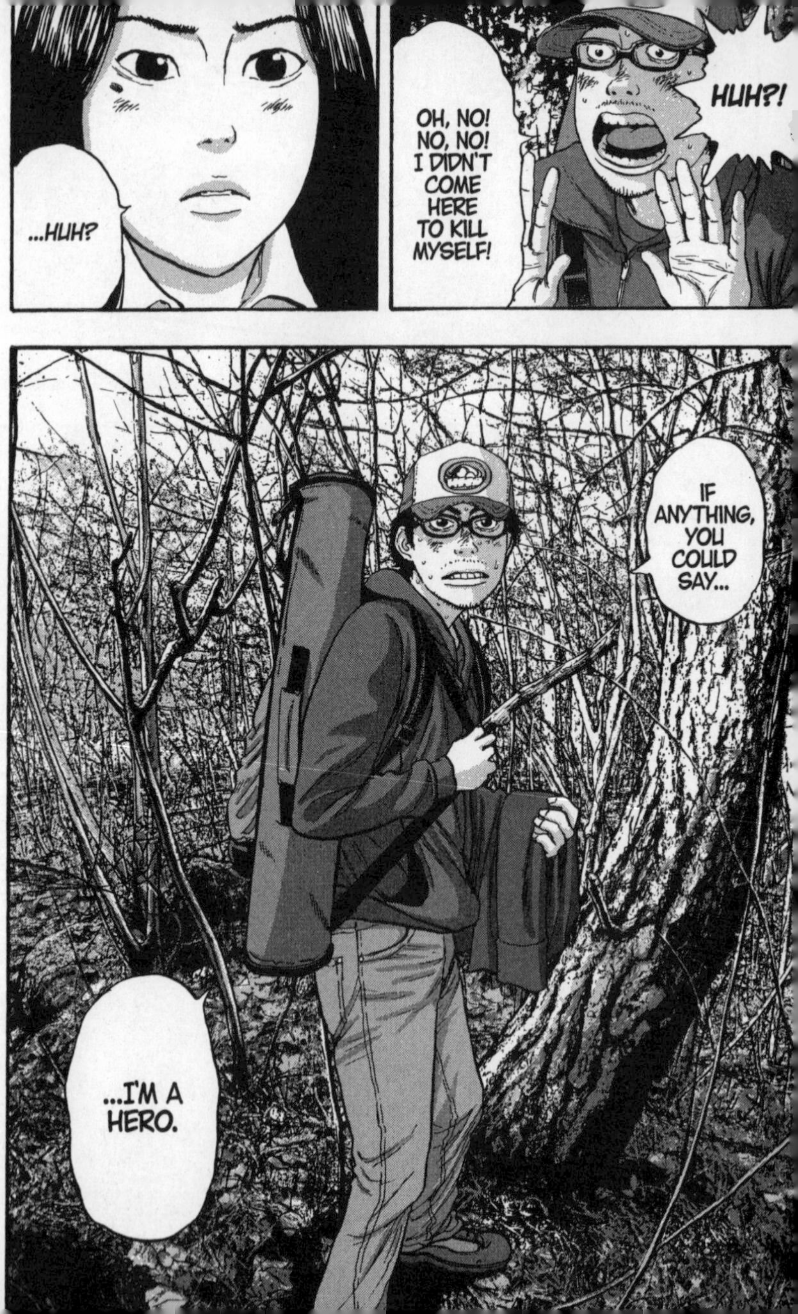
HUH?!
OH, NO! NO, NO! I DIDN'T COME HERE TO KILL MYSELF!
...HUH?
IF ANYTHING, YOU COULD SAY...
...I'M A HERO.

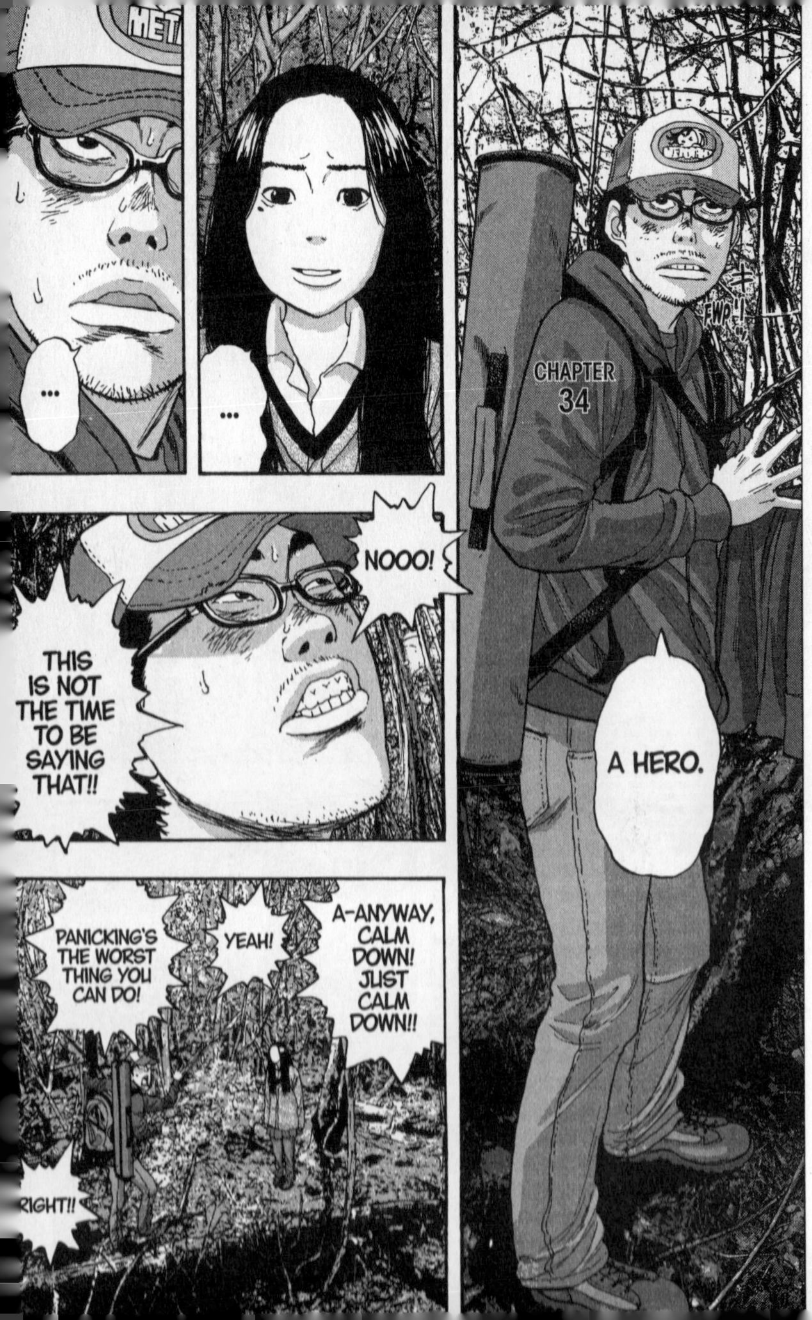
CHAPTER
34
A HERO.
...
...
NOOO!
THIS IS NOT THE TIME TO BE SAYING THAT!!
A-ANYWAY, CALM DOWN! JUST CALM DOWN!!
YEAH!
PANICKING'S THE WORST THING YOU CAN DO!
RIGHT!!

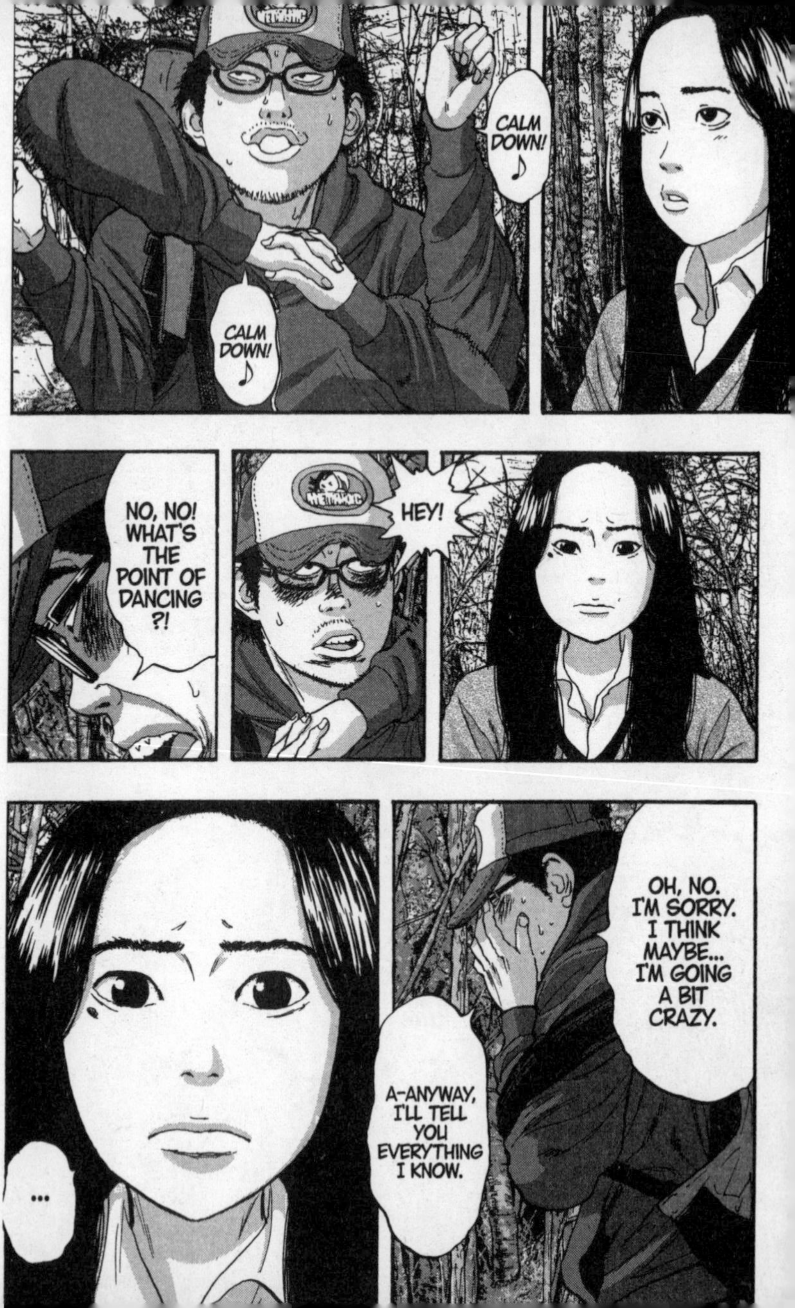
CALM DOWN! ♪
CALM DOWN! ♪
HEY!
NO, NO! WHAT'S THE POINT OF DANCING?!
OH, NO. I'M SORRY. I THINK MAYBE... I'M GOING A BIT CRAZY.
A-ANYWAY, I'LL TELL YOU EVERYTHING I KNOW.
...

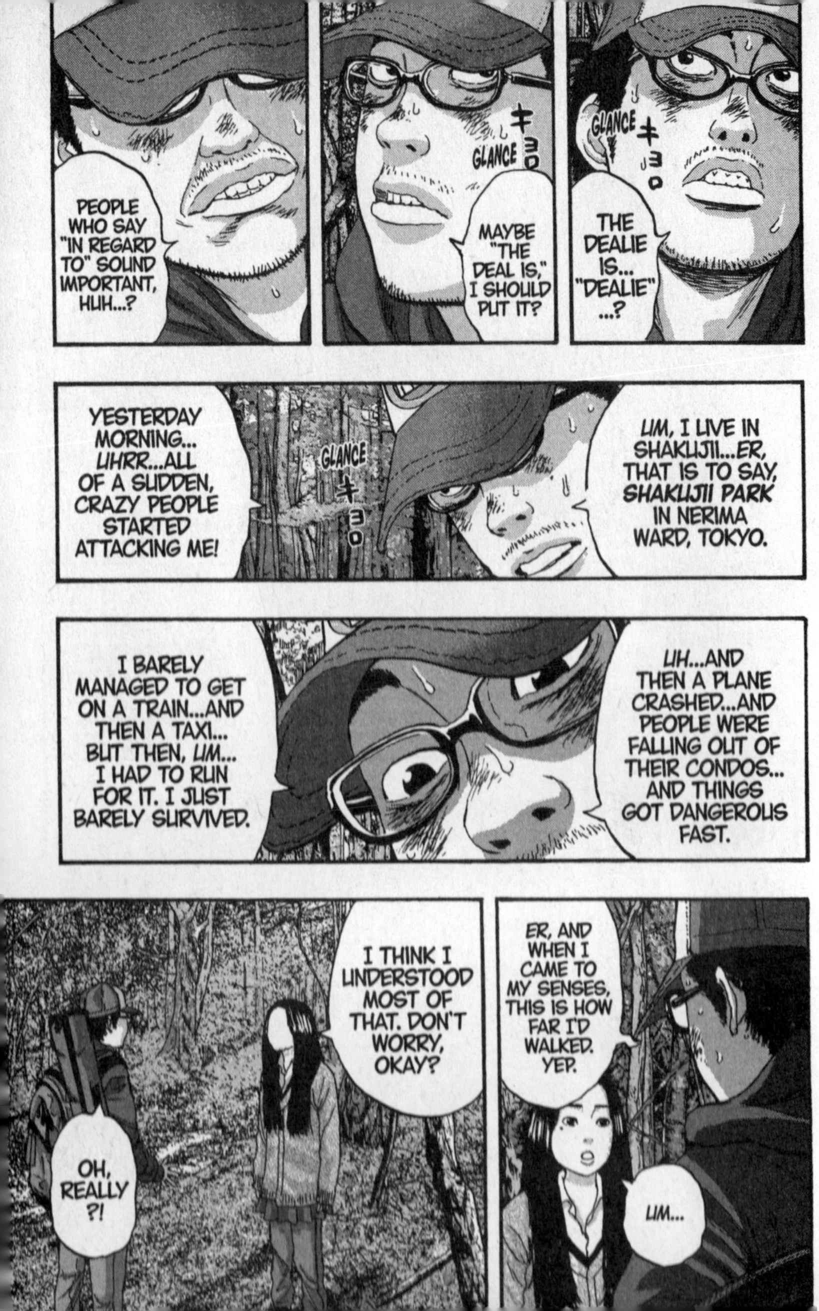
GLANCE
キョロ
THE DEALIE IS... "DEALIE" ...?
GLANCE
キョロ
MAYBE "THE DEAL IS," I SHOULD PUT IT?
PEOPLE WHO SAY "IN REGARD TO" SOUND IMPORTANT, HUH...?
UM, I LIVE IN SHAKUJII...ER, THAT IS TO SAY, SHAKUJII PARK IN NERIMA WARD, TOKYO.
GLANCE
キョロ
YESTERDAY MORNING... UHRR...ALL OF A SUDDEN, CRAZY PEOPLE STARTED ATTACKING ME!
UH...AND THEN A PLANE CRASHED...AND PEOPLE WERE FALLING OUT OF THEIR CONDOS... AND THINGS GOT DANGEROUS FAST.
I BARELY MANAGED TO GET ON A TRAIN...AND THEN A TAXI... BUT THEN, UM... I HAD TO RUN FOR IT. I JUST BARELY SURVIVED.
ER, AND WHEN I CAME TO MY SENSES, THIS IS HOW FAR I'D WALKED. YEP.
UM...
I THINK I UNDERSTOOD MOST OF THAT. DON'T WORRY, OKAY?
OH, REALLY ?!

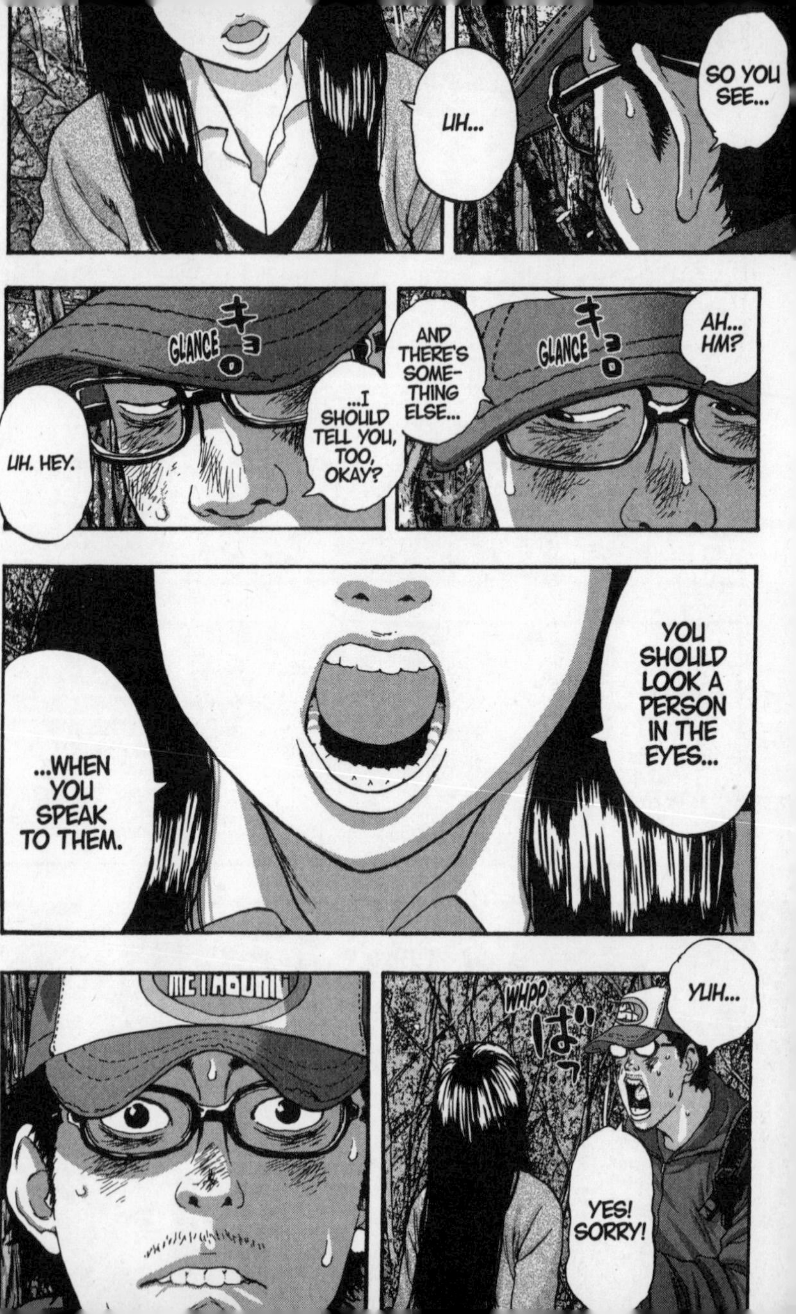
SO YOU SEE...
UH...
GLANCE キョロ
AH... HM?
AND THERE'S SOME-THING ELSE...
GLANCE キョロ
...I SHOULD TELL YOU, TOO, OKAY?
UH. HEY.
YOU SHOULD LOOK A PERSON IN THE EYES...
...WHEN YOU SPEAK TO THEM.
YUH...
WHPP ばっ
YES! SORRY!

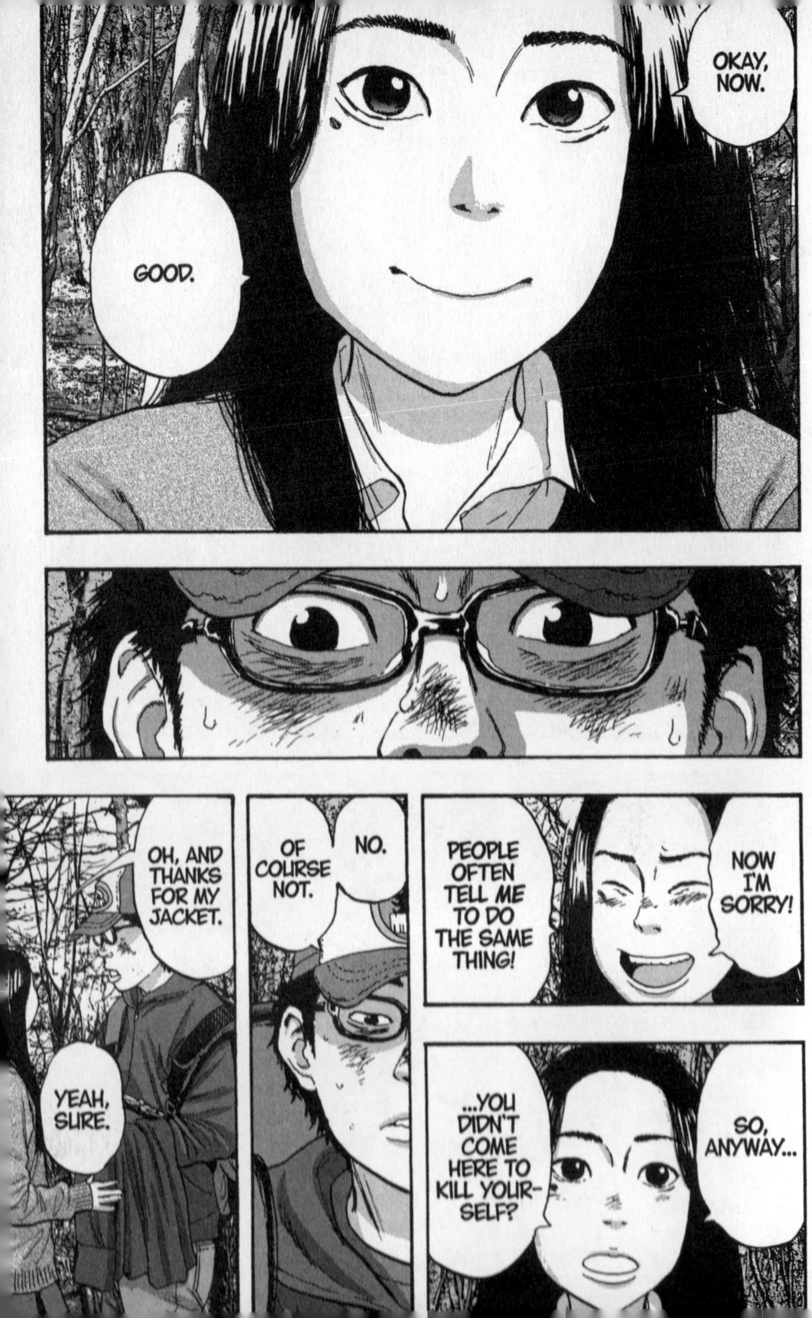
OKAY, NOW.
GOOD.
NOW I'M SORRY!
PEOPLE OFTEN TELL ME TO DO THE SAME THING!
SO, ANYWAY...
...YOU DIDN'T COME HERE TO KILL YOUR-SELF?
NO.
OF COURSE NOT.
OH, AND THANKS FOR MY JACKET.
YEAH, SURE.

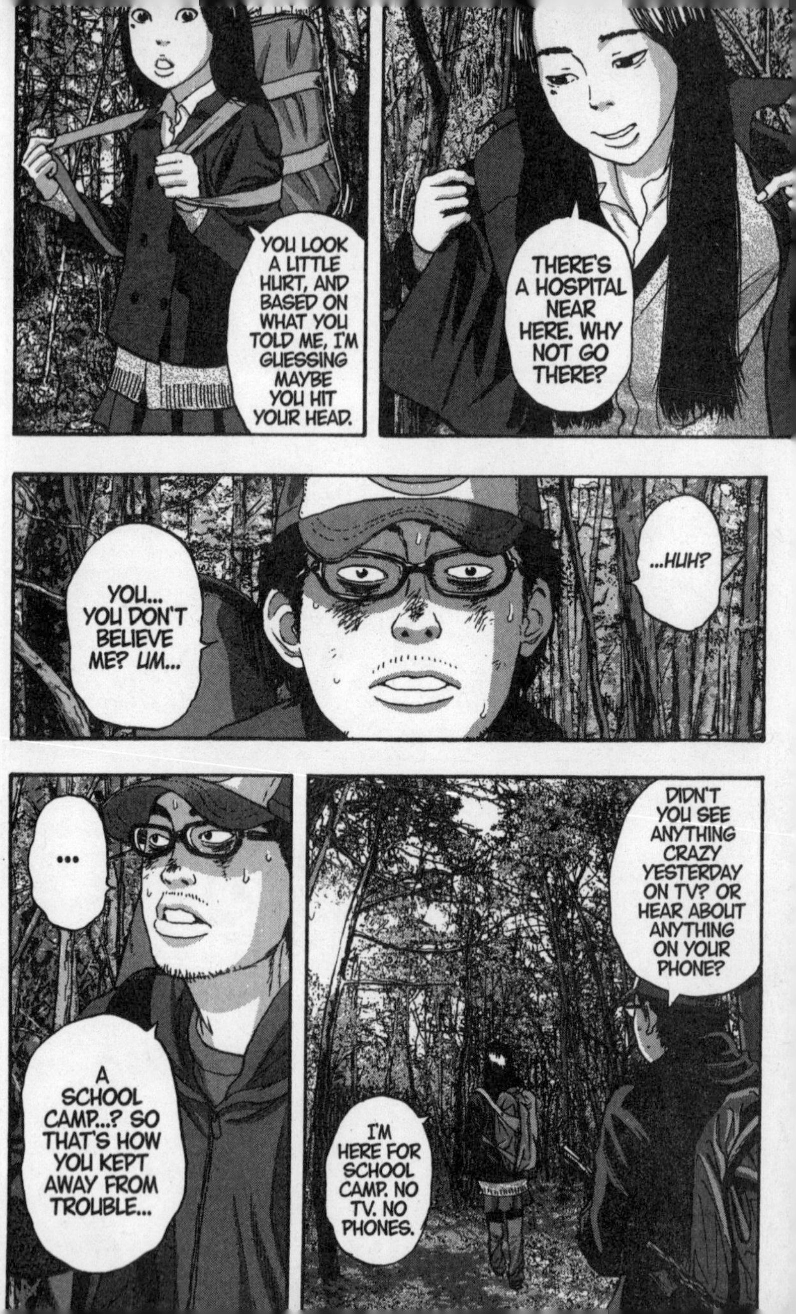
THERE'S A HOSPITAL NEAR HERE. WHY NOT GO THERE?
YOU LOOK A LITTLE HURT, AND BASED ON WHAT YOU TOLD ME, I'M GUESSING MAYBE YOU HIT YOUR HEAD.
...HUH?
YOU... YOU DON'T BELIEVE ME? UM...
DIDN'T YOU SEE ANYTHING CRAZY YESTERDAY ON TV? OR HEAR ABOUT ANYTHING ON YOUR PHONE?
I'M HERE FOR SCHOOL CAMP. NO TV. NO PHONES.
...
A SCHOOL CAMP...? SO THAT'S HOW YOU KEPT AWAY FROM TROUBLE...

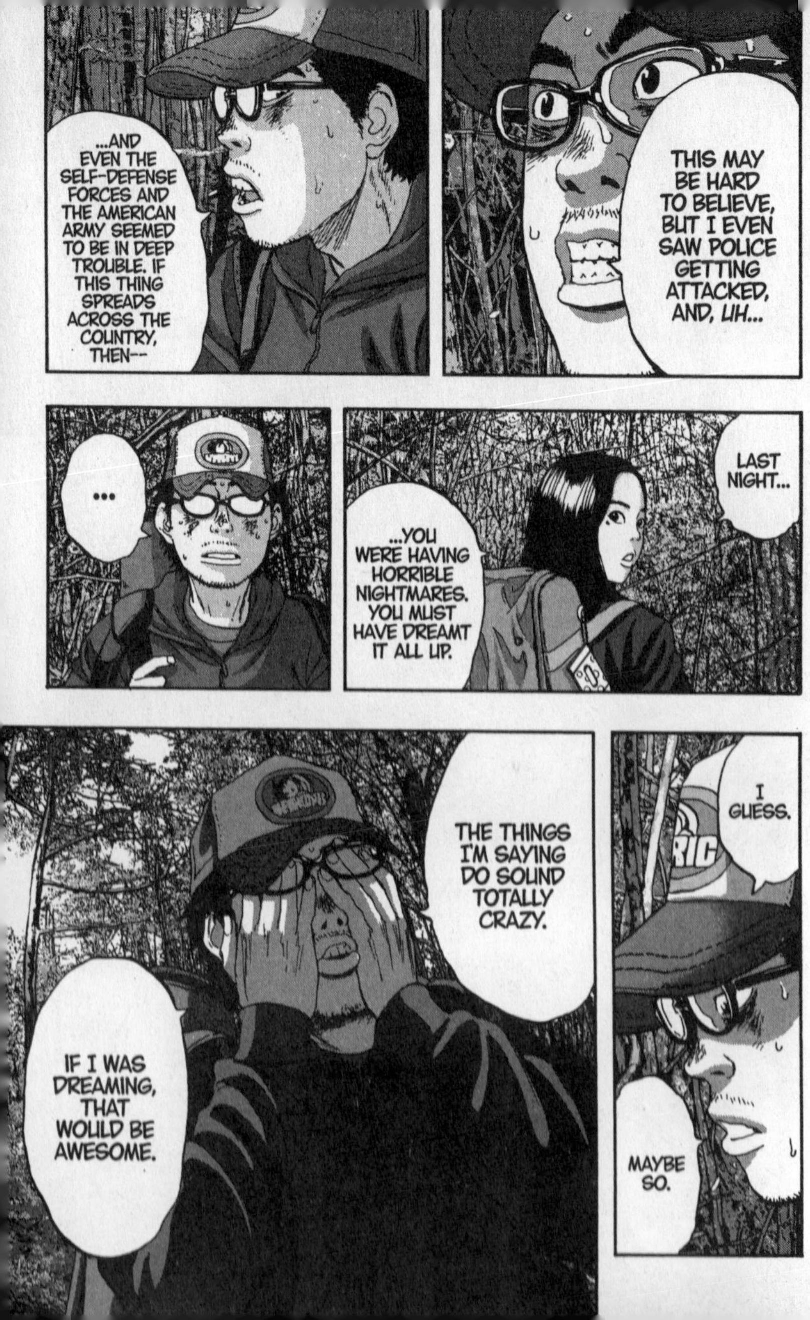
THIS MAY BE HARD TO BELIEVE, BUT I EVEN SAW POLICE GETTING ATTACKED, AND, UH...
...AND EVEN THE SELF-DEFENSE FORCES AND THE AMERICAN ARMY SEEMED TO BE IN DEEP TROUBLE. IF THIS THING SPREADS ACROSS THE COUNTRY, THEN--
LAST NIGHT...
...YOU WERE HAVING HORRIBLE NIGHTMARES. YOU MUST HAVE DREAMT IT ALL UP.
...
I GUESS.
MAYBE SO.
THE THINGS I'M SAYING DO SOUND TOTALLY CRAZY.
IF I WAS DREAMING, THAT WOULD BE AWESOME.

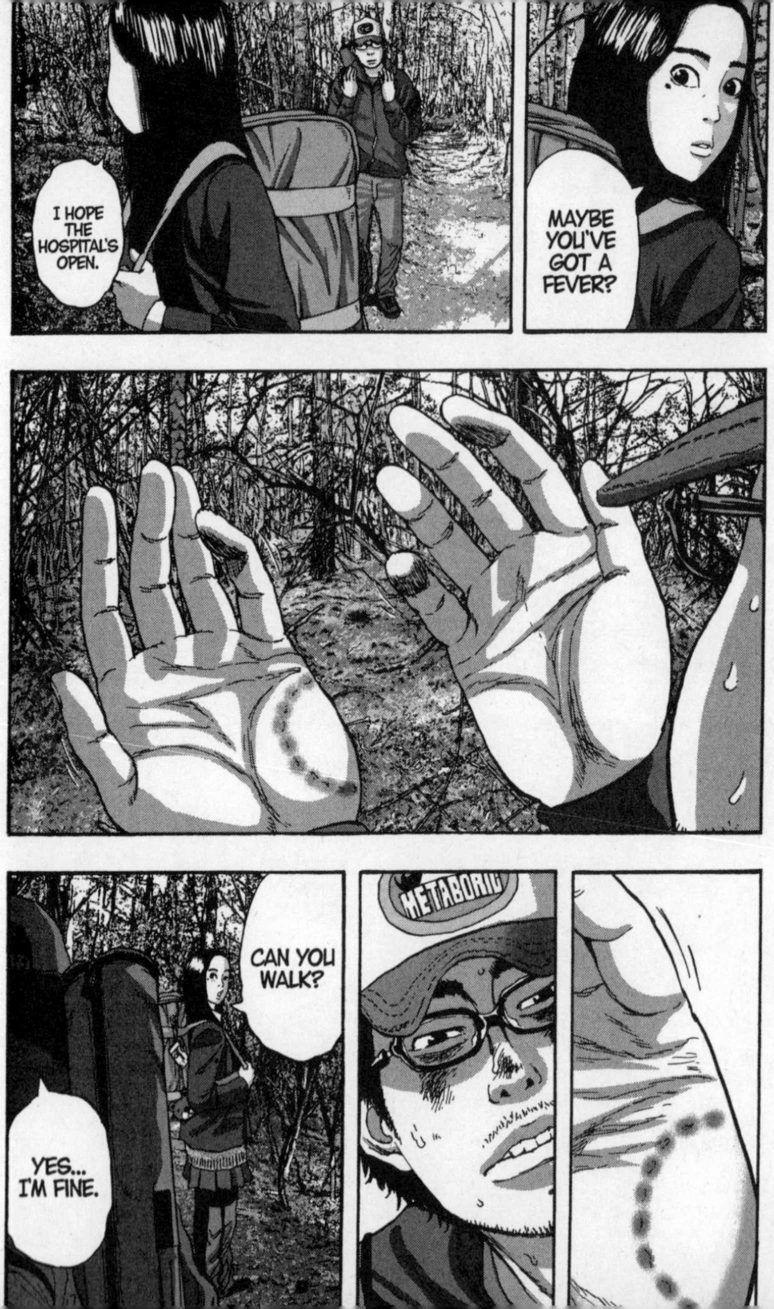
MAYBE YOU'VE GOT A FEVER?
I HOPE THE HOSPITAL'S OPEN.
METABORIC
CAN YOU WALK?
YES... I'M FINE.

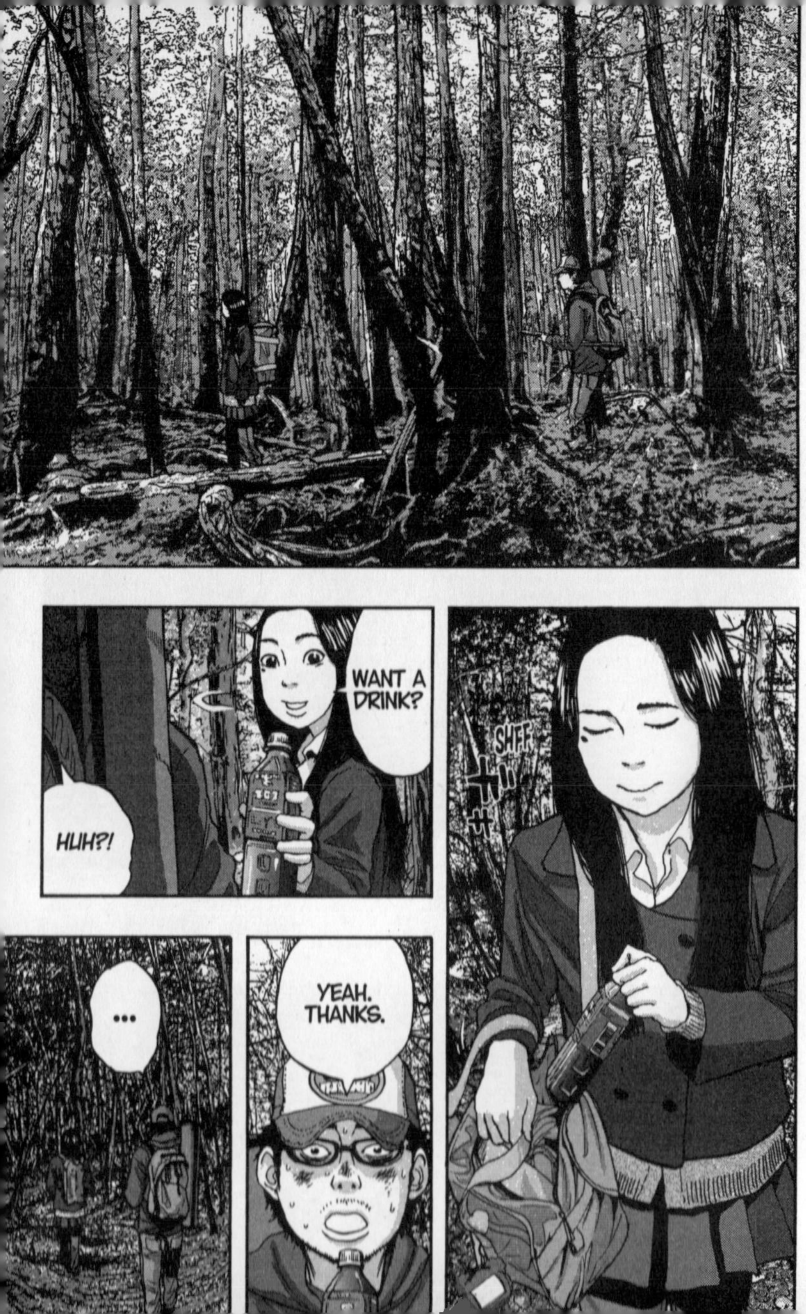
SHFF
WANT A DRINK?
HUH?!
YEAH. THANKS.
...

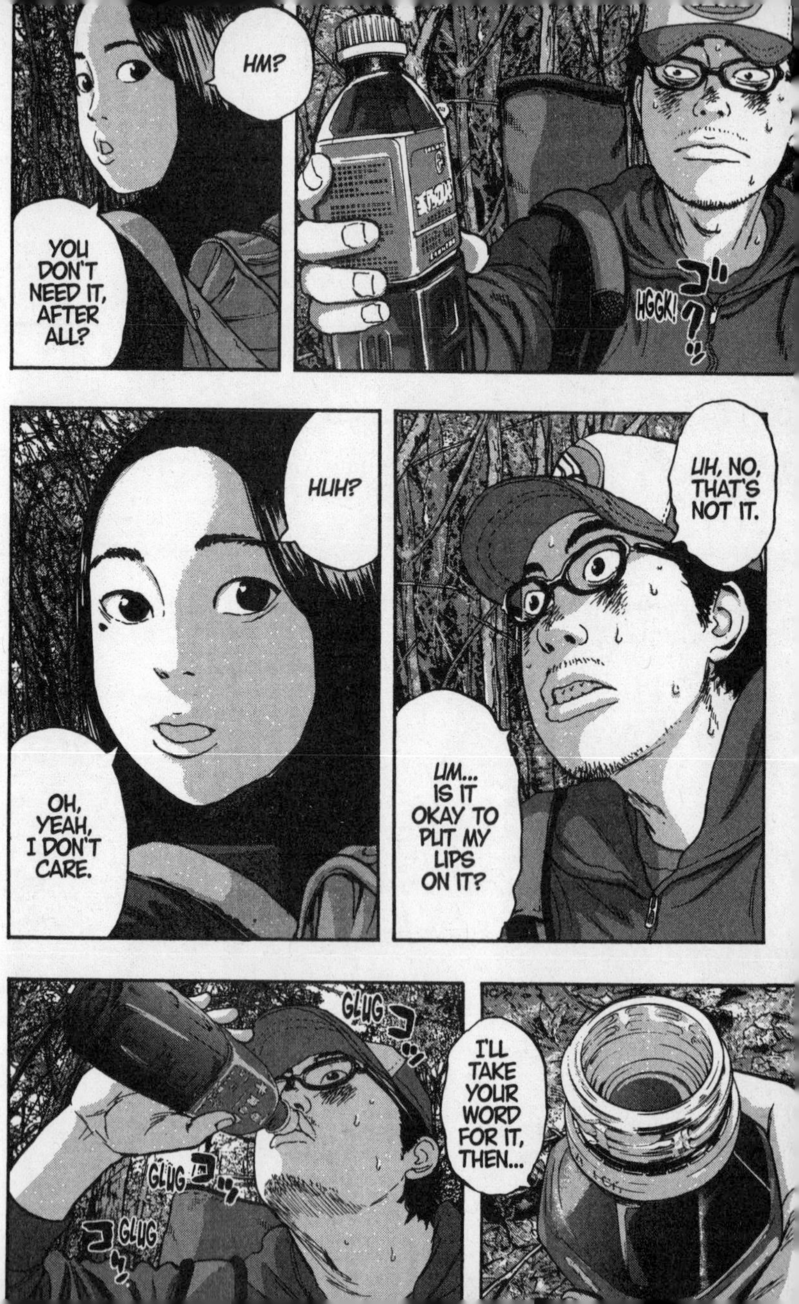
HGGK!
HM?
YOU DON'T NEED IT, AFTER ALL?
UH, NO, THAT'S NOT IT.
UM... IS IT OKAY TO PUT MY LIPS ON IT?
HUH?
OH, YEAH, I DON'T CARE.
I'LL TAKE YOUR WORD FOR IT, THEN...
GLUG
GLUG
GLUG

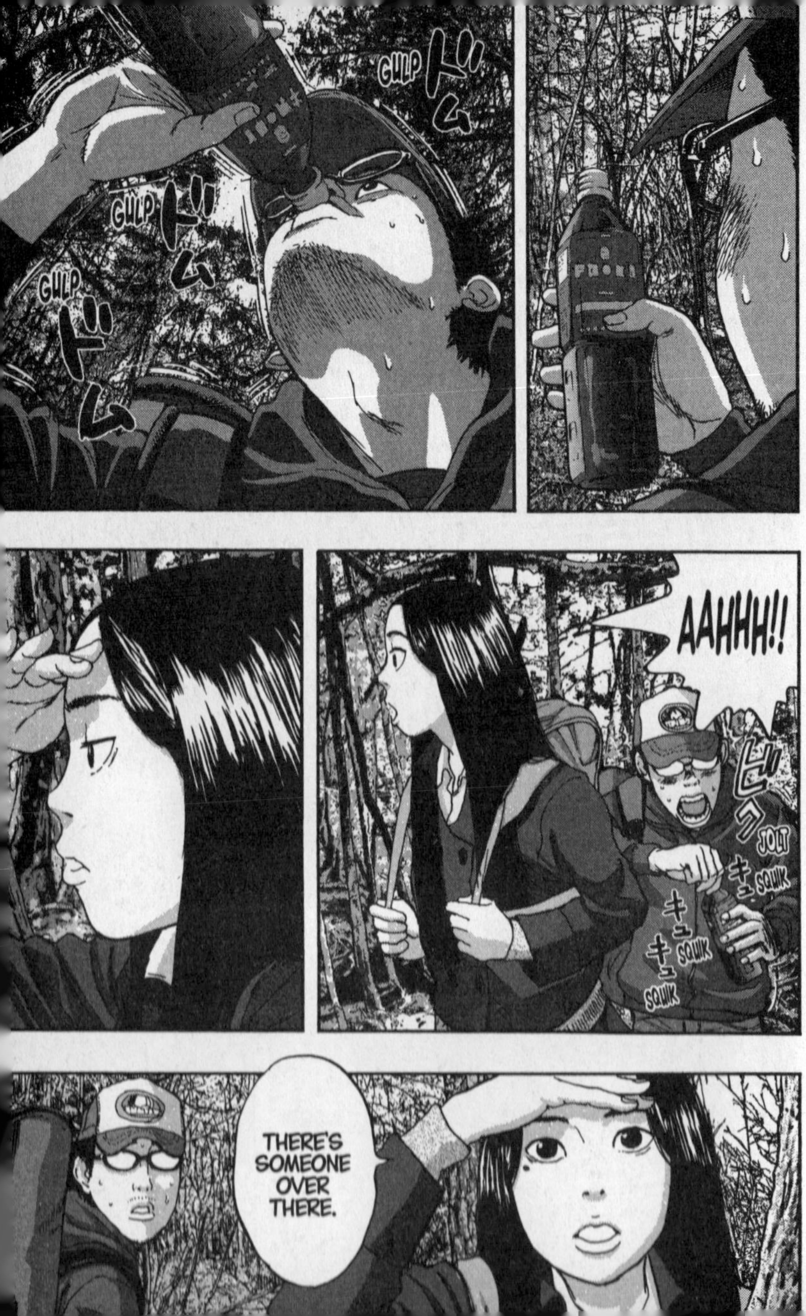
GULP
ドム
GULP
ドム
GULP
ドム
AAHHH!!
ビク
JOLT
キュ
SQUIK
キュ
SQUIK
キュ
SQUIK
THERE'S SOMEONE OVER THERE.

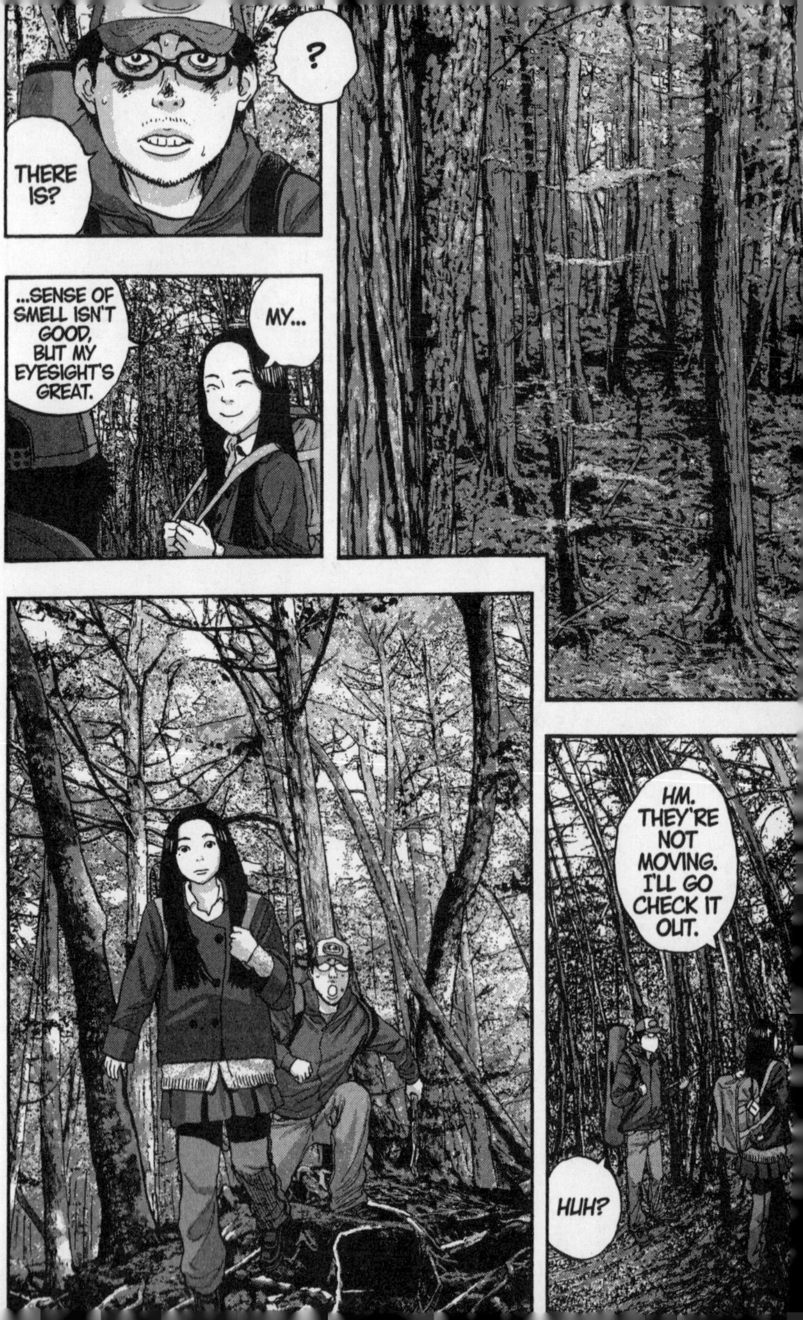
?
THERE IS?
MY...
...SENSE OF SMELL ISN'T GOOD, BUT MY EYESIGHT'S GREAT.
HM. THEY'RE NOT MOVING. I'LL GO CHECK IT OUT.
HUH?

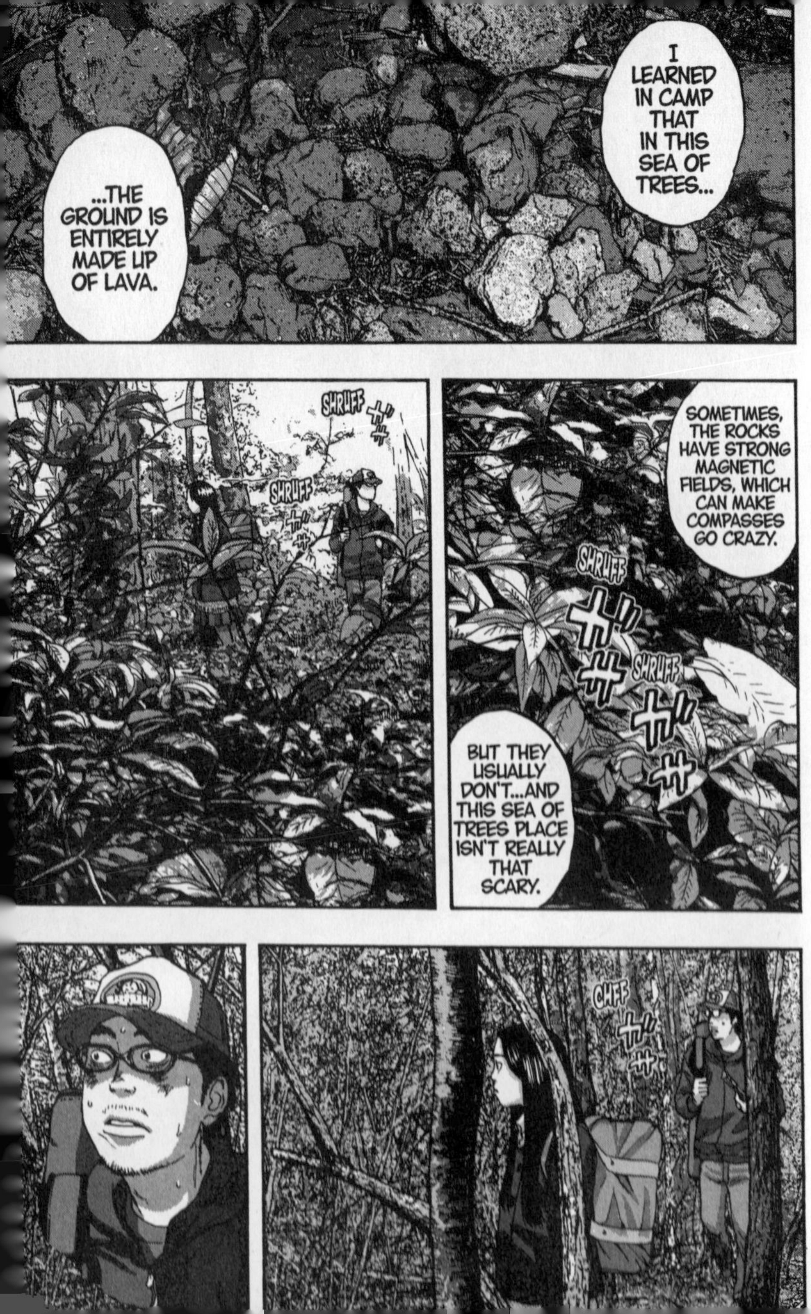
I LEARNED IN CAMP THAT IN THIS SEA OF TREES...
...THE GROUND IS ENTIRELY MADE UP OF LAVA.
SOMETIMES, THE ROCKS HAVE STRONG MAGNETIC FIELDS, WHICH CAN MAKE COMPASSES GO CRAZY.
SHRUFF
SHRUFF
BUT THEY USUALLY DON'T...AND THIS SEA OF TREES PLACE ISN'T REALLY THAT SCARY.
SHRUFF
SHRUFF
CHFF

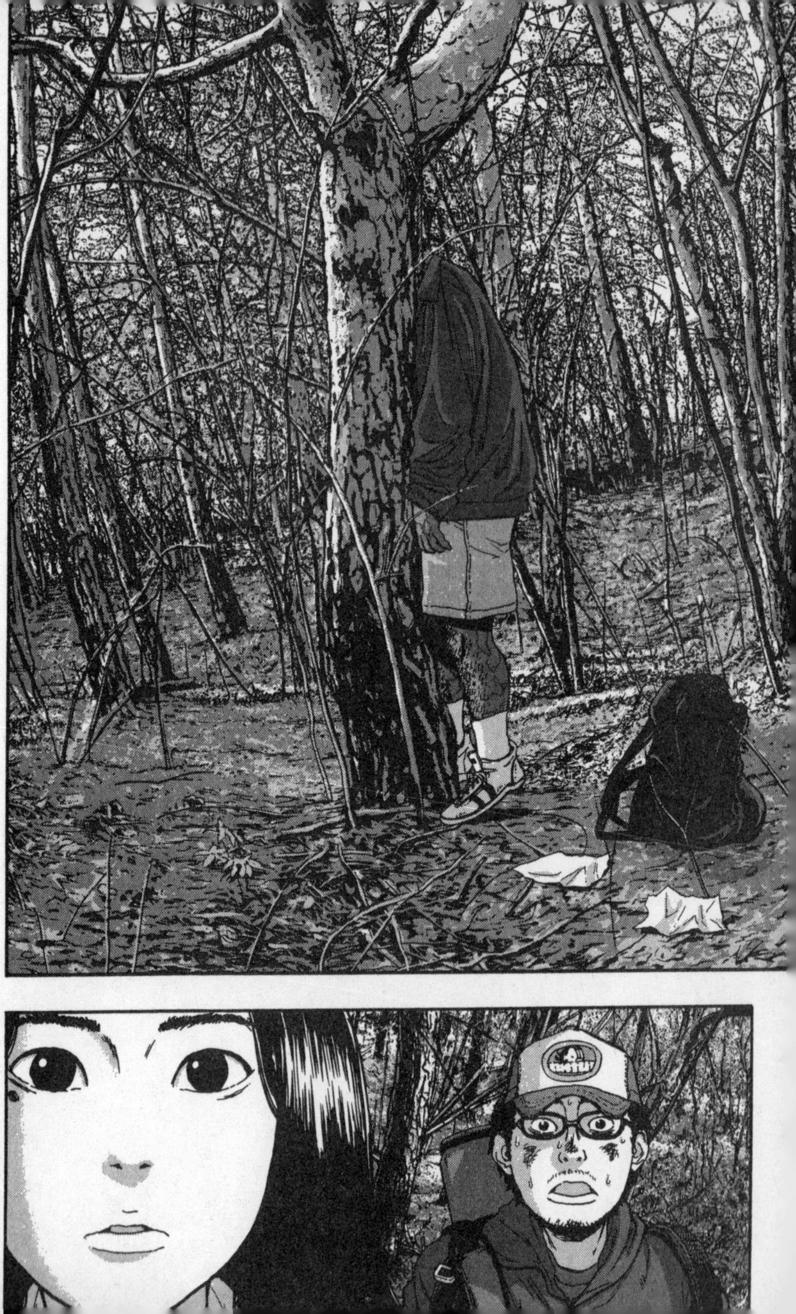

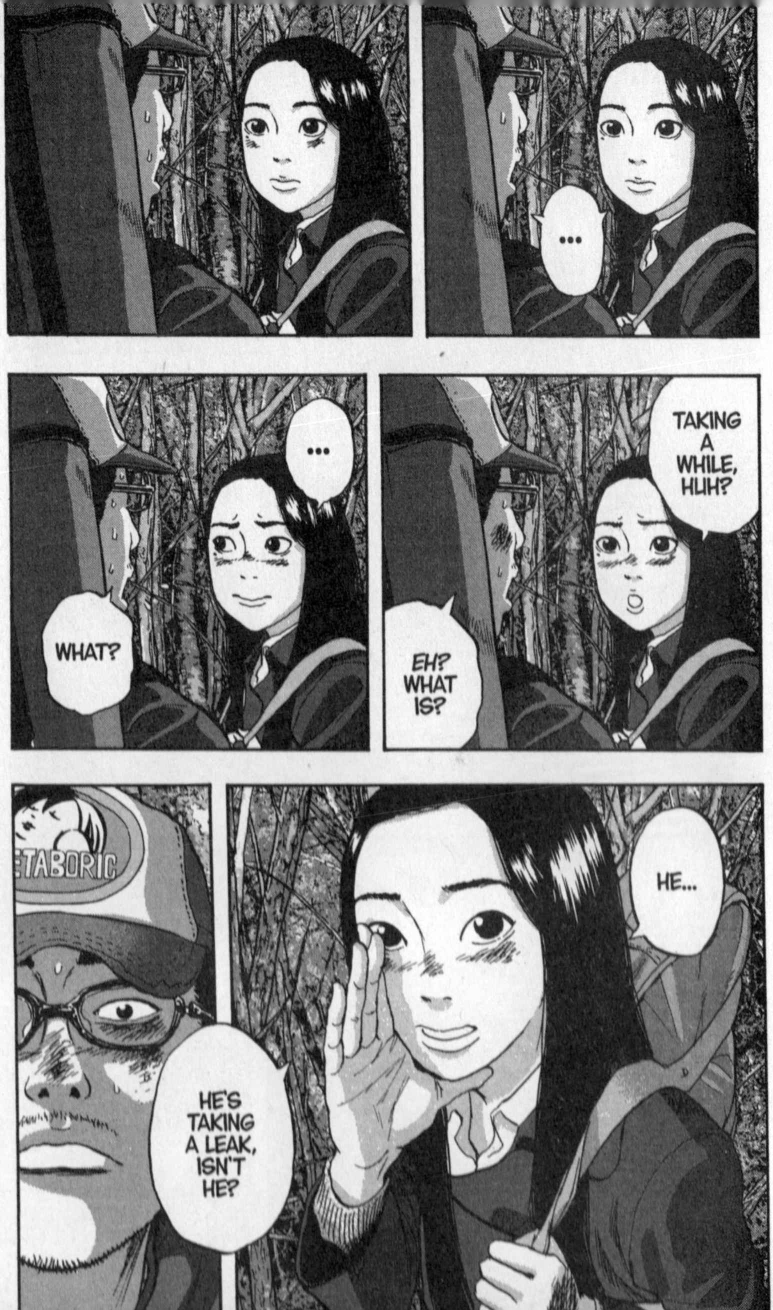
...
TAKING A WHILE, HUH?
EH? WHAT IS?
...
WHAT?
HE...
HE'S TAKING A LEAK, ISN'T HE?

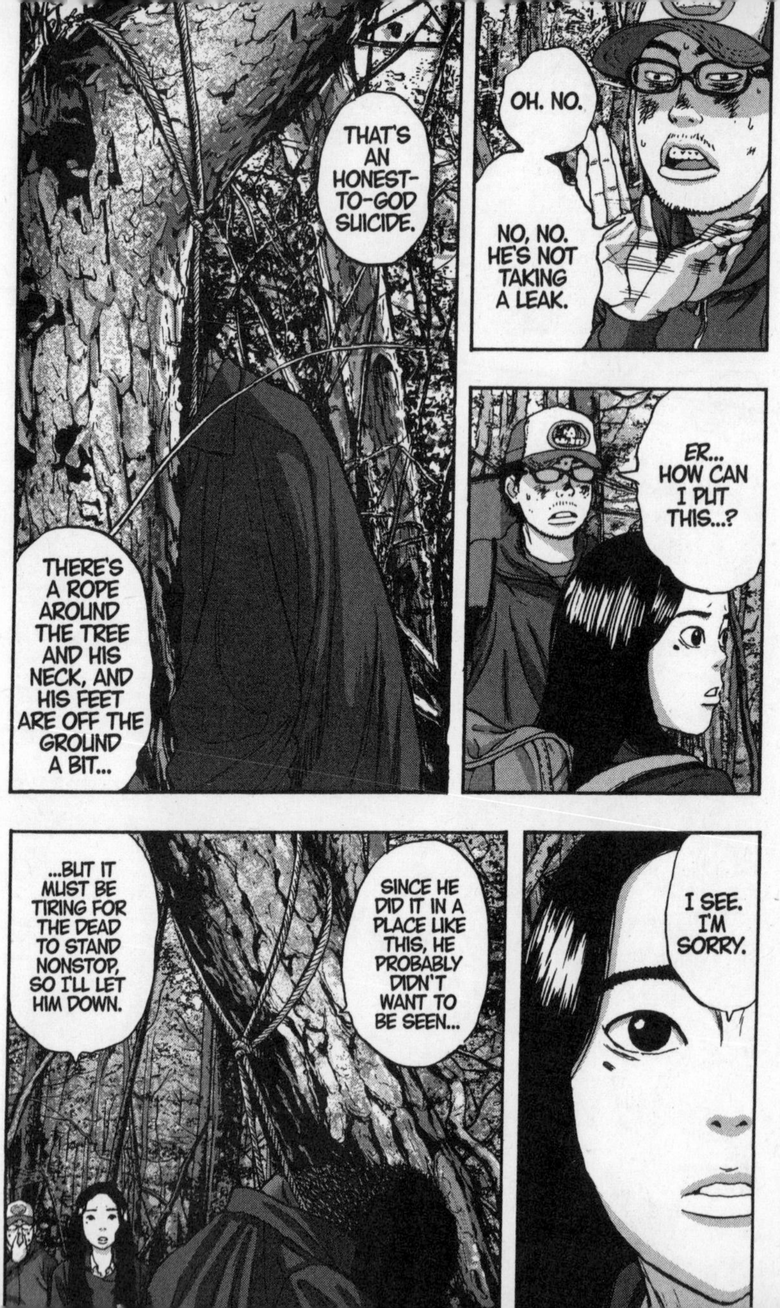
OH. NO.
NO, NO. HE'S NOT TAKING A LEAK.
ER... HOW CAN I PUT THIS...?
THAT'S AN HONEST-TO-GOD SUICIDE.
THERE'S A ROPE AROUND THE TREE AND HIS NECK, AND HIS FEET ARE OFF THE GROUND A BIT...
I SEE. I'M SORRY.
SINCE HE DID IT IN A PLACE LIKE THIS, HE PROBABLY DIDN'T WANT TO BE SEEN...
...BUT IT MUST BE TIRING FOR THE DEAD TO STAND NONSTOP, SO I'LL LET HIM DOWN.

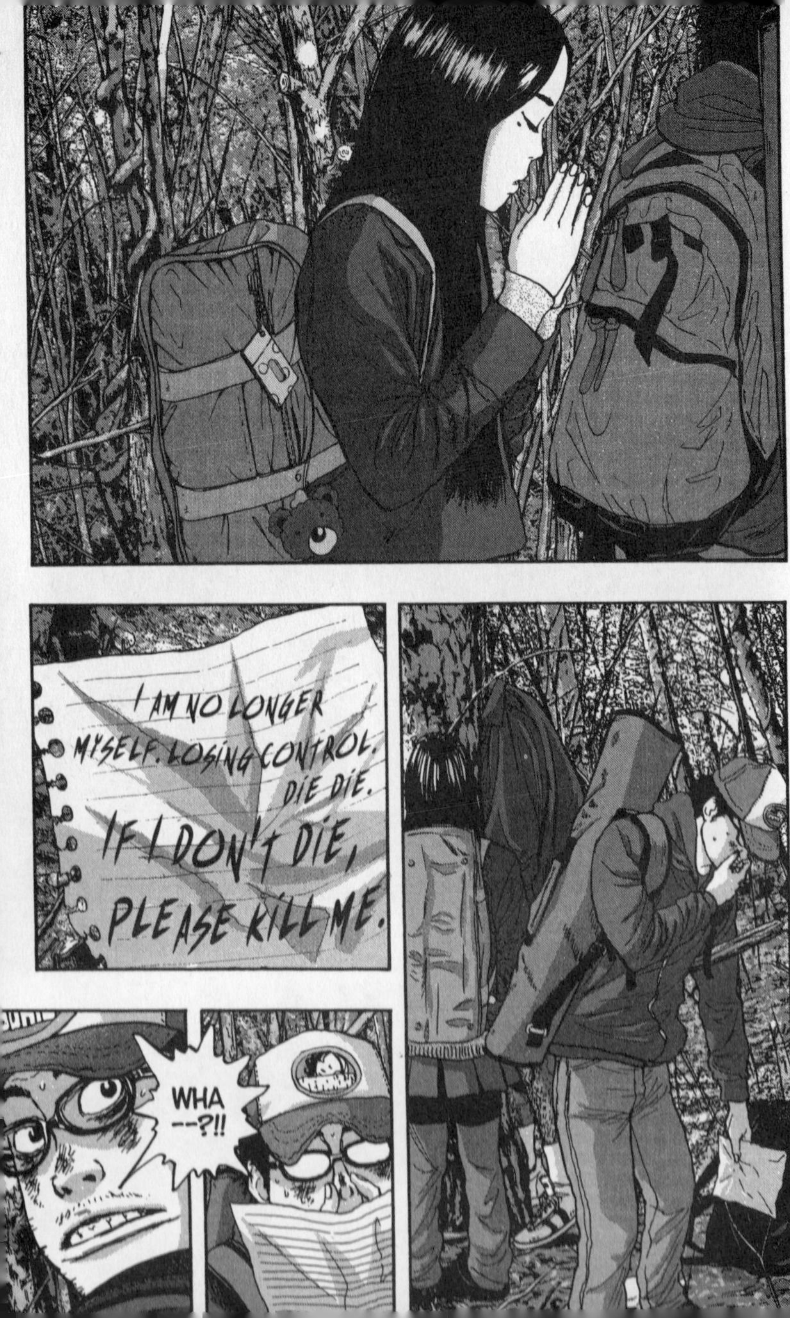
I AM NO LONGER MYSELF. LOSING CONTROL. DIE DIE.
IF I DON'T DIE, PLEASE KILL ME.
WHA--?!!

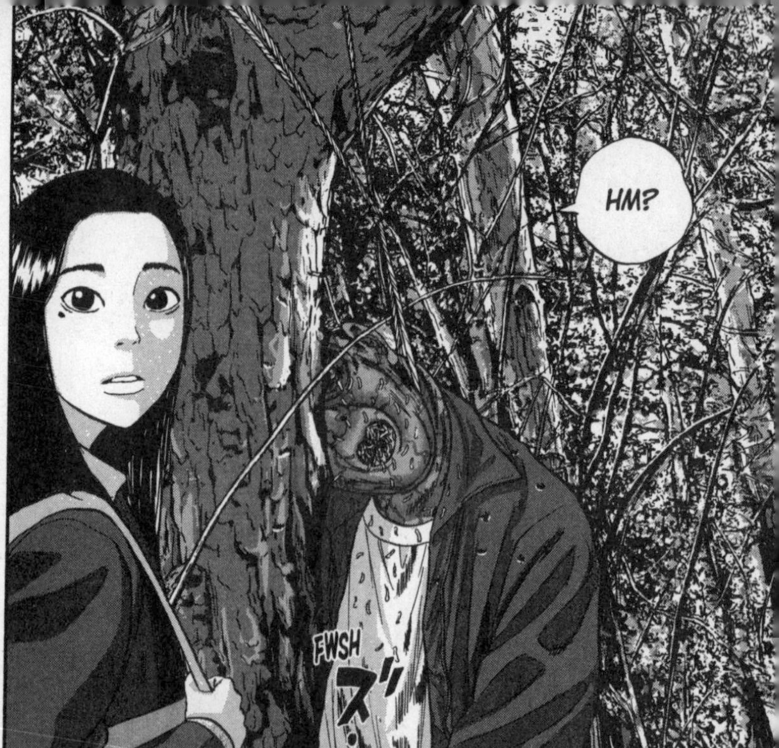
HM?
FWSH
ズッ
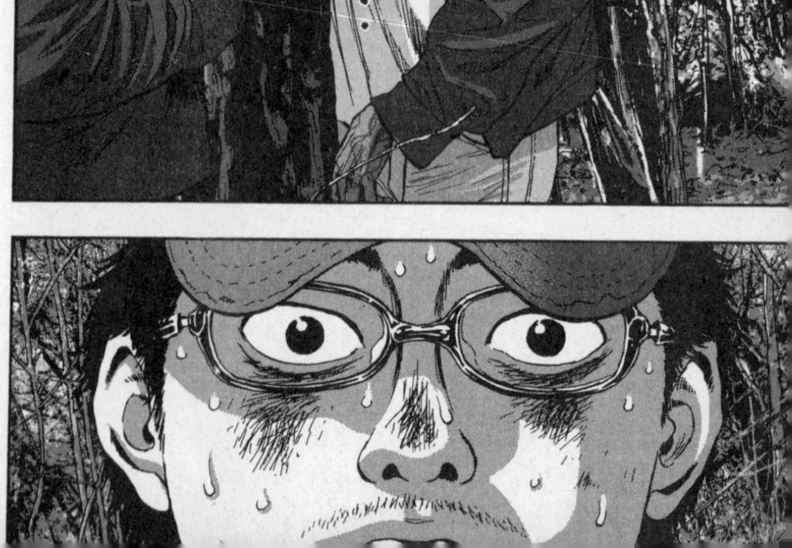

I AM
A HERO

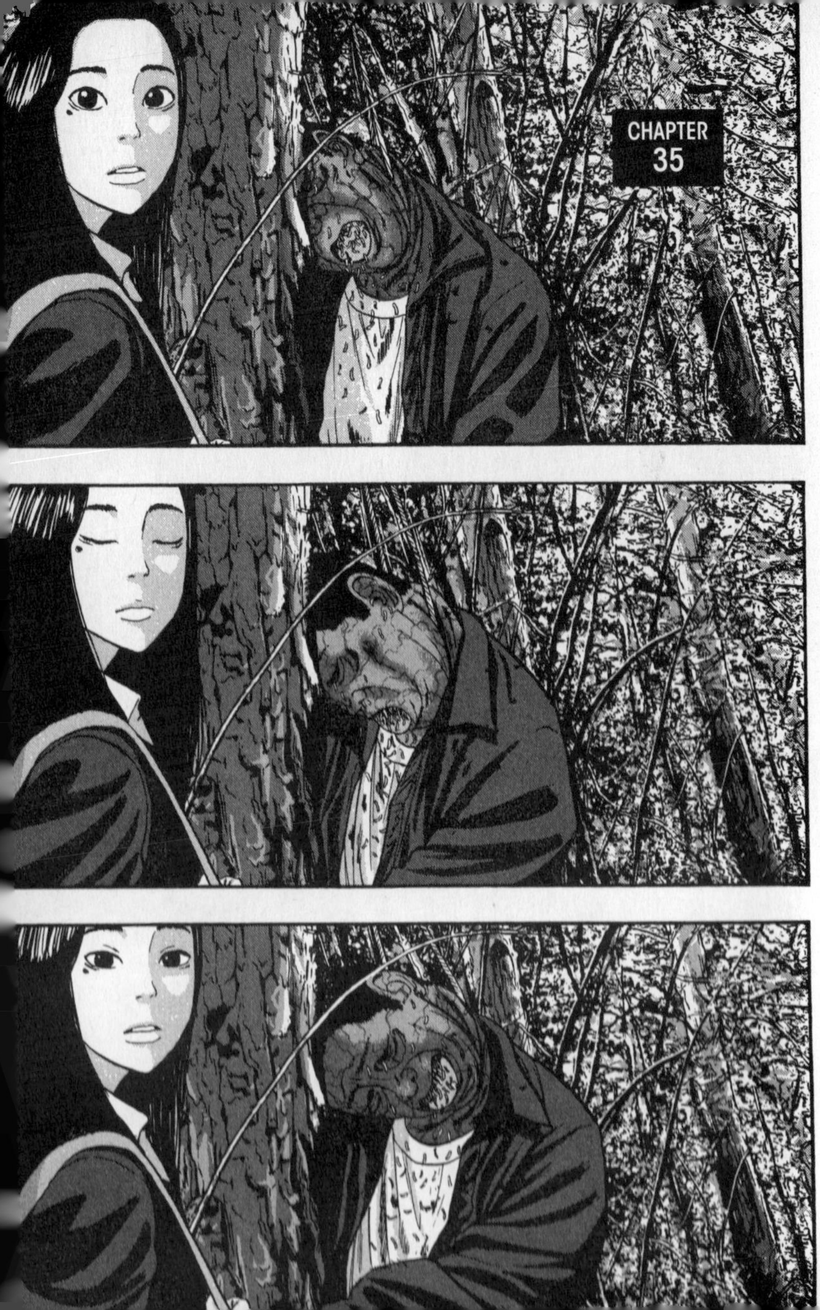
CHAPTER
35

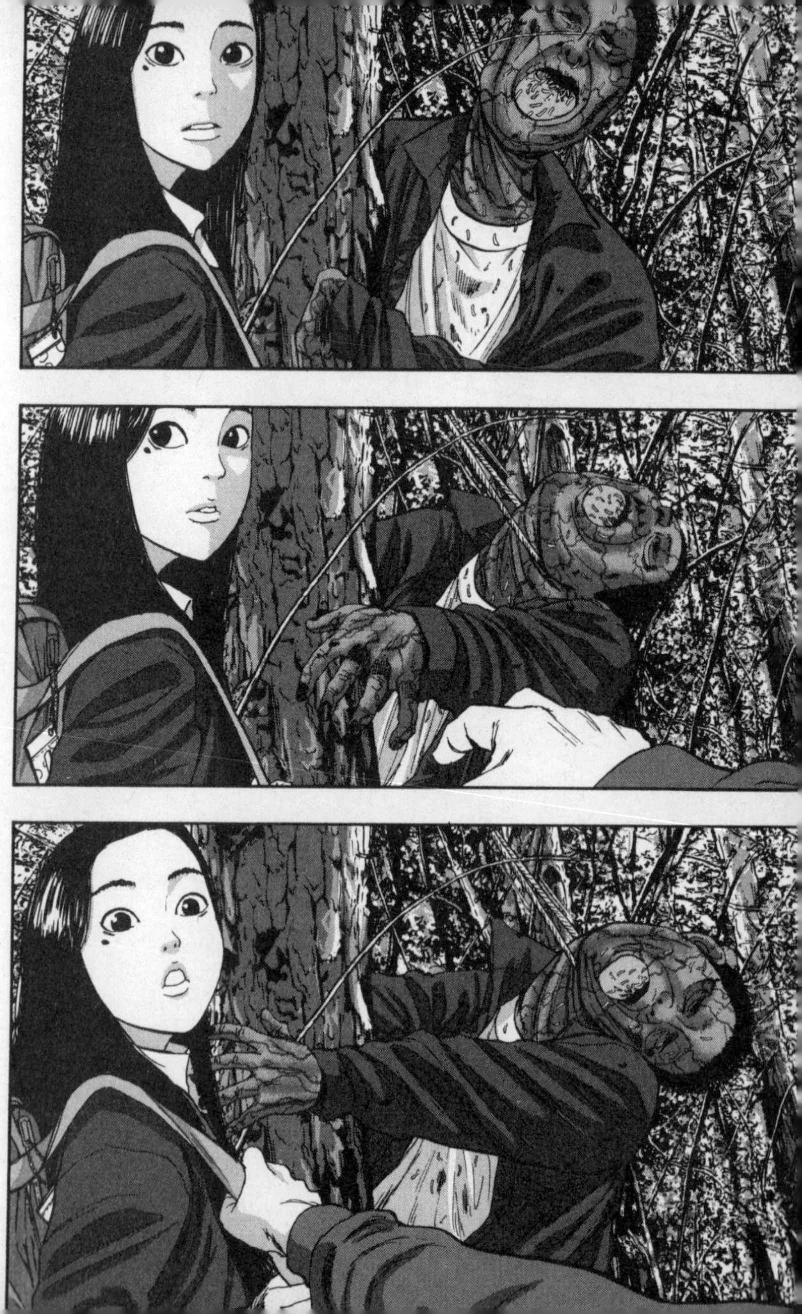

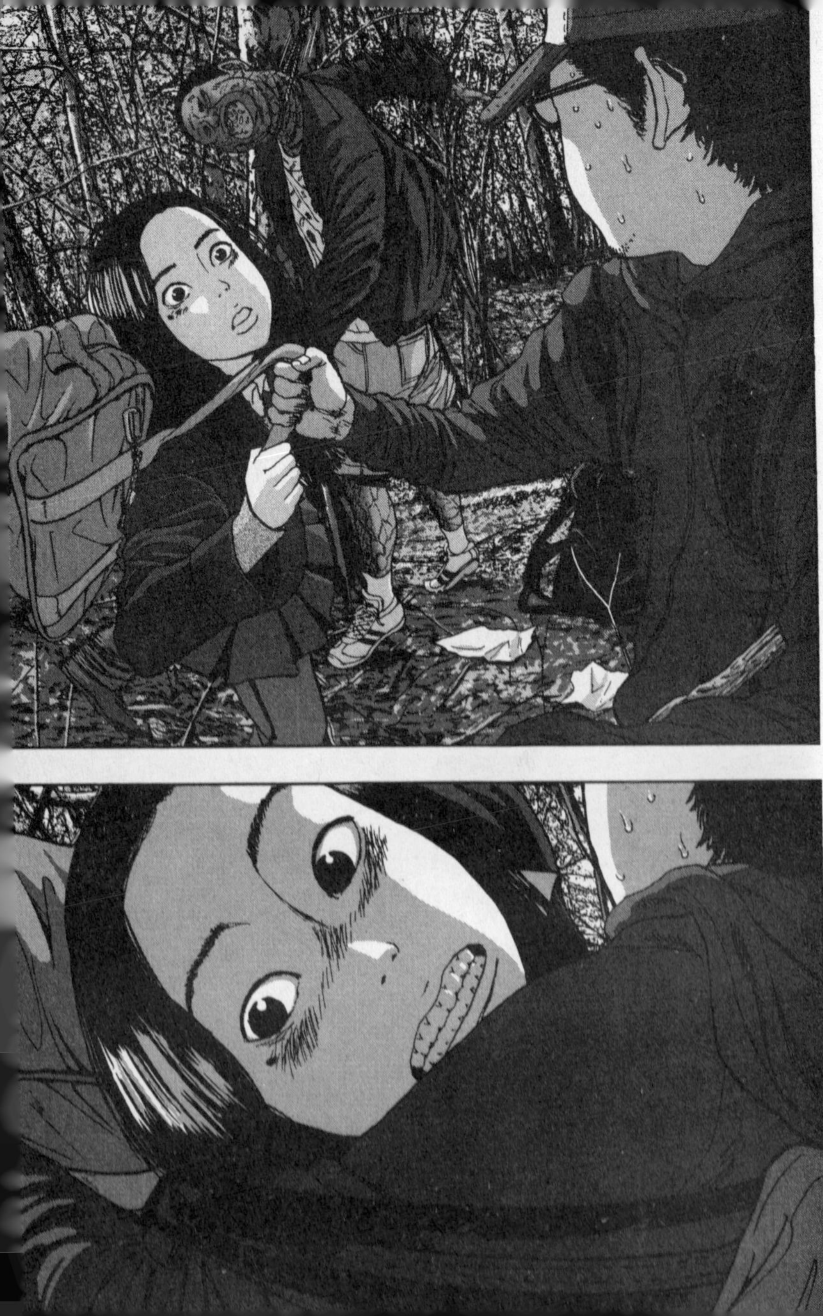

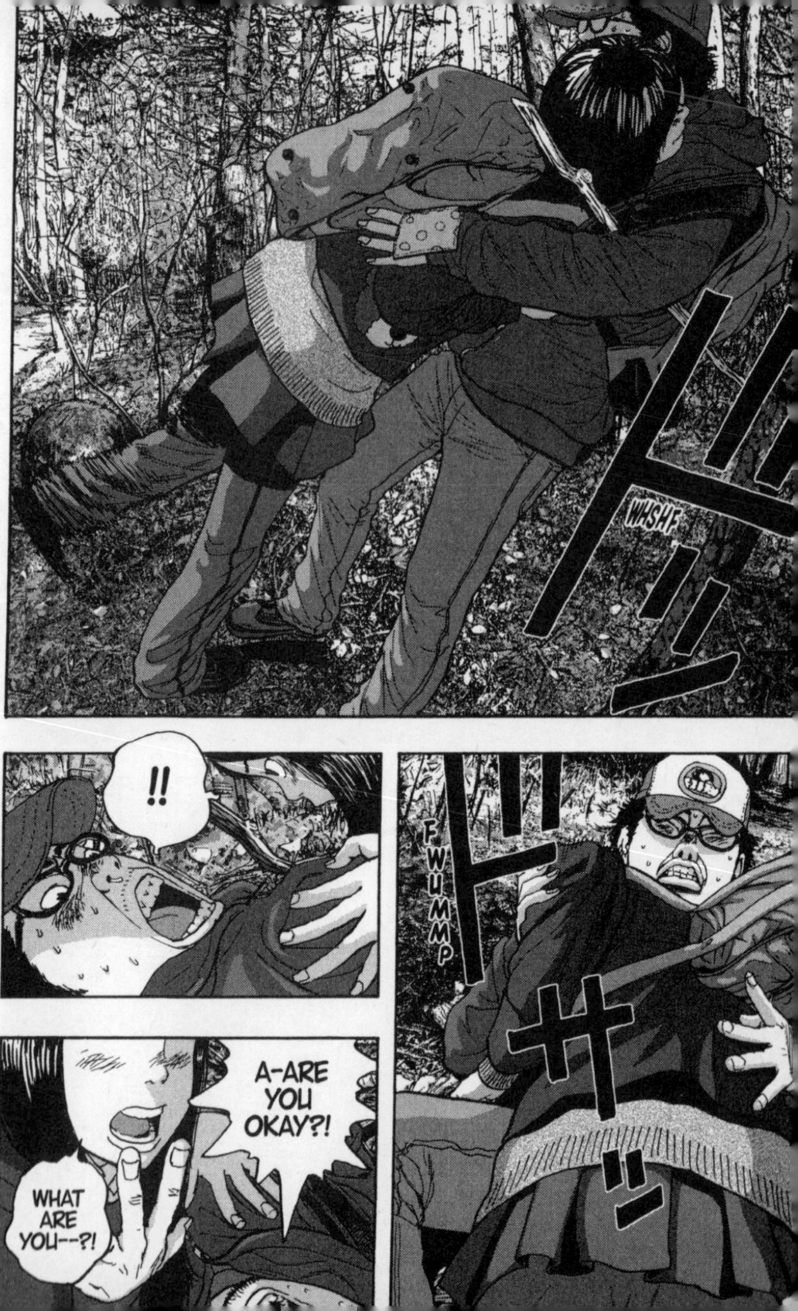
WHSHF
FWUMMP
!!
A-ARE YOU OKAY?!
WHAT ARE YOU--?!

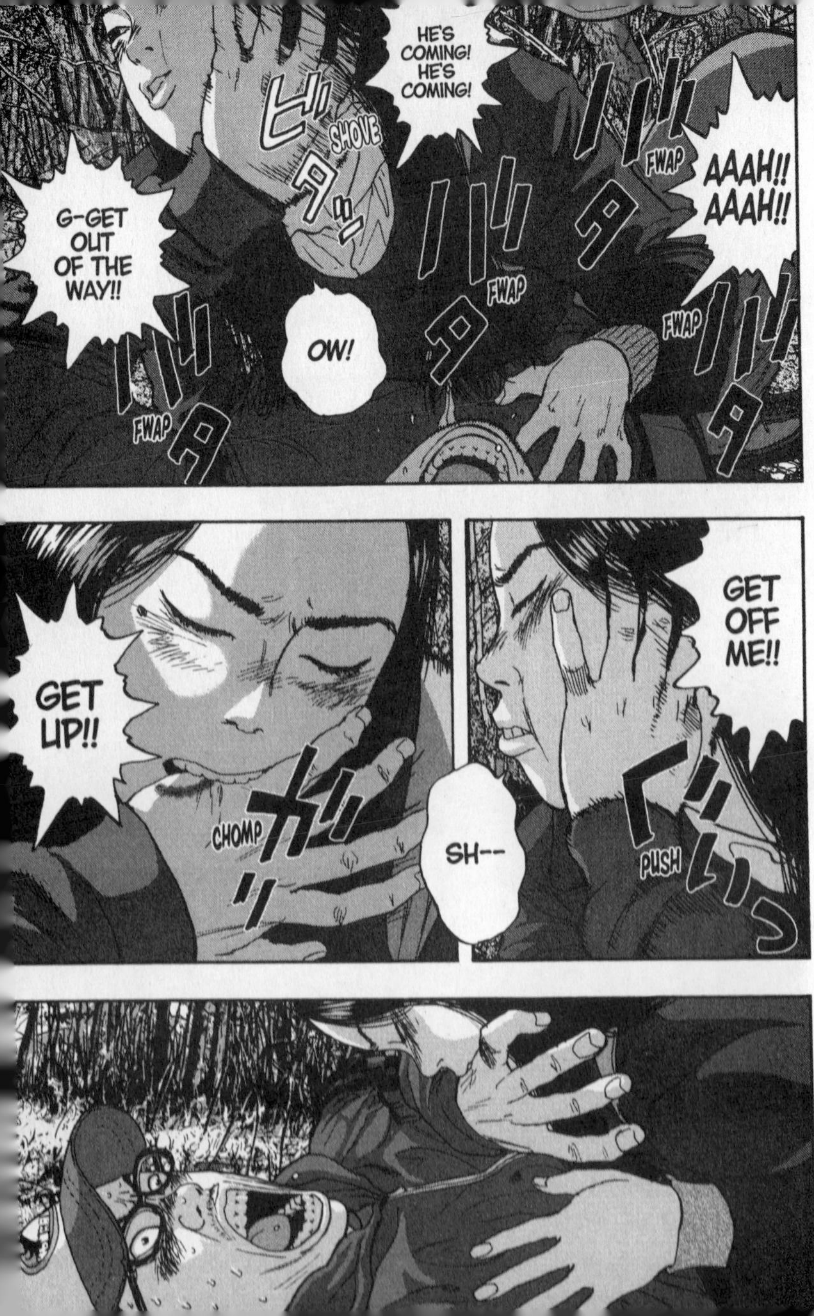

HE'S COMING! HE'S COMING!
AAAH!! AAAH!!
FWAP
SHOVE
FWAP
FWAP
G-GET OUT OF THE WAY!!
OW!
FWAP
GET OFF ME!!
PUSH
SH--
GET UP!!
CHOMP

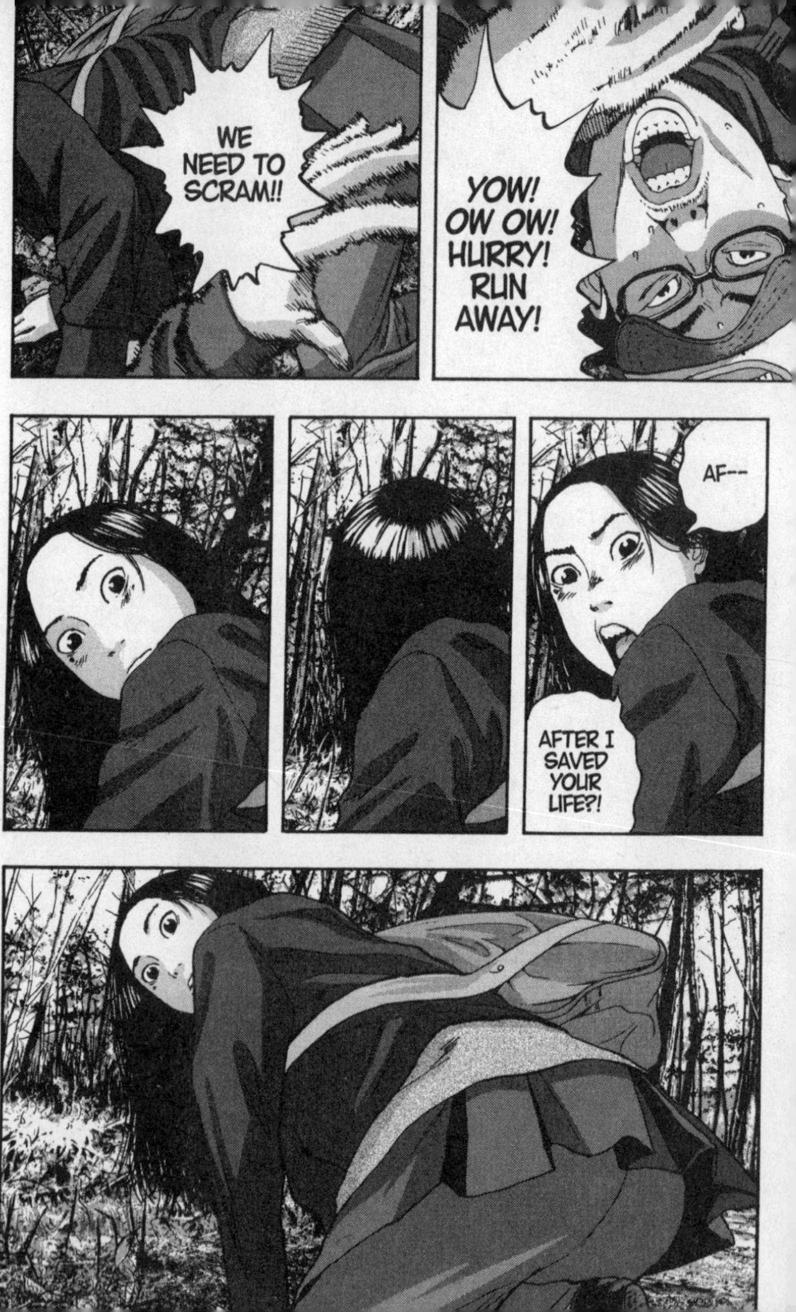
YOW! OW OW! HURRY! RUN AWAY!
WE NEED TO SCRAM!!
AF--
AFTER I SAVED YOUR LIFE?!

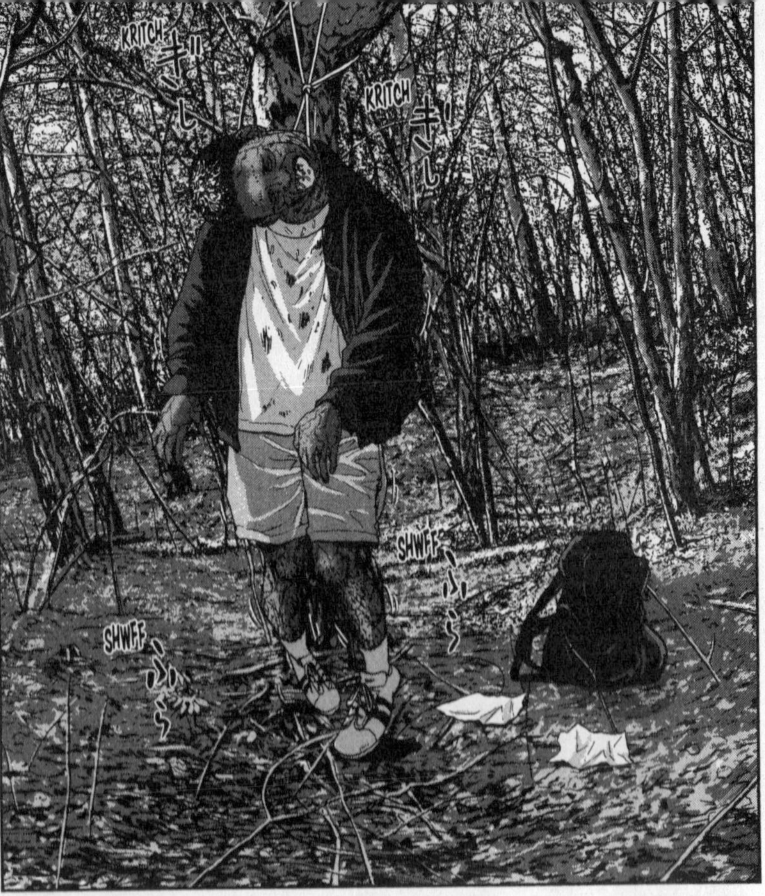
KRITCH
きし
KRITCH
ぎし
SHWFF
ふら
SHWFF
ふら

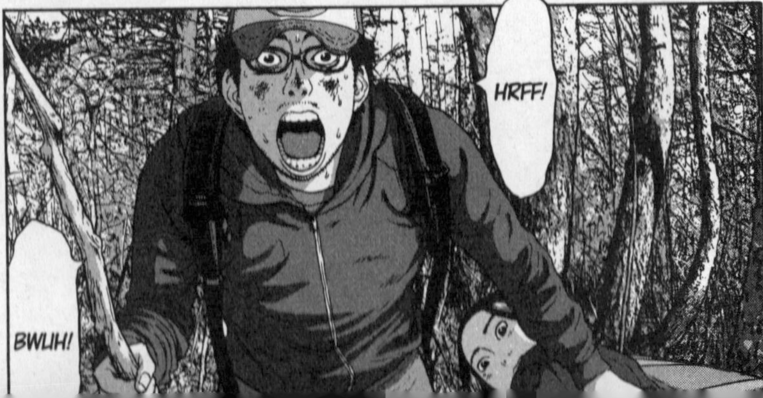
HRFF!
BWUH!

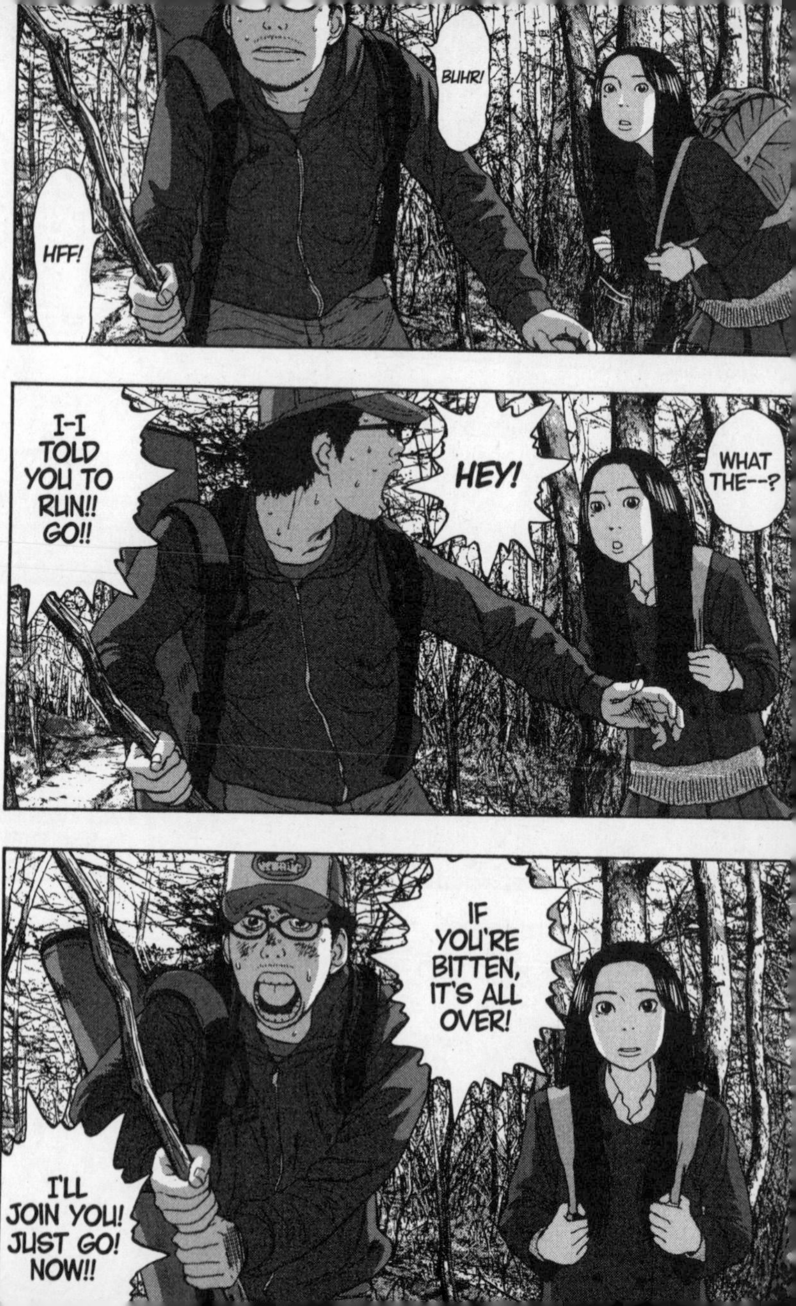
BUHR!
HFF!
WHAT THE--?
HEY!
I-I TOLD YOU TO RUN!! GO!!
IF YOU'RE BITTEN, IT'S ALL OVER!
I'LL JOIN YOU! JUST GO! NOW!!

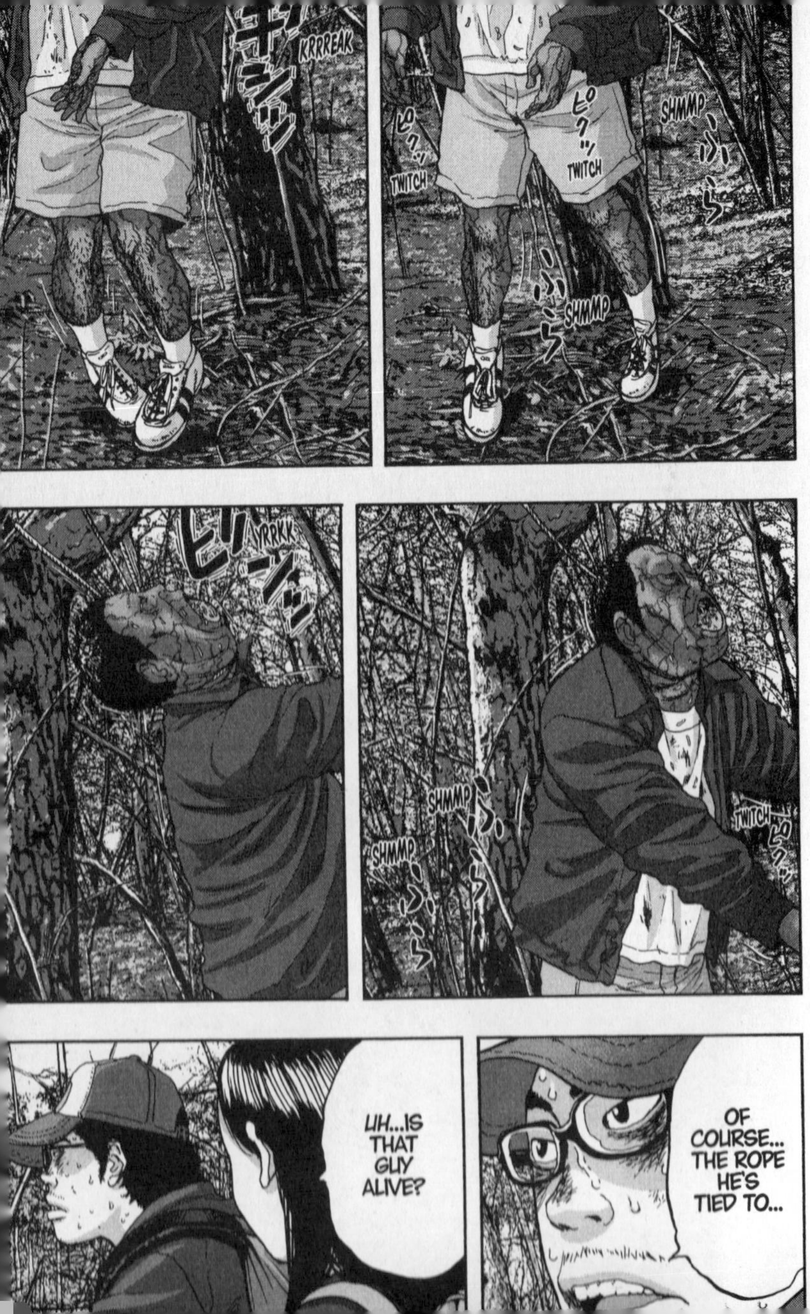
SHMMP
TWITCH
TWITCH
SHMMP
KRRREAK
TWITCH
SHMMP
SHMMP
YRRKK
OF COURSE... THE ROPE HE'S TIED TO...
UH...IS THAT GUY ALIVE?

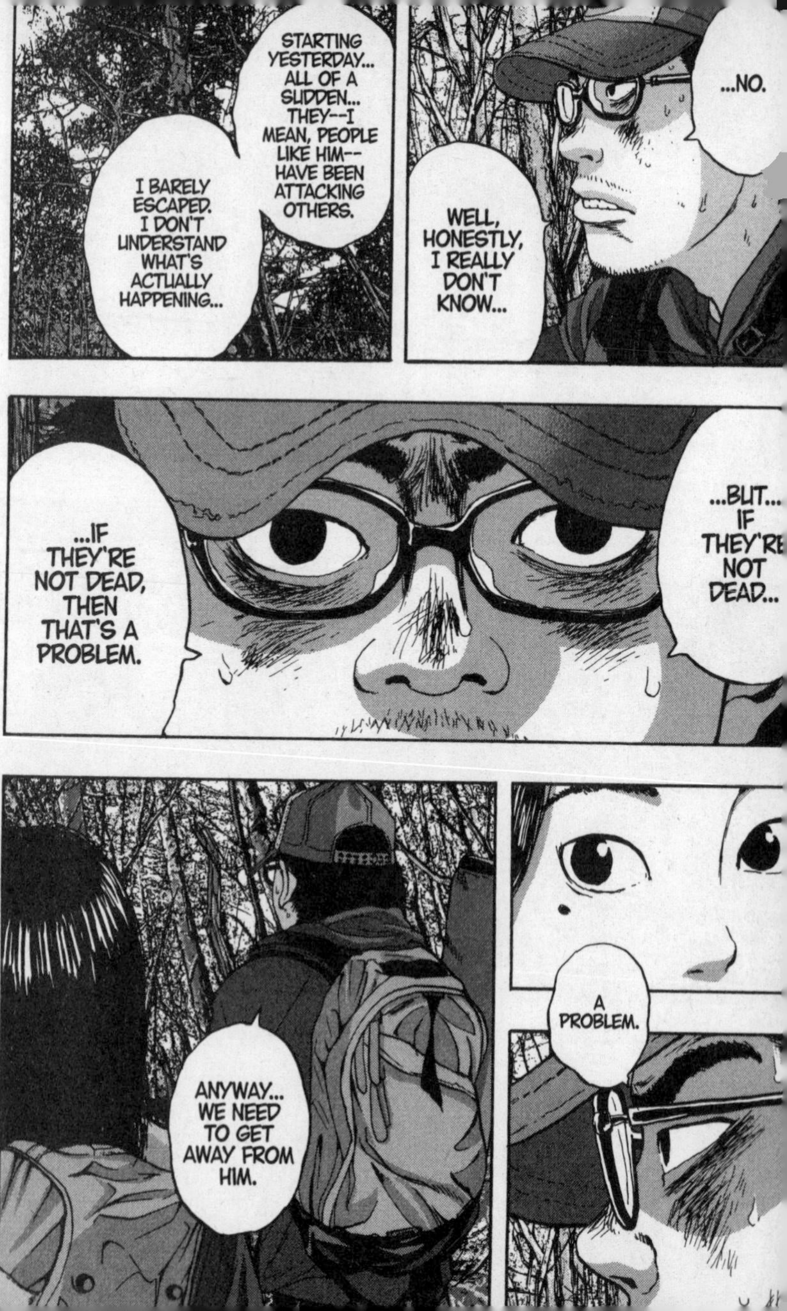
...NO.
WELL, HONESTLY, I REALLY DON'T KNOW...
STARTING YESTERDAY... ALL OF A SUDDEN... THEY--I MEAN, PEOPLE LIKE HIM--HAVE BEEN ATTACKING OTHERS.
I BARELY ESCAPED. I DON'T UNDERSTAND WHAT'S ACTUALLY HAPPENING...
...BUT... IF THEY'RE NOT DEAD...
...IF THEY'RE NOT DEAD, THEN THAT'S A PROBLEM.
A PROBLEM.
ANYWAY... WE NEED TO GET AWAY FROM HIM.

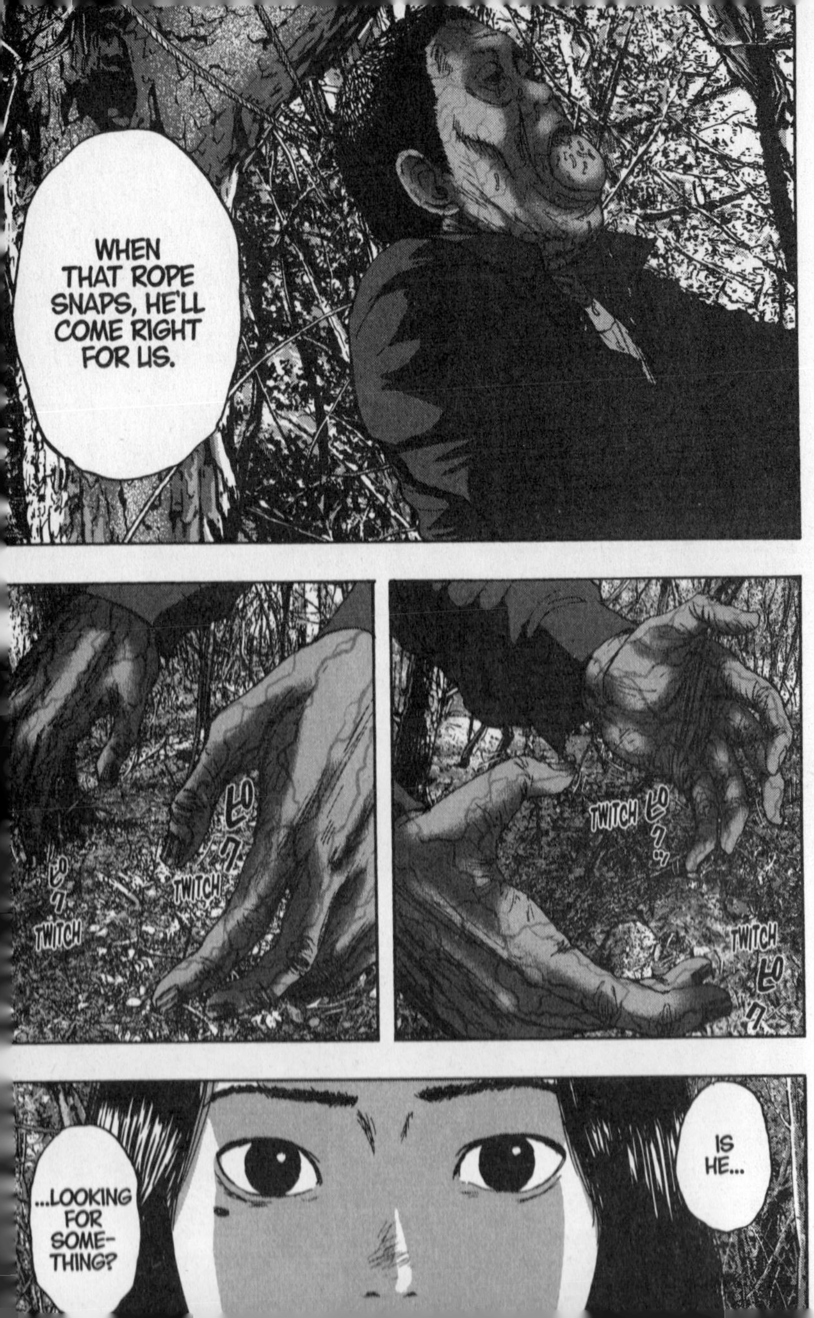
WHEN THAT ROPE SNAPS, HE'LL COME RIGHT FOR US.
TWITCH ピクッ
TWITCH ピク
ピク TWITCH
ピク TWITCH
IS HE...
...LOOKING FOR SOME-THING?

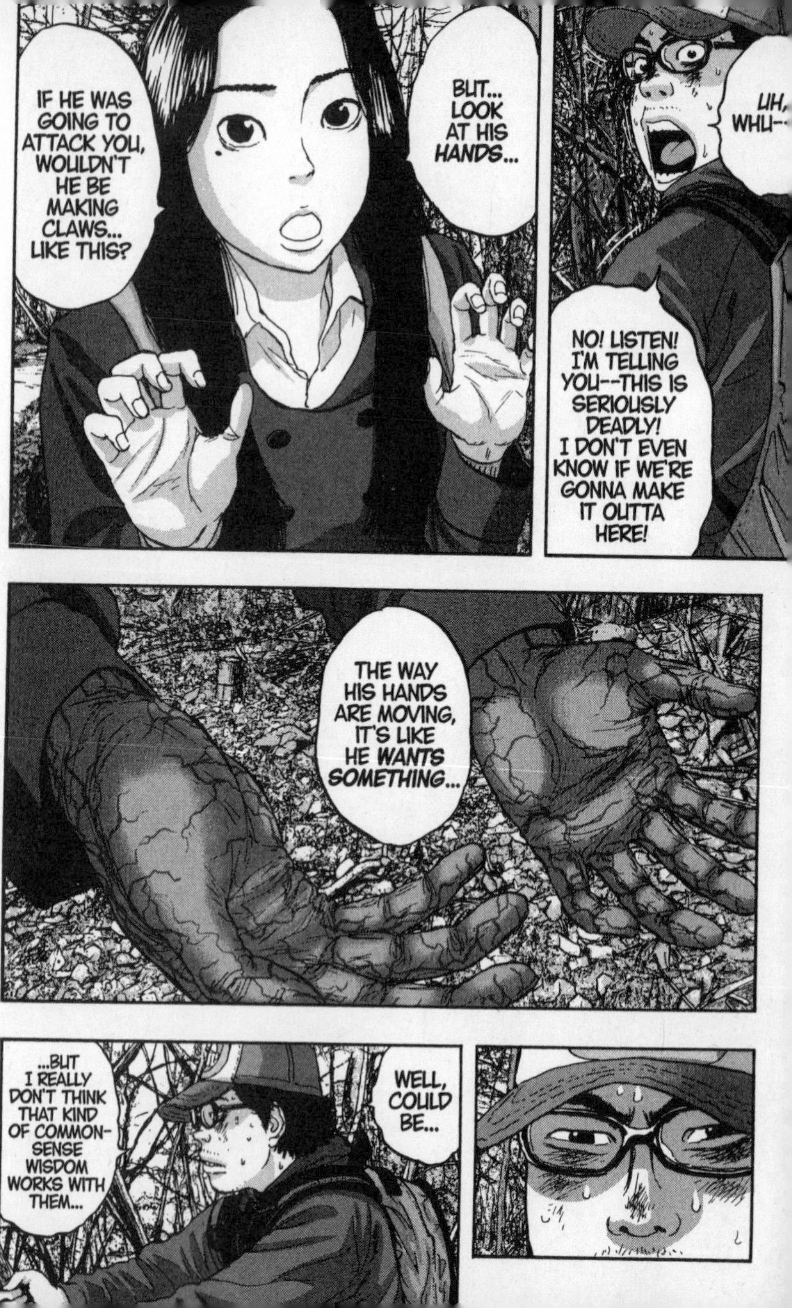
UH, WHU--
NO! LISTEN! I'M TELLING YOU--THIS IS SERIOUSLY DEADLY! I DON'T EVEN KNOW IF WE'RE GONNA MAKE IT OUTTA HERE!
BUT... LOOK AT HIS *HANDS*...
IF HE WAS GOING TO ATTACK YOU, WOULDN'T HE BE MAKING CLAWS... LIKE THIS?
THE WAY HIS HANDS ARE MOVING, IT'S LIKE HE *WANTS SOMETHING*...
WELL, COULD BE...
...BUT I REALLY DON'T THINK THAT KIND OF COMMON-SENSE WISDOM WORKS WITH THEM...

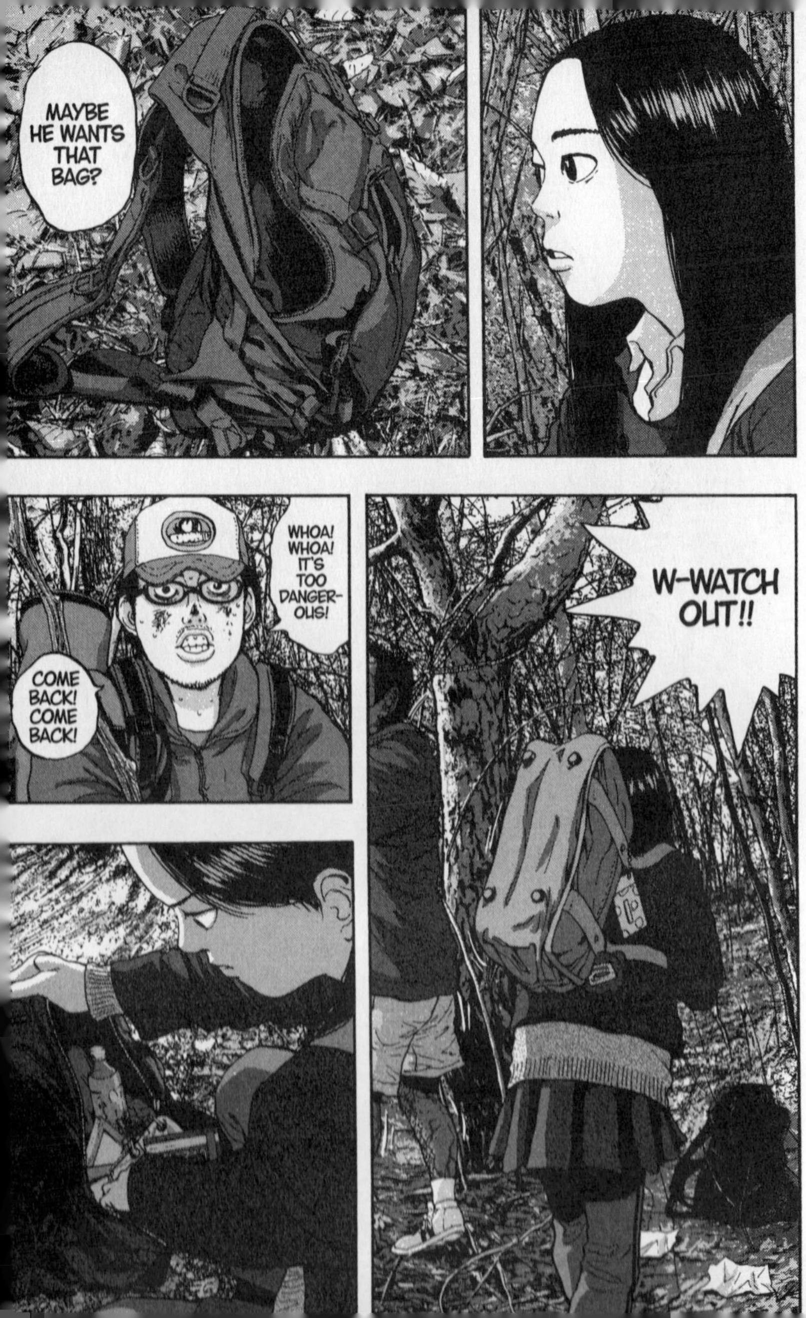
MAYBE HE WANTS THAT BAG?
W-WATCH OUT!!
WHOA! WHOA! IT'S TOO DANGER-OUS!
COME BACK! COME BACK!

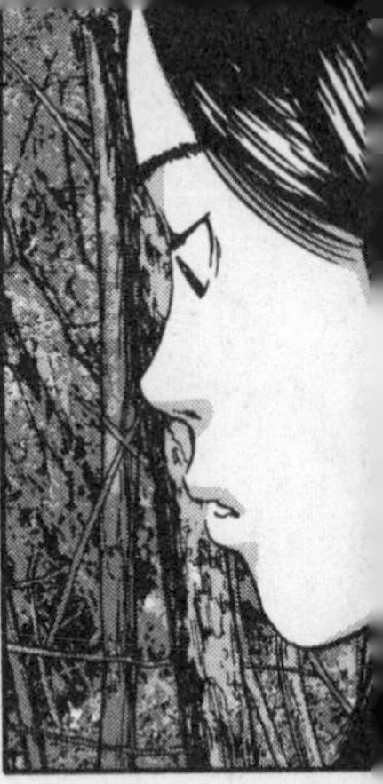

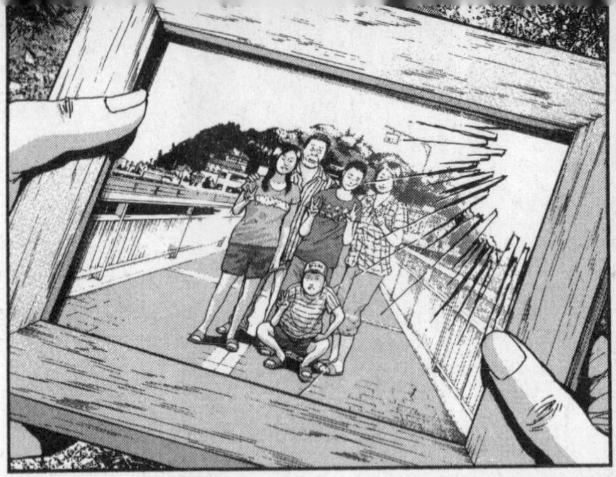

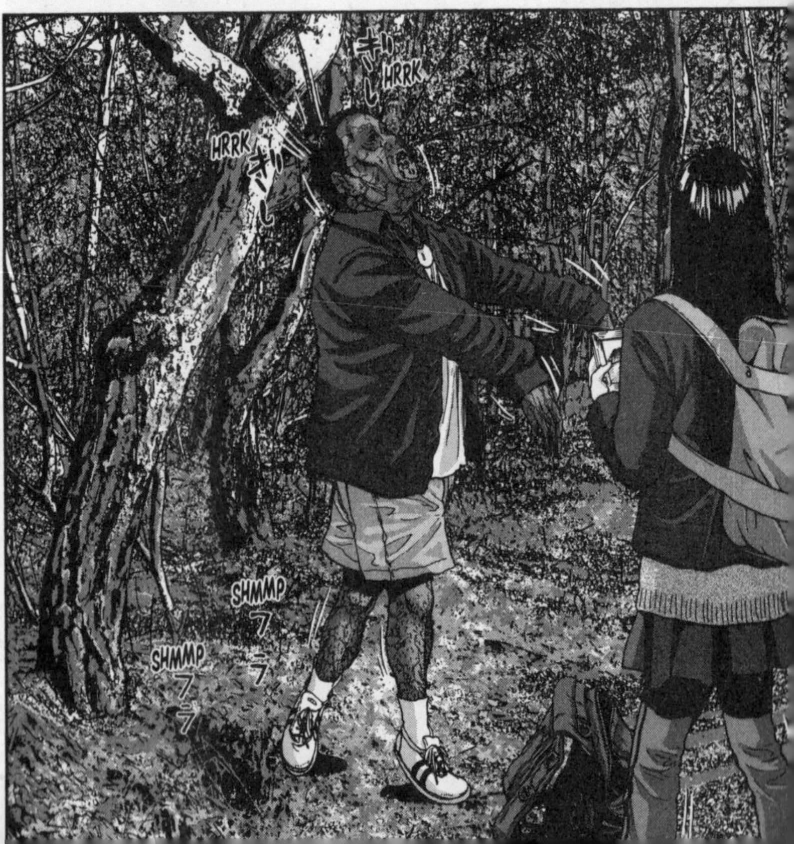
HRRK
HRRK
SHMMP
フラ
SHMMP
フラ

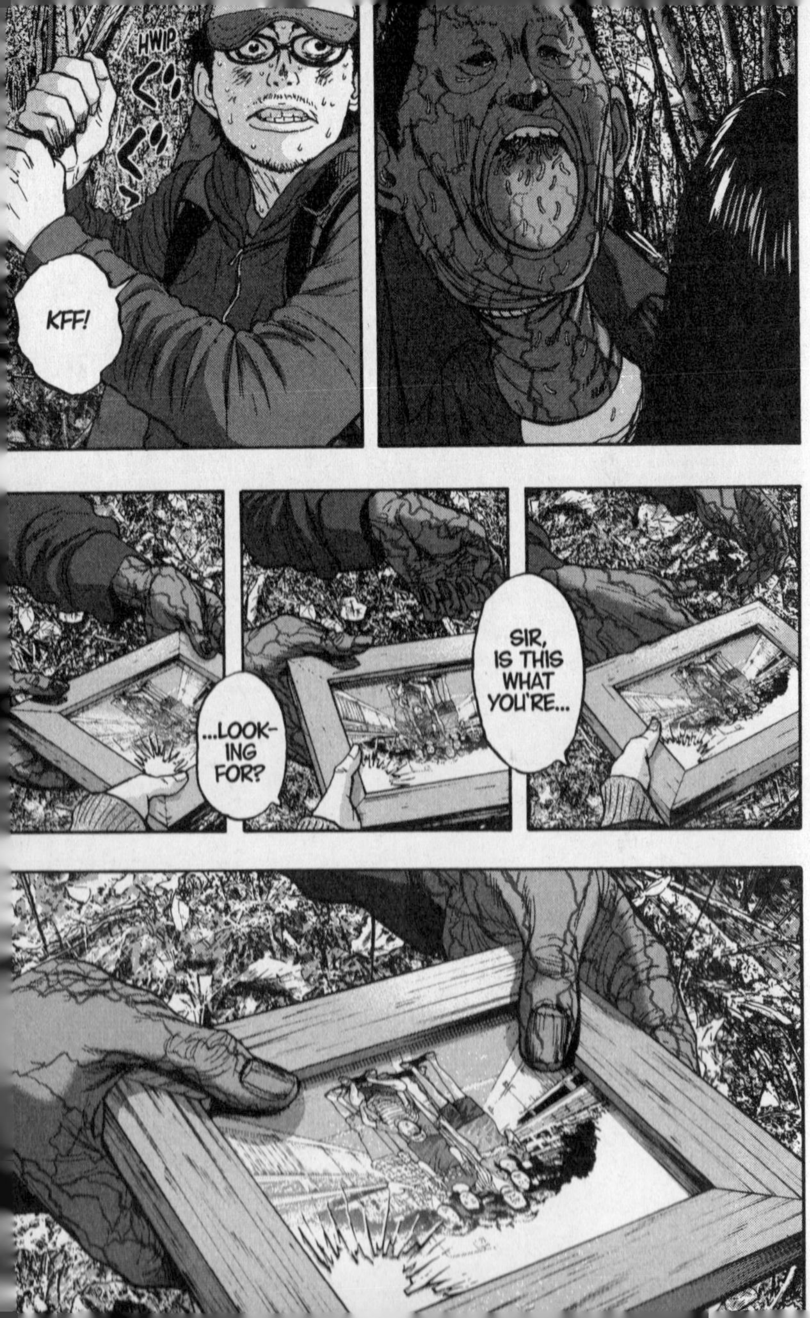
HWIP
KFF!
SIR, IS THIS WHAT YOU'RE...
...LOOKING FOR?

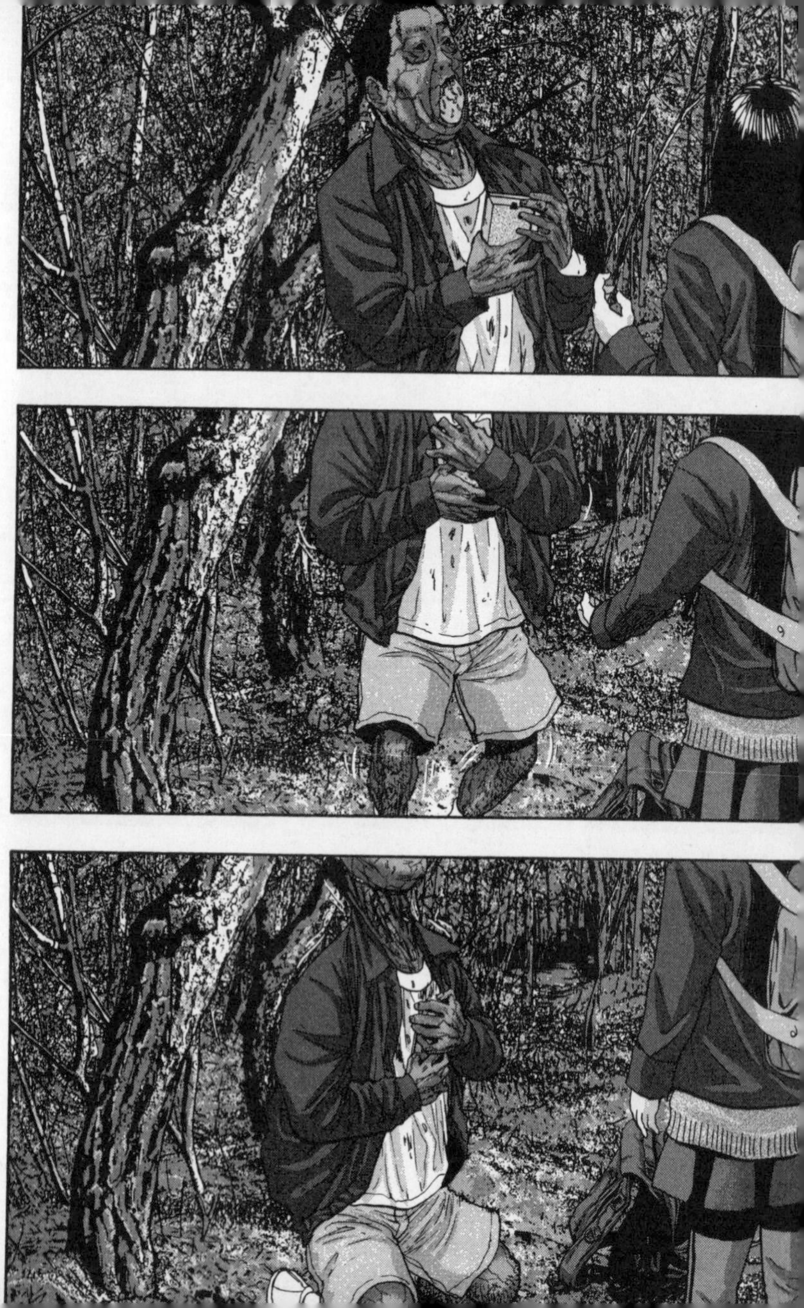

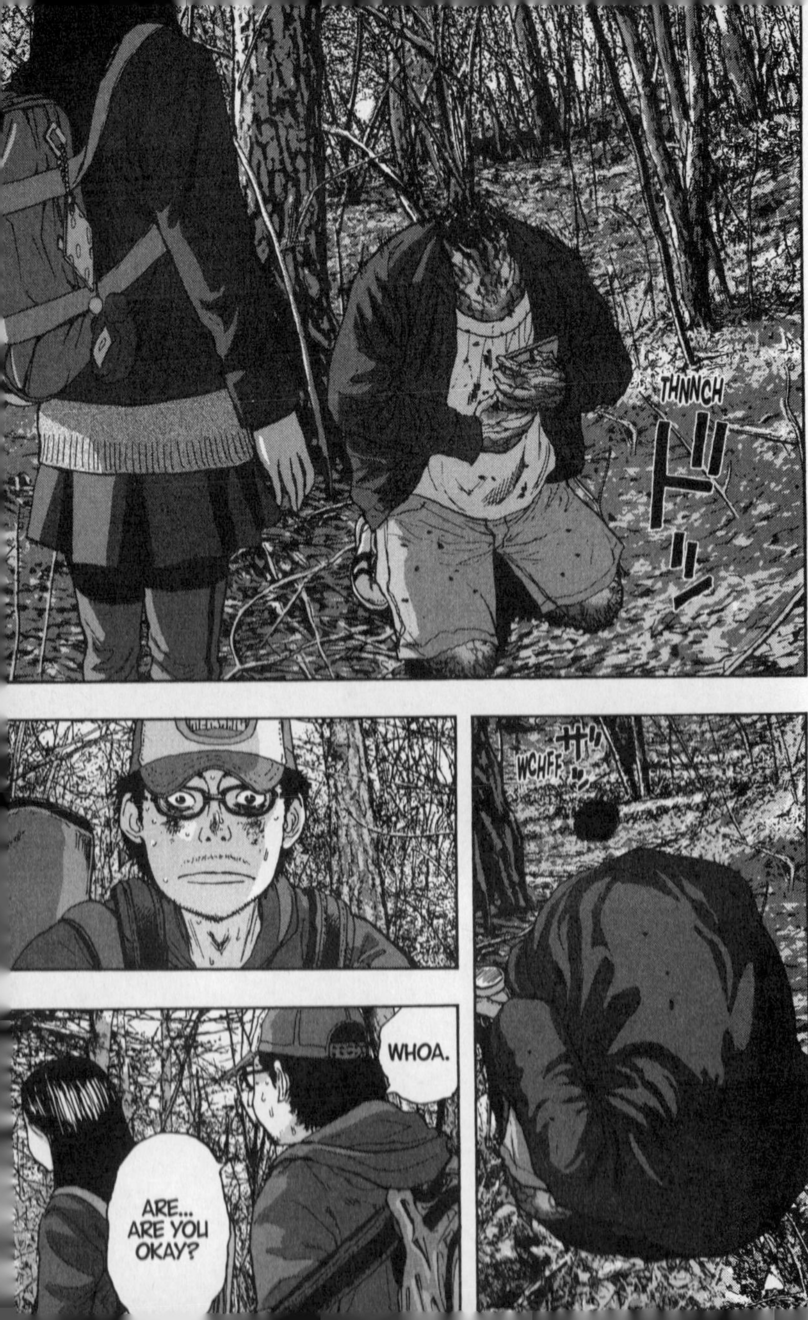
THNNCH
ドッ
WCHFF
ザッ
WHOA.
ARE... ARE YOU OKAY?

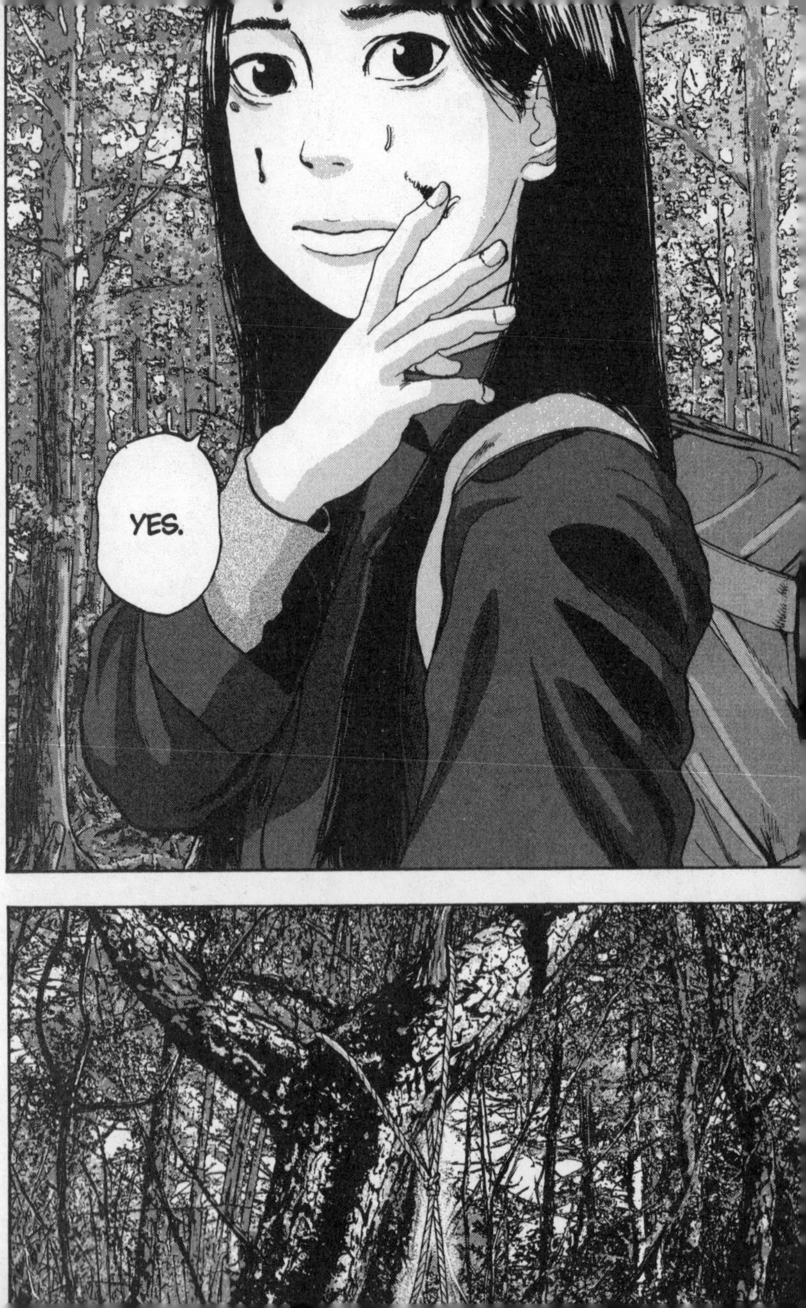
YES.

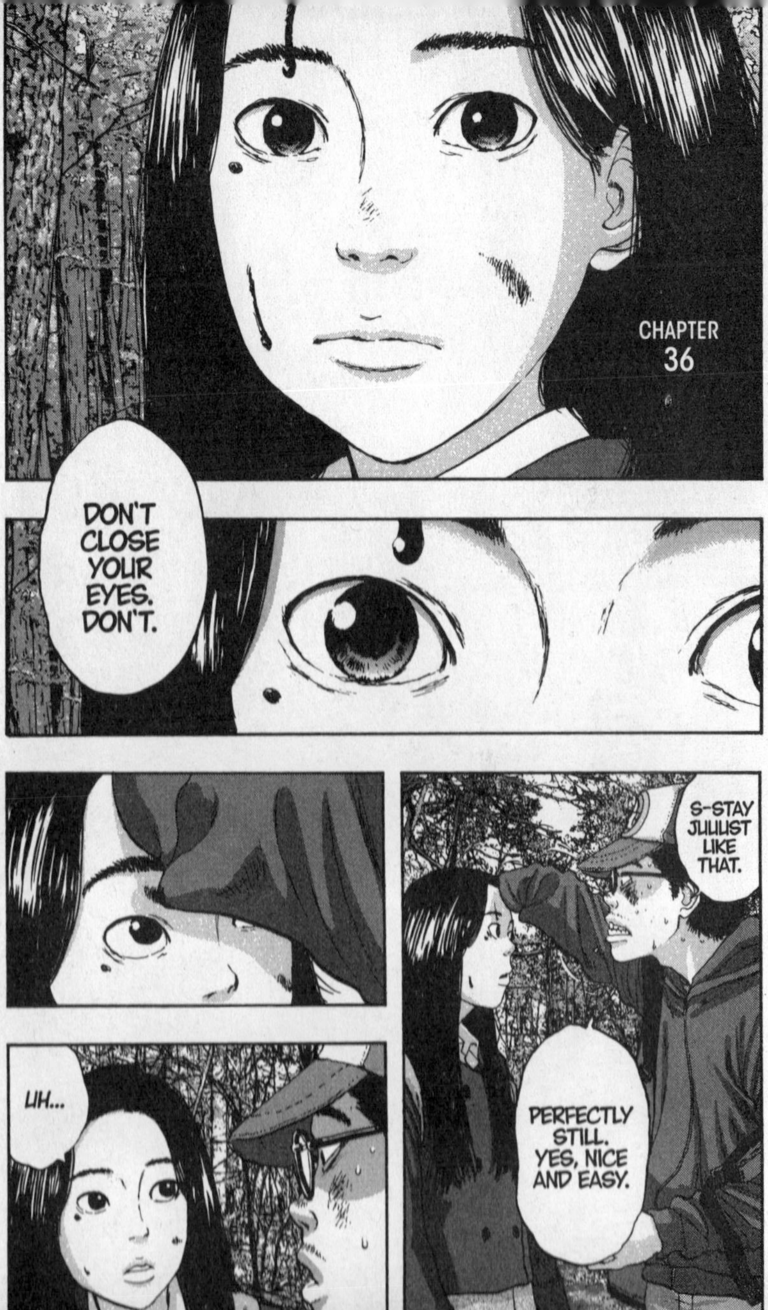
CHAPTER 36
DON'T CLOSE YOUR EYES. DON'T.
S-STAY JUUUST LIKE THAT.
PERFECTLY STILL. YES, NICE AND EASY.
UH...

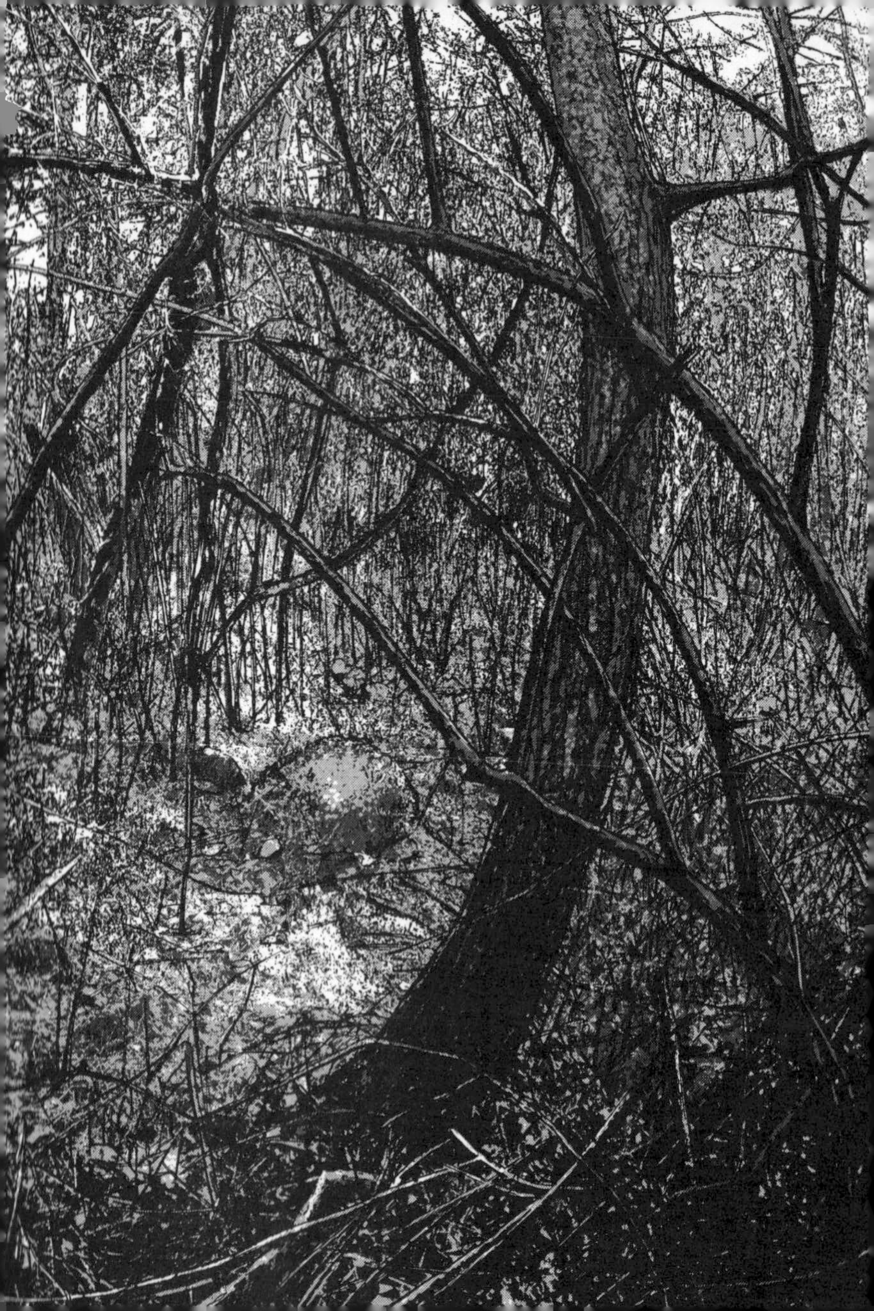

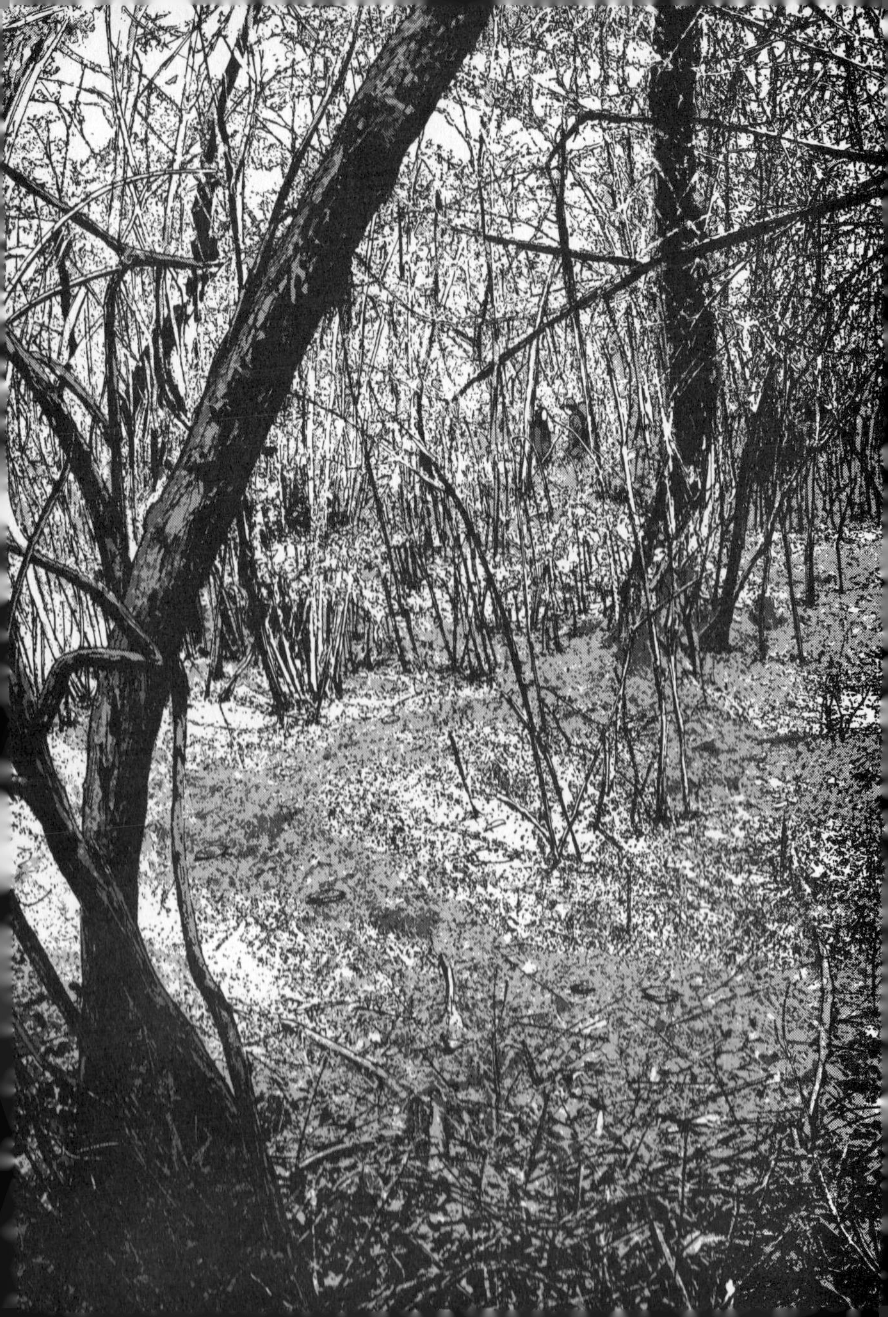

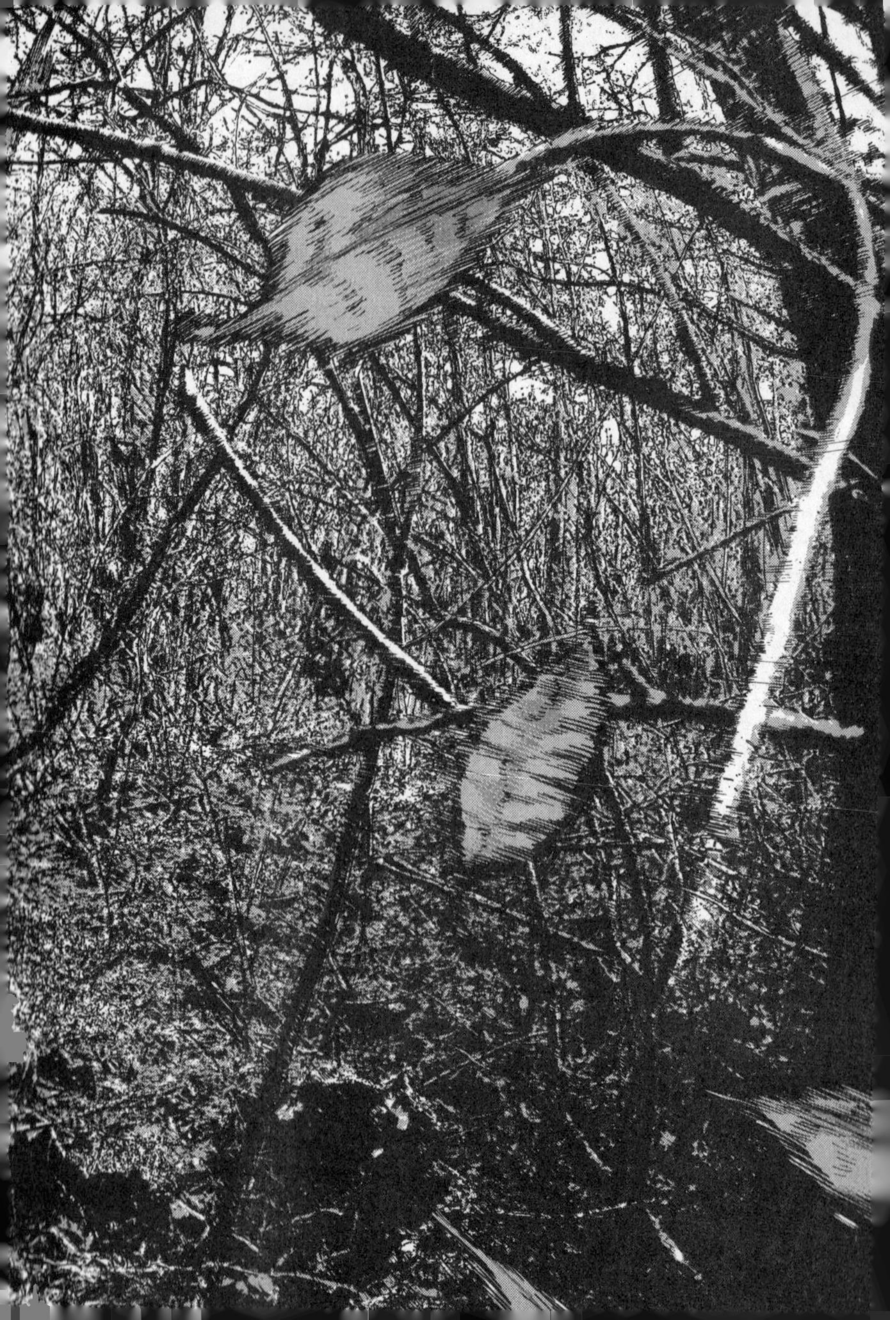

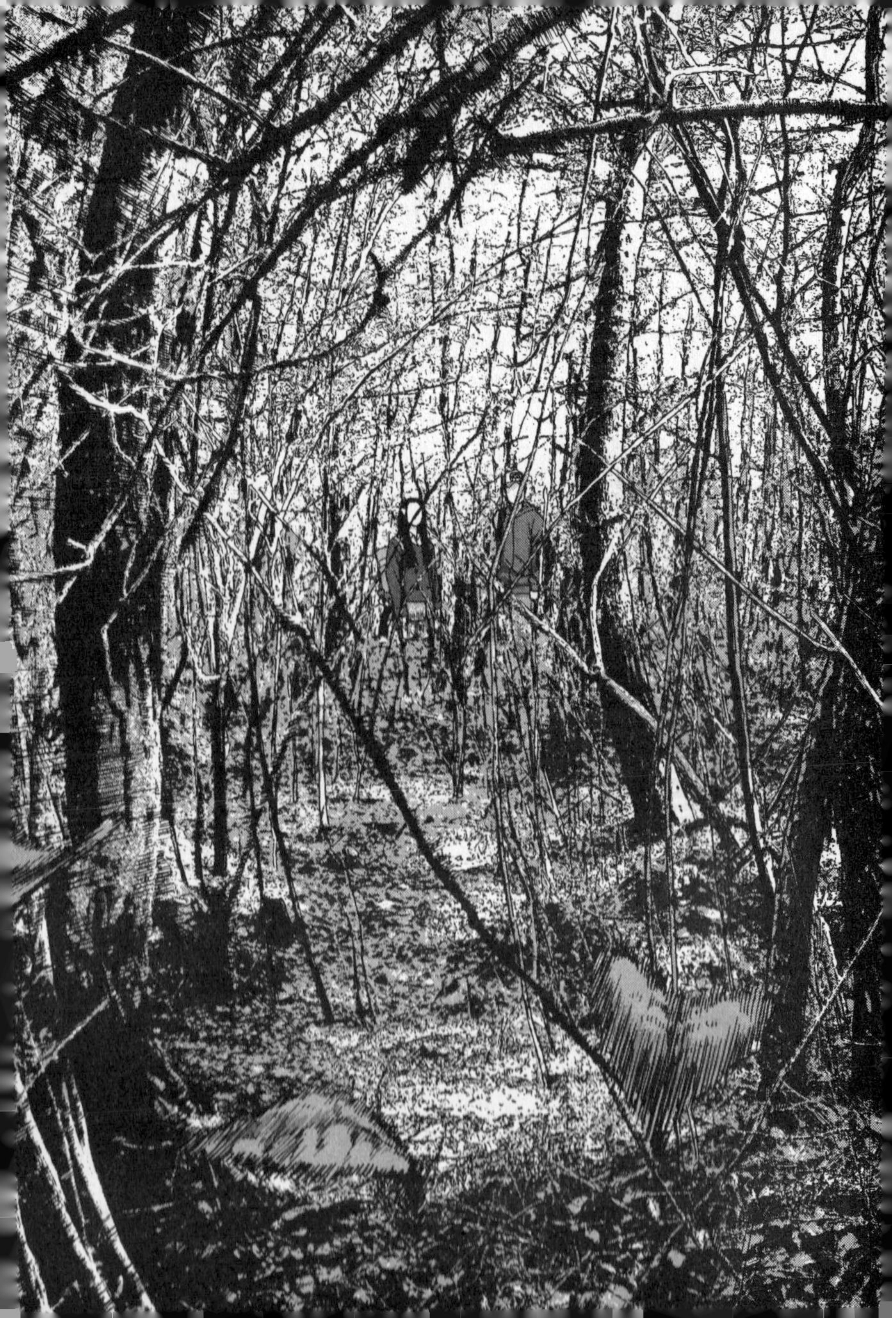

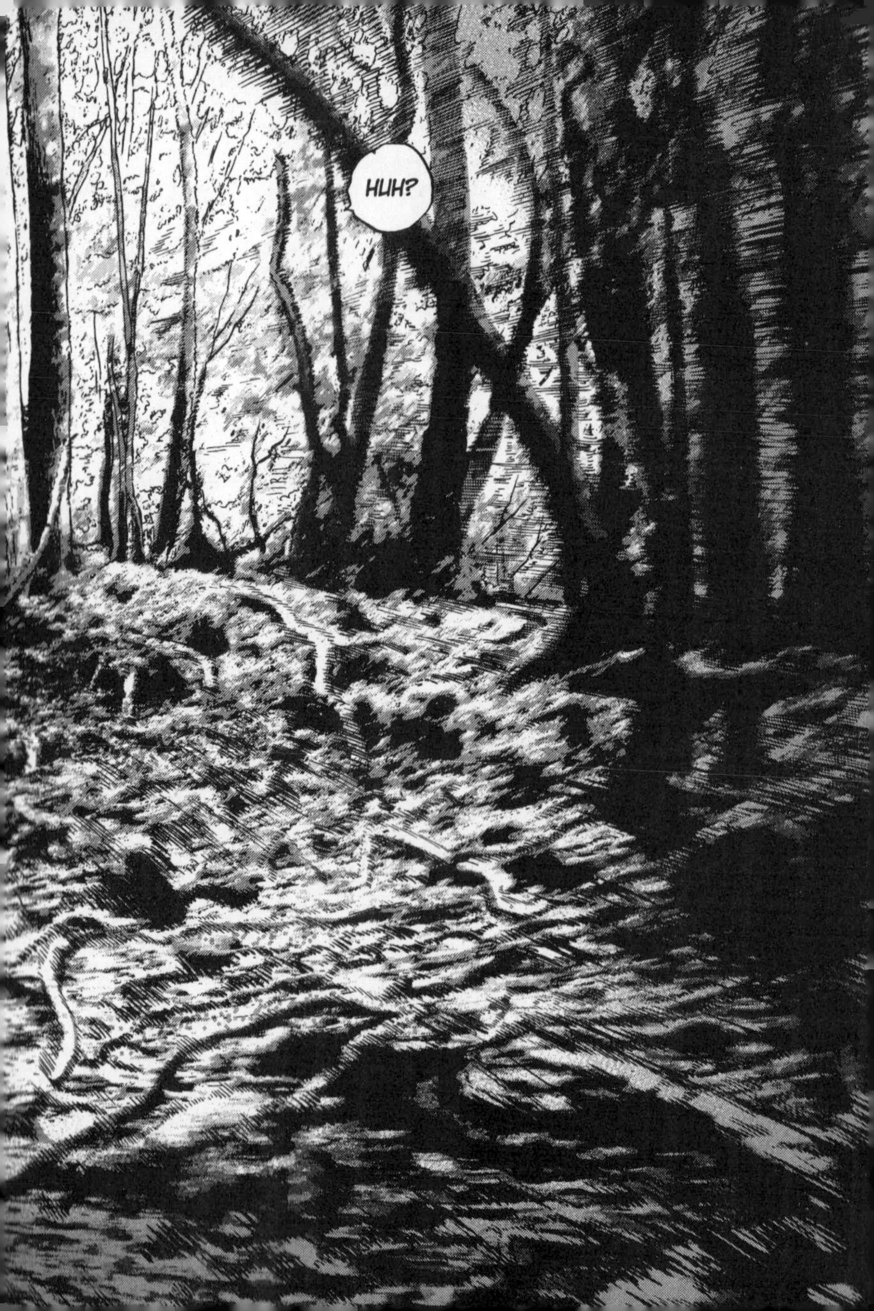
HUH?

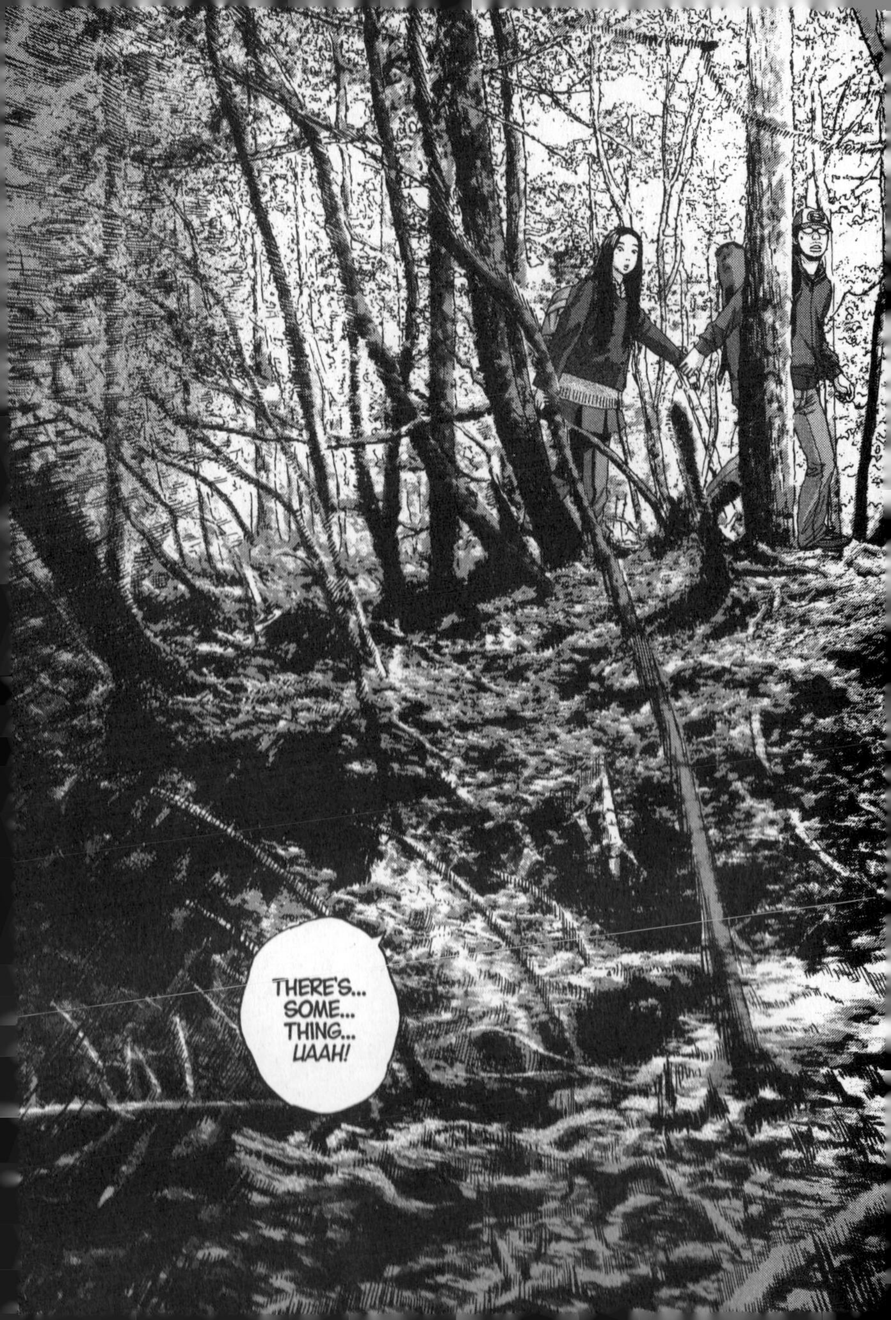
THERE'S... SOME... THING... UAAH!

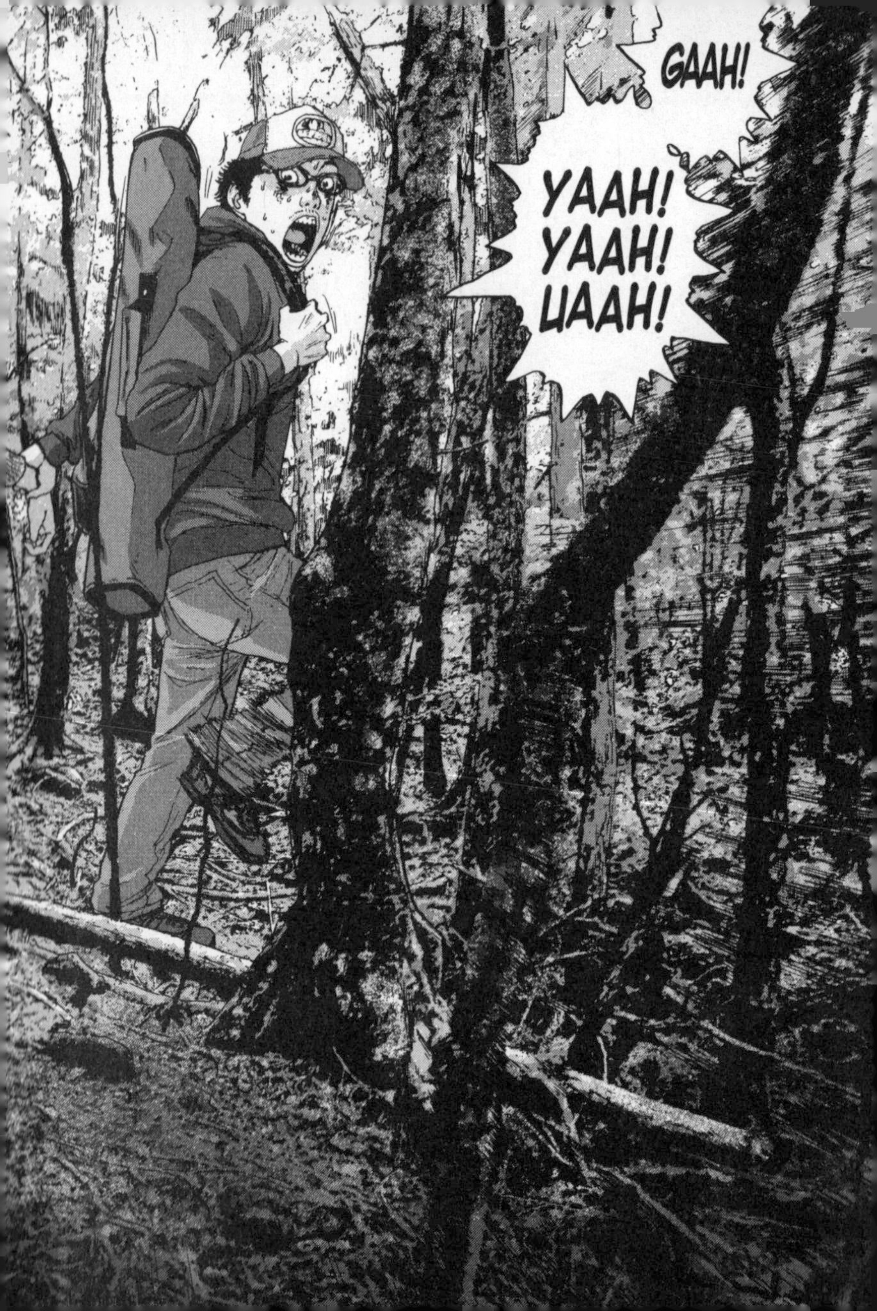
GAAH!
YAAH! YAAH! UAAH!

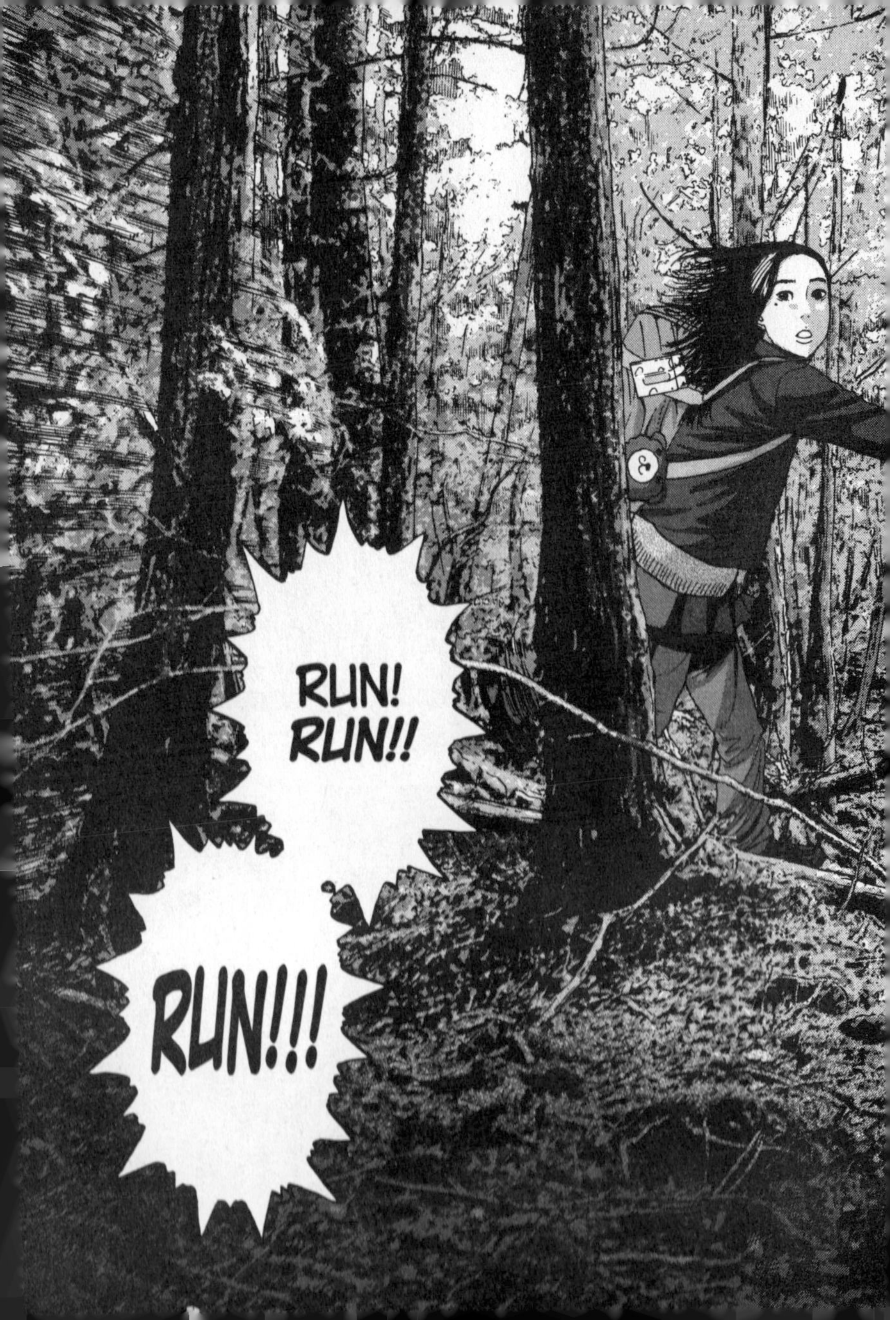
RUN! RUN!!
RUN!!!

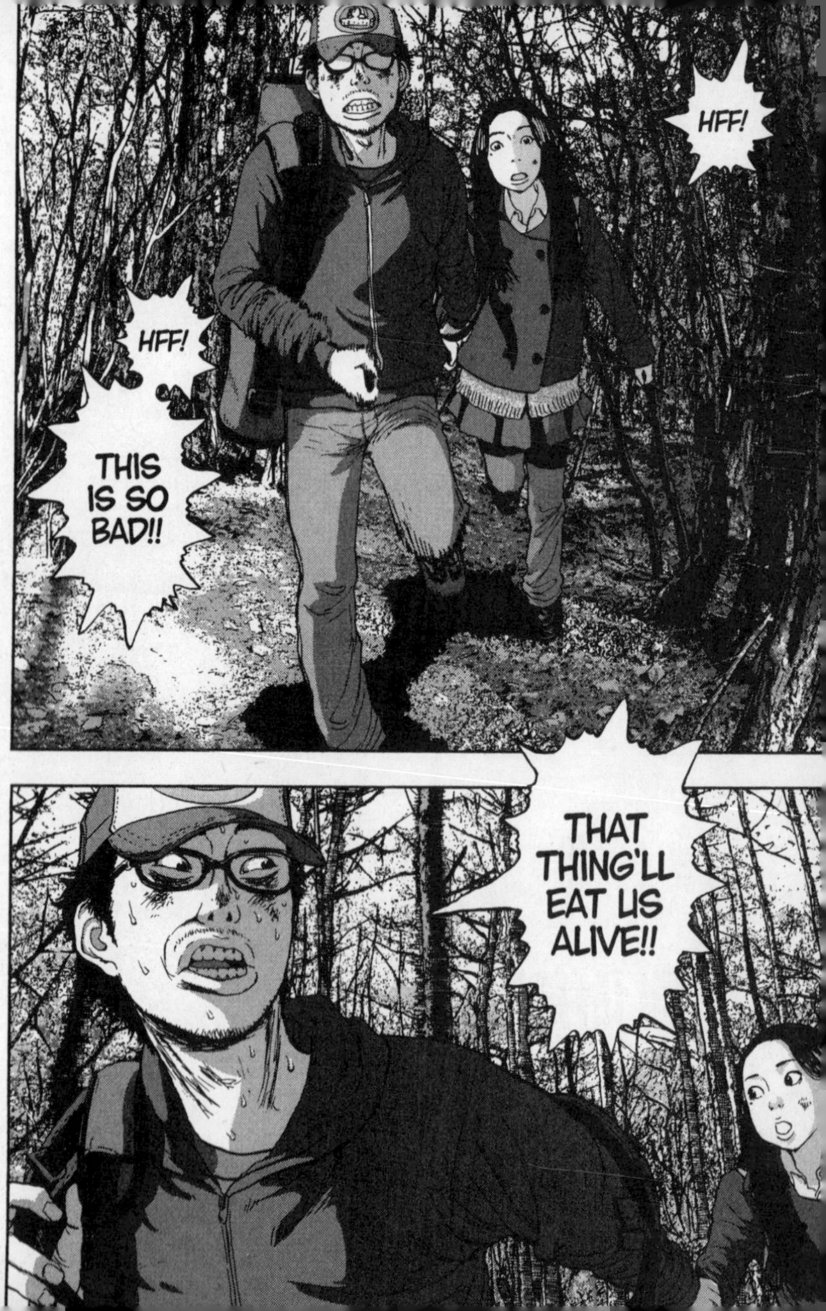
HFF!
HFF!
THIS IS SO BAD!!
THAT THING'LL EAT US ALIVE!!

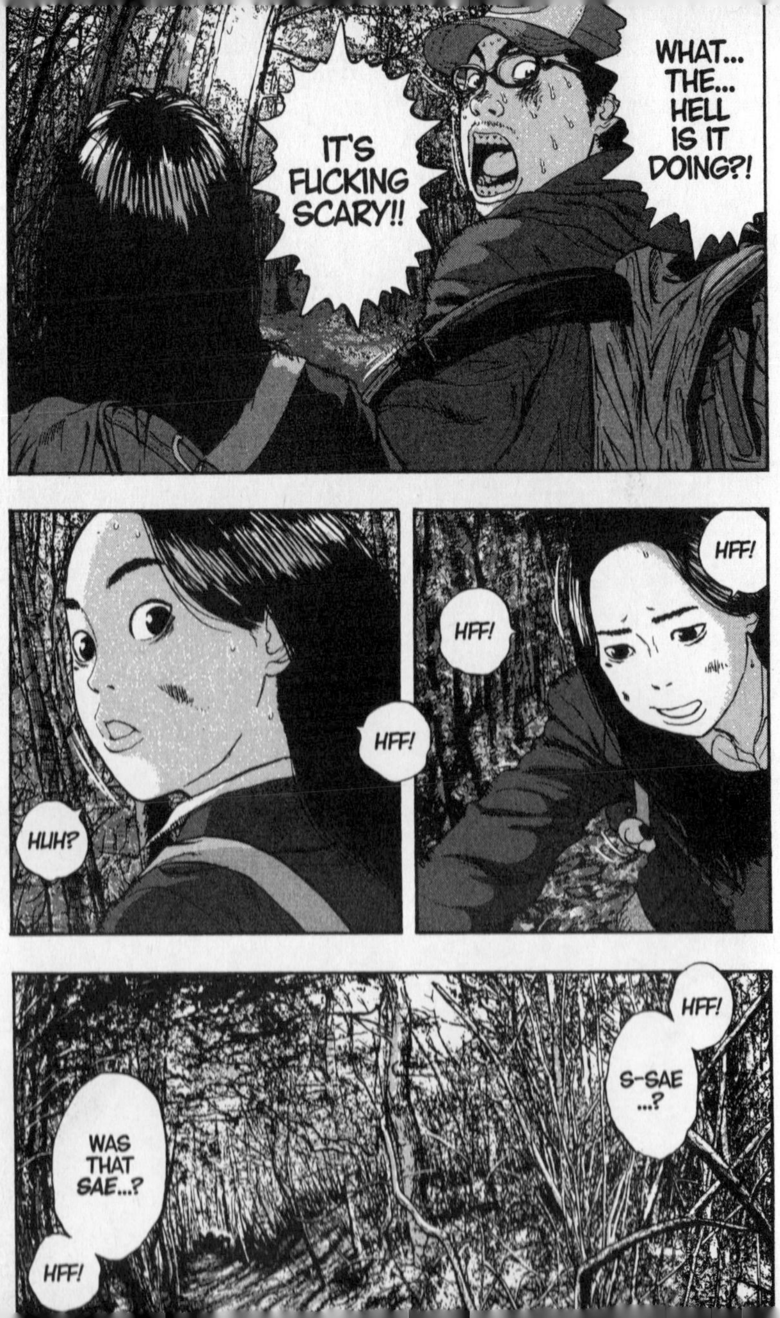
WHAT... THE... HELL IS IT DOING?!
IT'S FUCKING SCARY!!
HFF!
HFF!
HFF!
HUH?
HFF!
S-SAE ...?
WAS THAT SAE...?
HFF!

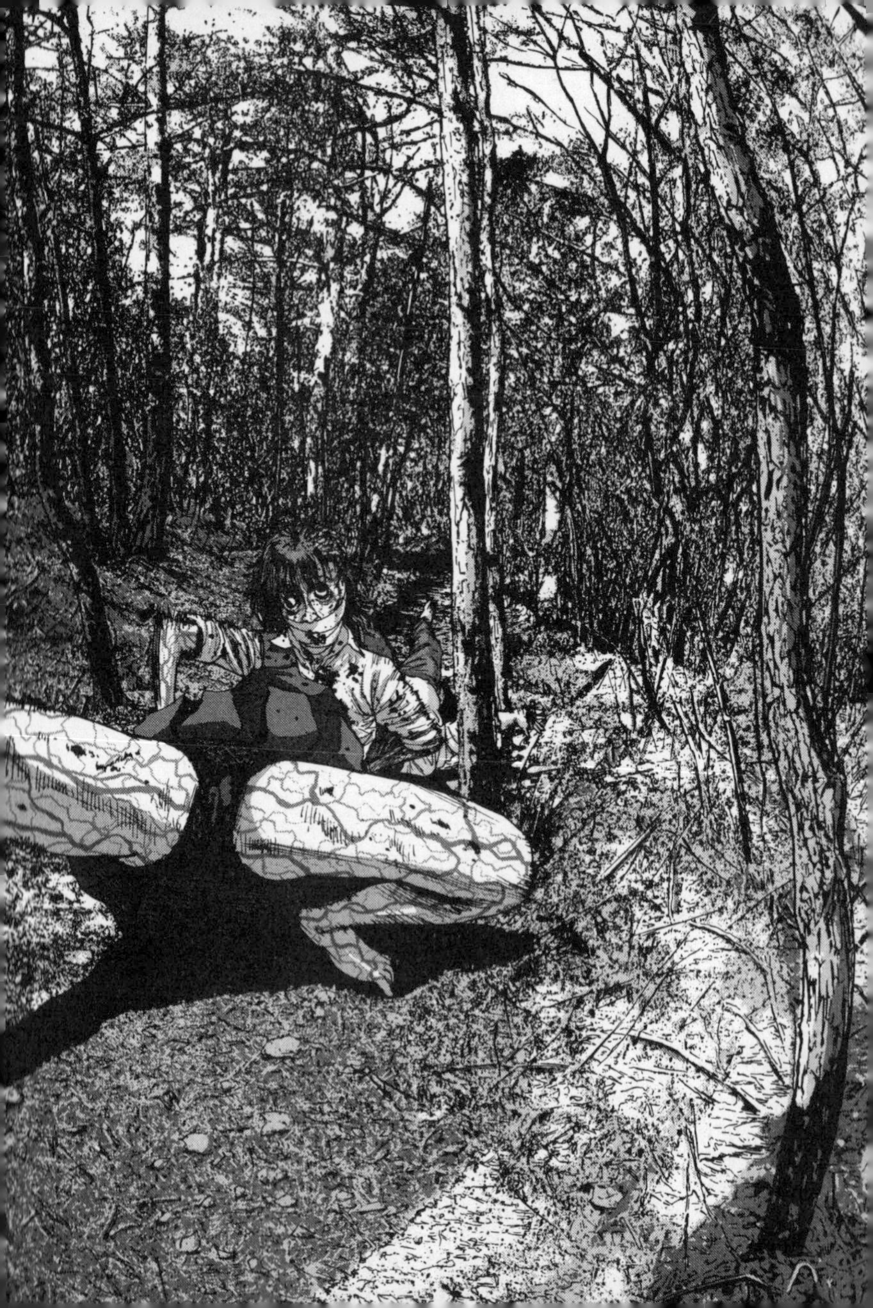

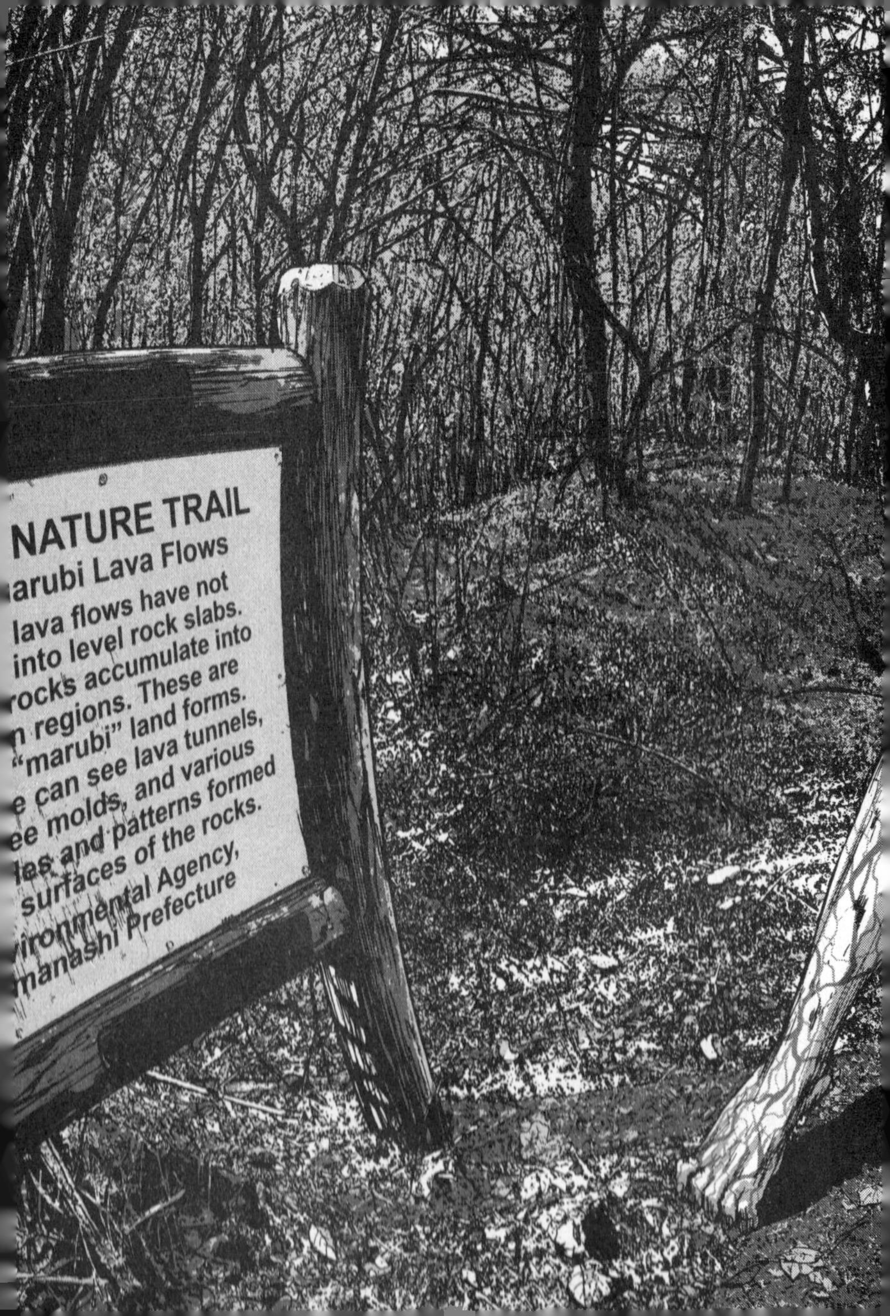
NATURE TRAIL
arubi Lava Flows
lava flows have not
into level rock slabs.
rocks accumulate into
n regions. These are
"marubi" land forms.
e can see lava tunnels,
ee molds, and various
les and patterns formed
surfaces of the rocks.
ironmental Agency,
manashi Prefecture

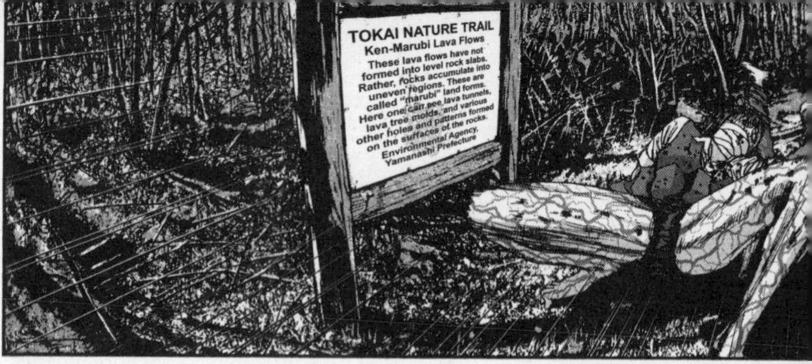
TOKAI NATURE TRAIL
Ken-Marubi Lava Flows
These lava flows have not formed into level rock slabs. Rather, rocks accumulate into uneven regions. These are called "marubi" land forms. Here one can see lava tunnels, lava tree molds, and various other holes and patterns formed on the surfaces of the rocks.
Environmental Agency, Yamanashi Prefecture

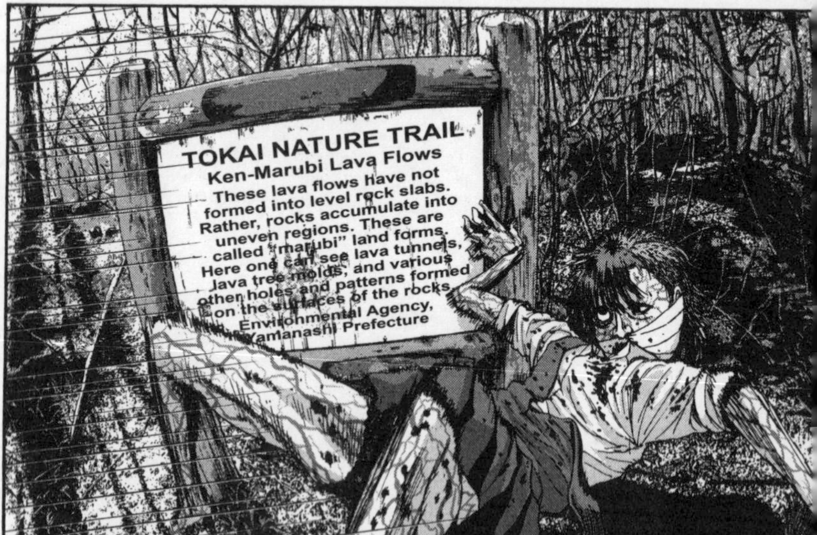
TOKAI NATURE TRAIL
Ken-Marubi Lava Flows
These lava flows have not formed into level rock slabs. Rather, rocks accumulate into uneven regions. These are called "marubi" land forms. Here one can see lava tunnels, lava tree molds, and various other holes and patterns formed on the surfaces of the rocks.
Environmental Agency, Yamanashi Prefecture

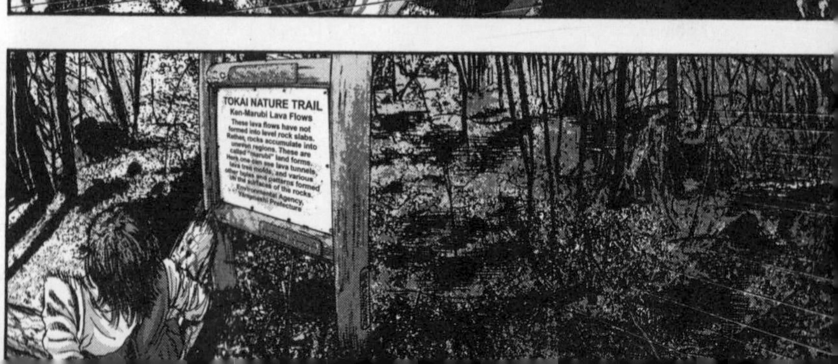
TOKAI NATURE TRAIL
Ken-Marubi Lava Flows
These lava flows have not formed into level rock slabs. Rather, rocks accumulate into uneven regions. These are called "marubi" land forms. Here one can see lava tunnels, lava tree molds, and various other holes and patterns formed on the surfaces of the rocks.
Environmental Agency, Yamanashi Prefecture

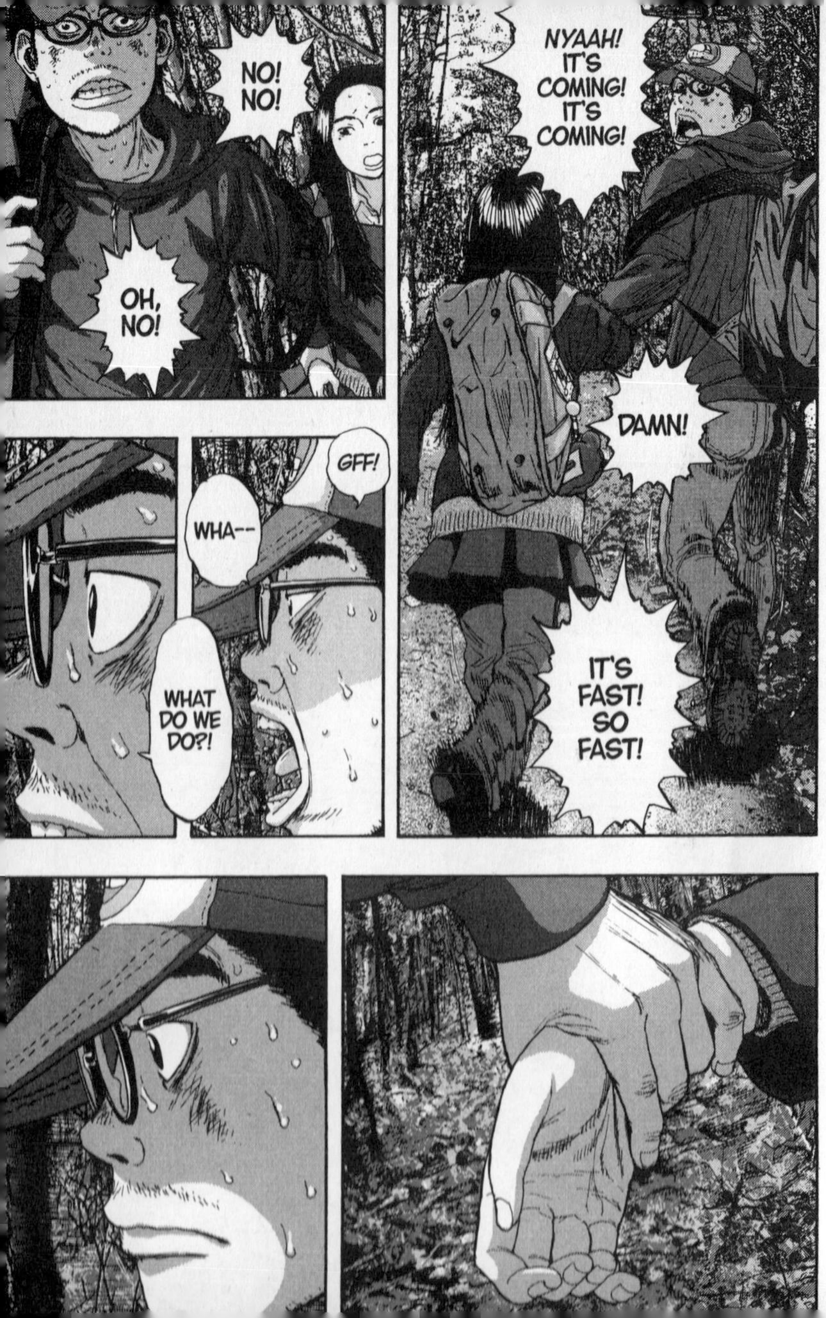
NYAAH! IT'S COMING! IT'S COMING!
DAMN!
IT'S FAST! SO FAST!
NO! NO!
OH, NO!
GFF!
WHA--
WHAT DO WE DO?!

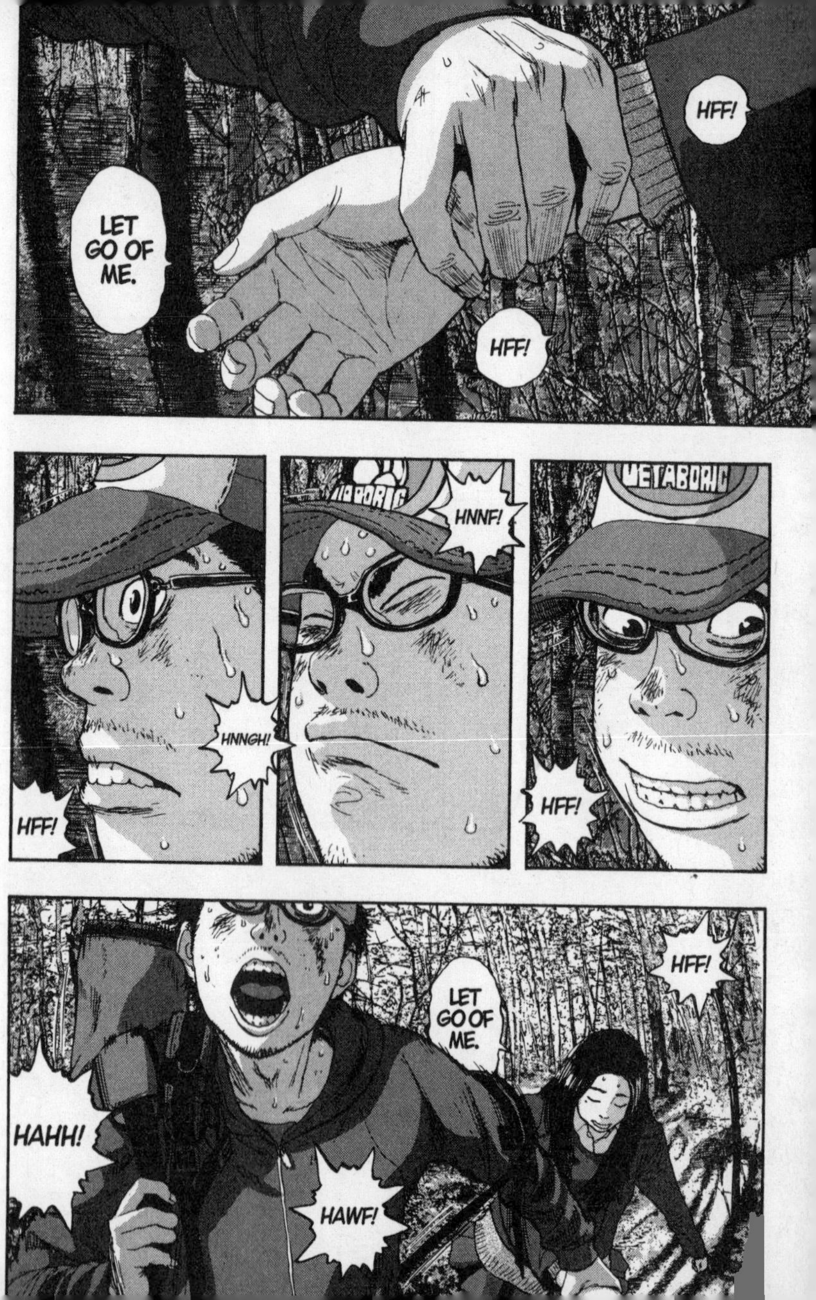
HFF!
LET GO OF ME.
HFF!
METABORIC
HFF!
HNNF!
HNNGH!
HFF!
HFF!
LET GO OF ME.
HAHH!
HAWF!

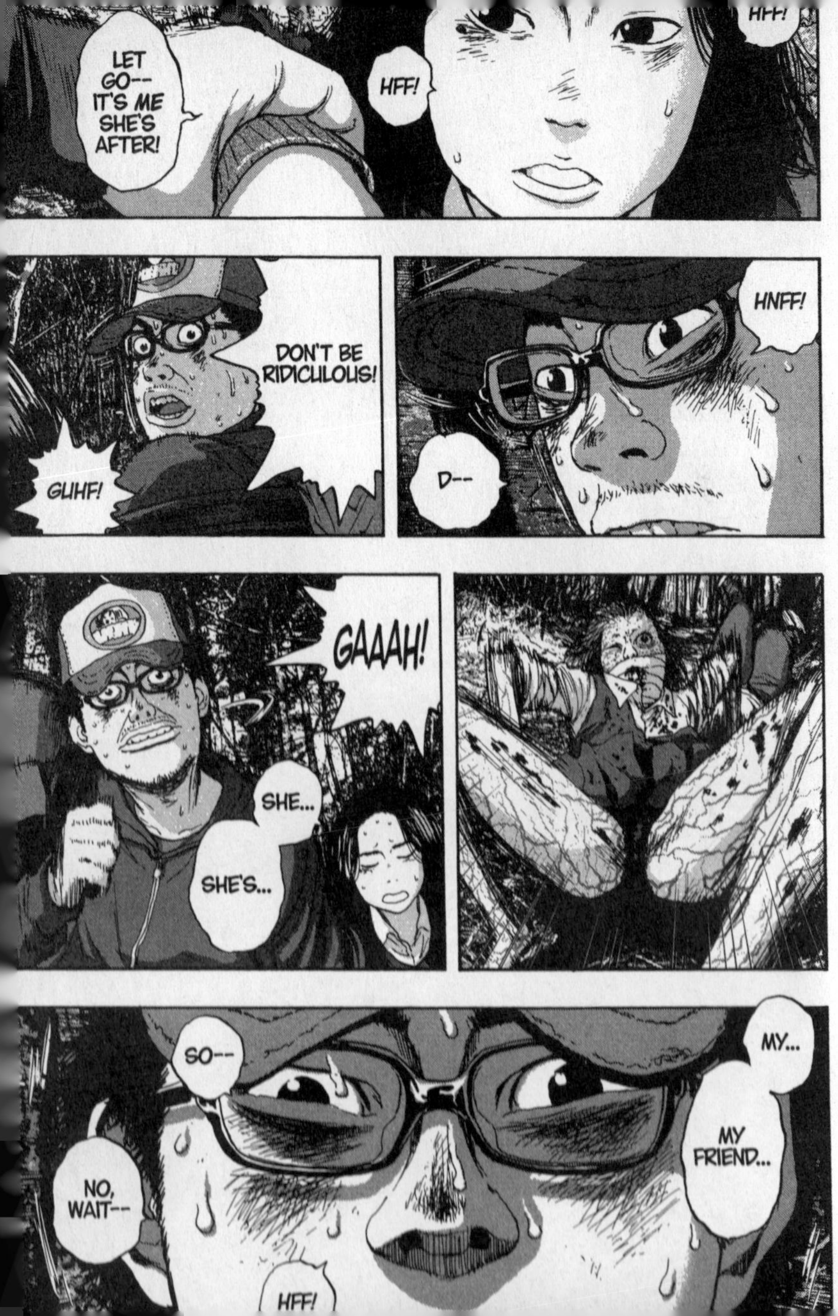
HFF!
HFF!
LET GO-- IT'S ME SHE'S AFTER!
HNFF!
D--
DON'T BE RIDICULOUS!
GUHF!
GAAAH!
SHE...
SHE'S...
MY...
MY FRIEND...
SO--
NO, WAIT--
HFF!

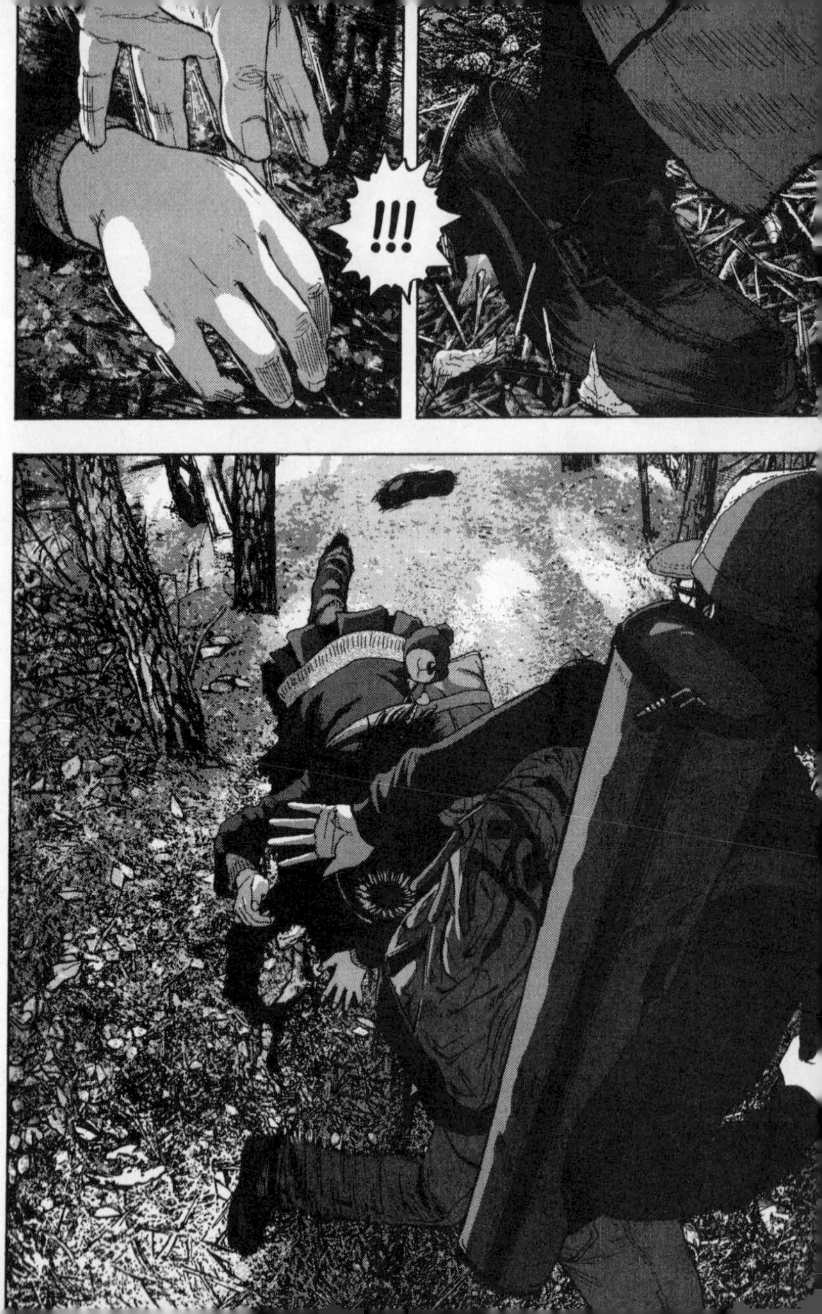
!!!

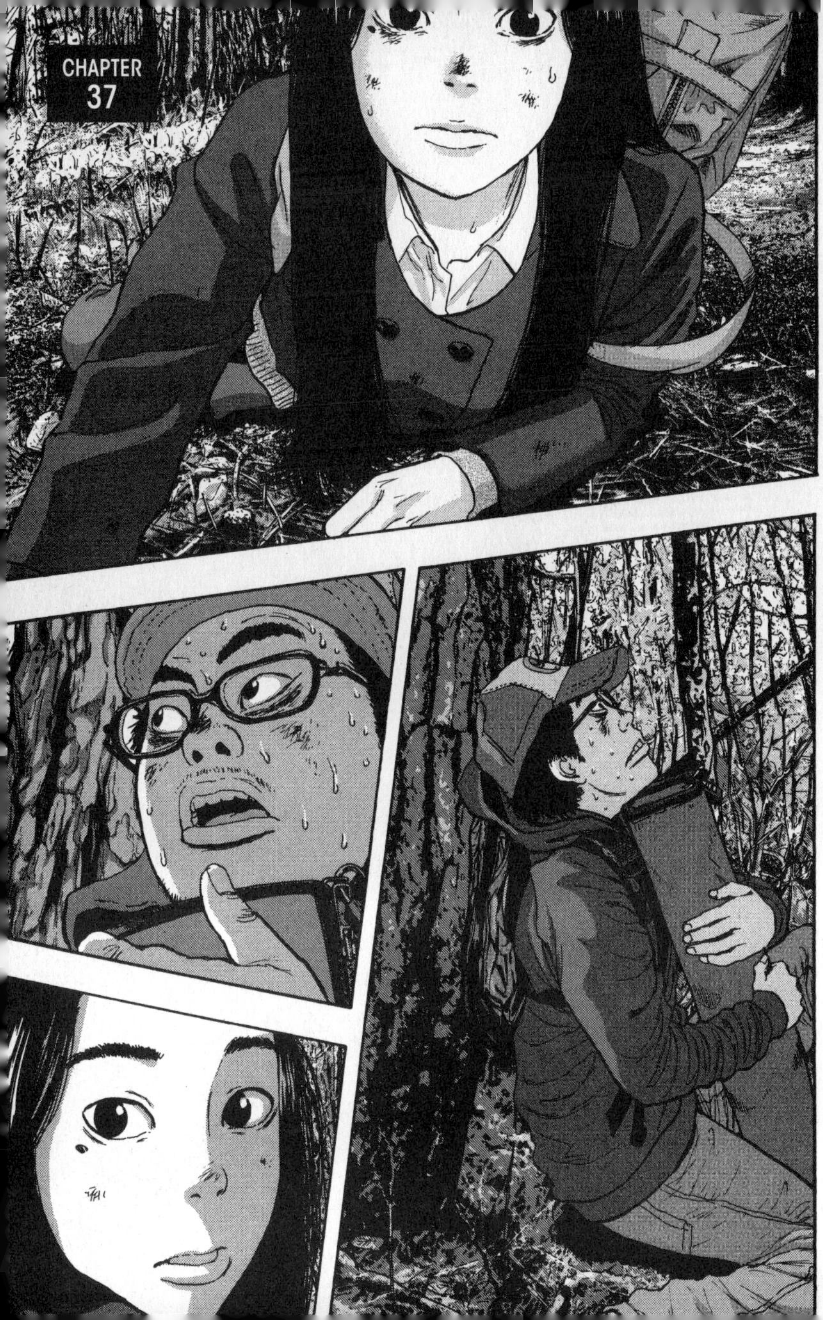
CHAPTER
37

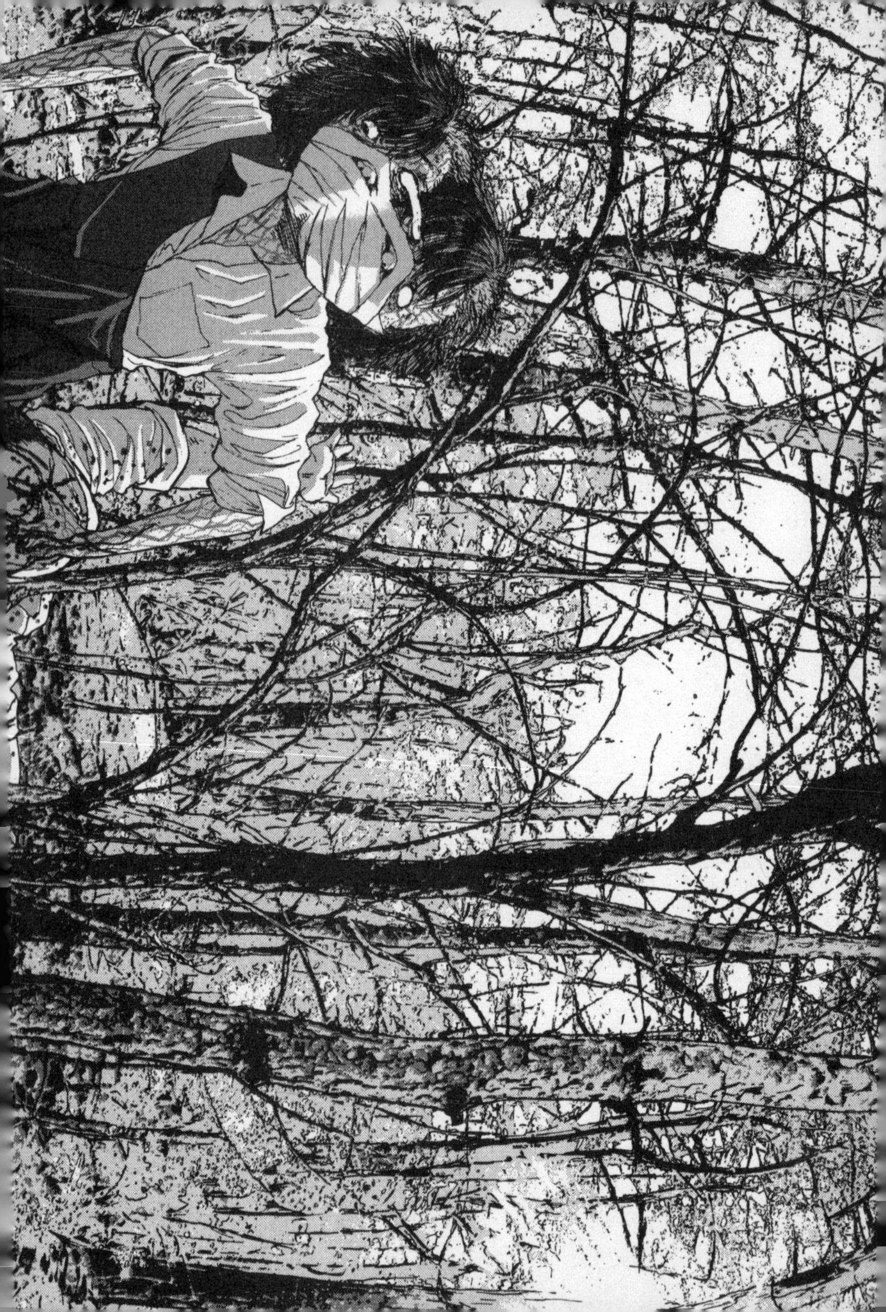

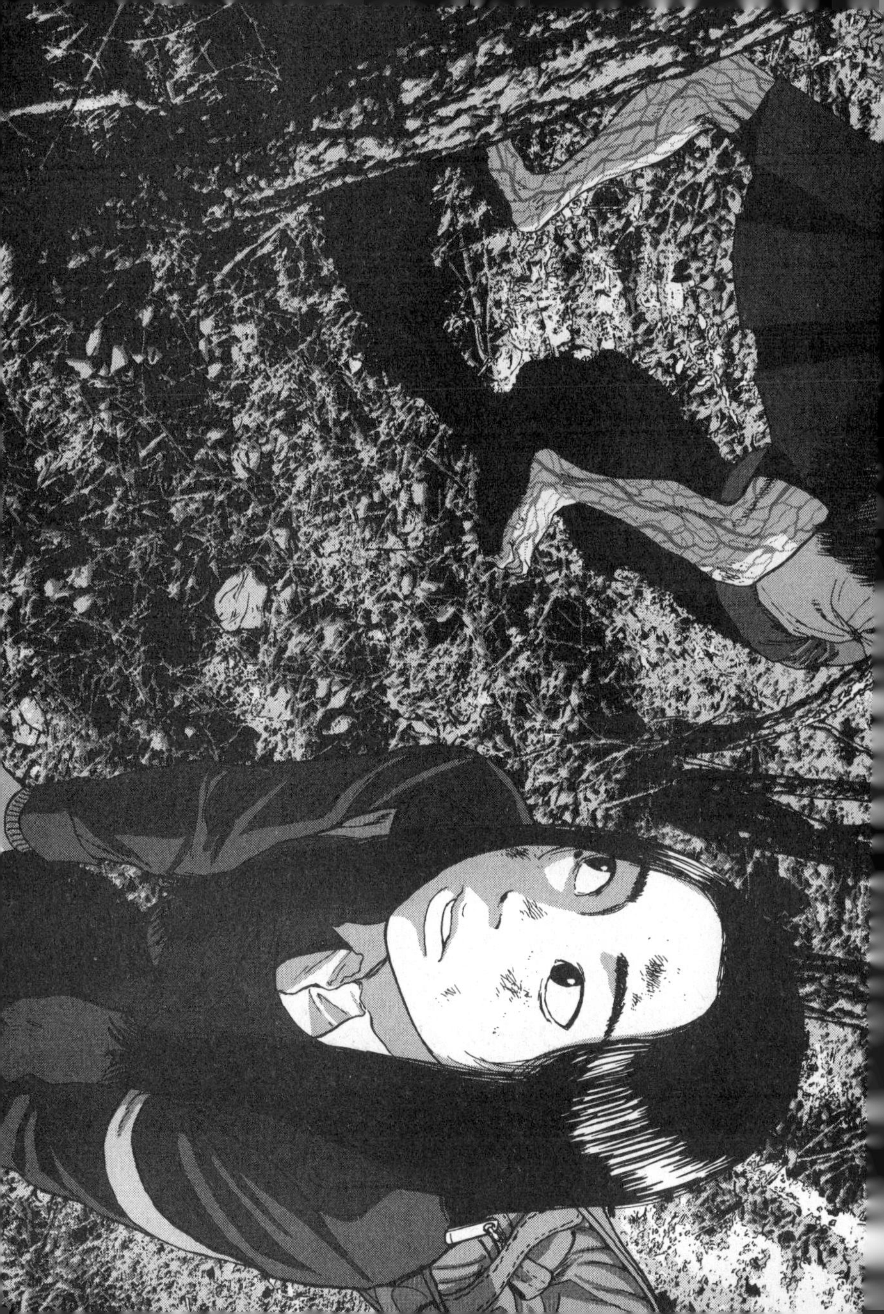

I AM
A HERO

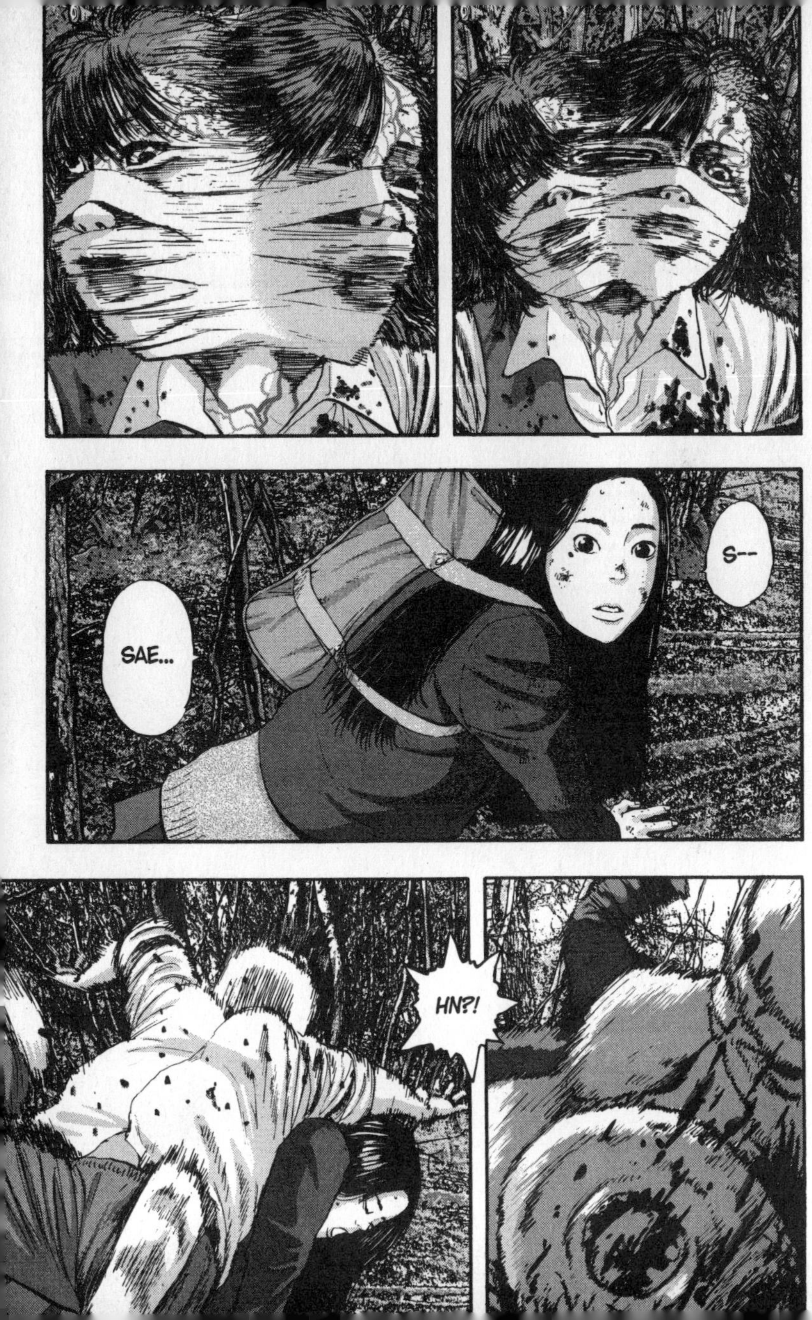
S--
SAE...
HN?!

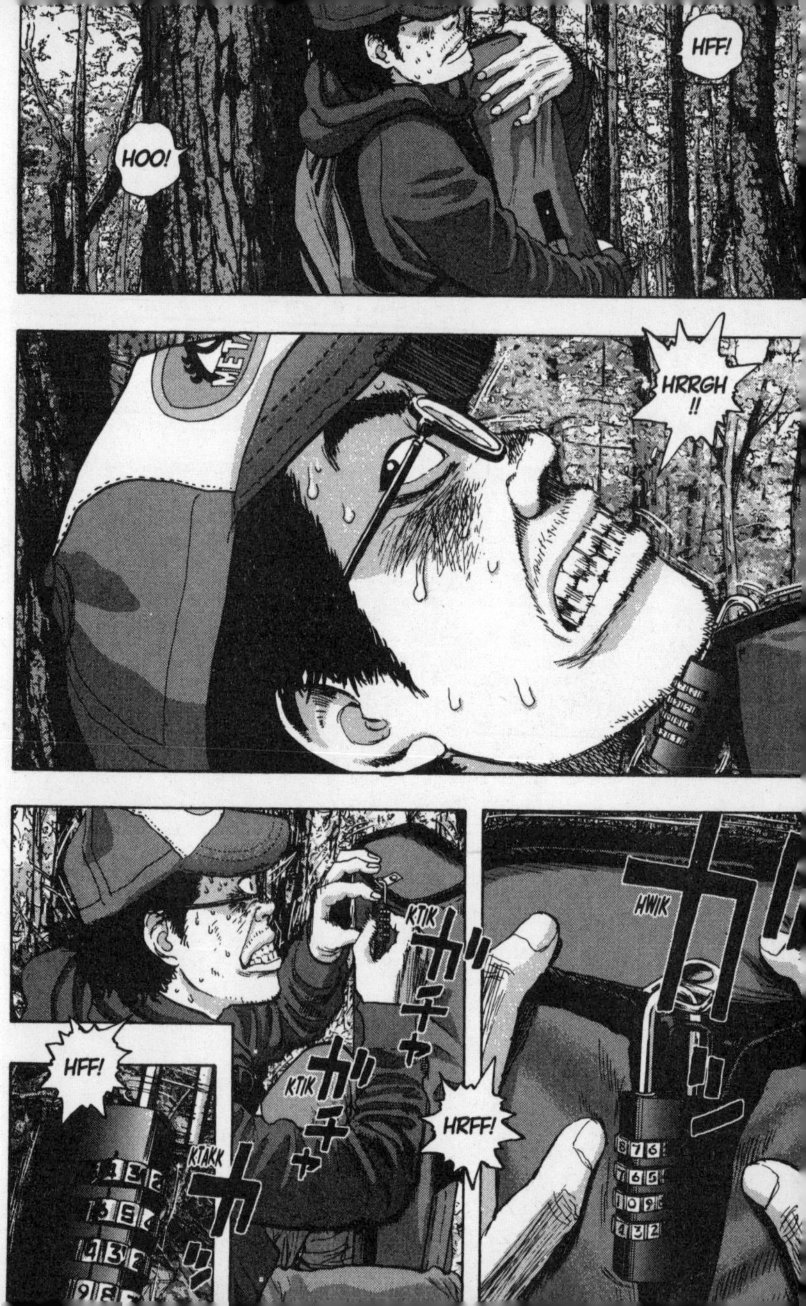
HFF!
HOO!
HRRGH !!
HWIK
KTIK
KTIK
HRFF!
HFF!
KTAKK

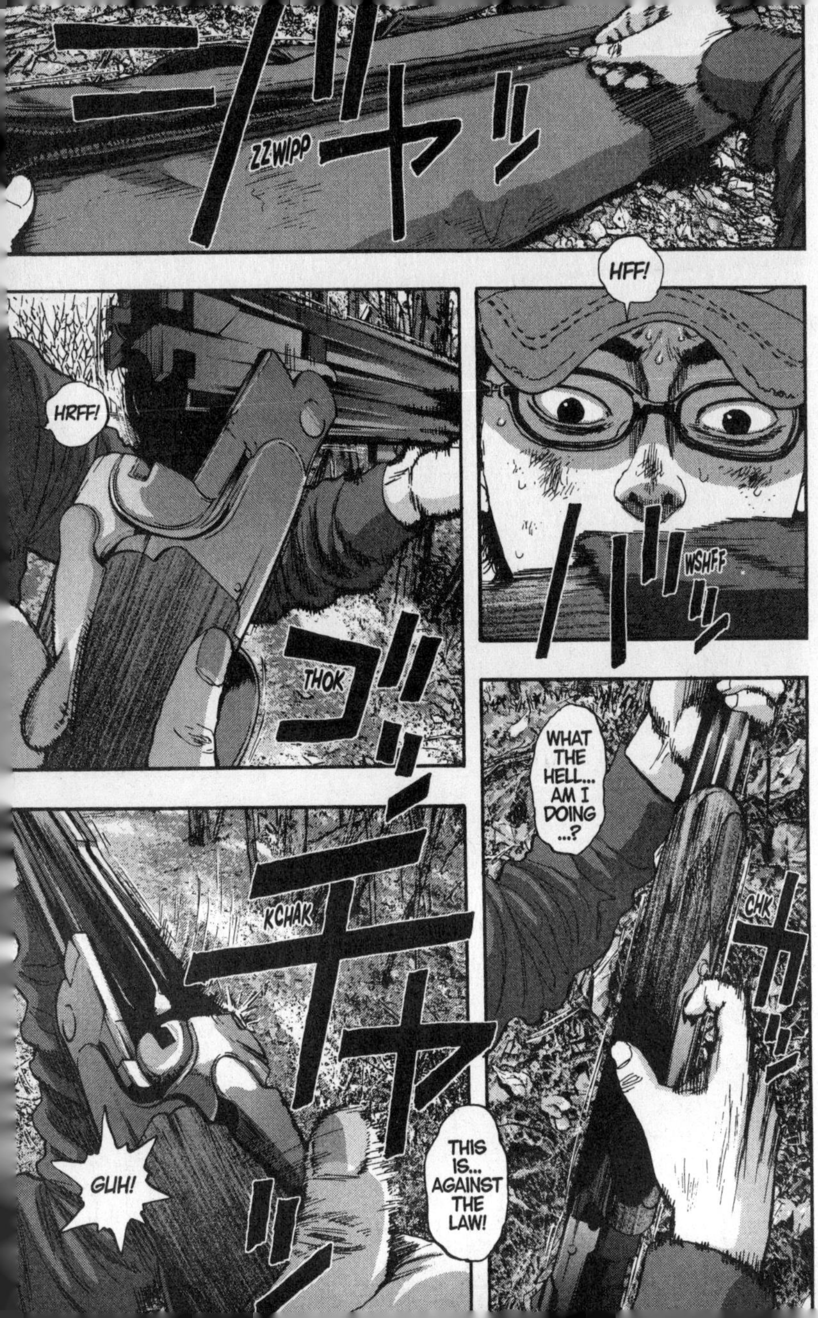
ZZWIPP
HFF!
WSHFF
HRFF!
THOK
WHAT THE HELL... AM I DOING ...?
CHK
THIS IS... AGAINST THE LAW!
KCHAK
GUH!

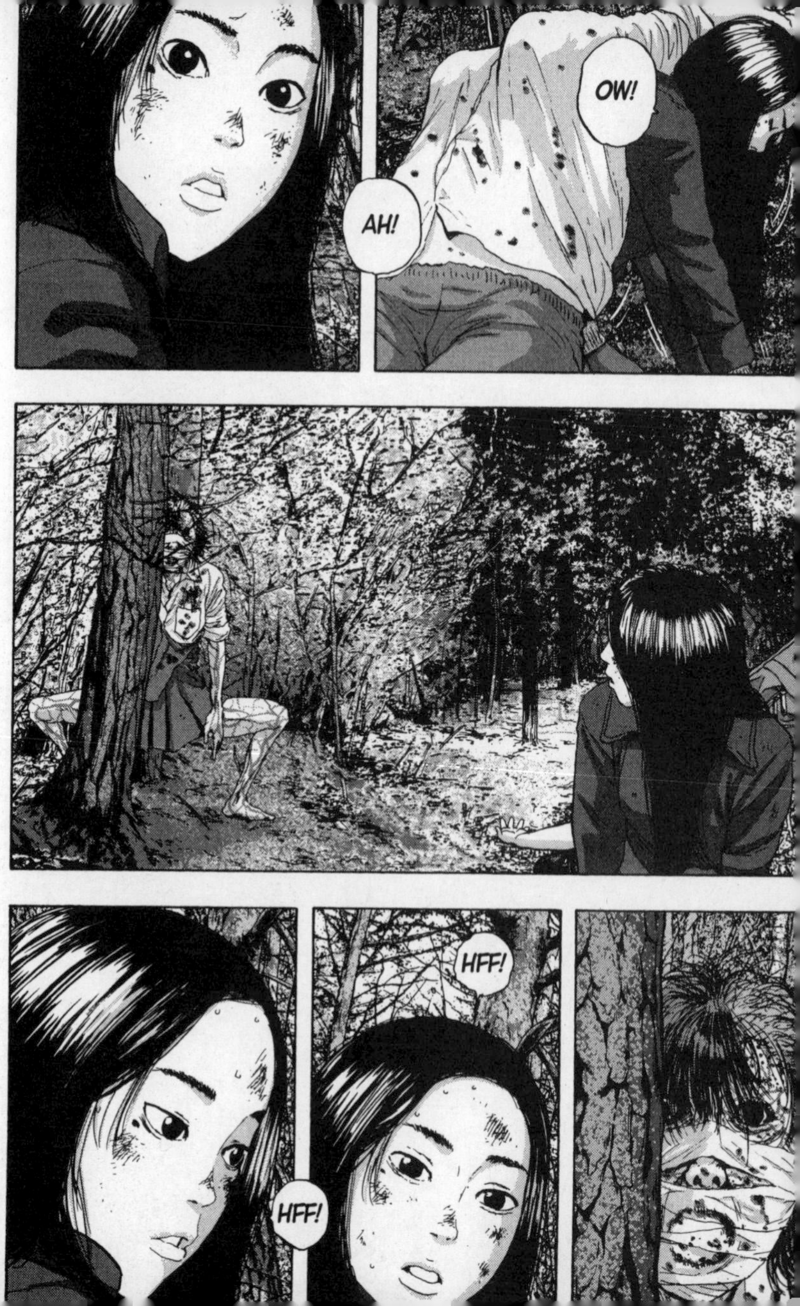
OW!
AH!
HFF!
HFF!

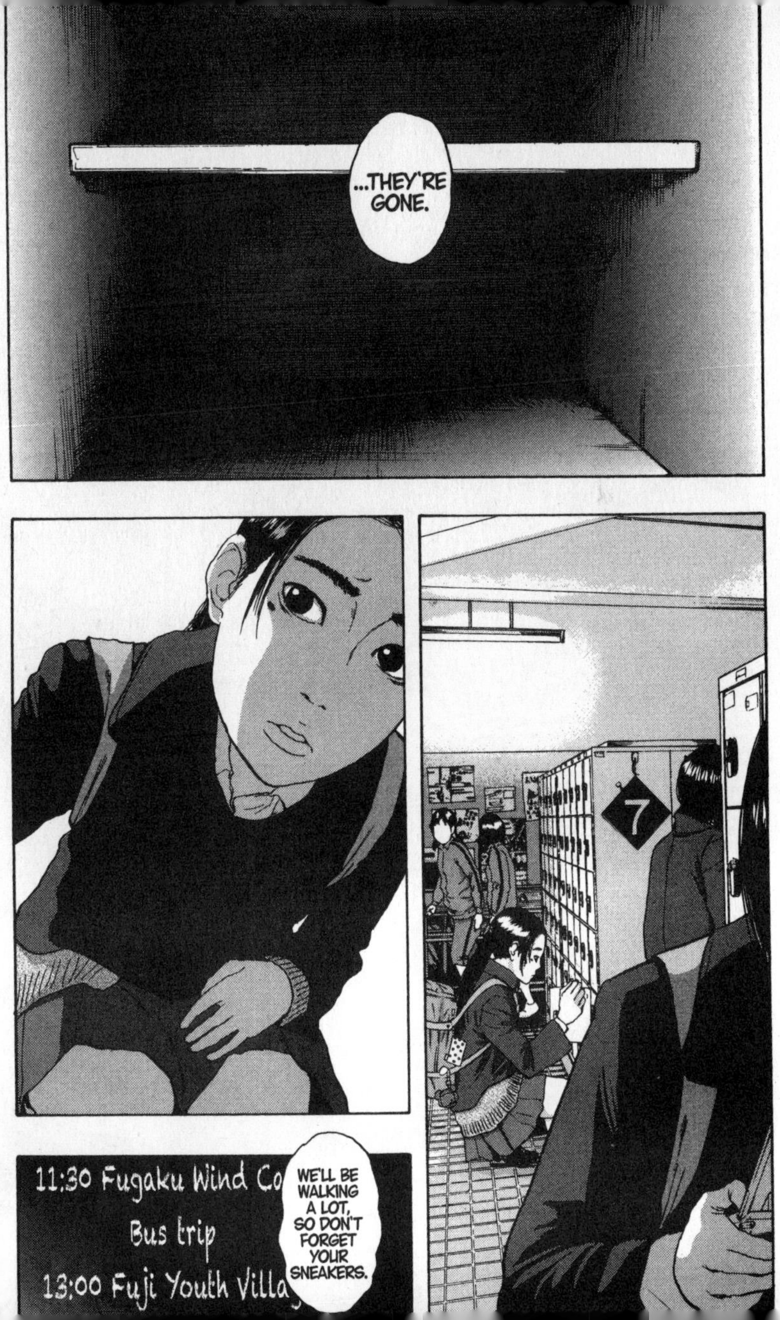
...THEY'RE GONE.
7
WE'LL BE WALKING A LOT, SO DON'T FORGET YOUR SNEAKERS.
11:30 Fugaku Wind Co
Bus trip
13:00 Fuji Youth Villa

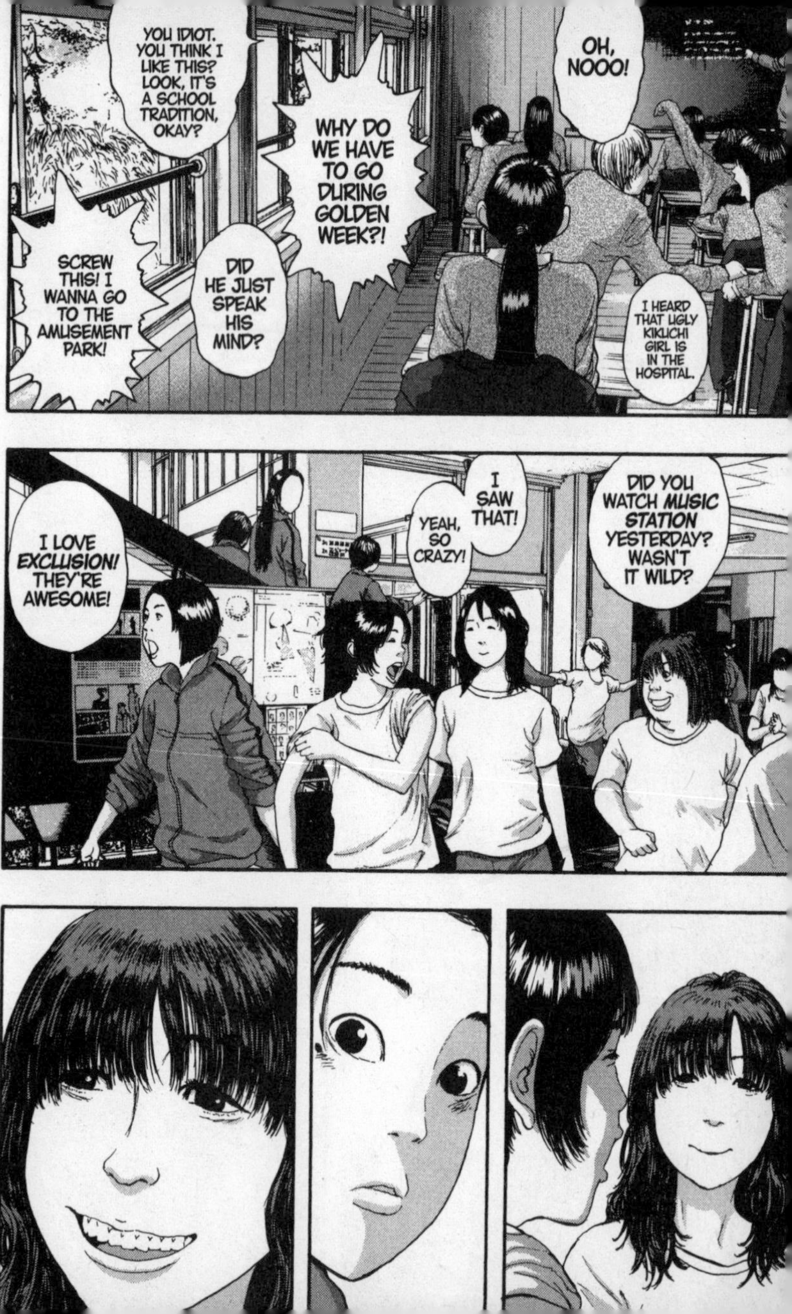
OH, NOOO!
WHY DO WE HAVE TO GO DURING GOLDEN WEEK?!
YOU IDIOT. YOU THINK I LIKE THIS? LOOK, IT'S A SCHOOL TRADITION, OKAY?
SCREW THIS! I WANNA GO TO THE AMUSEMENT PARK!
DID HE JUST SPEAK HIS MIND?
I HEARD THAT UGLY KIKUCHI GIRL IS IN THE HOSPITAL.
DID YOU WATCH *MUSIC STATION* YESTERDAY? WASN'T IT WILD?
I SAW THAT!
YEAH, SO CRAZY!
I LOVE *EXCLUSION*! THEY'RE AWESOME!

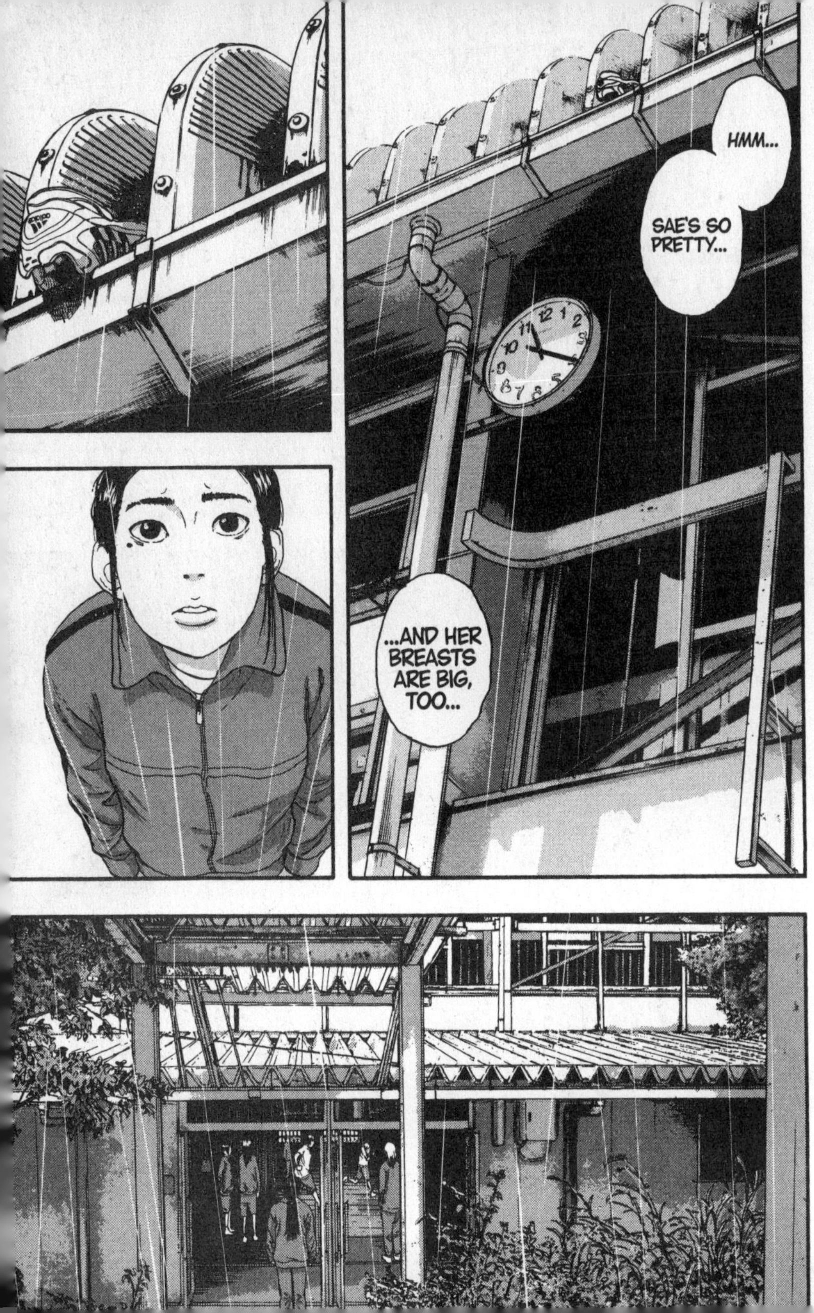
HMM...
SAE'S SO PRETTY...
...AND HER BREASTS ARE BIG, TOO...

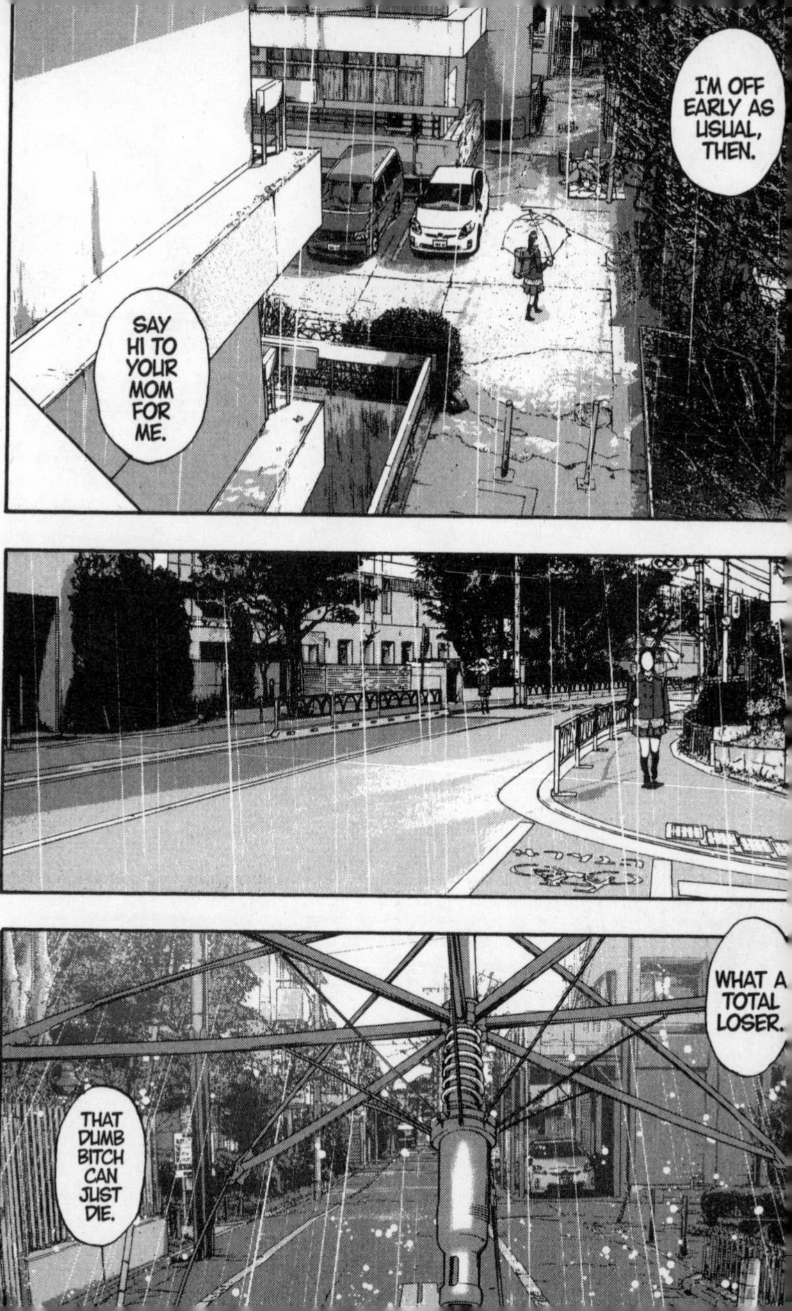
I'M OFF EARLY AS USUAL, THEN.
SAY HI TO YOUR MOM FOR ME.
WHAT A TOTAL LOSER.
THAT DUMB BITCH CAN JUST DIE.

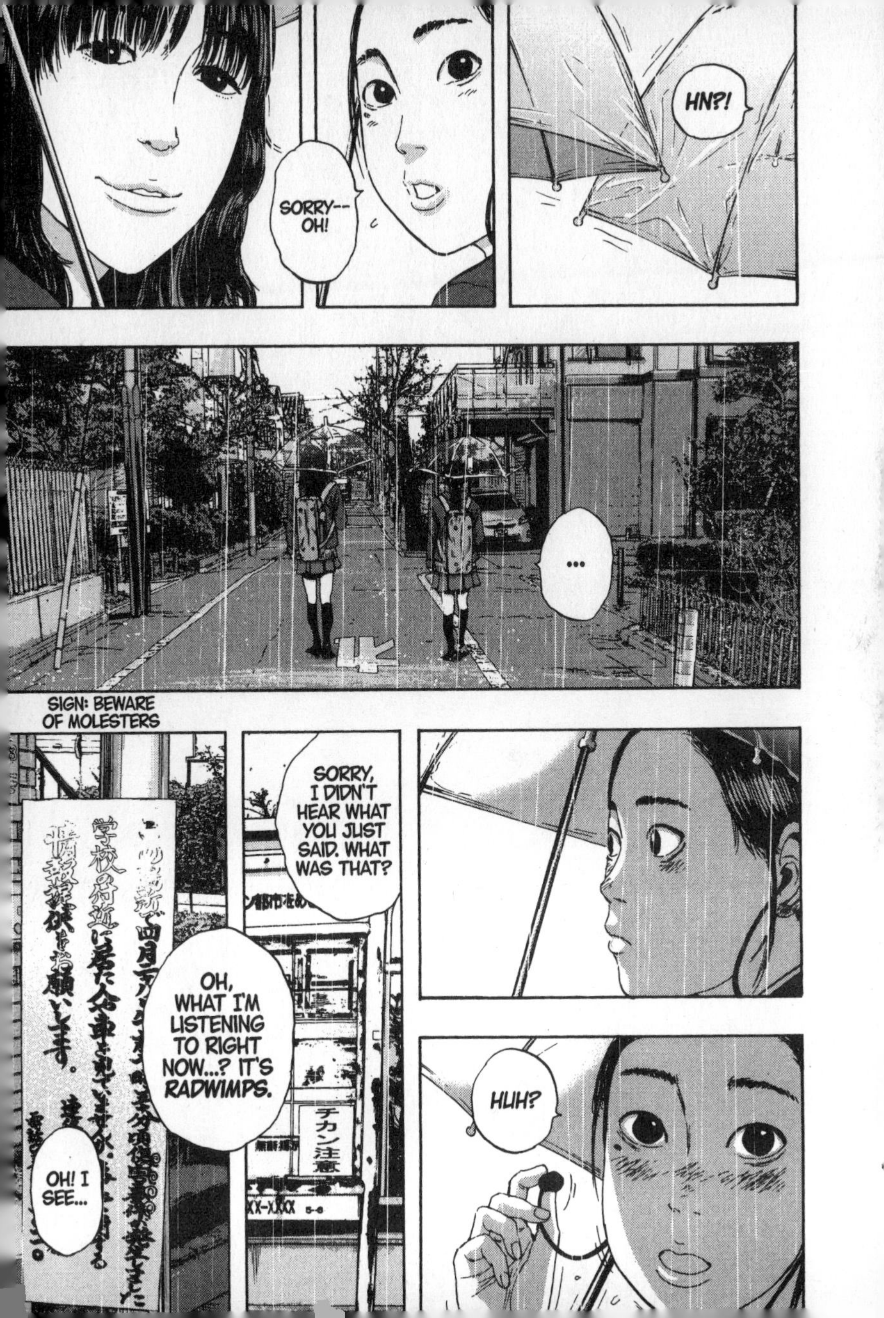
HN?!
SORRY-- OH!
...
SIGN: BEWARE OF MOLESTERS
SORRY, I DIDN'T HEAR WHAT YOU JUST SAID. WHAT WAS THAT?
OH, WHAT I'M LISTENING TO RIGHT NOW...? IT'S RADWIMPS.
HUH?
OH! I SEE...
チカン注意

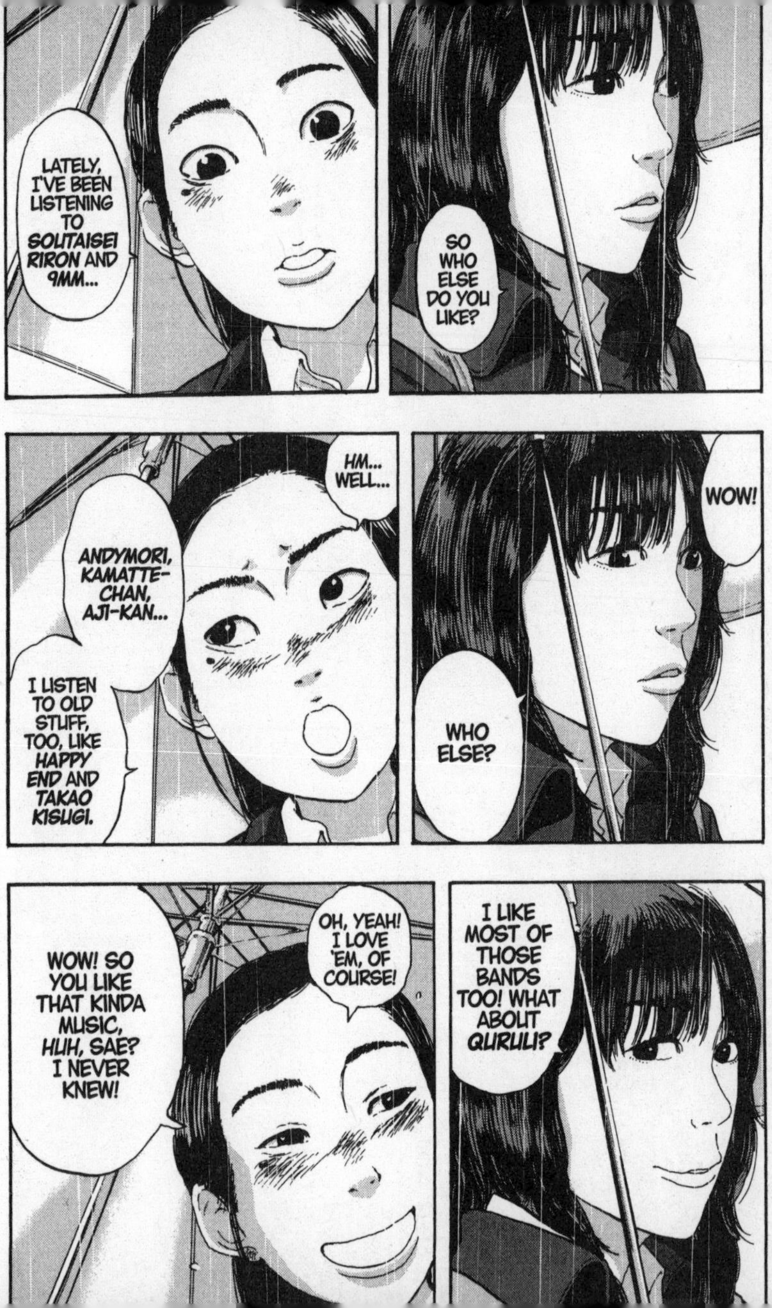
SO WHO ELSE DO YOU LIKE?
LATELY, I'VE BEEN LISTENING TO SOUTAISEI RIRON AND 9MM...
WOW!
WHO ELSE?
HM... WELL...
ANDYMORI, KAMATTE-CHAN, AJI-KAN...
I LISTEN TO OLD STUFF, TOO, LIKE HAPPY END AND TAKAO KISUGI.
I LIKE MOST OF THOSE BANDS TOO! WHAT ABOUT QURULI?
OH, YEAH! I LOVE 'EM, OF COURSE!
WOW! SO YOU LIKE THAT KINDA MUSIC, HUH, SAE? I NEVER KNEW!

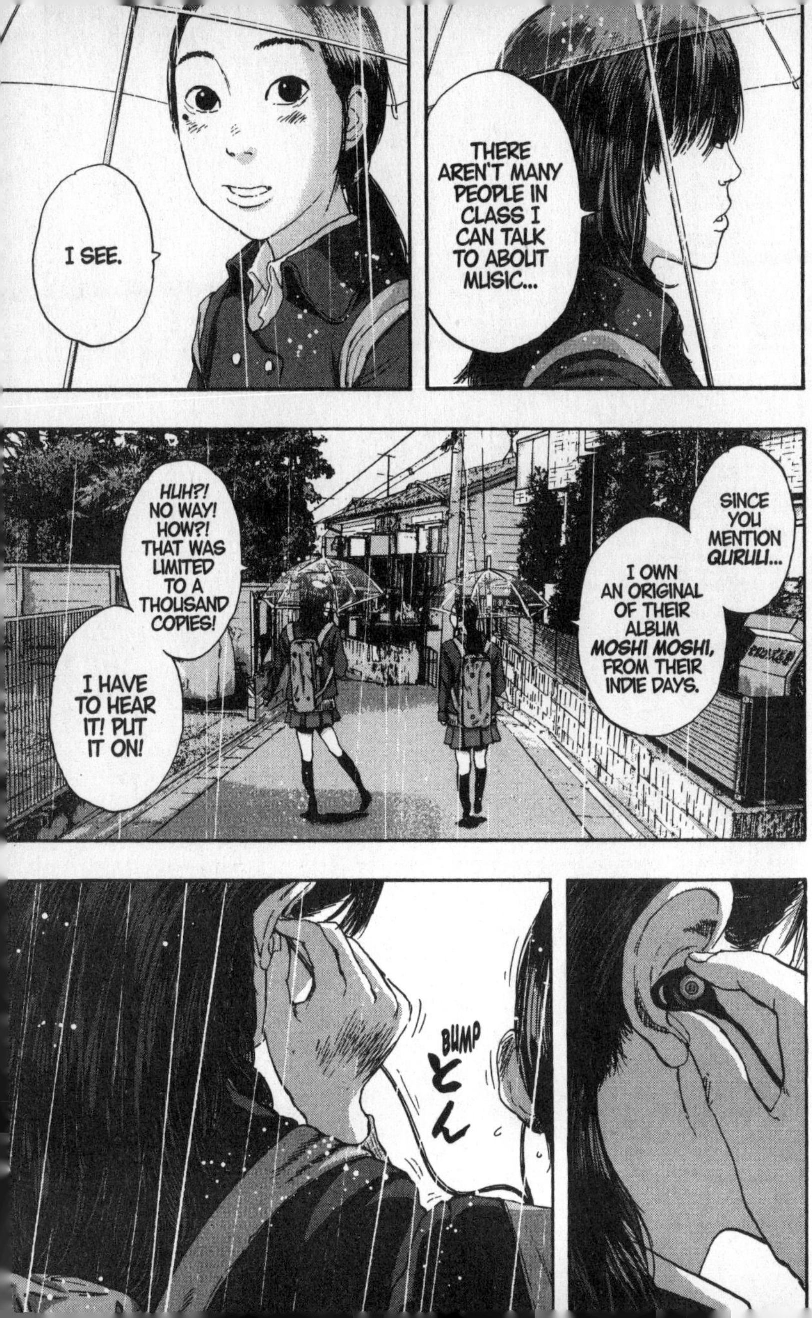
THERE AREN'T MANY PEOPLE IN CLASS I CAN TALK TO ABOUT MUSIC...
I SEE.
SINCE YOU MENTION *QURULI*...
I OWN AN ORIGINAL OF THEIR ALBUM *MOSHI MOSHI*, FROM THEIR INDIE DAYS.
HUH?! NO WAY! HOW?! THAT WAS LIMITED TO A THOUSAND COPIES!
I HAVE TO HEAR IT! PUT IT ON!
BUMP
とん

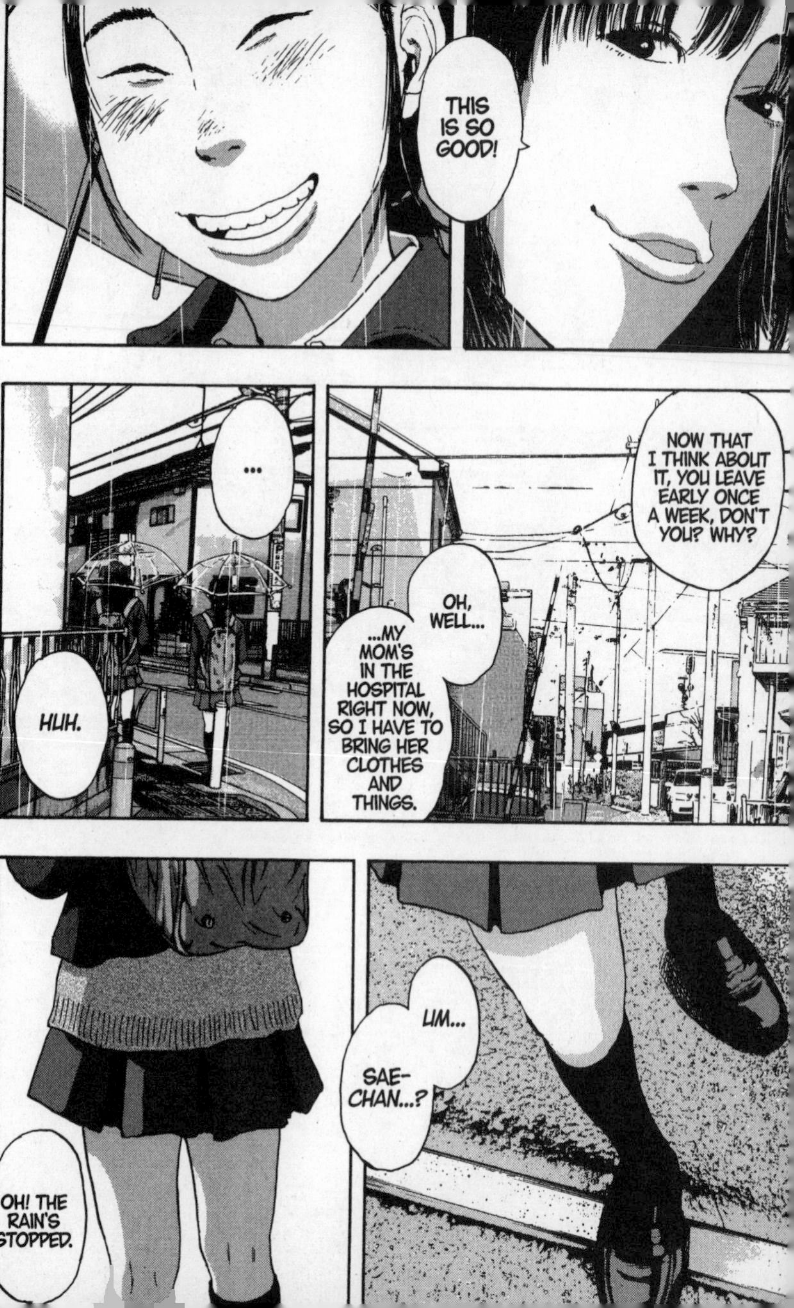
THIS IS SO GOOD!
NOW THAT I THINK ABOUT IT, YOU LEAVE EARLY ONCE A WEEK, DON'T YOU? WHY?
OH, WELL...
...MY MOM'S IN THE HOSPITAL RIGHT NOW, SO I HAVE TO BRING HER CLOTHES AND THINGS.
...
HUH.
UM...
SAE-CHAN...?
OH! THE RAIN'S STOPPED.

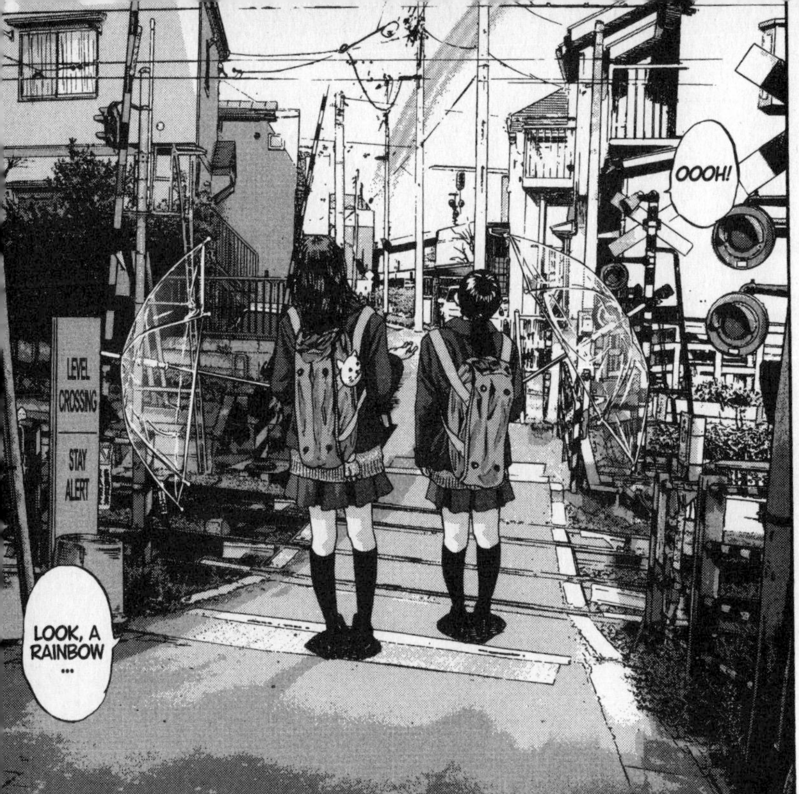
OOOH!
LEVEL CROSSING
STAY ALERT
LOOK, A RAINBOW ...
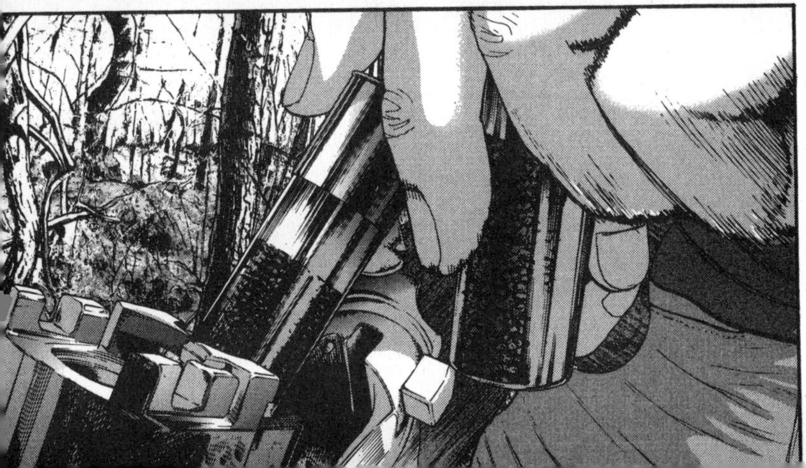

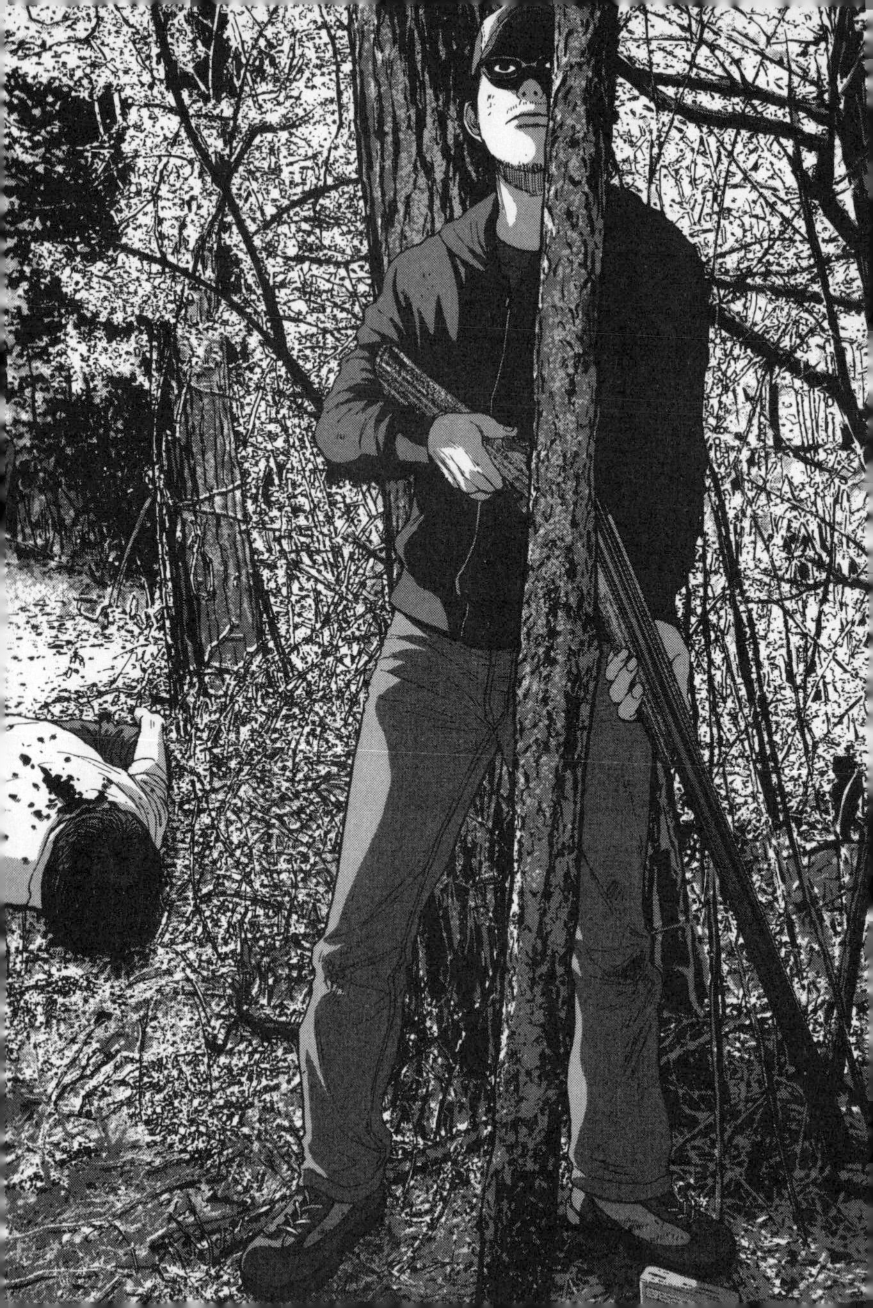

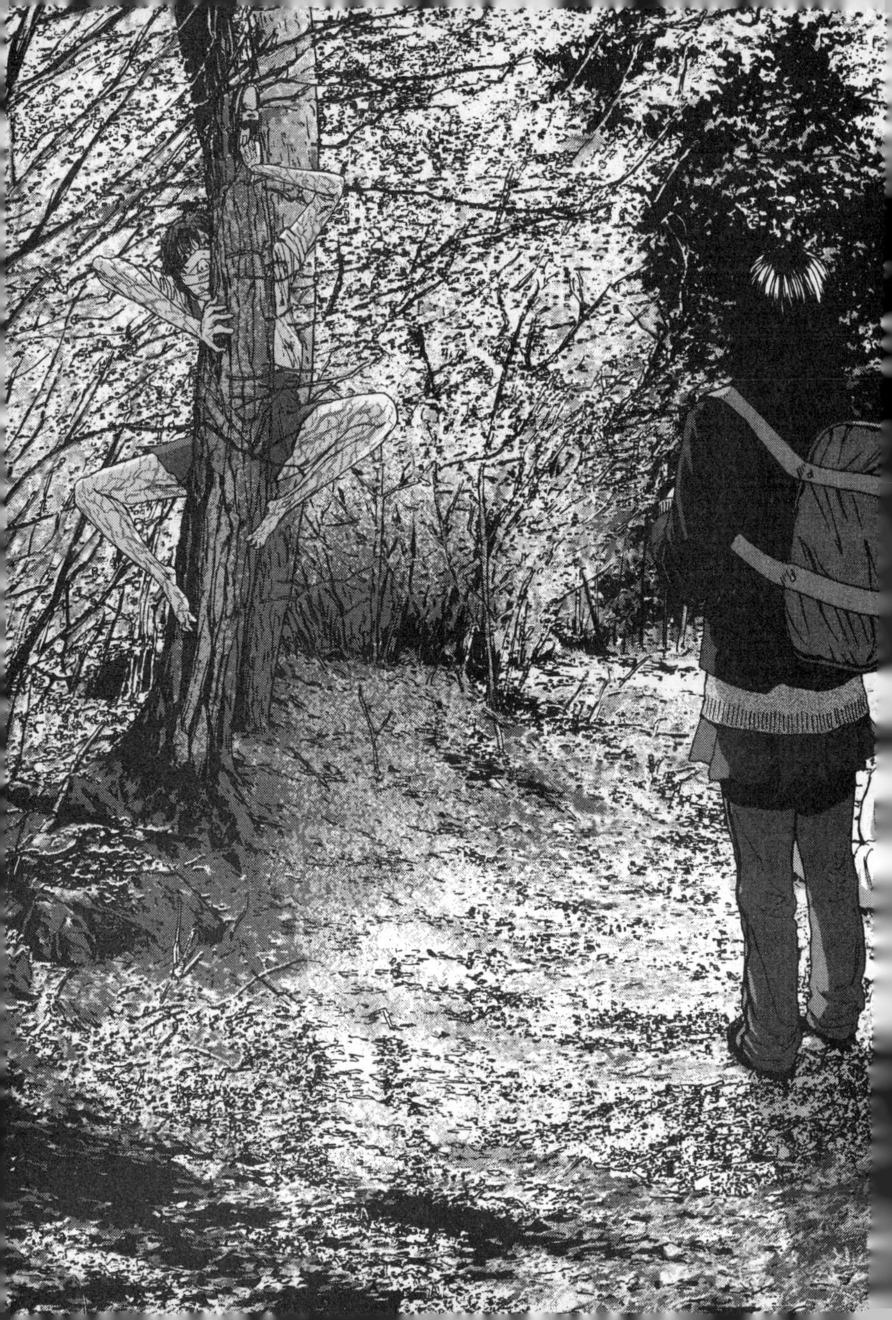

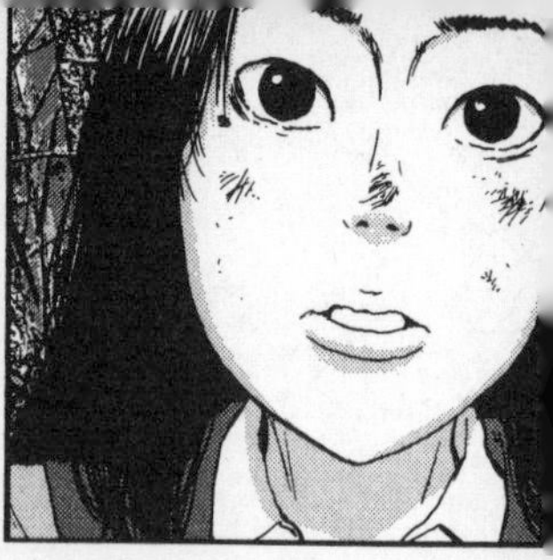
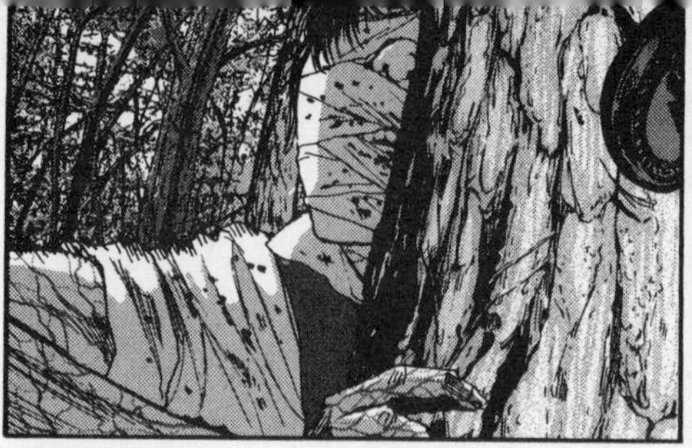
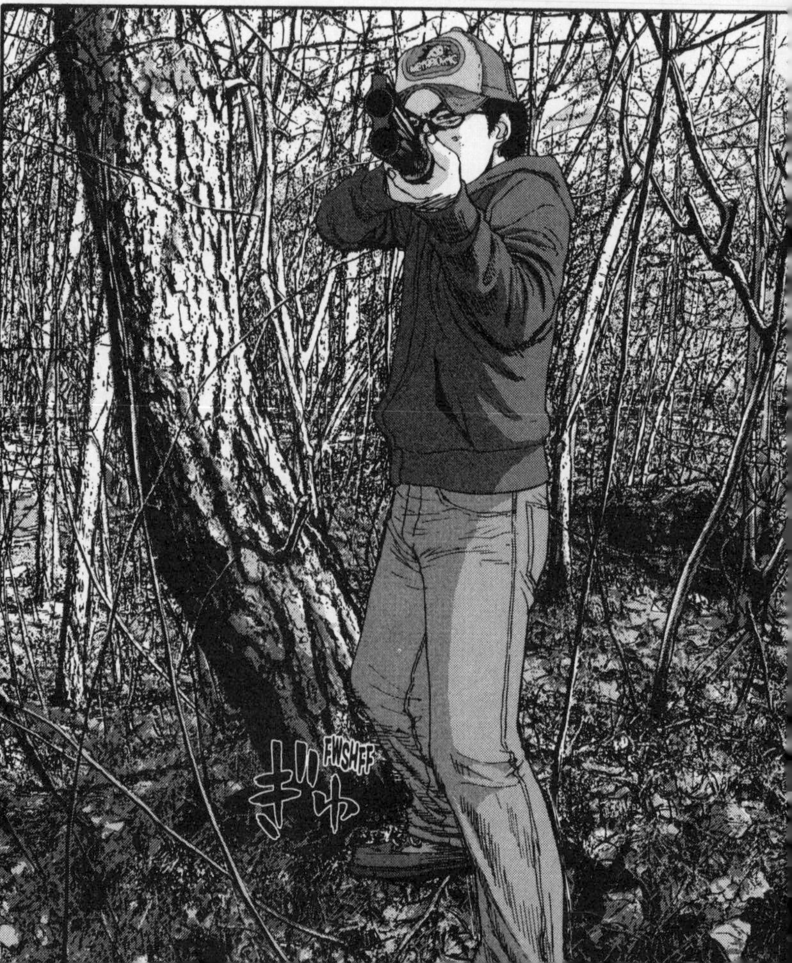
ぎゅ
FWSHFF

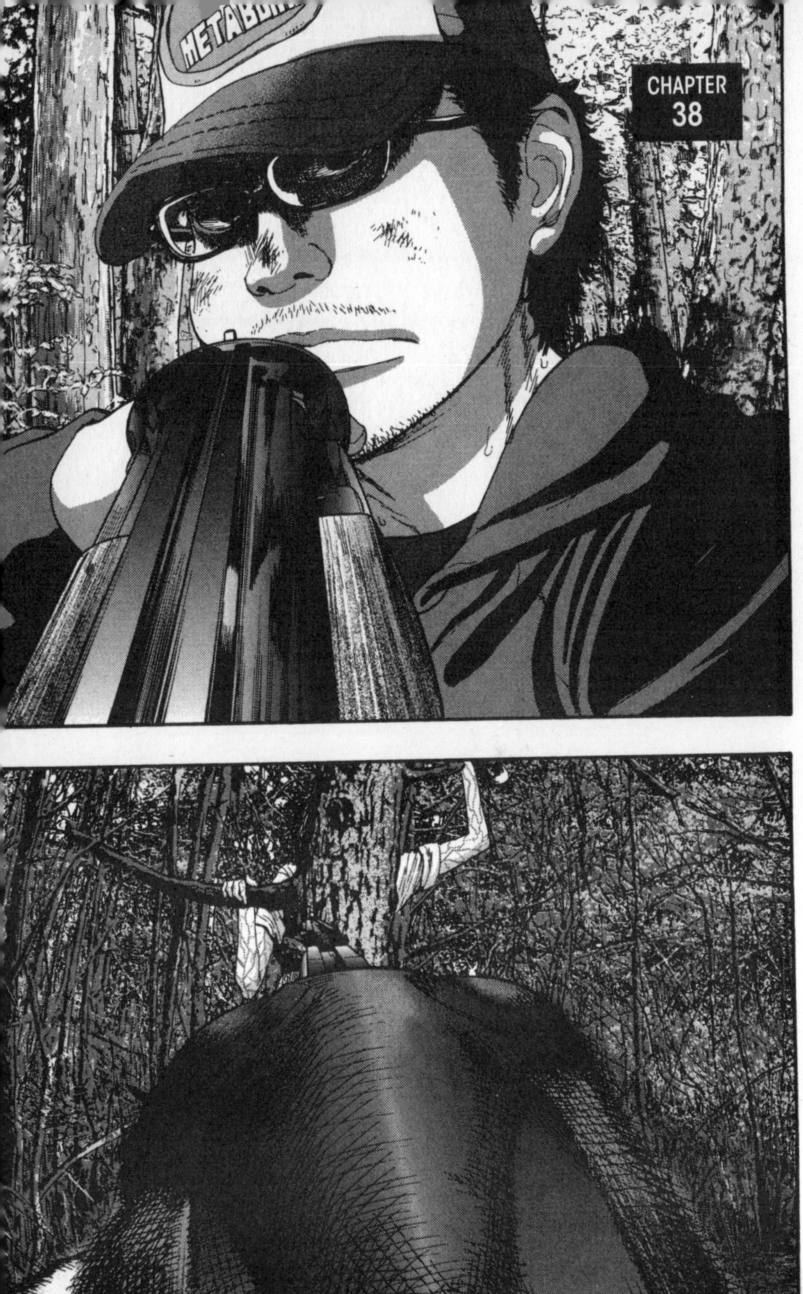
CHAPTER
38

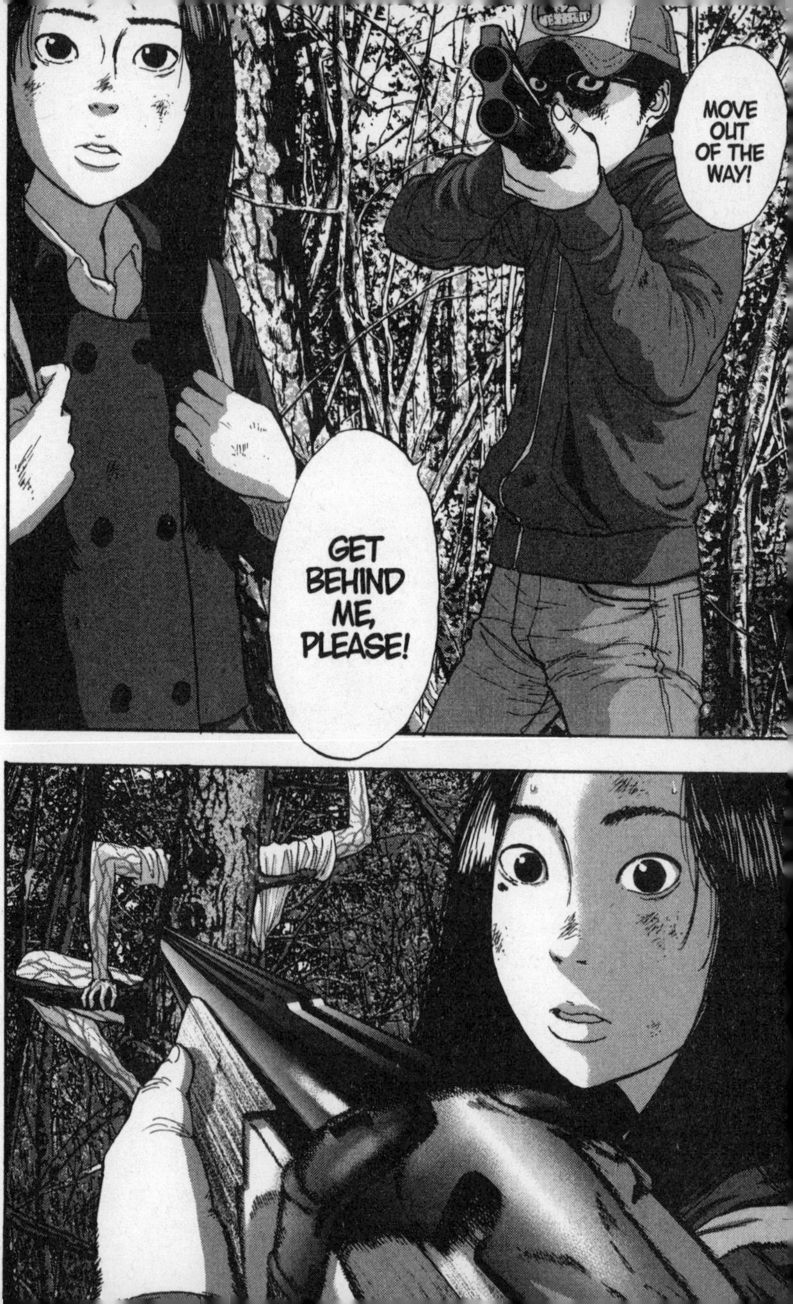
MOVE OUT OF THE WAY!
GET BEHIND ME, PLEASE!

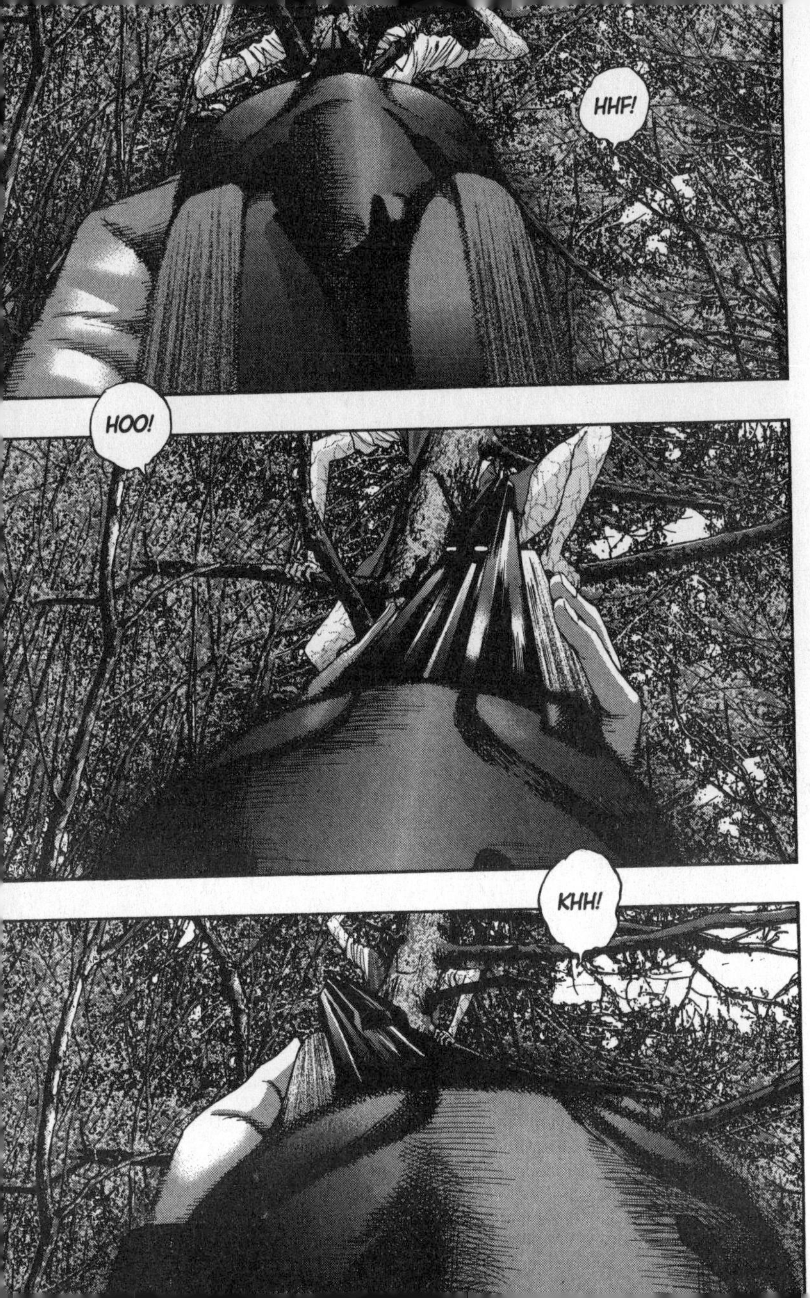
HHF!
HOO!
KHH!

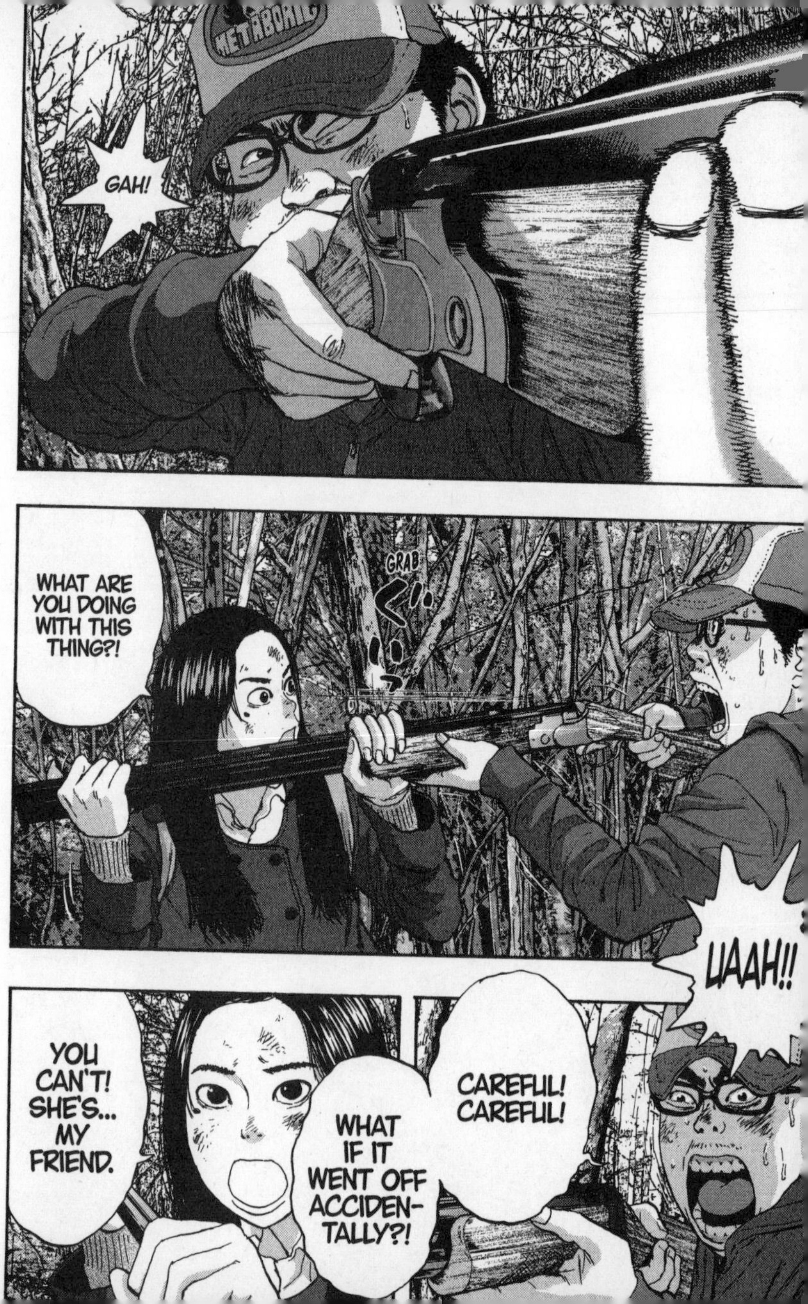
GAH!
GRAB
WHAT ARE YOU DOING WITH THIS THING?!
UAAH!!
CAREFUL! CAREFUL!
WHAT IF IT WENT OFF ACCIDENTALLY?!
YOU CAN'T! SHE'S... MY FRIEND.

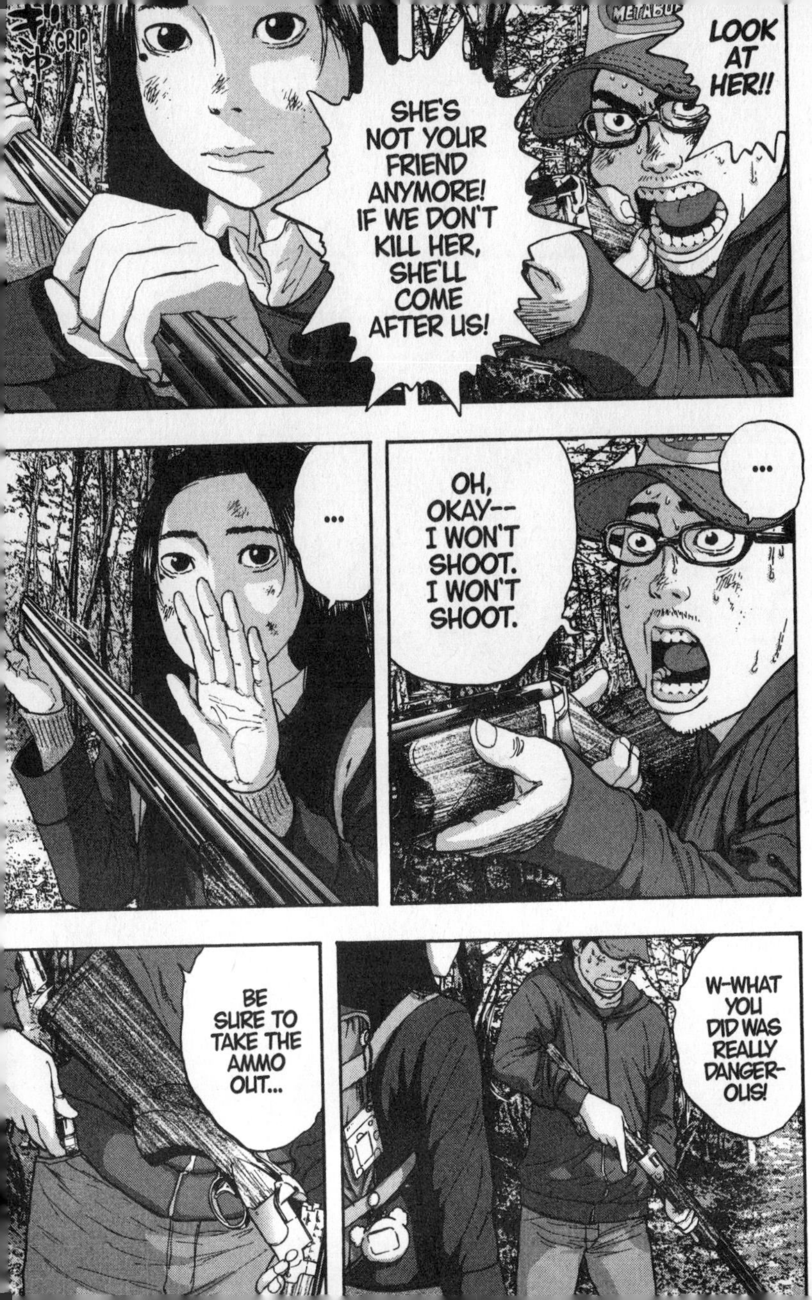
LOOK AT HER!!
SHE'S NOT YOUR FRIEND ANYMORE! IF WE DON'T KILL HER, SHE'LL COME AFTER US!
GRIP
...
OH, OKAY-- I WON'T SHOOT. I WON'T SHOOT.
...
W-WHAT YOU DID WAS REALLY DANGER-OUS!
BE SURE TO TAKE THE AMMO OUT...

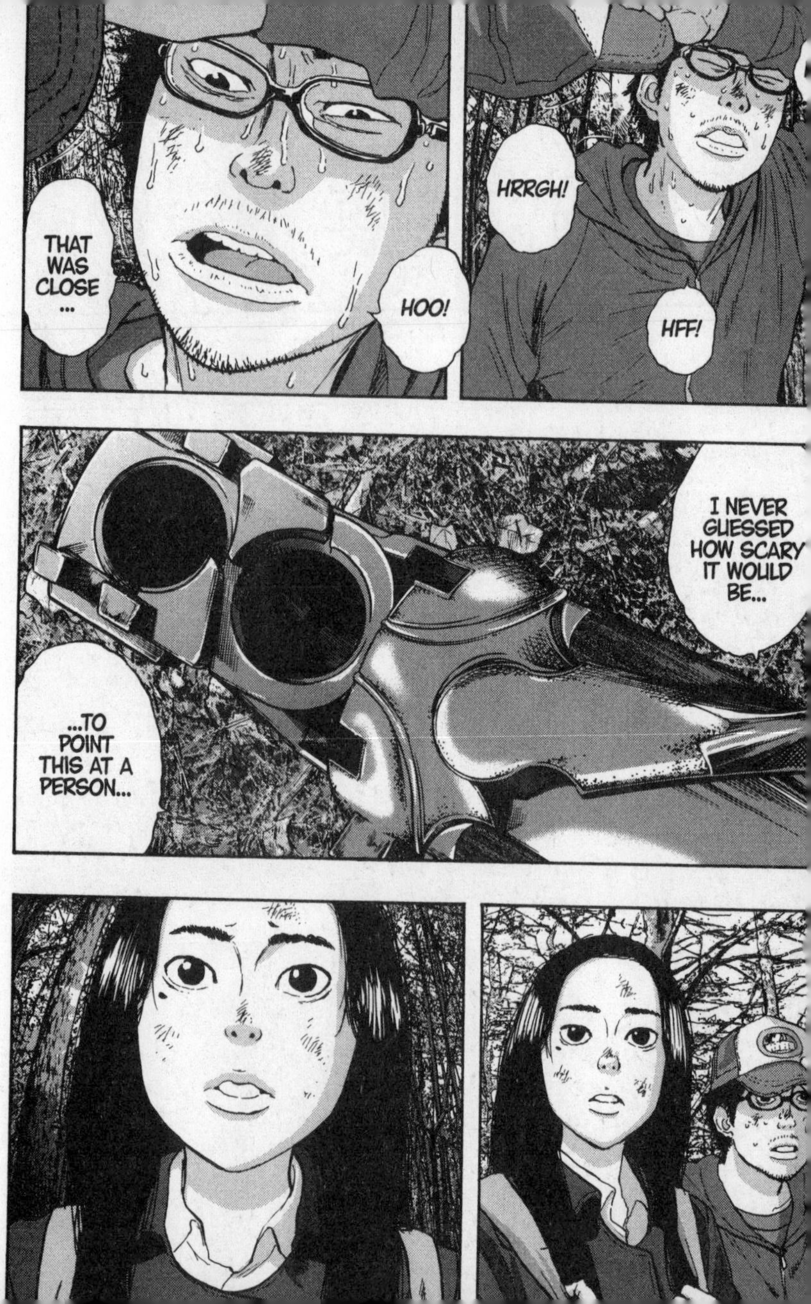
HRRGH!
HFF!
HOO!
THAT WAS CLOSE ...
I NEVER GUESSED HOW SCARY IT WOULD BE...
...TO POINT THIS AT A PERSON...

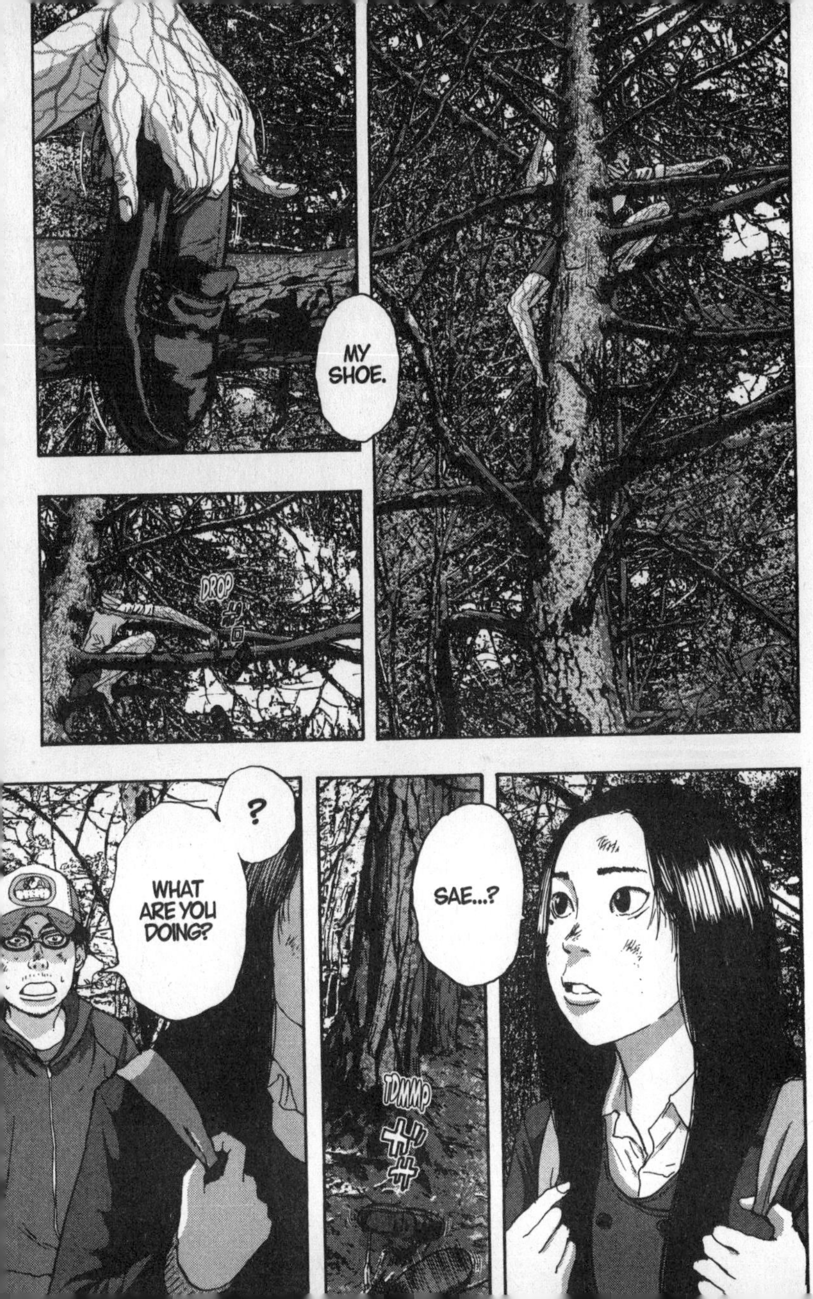
MY SHOE.
DROP
SAE...?
TDMMP
?
WHAT ARE YOU DOING?

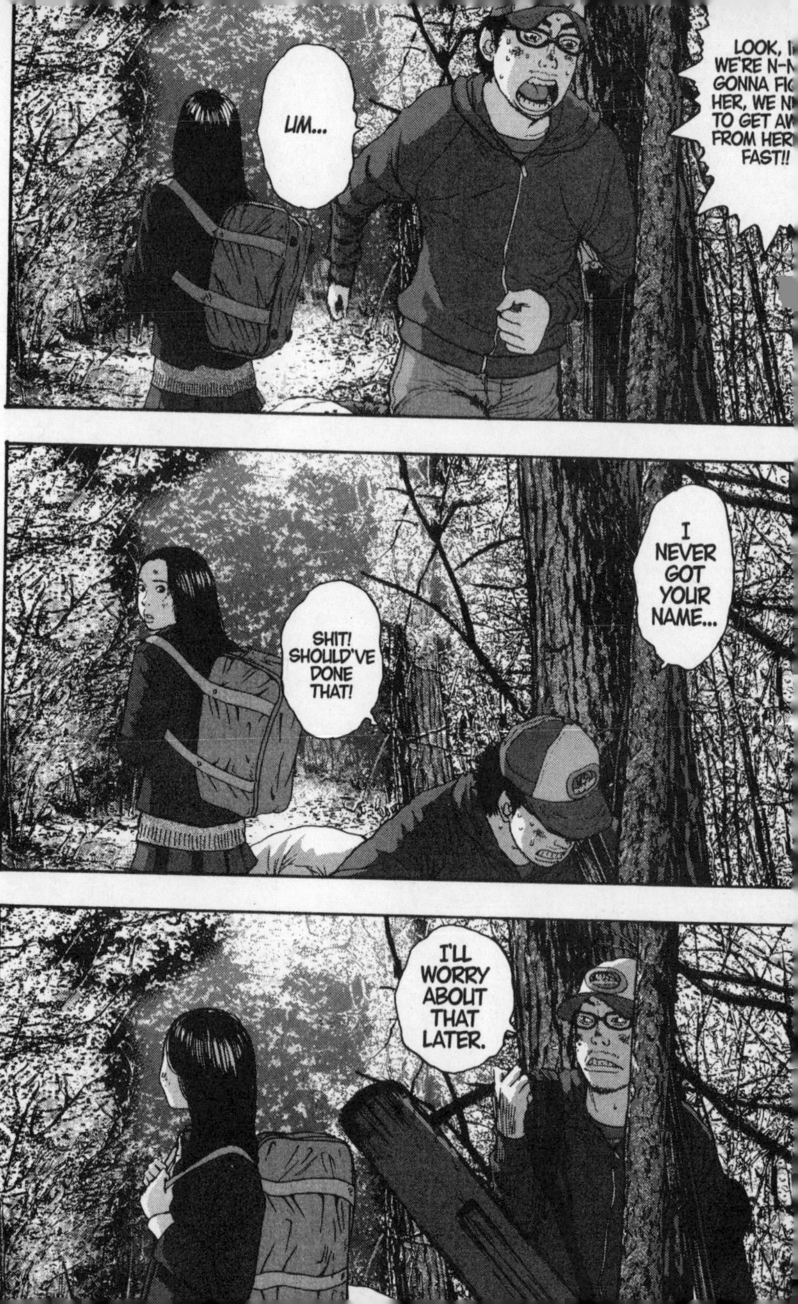
LOOK, I WE'RE N-N GONNA FIG HER, WE N TO GET AW FROM HER FAST!!
UM...
I NEVER GOT YOUR NAME...
SHIT! SHOULD'VE DONE THAT!
I'LL WORRY ABOUT THAT LATER.

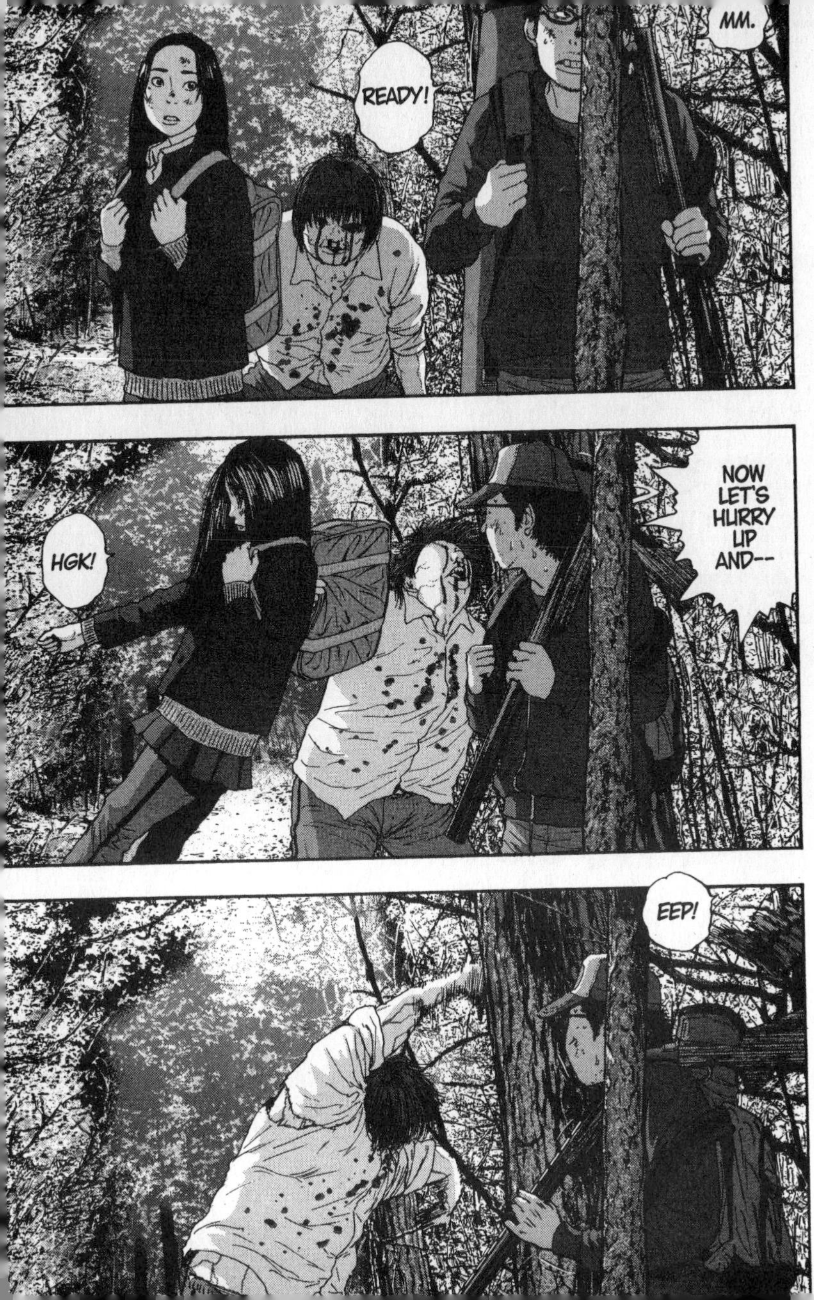
MM.
READY!
NOW LET'S HURRY UP AND--
HGK!
EEP!

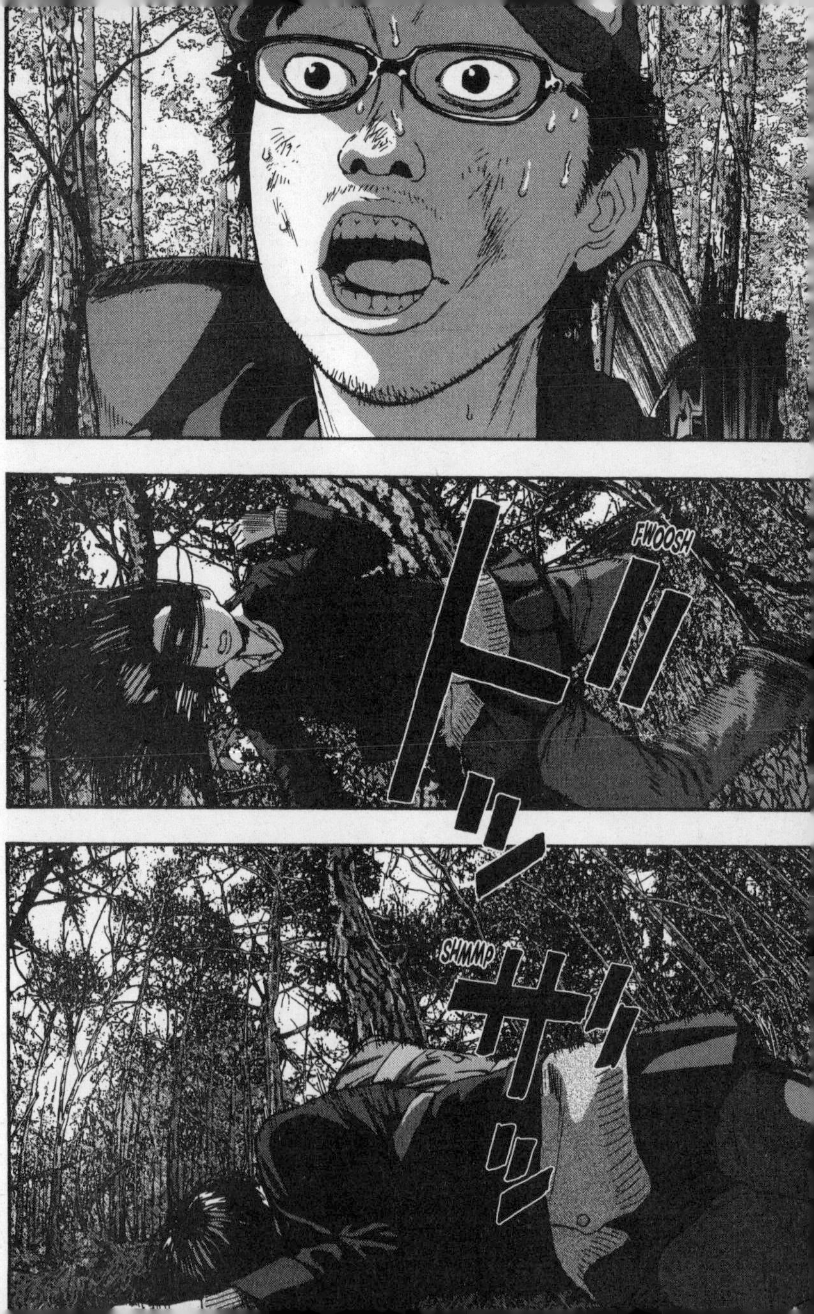
FWOOSH
SHMMP

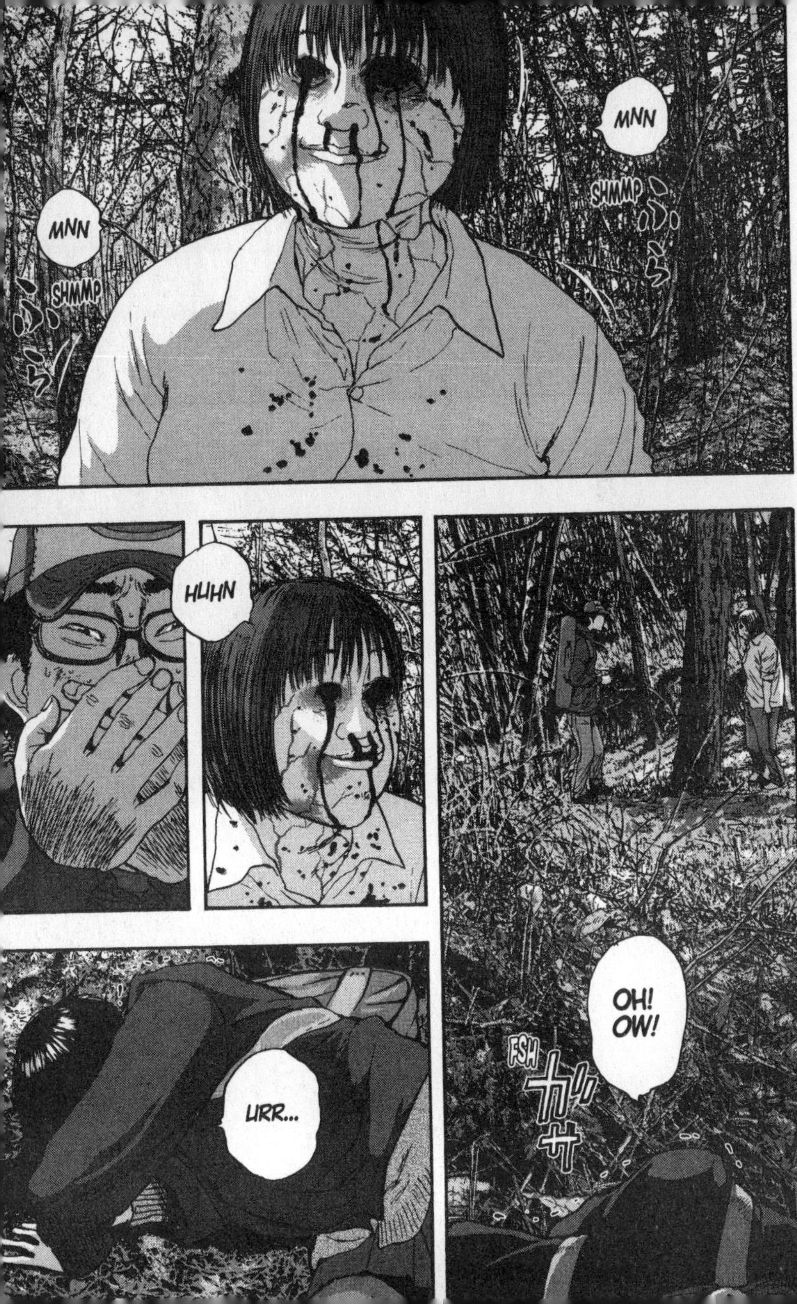
MNN
SHMMP
MNN
SHMMP
OH! OW!
FSH
HUHN
URR...

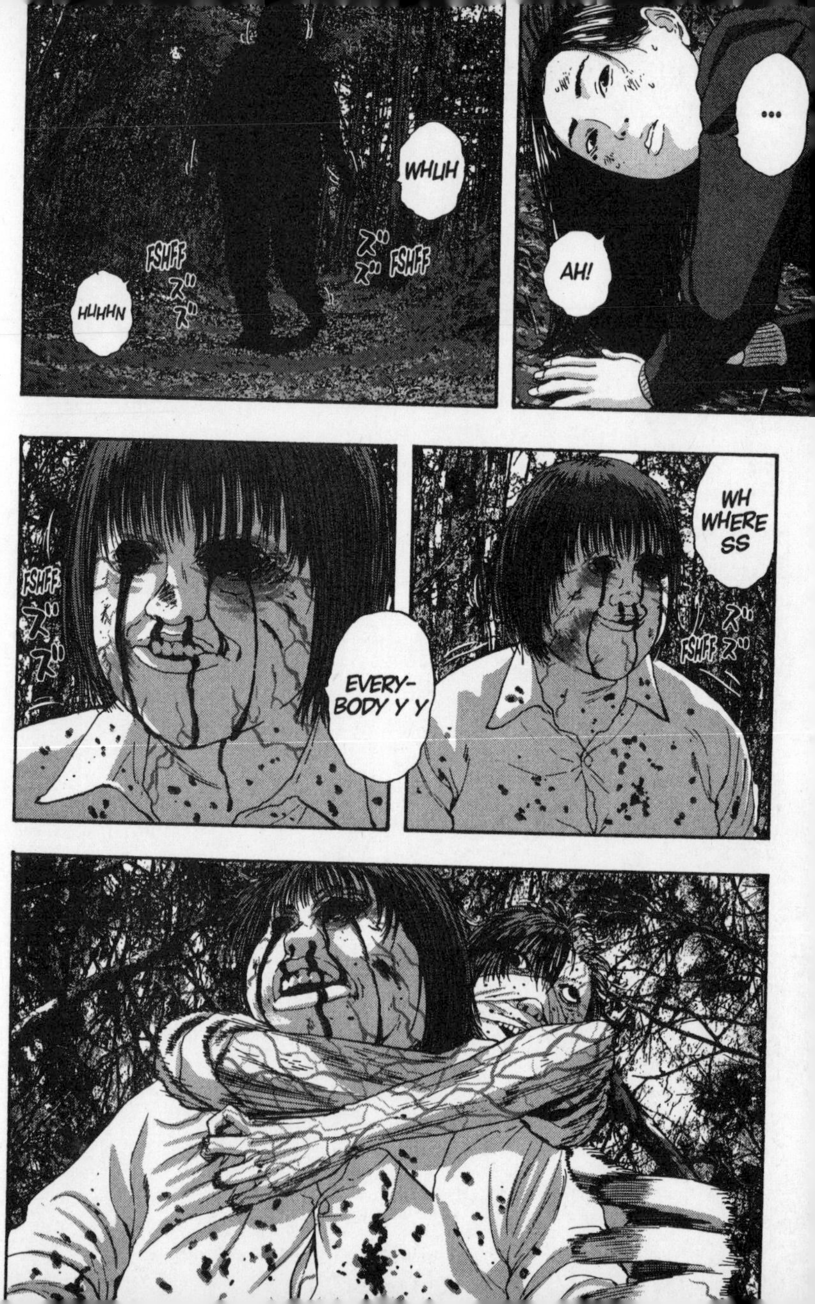
...
AH!
WHUH
ズズ
FSHFF
FSHFF
ズズ
HUHHN
WH WHERE SS
ズズ
FSHFF
ズズ
EVERY-BODY Y Y
FSHFF
ズズ

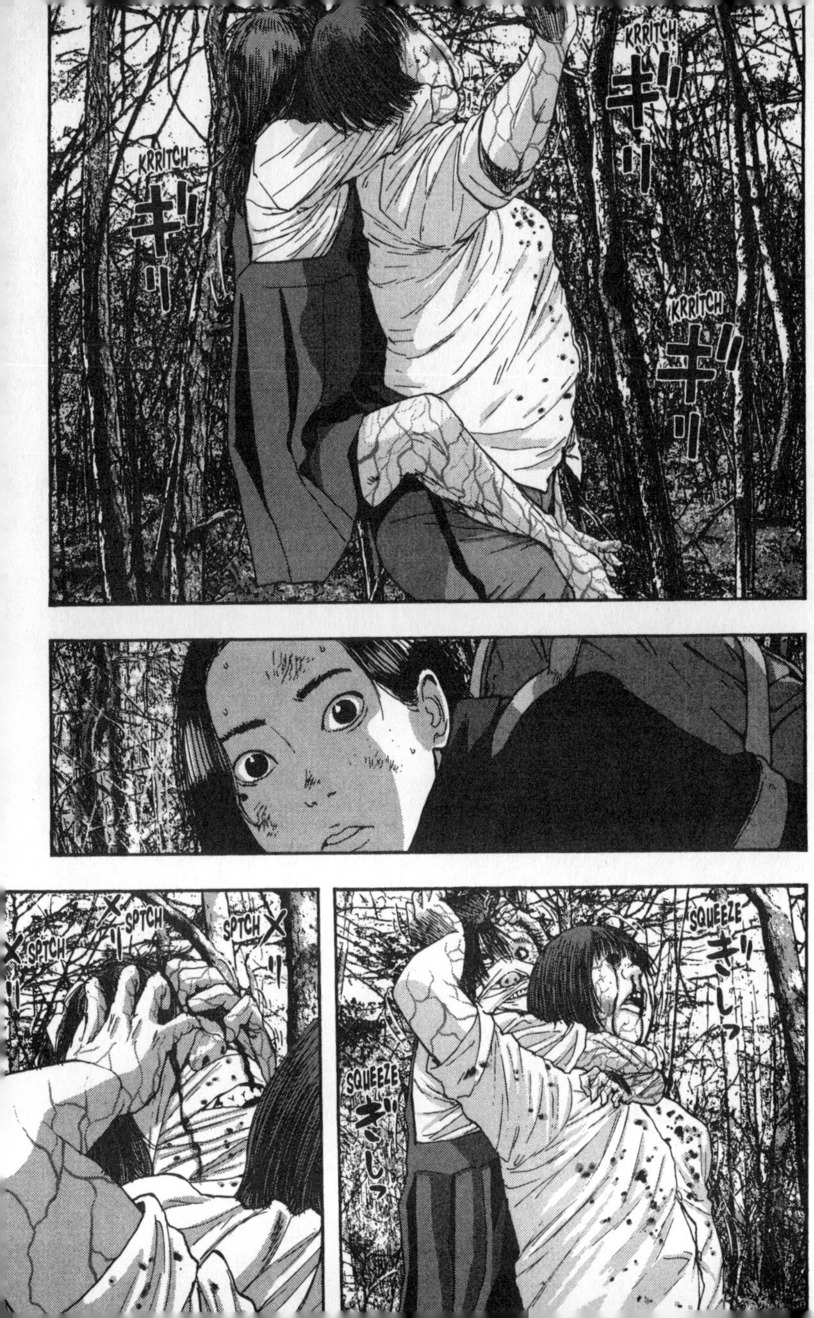
KRRITCH
KRRITCH
KRRITCH
SQUEEZE
SQUEEZE
SPTCH
SPTCH
SPTCH

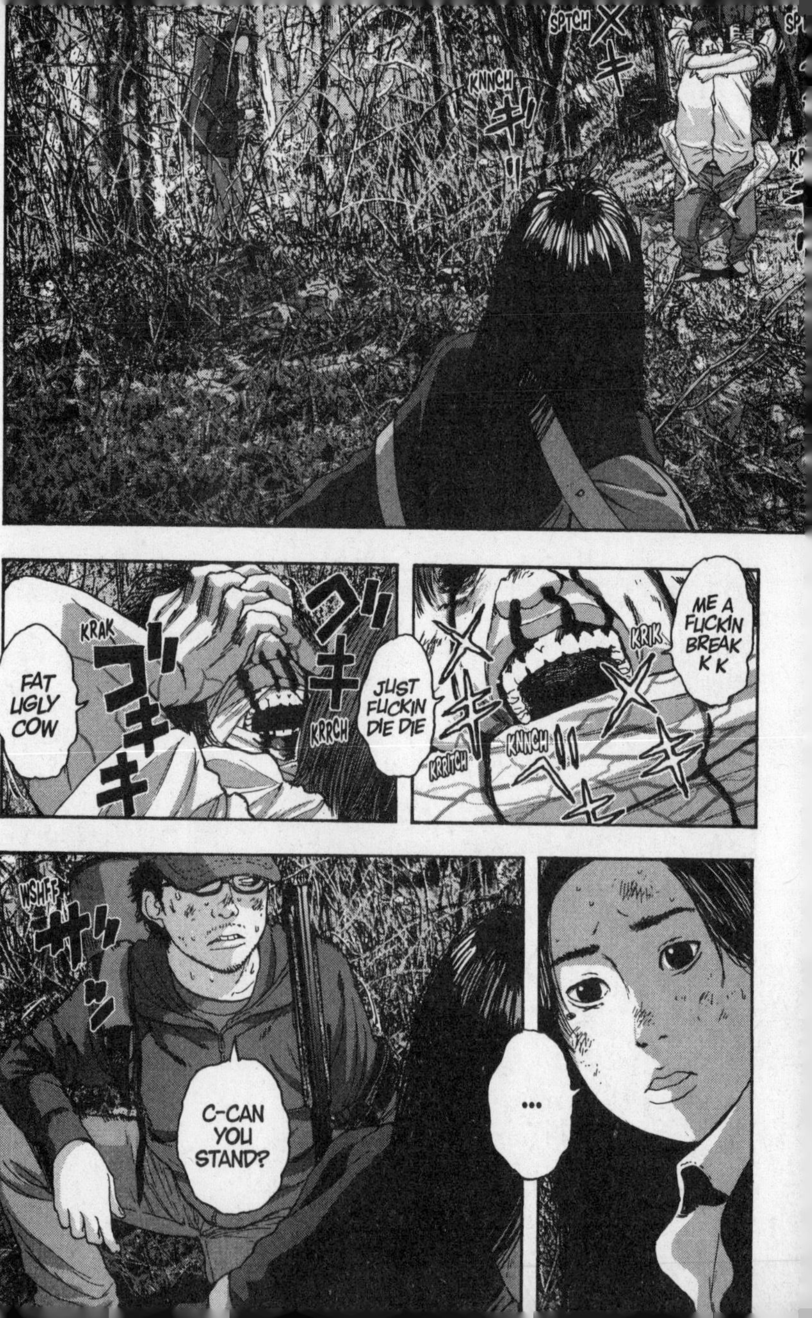
SPTCH
KNNCH
ME A FUCKIN BREAK K K
KRIK
JUST FUCKIN DIE DIE
KNNCH
KRRITCH
KRAK
FAT UGLY COW
KRRCH
...
WSHFF
C-CAN YOU STAND?

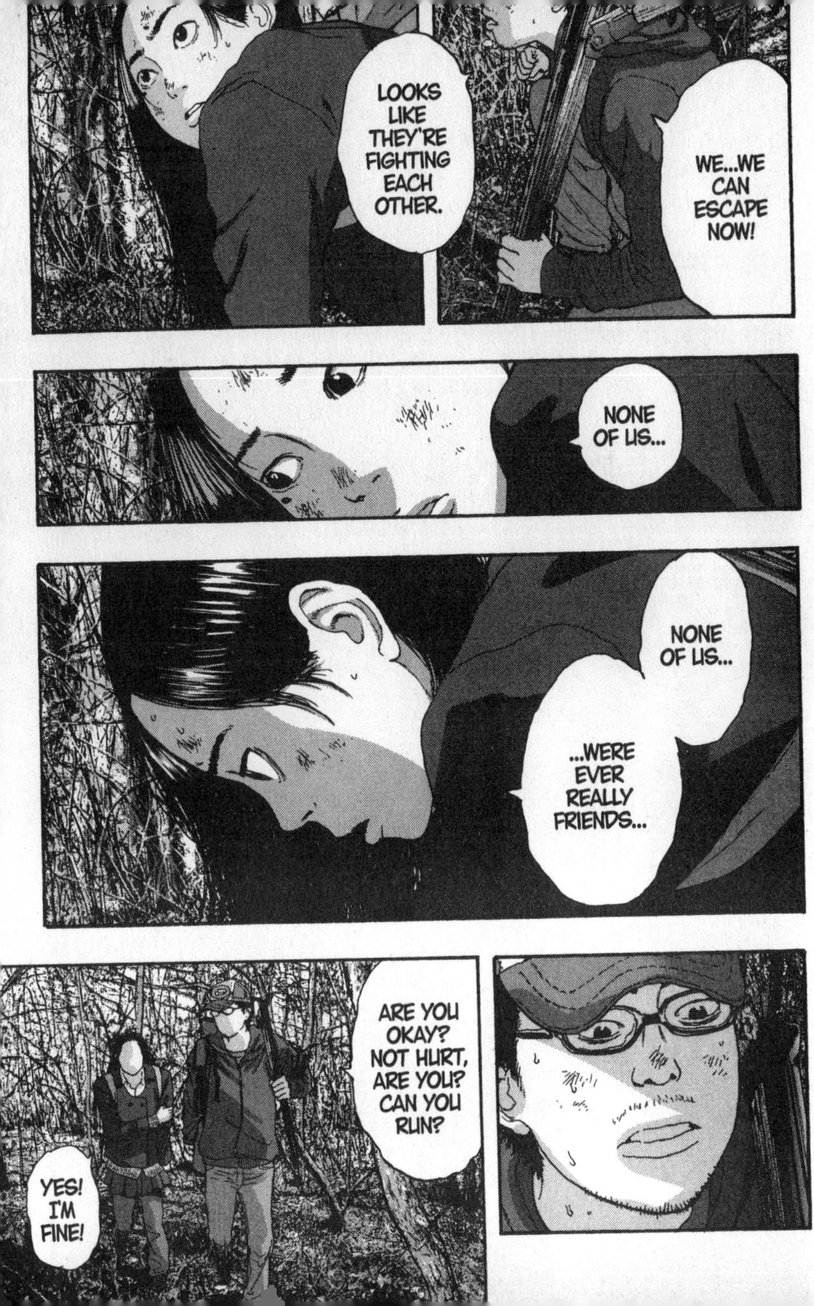
WE...WE CAN ESCAPE NOW!
LOOKS LIKE THEY'RE FIGHTING EACH OTHER.
NONE OF US...
NONE OF US...
...WERE EVER REALLY FRIENDS...
ARE YOU OKAY? NOT HURT, ARE YOU? CAN YOU RUN?
YES! I'M FINE!

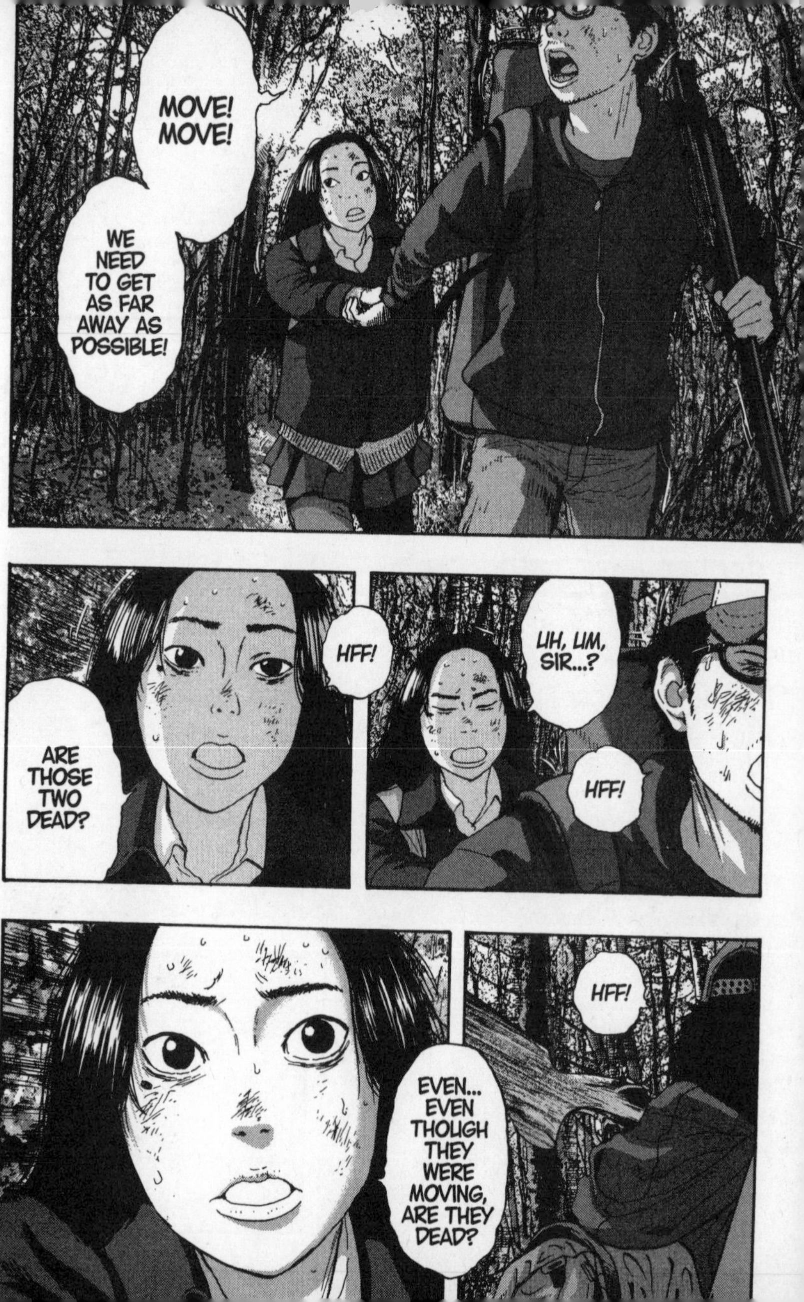
MOVE! MOVE!
WE NEED TO GET AS FAR AWAY AS POSSIBLE!
UH, UM, SIR...?
HFF!
HFF!
ARE THOSE TWO DEAD?
HFF!
EVEN... EVEN THOUGH THEY WERE MOVING, ARE THEY DEAD?

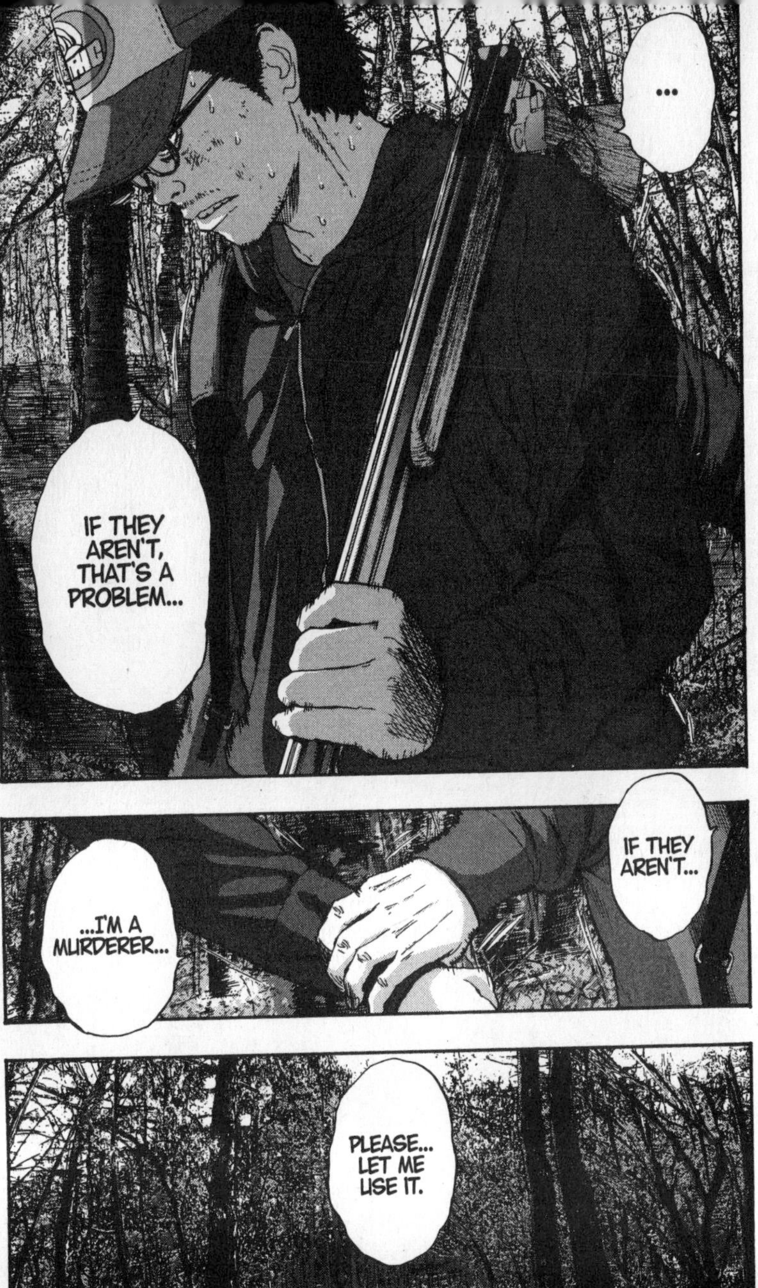
...
IF THEY AREN'T, THAT'S A PROBLEM...
IF THEY AREN'T...
...I'M A MURDERER...
PLEASE... LET ME USE IT.

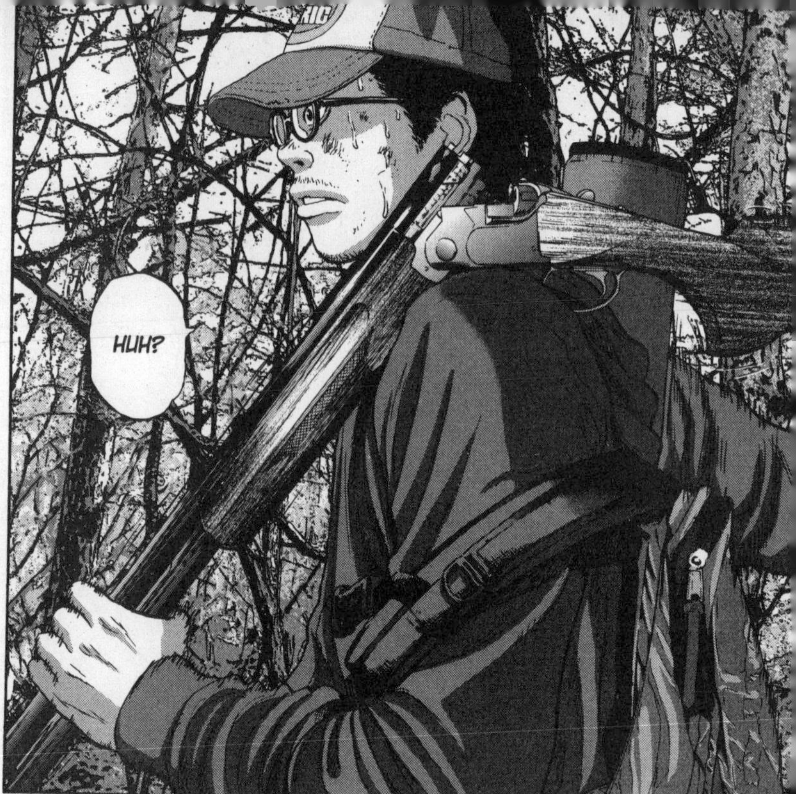
HUH?
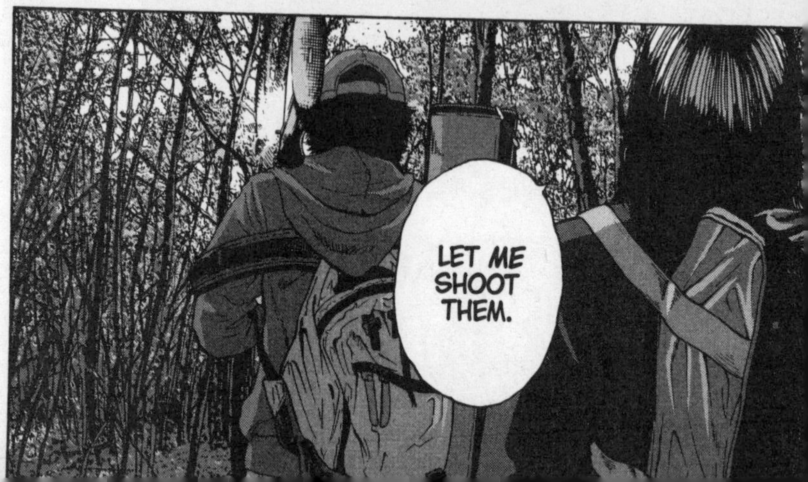
LET ME SHOOT THEM.

CHAPTER 39

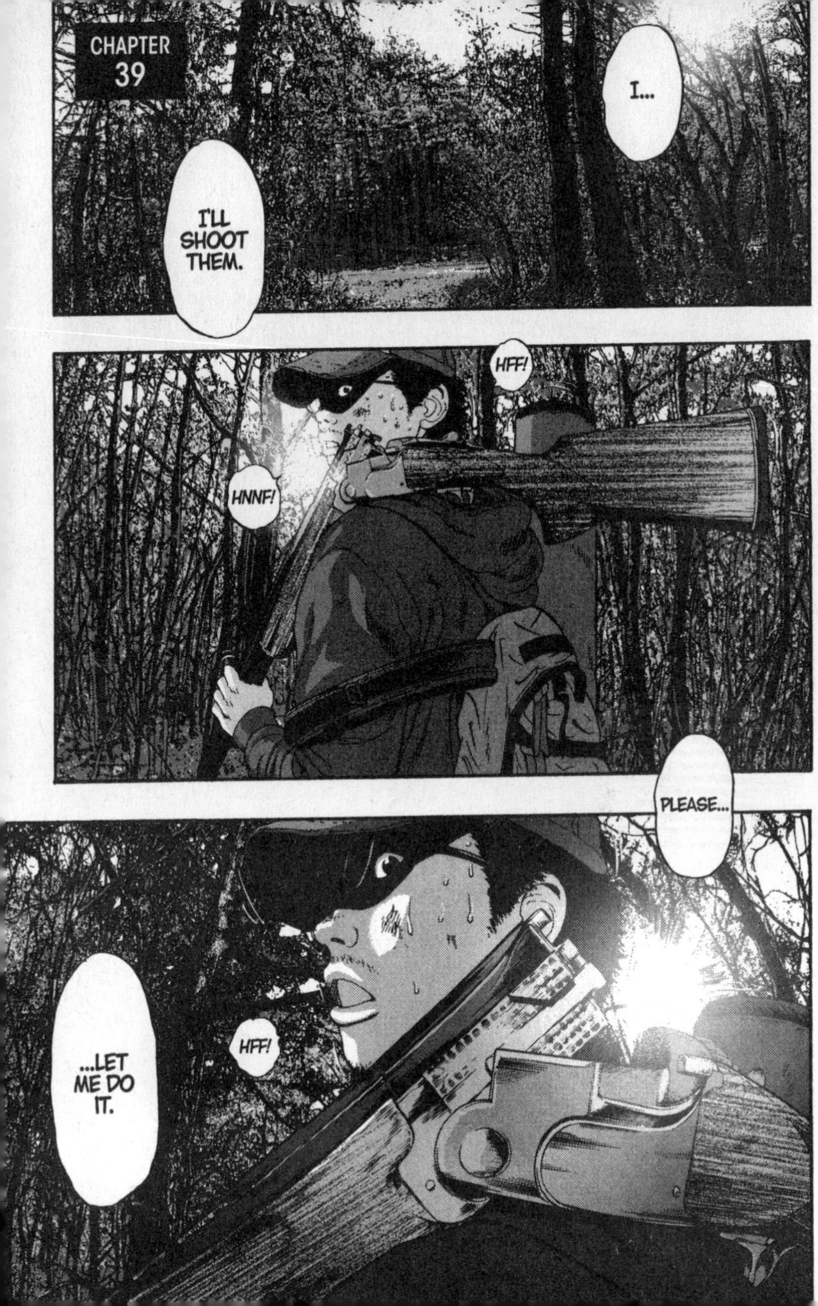
I...
I'LL SHOOT THEM.
HFF!
HNNF!
PLEASE...
HFF!
...LET ME DO IT.

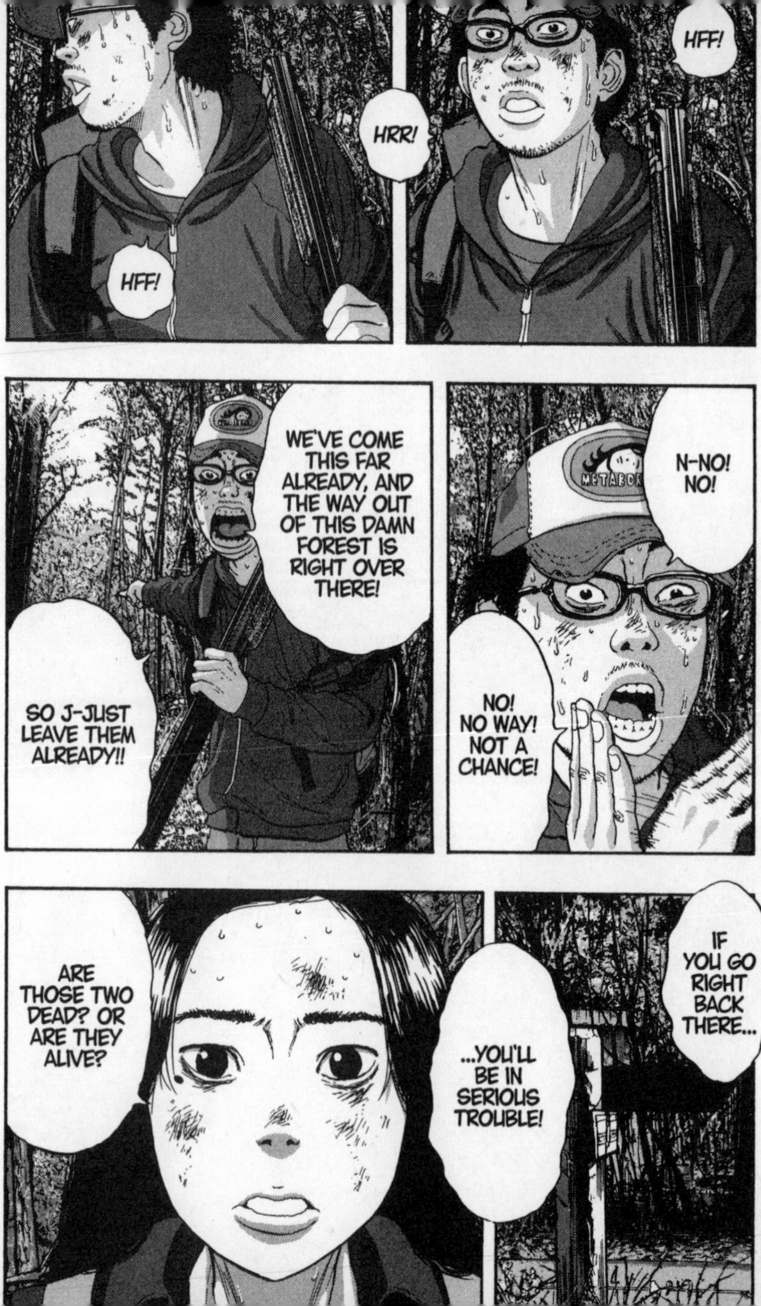
HFF!
HRR!
HFF!
N-NO! NO!
NO! NO WAY! NOT A CHANCE!
WE'VE COME THIS FAR ALREADY, AND THE WAY OUT OF THIS DAMN FOREST IS RIGHT OVER THERE!
SO J-JUST LEAVE THEM ALREADY!!
IF YOU GO RIGHT BACK THERE...
...YOU'LL BE IN SERIOUS TROUBLE!
ARE THOSE TWO DEAD? OR ARE THEY ALIVE?

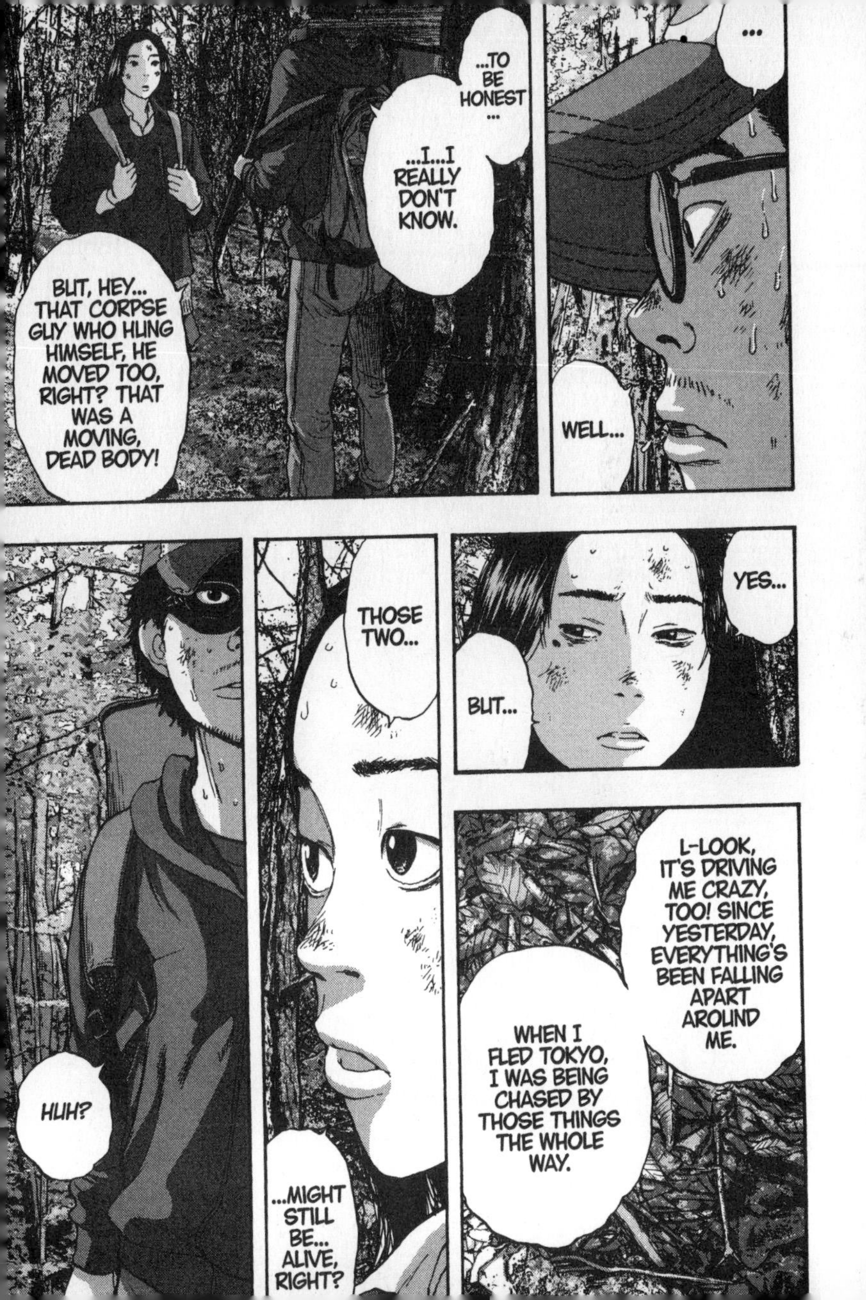
...
WELL...
...TO BE HONEST...
...I...I REALLY DON'T KNOW.
BUT, HEY... THAT CORPSE GUY WHO HUNG HIMSELF, HE MOVED TOO, RIGHT? THAT WAS A MOVING, DEAD BODY!
YES...
BUT...
L-LOOK, IT'S DRIVING ME CRAZY, TOO! SINCE YESTERDAY, EVERYTHING'S BEEN FALLING APART AROUND ME.
WHEN I FLED TOKYO, I WAS BEING CHASED BY THOSE THINGS THE WHOLE WAY.
THOSE TWO...
...MIGHT STILL BE... ALIVE, RIGHT?
HUH?

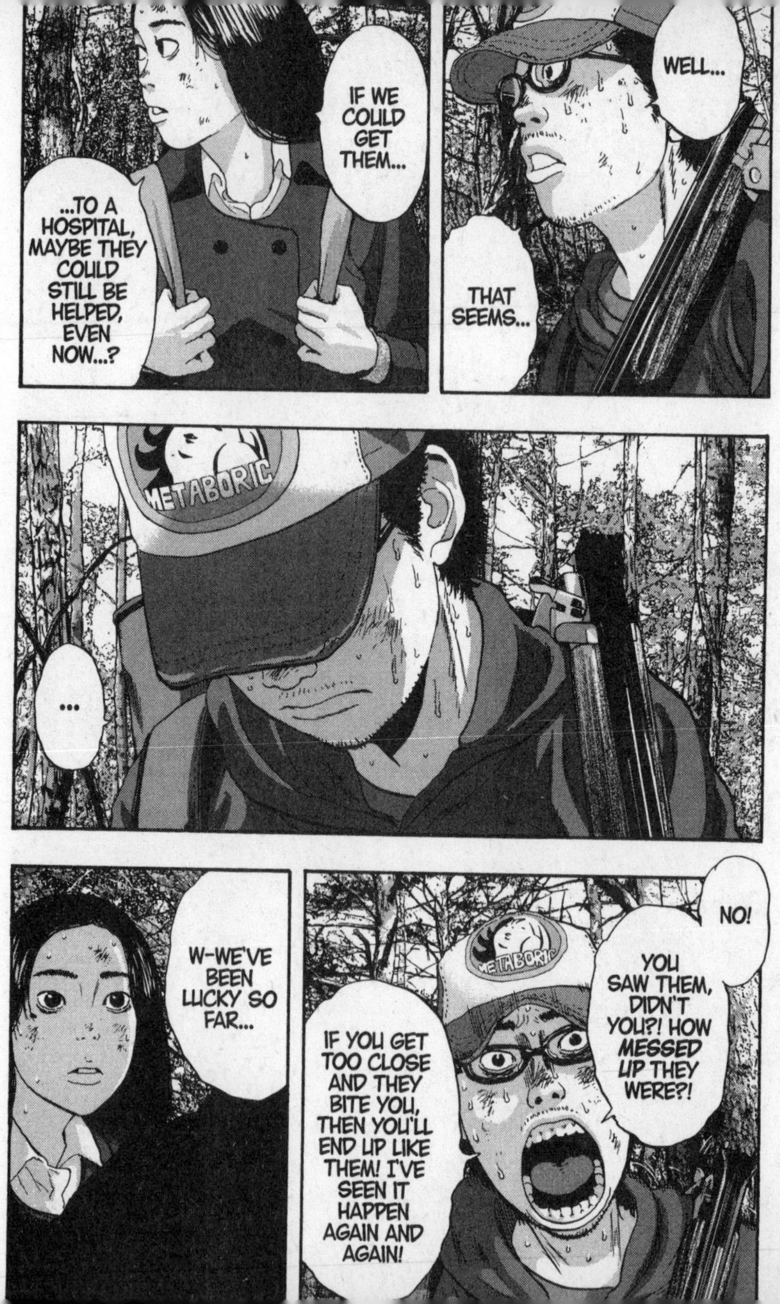
WELL...
THAT SEEMS...
IF WE COULD GET THEM...
...TO A HOSPITAL, MAYBE THEY COULD STILL BE HELPED, EVEN NOW...?
...
NO!
YOU SAW THEM, DIDN'T YOU?! HOW MESSED UP THEY WERE?!
IF YOU GET TOO CLOSE AND THEY BITE YOU, THEN YOU'LL END UP LIKE THEM! I'VE SEEN IT HAPPEN AGAIN AND AGAIN!
W-WE'VE BEEN LUCKY SO FAR...

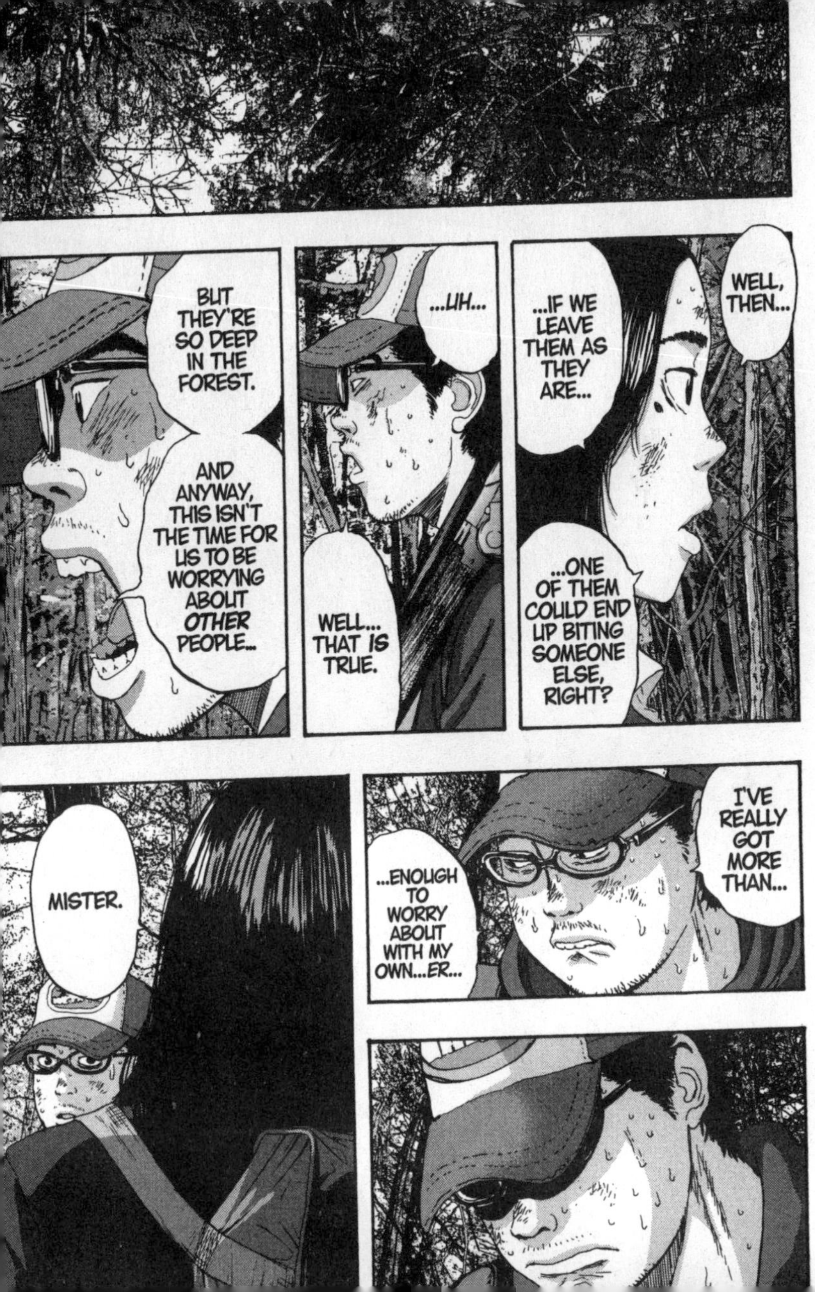
WELL, THEN...
...IF WE LEAVE THEM AS THEY ARE...
...ONE OF THEM COULD END UP BITING SOMEONE ELSE, RIGHT?
...UH...
WELL... THAT IS TRUE.
BUT THEY'RE SO DEEP IN THE FOREST.
AND ANYWAY, THIS ISN'T THE TIME FOR US TO BE WORRYING ABOUT OTHER PEOPLE...
I'VE REALLY GOT MORE THAN...
...ENOUGH TO WORRY ABOUT WITH MY OWN...ER...
MISTER.

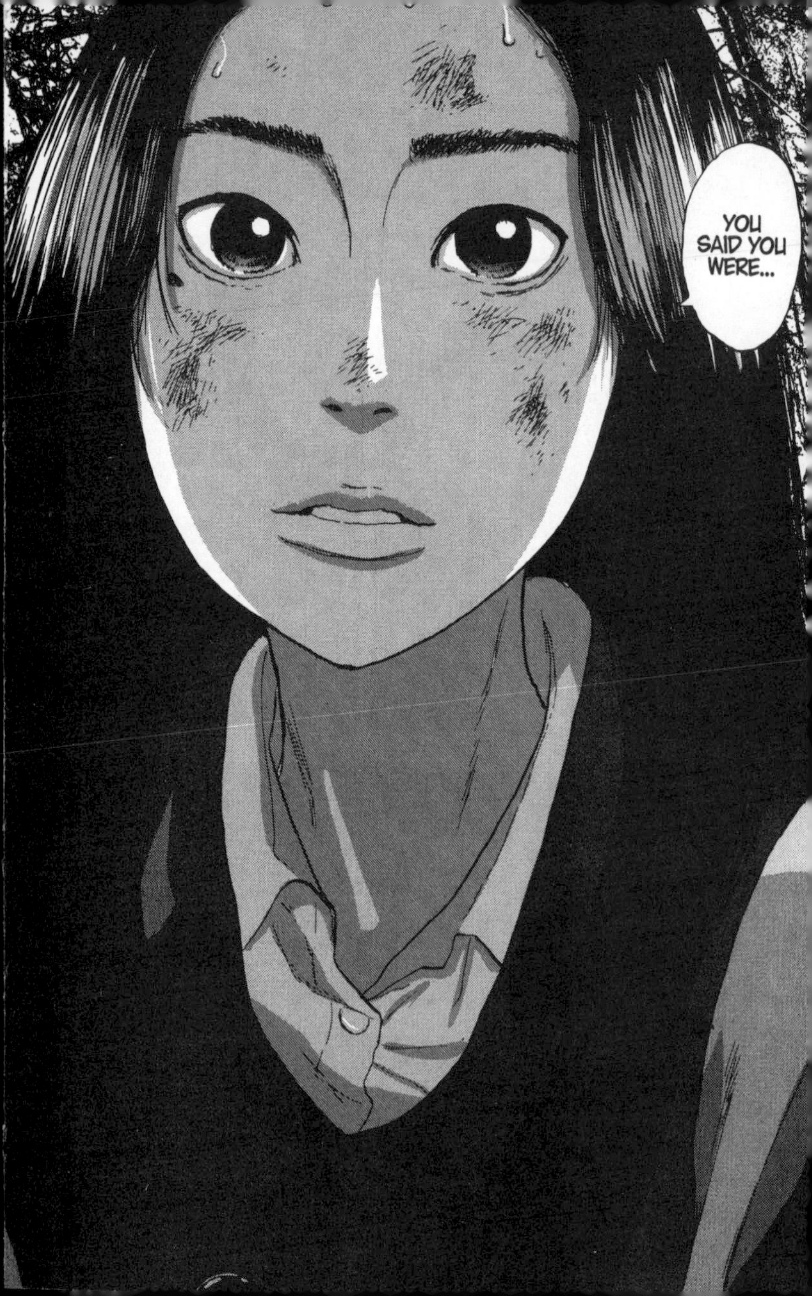
YOU SAID YOU WERE...

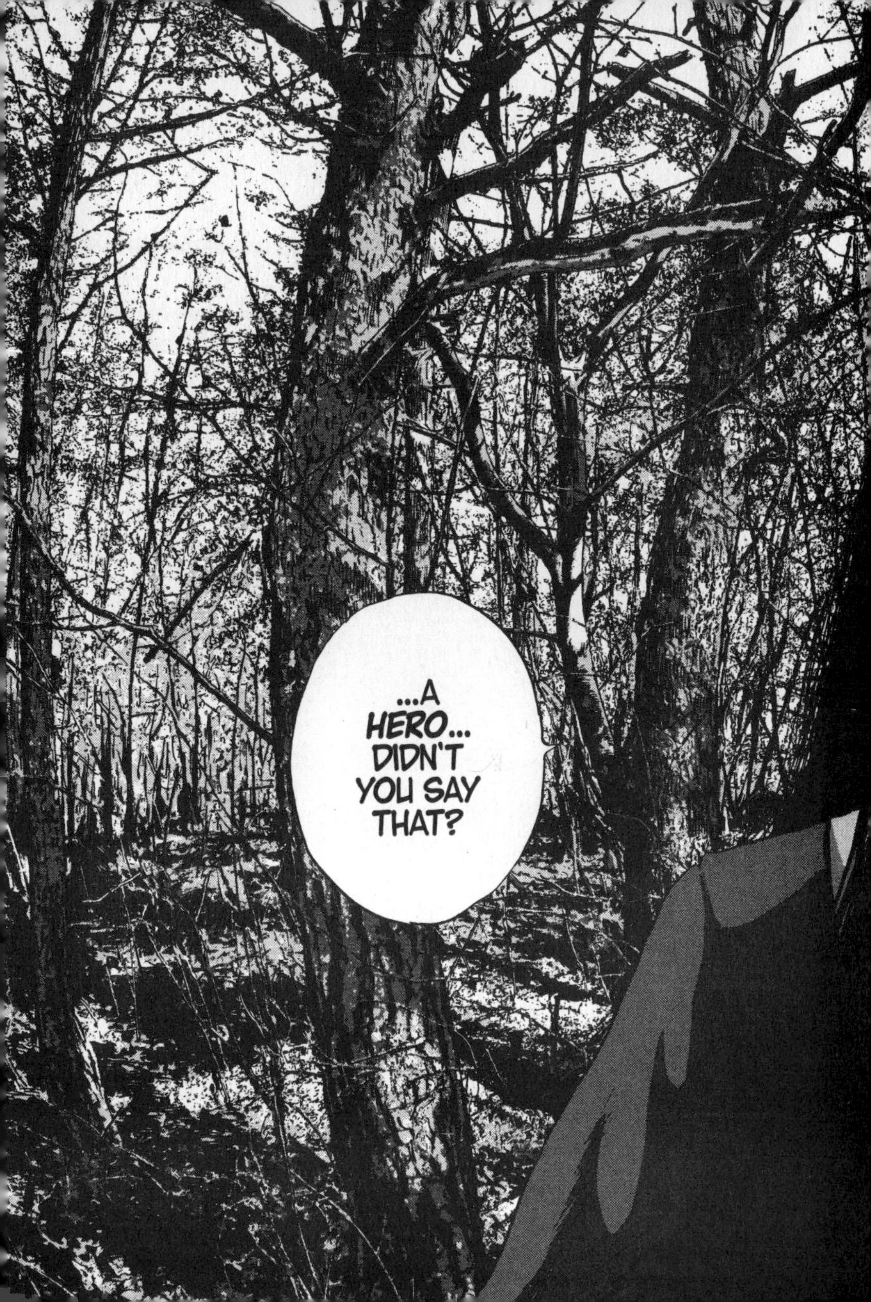
...A HERO... DIDN'T YOU SAY THAT?

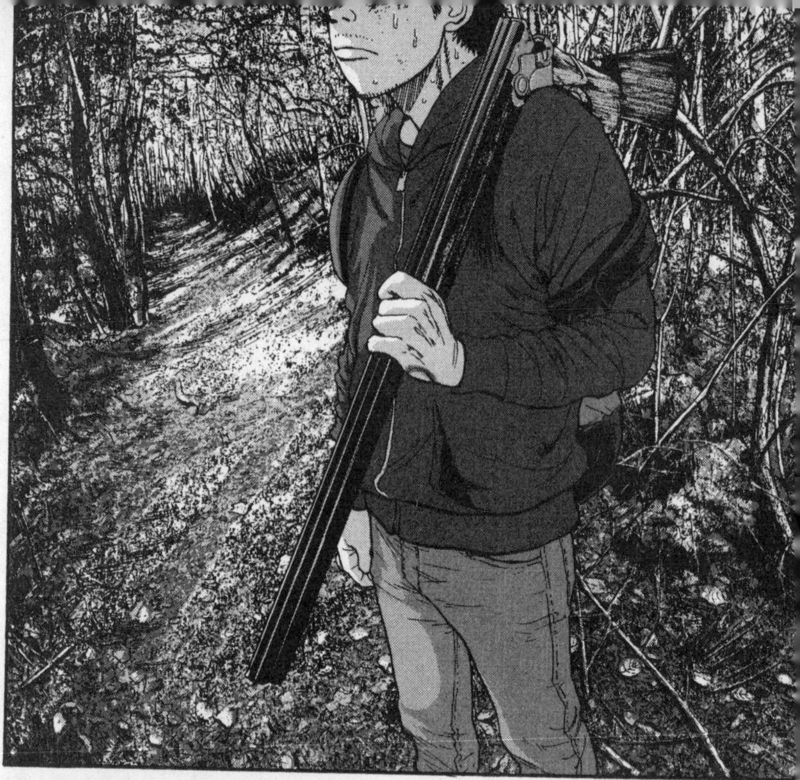
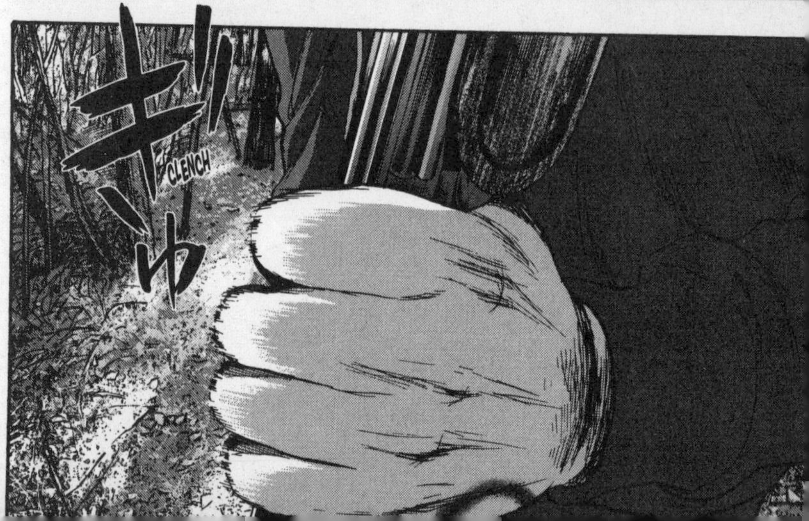
CLENCH

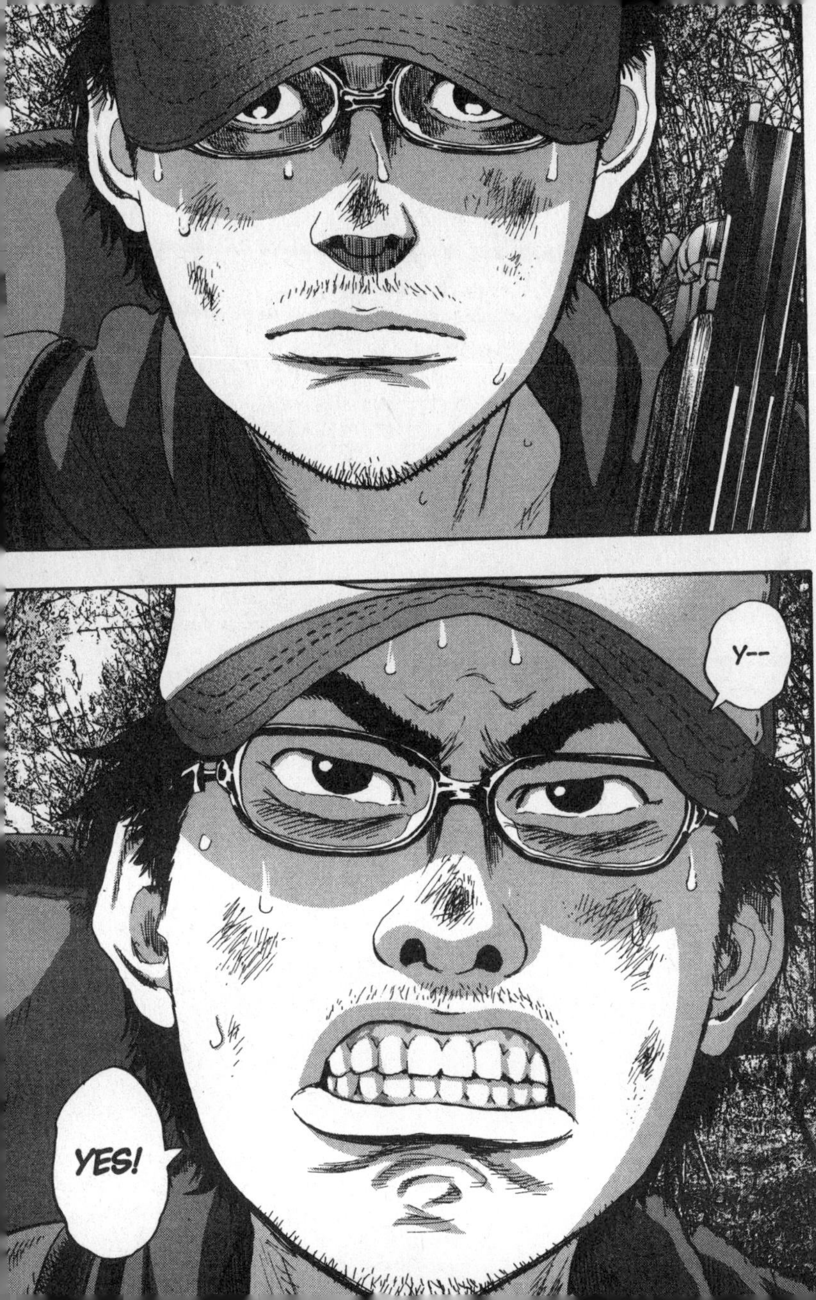
Y--
YES!

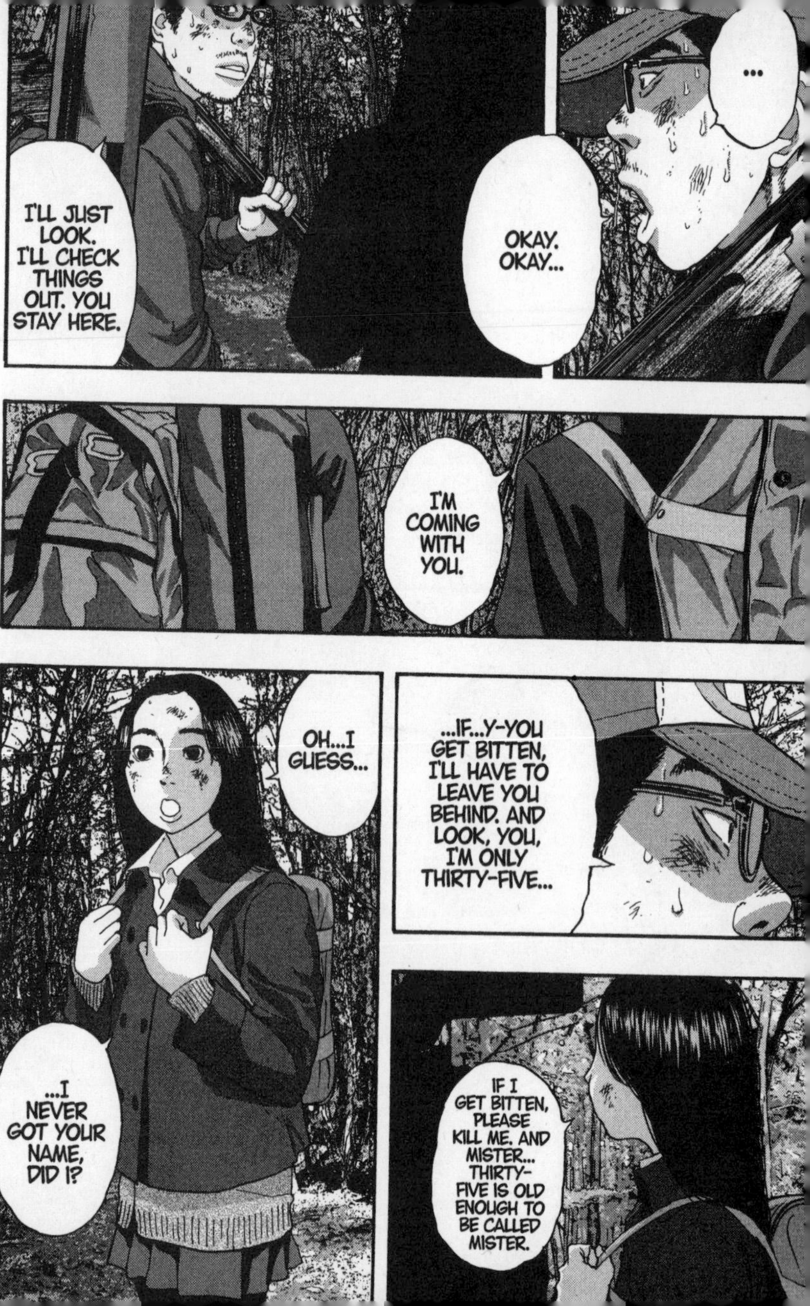
...
OKAY. OKAY...
I'LL JUST LOOK. I'LL CHECK THINGS OUT. YOU STAY HERE.
I'M COMING WITH YOU.
...IF...Y-YOU GET BITTEN, I'LL HAVE TO LEAVE YOU BEHIND. AND LOOK, YOU, I'M ONLY THIRTY-FIVE...
IF I GET BITTEN, PLEASE KILL ME. AND MISTER... THIRTY-FIVE IS OLD ENOUGH TO BE CALLED MISTER.
OH...I GUESS...
...I NEVER GOT YOUR NAME, DID I?

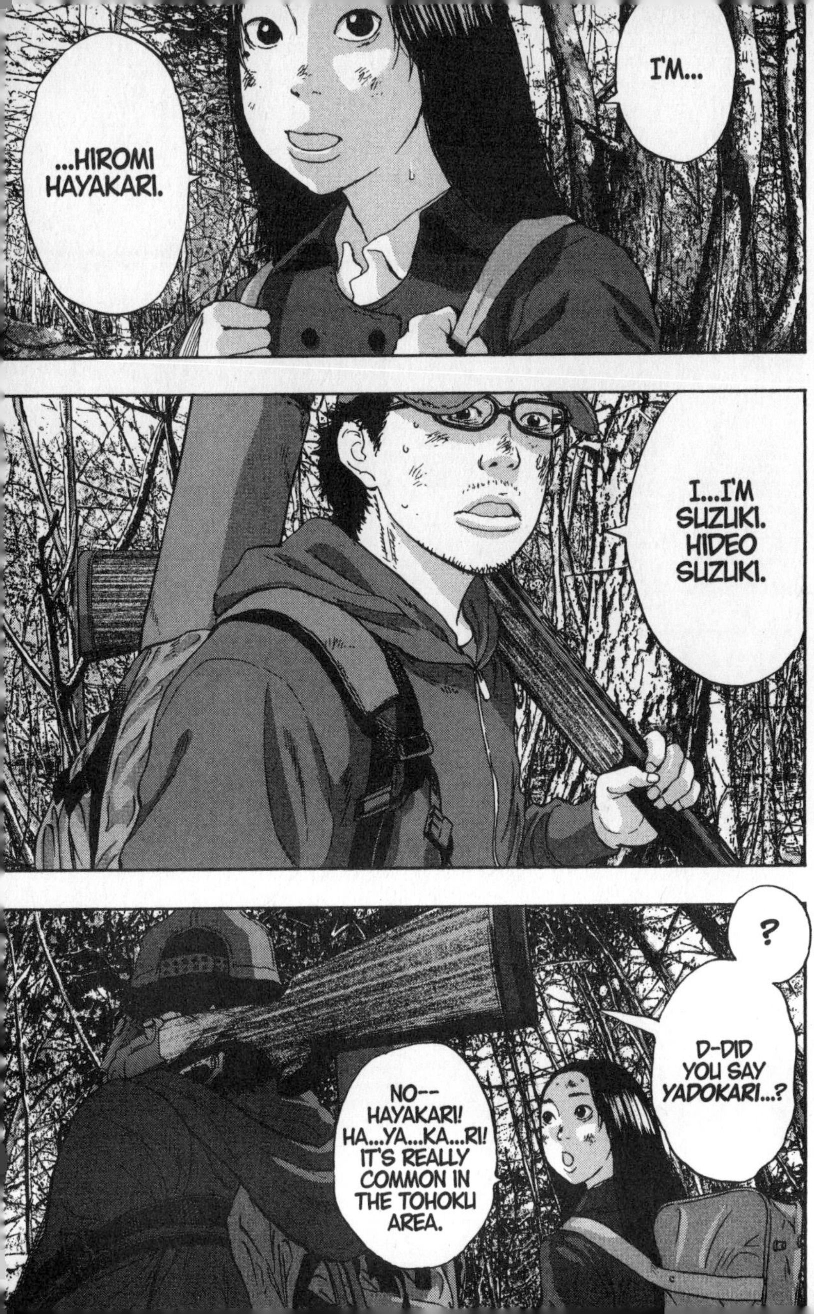
I'M...
...HIROMI HAYAKARI.
I...I'M SUZUKI. HIDEO SUZUKI.
?
D-DID YOU SAY YADOKARI...?
NO-- HAYAKARI! HA...YA...KA...RI! IT'S REALLY COMMON IN THE TOHOKU AREA.

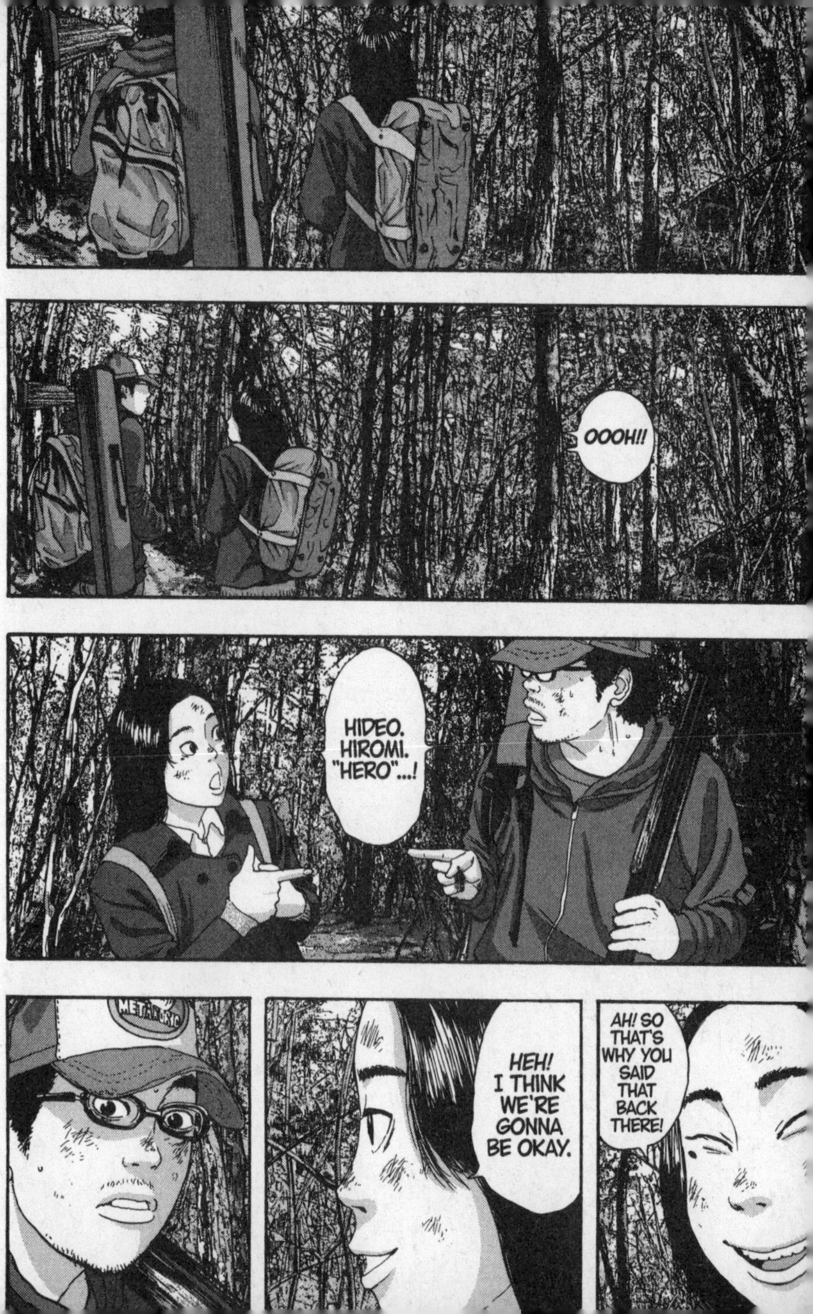
OOOH!!
HIDEO. HIROMI. "HERO"...!
AH! SO THAT'S WHY YOU SAID THAT BACK THERE!
HEH! I THINK WE'RE GONNA BE OKAY.

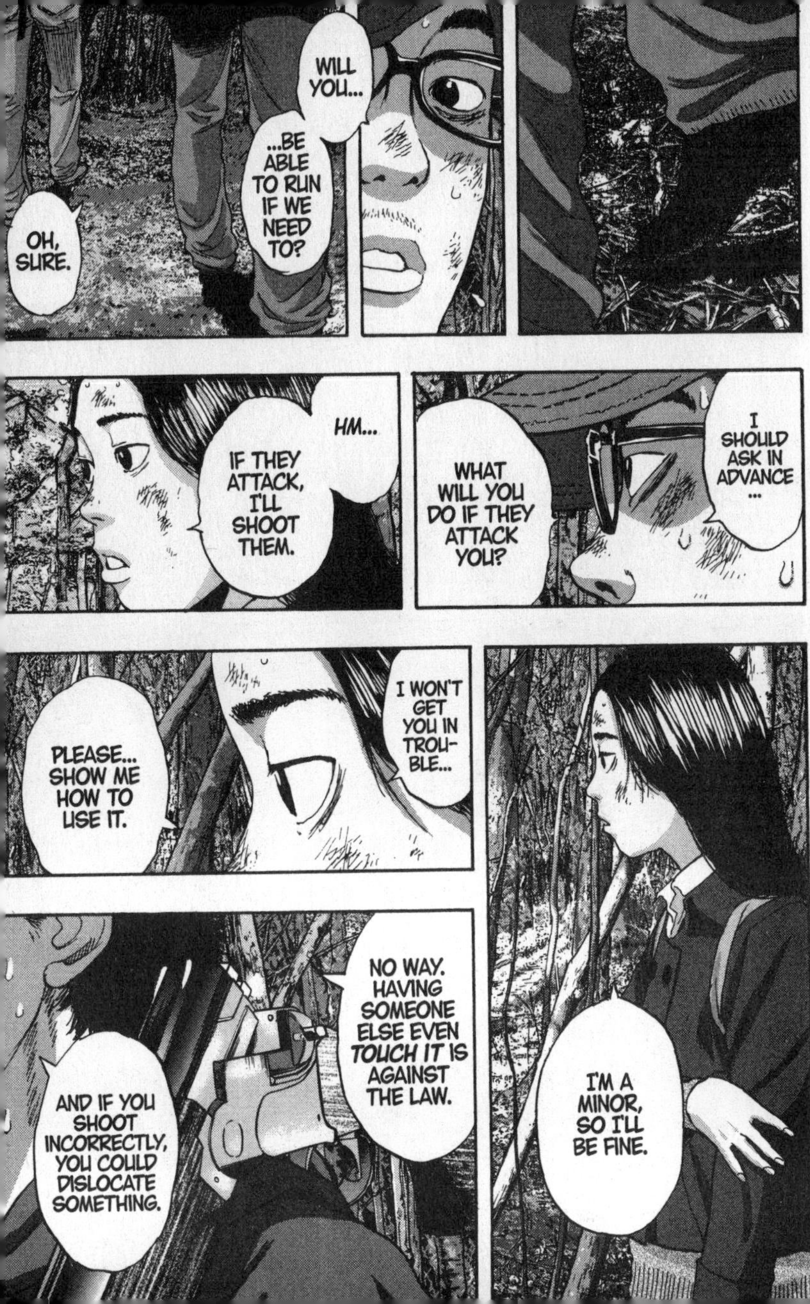
WILL YOU...
...BE ABLE TO RUN IF WE NEED TO?
OH, SURE.
I SHOULD ASK IN ADVANCE ...
WHAT WILL YOU DO IF THEY ATTACK YOU?
HM...
IF THEY ATTACK, I'LL SHOOT THEM.
I'M A MINOR, SO I'LL BE FINE.
I WON'T GET YOU IN TROU-BLE...
PLEASE... SHOW ME HOW TO USE IT.
NO WAY. HAVING SOMEONE ELSE EVEN *TOUCH IT* IS AGAINST THE LAW.
AND IF YOU SHOOT INCORRECTLY, YOU COULD DISLOCATE SOMETHING.

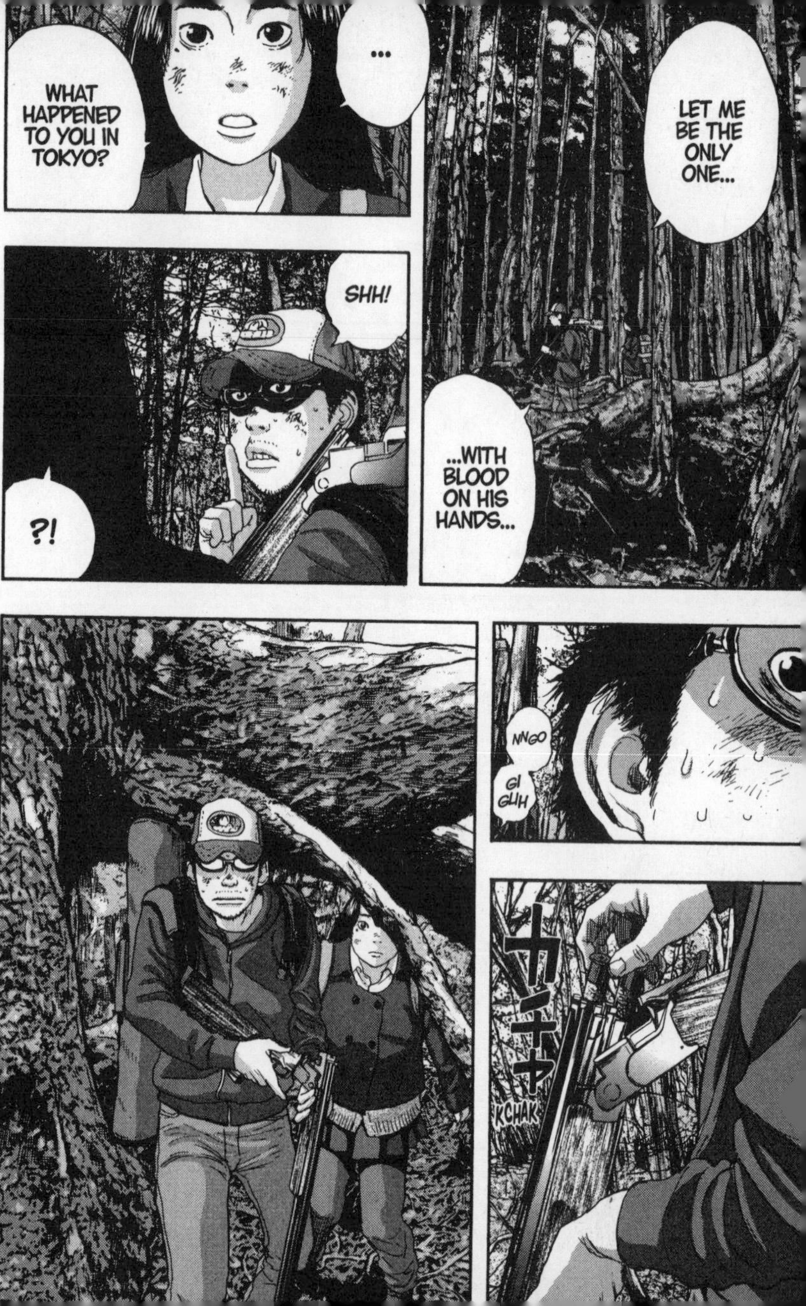
LET ME BE THE ONLY ONE...
...WITH BLOOD ON HIS HANDS...
...
WHAT HAPPENED TO YOU IN TOKYO?
SHH!
?!
NNGO
GI GUH
カチャ
KCHAK

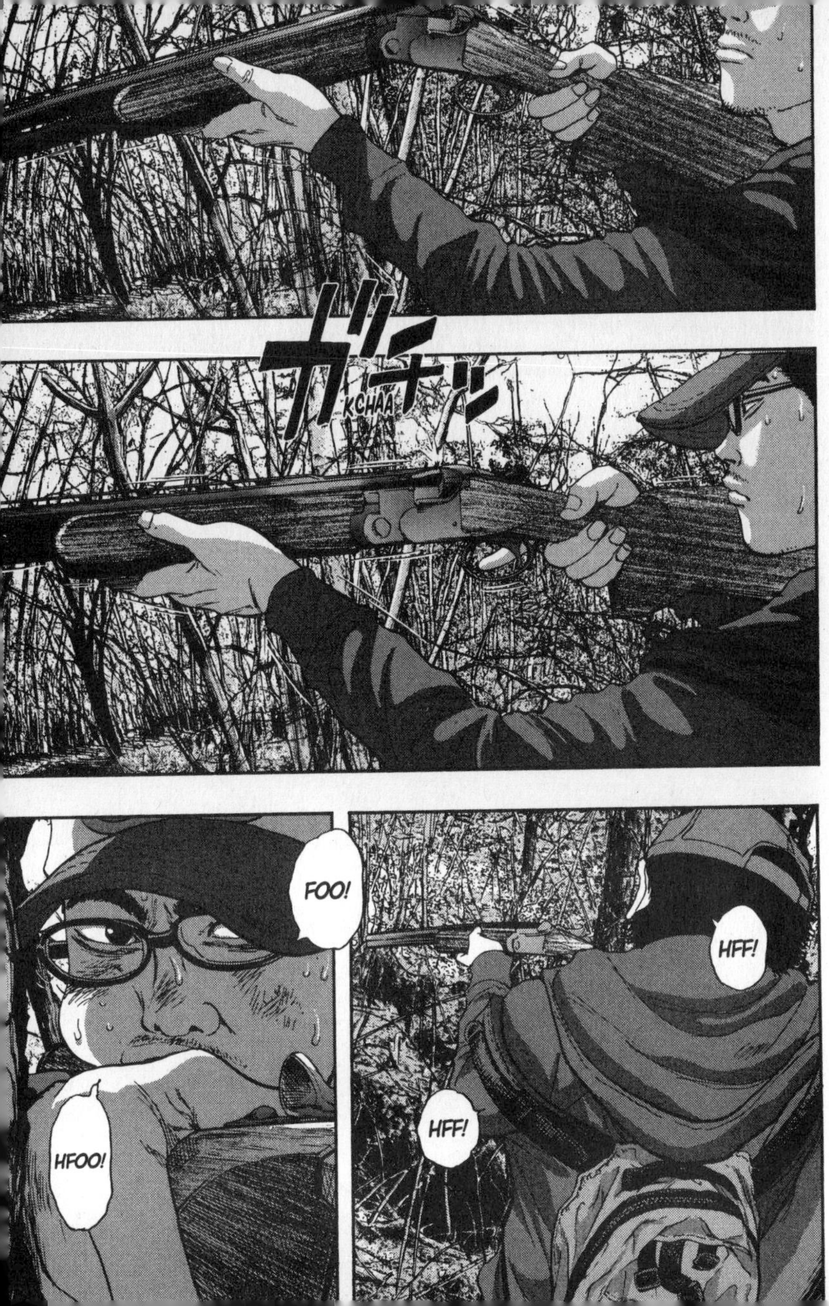
ガチャッ
KCHAA
HFF!
HFF!
FOO!
HFOO!

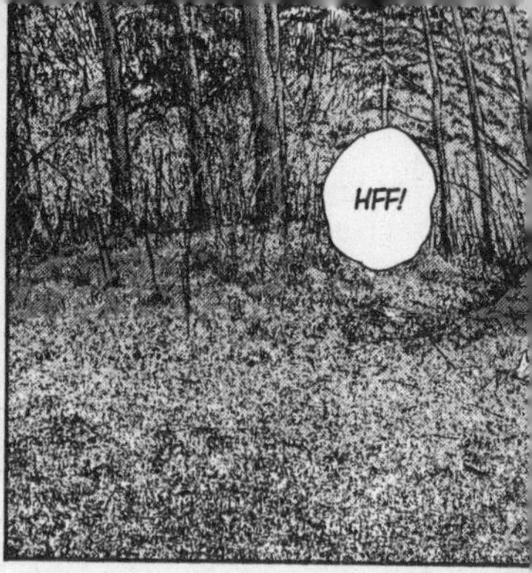
HFF!

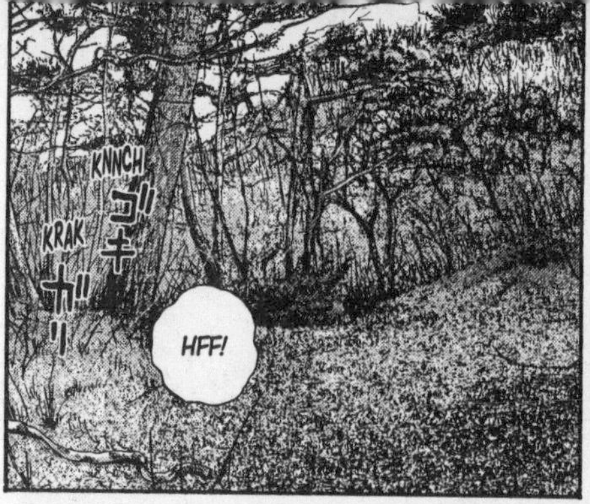
KNNCH
ゴキ
KRAK
ガリ
HFF!

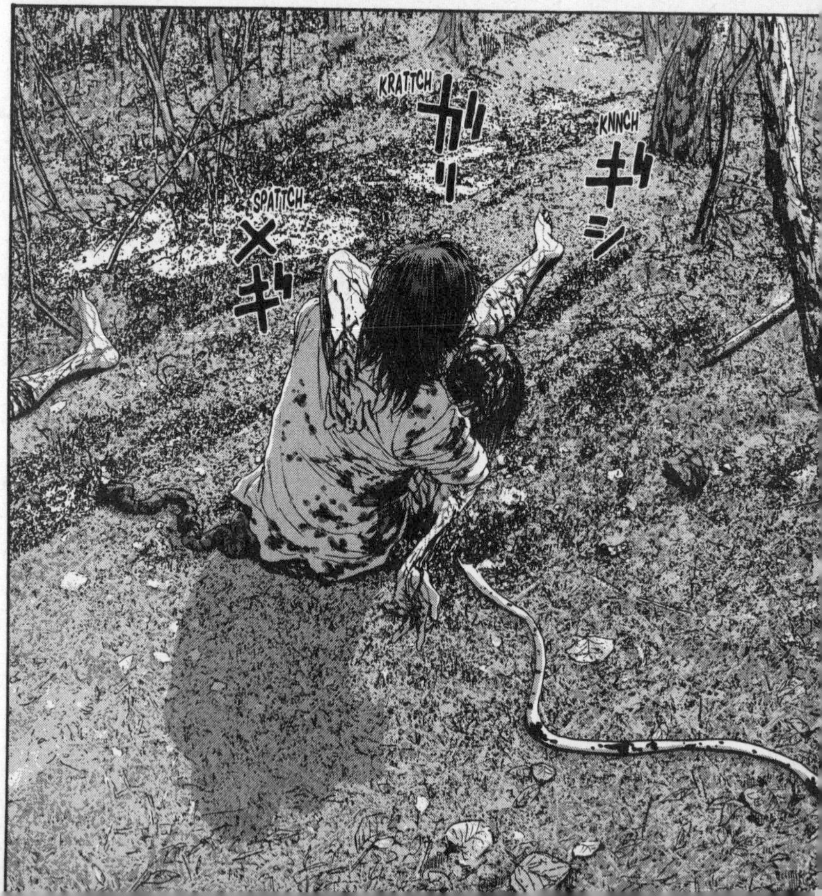
KNNCH
ギシ
KRATTCH
ガリ
SPATTCH
メキ

HRRK!

CHRRK

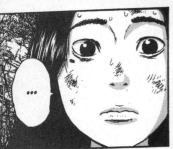

...

WHUH-- WHAT DO WE DO? TH-THEY'RE EATING EACH OTHER! CAN'T WE JUST LEAVE THEM ALONE?

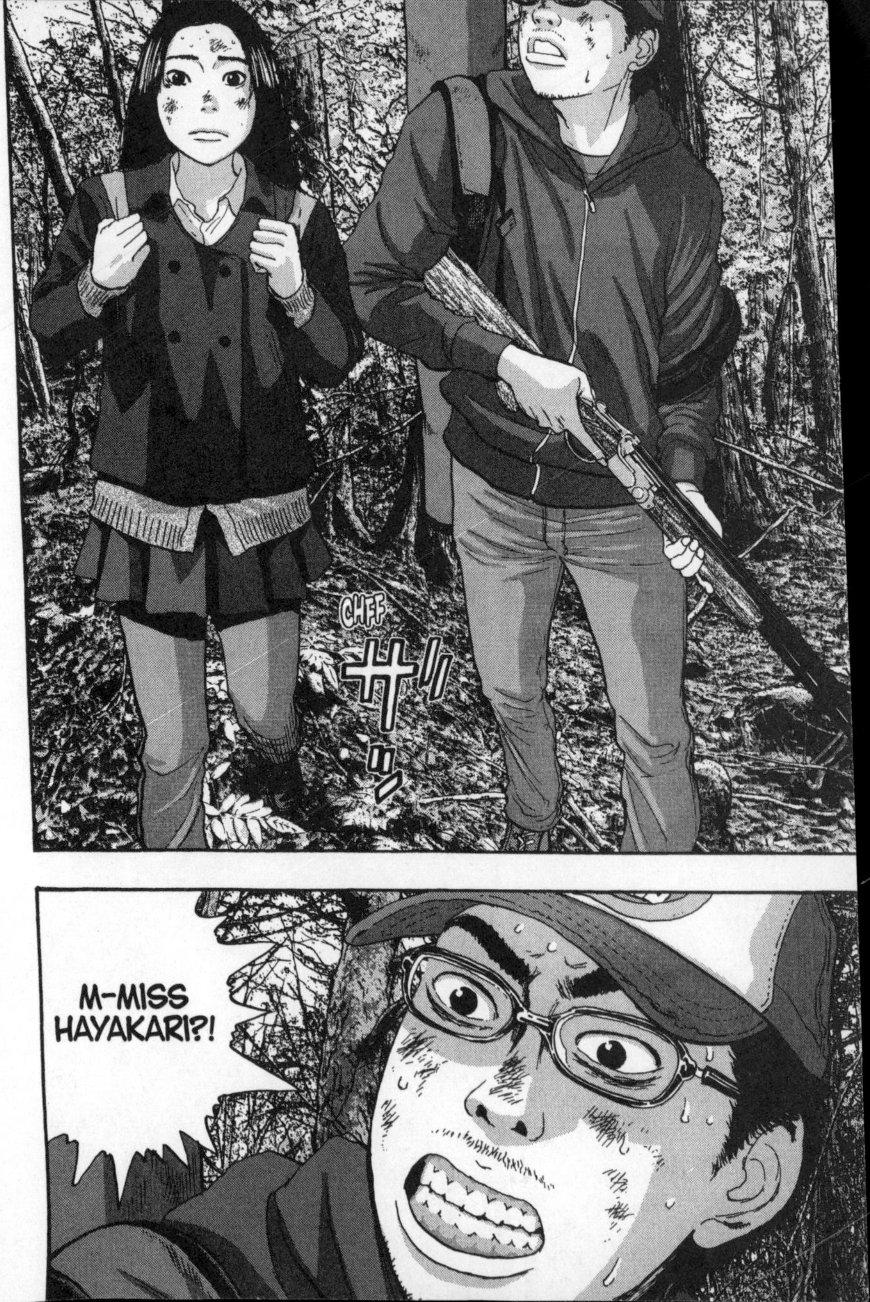
CHFF
M-MISS HAYAKARI?!

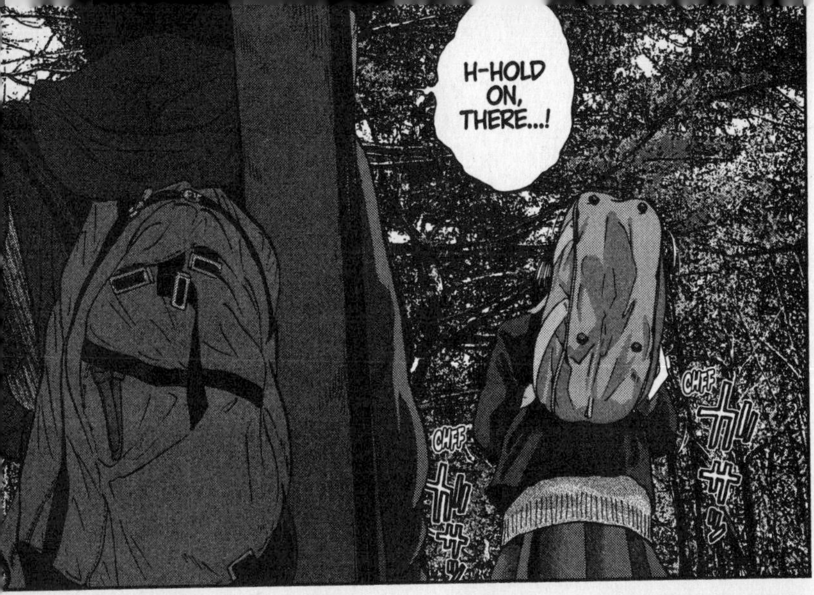
H-HOLD ON, THERE...!
CHFF
CHFF

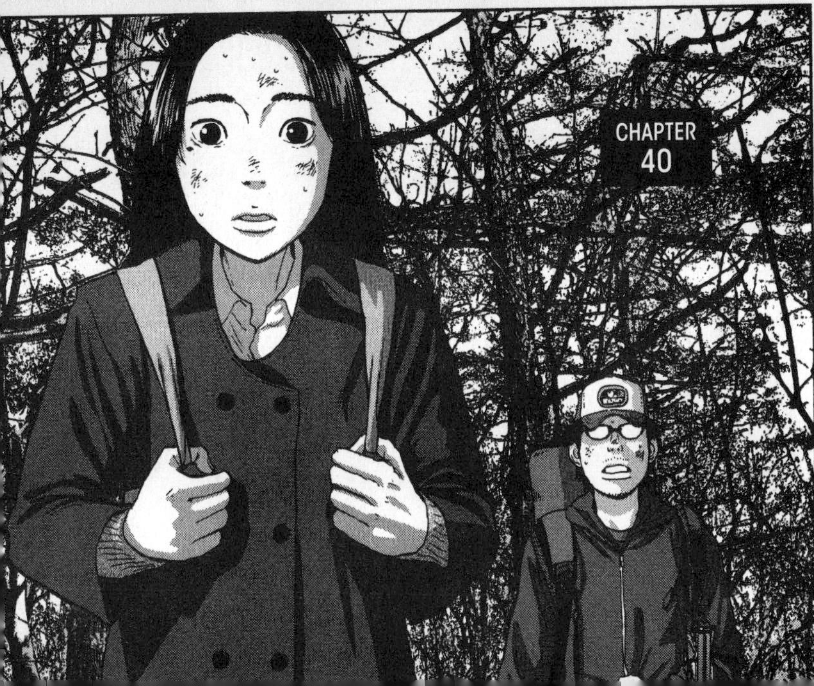
CHAPTER 40

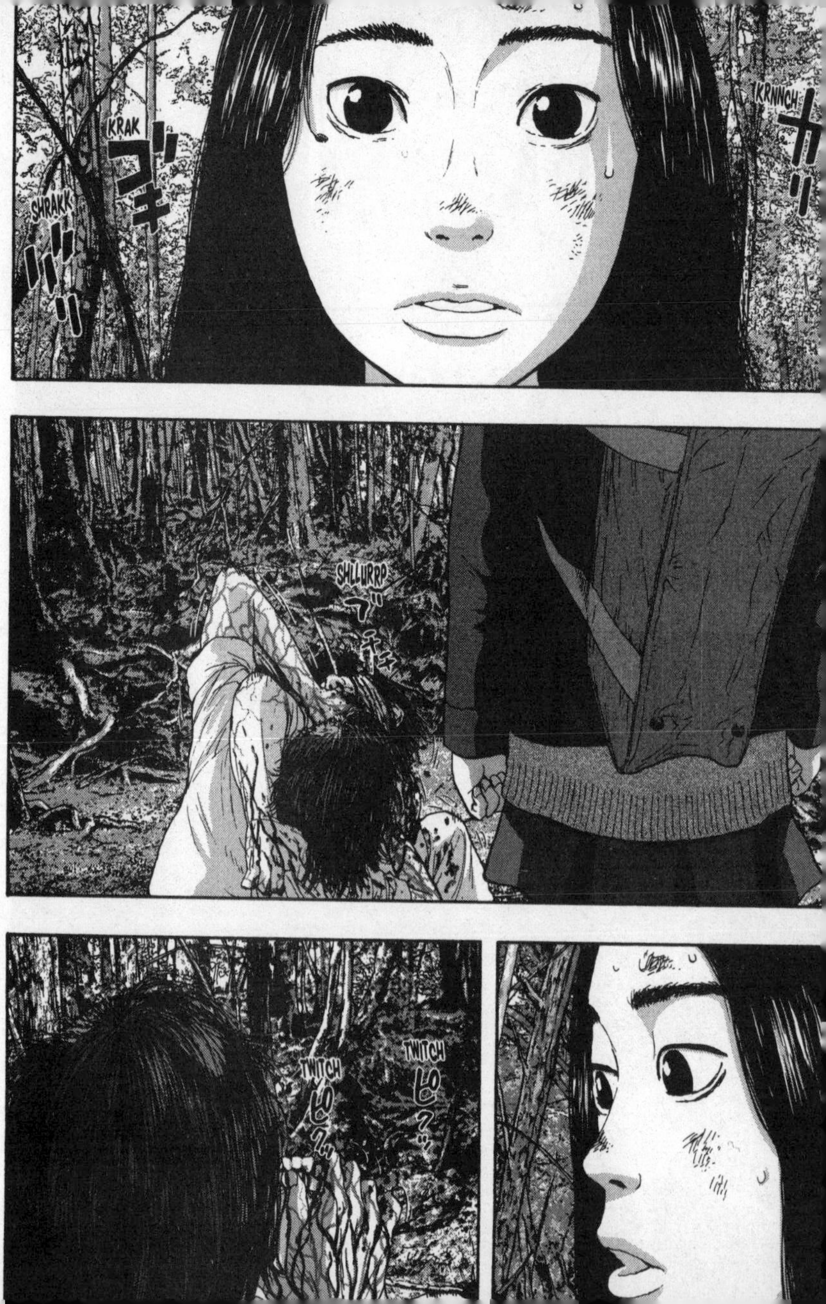
KRNNCH
KRAK
SHRAKK
SHLLURRP
TWITCH
TWITCH

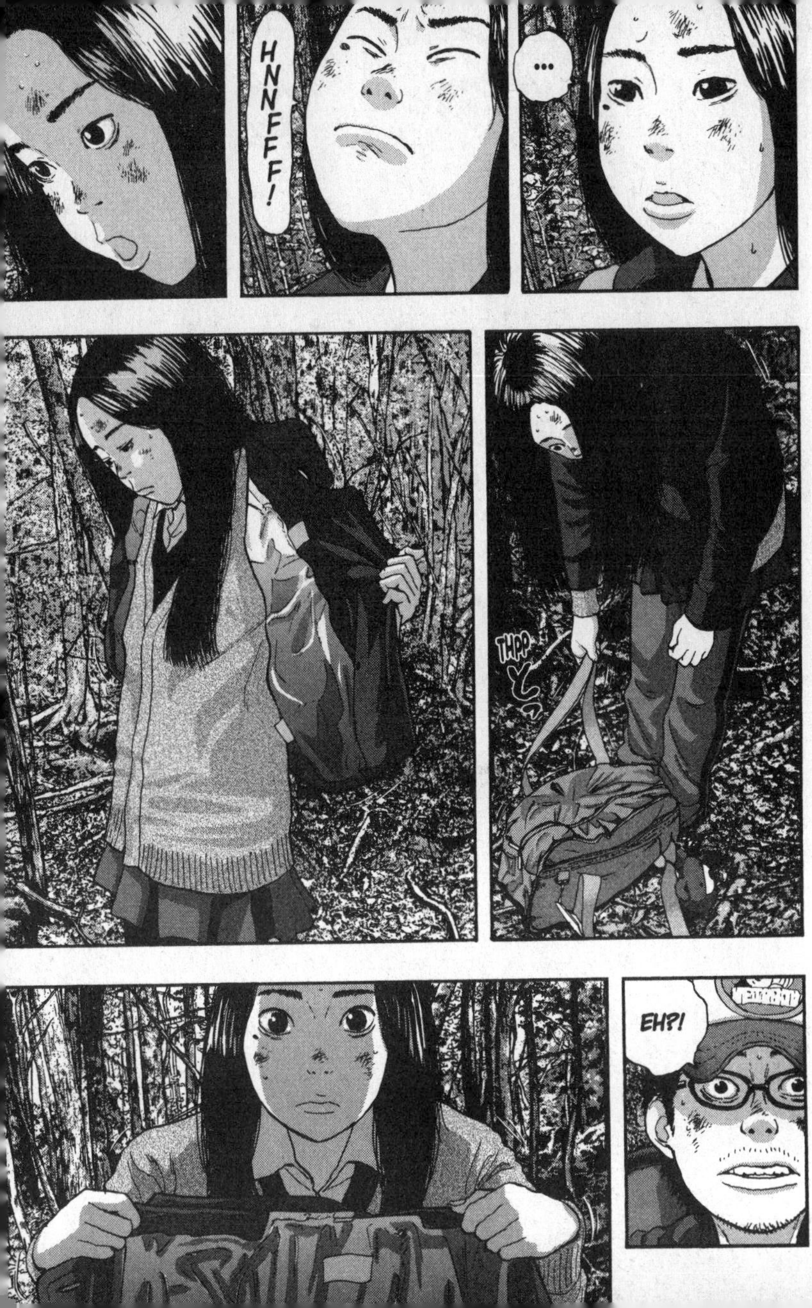
...
HNNFFF!
THPP
EH?!

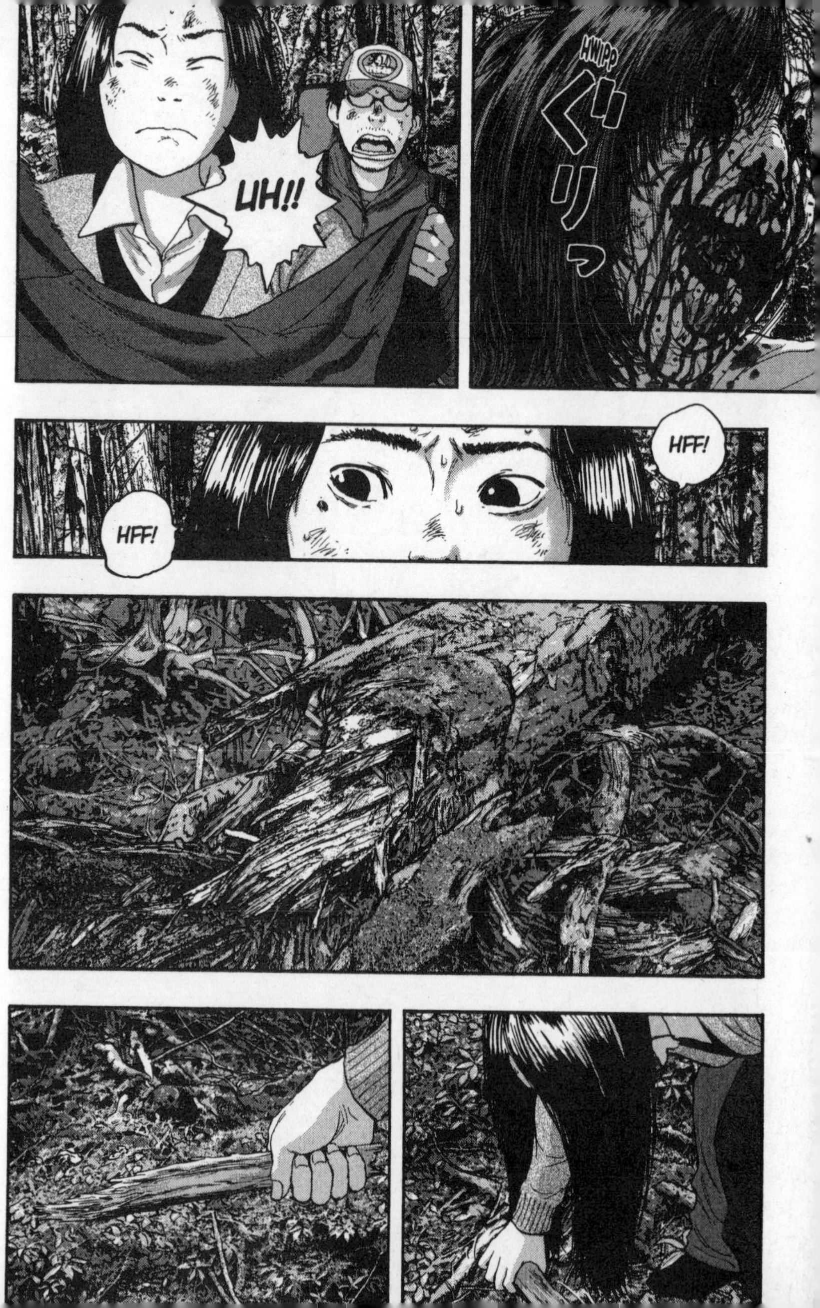
HWIPP
ぐリッ
UH!!
HFF!
HFF!

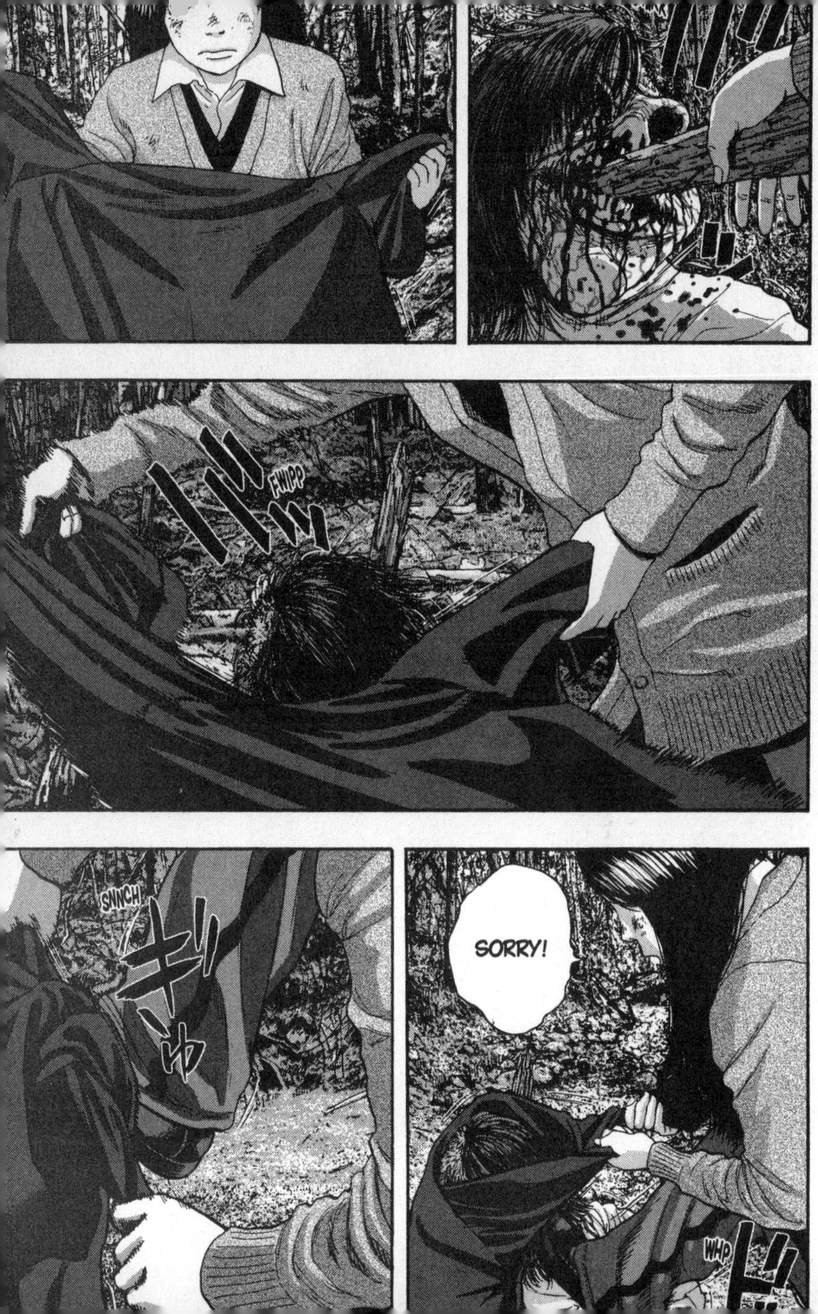
FWIPP
SORRY!
WHP
SNNCH

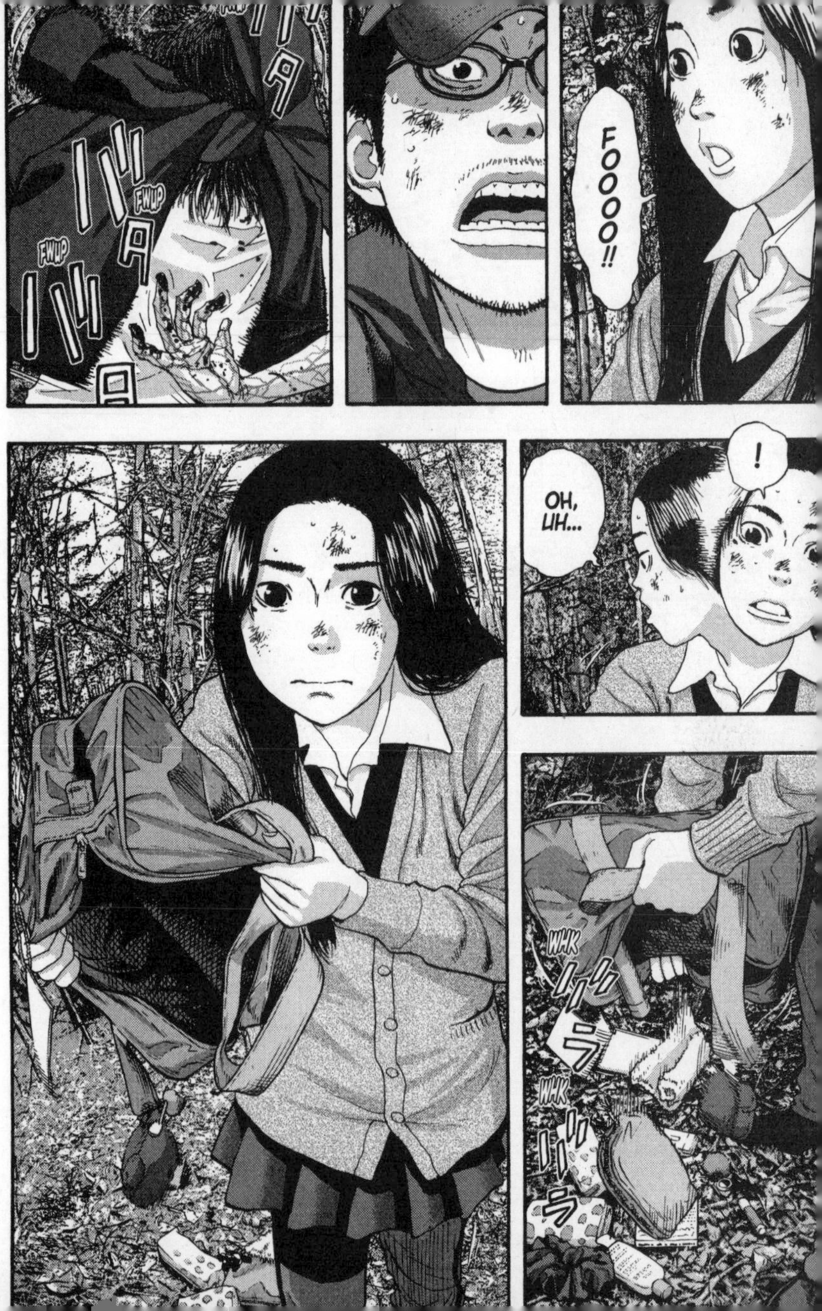

FOOOOO!!
FWUP
FWUP
!
OH, UH...
WHK
WHK

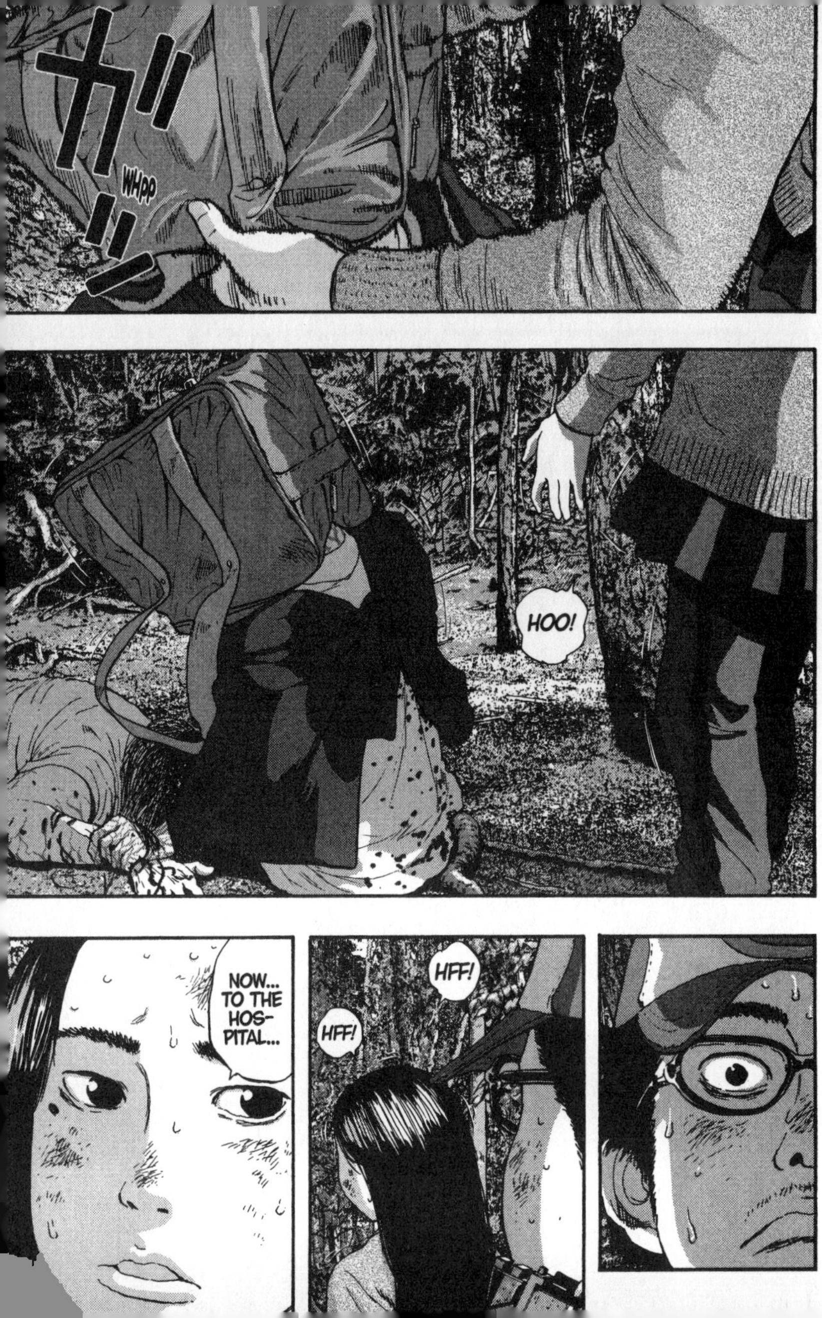
WHPP
HOO!
HFF!
HFF!
NOW... TO THE HOS-PITAL...

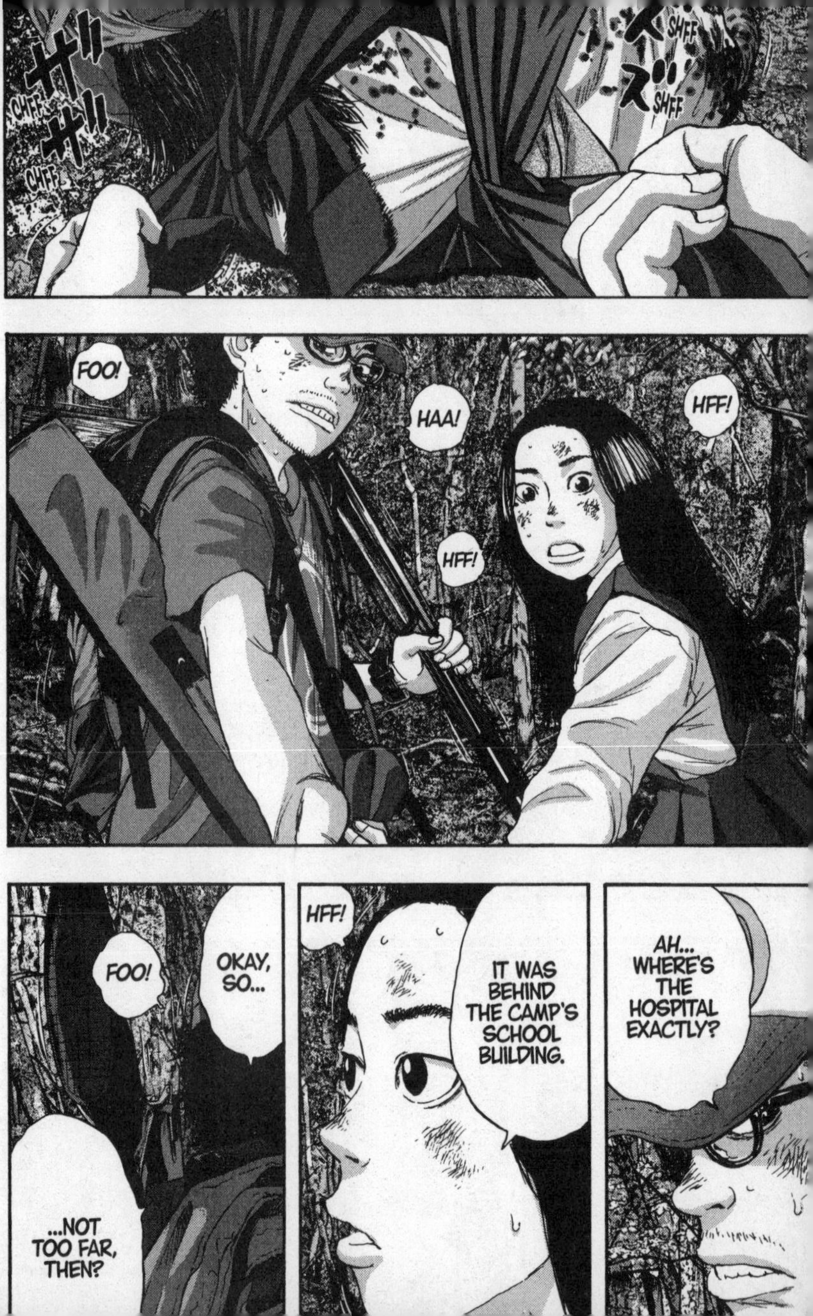
SHFF
SHFF
CHFF
CHFF
HFF!
HAA!
HFF!
FOO!
AH... WHERE'S THE HOSPITAL EXACTLY?
IT WAS BEHIND THE CAMP'S SCHOOL BUILDING.
HFF!
OKAY, SO...
FOO!
...NOT TOO FAR, THEN?

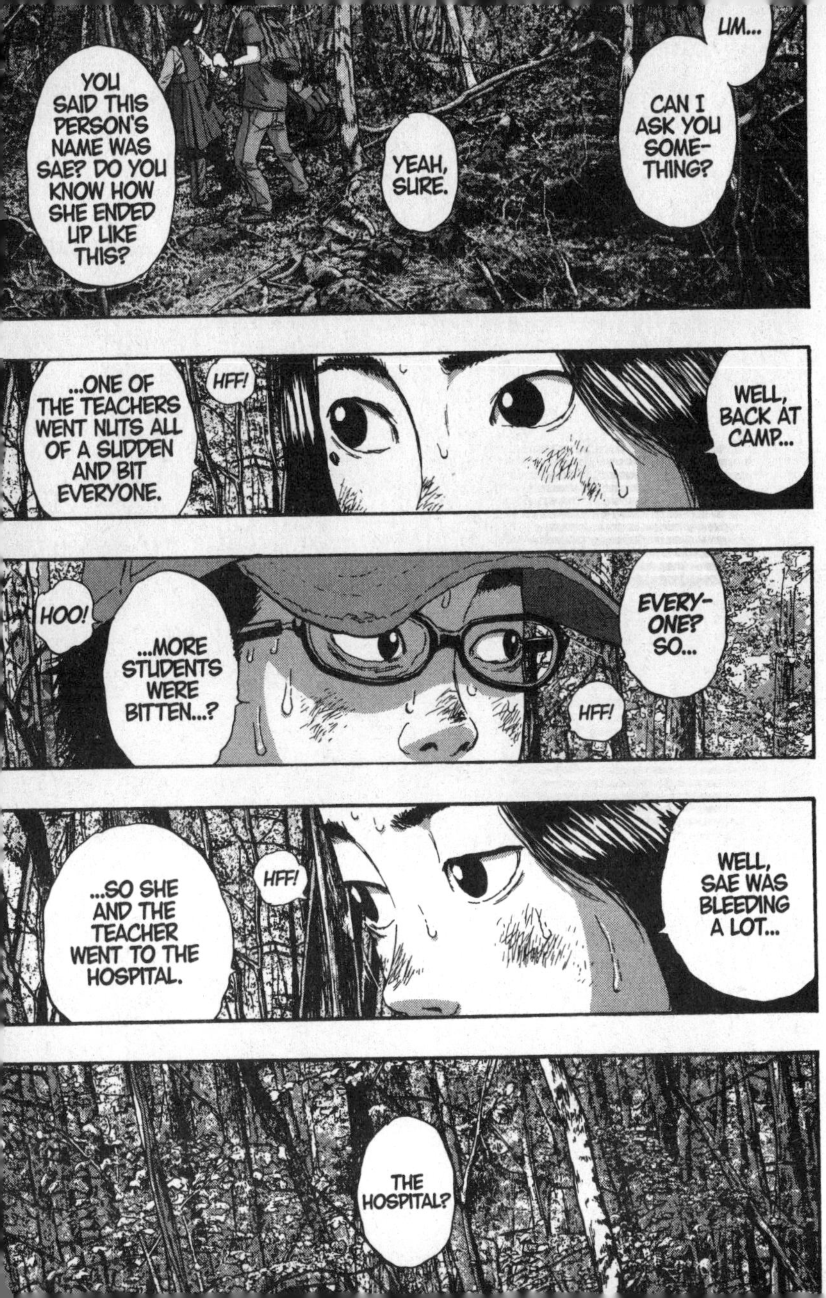
UM...
CAN I ASK YOU SOME-THING?
YEAH, SURE.
YOU SAID THIS PERSON'S NAME WAS SAE? DO YOU KNOW HOW SHE ENDED UP LIKE THIS?
WELL, BACK AT CAMP...
HFF!
...ONE OF THE TEACHERS WENT NUTS ALL OF A SUDDEN AND BIT EVERYONE.
EVERY-ONE? SO...
HFF!
...MORE STUDENTS WERE BITTEN...?
HOO!
WELL, SAE WAS BLEEDING A LOT...
HFF!
...SO SHE AND THE TEACHER WENT TO THE HOSPITAL.
THE HOSPITAL?

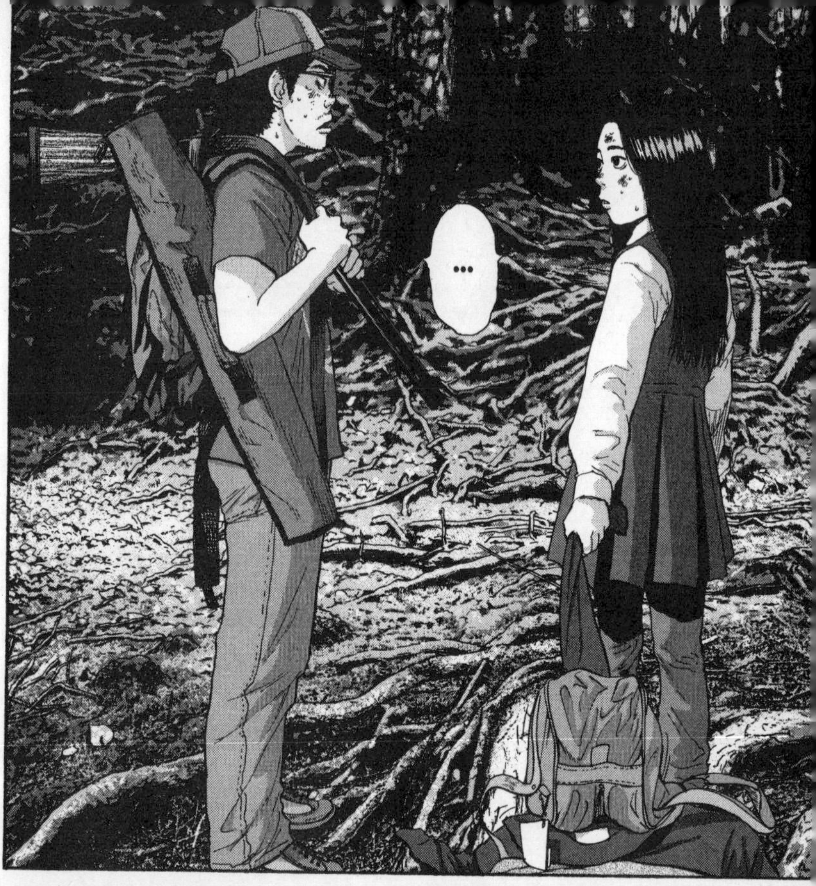
...
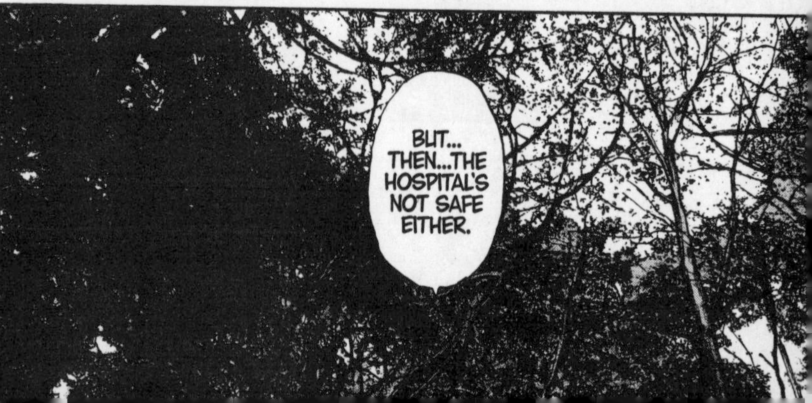
BUT... THEN...THE HOSPITAL'S NOT SAFE EITHER.

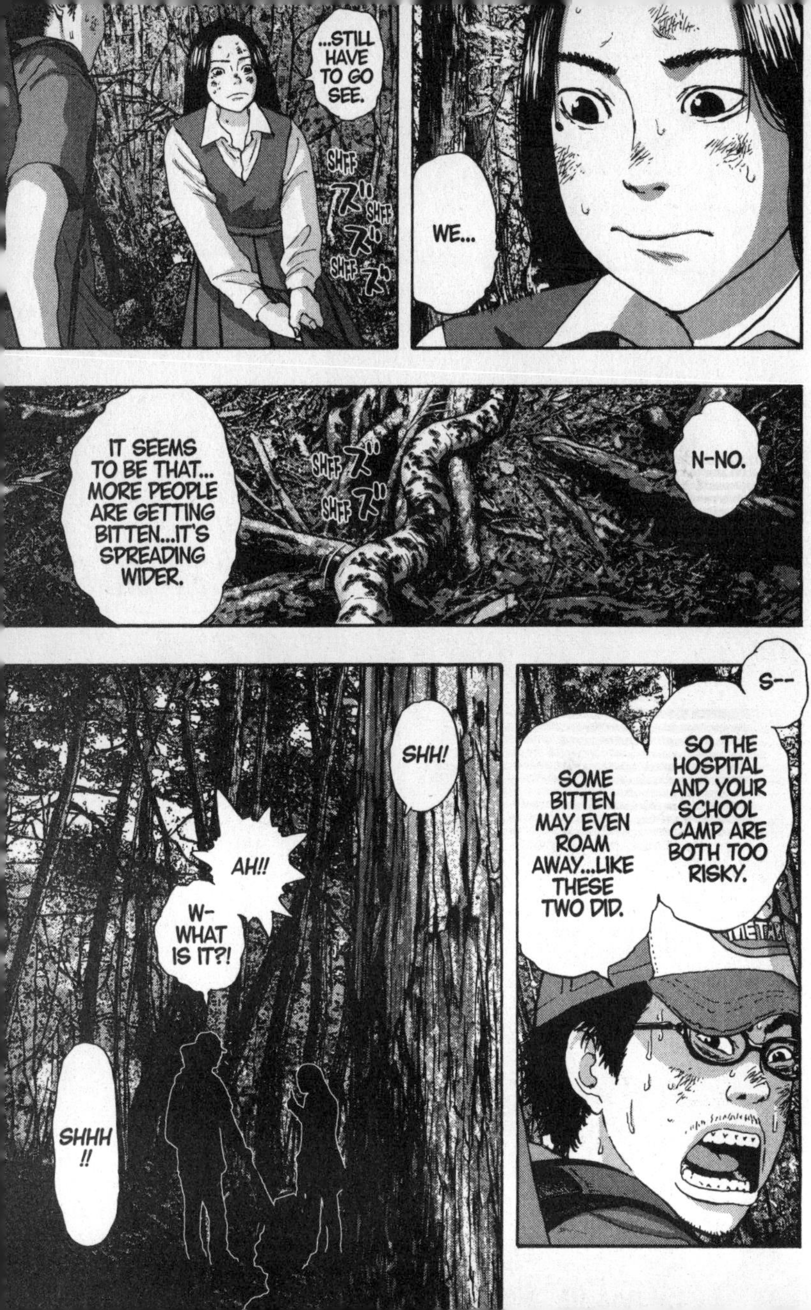
WE...
...STILL HAVE TO GO SEE.
SHFF ズ
SHFF ズ
SHFF ズ
N-NO.
SHFF ズ
SHFF ズ
IT SEEMS TO BE THAT... MORE PEOPLE ARE GETTING BITTEN...IT'S SPREADING WIDER.
S--
SO THE HOSPITAL AND YOUR SCHOOL CAMP ARE BOTH TOO RISKY.
SOME BITTEN MAY EVEN ROAM AWAY...LIKE THESE TWO DID.
SHH!
AH!!
W- WHAT IS IT?!
SHHH !!

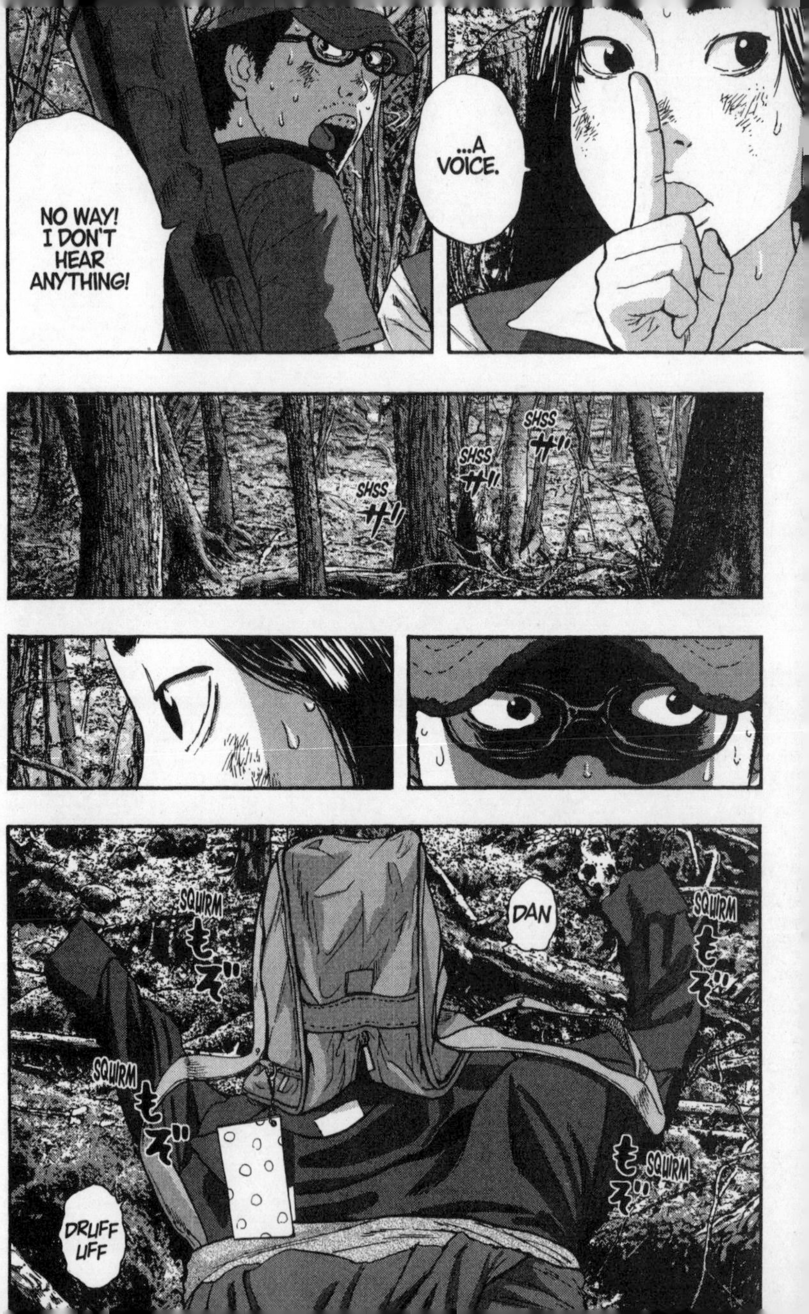

...A VOICE.
NO WAY! I DON'T HEAR ANYTHING!
SHSS ザッ
SHSS ザッ
SHSS ザッ
DAN
SQUIRM もぞ
SQUIRM もぞ
SQUIRM もぞ
SQUIRM もぞ
DRUFF LIFF

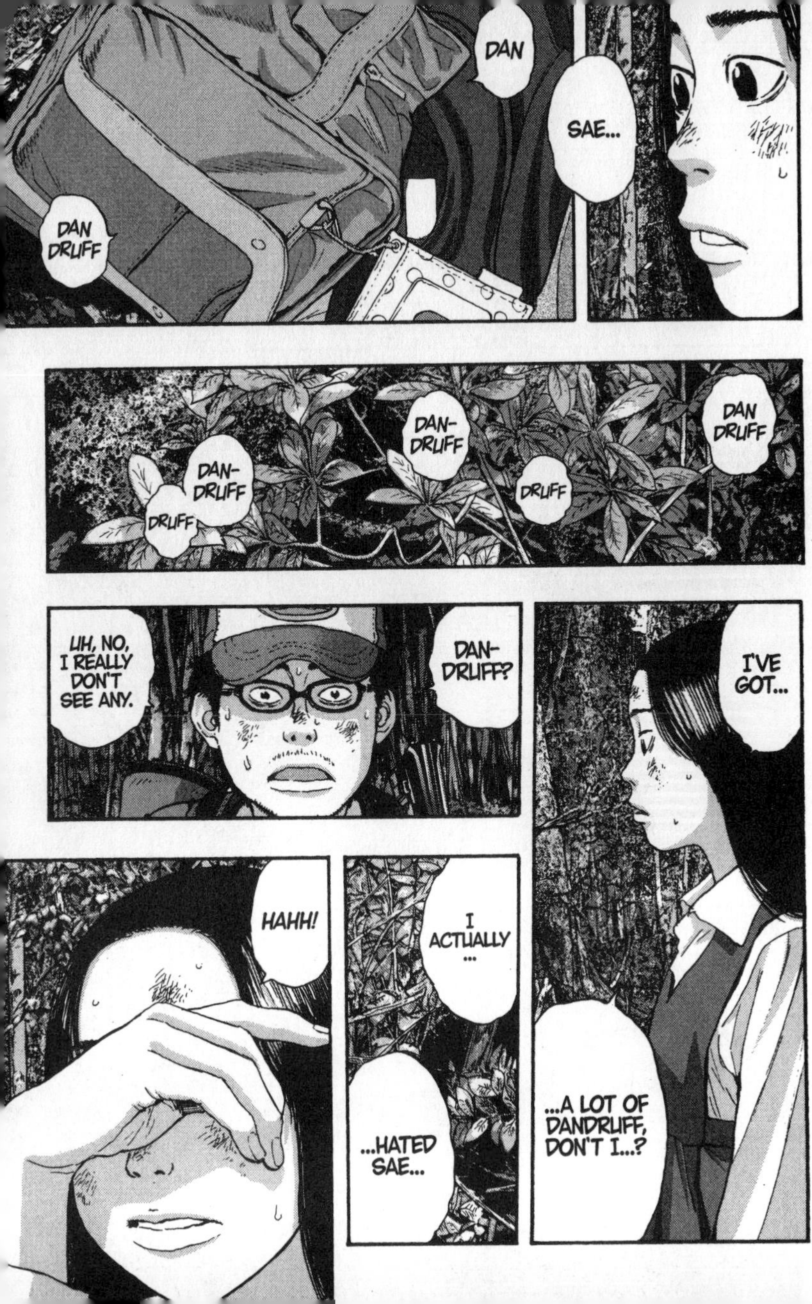
SAE...
DAN
DAN DRUFF
DAN DRUFF
DAN-DRUFF
DRUFF
DAN-DRUFF
DRUFF
I'VE GOT...
...A LOT OF DANDRUFF, DON'T I...?
DAN-DRUFF?
UH, NO, I REALLY DON'T SEE ANY.
I ACTUALLY ...
...HATED SAE...
HAHH!

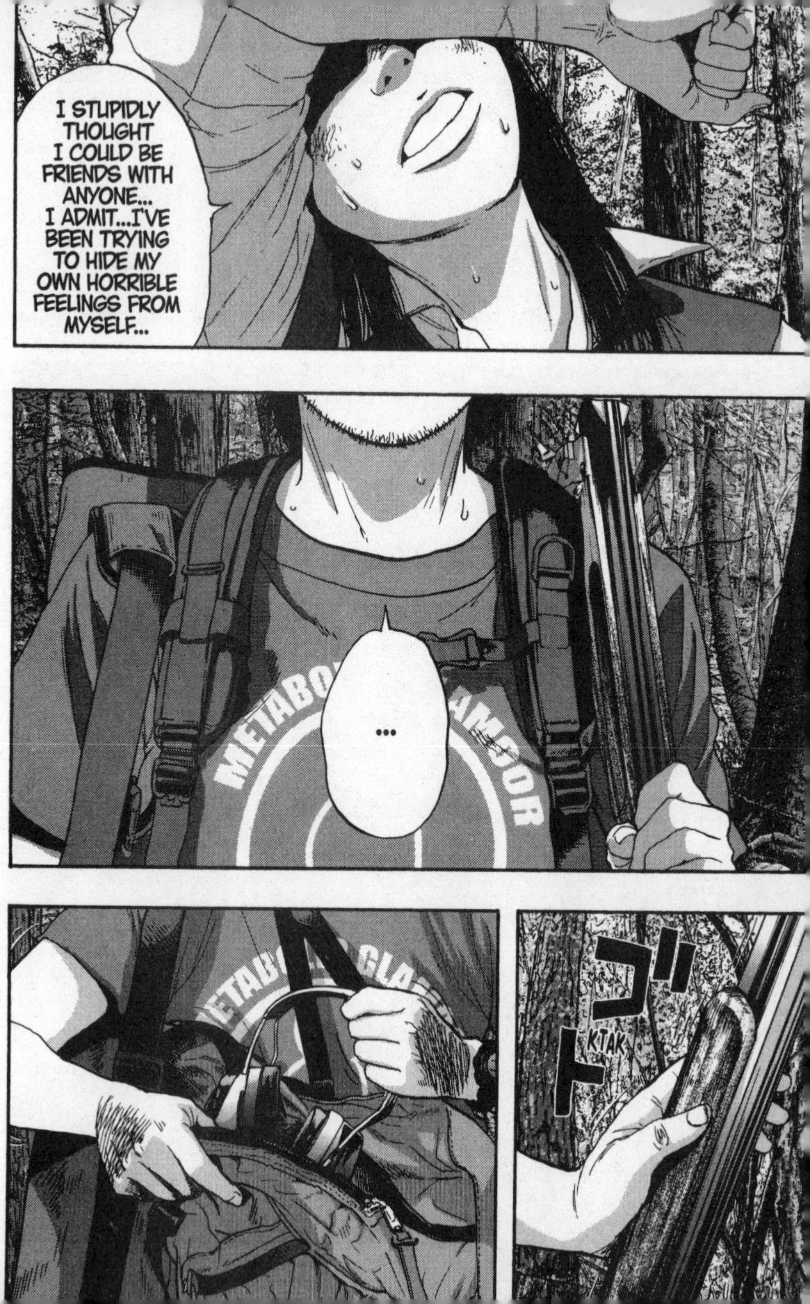
I STUPIDLY THOUGHT I COULD BE FRIENDS WITH ANYONE... I ADMIT...I'VE BEEN TRYING TO HIDE MY OWN HORRIBLE FEELINGS FROM MYSELF...
...
ゴット
K'TAK

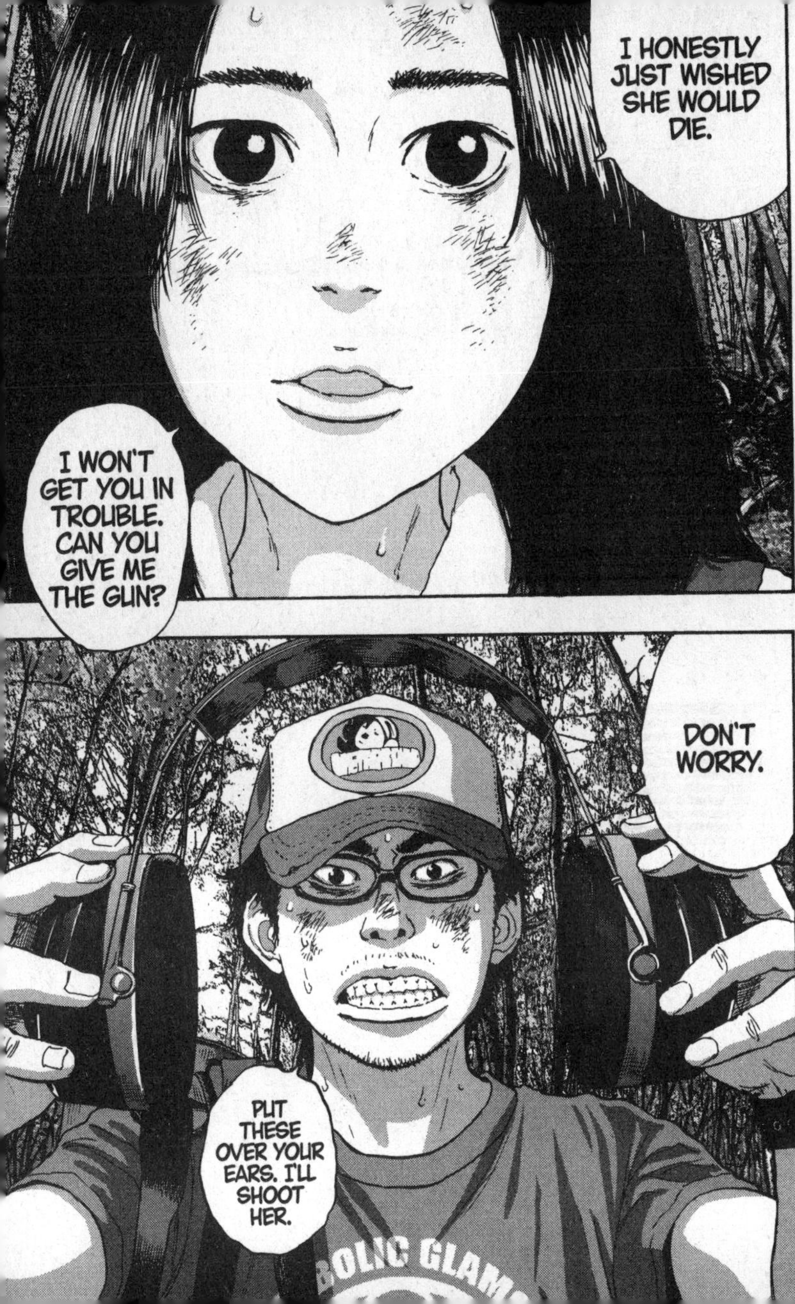
I HONESTLY JUST WISHED SHE WOULD DIE.
I WON'T GET YOU IN TROUBLE. CAN YOU GIVE ME THE GUN?
DON'T WORRY.
PUT THESE OVER YOUR EARS. I'LL SHOOT HER.

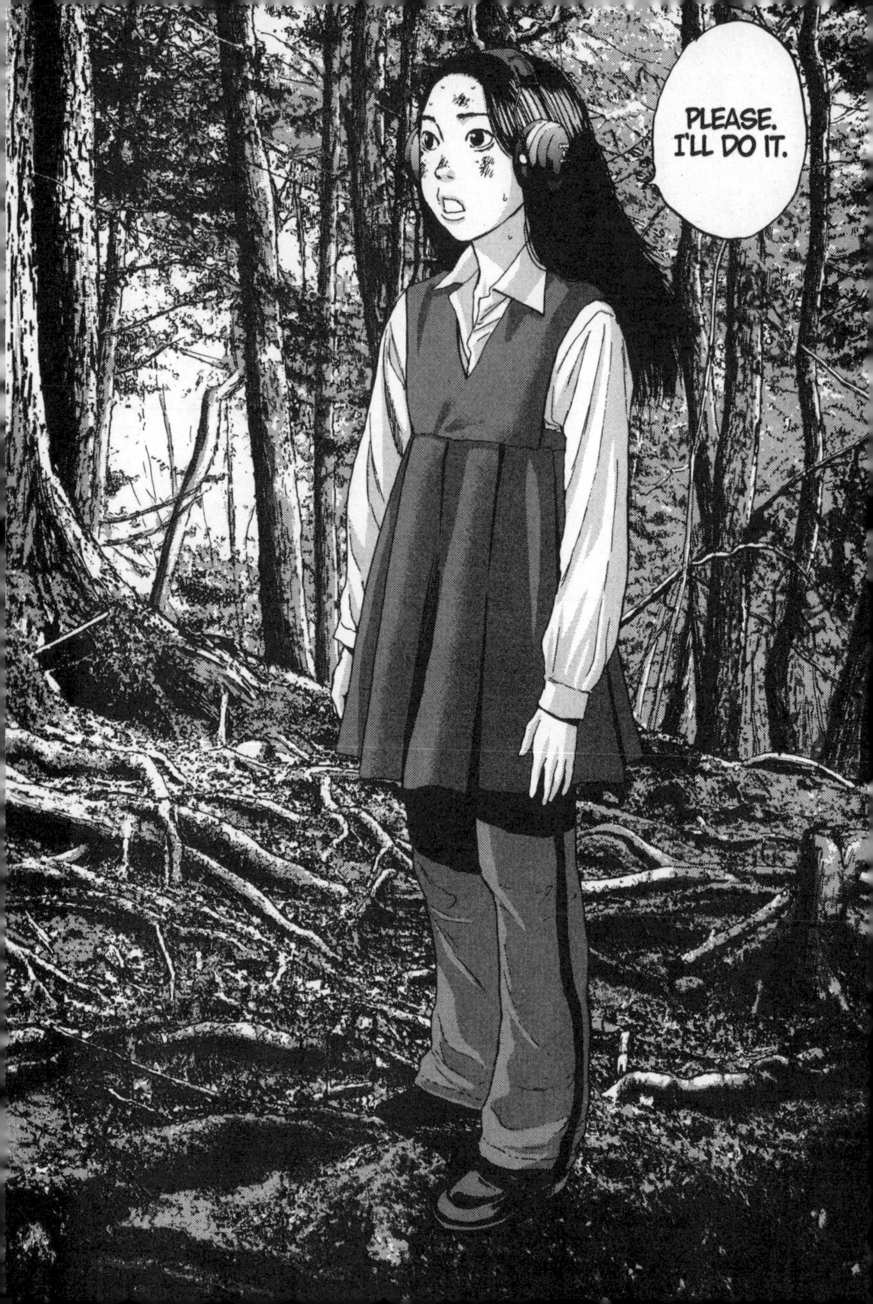
PLEASE. I'LL DO IT.

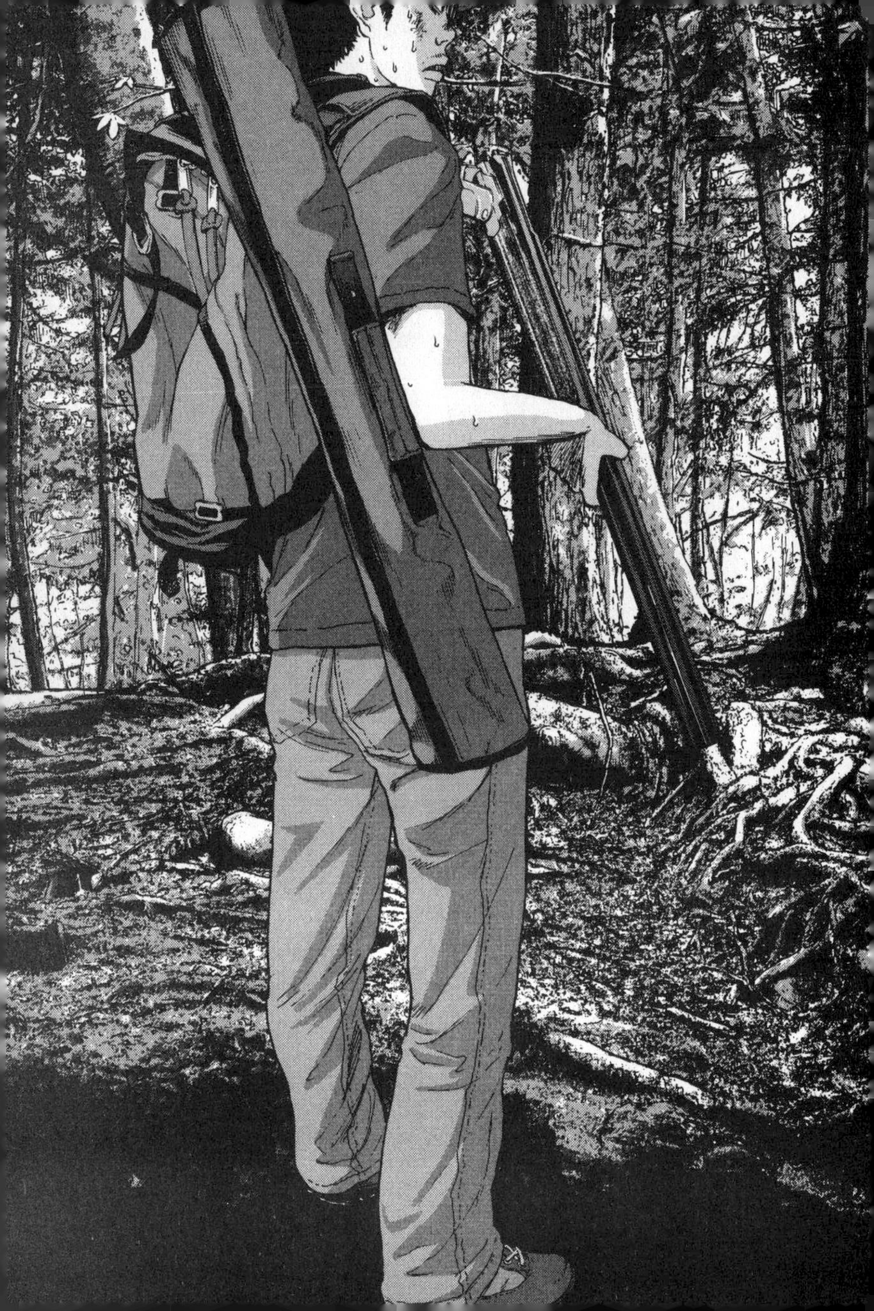

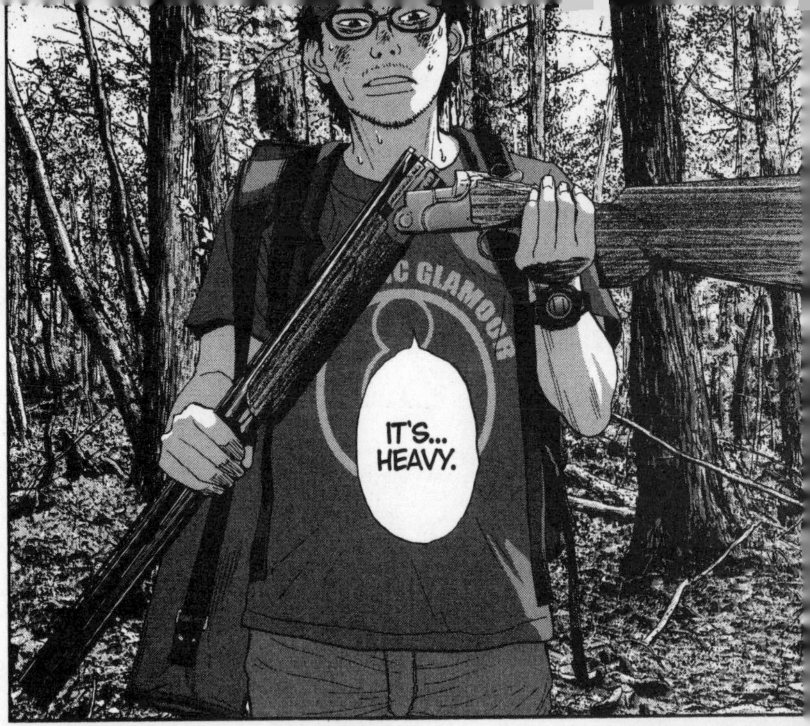
IT'S... HEAVY.
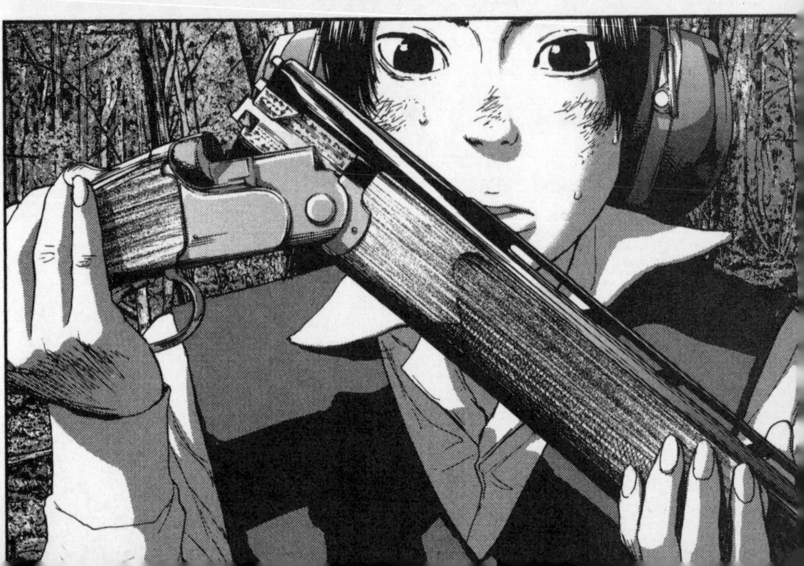

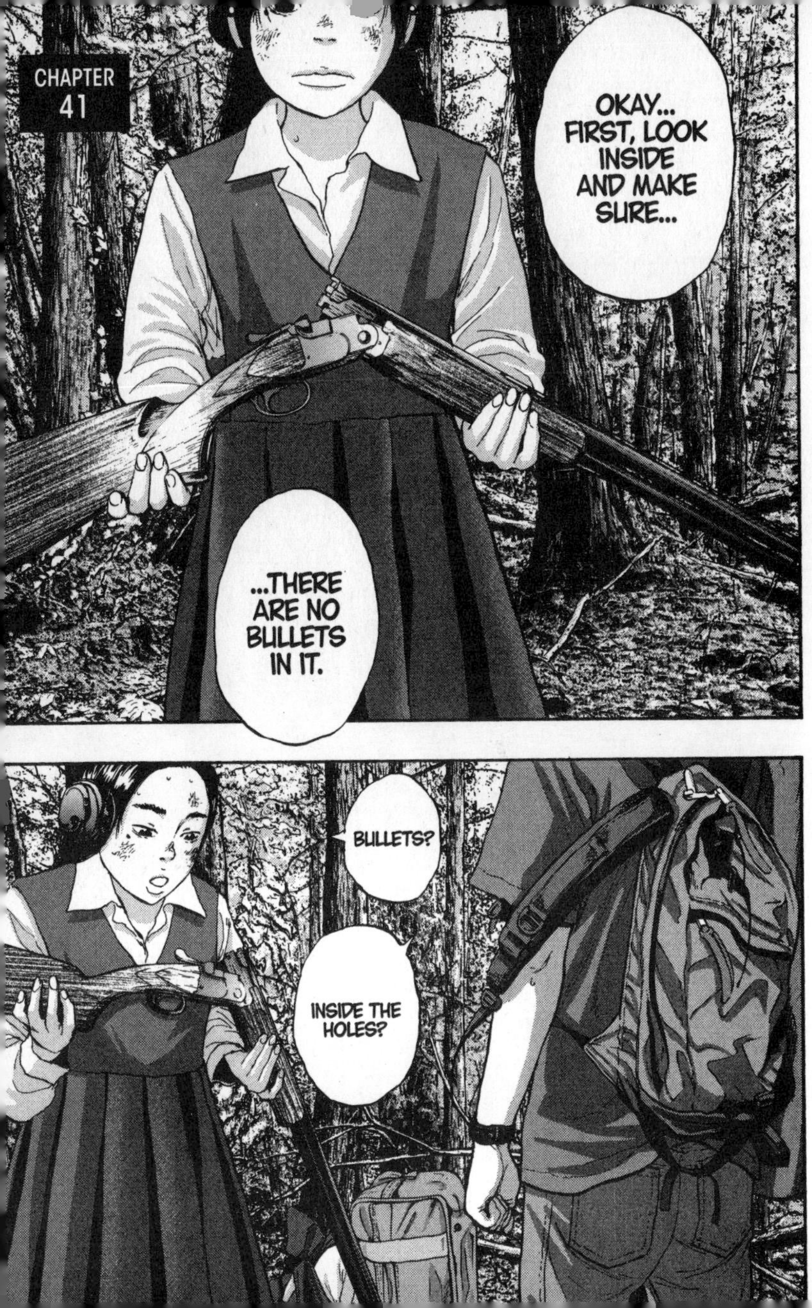
CHAPTER 41
OKAY... FIRST, LOOK INSIDE AND MAKE SURE...
...THERE ARE NO BULLETS IN IT.
BULLETS?
INSIDE THE HOLES?

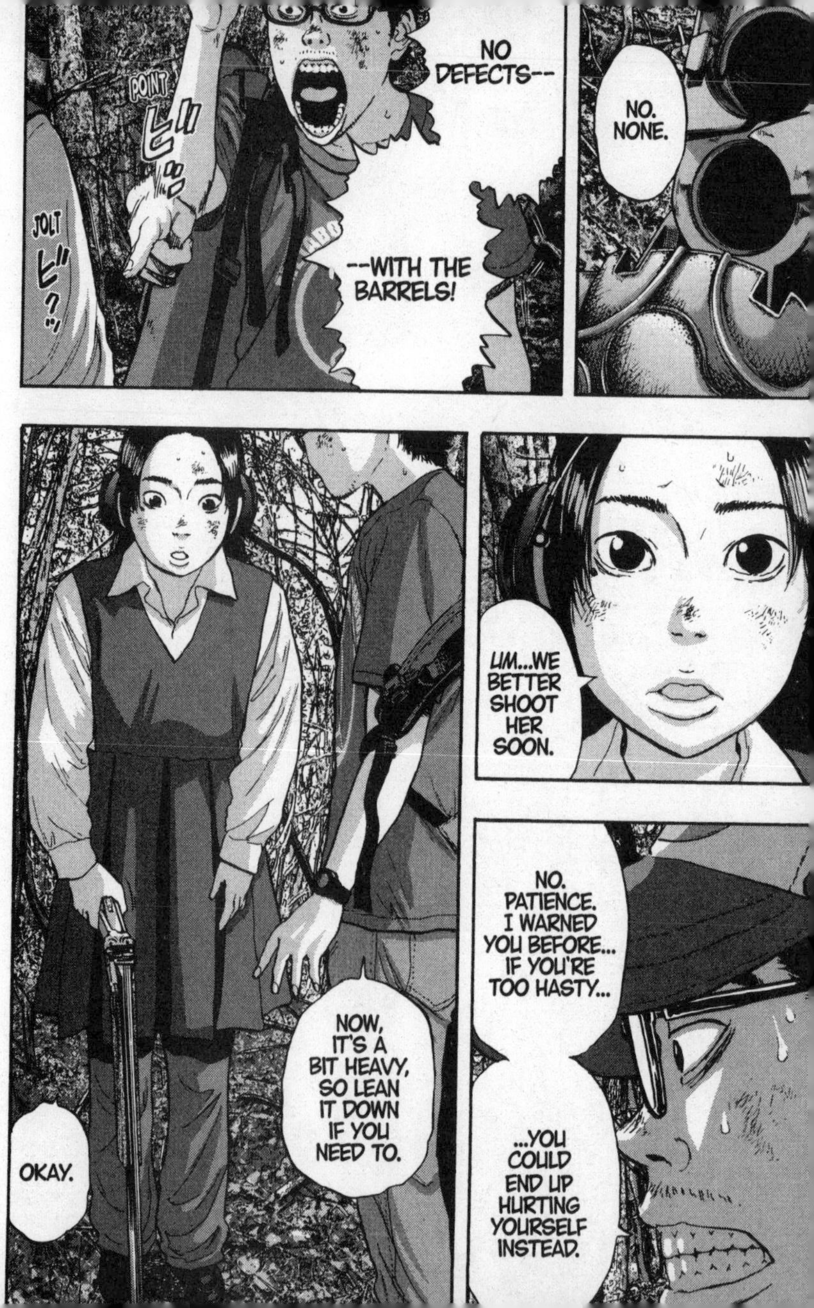
NO. NONE.
NO DEFECTS--
POINT
--WITH THE BARRELS!
JOLT
UM...WE BETTER SHOOT HER SOON.
NO. PATIENCE. I WARNED YOU BEFORE... IF YOU'RE TOO HASTY...
...YOU COULD END UP HURTING YOURSELF INSTEAD.
NOW, IT'S A BIT HEAVY, SO LEAN IT DOWN IF YOU NEED TO.
OKAY.

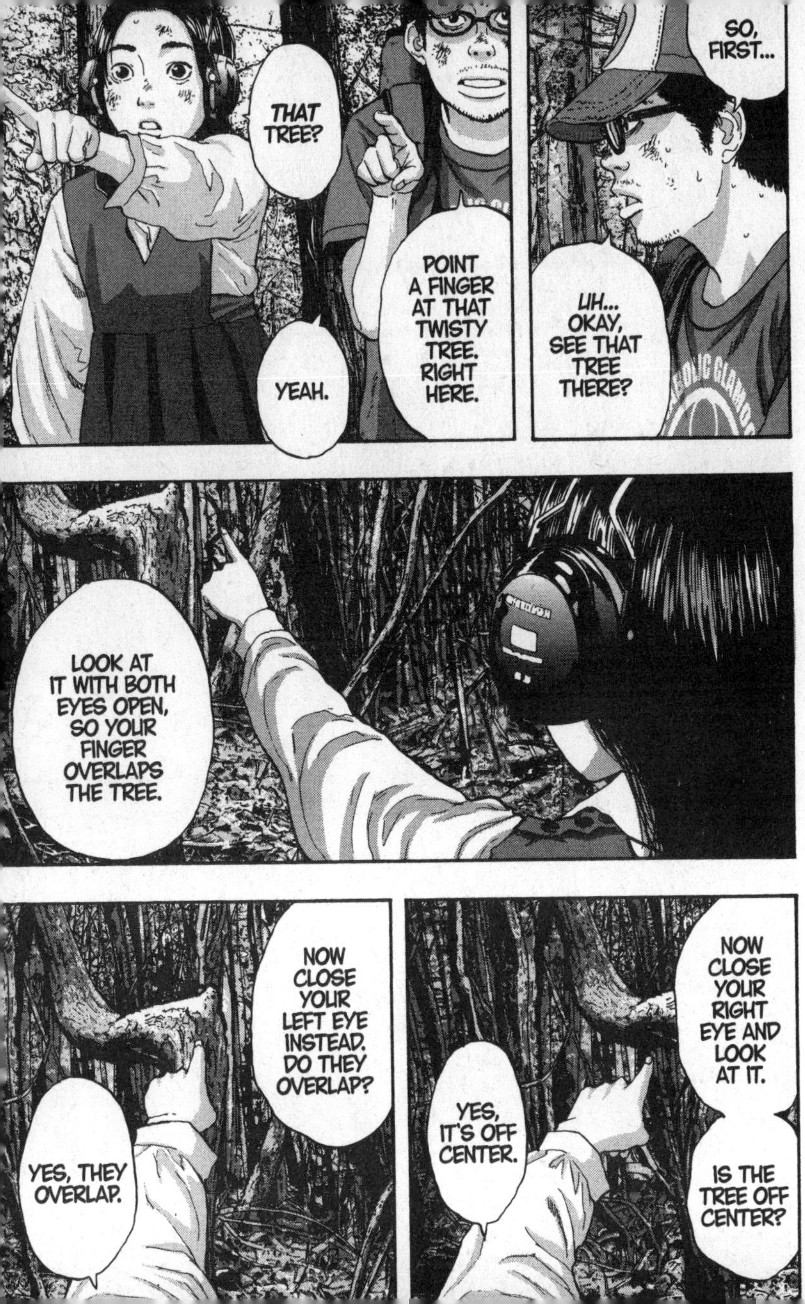
SO, FIRST...
UH... OKAY, SEE THAT TREE THERE?
POINT A FINGER AT THAT TWISTY TREE. RIGHT HERE.
THAT TREE?
YEAH.
LOOK AT IT WITH BOTH EYES OPEN, SO YOUR FINGER OVERLAPS THE TREE.
NOW CLOSE YOUR RIGHT EYE AND LOOK AT IT.
IS THE TREE OFF CENTER?
YES, IT'S OFF CENTER.
NOW CLOSE YOUR LEFT EYE INSTEAD. DO THEY OVERLAP?
YES, THEY OVERLAP.

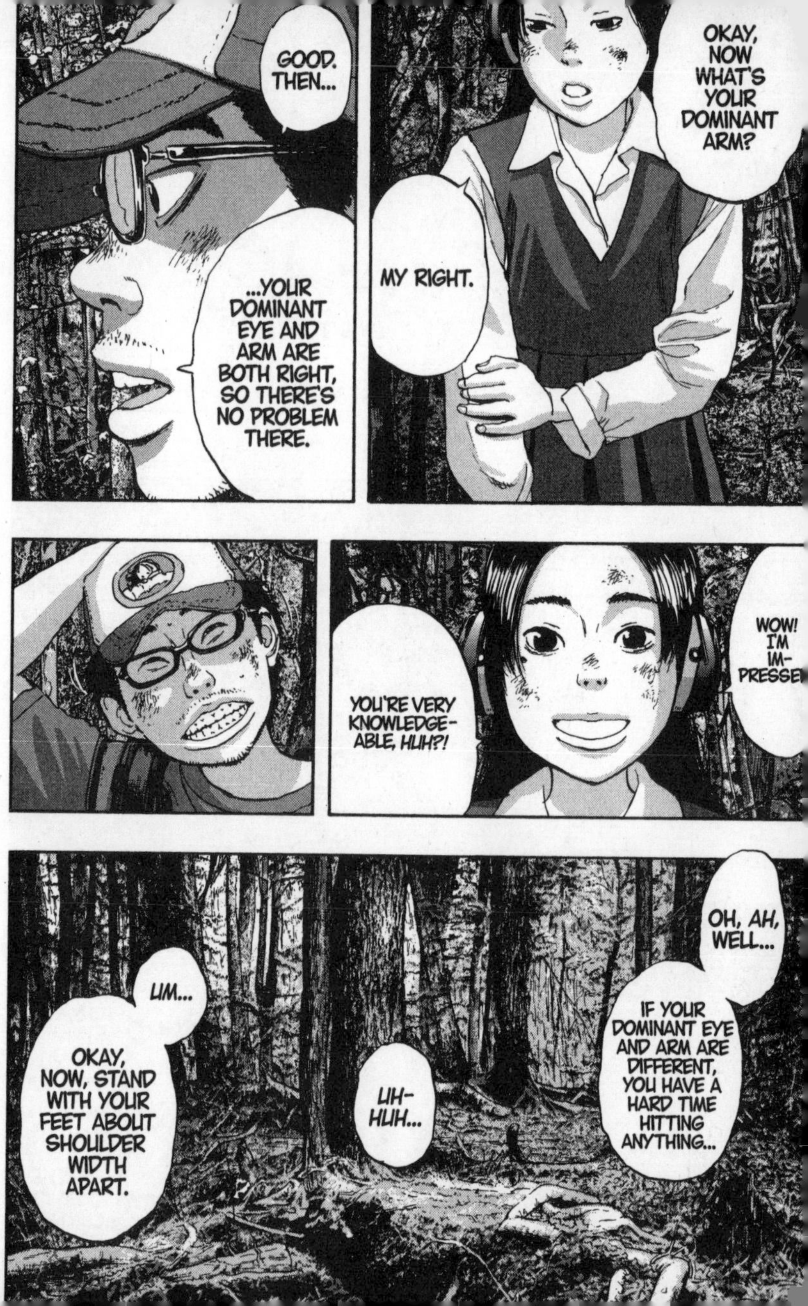
OKAY, NOW WHAT'S YOUR DOMINANT ARM?
MY RIGHT.
GOOD. THEN...
...YOUR DOMINANT EYE AND ARM ARE BOTH RIGHT, SO THERE'S NO PROBLEM THERE.
WOW! I'M IM-PRESSE
YOU'RE VERY KNOWLEDGE-ABLE, HUH?!
OH, AH, WELL...
IF YOUR DOMINANT EYE AND ARM ARE DIFFERENT, YOU HAVE A HARD TIME HITTING ANYTHING...
UH-HUH...
UM...
OKAY, NOW, STAND WITH YOUR FEET ABOUT SHOULDER WIDTH APART.

KEEP YOUR FEET THERE... AND TURN TOWARD ME.

GOOD.

NOW I'LL LOAD IT.

UH-HUH.

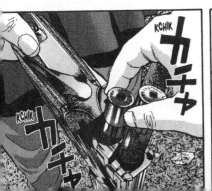

KCHIK

KCHIK

OKAY.

DO NOT TOUCH THE TRIGGER, NO MATTER WHAT.

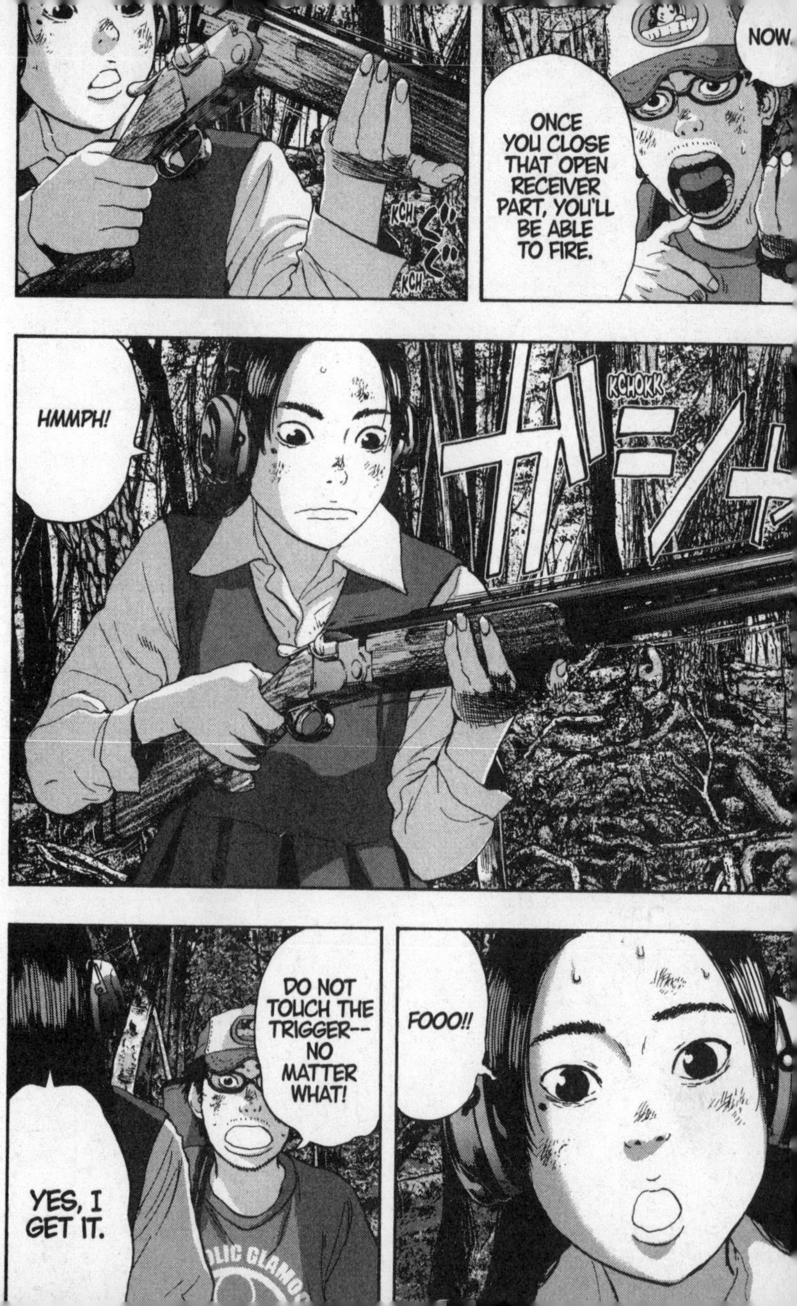

NOW.
ONCE YOU CLOSE THAT OPEN RECEIVER PART, YOU'LL BE ABLE TO FIRE.
KCH
KCH
KCHOKK
HMMPH!
FOOO!!
DO NOT TOUCH THE TRIGGER-- NO MATTER WHAT!
YES, I GET IT.

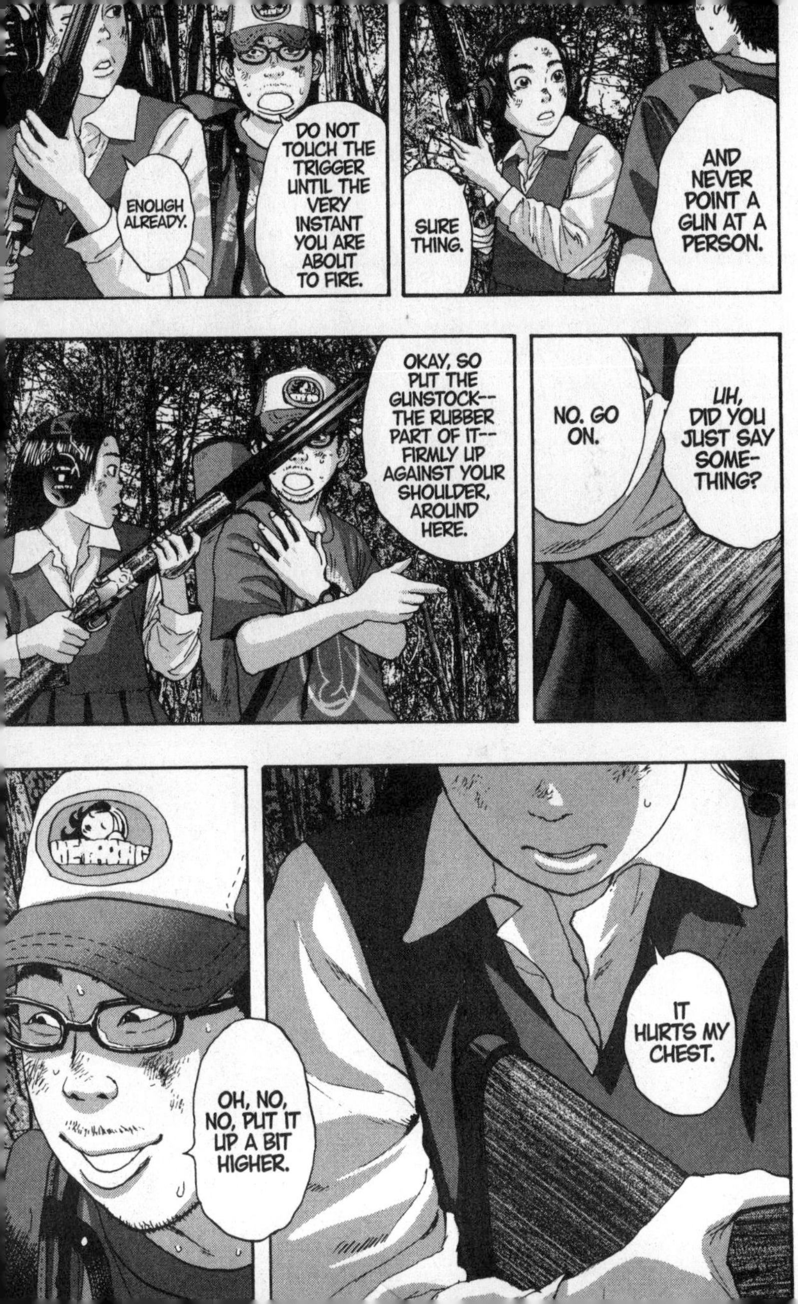
AND NEVER POINT A GUN AT A PERSON.
SURE THING.
DO NOT TOUCH THE TRIGGER UNTIL THE VERY INSTANT YOU ARE ABOUT TO FIRE.
ENOUGH ALREADY.
UH, DID YOU JUST SAY SOME-THING?
NO. GO ON.
OKAY, SO PUT THE GUNSTOCK-- THE RUBBER PART OF IT-- FIRMLY UP AGAINST YOUR SHOULDER, AROUND HERE.
IT HURTS MY CHEST.
OH, NO, NO, PUT IT UP A BIT HIGHER.

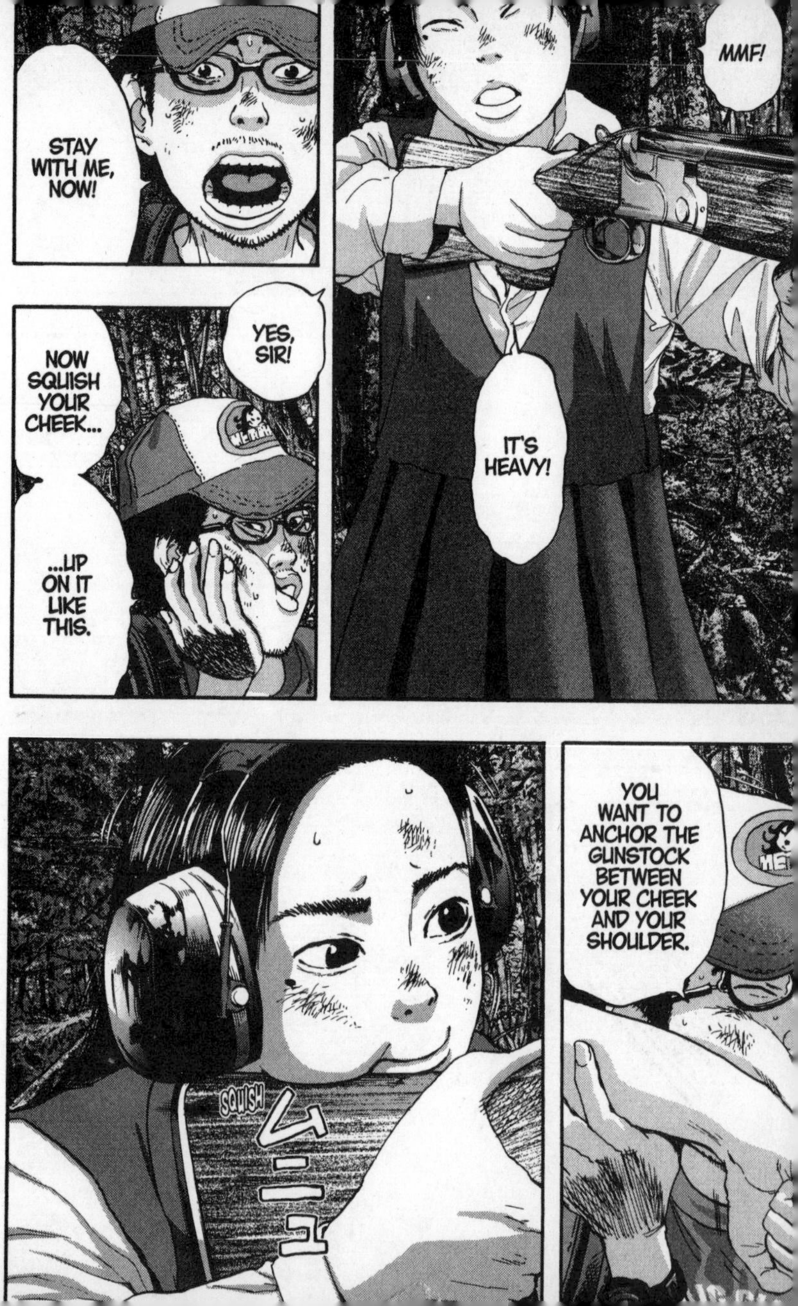
MMF!
IT'S HEAVY!
STAY WITH ME, NOW!
YES, SIR!
NOW SQUISH YOUR CHEEK...
...UP ON IT LIKE THIS.
YOU WANT TO ANCHOR THE GUNSTOCK BETWEEN YOUR CHEEK AND YOUR SHOULDER.
SQUISH

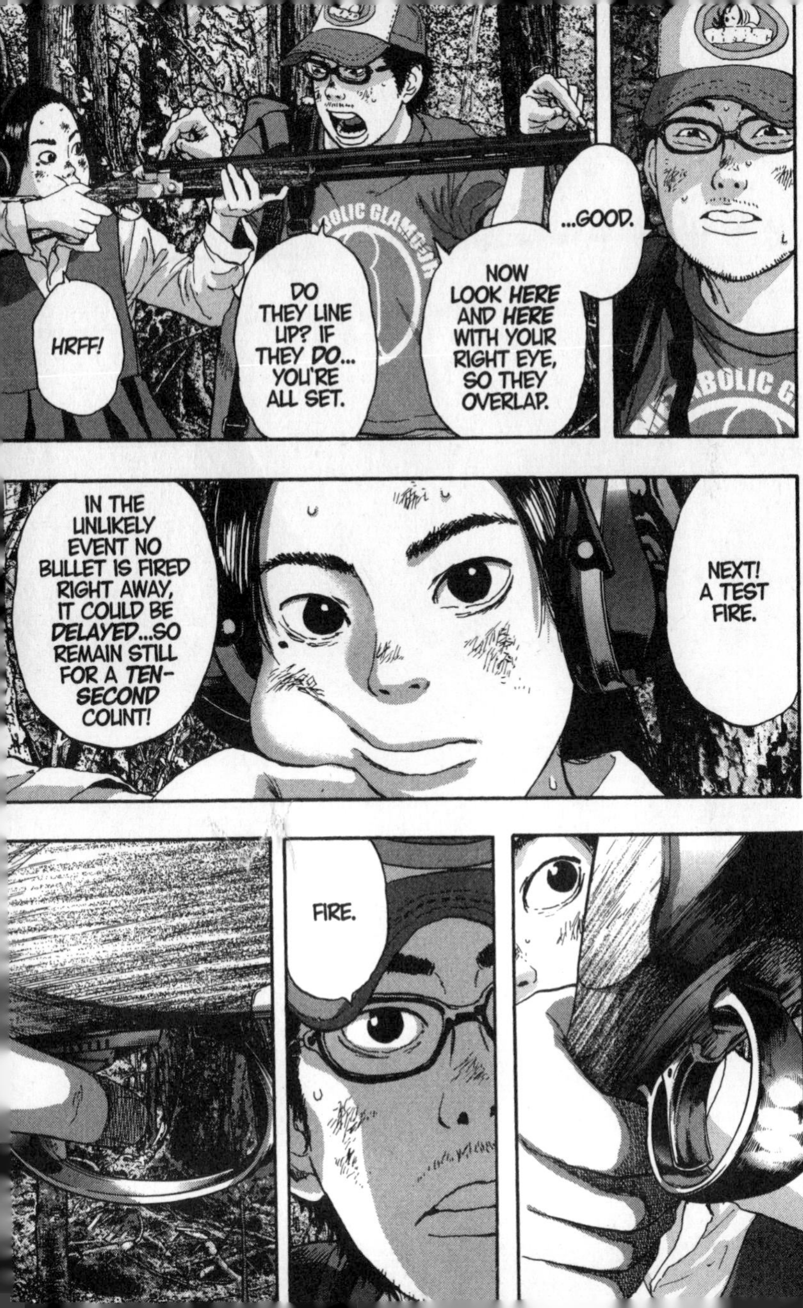
...GOOD.
NOW LOOK HERE AND HERE WITH YOUR RIGHT EYE, SO THEY OVERLAP.
DO THEY LINE UP? IF THEY DO... YOU'RE ALL SET.
HRFF!
NEXT! A TEST FIRE.
IN THE UNLIKELY EVENT NO BULLET IS FIRED RIGHT AWAY, IT COULD BE DELAYED...SO REMAIN STILL FOR A TEN-SECOND COUNT!
FIRE.

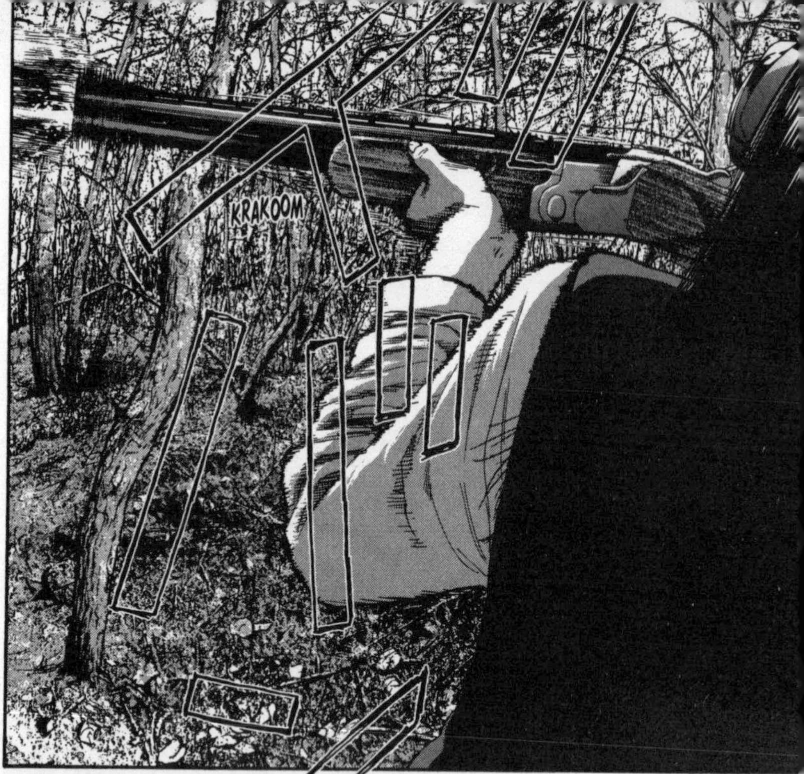
KRAKOOM
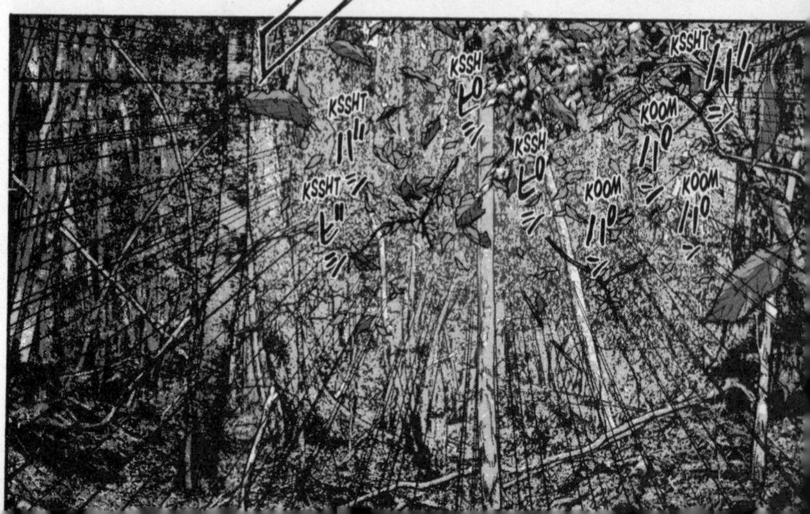
KSSHT
KOOM
KOOM
KSSH
KOOM
KSSH
KSSHT
KSSHT

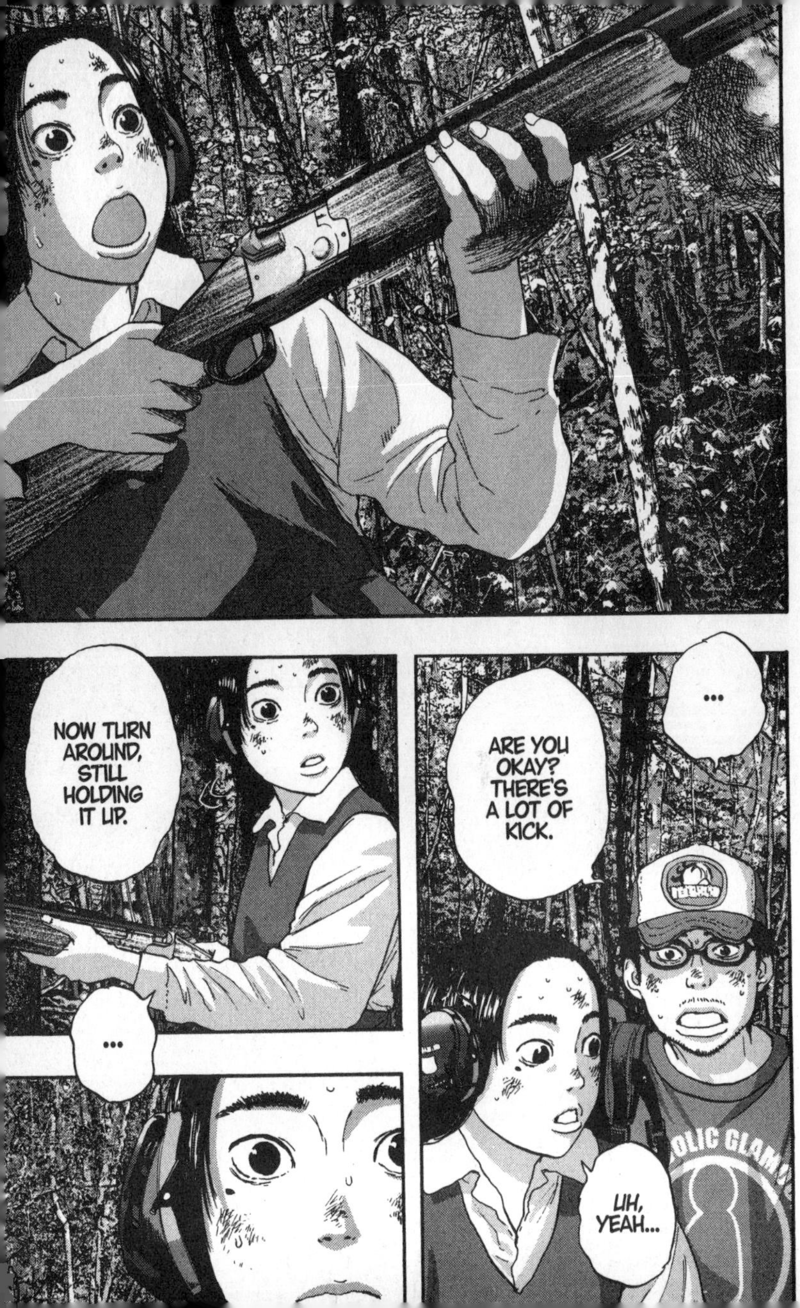
...
ARE YOU OKAY? THERE'S A LOT OF KICK.
UH, YEAH...
NOW TURN AROUND, STILL HOLDING IT UP.
...

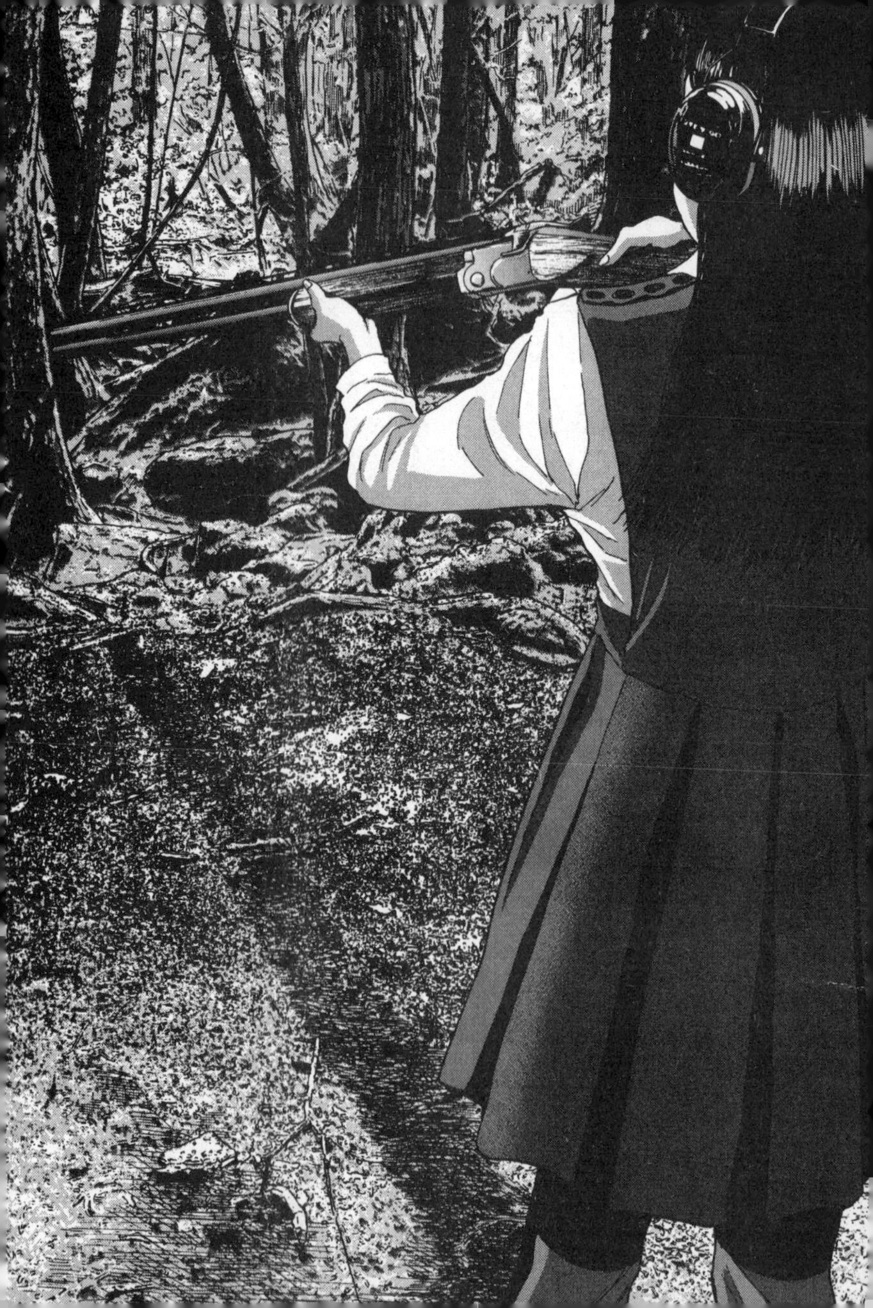

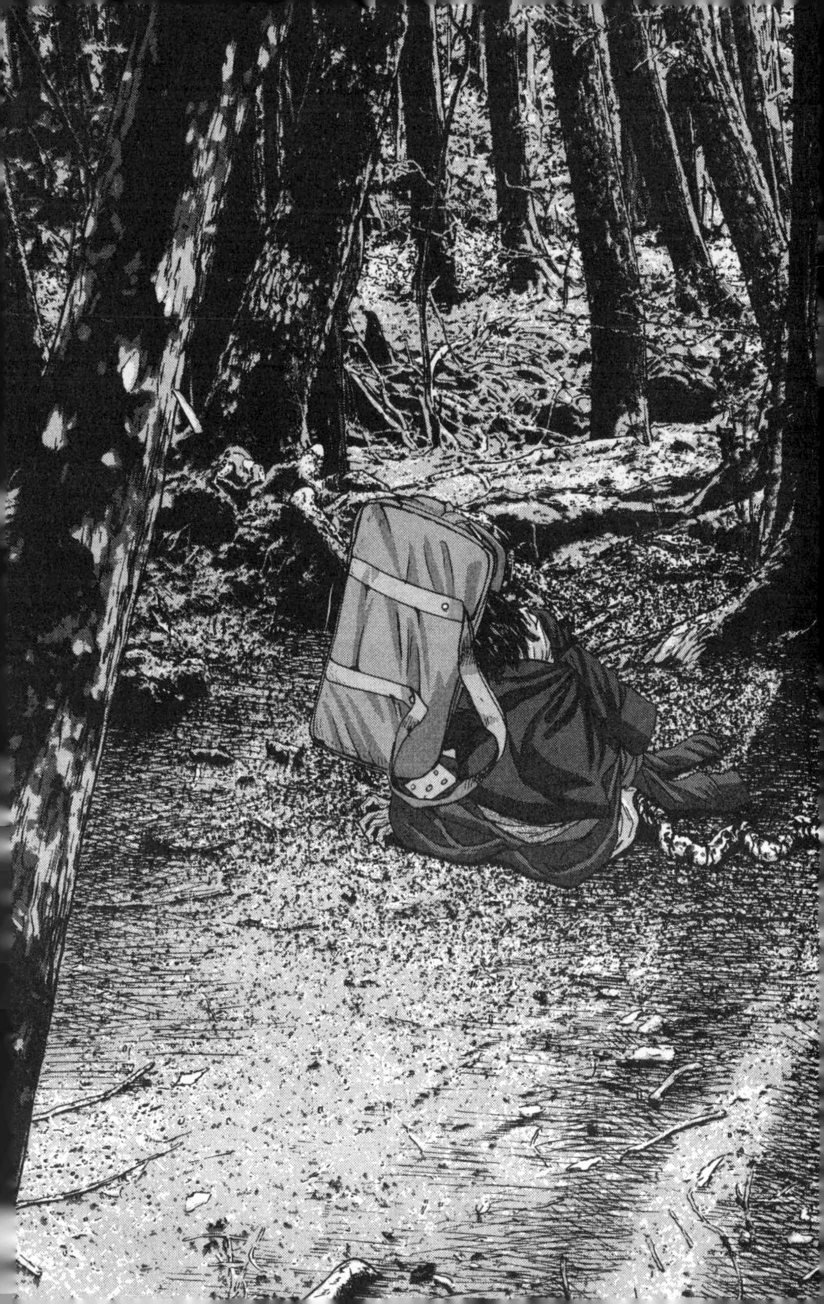

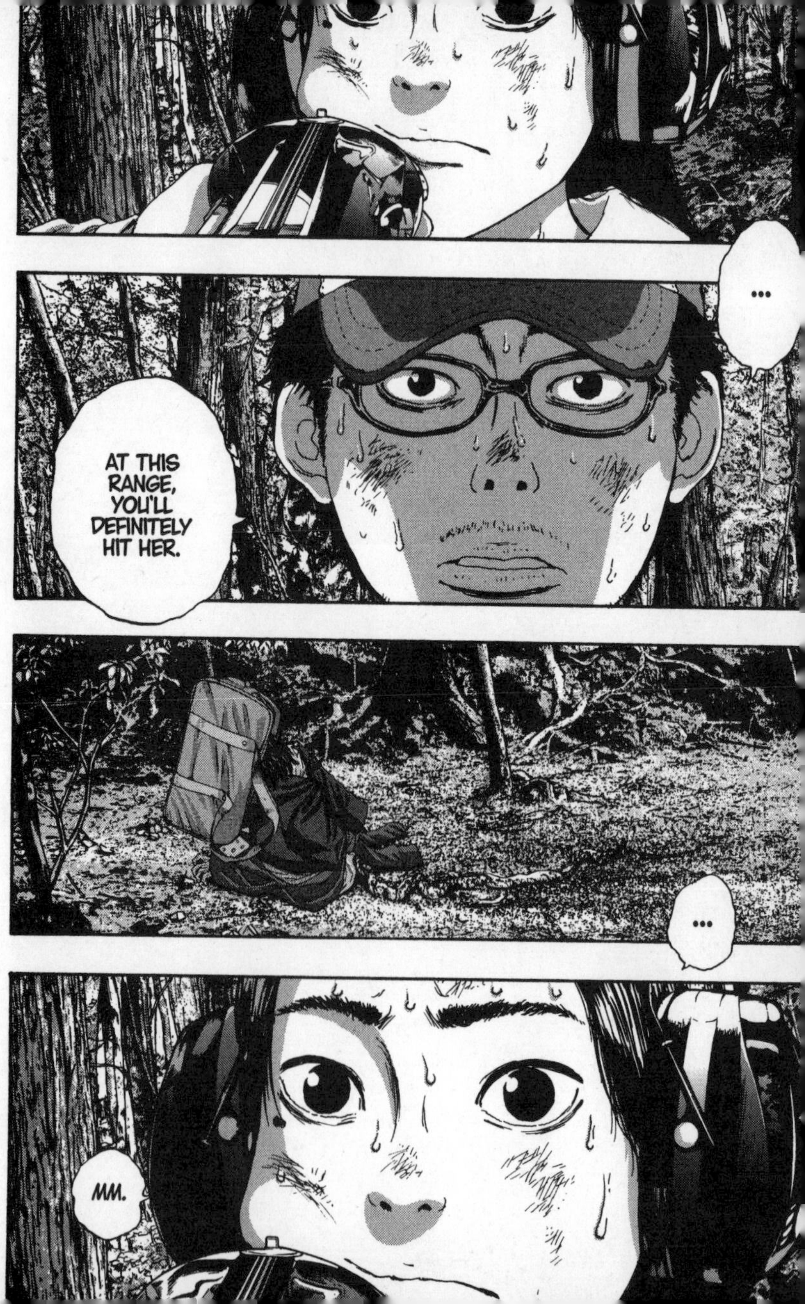
...
AT THIS RANGE, YOU'LL DEFINITELY HIT HER.
...
MM.

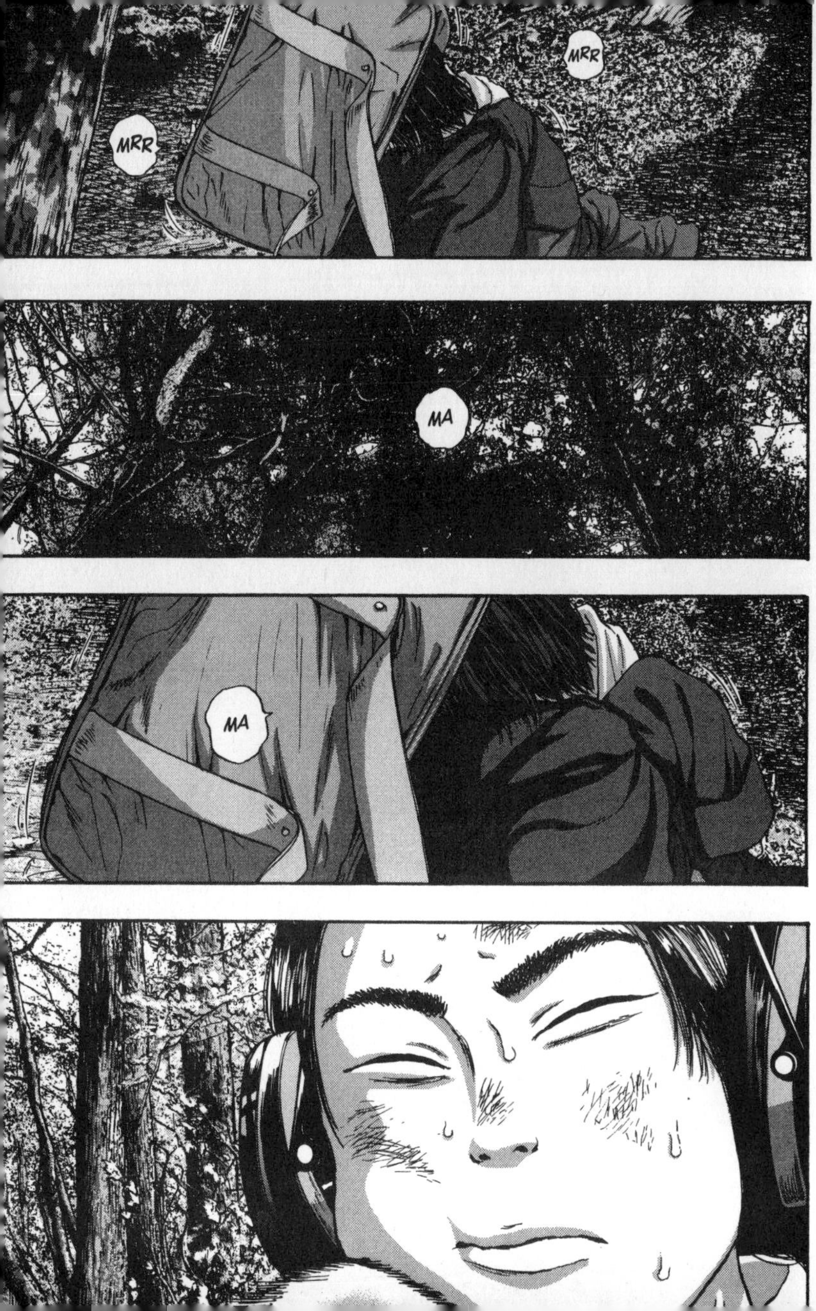
MRR
MRR
MA
MA

SAE...?

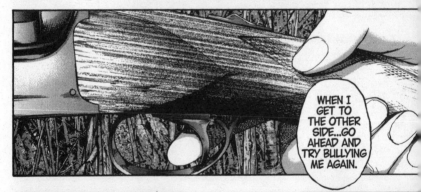

WHEN I GET TO THE OTHER SIDE...GO AHEAD AND TRY BULLYING ME AGAIN.

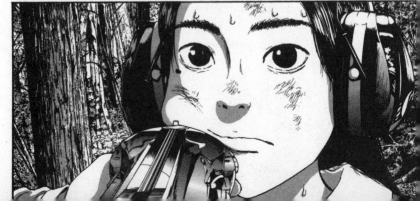

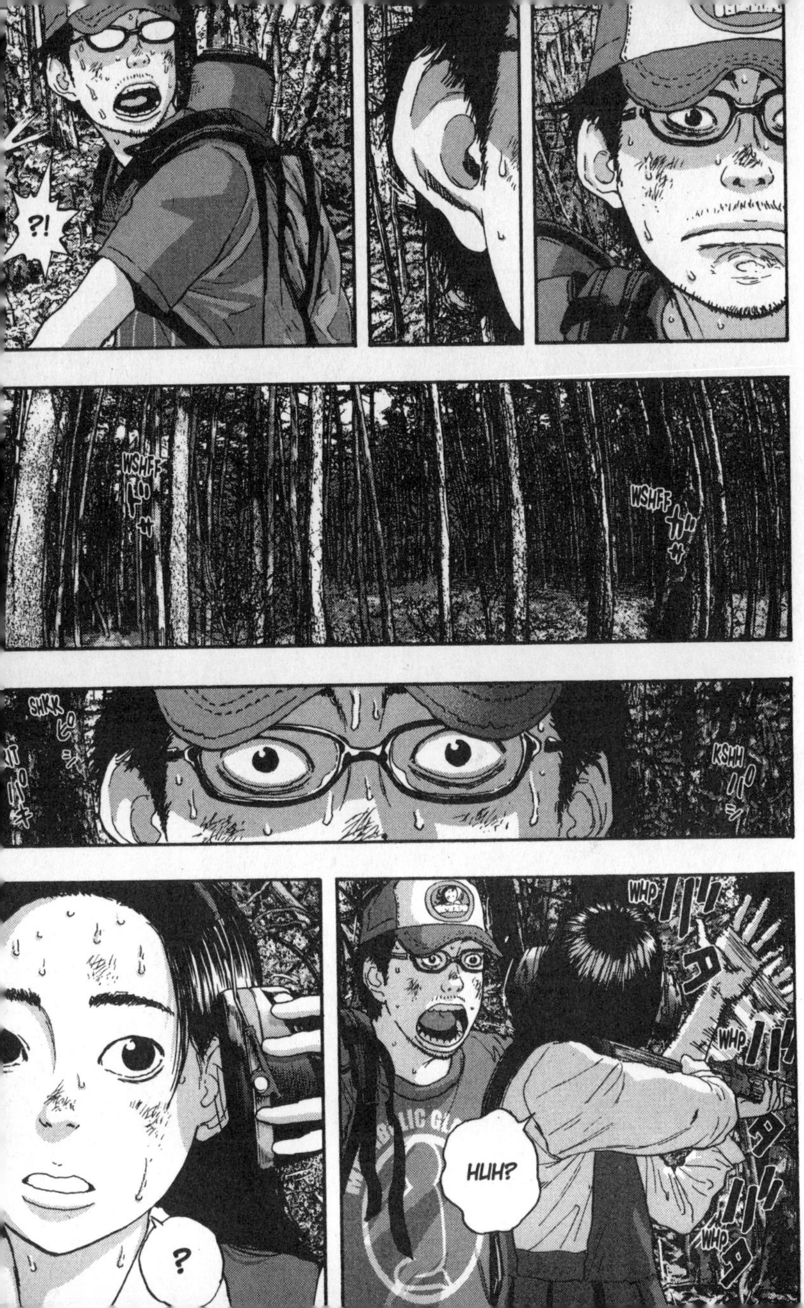

?!
WSHFF
WSHFF
KSHH
SHKK
WHP
WHP
HUH?
WHP
?

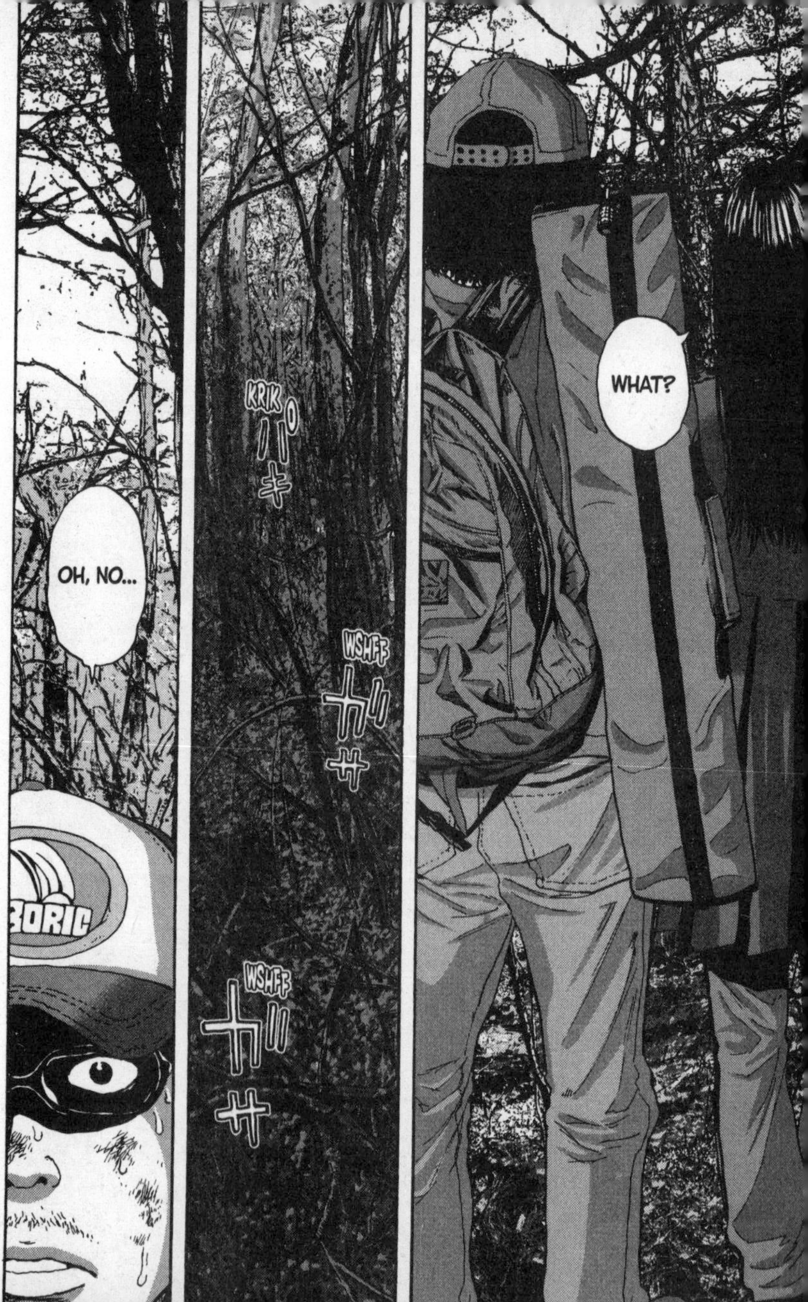
WHAT?
KRIK
WSHFF
WSHFF
OH, NO...

CHAPTER 42

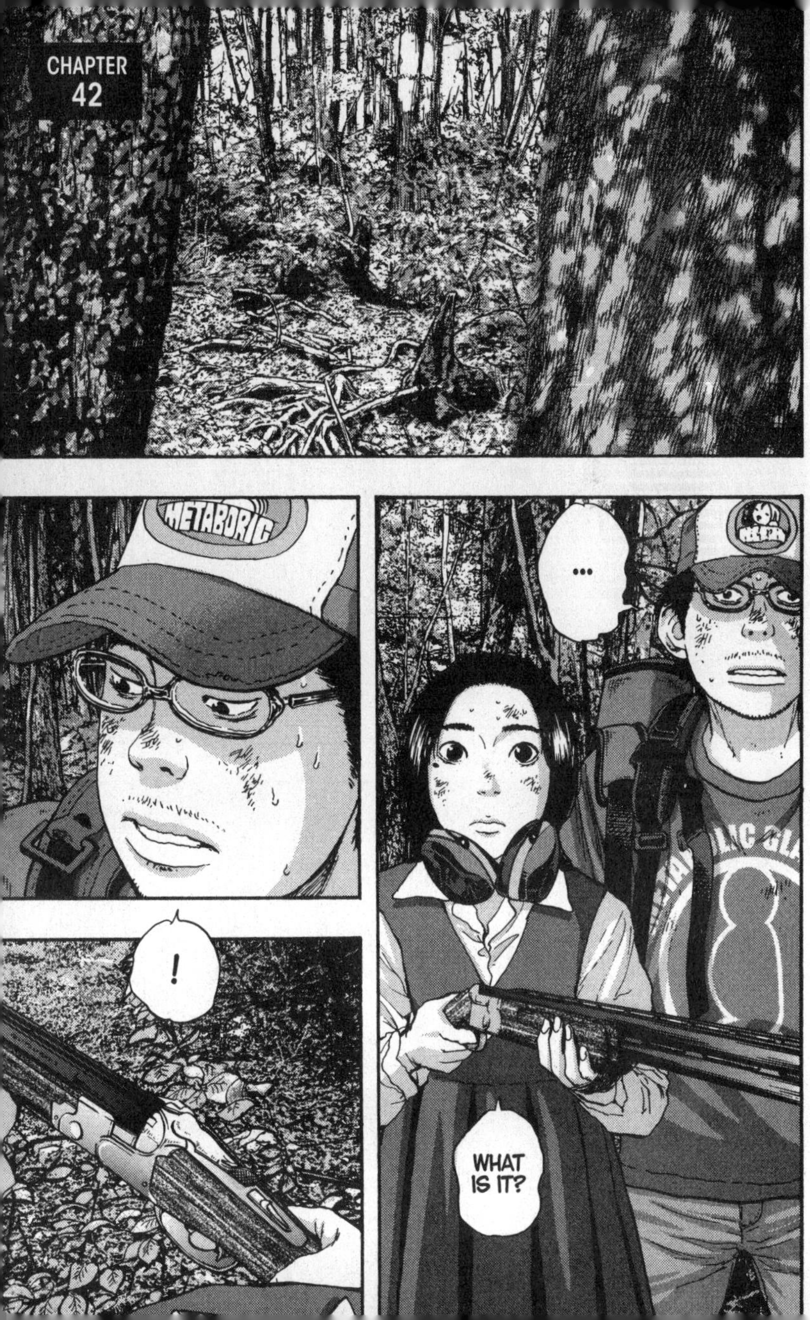
...
WHAT IS IT?
!

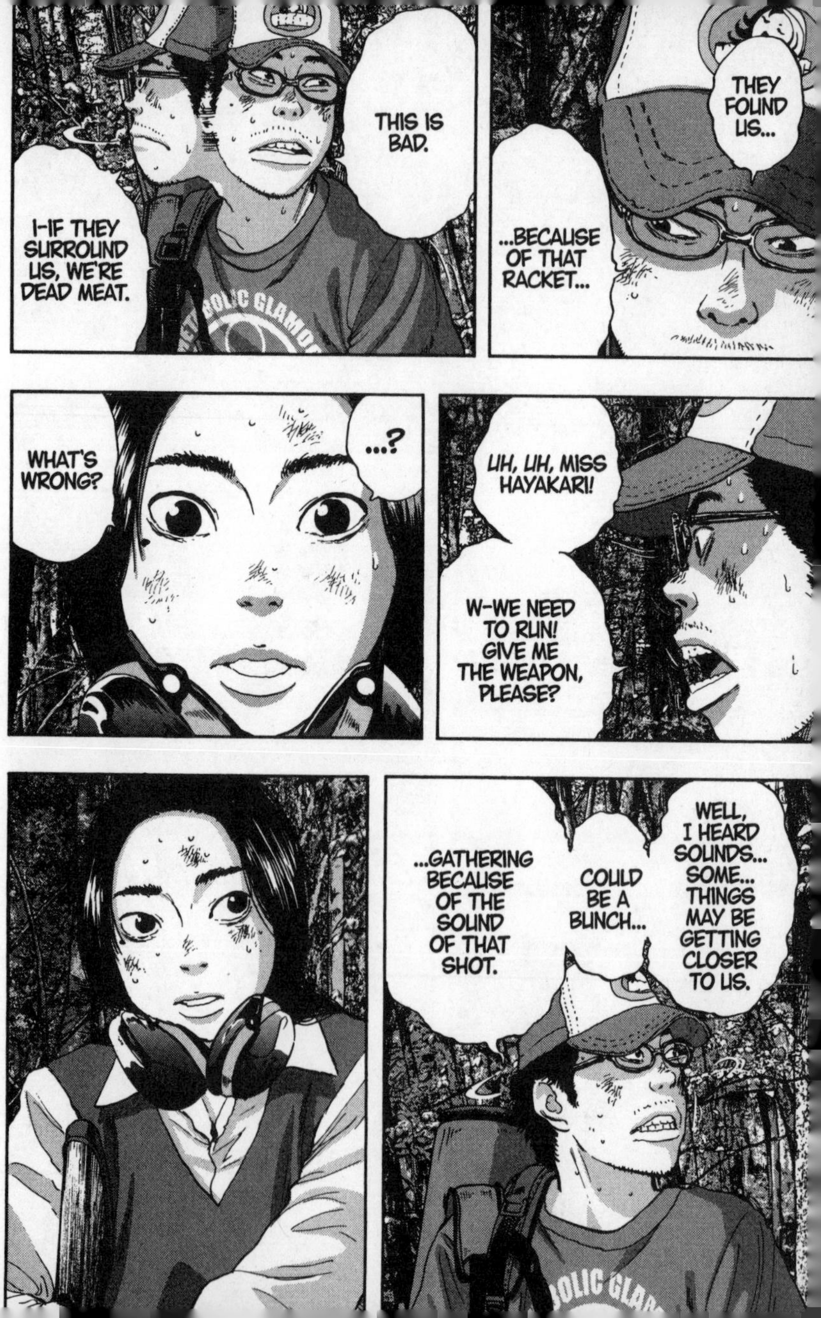
THEY FOUND US...
...BECAUSE OF THAT RACKET...
THIS IS BAD.
I-IF THEY SURROUND US, WE'RE DEAD MEAT.
UH, UH, MISS HAYAKARI!
W-WE NEED TO RUN! GIVE ME THE WEAPON, PLEASE?
...?
WHAT'S WRONG?
WELL, I HEARD SOUNDS... SOME... THINGS MAY BE GETTING CLOSER TO US.
COULD BE A BUNCH...
...GATHERING BECAUSE OF THE SOUND OF THAT SHOT.

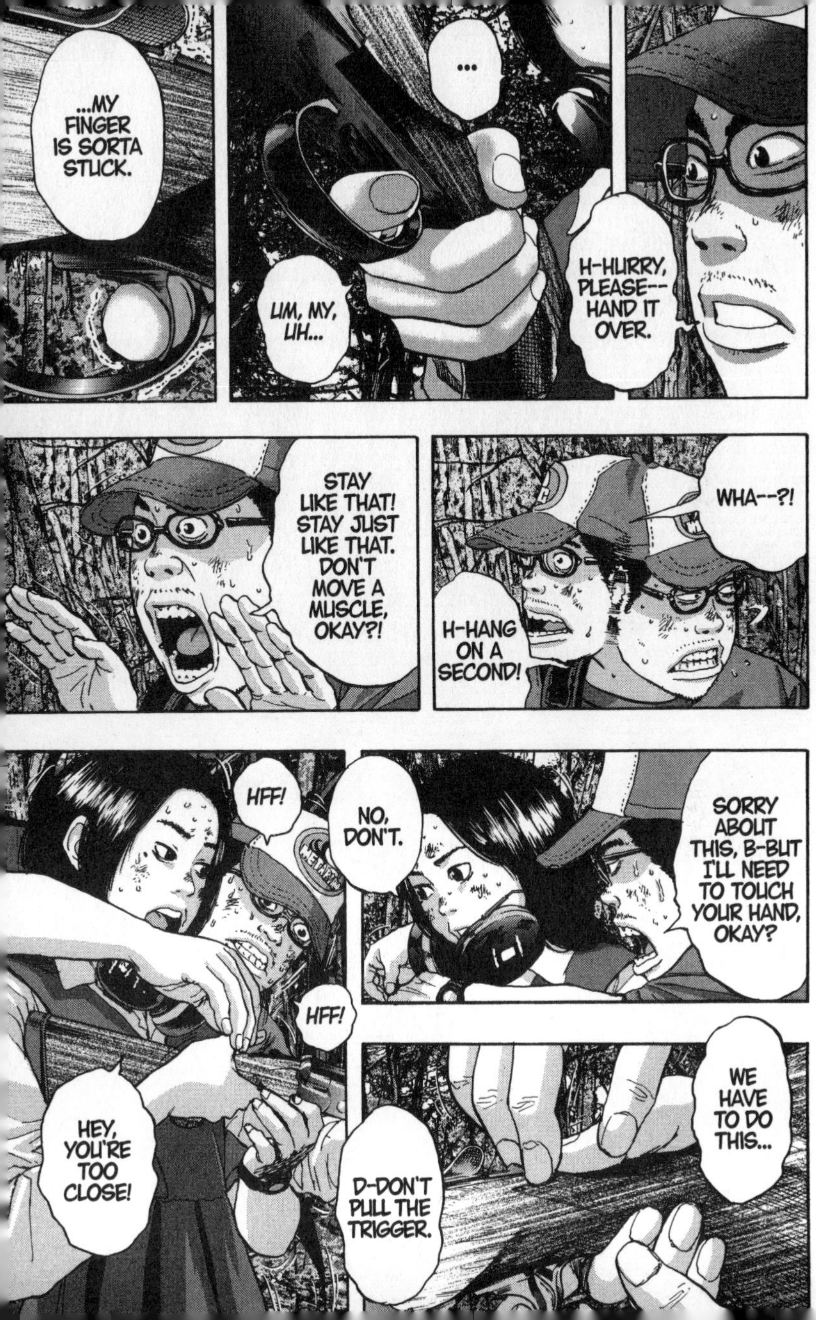
H-HURRY, PLEASE-- HAND IT OVER.
...
UM, MY, UH...
...MY FINGER IS SORTA STUCK.
WHA--?!
H-HANG ON A SECOND!
STAY LIKE THAT! STAY JUST LIKE THAT. DON'T MOVE A MUSCLE, OKAY?!
SORRY ABOUT THIS, B-BUT I'LL NEED TO TOUCH YOUR HAND, OKAY?
NO, DON'T.
HFF!
HFF!
WE HAVE TO DO THIS...
D-DON'T PULL THE TRIGGER.
HEY, YOU'RE TOO CLOSE!

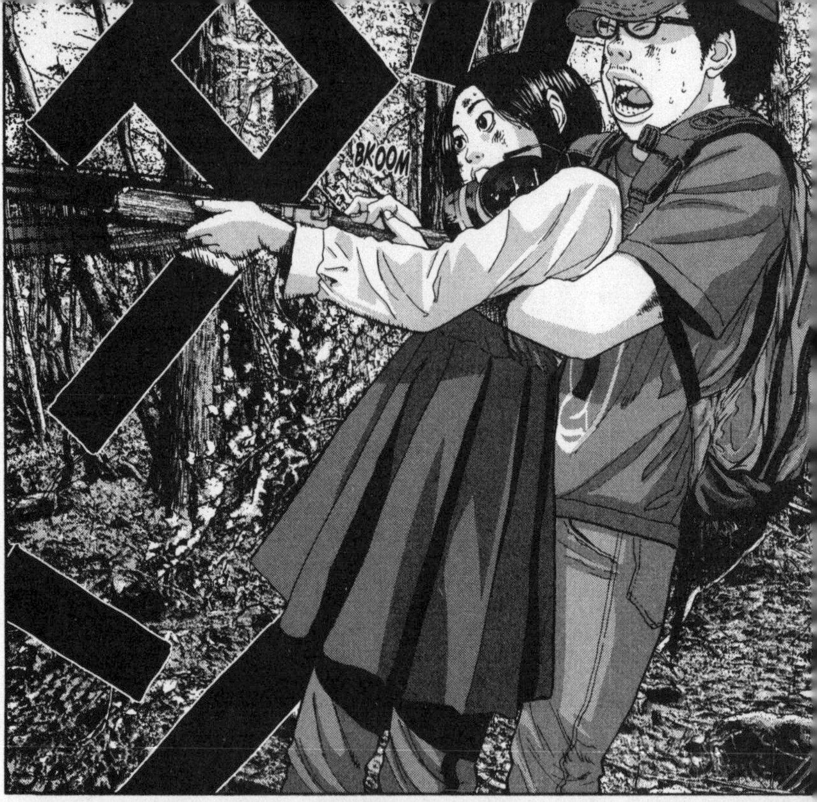
BKOOM
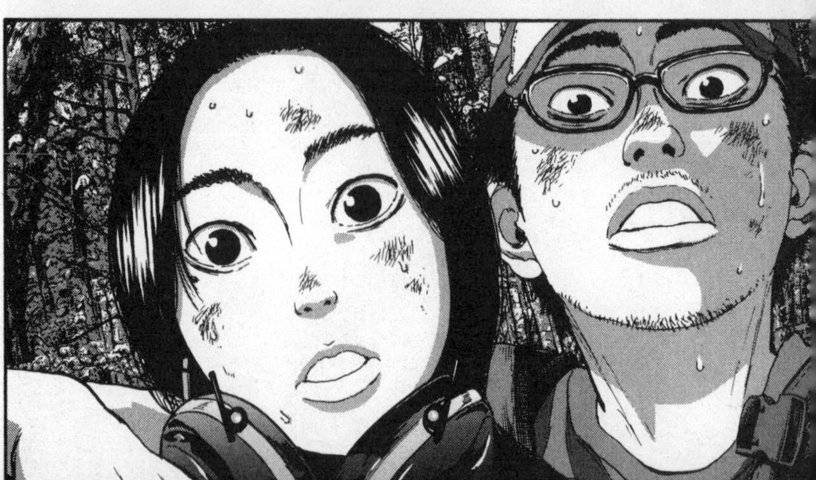

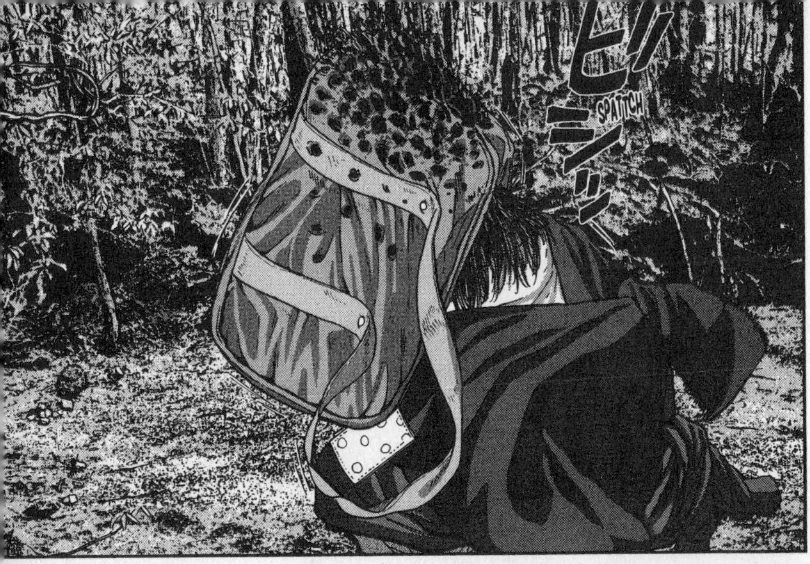
ビ!!
SPATTCH
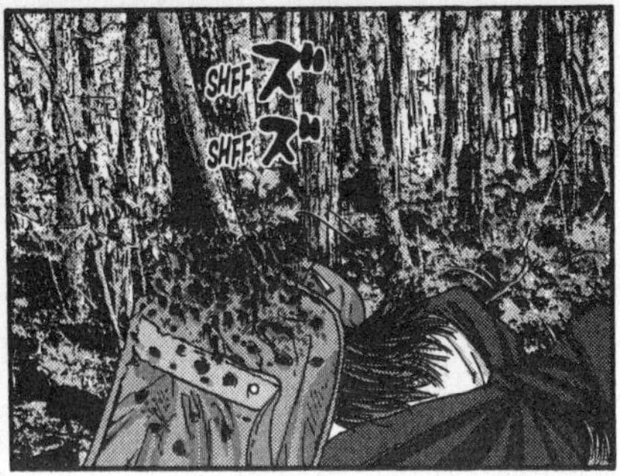
SHFF
SHFF
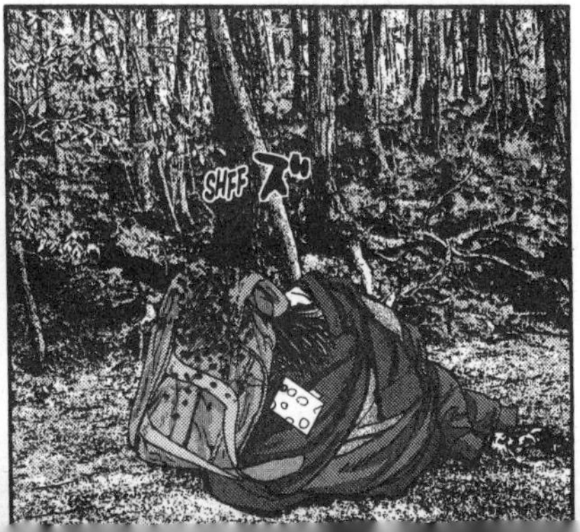
SHFF
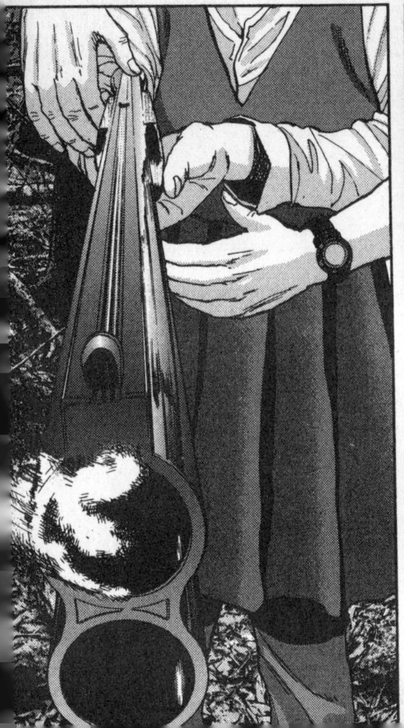

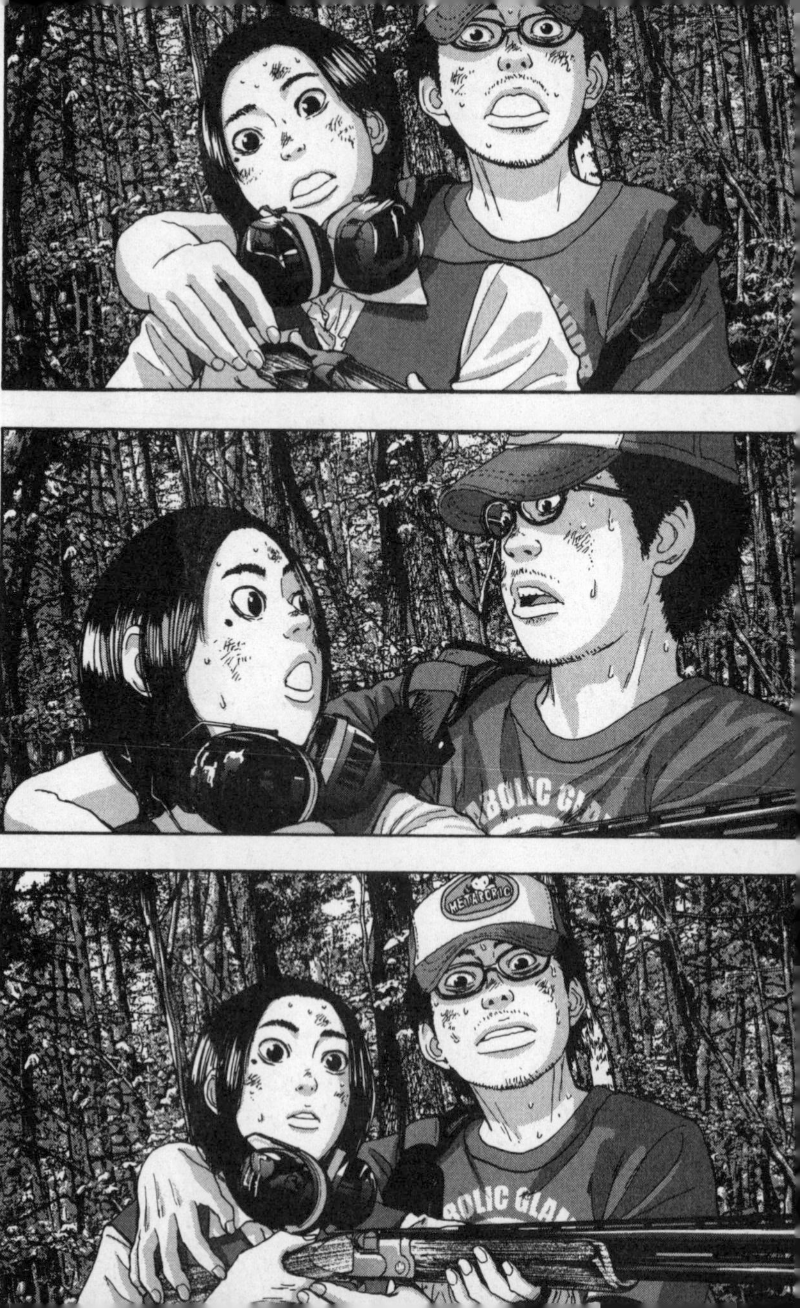
METABORIC

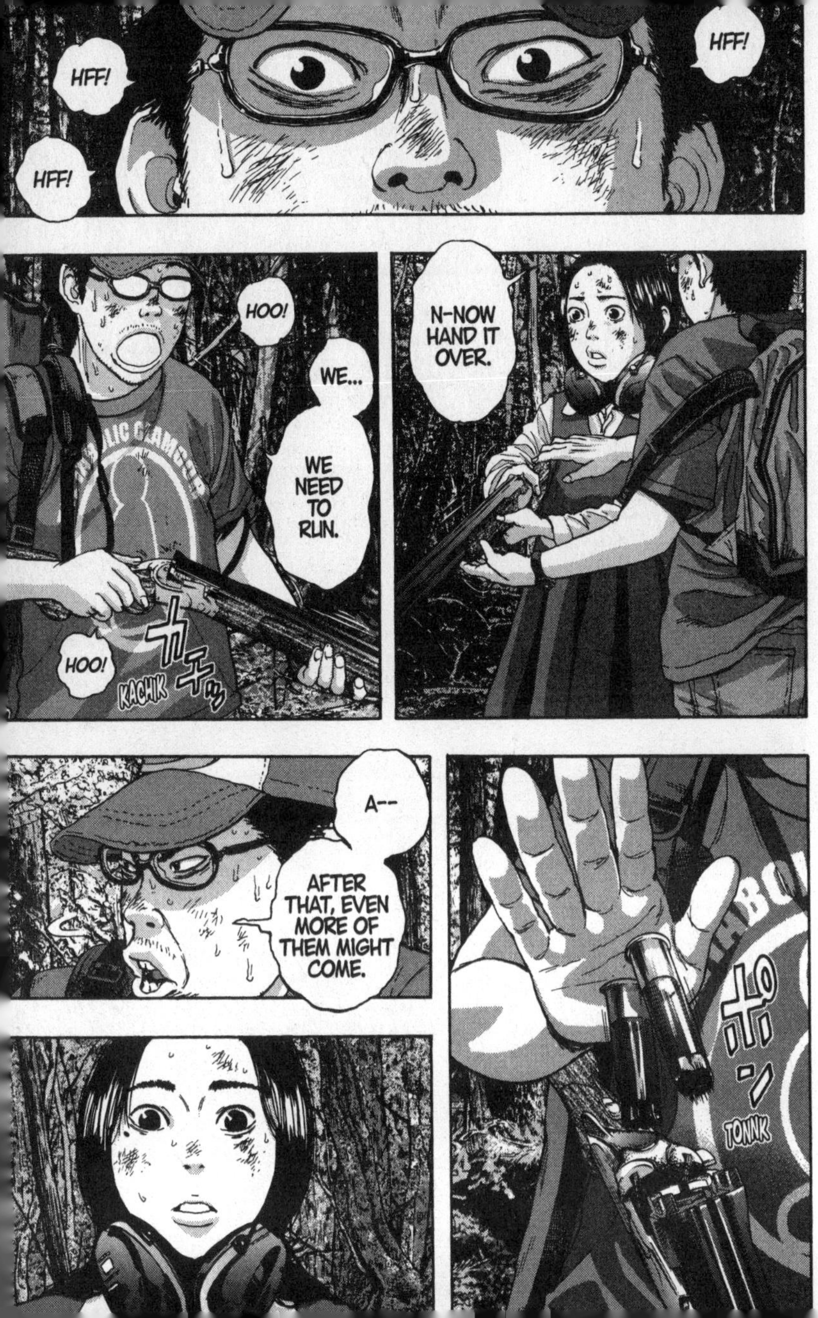
HFF!
HFF!
HFF!
N-NOW HAND IT OVER.
HOO!
WE...
WE NEED TO RUN.
HOO!
KACHIK
TONNK
A--
AFTER THAT, EVEN MORE OF THEM MIGHT COME.

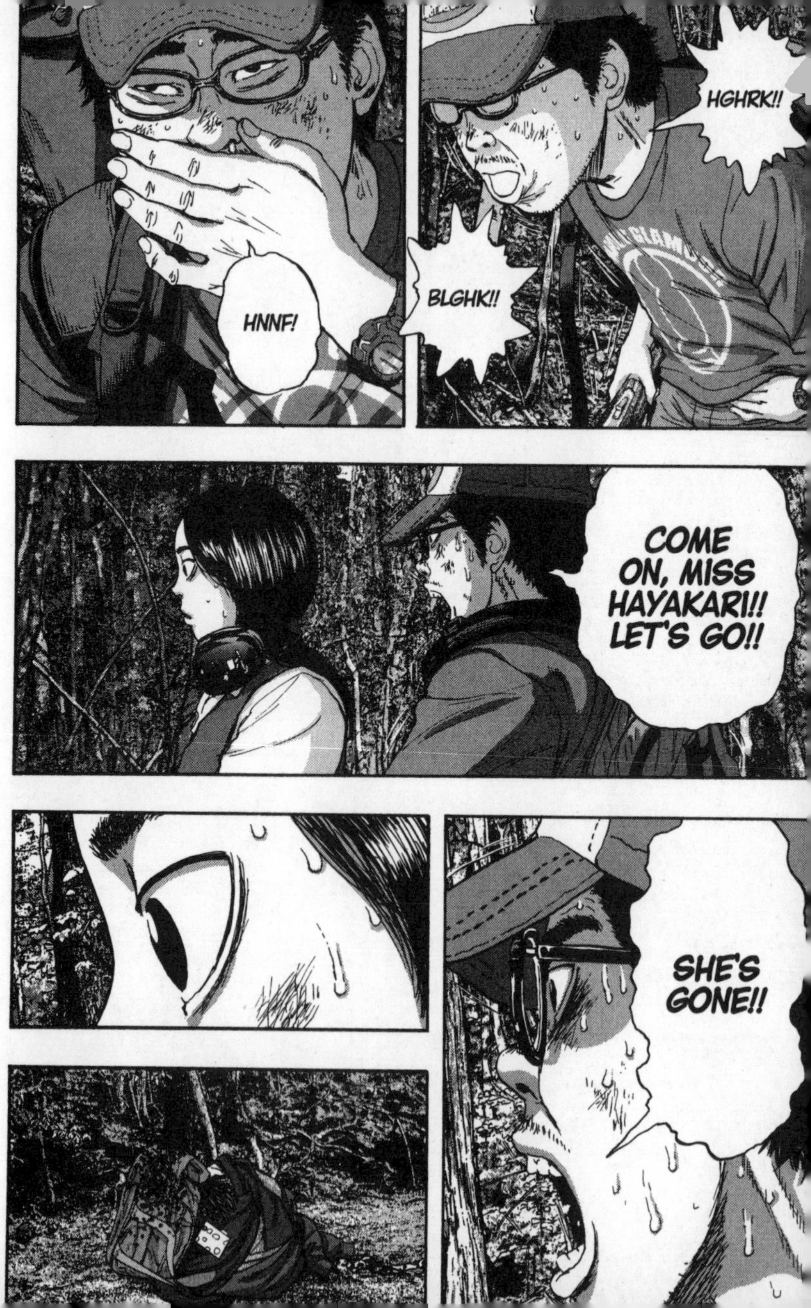
HGHRK!!
BLGHK!!
HNNF!
COME ON, MISS HAYAKARI!! LET'S GO!!
SHE'S GONE!!

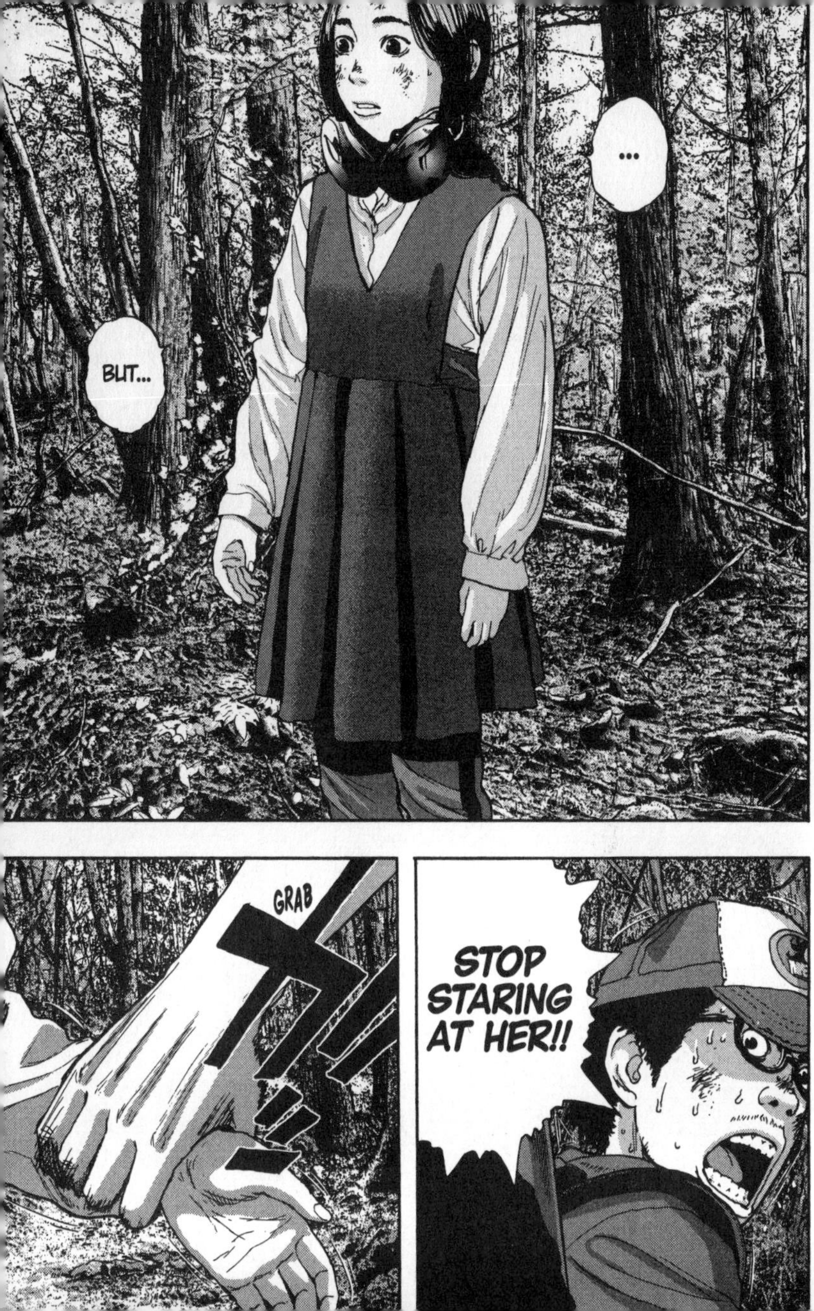
...
BUT...
STOP STARING AT HER!!
GRAB

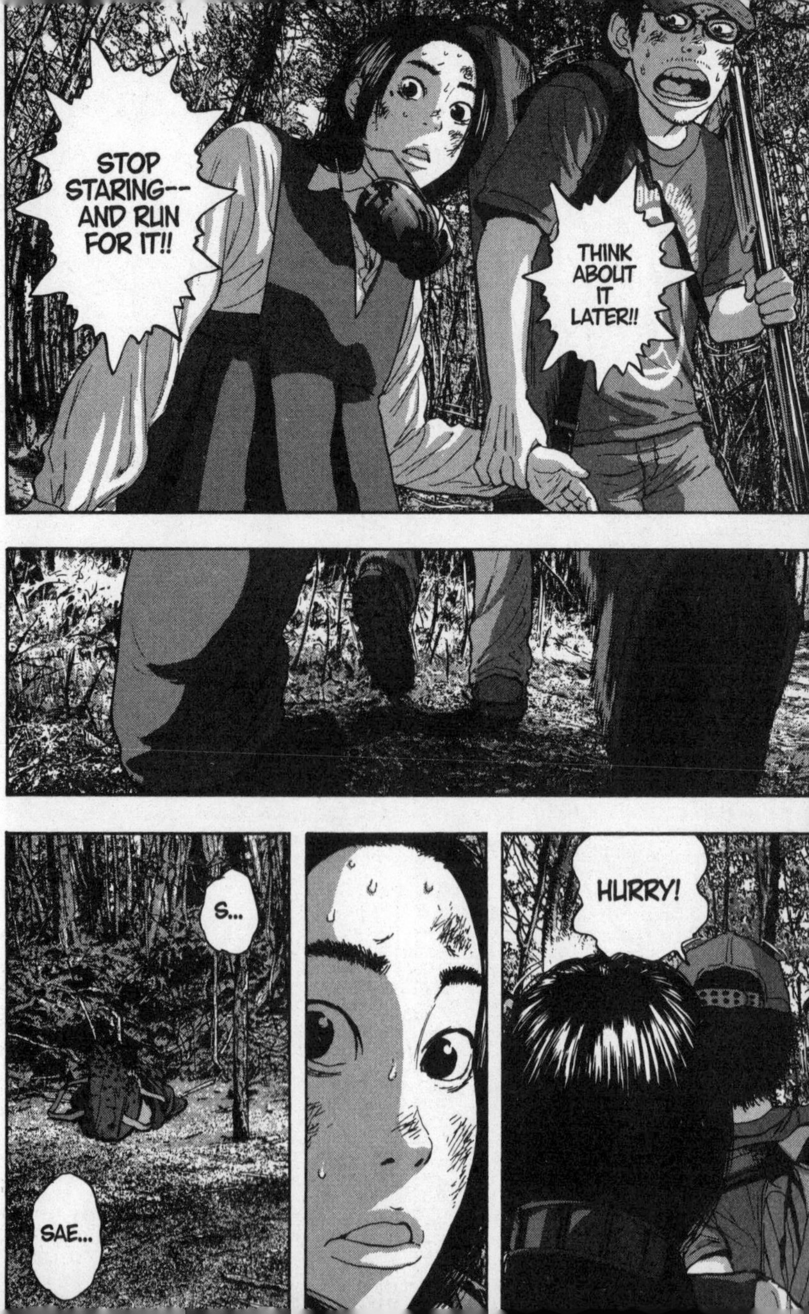
THINK ABOUT IT LATER!!
STOP STARING-- AND RUN FOR IT!!
HURRY!
S...
SAE...

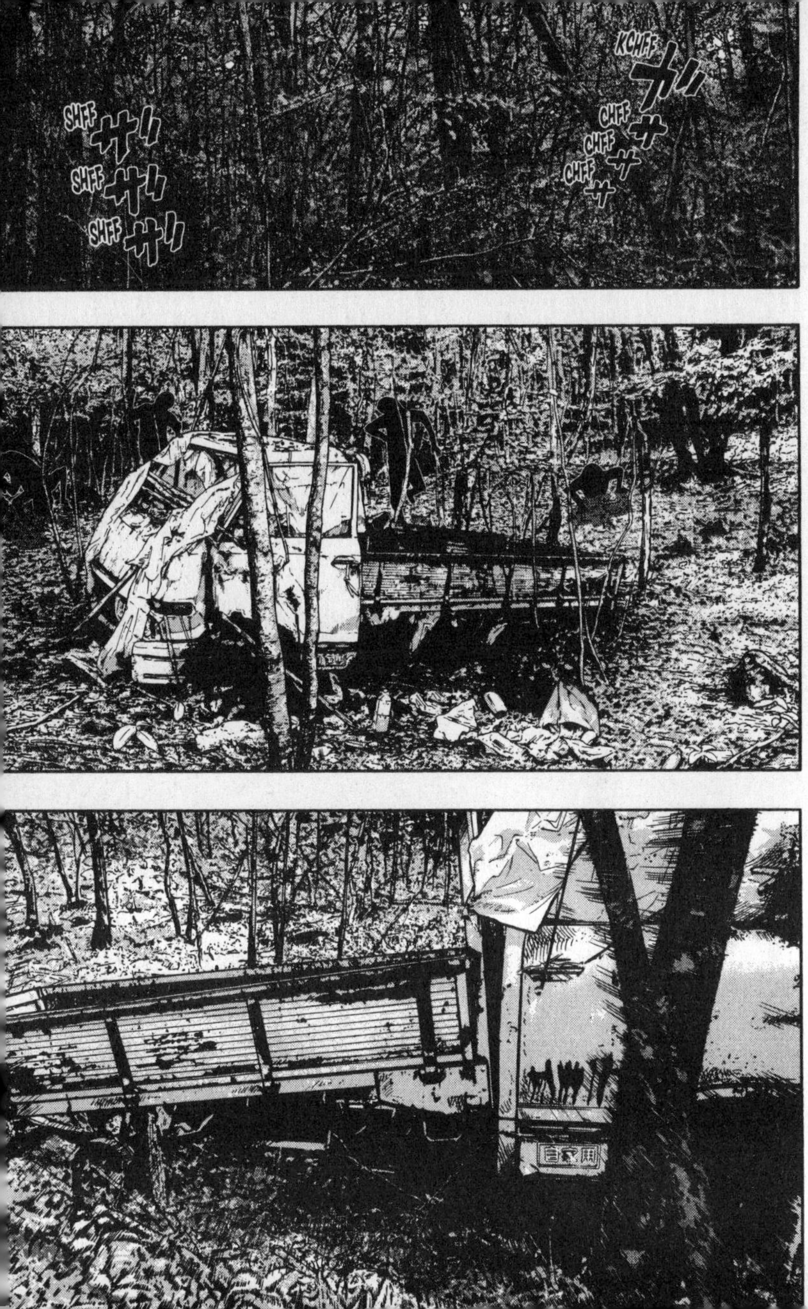
KCHFF
CHFF
CHFF
CHFF
SHFF
SHFF
SHFF

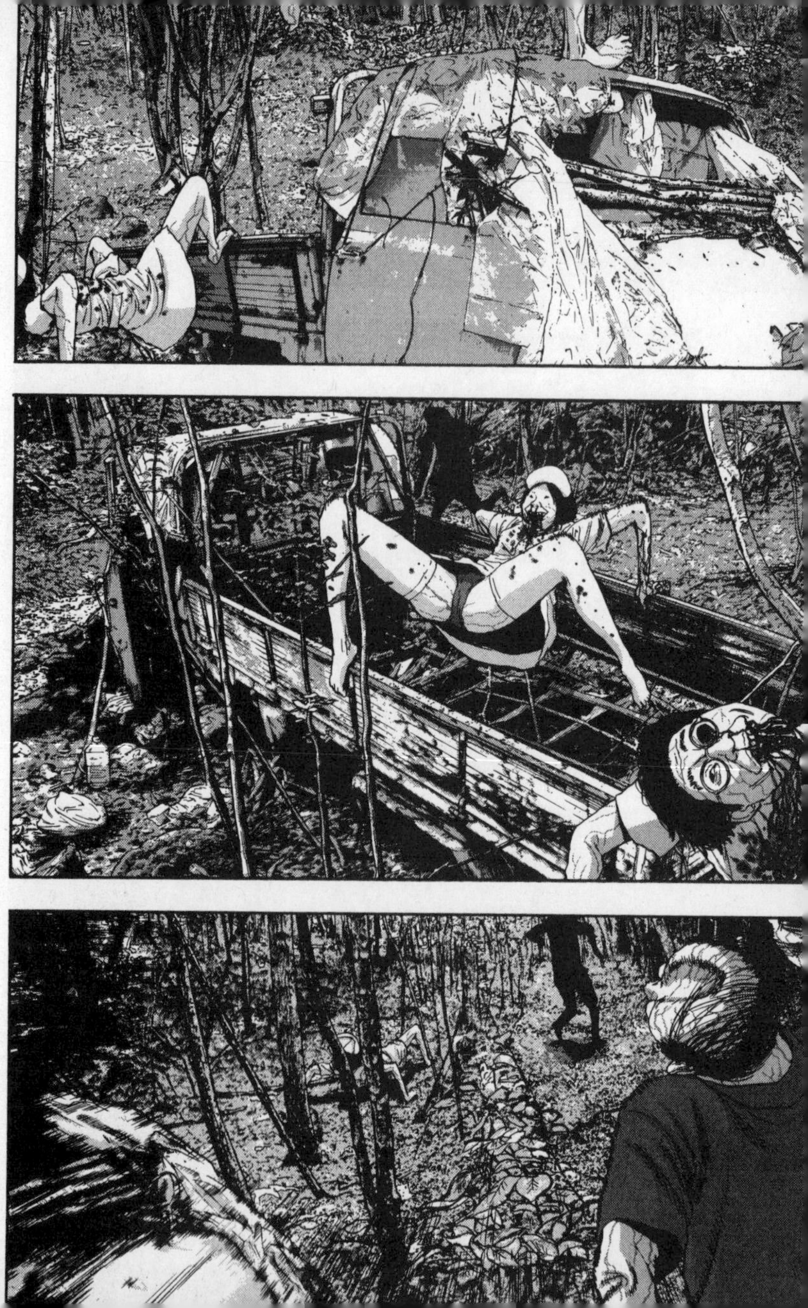

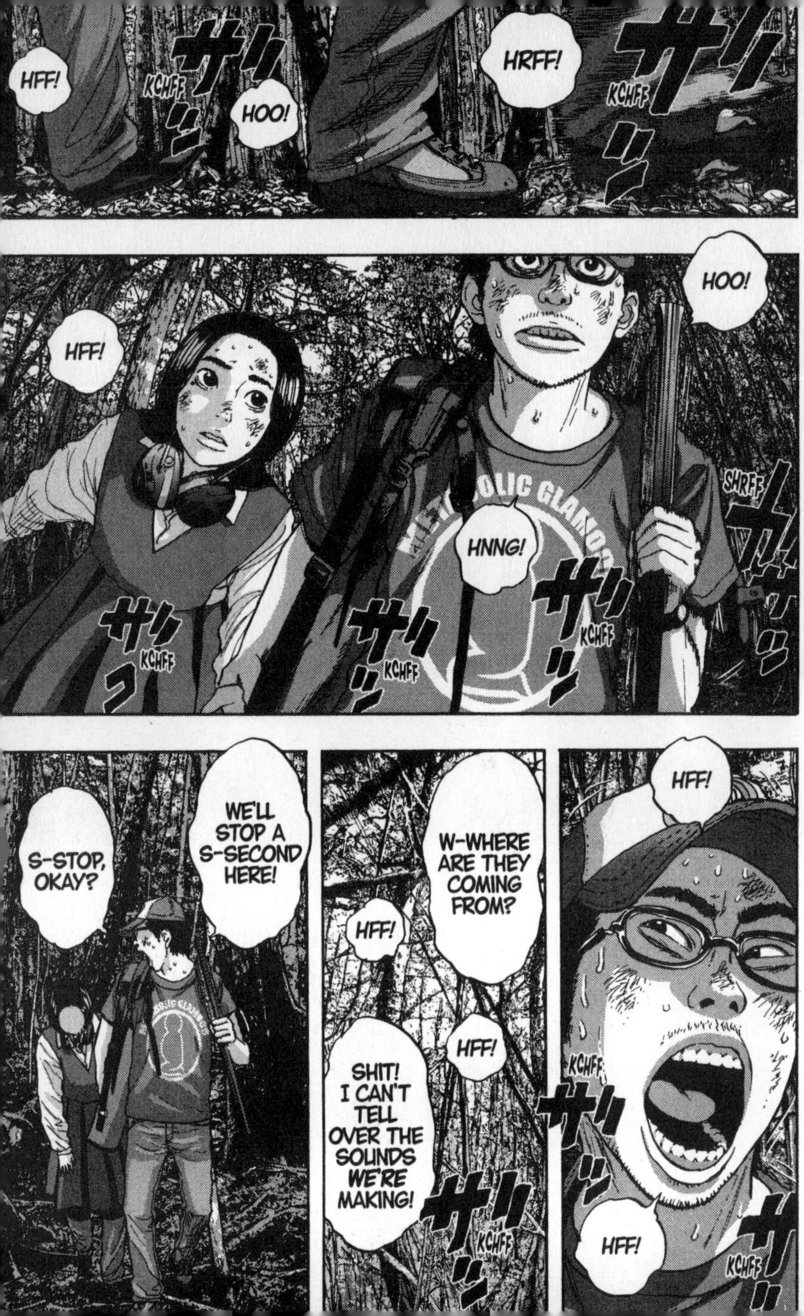
HRFF!
KCHFF
HOO!
KCHFF
HFF!
HOO!
HFF!
SHRFF
HNNG!
KCHFF
KCHFF
KCHFF
HFF!
KCHFF
HFF!
KCHFF
W-WHERE ARE THEY COMING FROM?
HFF!
HFF!
SHIT! I CAN'T TELL OVER THE SOUNDS WE'RE MAKING!
KCHFF
WE'LL STOP A S-SECOND HERE!
S-STOP, OKAY?

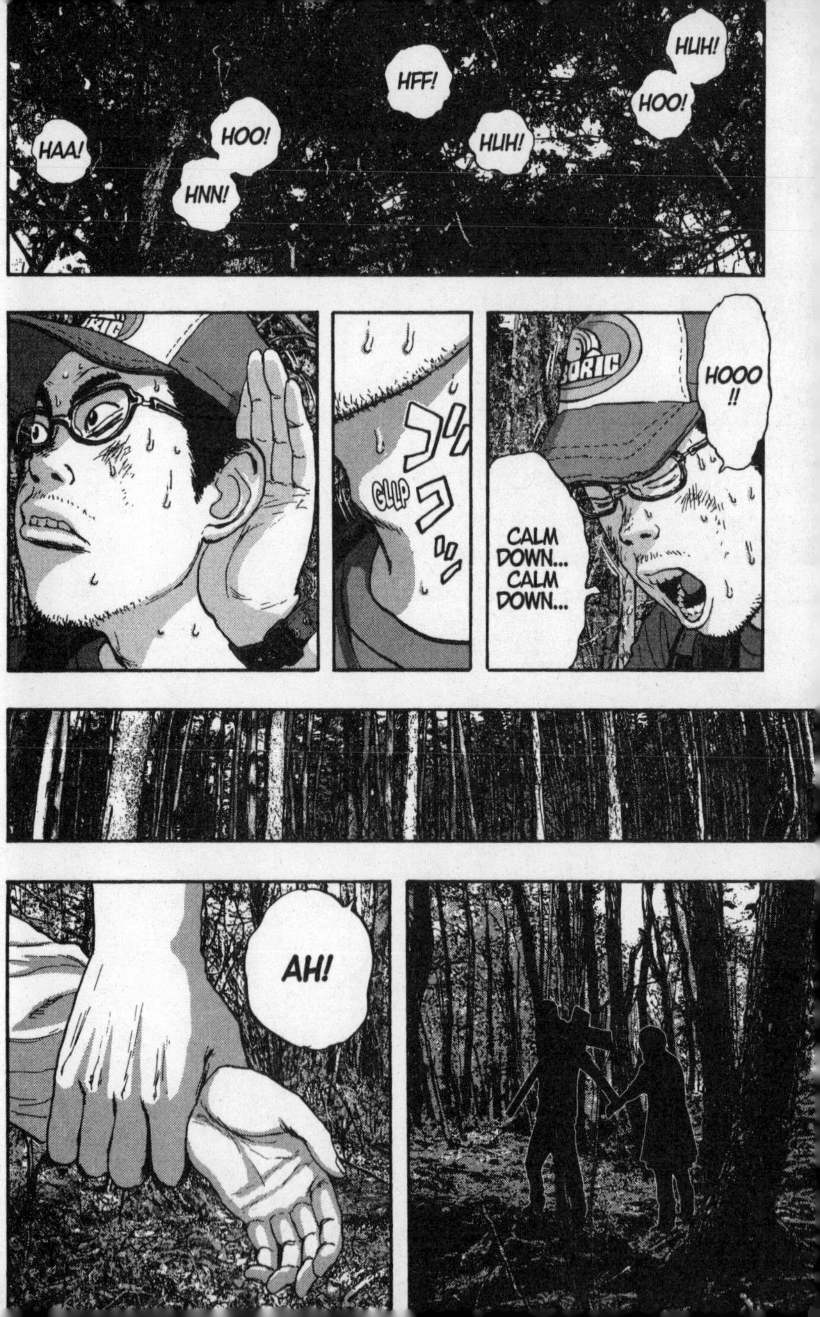
HUH!
HOO!
HUH!
HFF!
HOO!
HNN!
HAA!
HOOO !!
CALM DOWN... CALM DOWN...
GULP
AH!

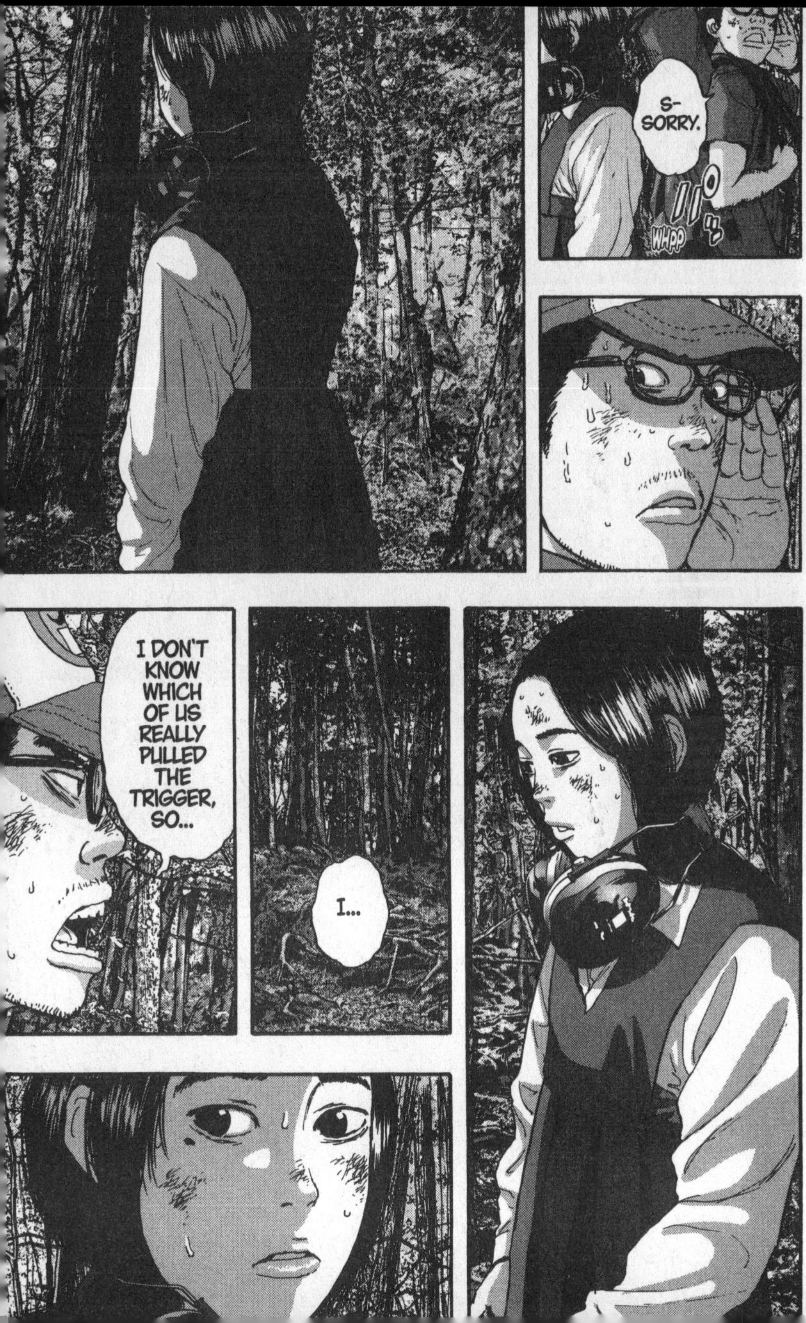
S-
SORRY.
WHPP
I DON'T KNOW WHICH OF US REALLY PULLED THE TRIGGER, SO...
I...

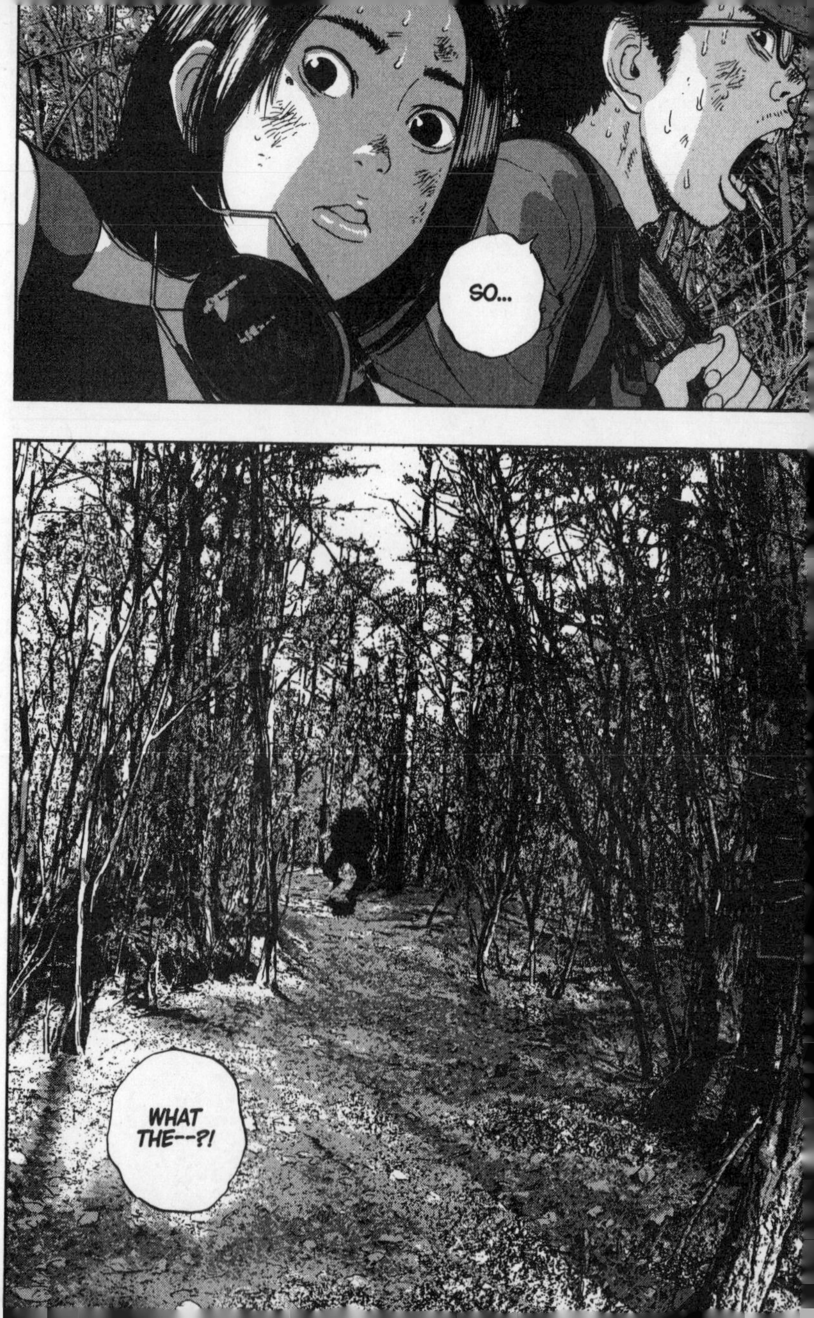
SO...
WHAT THE--?!

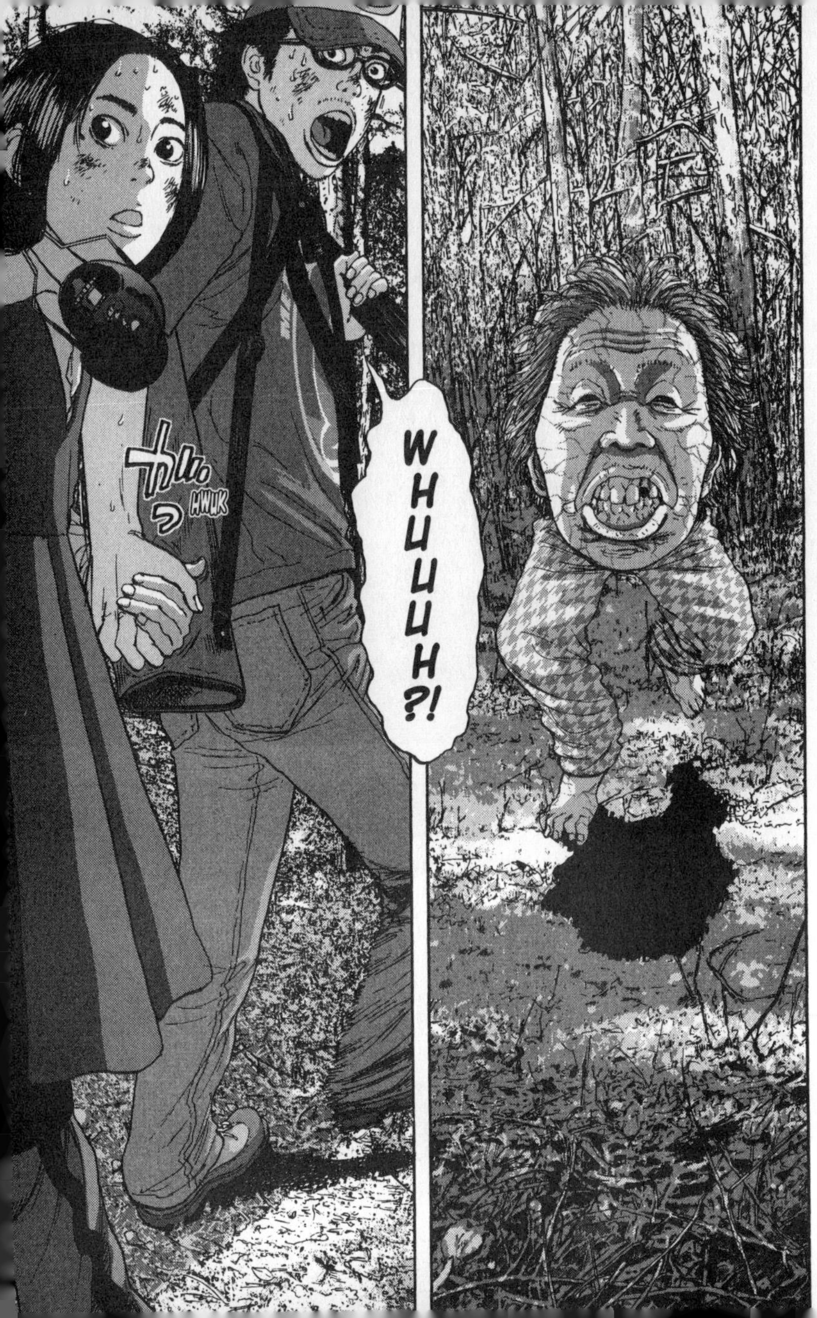
WHUUUUH?!
ガっ
HWK

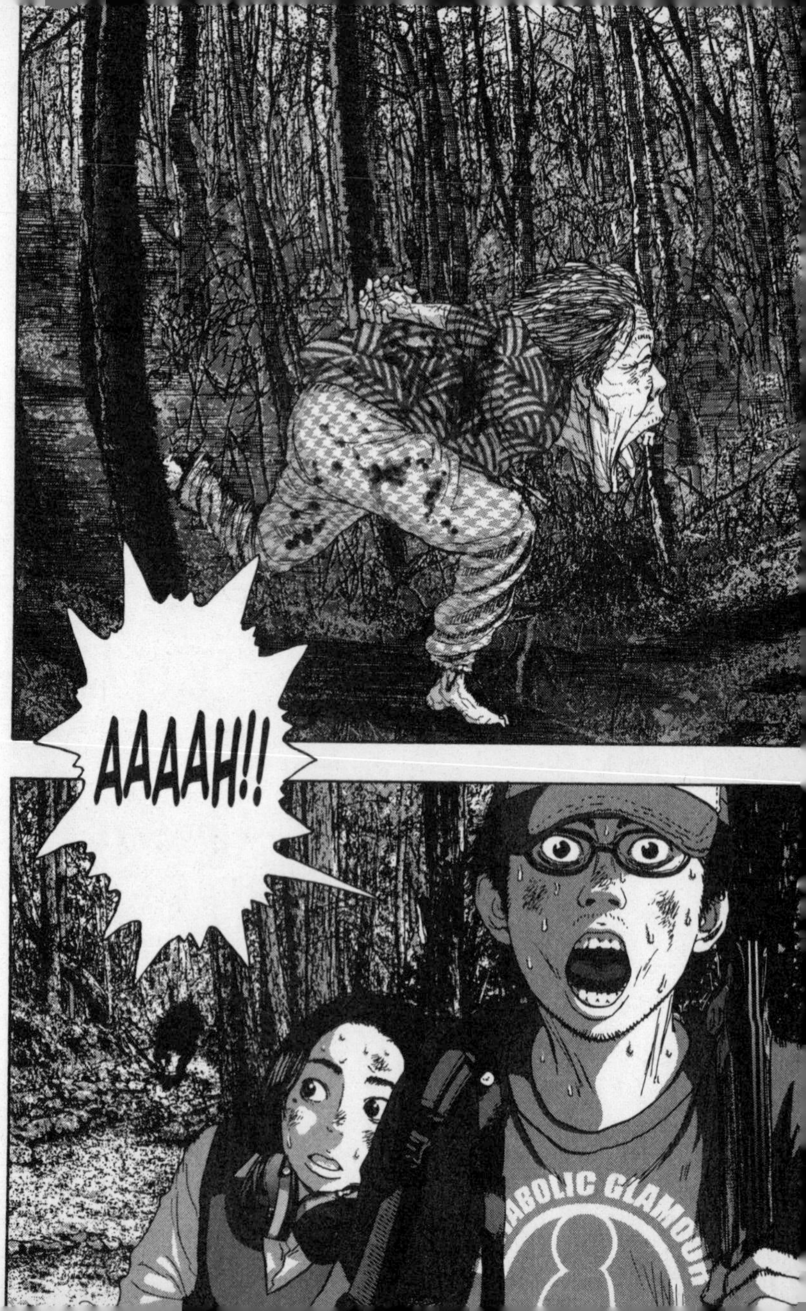
AAAAH!!
ABOLIC GLAMOUR

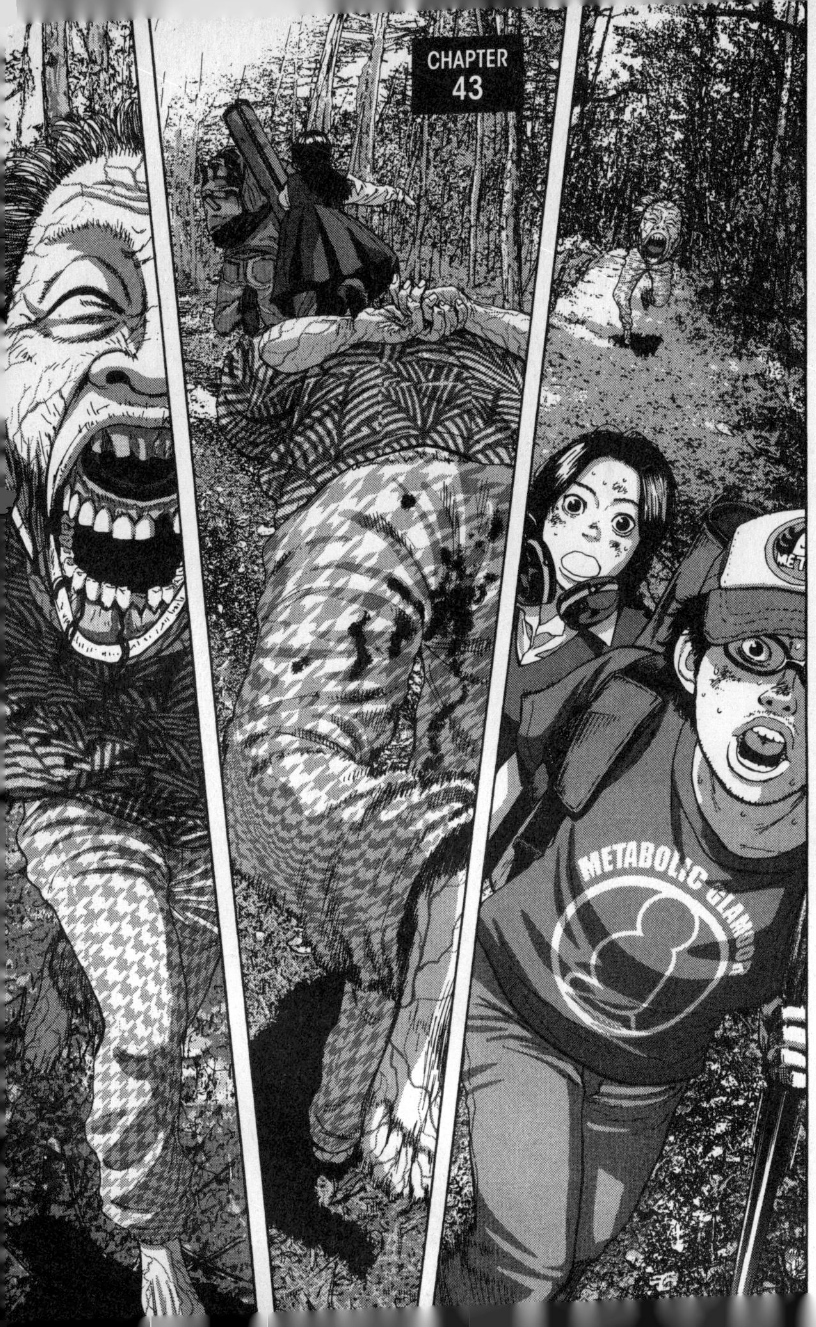
CHAPTER
43

GUAAH!!

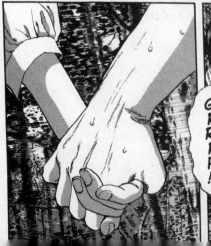

HNNF!

GRRRF!!

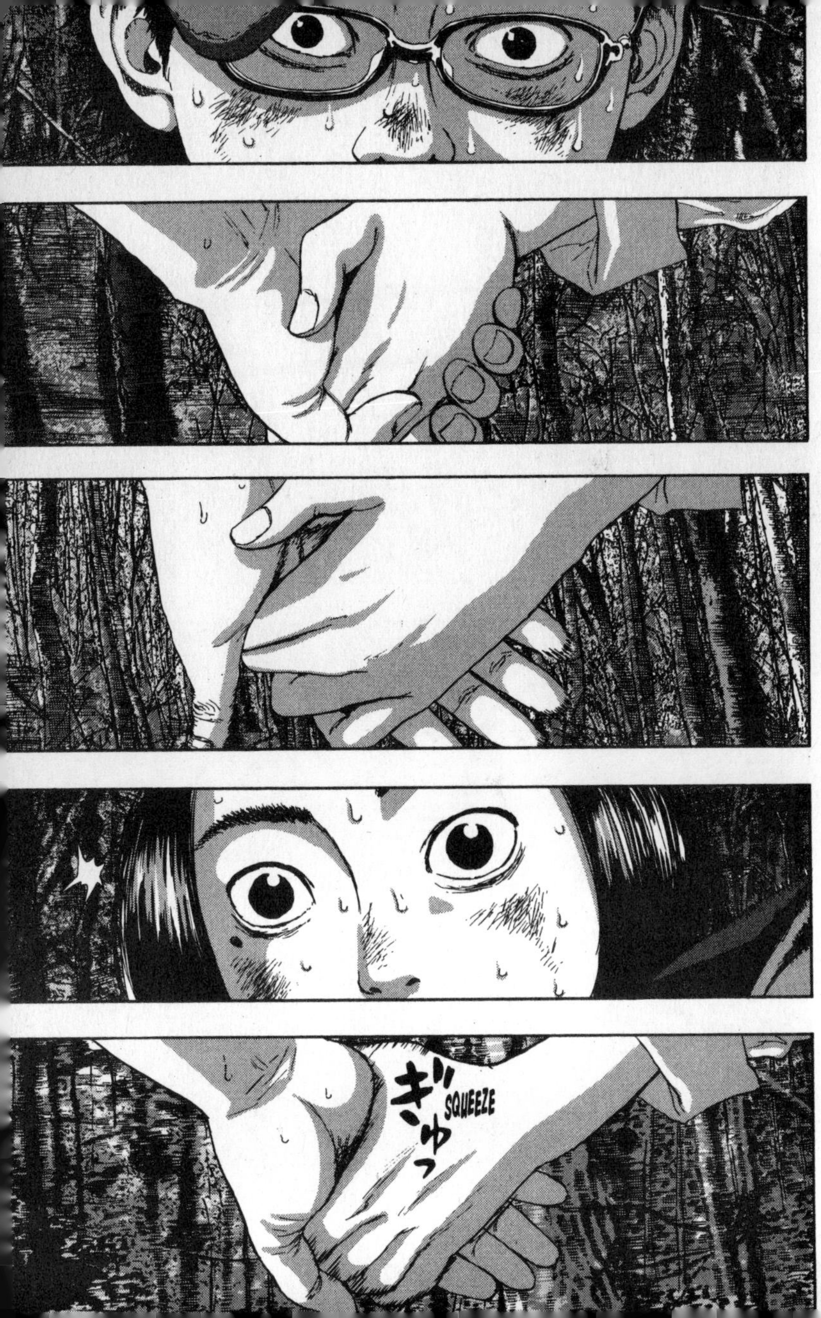
ぎゅっ
SQUEEZE

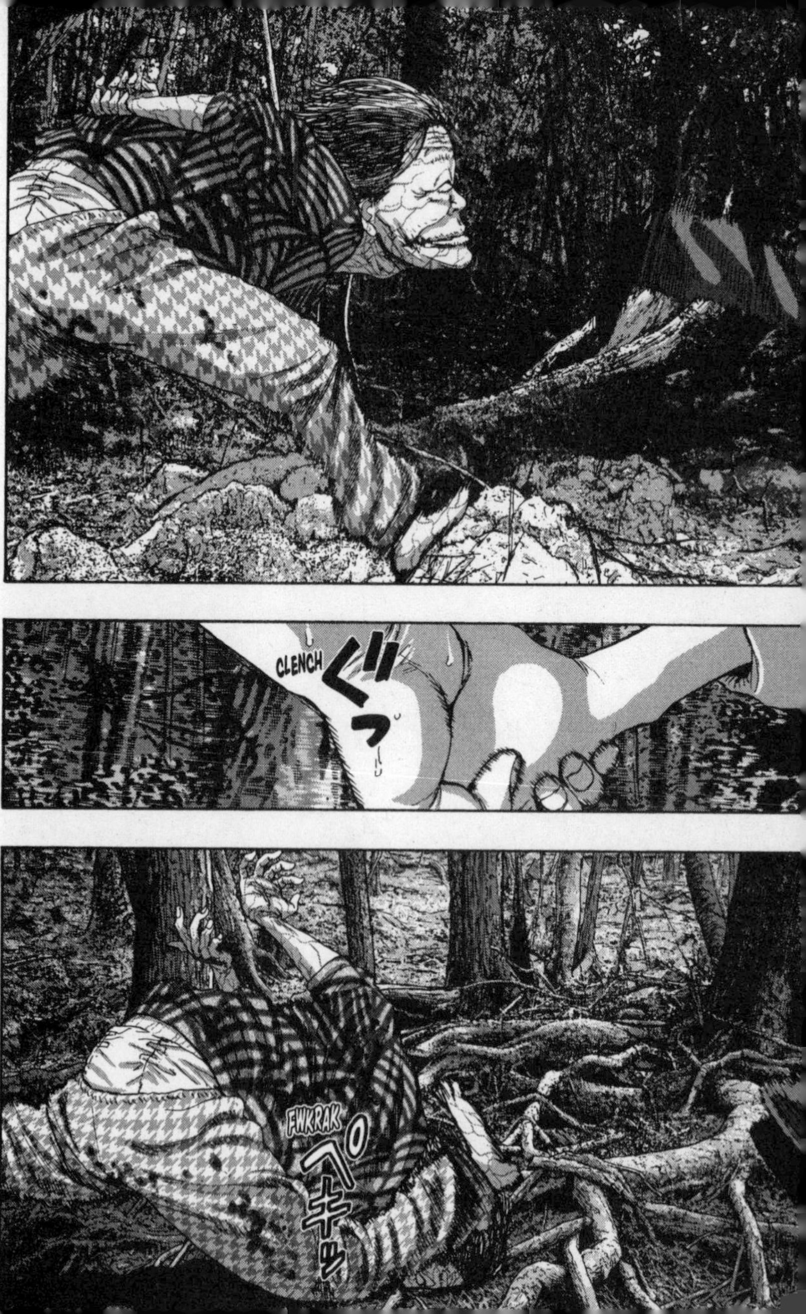
CLENCH
ぐっ
FWKRAK
ペキッ

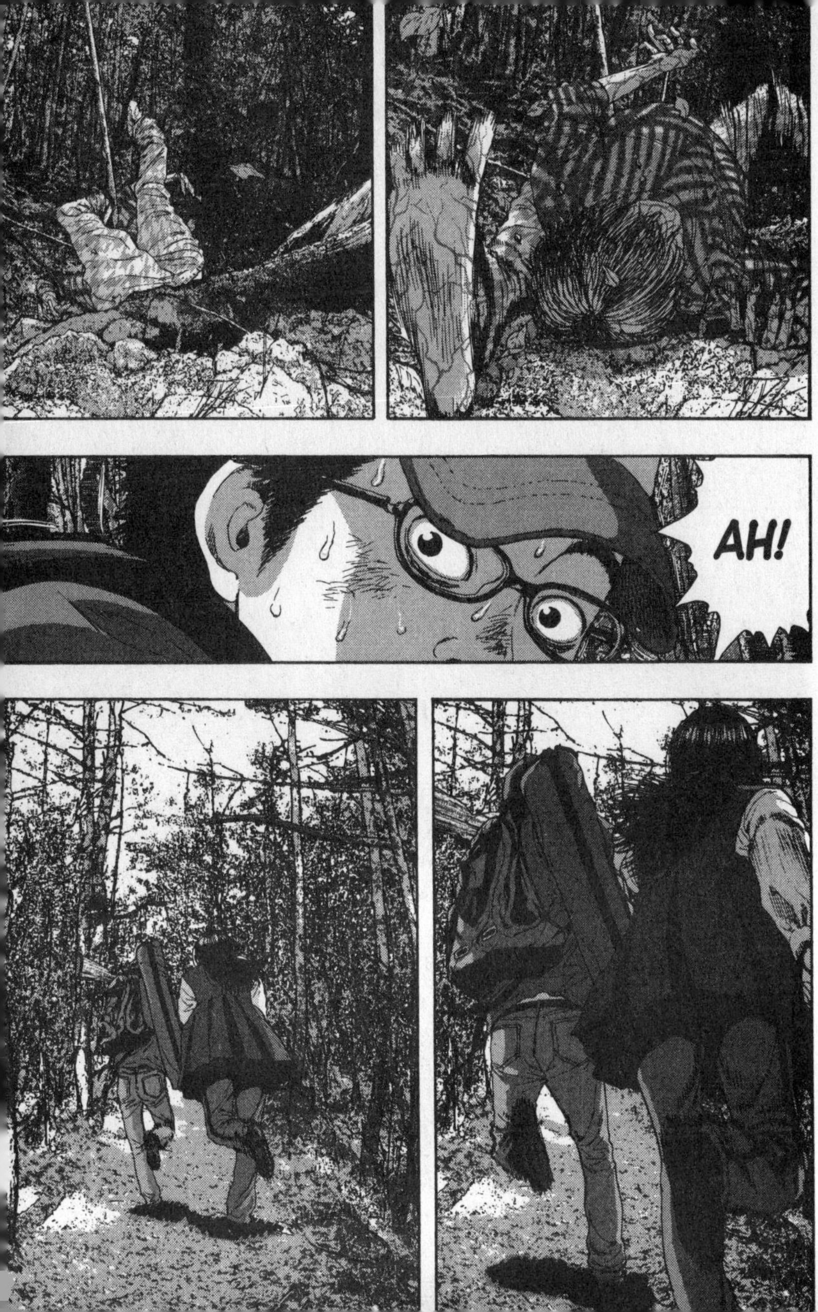
AH!

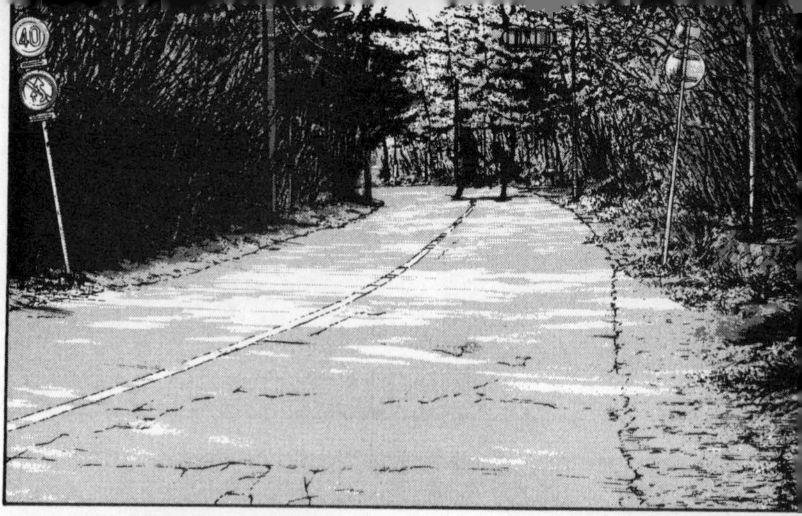

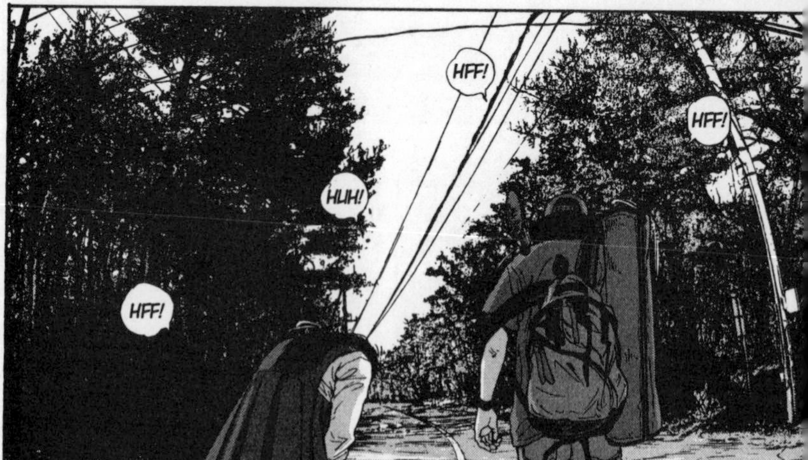
HFF!
HFF!
HUH!
HFF!

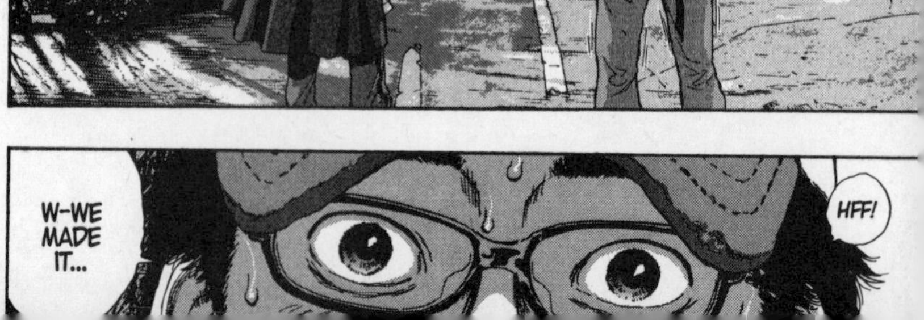
HFF!
W-WE MADE IT...

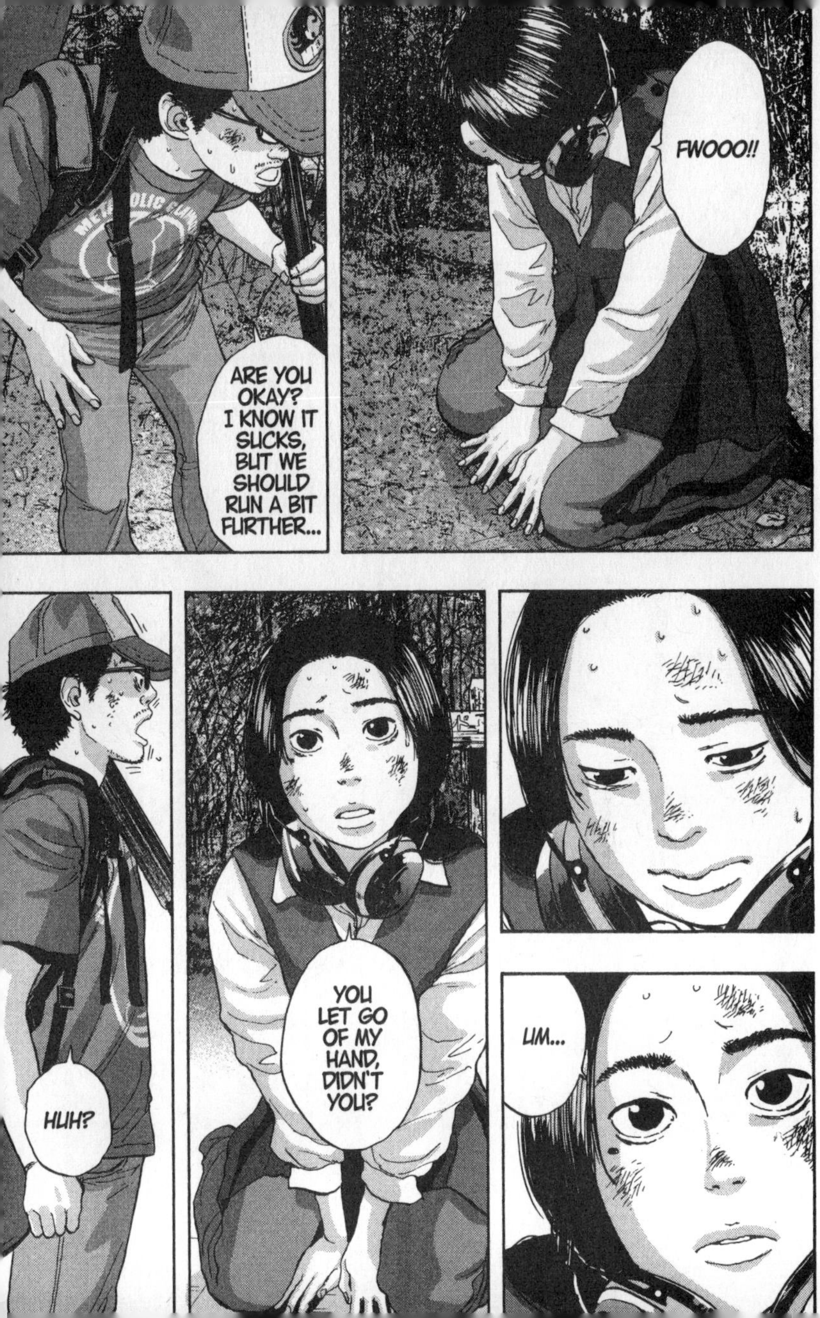
FWOOO!!
ARE YOU OKAY? I KNOW IT SUCKS, BUT WE SHOULD RUN A BIT FURTHER...
UM...
YOU LET GO OF MY HAND, DIDN'T YOU?
HUH?

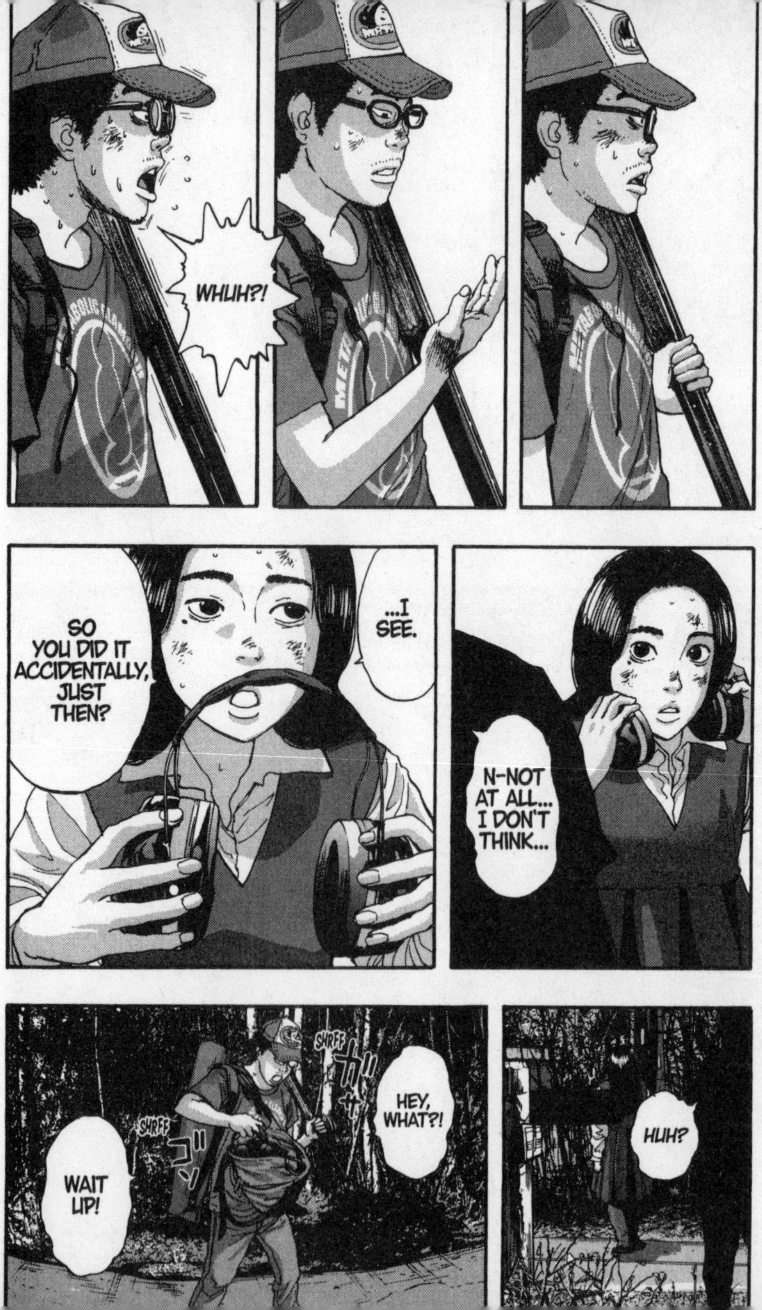

WHUH?!
N-NOT AT ALL... I DON'T THINK...
...I SEE.
SO YOU DID IT ACCIDENTALLY, JUST THEN?
HUH?
SHRFF
HEY, WHAT?!
SHRFF
WAIT UP!

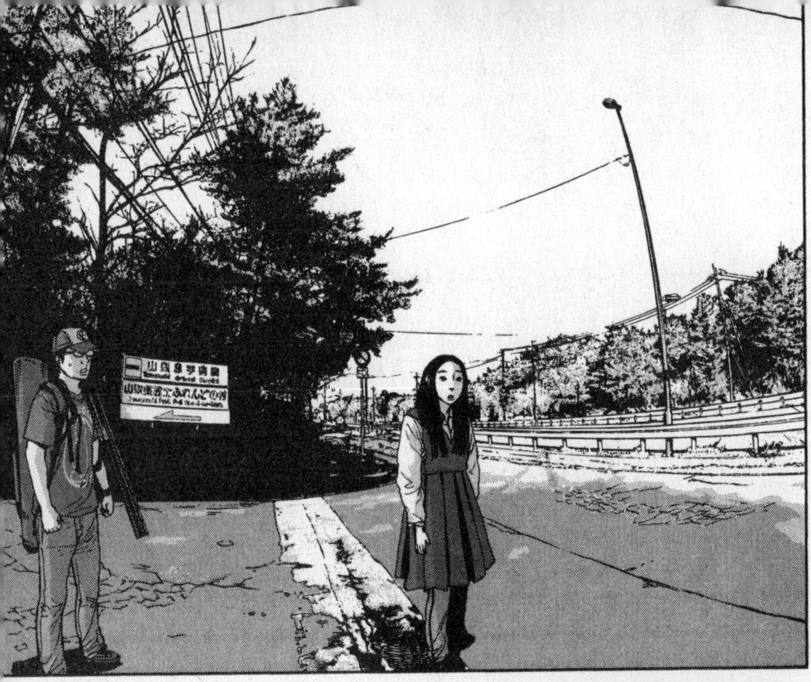
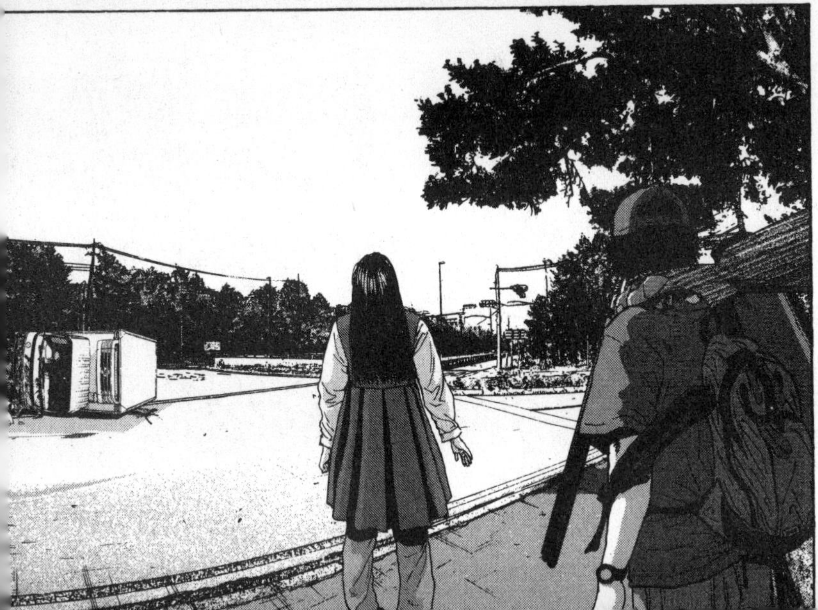

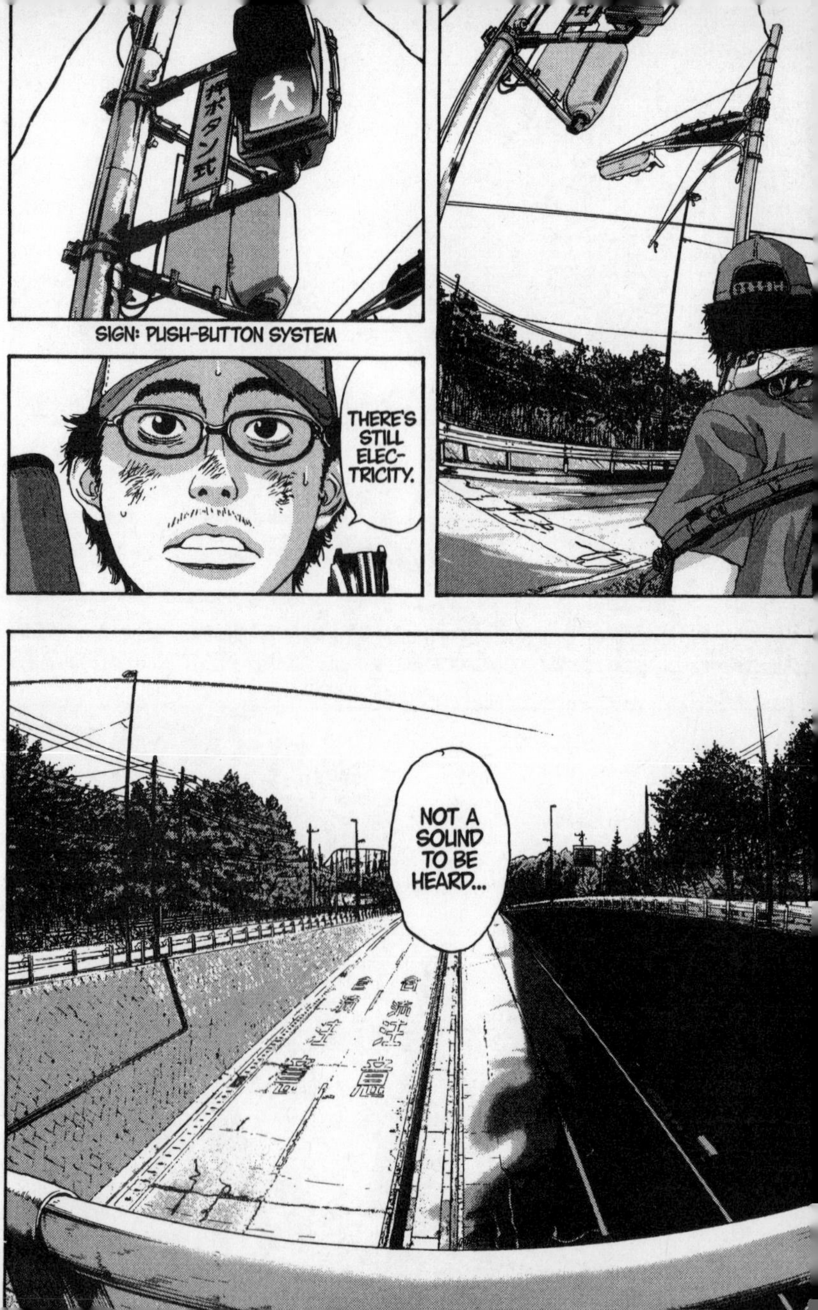
押ボタン式
SIGN: PUSH-BUTTON SYSTEM
THERE'S STILL ELECTRICITY.
NOT A SOUND TO BE HEARD...

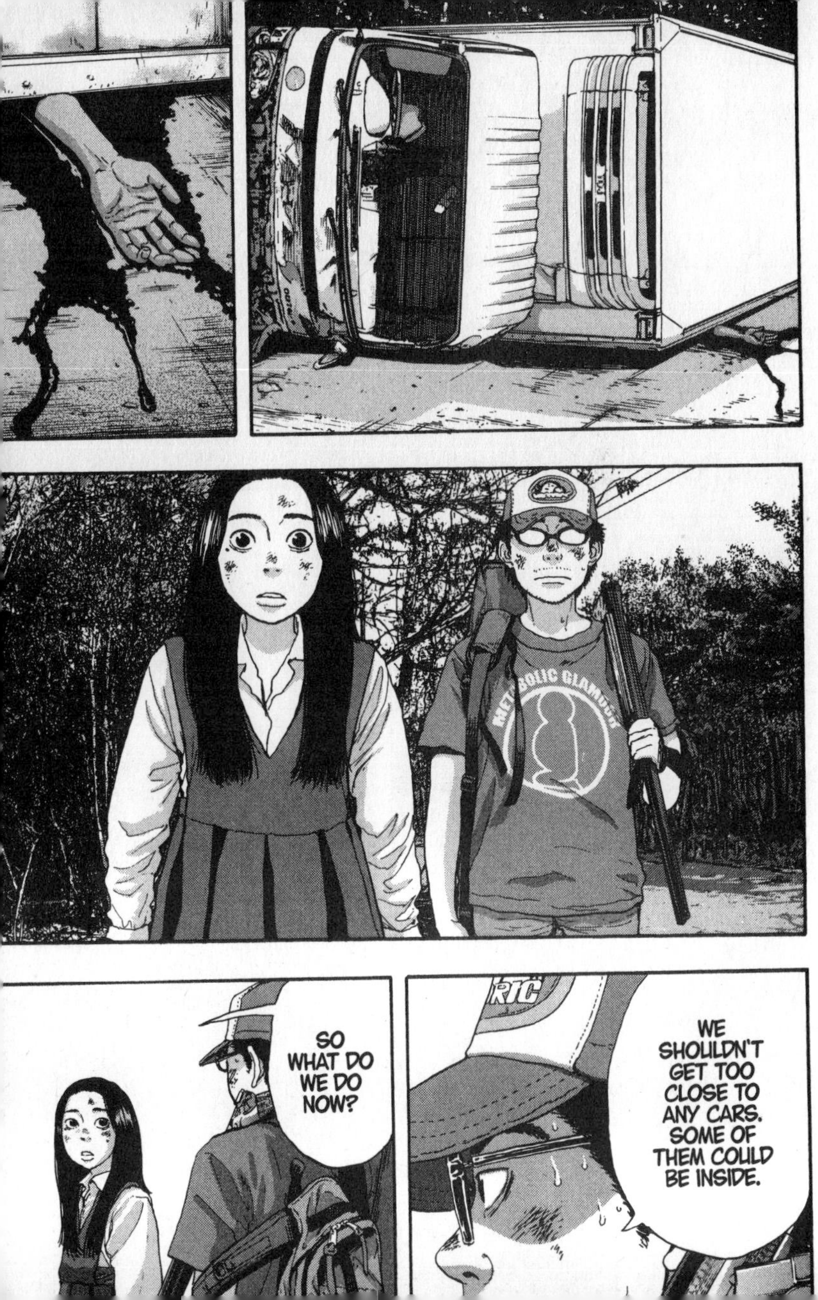
WE SHOULDN'T GET TOO CLOSE TO ANY CARS. SOME OF THEM COULD BE INSIDE.
SO WHAT DO WE DO NOW?

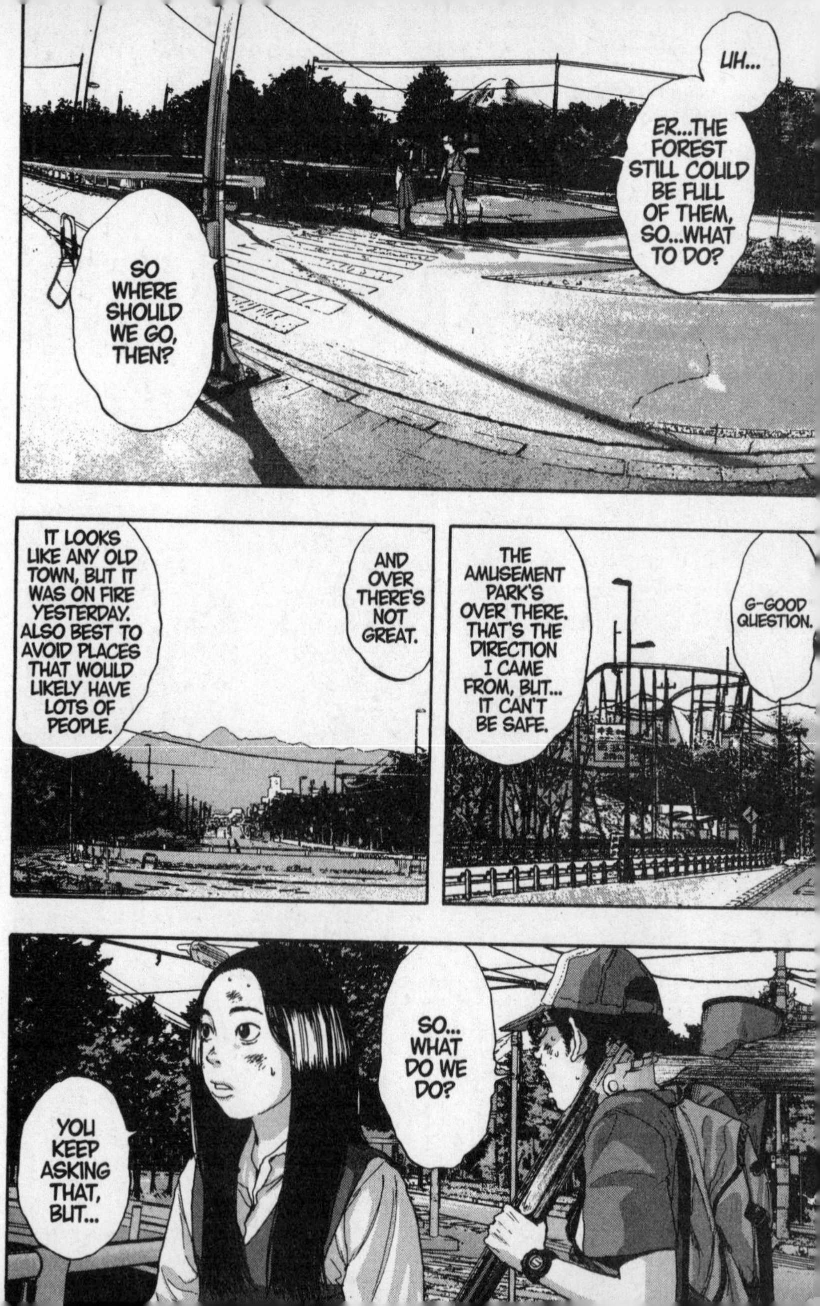
UH...
ER...THE FOREST STILL COULD BE FULL OF THEM, SO...WHAT TO DO?
SO WHERE SHOULD WE GO, THEN?
G-GOOD QUESTION.
THE AMUSEMENT PARK'S OVER THERE. THAT'S THE DIRECTION I CAME FROM, BUT... IT CAN'T BE SAFE.
AND OVER THERE'S NOT GREAT.
IT LOOKS LIKE ANY OLD TOWN, BUT IT WAS ON FIRE YESTERDAY. ALSO BEST TO AVOID PLACES THAT WOULD LIKELY HAVE LOTS OF PEOPLE.
SO... WHAT DO WE DO?
YOU KEEP ASKING THAT, BUT...

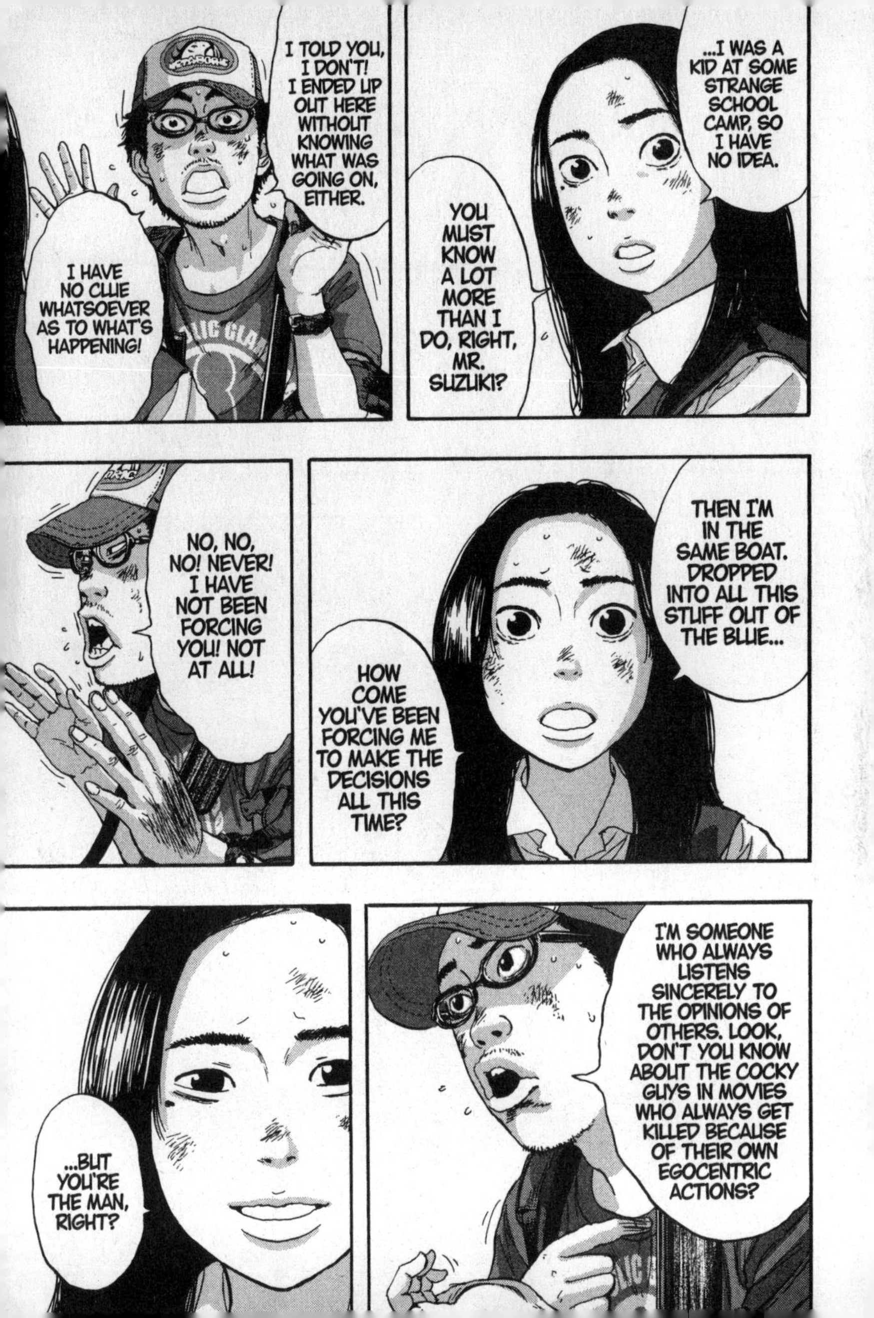
...I WAS A KID AT SOME STRANGE SCHOOL CAMP, SO I HAVE NO IDEA.
YOU MUST KNOW A LOT MORE THAN I DO, RIGHT, MR. SUZUKI?
I TOLD YOU, I DON'T! I ENDED UP OUT HERE WITHOUT KNOWING WHAT WAS GOING ON, EITHER.
I HAVE NO CLUE WHATSOEVER AS TO WHAT'S HAPPENING!
THEN I'M IN THE SAME BOAT. DROPPED INTO ALL THIS STUFF OUT OF THE BLUE...
HOW COME YOU'VE BEEN FORCING ME TO MAKE THE DECISIONS ALL THIS TIME?
NO, NO, NO! NEVER! I HAVE NOT BEEN FORCING YOU! NOT AT ALL!
I'M SOMEONE WHO ALWAYS LISTENS SINCERELY TO THE OPINIONS OF OTHERS. LOOK, DON'T YOU KNOW ABOUT THE COCKY GUYS IN MOVIES WHO ALWAYS GET KILLED BECAUSE OF THEIR OWN EGOCENTRIC ACTIONS?
...BUT YOU'RE THE MAN, RIGHT?

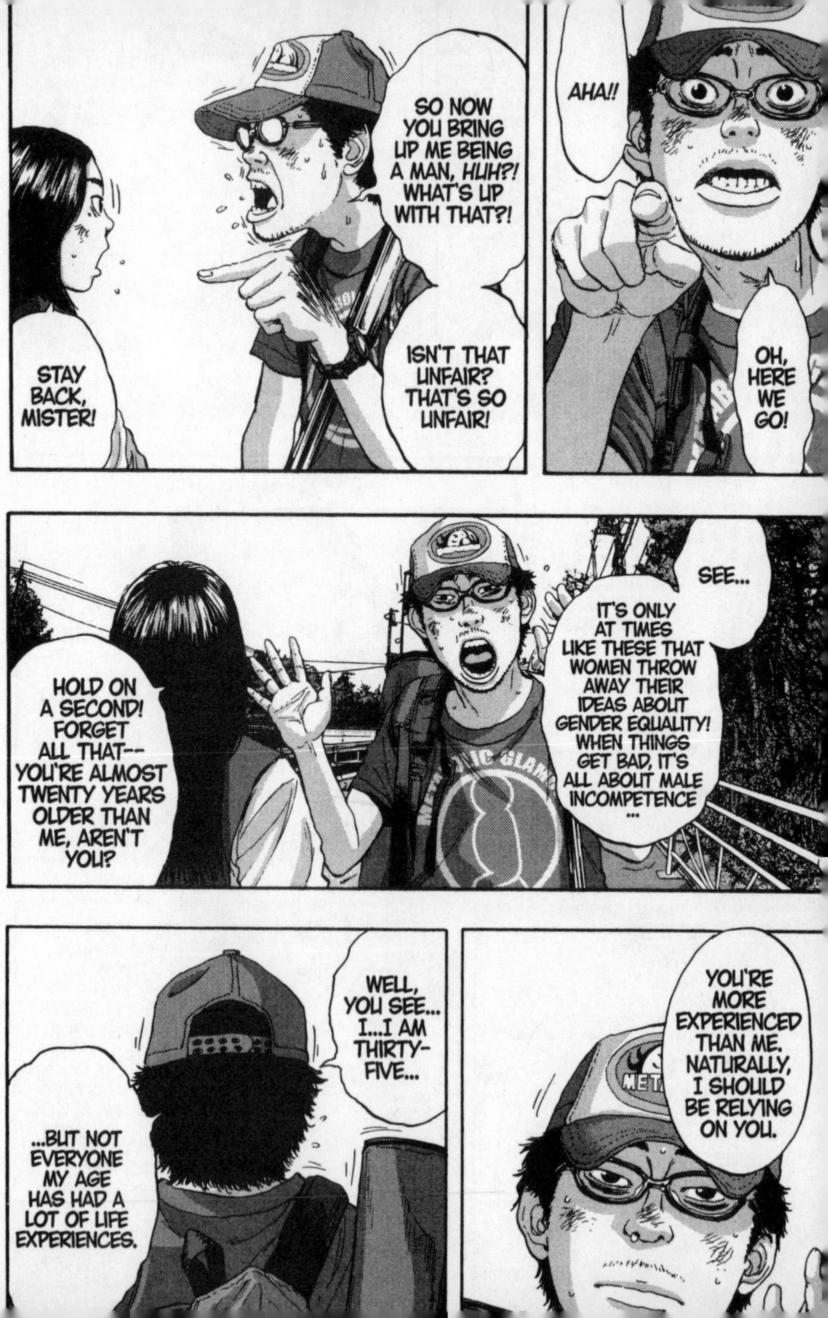
AHA!!
OH, HERE WE GO!
SO NOW YOU BRING UP ME BEING A MAN, HUH?! WHAT'S UP WITH THAT?!
ISN'T THAT UNFAIR? THAT'S SO UNFAIR!
STAY BACK, MISTER!
SEE...
IT'S ONLY AT TIMES LIKE THESE THAT WOMEN THROW AWAY THEIR IDEAS ABOUT GENDER EQUALITY! WHEN THINGS GET BAD, IT'S ALL ABOUT MALE INCOMPETENCE ...
HOLD ON A SECOND! FORGET ALL THAT-- YOU'RE ALMOST TWENTY YEARS OLDER THAN ME, AREN'T YOU?
YOU'RE MORE EXPERIENCED THAN ME. NATURALLY, I SHOULD BE RELYING ON YOU.
WELL, YOU SEE... I...I AM THIRTY-FIVE...
...BUT NOT EVERYONE MY AGE HAS HAD A LOT OF LIFE EXPERIENCES.

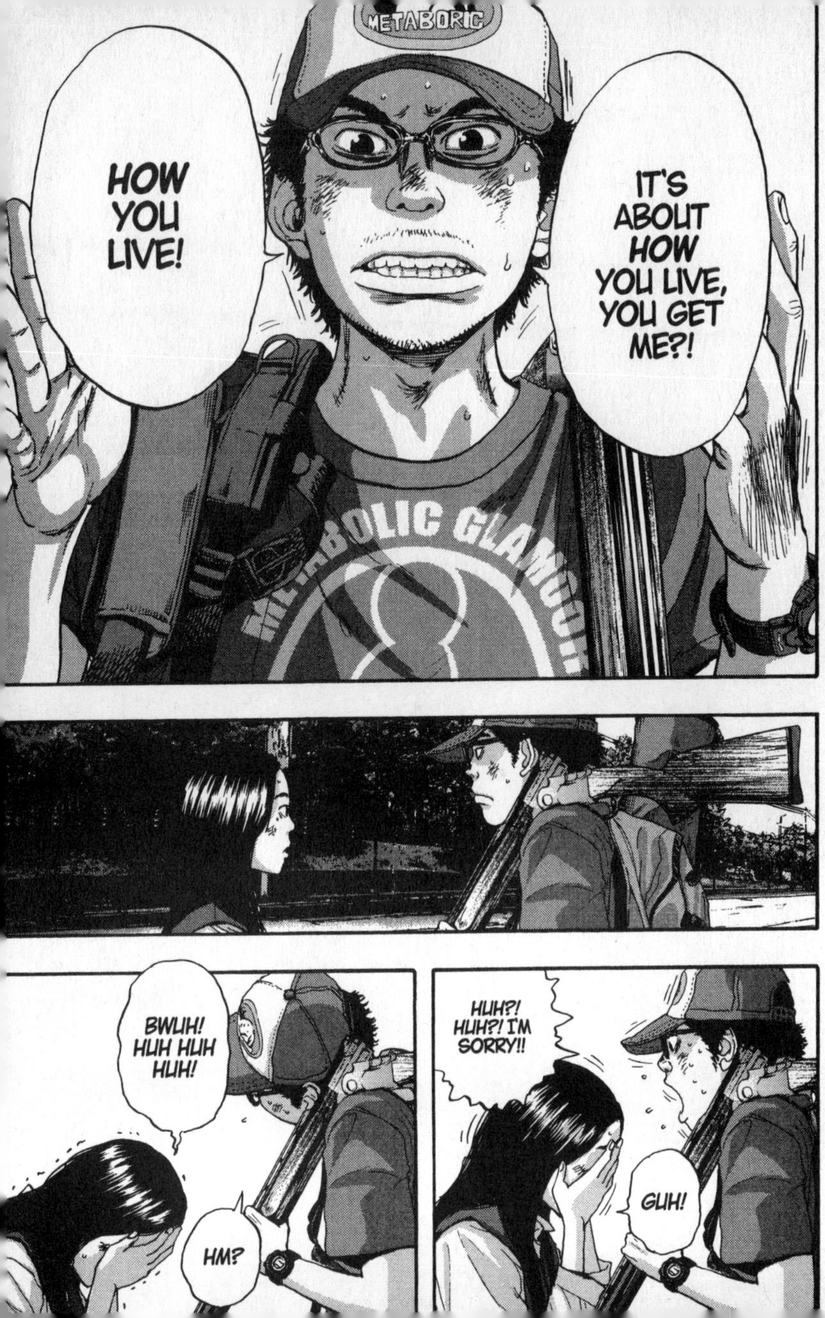
METABORIC
IT'S ABOUT HOW YOU LIVE, YOU GET ME?!
HOW YOU LIVE!
HUH?! HUH?! I'M SORRY!!
GUH!
BWUH! HUH HUH HUH!
HM?

OH, I'M SORRY.

IT MAKES ME FEEL BETTER TO KNOW THAT SOME ADULTS ARE LIKE YOU, TOO.

BMMP
BMMP
BMMP

!!!

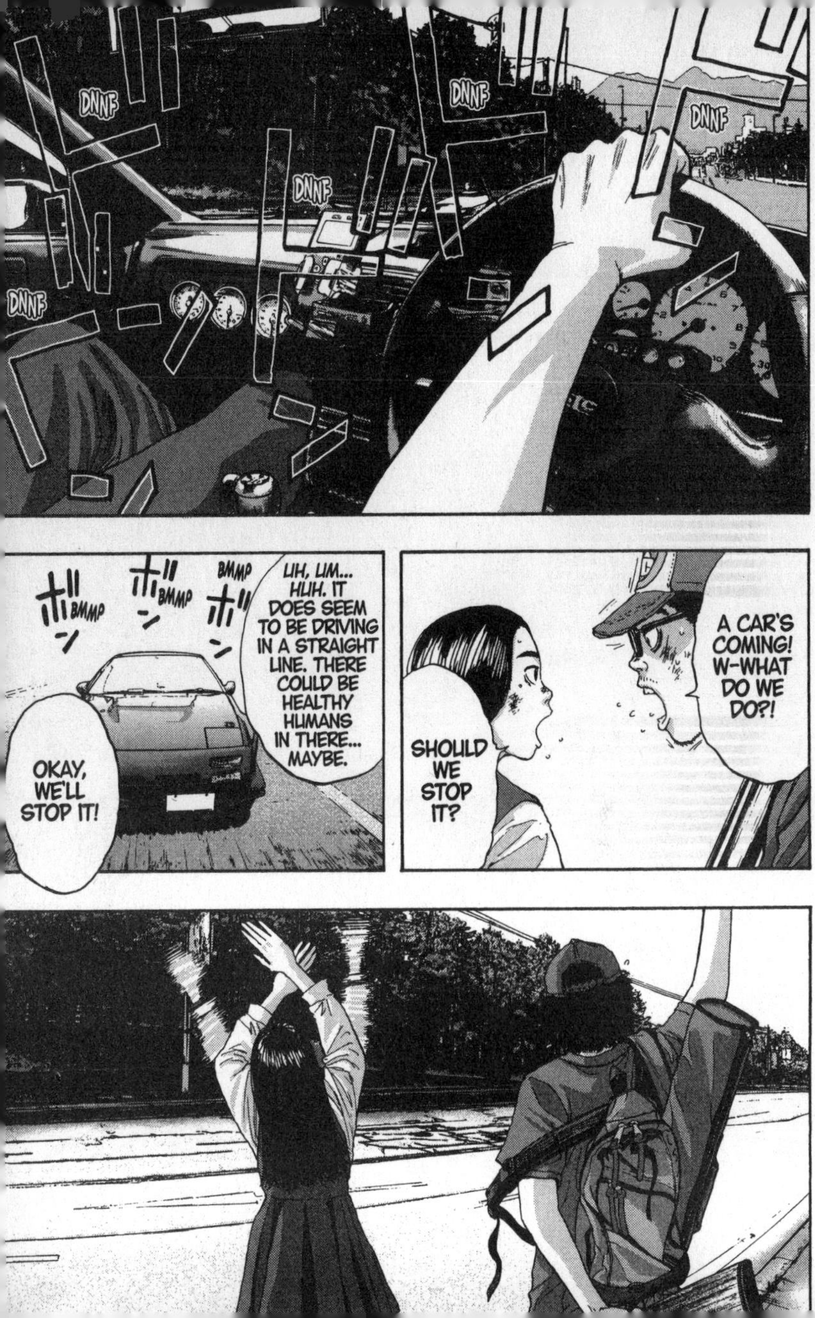
DNNF
DNNF
DNNF
DNNF
DNNF
A CAR'S COMING! W-WHAT DO WE DO?!
SHOULD WE STOP IT?
BMMP
BMMP
BMMP
UH, UM... HUH. IT DOES SEEM TO BE DRIVING IN A STRAIGHT LINE. THERE COULD BE HEALTHY HUMANS IN THERE... MAYBE.
OKAY, WE'LL STOP IT!

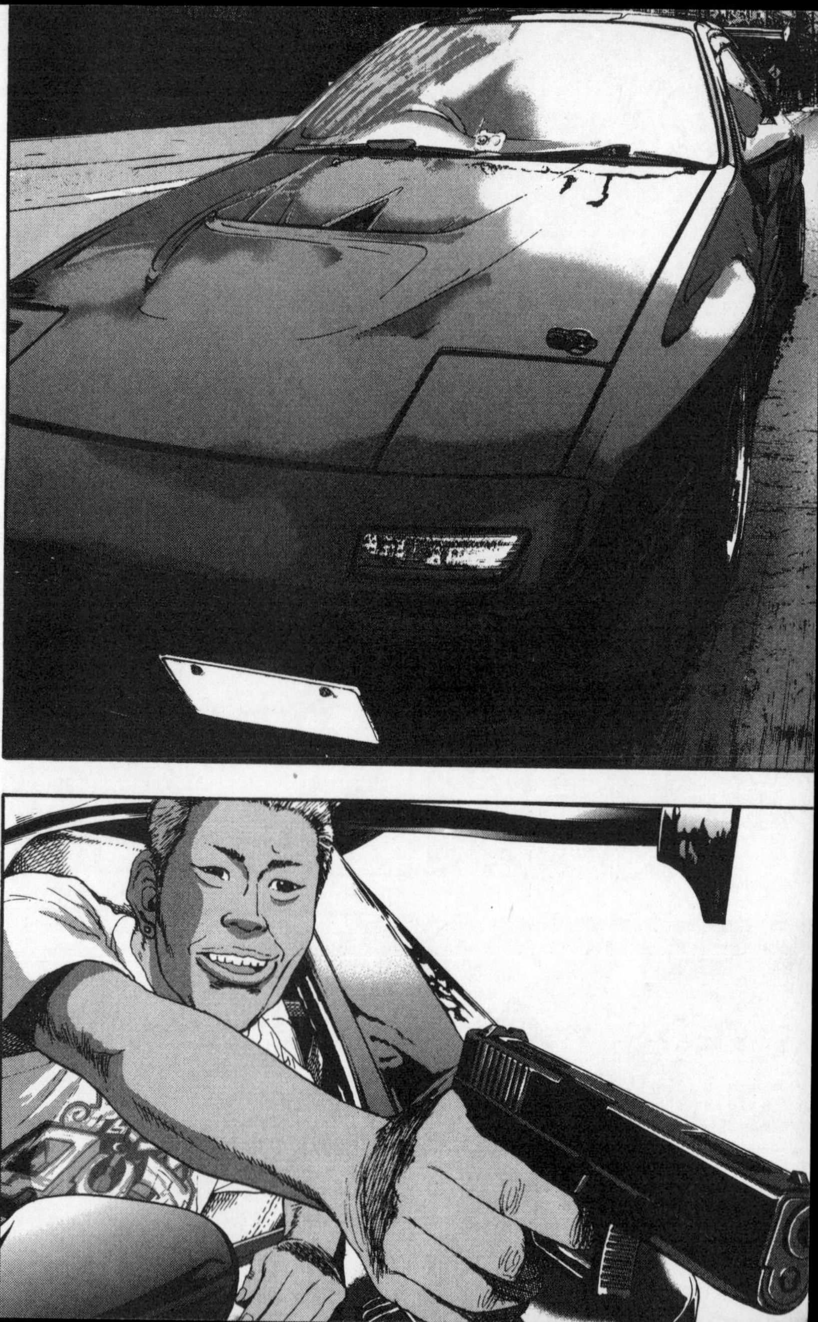

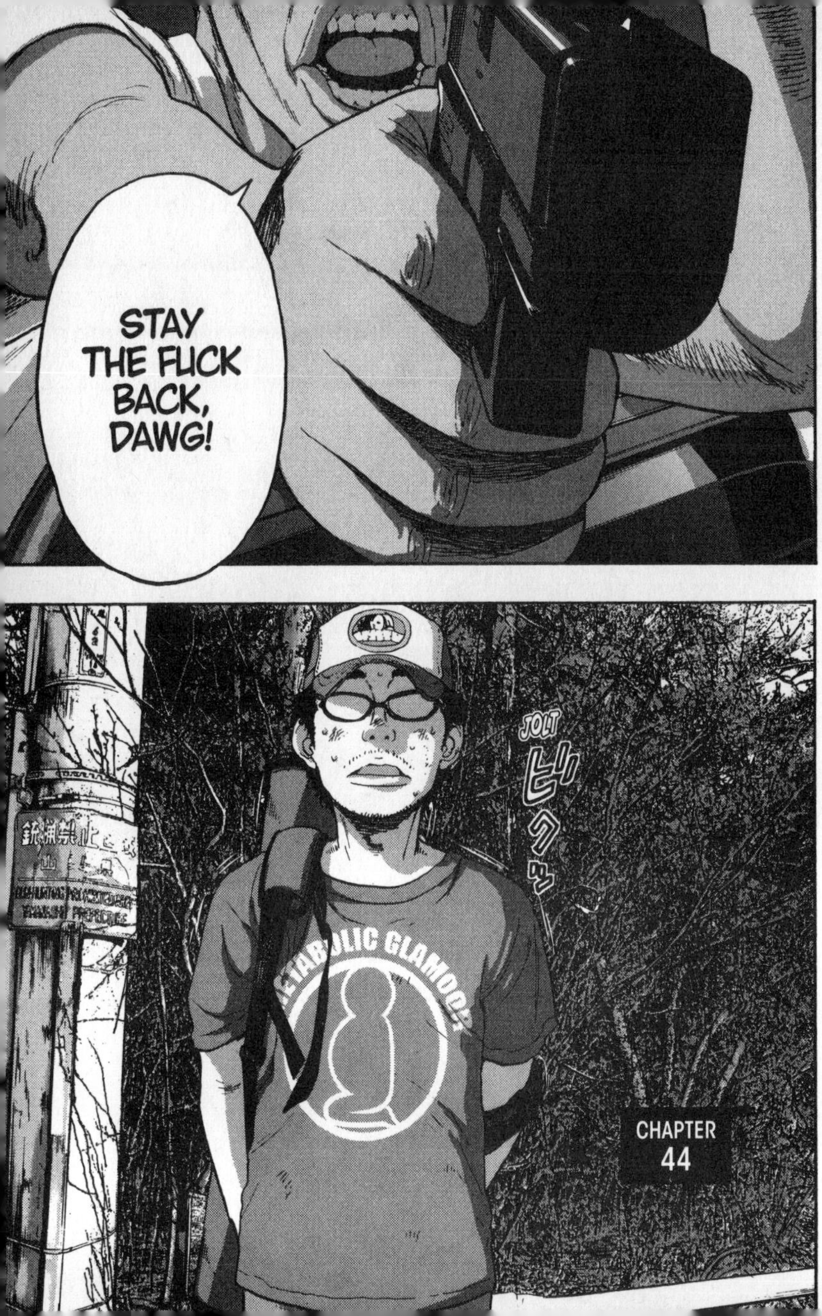
STAY THE FUCK BACK, DAWG!
JOLT
CHAPTER 44

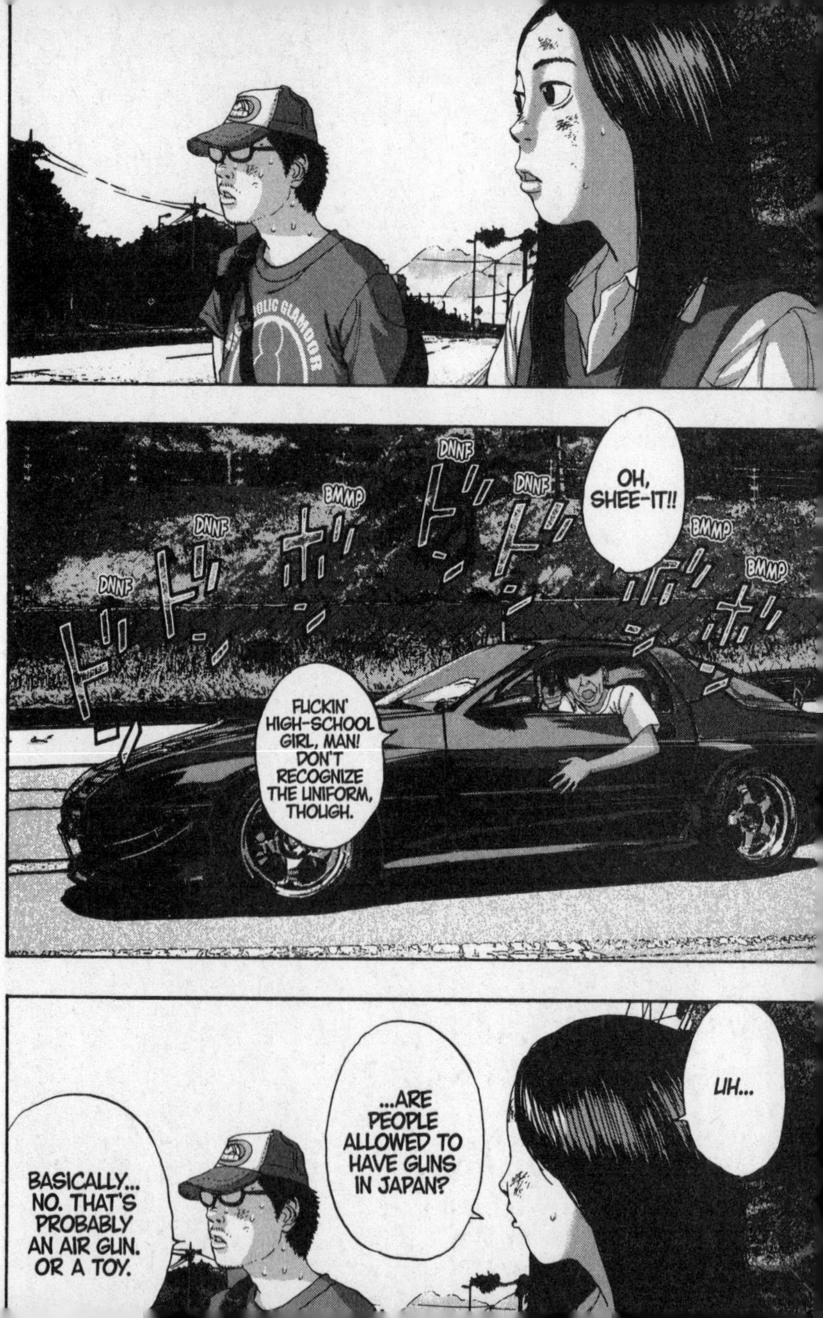
OH, SHEE-IT!!
BMMP
BMMP
DNNF
DNNF
BMMP
DNNF
DNNF
FUCKIN' HIGH-SCHOOL GIRL, MAN! DON'T RECOGNIZE THE UNIFORM, THOUGH.
UH...
...ARE PEOPLE ALLOWED TO HAVE GUNS IN JAPAN?
BASICALLY... NO. THAT'S PROBABLY AN AIR GUN. OR A TOY.

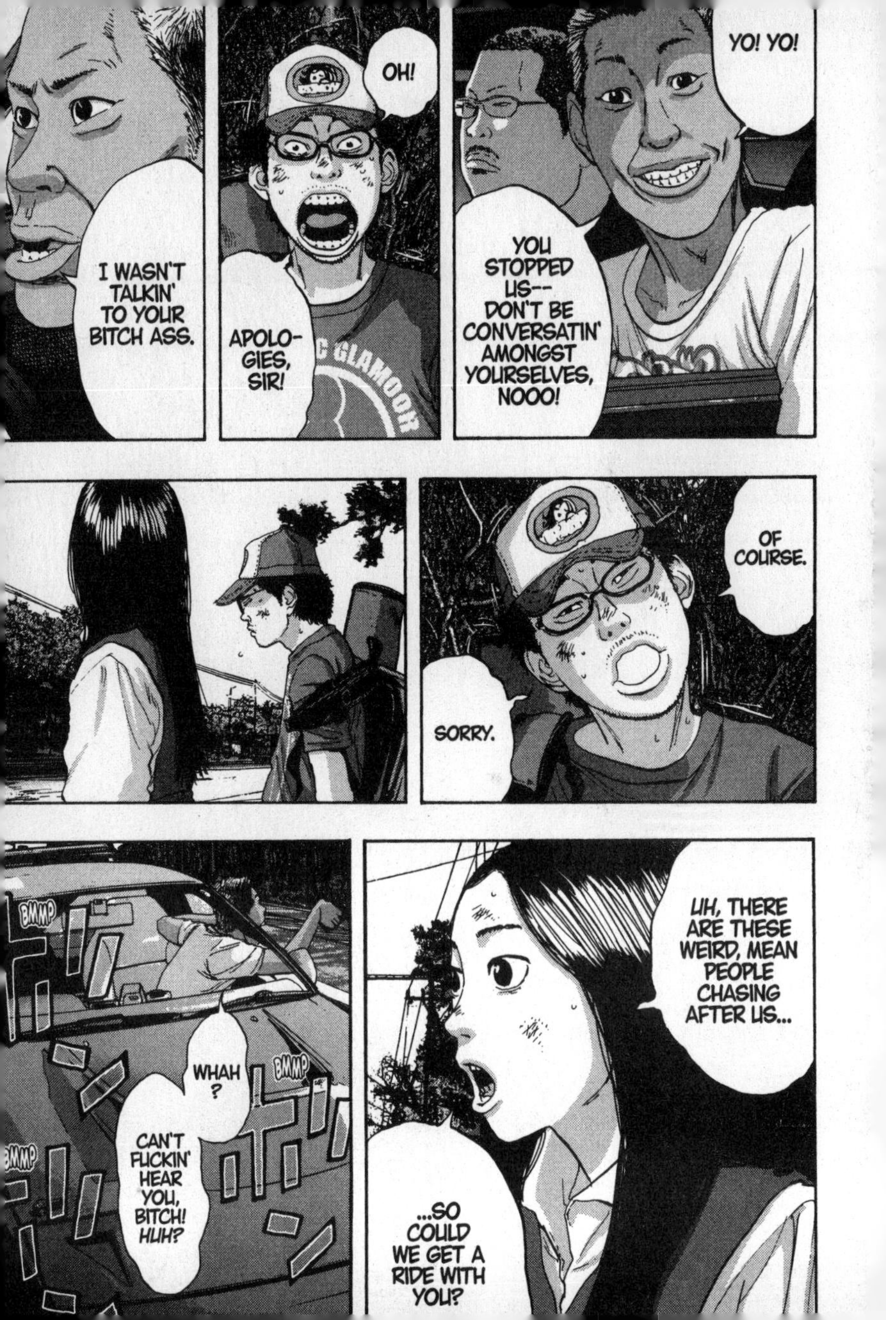
YO! YO!
YOU STOPPED US-- DON'T BE CONVERSATIN' AMONGST YOURSELVES, NOOO!
OH!
APOLO-GIES, SIR!
I WASN'T TALKIN' TO YOUR BITCH ASS.
OF COURSE.
SORRY.
UH, THERE ARE THESE WEIRD, MEAN PEOPLE CHASING AFTER US...
...SO COULD WE GET A RIDE WITH YOU?
BMMP
BMMP
BMMP
WHAH?
CAN'T FUCKIN' HEAR YOU, BITCH! HUH?

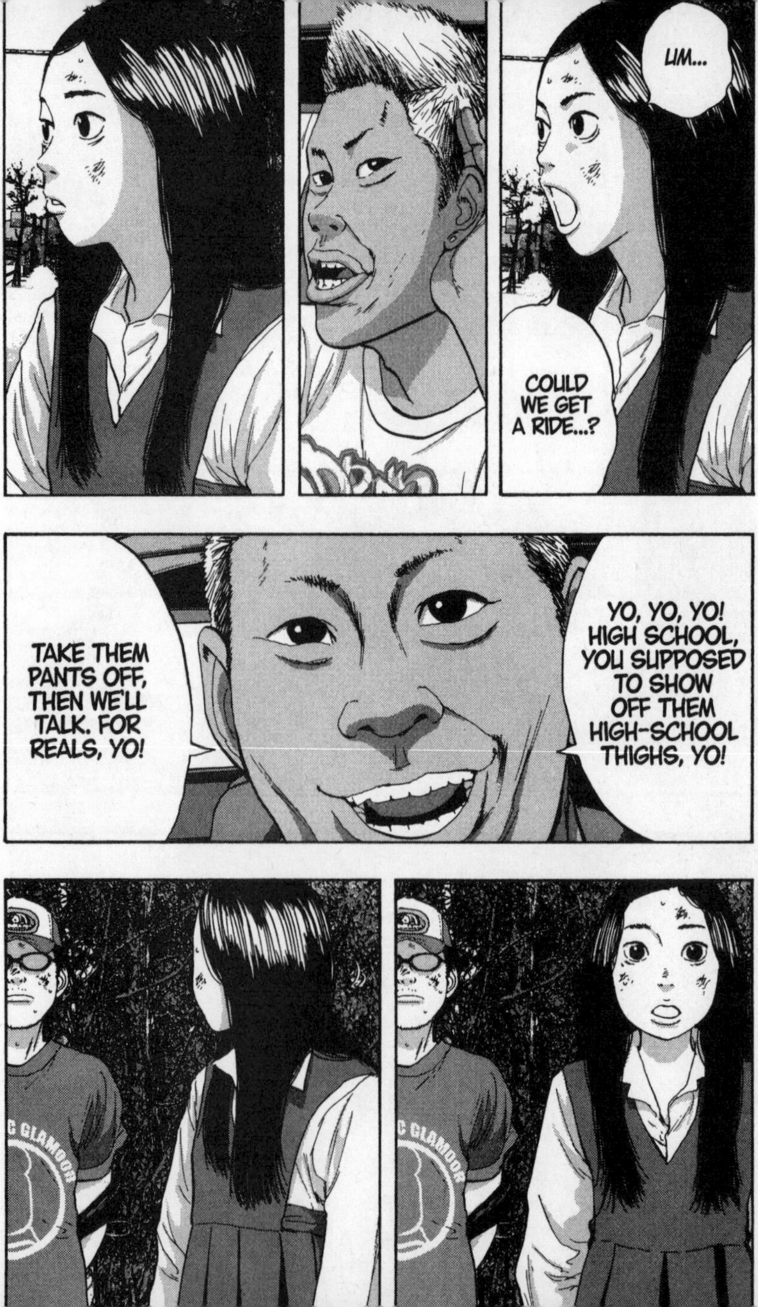
UM...
COULD WE GET A RIDE...?
YO, YO, YO! HIGH SCHOOL, YOU SUPPOSED TO SHOW OFF THEM HIGH-SCHOOL THIGHS, YO!
TAKE THEM PANTS OFF, THEN WE'LL TALK. FOR REALS, YO!

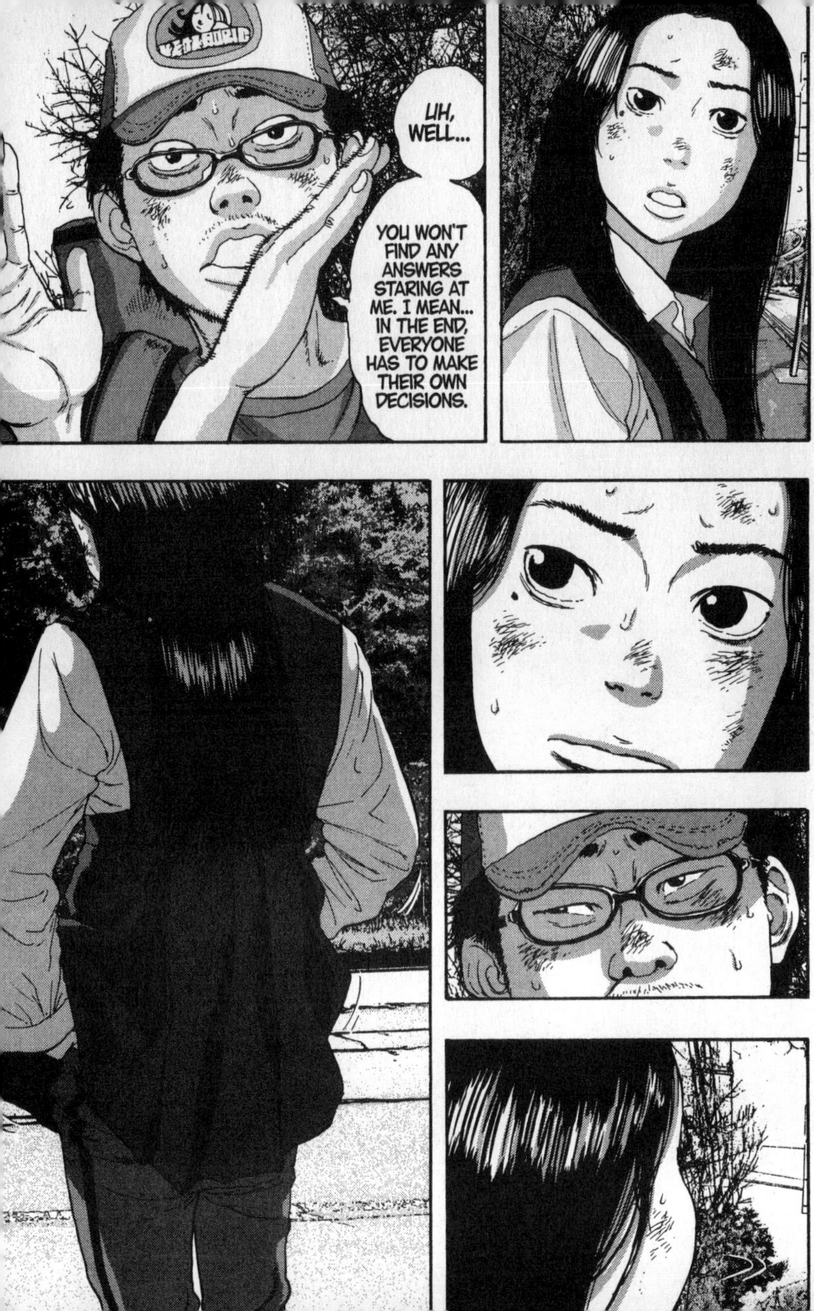
UH, WELL...
YOU WON'T FIND ANY ANSWERS STARING AT ME. I MEAN... IN THE END, EVERYONE HAS TO MAKE THEIR OWN DECISIONS.

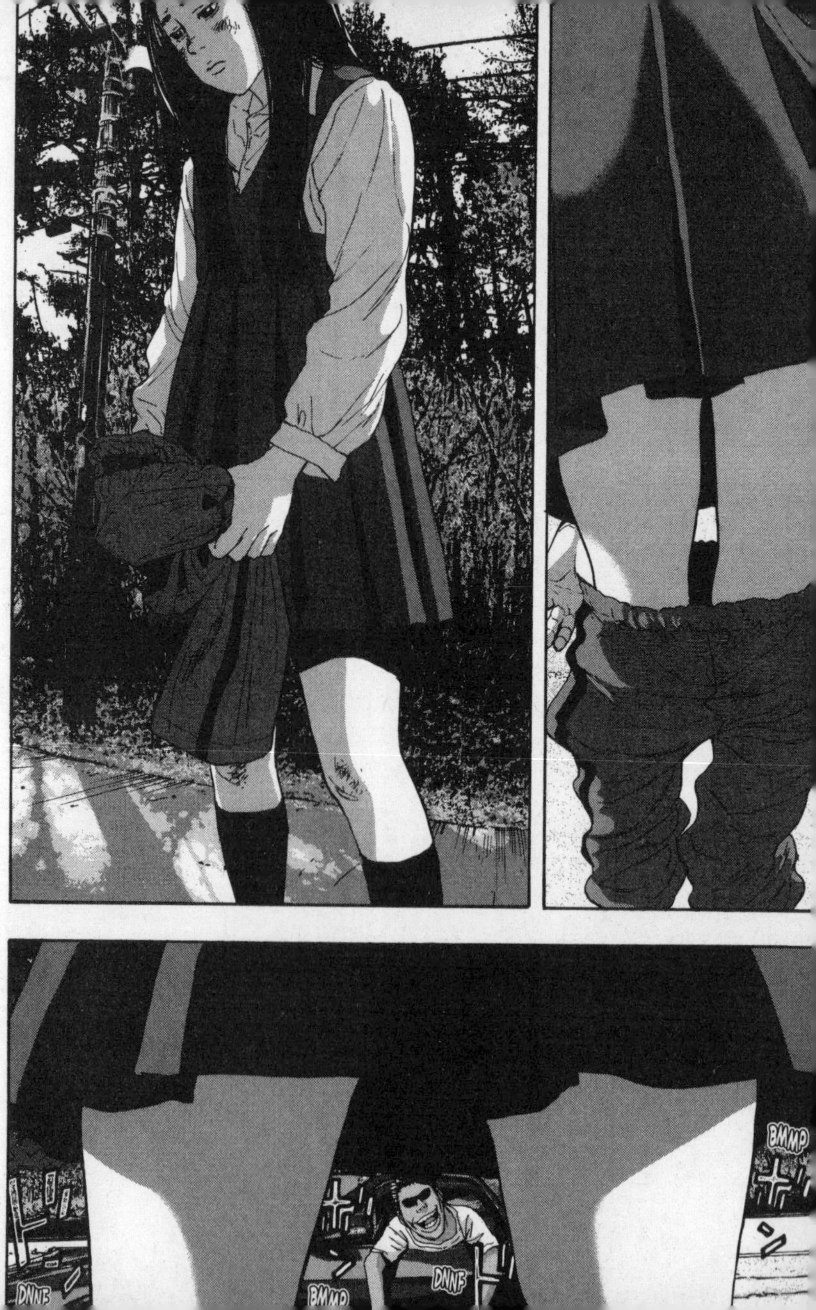
BMMP
DNNF
BMMP
DNNF

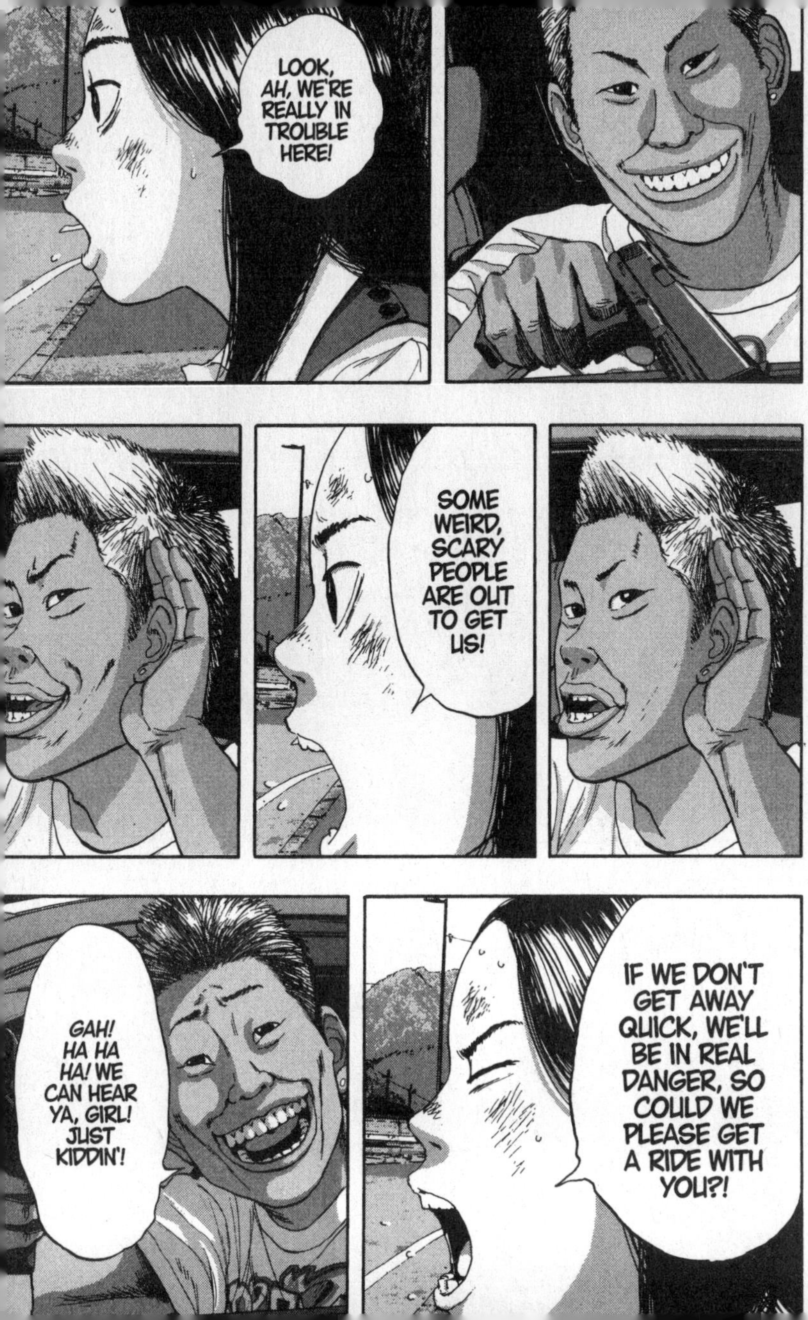
LOOK, AH, WE'RE REALLY IN TROUBLE HERE!
SOME WEIRD, SCARY PEOPLE ARE OUT TO GET US!
IF WE DON'T GET AWAY QUICK, WE'LL BE IN REAL DANGER, SO COULD WE PLEASE GET A RIDE WITH YOU?!
GAH! HA HA HA! WE CAN HEAR YA, GIRL! JUST KIDDIN'!

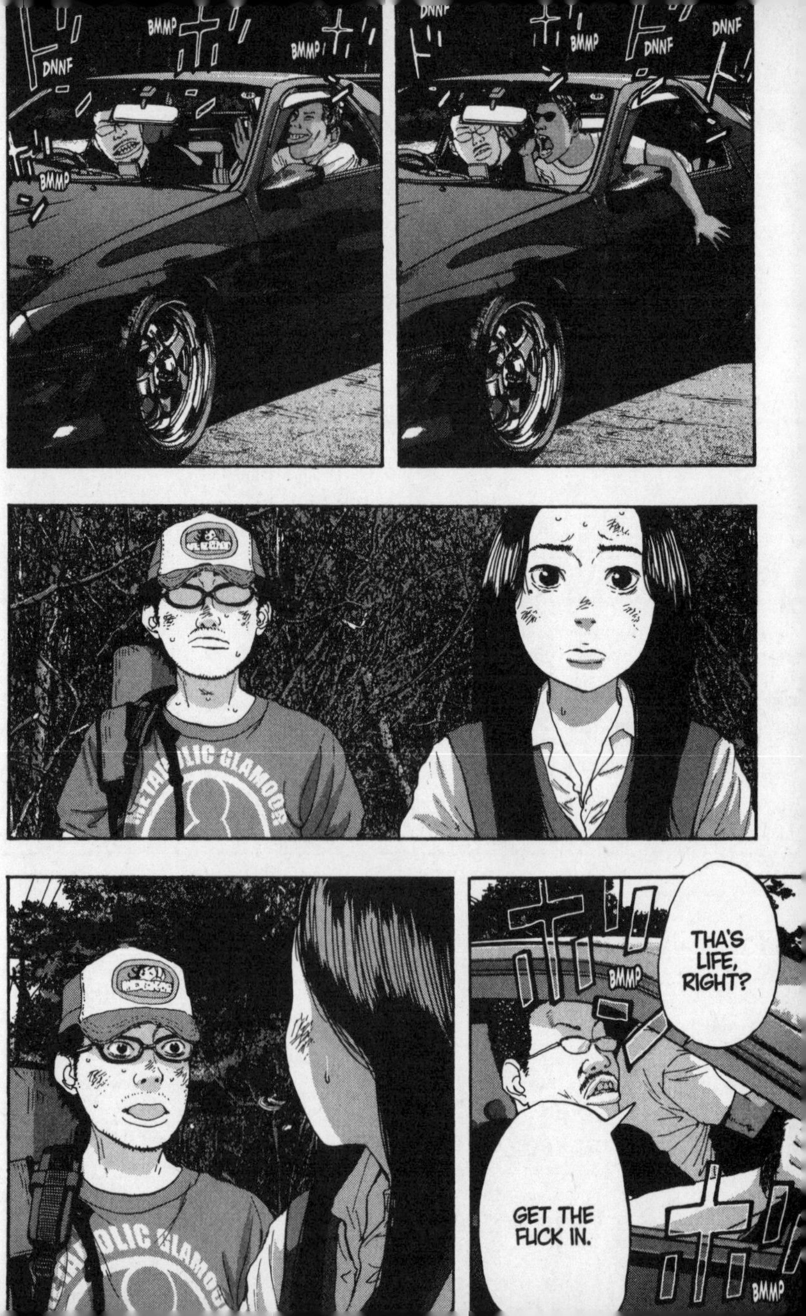
DNNF
BMMP
DNNF
DNNF
BMMP
DNNF
BMMP
BMMP
THA'S LIFE, RIGHT?
BMMP
GET THE FUCK IN.
BMMP

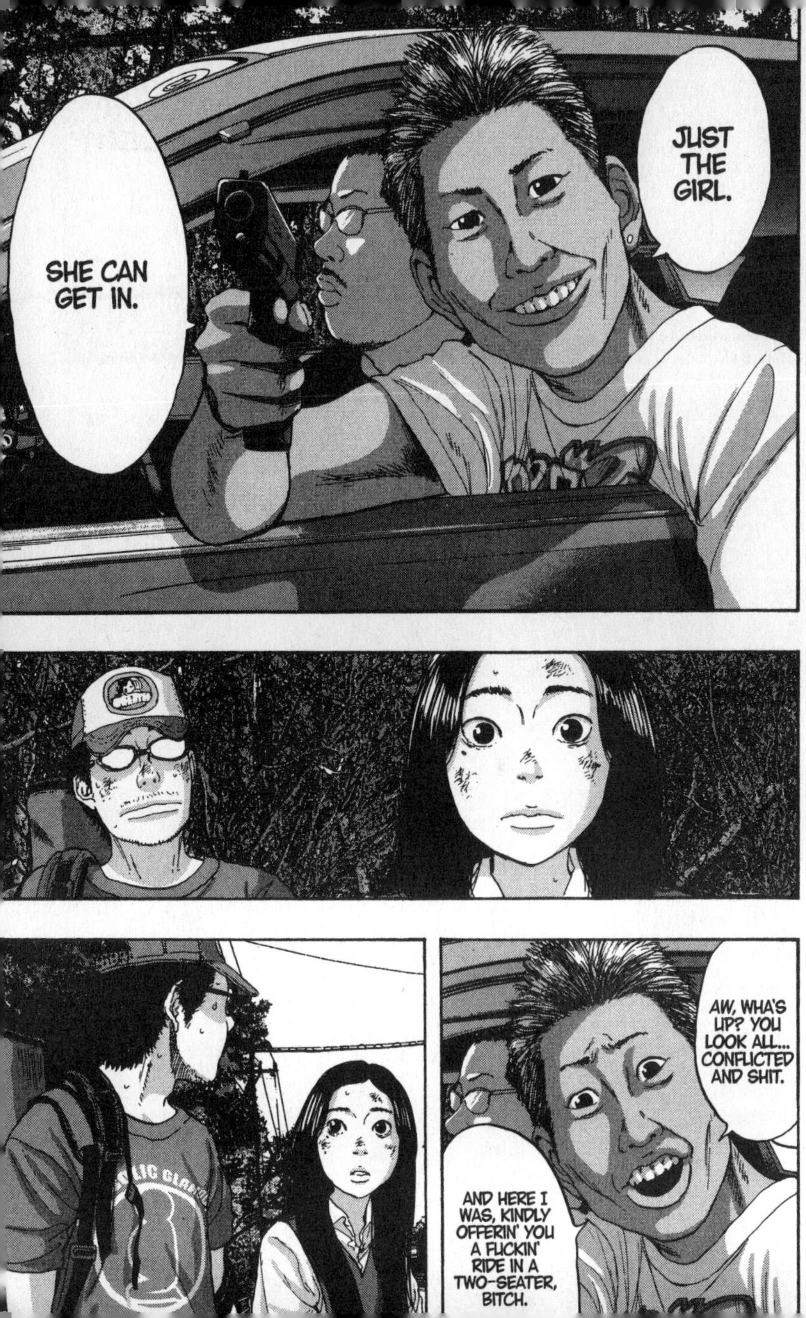
JUST THE GIRL.
SHE CAN GET IN.
AW, WHA'S UP? YOU LOOK ALL... CONFLICTED AND SHIT.
AND HERE I WAS, KINDLY OFFERIN' YOU A FUCKIN' RIDE IN A TWO-SEATER, BITCH.

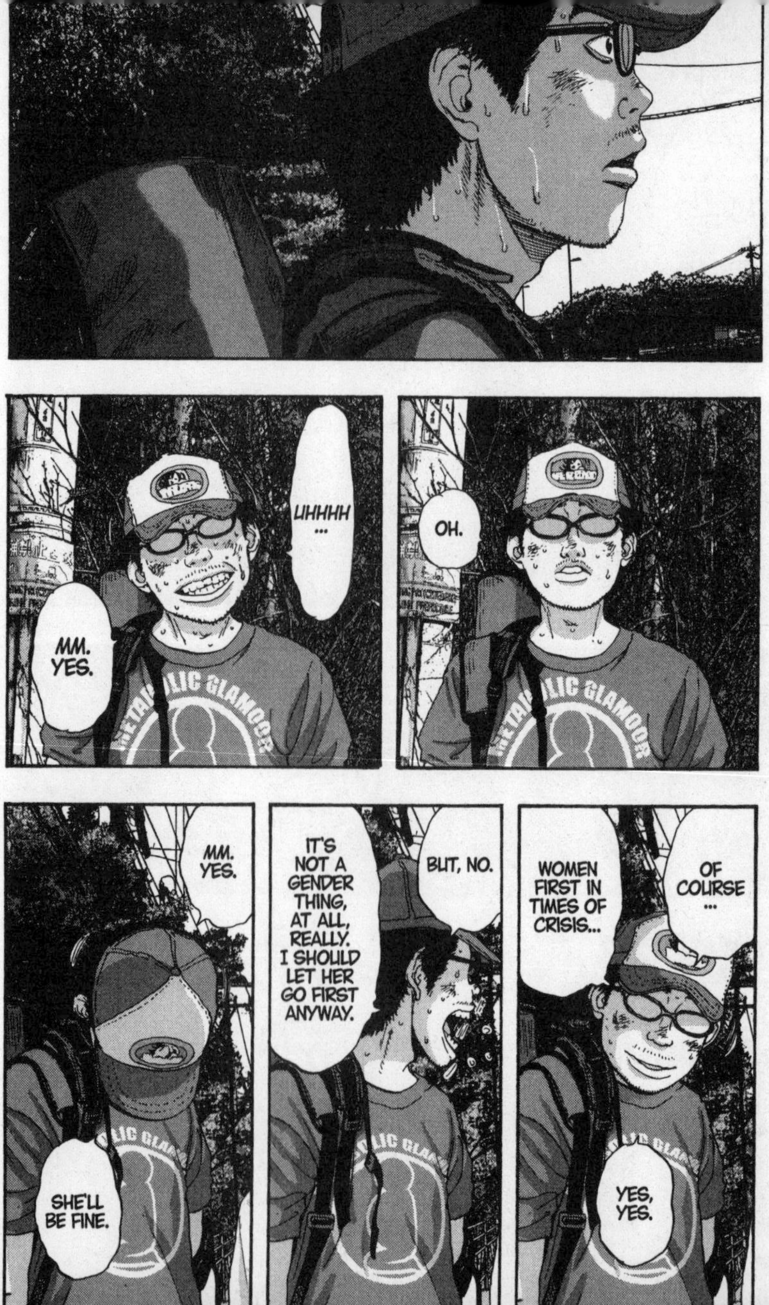
OH.
UHHHH ...
MM. YES.
OF COURSE ...
WOMEN FIRST IN TIMES OF CRISIS...
YES, YES.
BUT, NO.
IT'S NOT A GENDER THING, AT ALL, REALLY. I SHOULD LET HER GO FIRST ANYWAY.
MM. YES.
SHE'LL BE FINE.

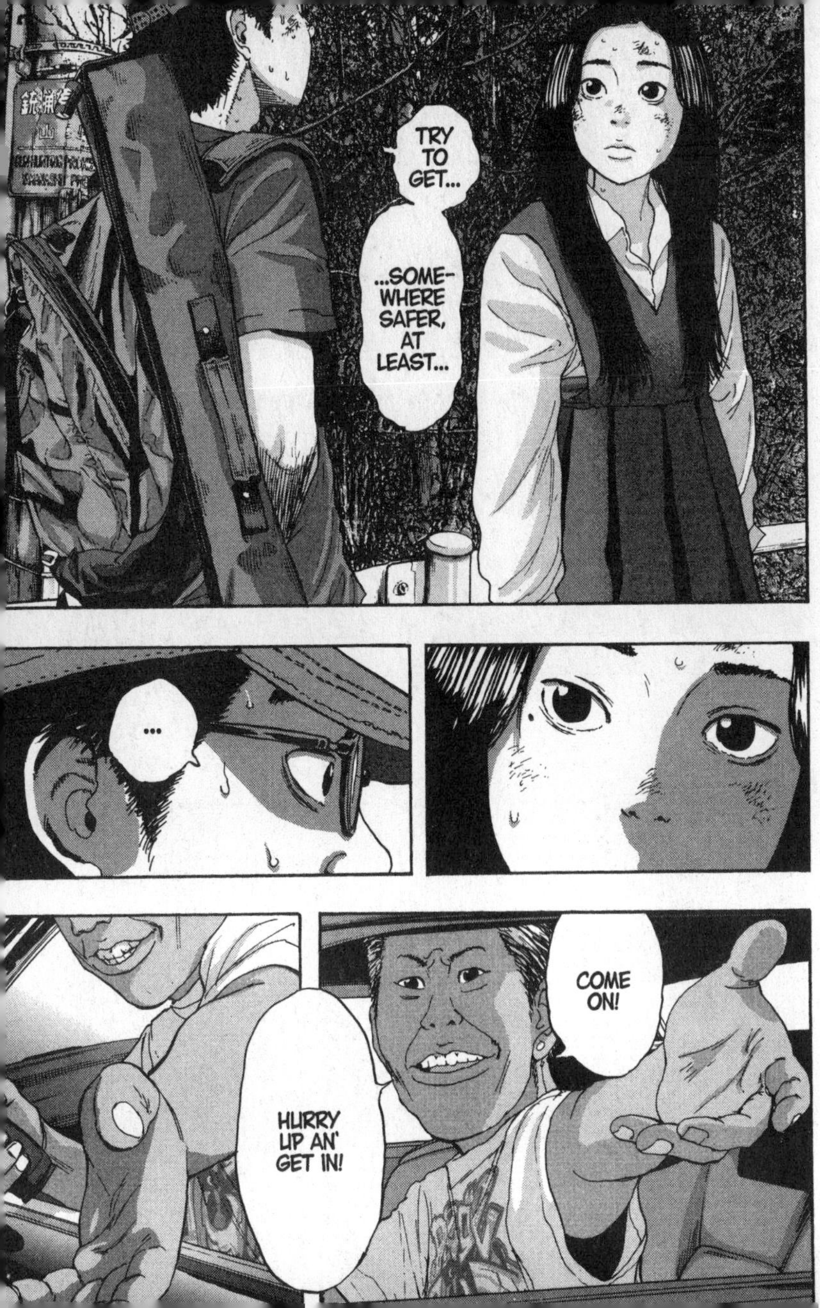
TRY TO GET...
...SOME-WHERE SAFER, AT LEAST...
...
COME ON!
HURRY UP AN' GET IN!

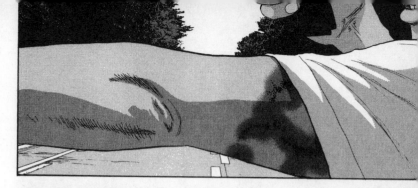

NO, MISS HAYAKARI!! GET AWAY FROM THE CAR!!

HE'S BEEN BITTEN!!

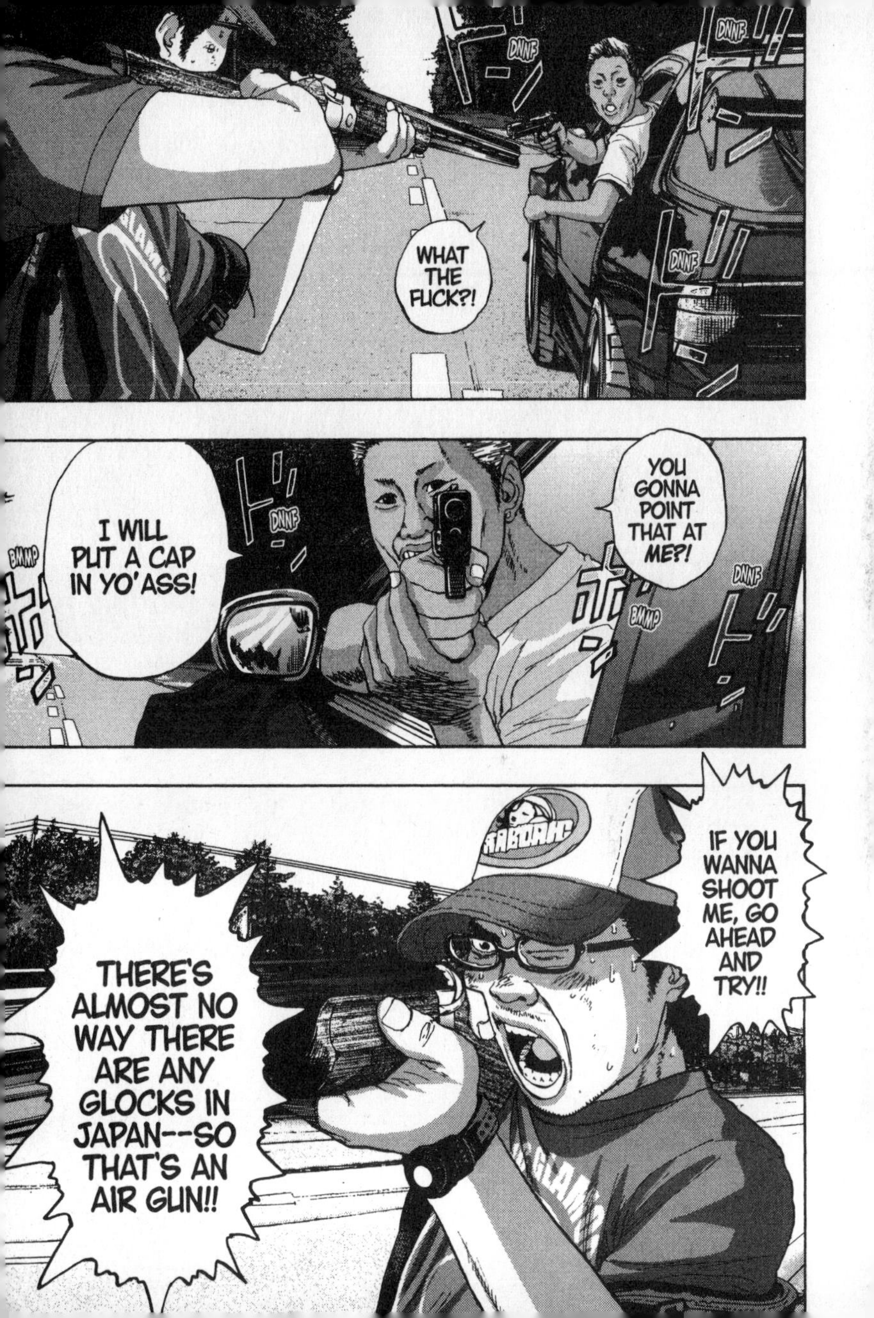
DNNF
DNNF
WHAT THE FUCK?!
DNNF
DNNF
BMMP
YOU GONNA POINT THAT AT ME?!
DNNF
I WILL PUT A CAP IN YO'ASS!
BMMP
IF YOU WANNA SHOOT ME, GO AHEAD AND TRY!!
THERE'S ALMOST NO WAY THERE ARE ANY GLOCKS IN JAPAN--SO THAT'S AN AIR GUN!!

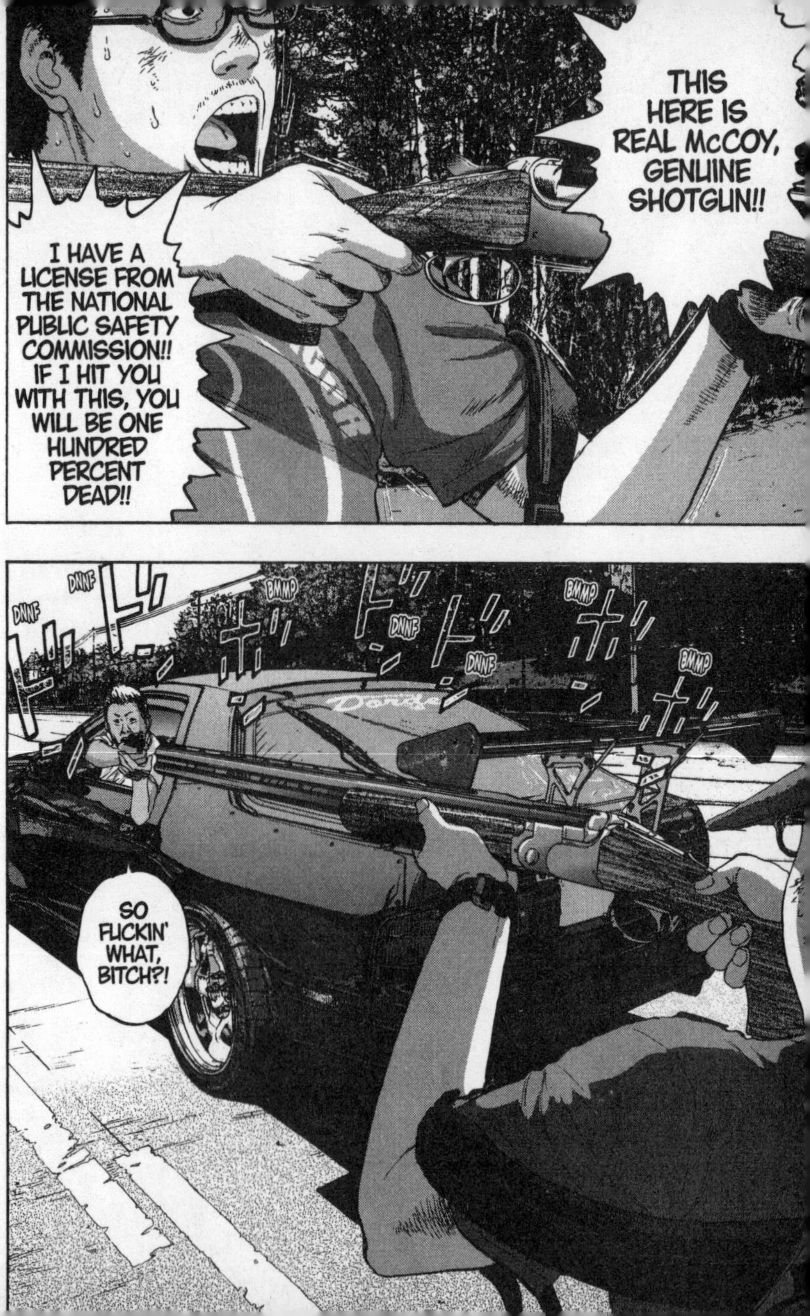
THIS HERE IS REAL McCOY, GENUINE SHOTGUN!!
I HAVE A LICENSE FROM THE NATIONAL PUBLIC SAFETY COMMISSION!! IF I HIT YOU WITH THIS, YOU WILL BE ONE HUNDRED PERCENT DEAD!!
BMMP
BMMP
DNNF
DNNF
BMMP
DNNF
DNNF
SO FUCKIN' WHAT, BITCH?!

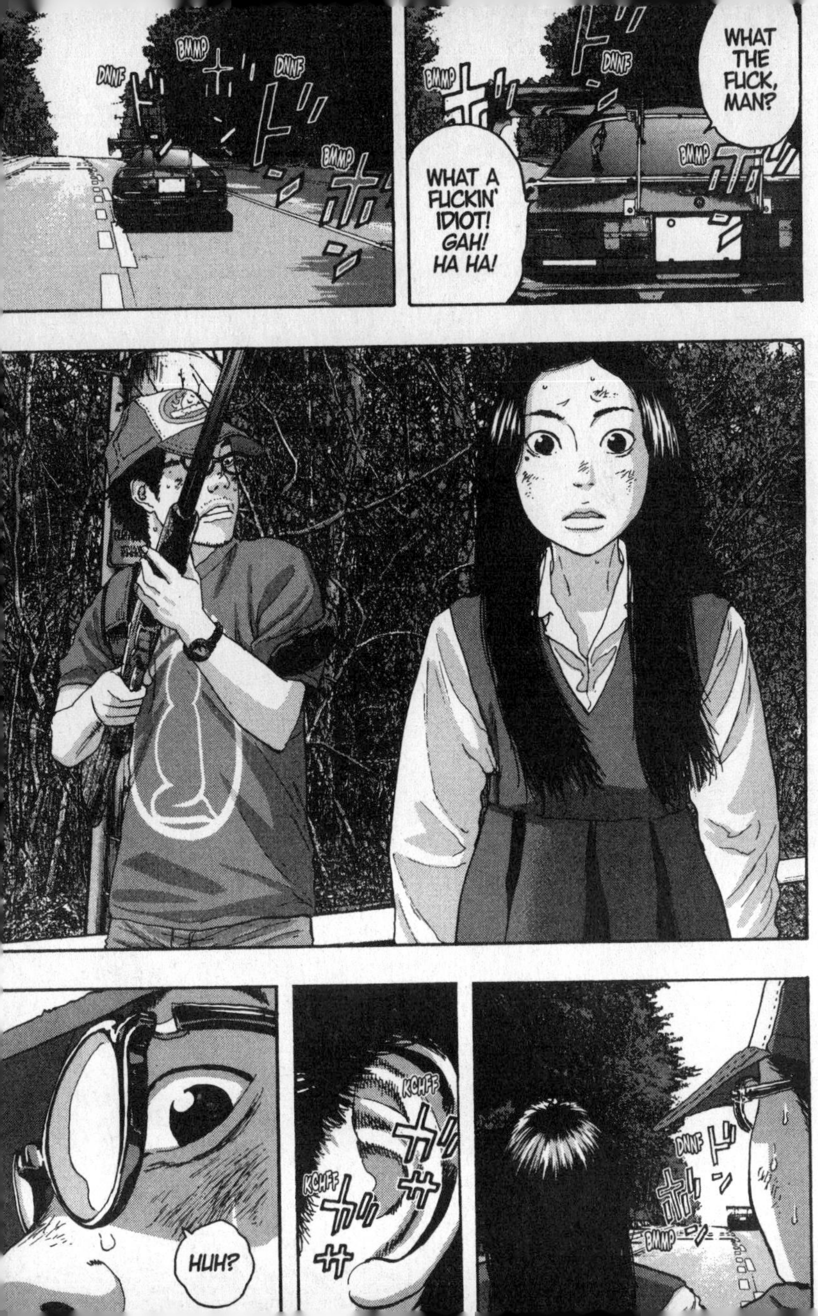
WHAT THE FUCK, MAN?
DNNF
BMMP
WHAT A FUCKIN' IDIOT! GAH! HA HA!
BMMP
DNNF
BMMP
DNNF
BMMP
DNNF
BMMP
KCHFF
KCHFF
HUH?

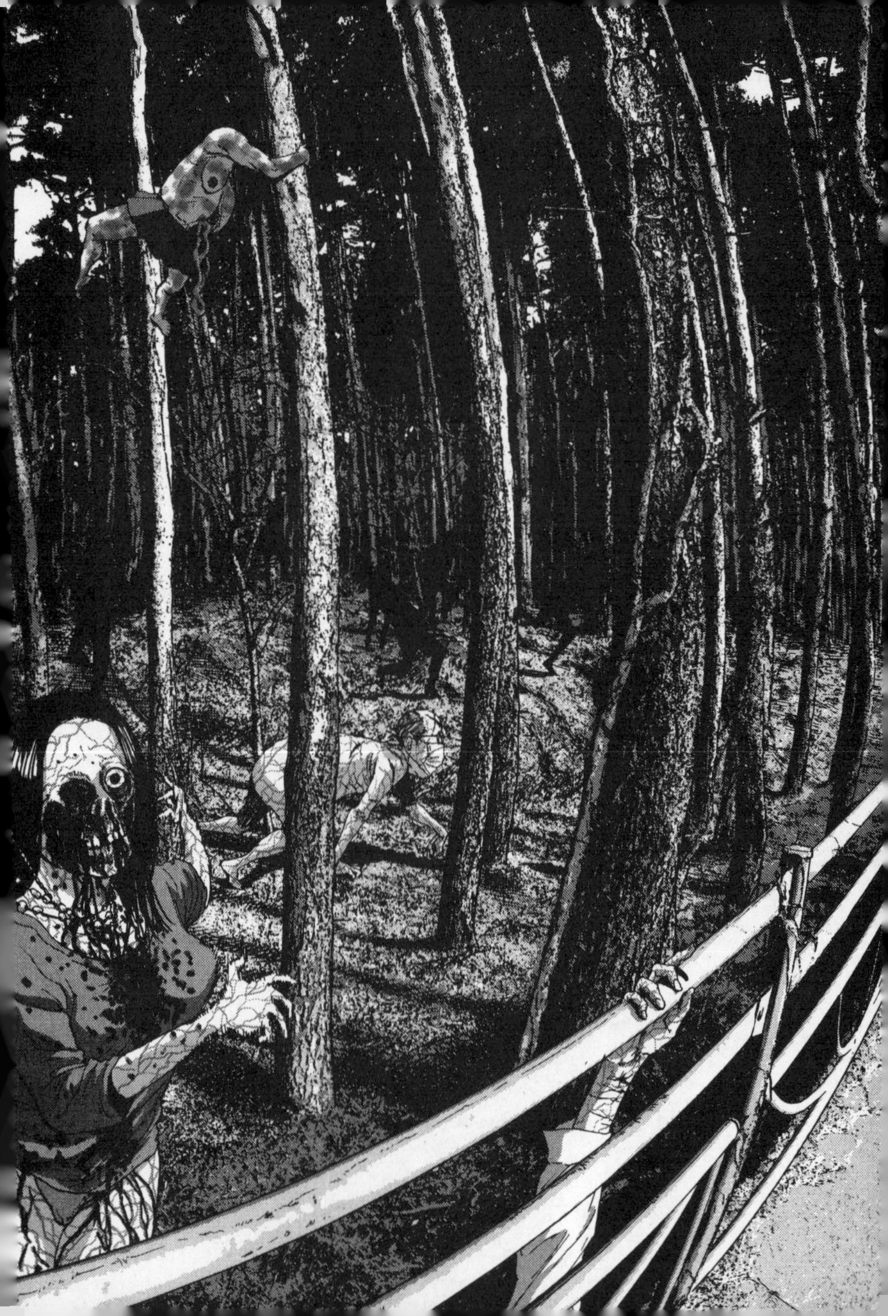

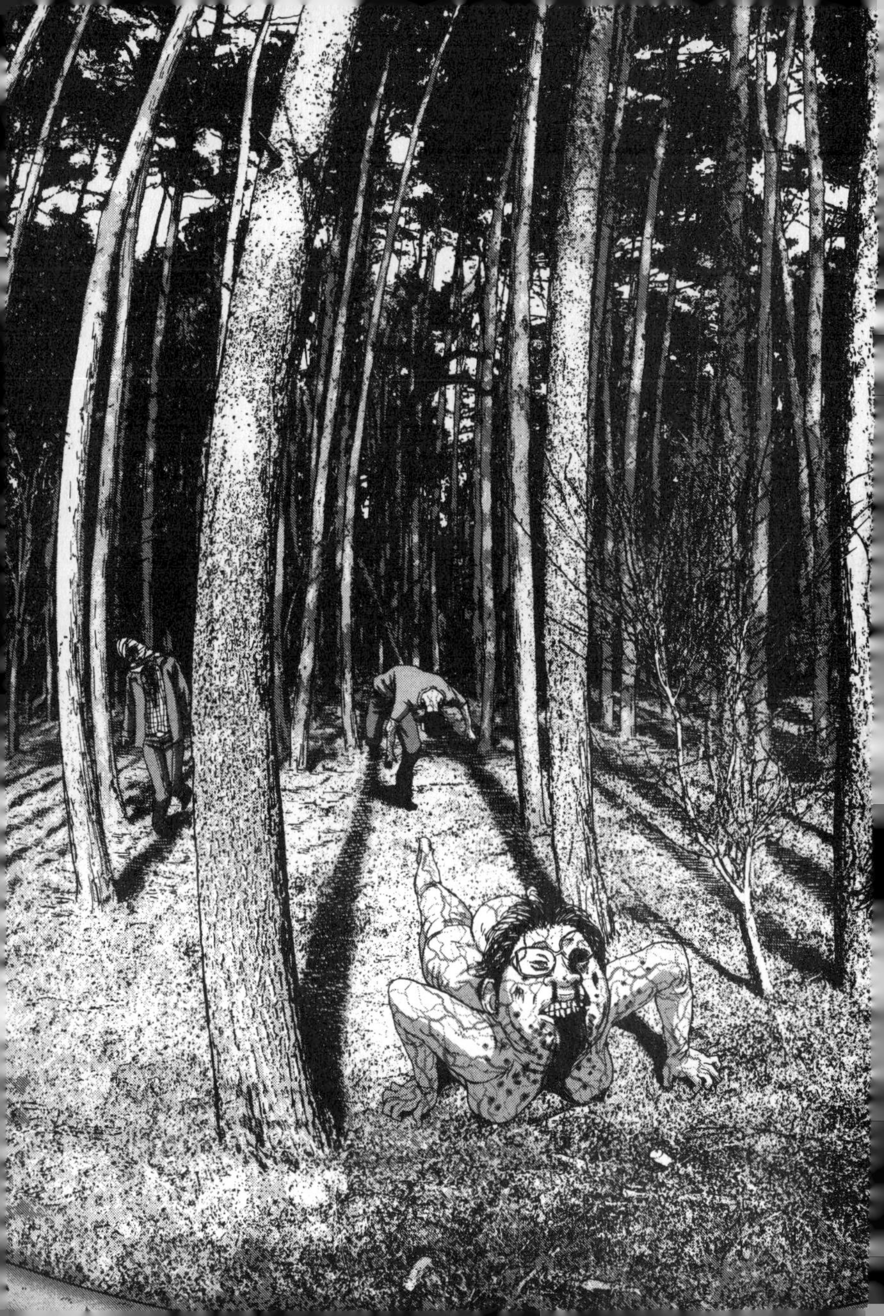

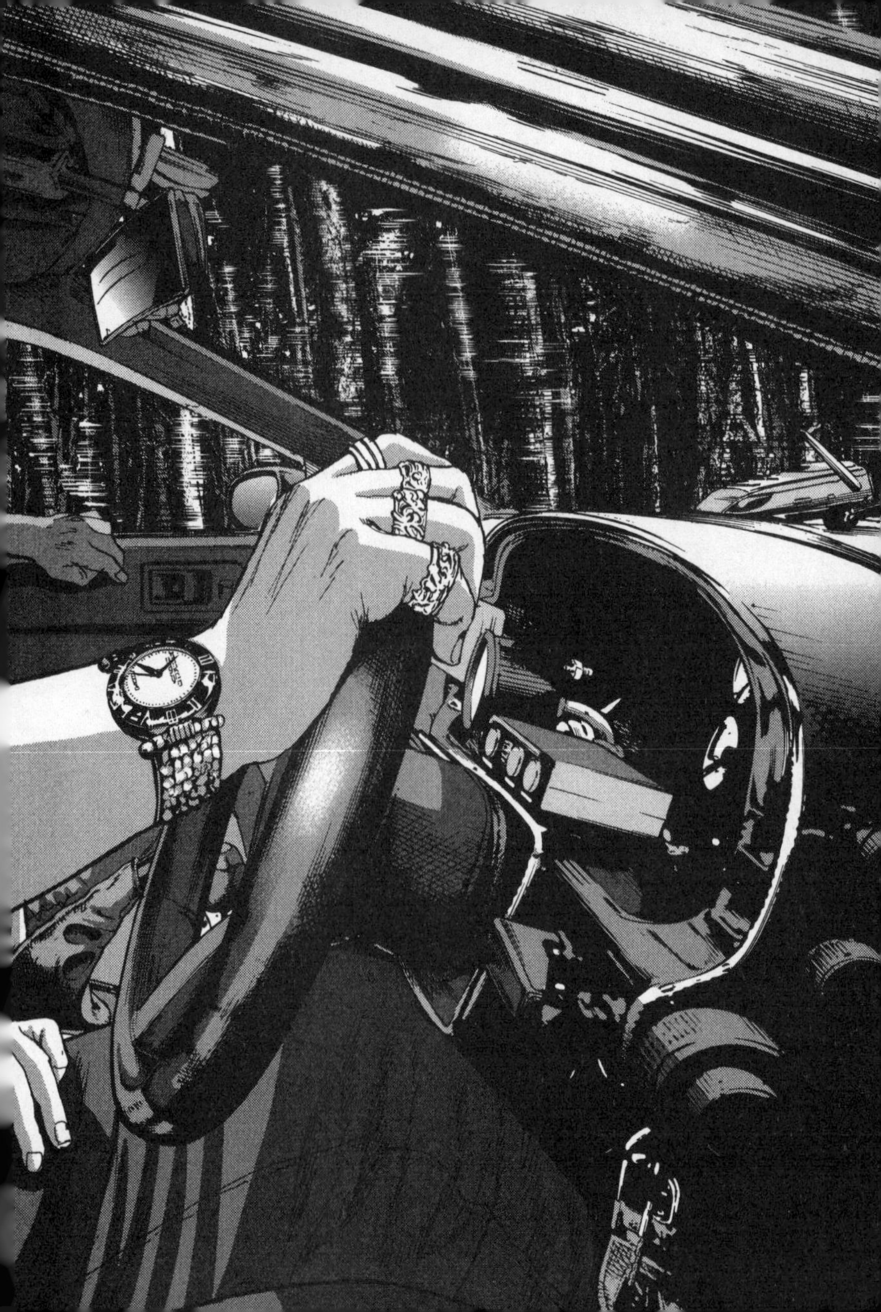

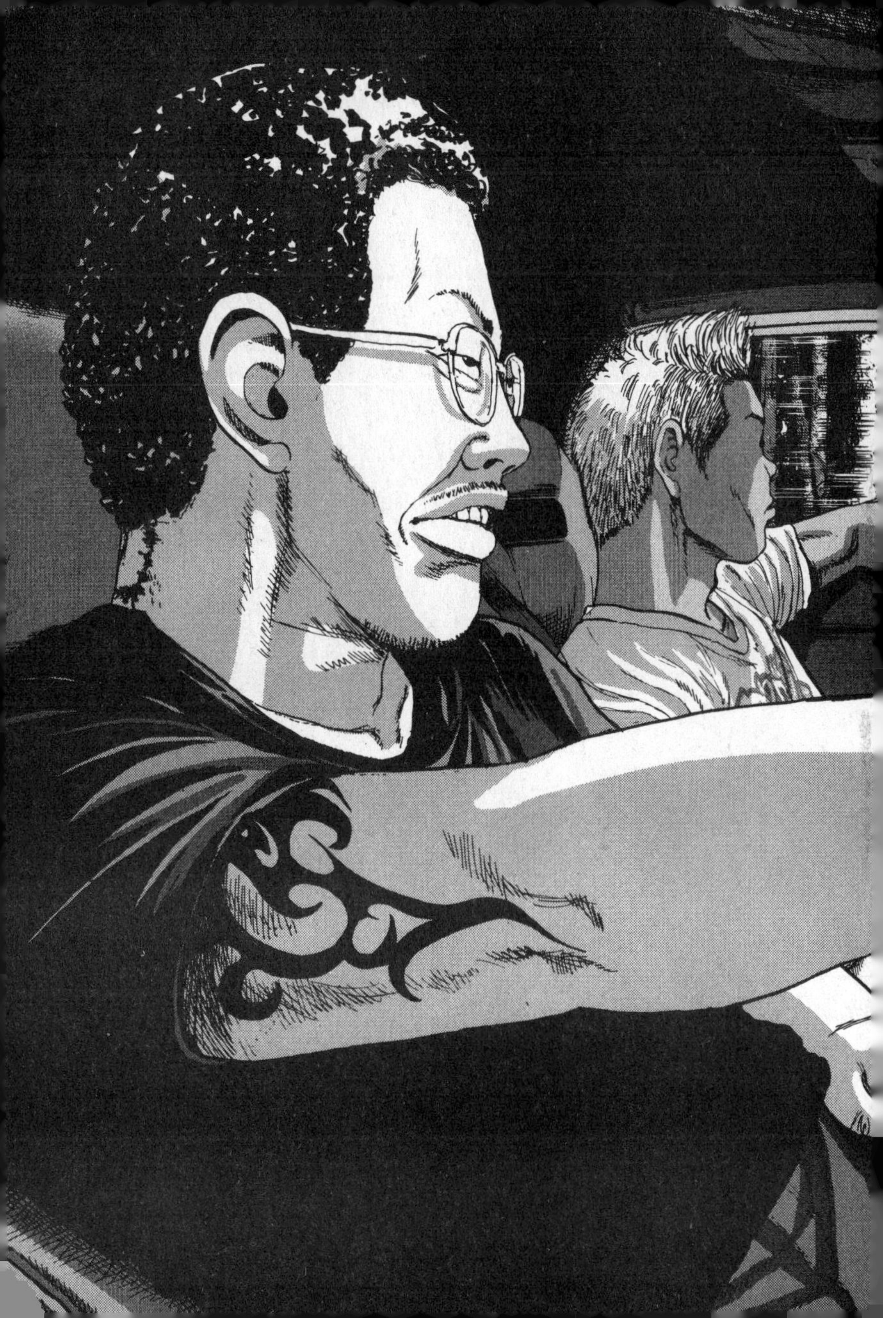

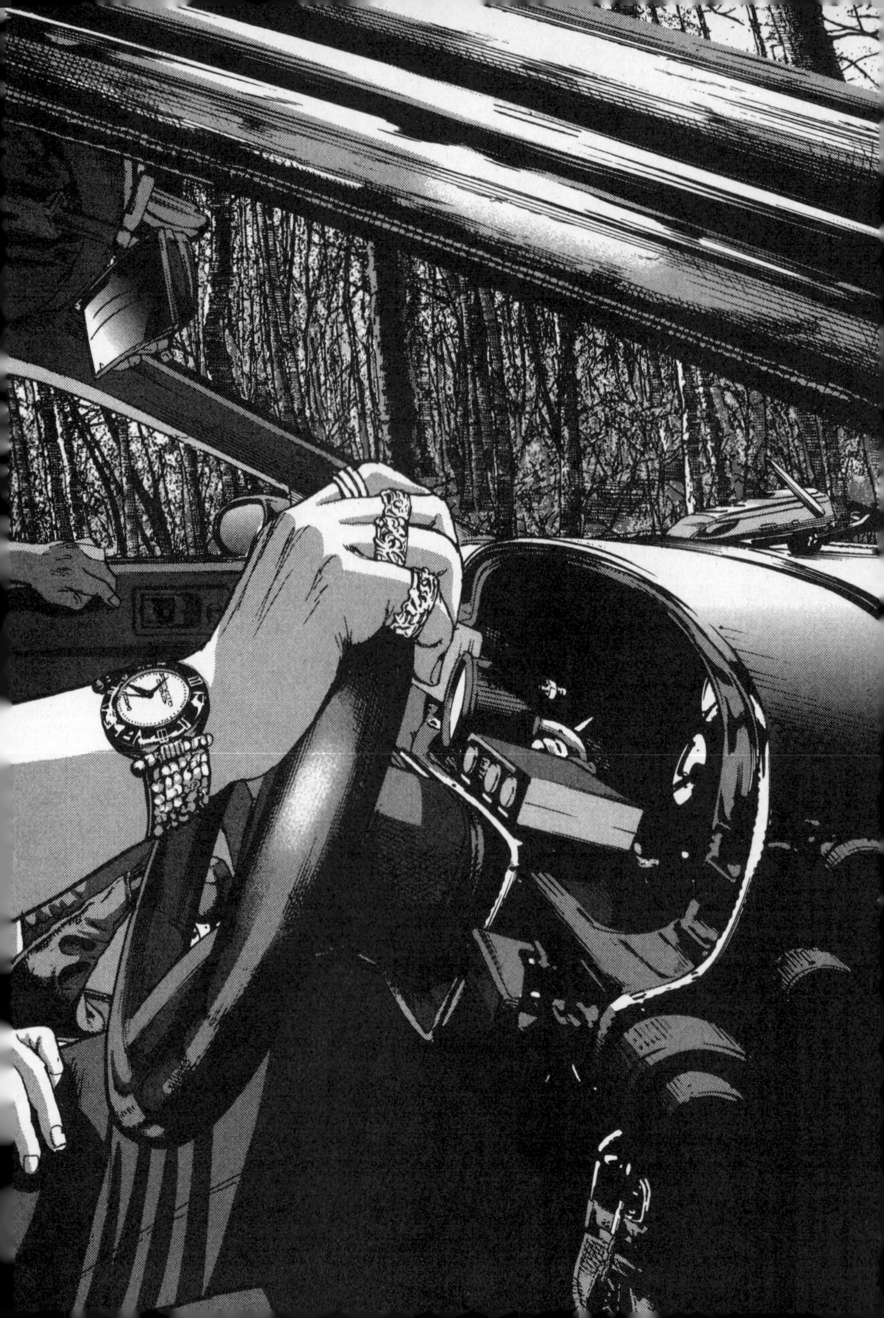

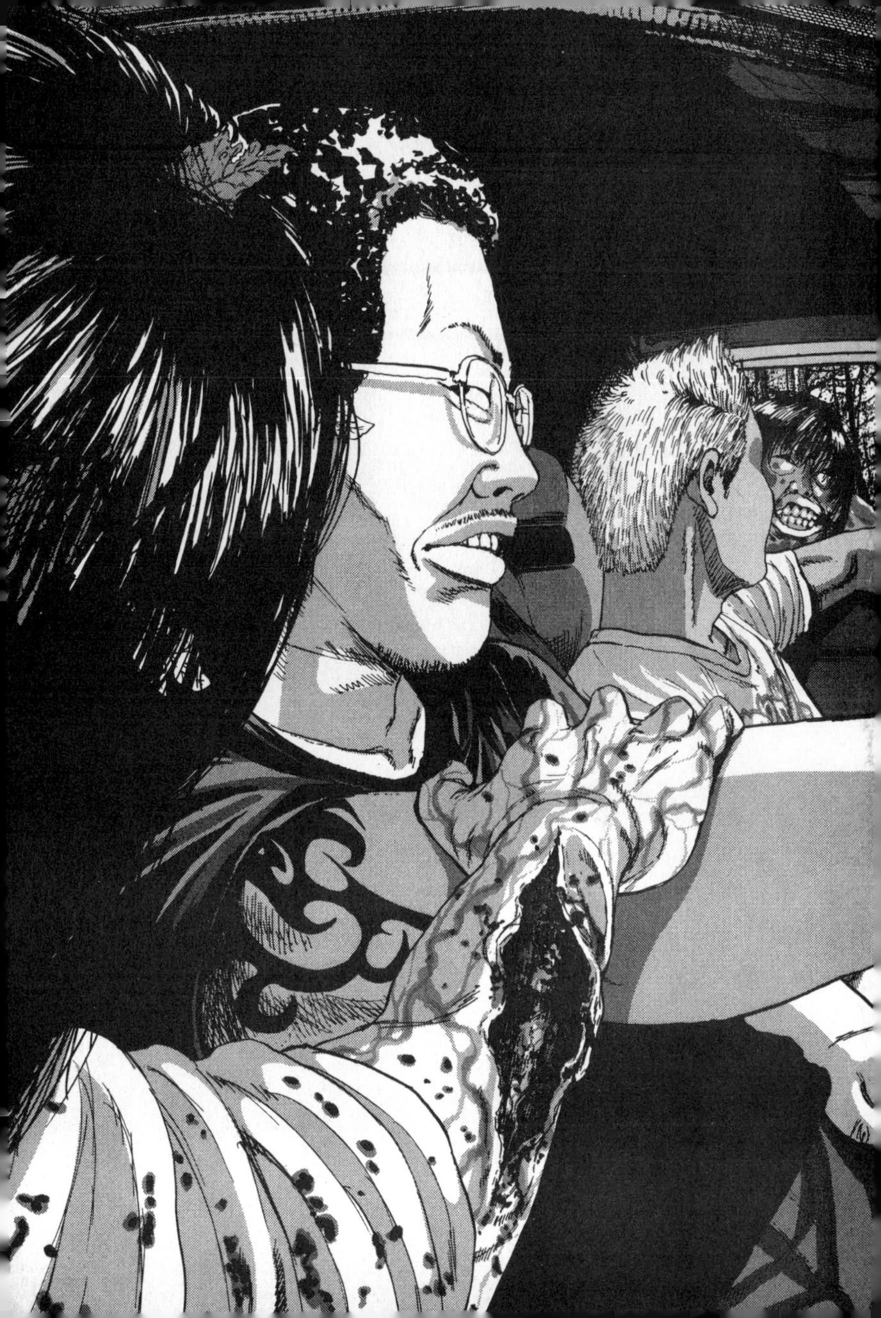

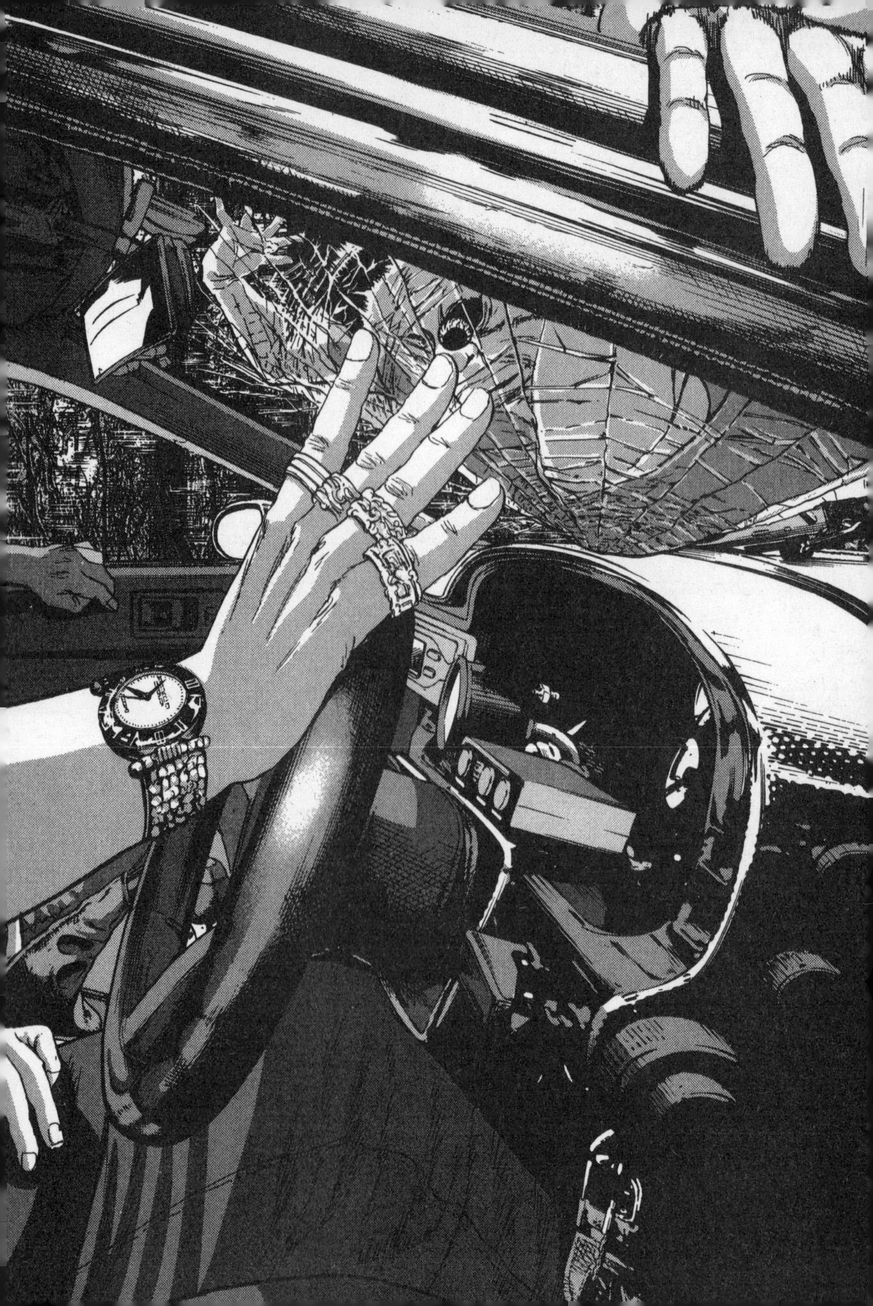

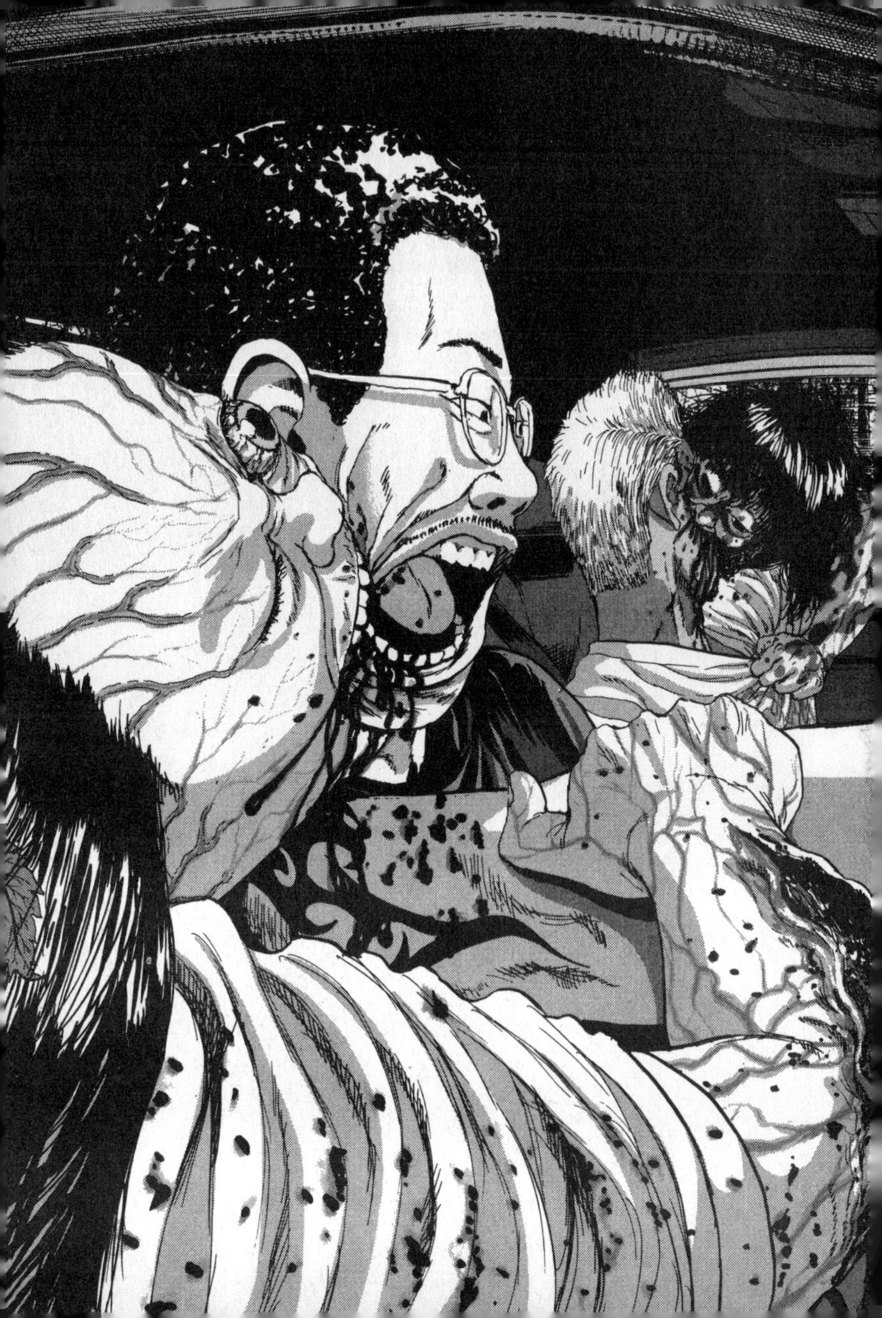

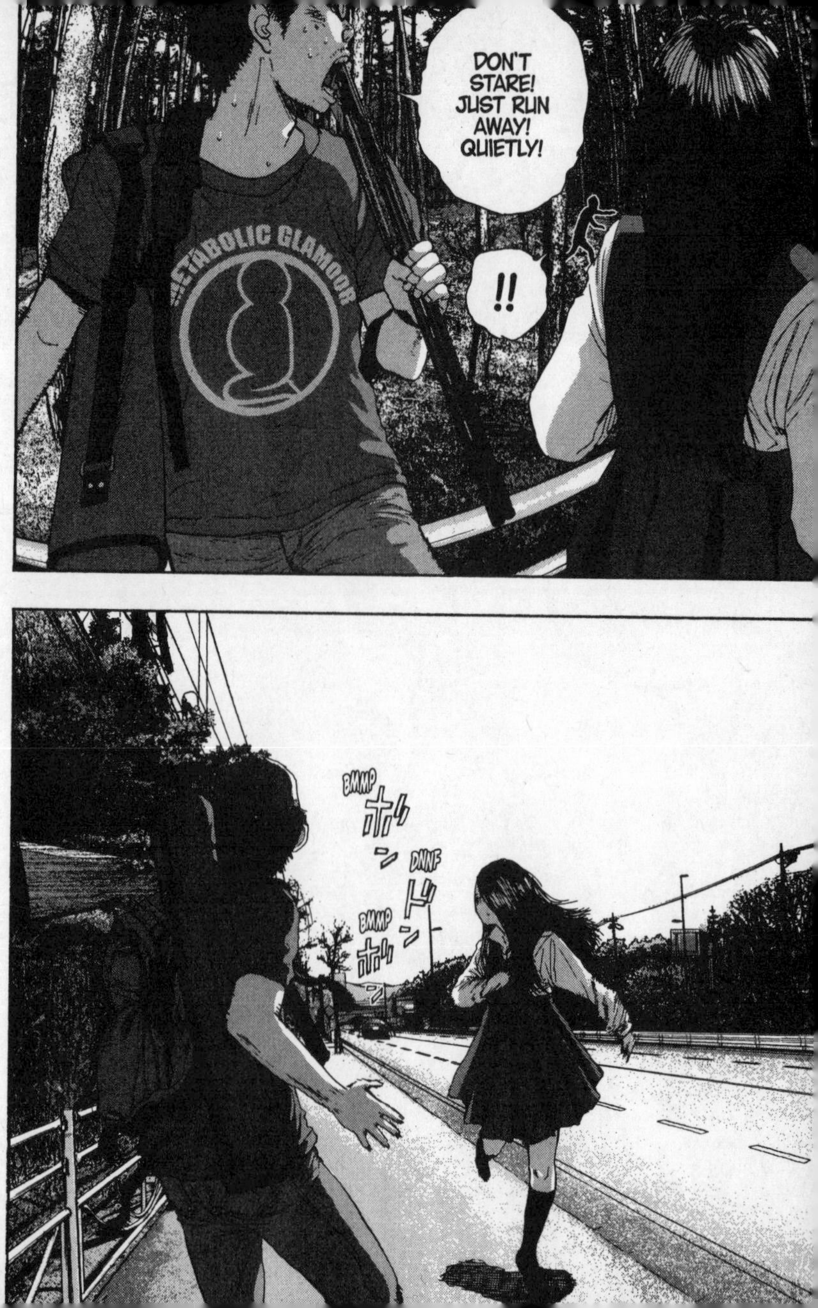
DON'T STARE! JUST RUN AWAY! QUIETLY!
!!
METABOLIC GLAMOUR
BMMP
ボン
DNNF
ドン
BMMP
ボン

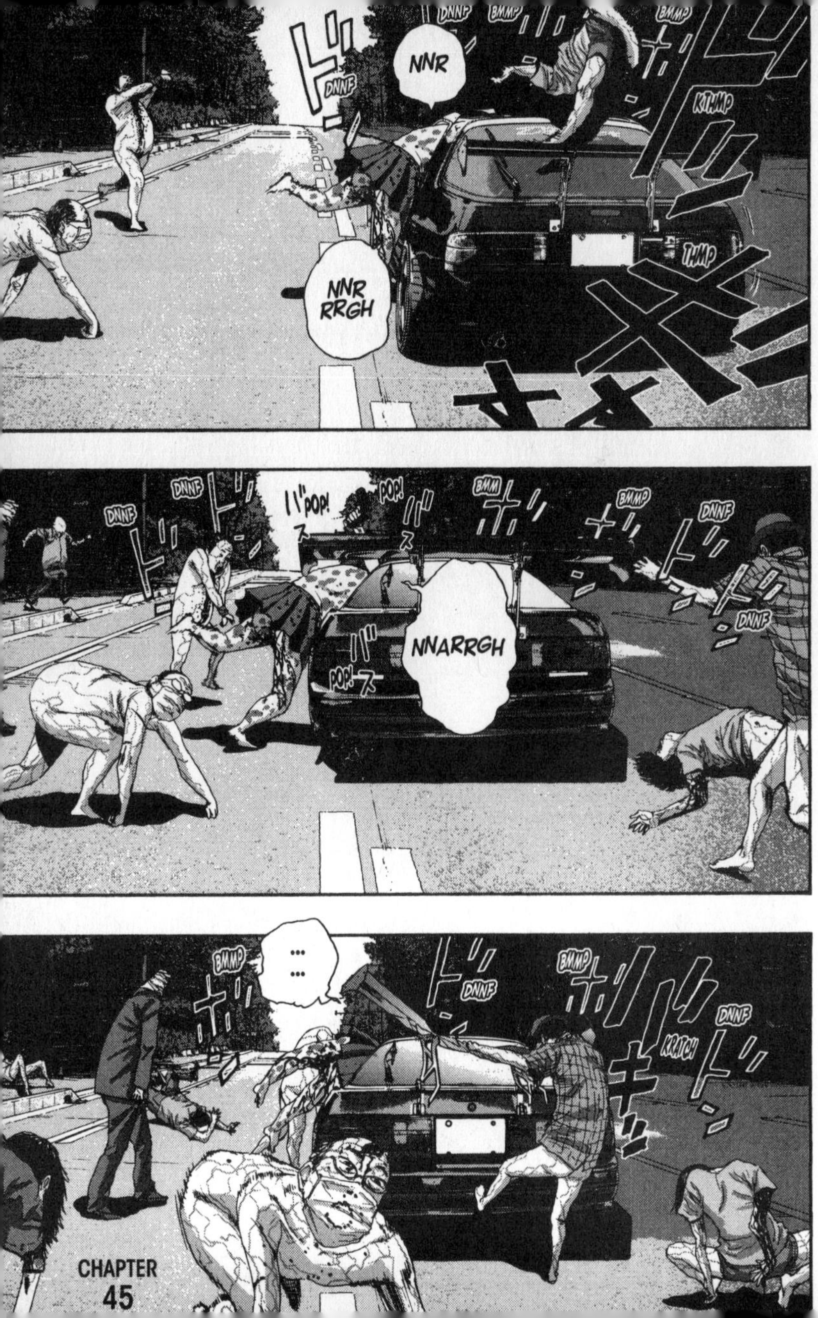
BMMP
BMMP
DNNP
NNR
DNNF
KTHMP
THMP
NNR RRGH
DNNF
DNNF
BMMP
BMMP
POP!
POP!
DNNF
DNNF
NNARRGH
POP!
DNNF
BMMP
DNNF
KRATCH
...
...
BMMP
CHAPTER 45

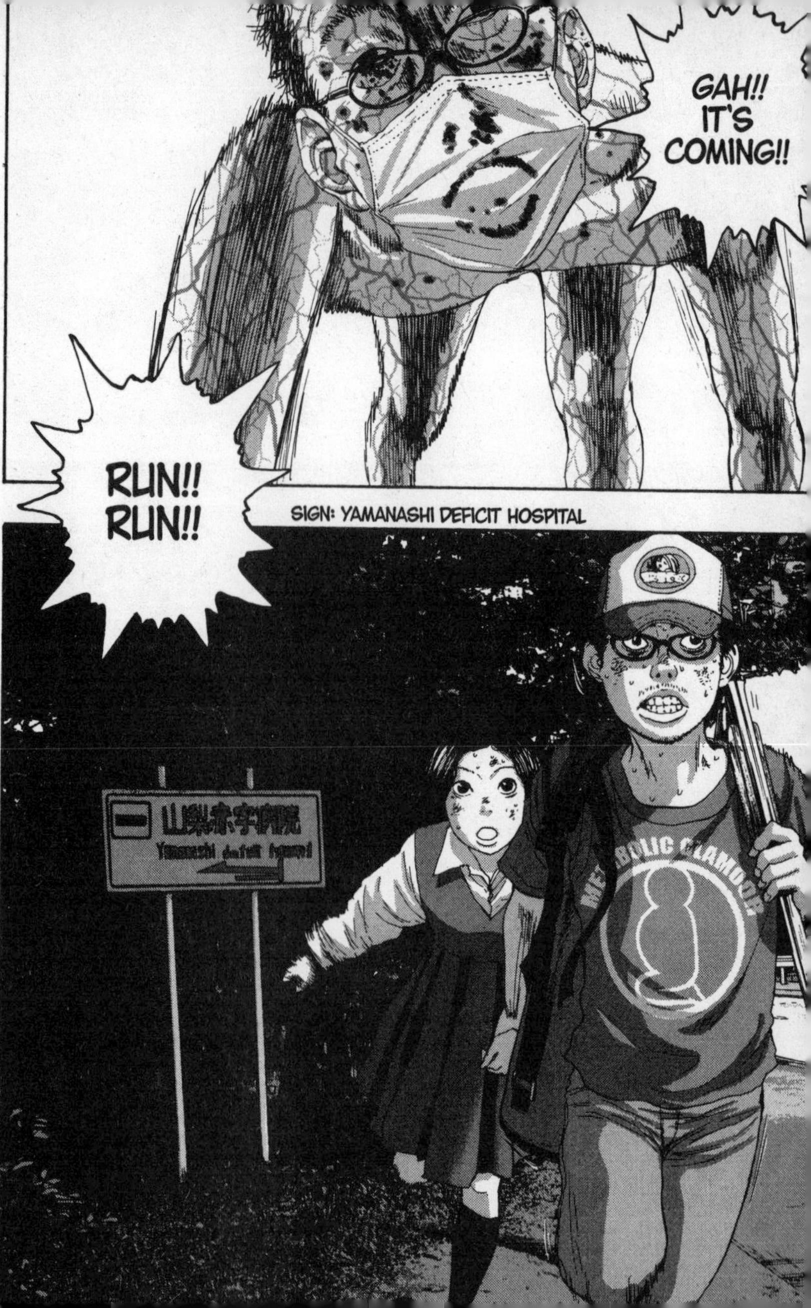
GAH!! IT'S COMING!!
RUN!! RUN!!
SIGN: YAMANASHI DEFICIT HOSPITAL
山梨赤字病院

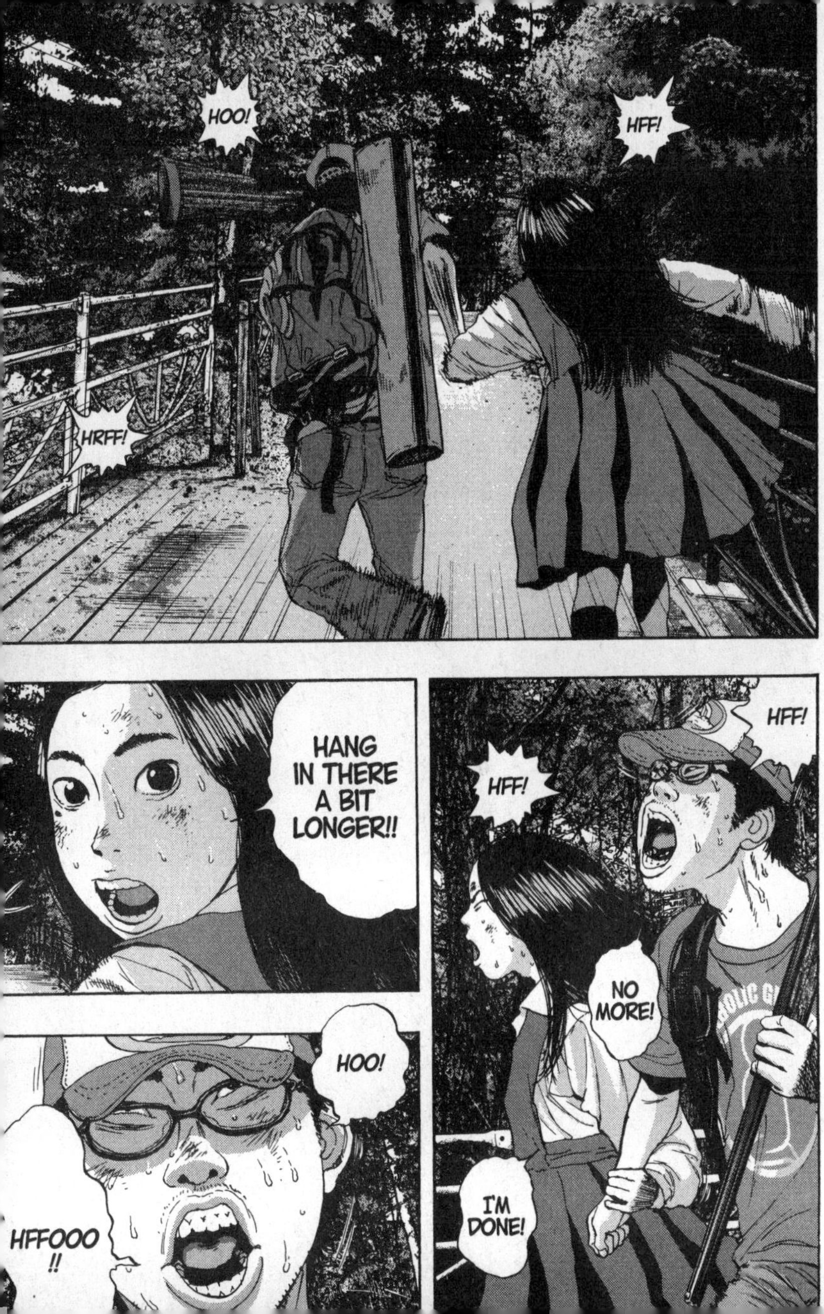
HFF!
HOO!
HRFF!
HFF!
HFF!
NO MORE!
I'M DONE!
HANG IN THERE A BIT LONGER!!
HOO!
HFFOOO !!

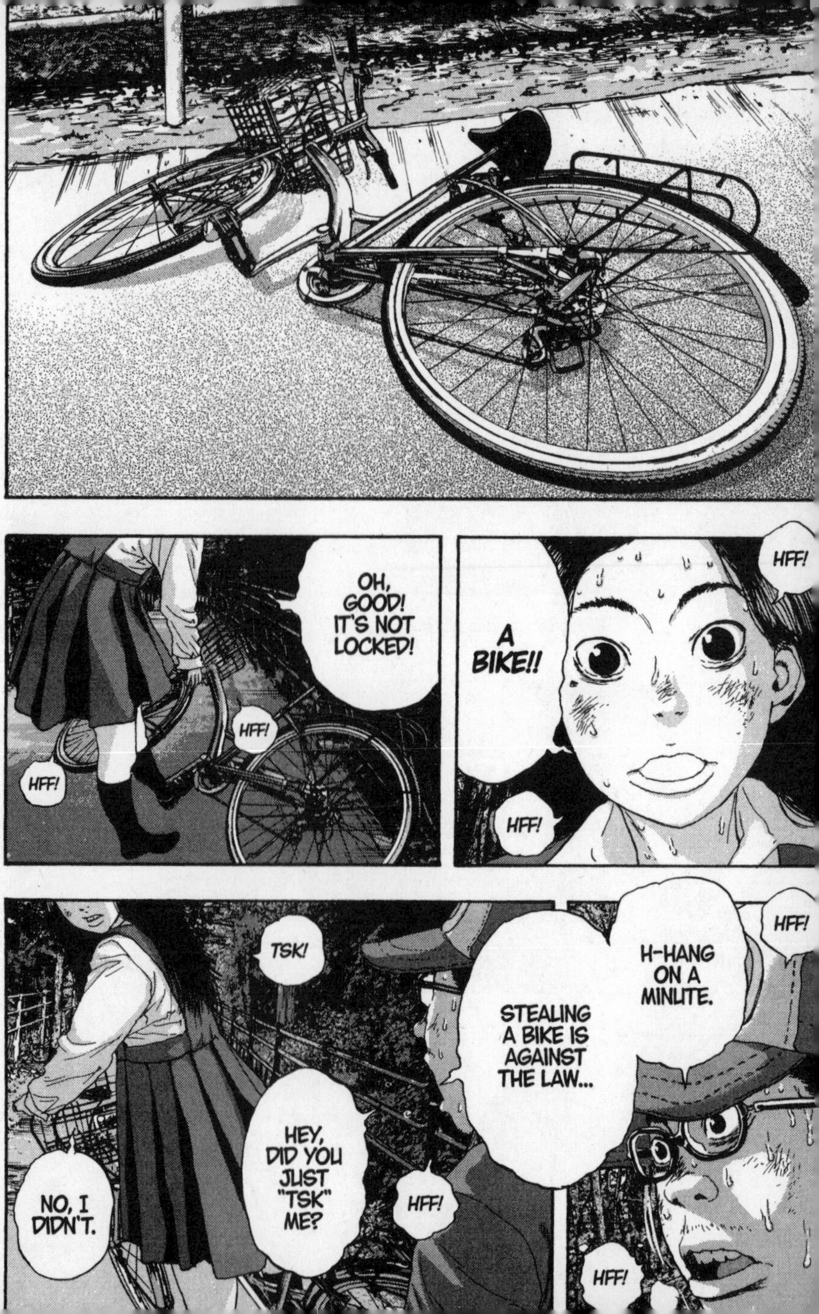
HFF!
A BIKE!!
HFF!
OH, GOOD! IT'S NOT LOCKED!
HFF!
HFF!
HFF!
H-HANG ON A MINUTE.
STEALING A BIKE IS AGAINST THE LAW...
HFF!
TSK!
HEY, DID YOU JUST "TSK" ME?
HFF!
NO, I DIDN'T.

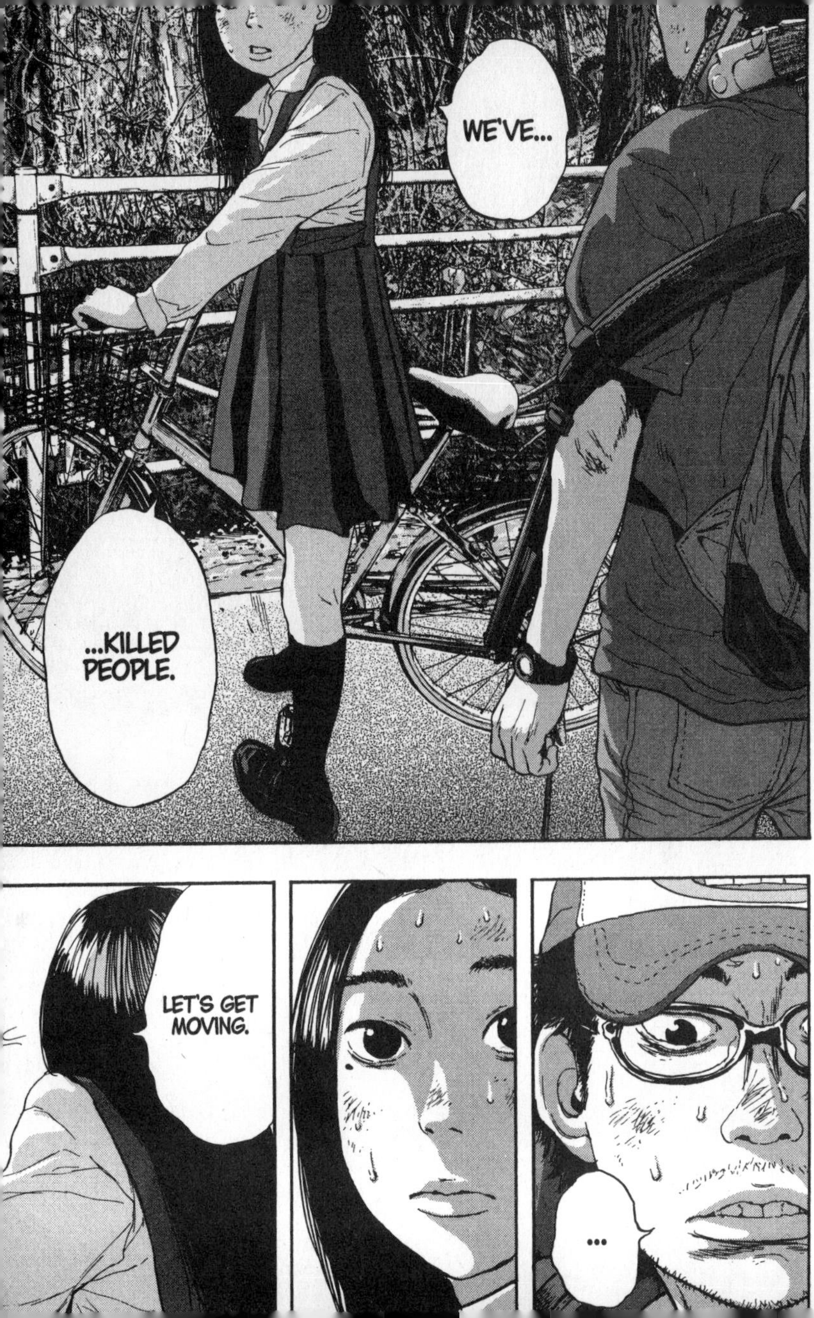
WE'VE...
...KILLED PEOPLE.
...
LET'S GET MOVING.

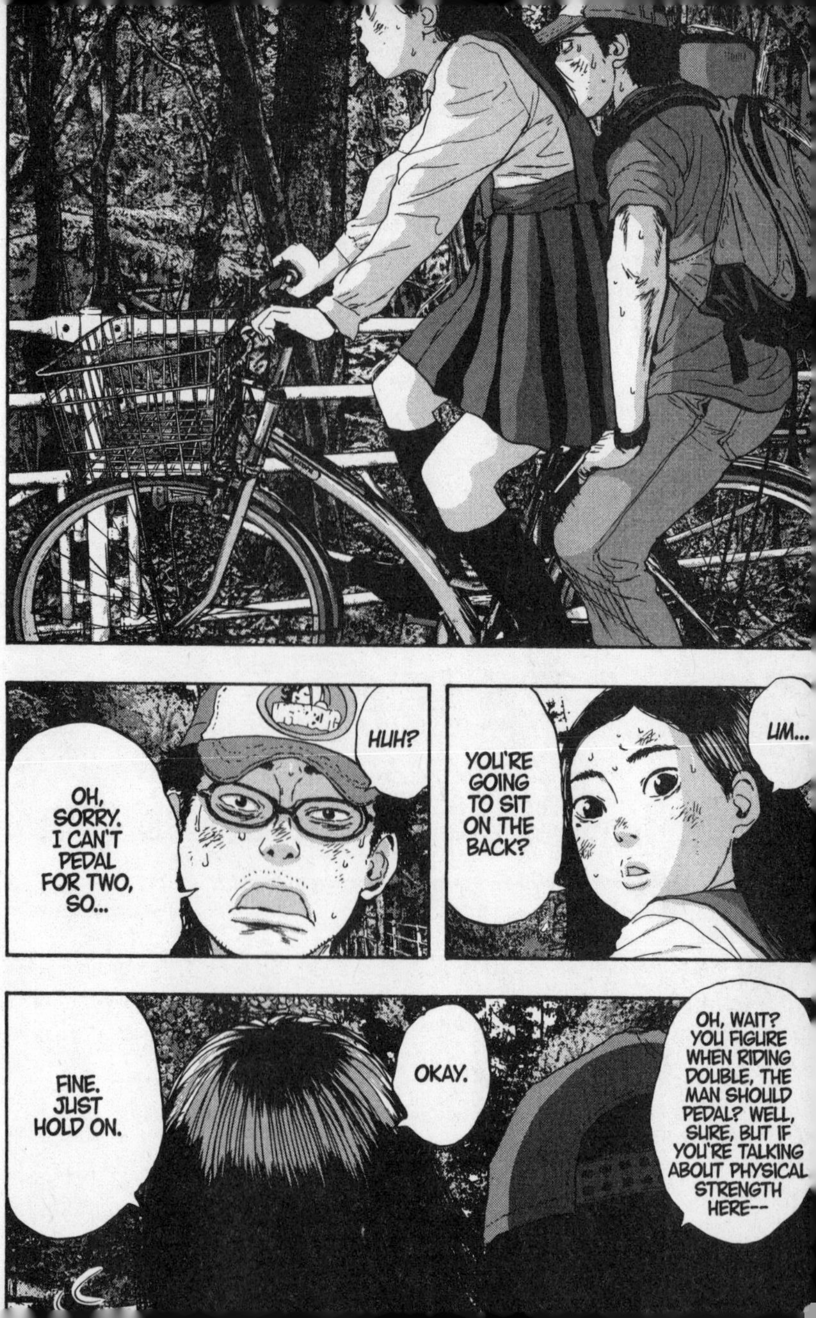
UM...
YOU'RE GOING TO SIT ON THE BACK?
HUH?
OH, SORRY. I CAN'T PEDAL FOR TWO, SO...
OH, WAIT? YOU FIGURE WHEN RIDING DOUBLE, THE MAN SHOULD PEDAL? WELL, SURE, BUT IF YOU'RE TALKING ABOUT PHYSICAL STRENGTH HERE--
OKAY.
FINE. JUST HOLD ON.

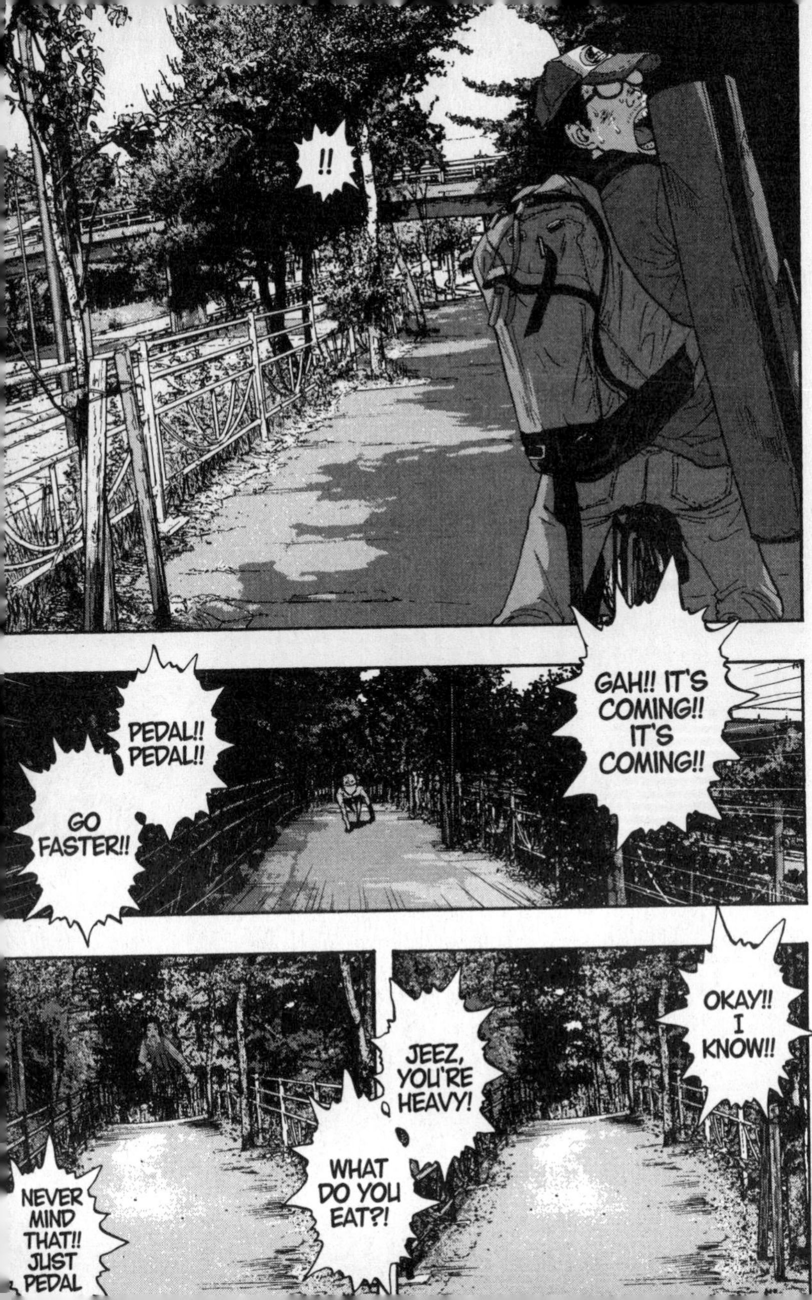
!!
GAH!! IT'S COMING!! IT'S COMING!!
PEDAL!! PEDAL!!
GO FASTER!!
OKAY!! I KNOW!!
JEEZ, YOU'RE HEAVY!
WHAT DO YOU EAT?!
NEVER MIND THAT!! JUST PEDAL

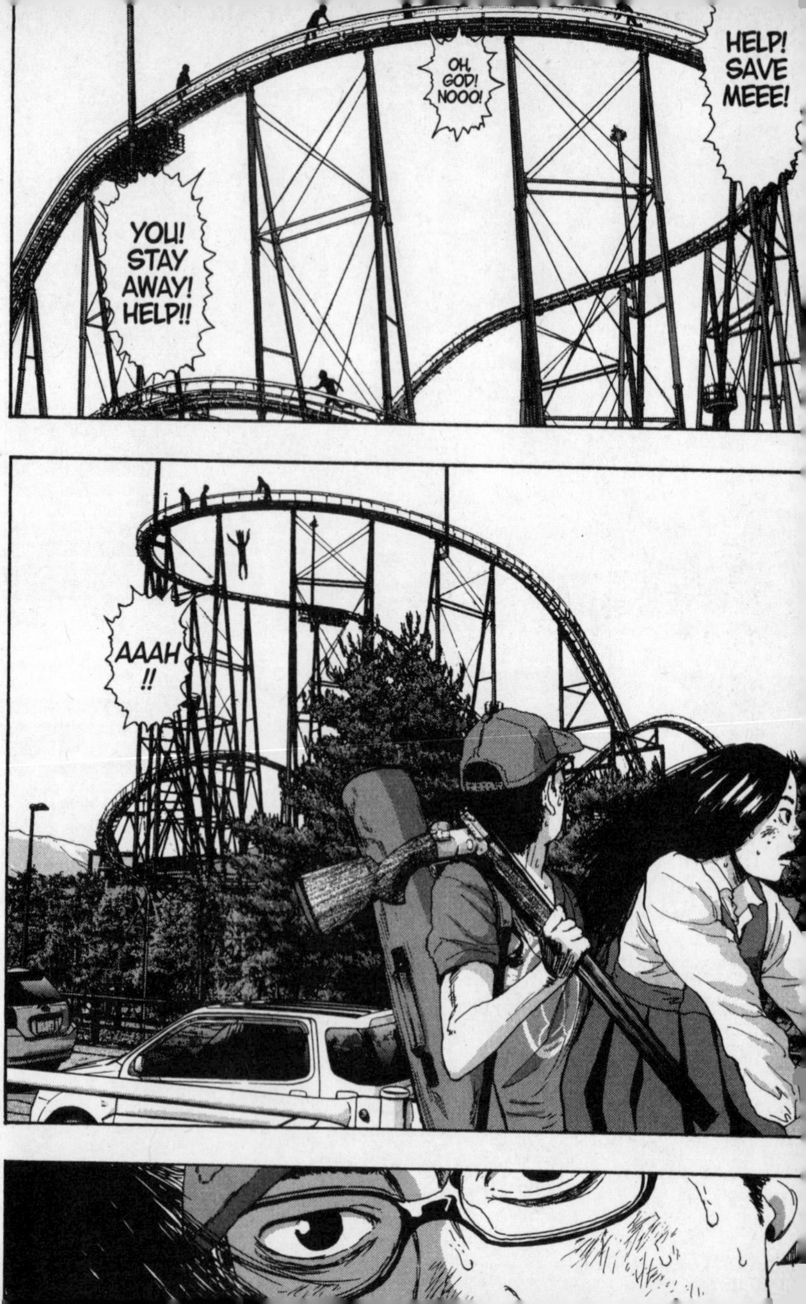
HELP! SAVE MEEE!
OH, GOD! NOOO!
YOU! STAY AWAY! HELP!!
AAAH !!

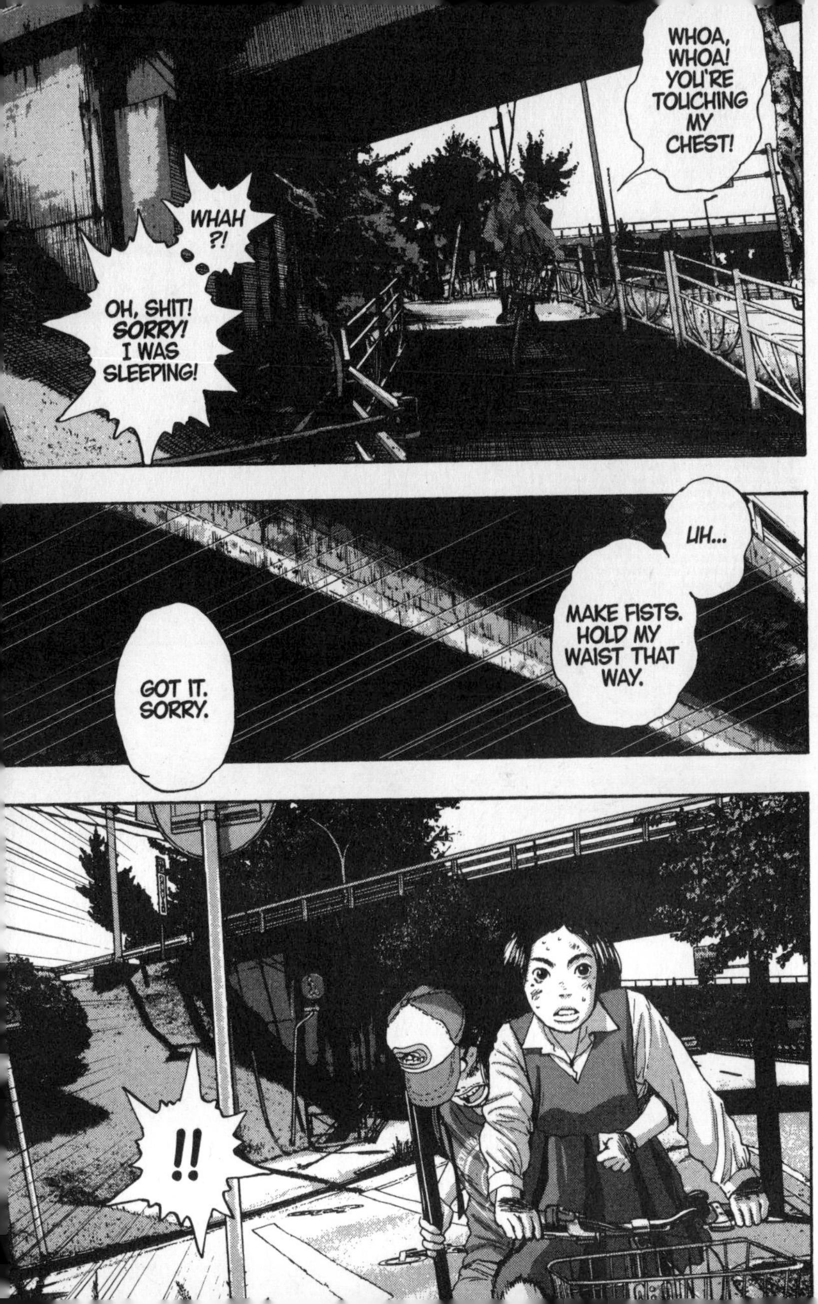
WHOA, WHOA! YOU'RE TOUCHING MY CHEST!
WHAH ?!
OH, SHIT! SORRY! I WAS SLEEPING!
UH...
MAKE FISTS. HOLD MY WAIST THAT WAY.
GOT IT. SORRY.
!!

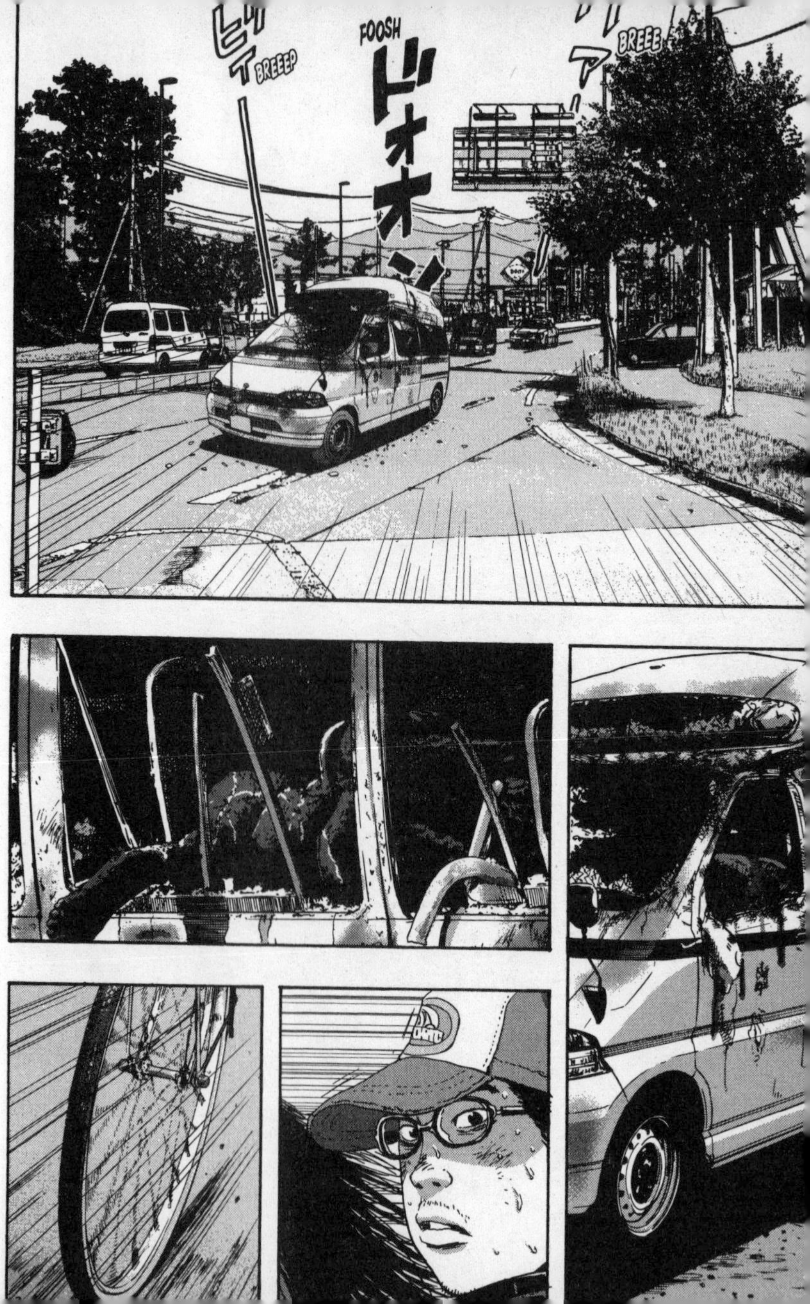
BREEE
FOOSH
ドォオーン
BREEEP

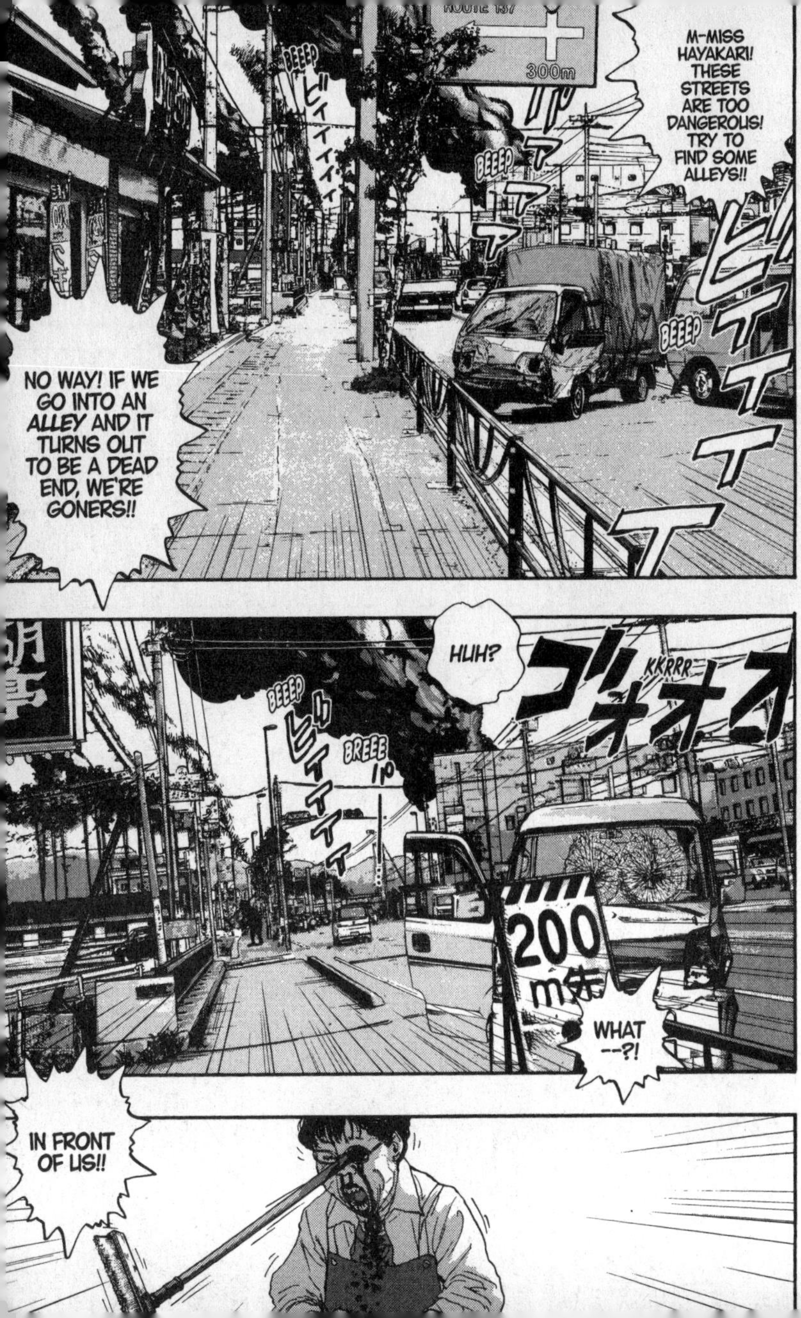
ROUTE 137
300m
M-MISS HAYAKARI! THESE STREETS ARE TOO DANGEROUS! TRY TO FIND SOME ALLEYS!!
BEEEP
BEEEP
BEEEP
NO WAY! IF WE GO INTO AN ALLEY AND IT TURNS OUT TO BE A DEAD END, WE'RE GONERS!!
KKRRR
HUH?
BREEE
BEEEP
200m
WHAT--?!
IN FRONT OF US!!

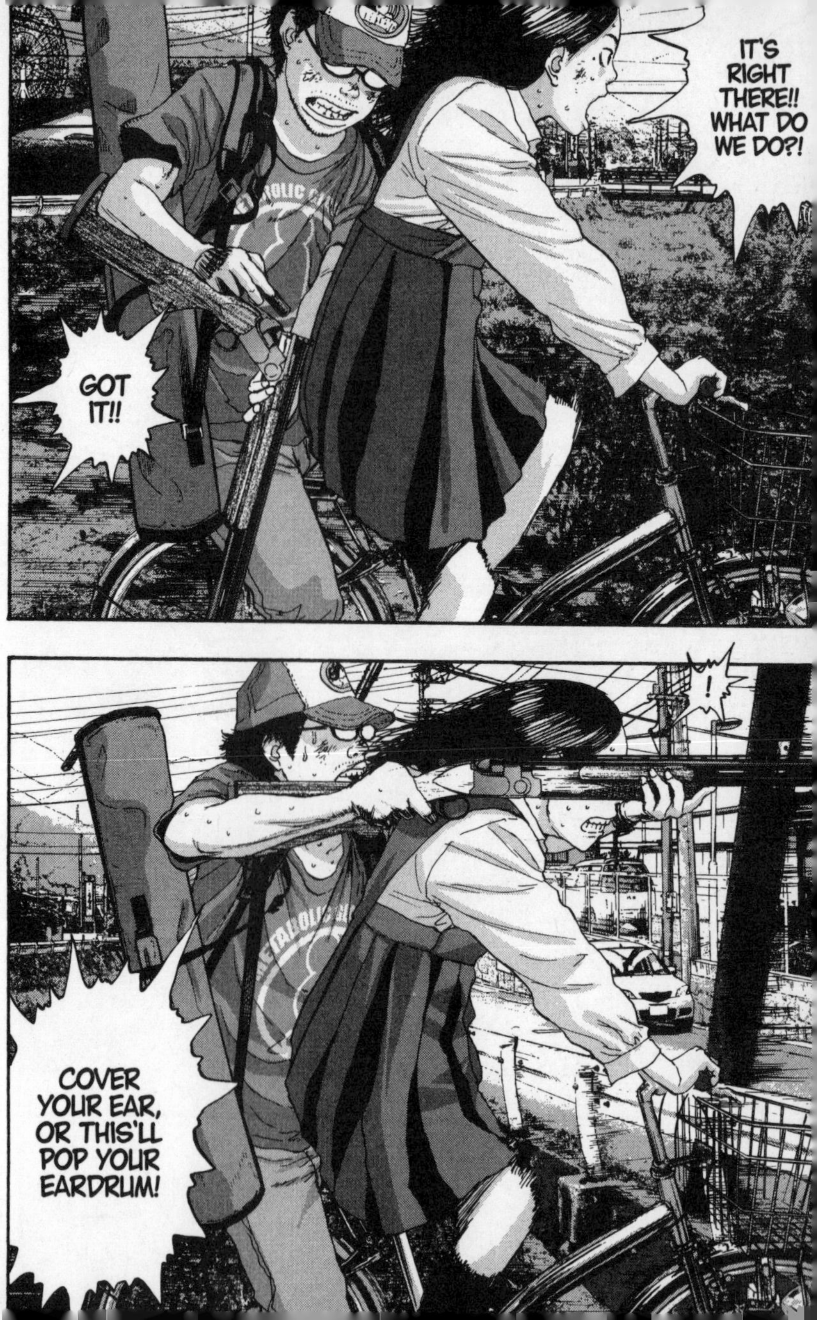
IT'S RIGHT THERE!! WHAT DO WE DO?!
GOT IT!!
!
COVER YOUR EAR, OR THIS'LL POP YOUR EARDRUM!

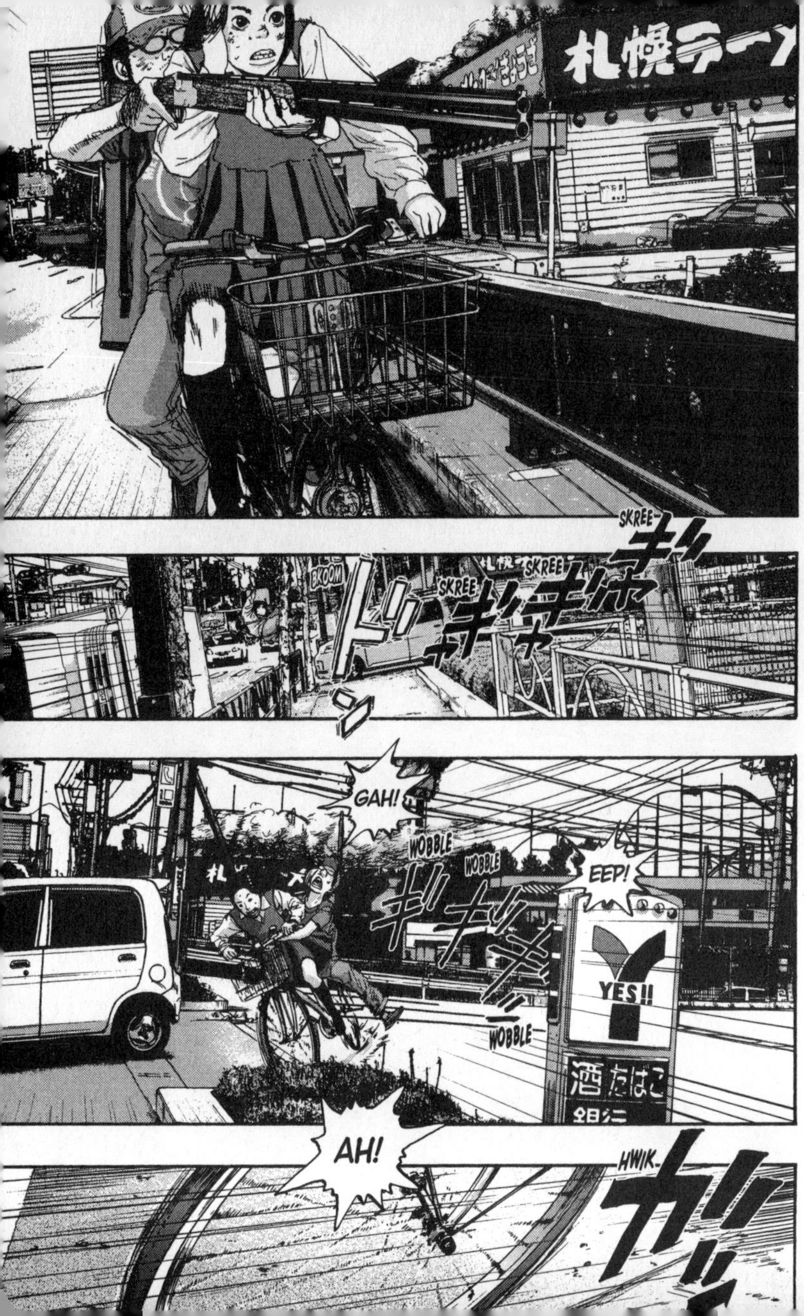
SKREE-
SKREE
SKREE
BROOM
EEP!
GAH!
WOBBLE
WOBBLE
YES!!
酒 たばこ
WOBBLE
HWIK-
AH!

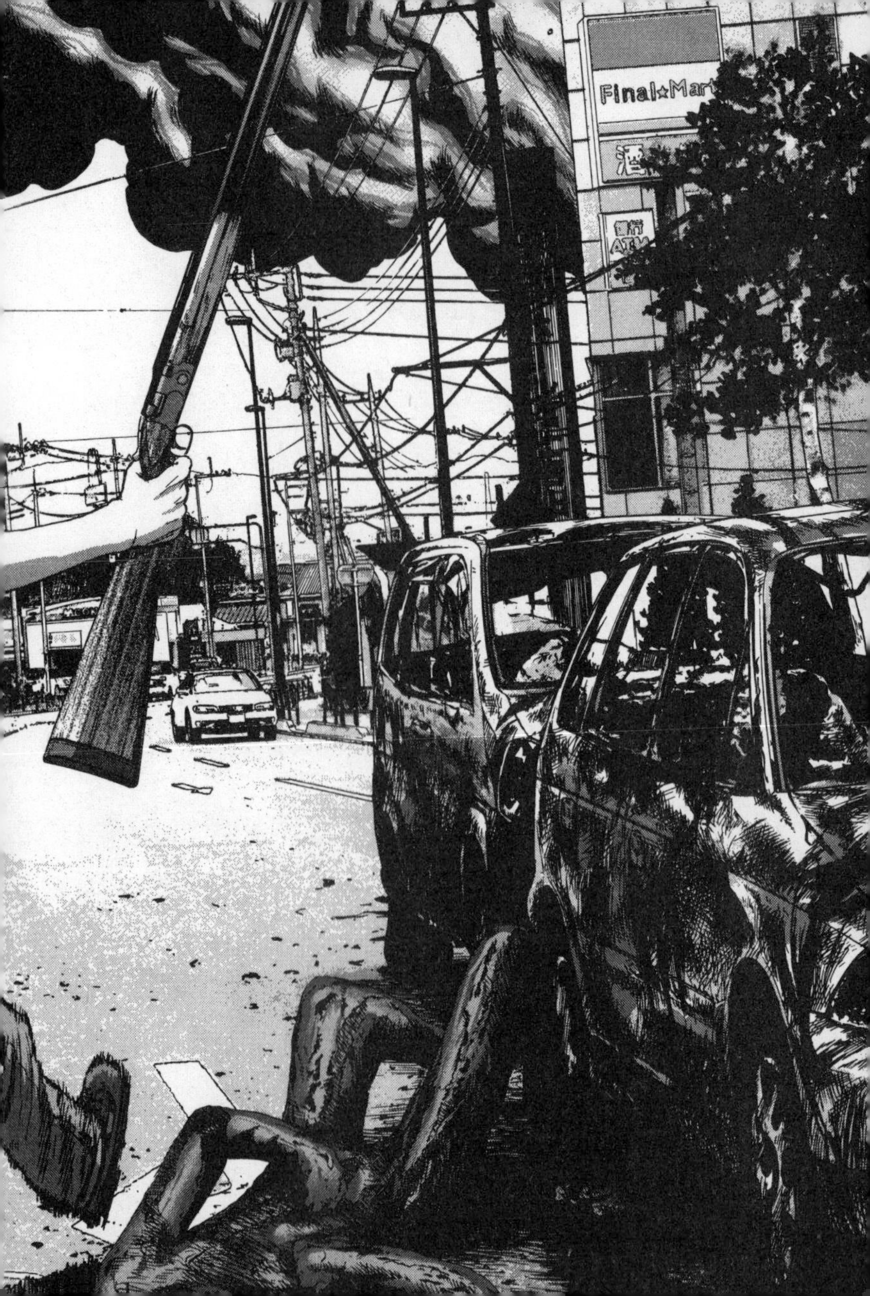
Final☆Mart
酒

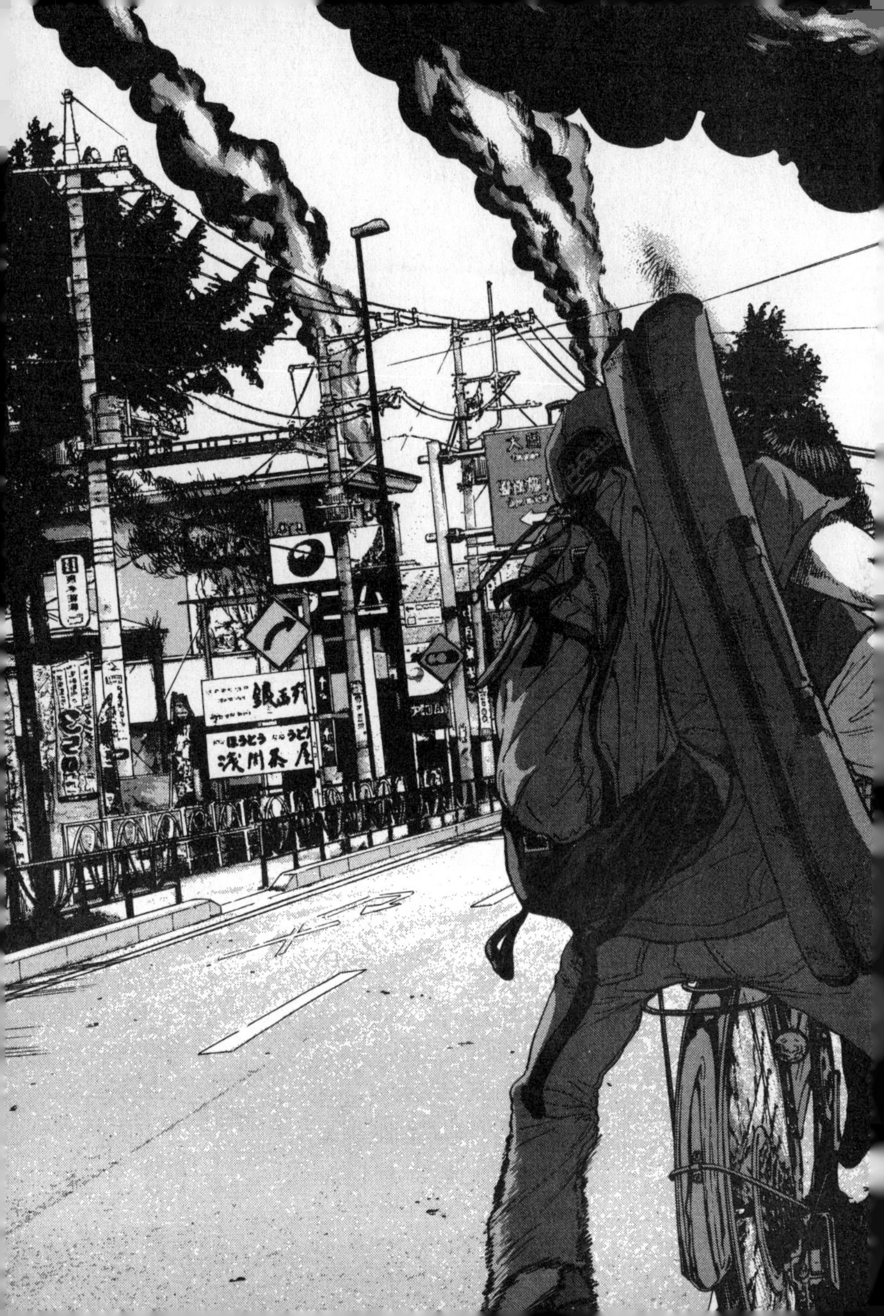
ほうとう
浅間茶屋

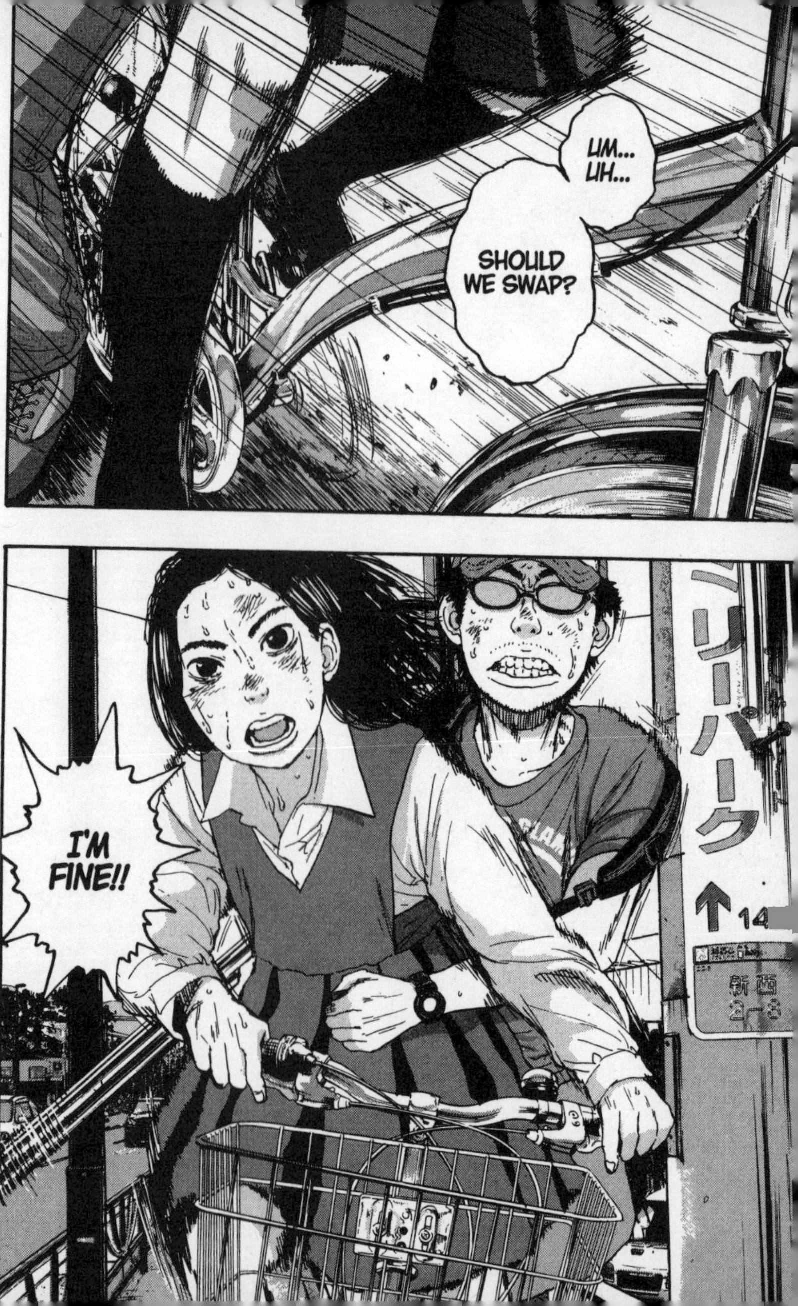
UM... UH...
SHOULD WE SWAP?
I'M FINE!!

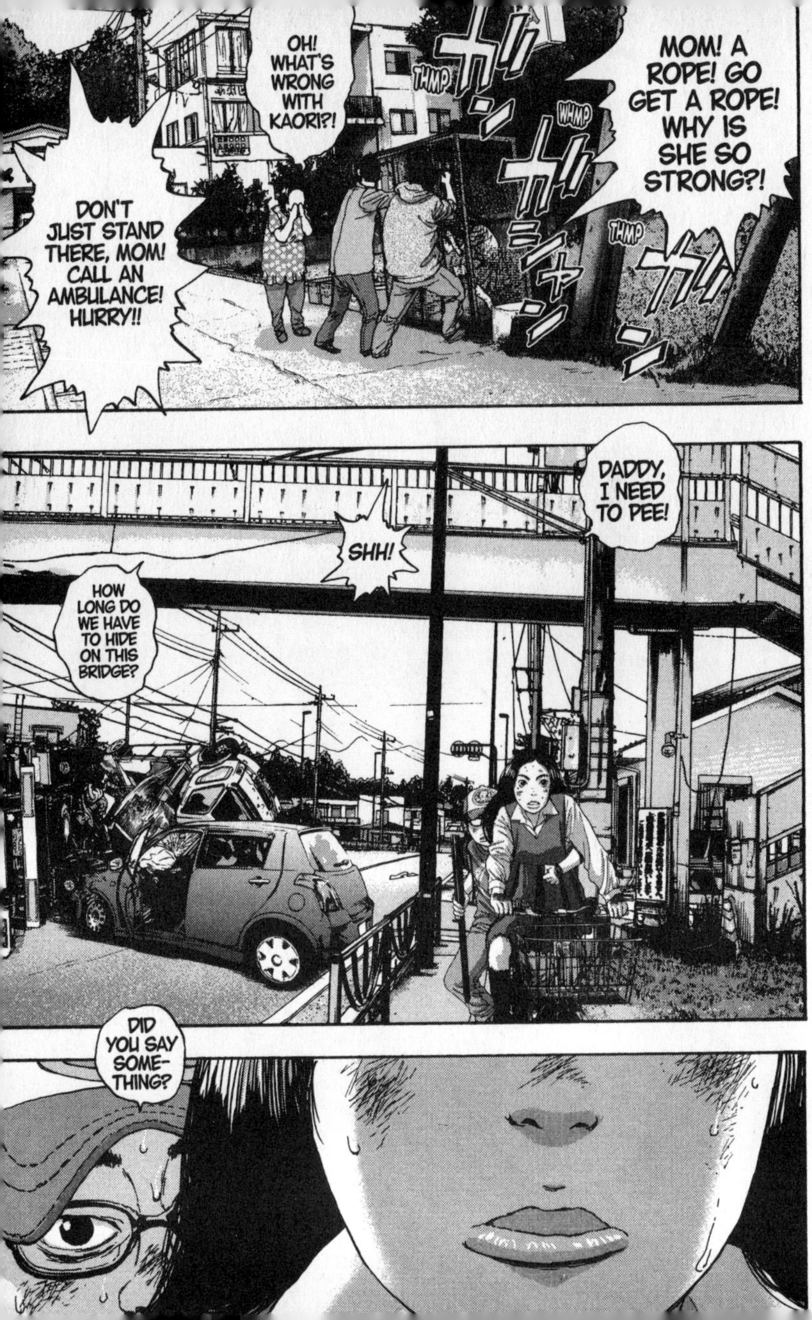
MOM! A ROPE! GO GET A ROPE! WHY IS SHE SO STRONG?!
THMP
WHMP
THMP
OH! WHAT'S WRONG WITH KAORI?!
DON'T JUST STAND THERE, MOM! CALL AN AMBULANCE! HURRY!!
DADDY, I NEED TO PEE!
SHH!
HOW LONG DO WE HAVE TO HIDE ON THIS BRIDGE?
DID YOU SAY SOME-THING?

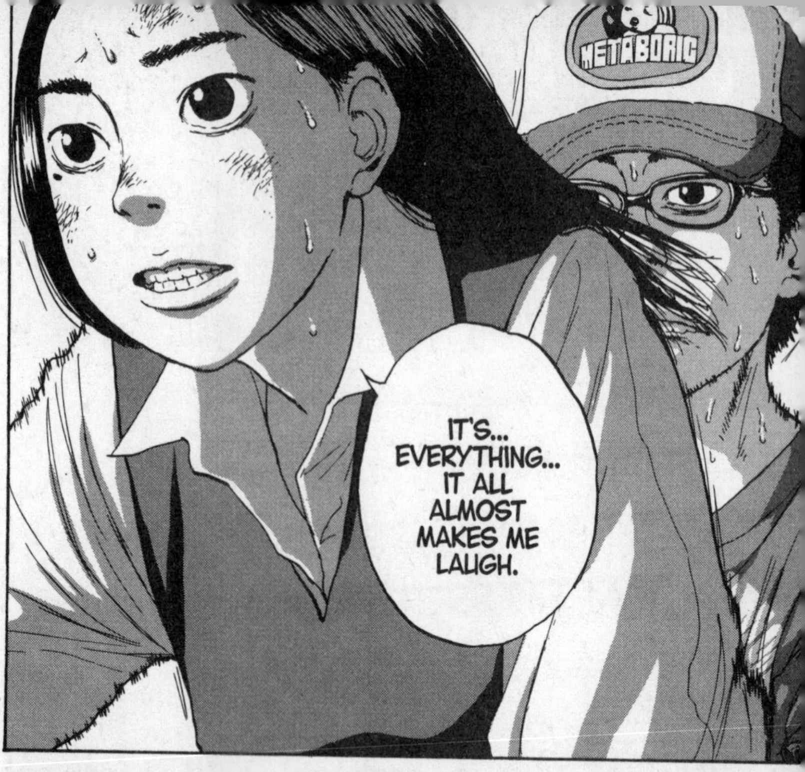
METABORIC
IT'S... EVERYTHING... IT ALL ALMOST MAKES ME LAUGH.
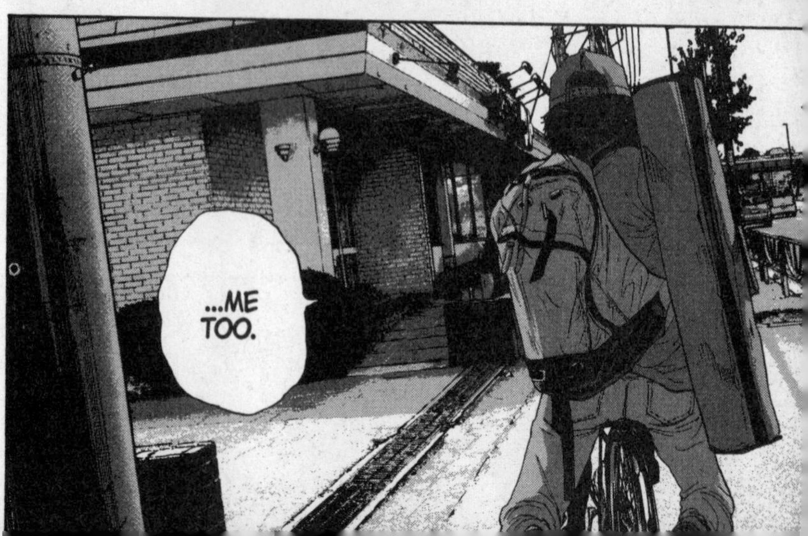
...ME TOO.

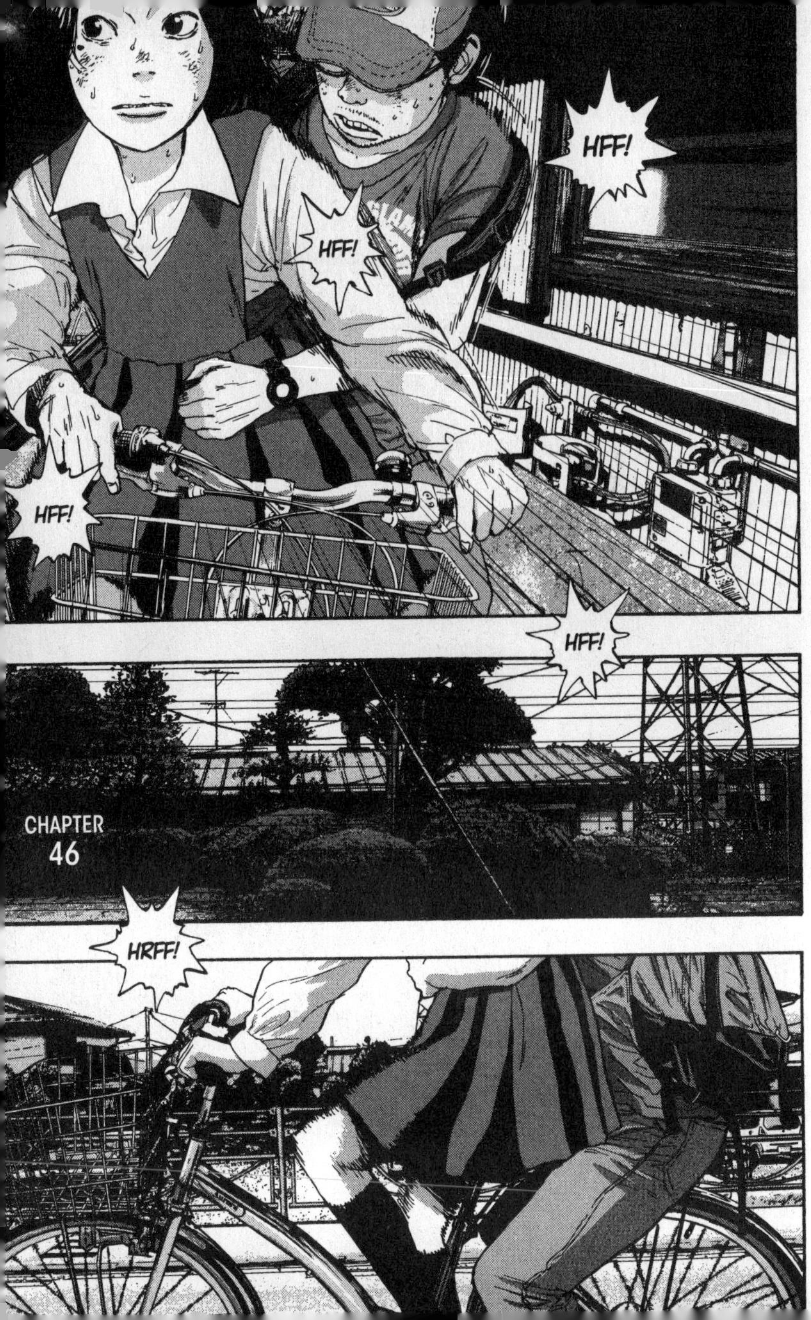
HFF!
HFF!
HFF!
HFF!
CHAPTER 46
HRFF!

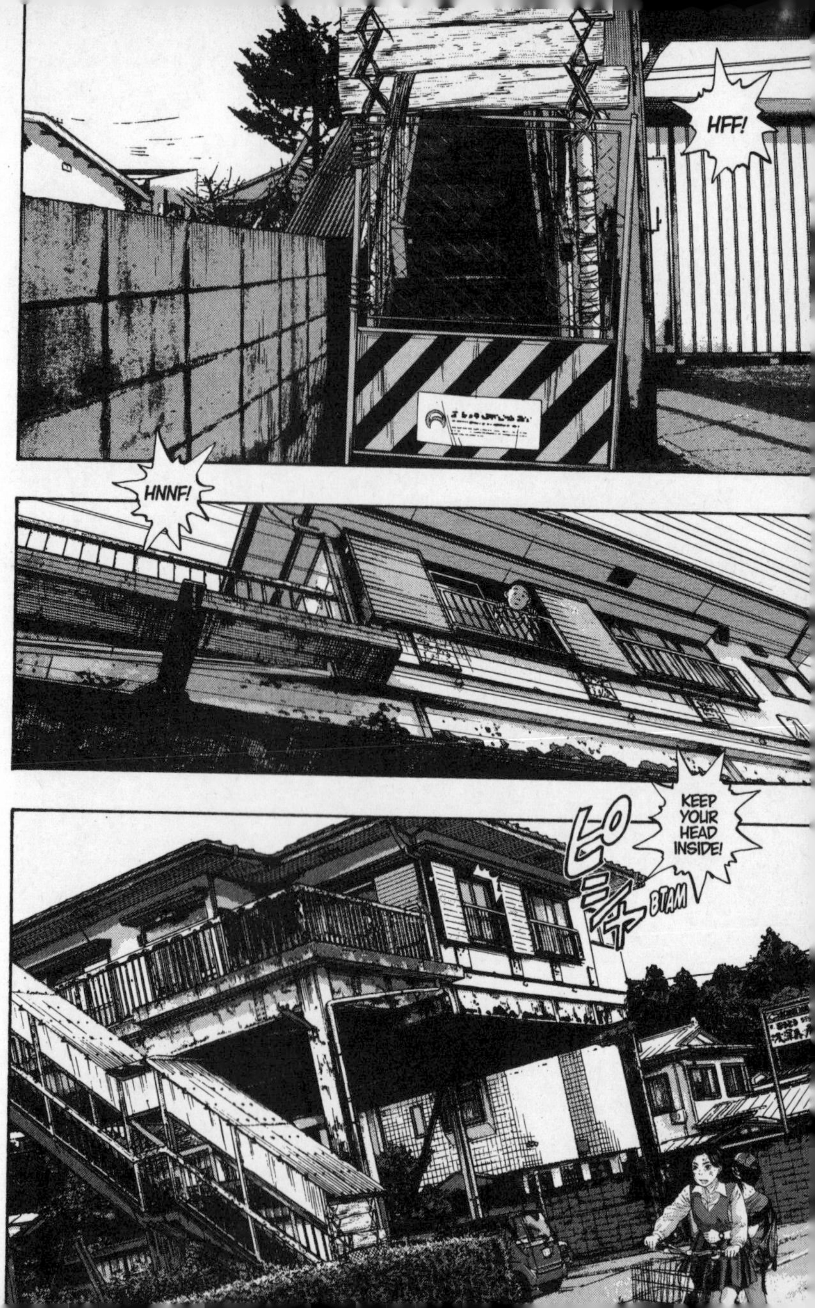
HFF!
HNNF!
KEEP YOUR HEAD INSIDE!
BTAM

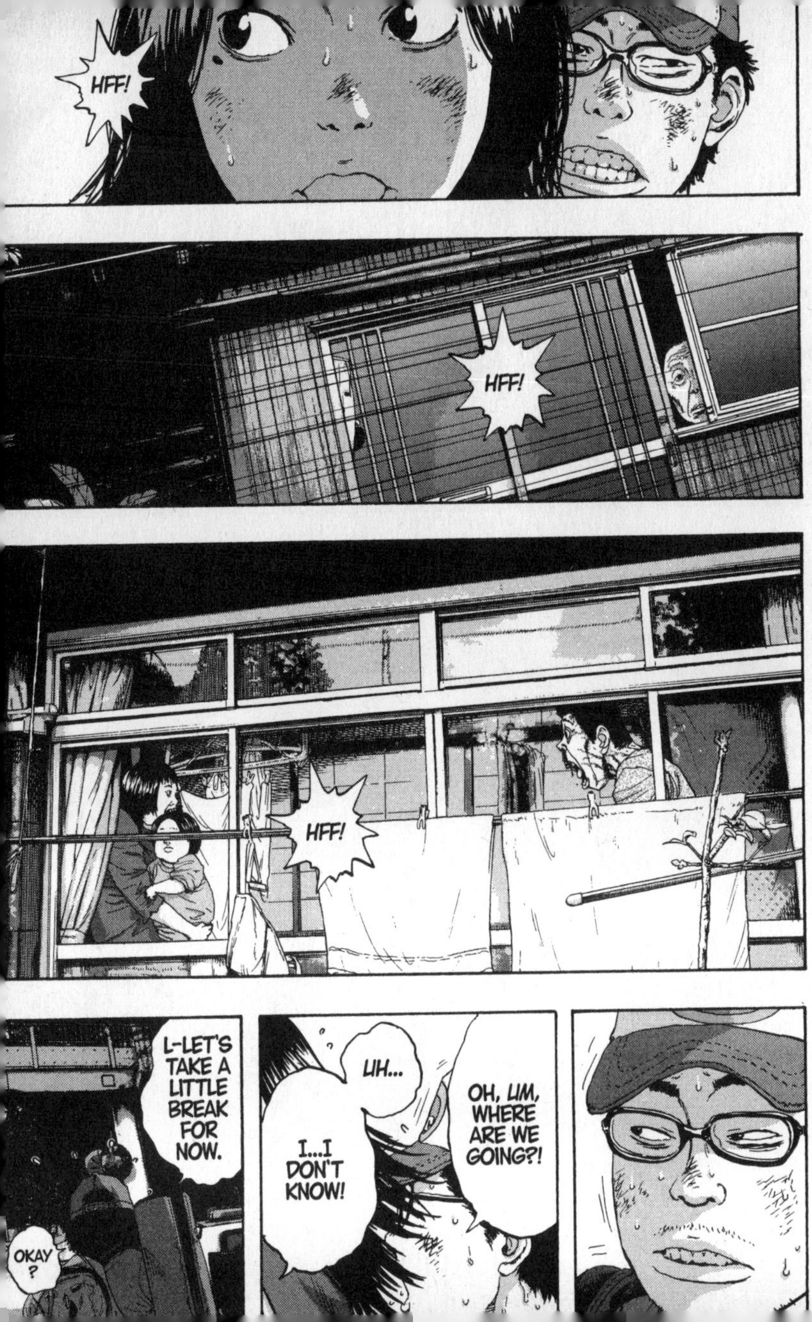
HFF!
HFF!
HFF!
L-LET'S TAKE A LITTLE BREAK FOR NOW.
OKAY?
OH, UM, WHERE ARE WE GOING?!
UH...
I...I DON'T KNOW!

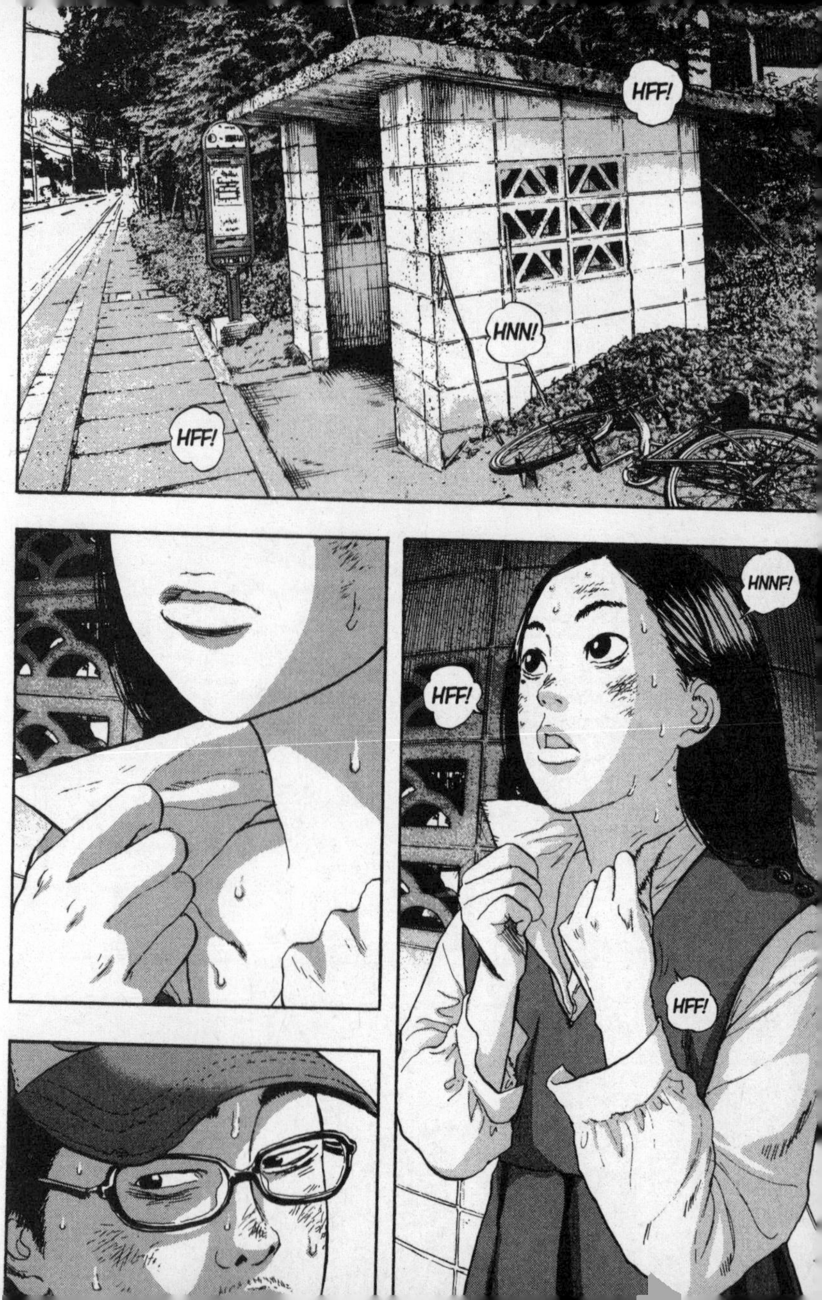
HFF!
HNN!
HFF!
HNNF!
HFF!
HFF!

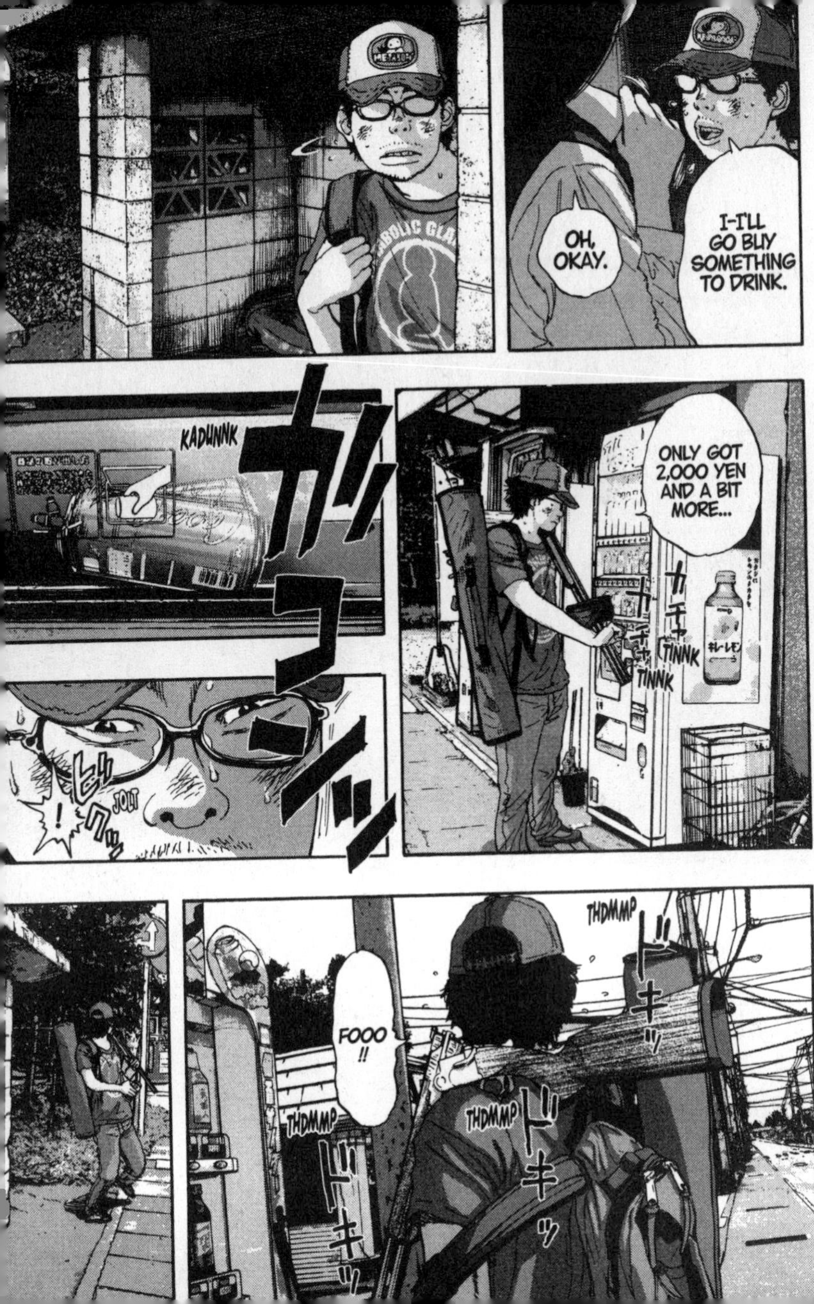
I-I'LL GO BUY SOMETHING TO DRINK.
OH, OKAY.
ONLY GOT 2,000 YEN AND A BIT MORE...
カチャ TINNK
カチャ TINNK
KADUNNK
ガコーン
ビクッ JOLT
!
THDMMP ドキッ
FOOO !!
THDMMP ドキッ
THDMMP ドキッ

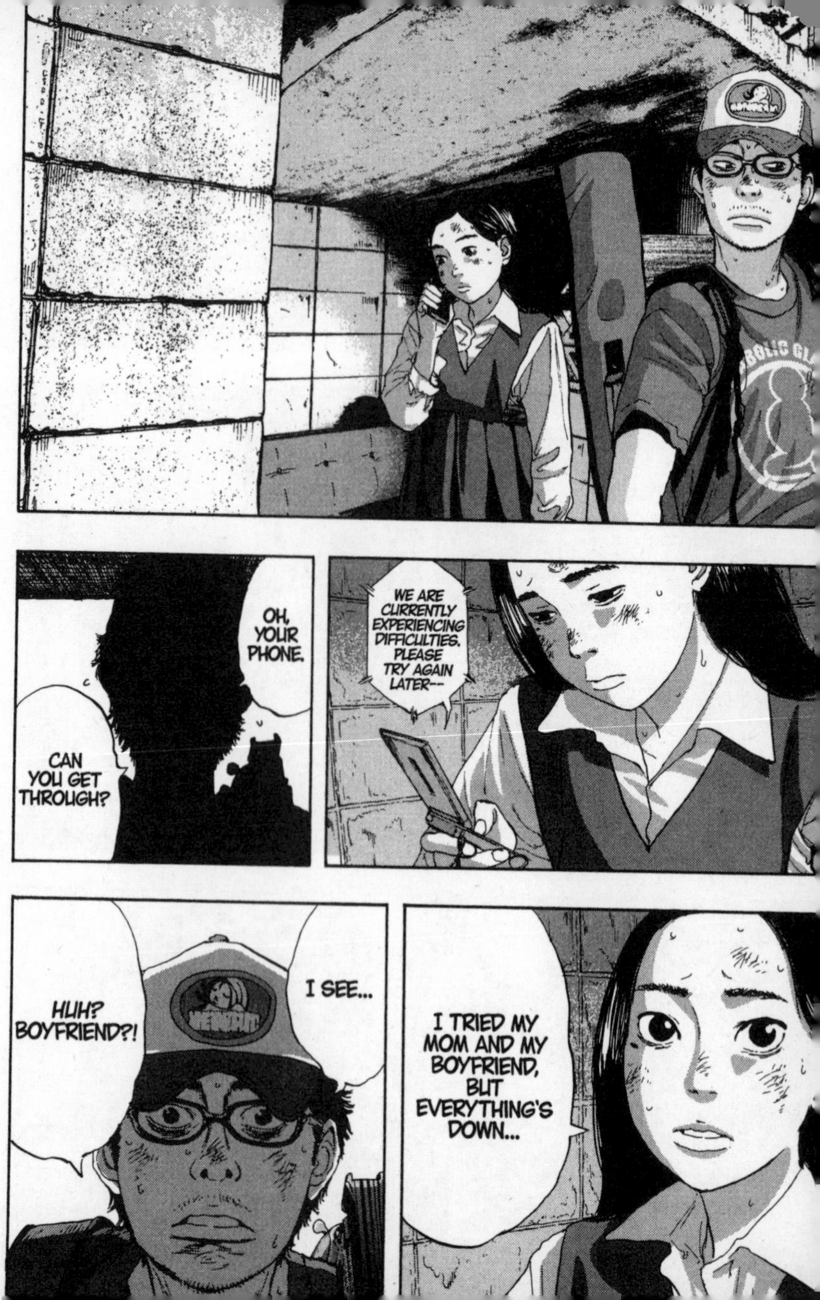
WE ARE CURRENTLY EXPERIENCING DIFFICULTIES. PLEASE TRY AGAIN LATER--
OH, YOUR PHONE.
CAN YOU GET THROUGH?
I TRIED MY MOM AND MY BOYFRIEND, BUT EVERYTHING'S DOWN...
I SEE...
HUH? BOYFRIEND?!

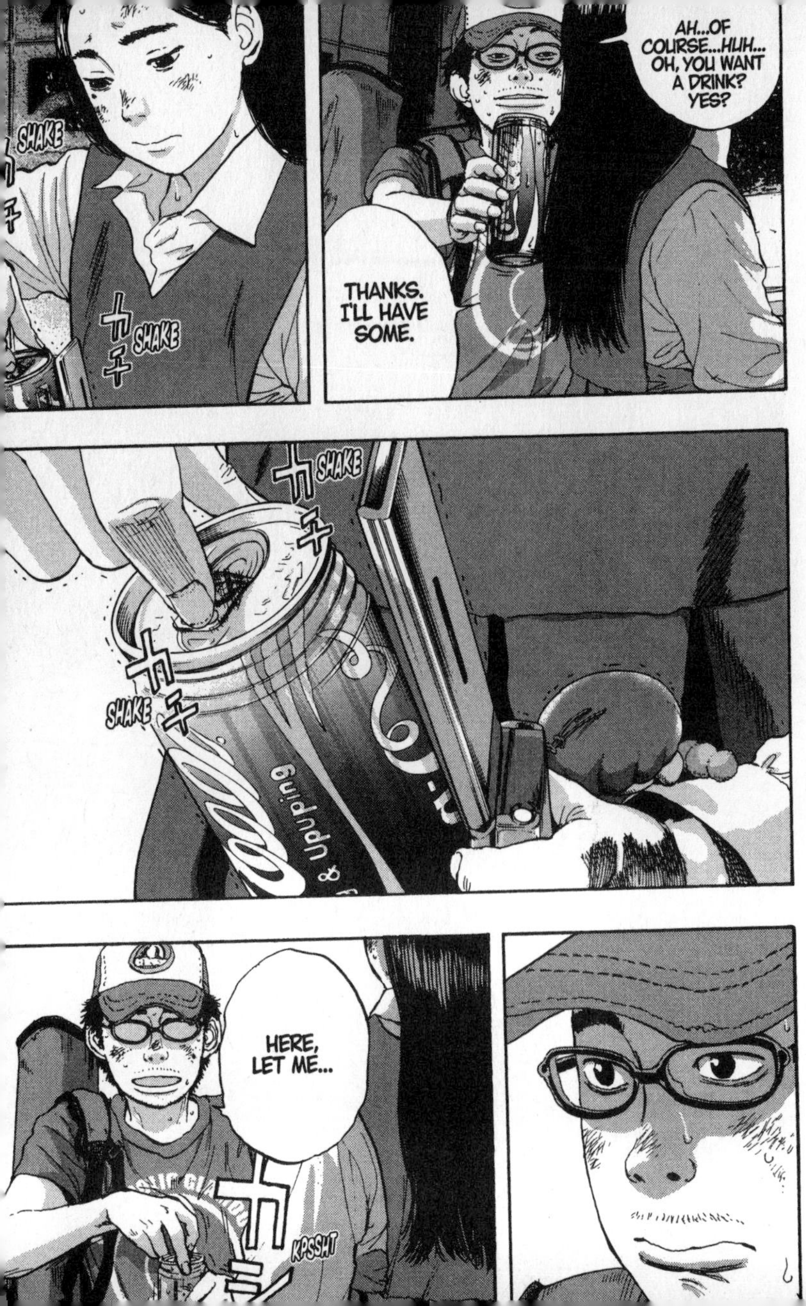
AH...OF COURSE...HUH... OH, YOU WANT A DRINK? YES?
THANKS. I'LL HAVE SOME.
SHAKE
SHAKE
SHAKE
SHAKE
HERE, LET ME...
KPSSHT

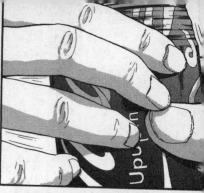

OH!

SHOULD YOU CALL SOMEONE, MR. SUZUKI? A GIRLFRIEND OR SOME-ONE?

THANKS FOR THE SODA.

HUH? OH! HM, MAYBE I SHOULD.

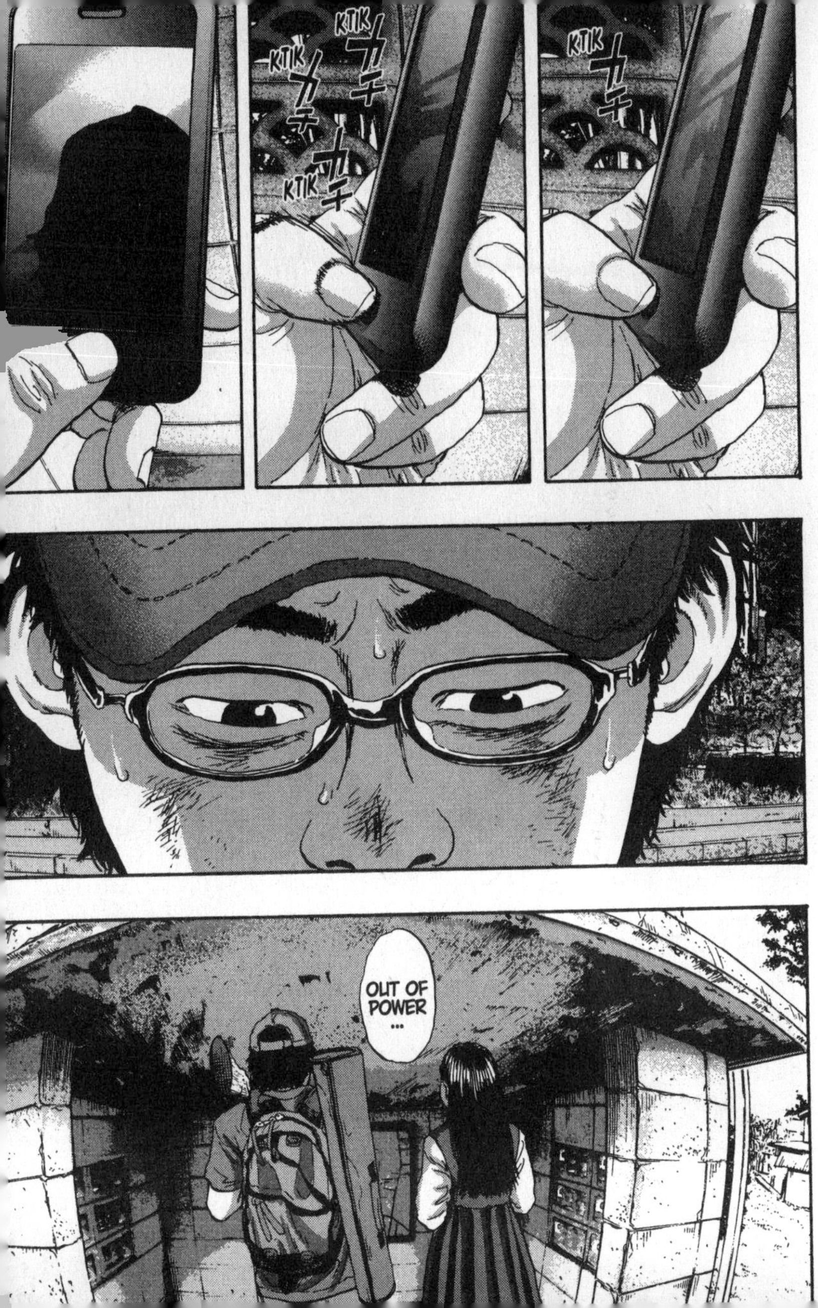

KTIK
カチ
KTIK
カチ
KTIK
カチ
OUT OF POWER ...

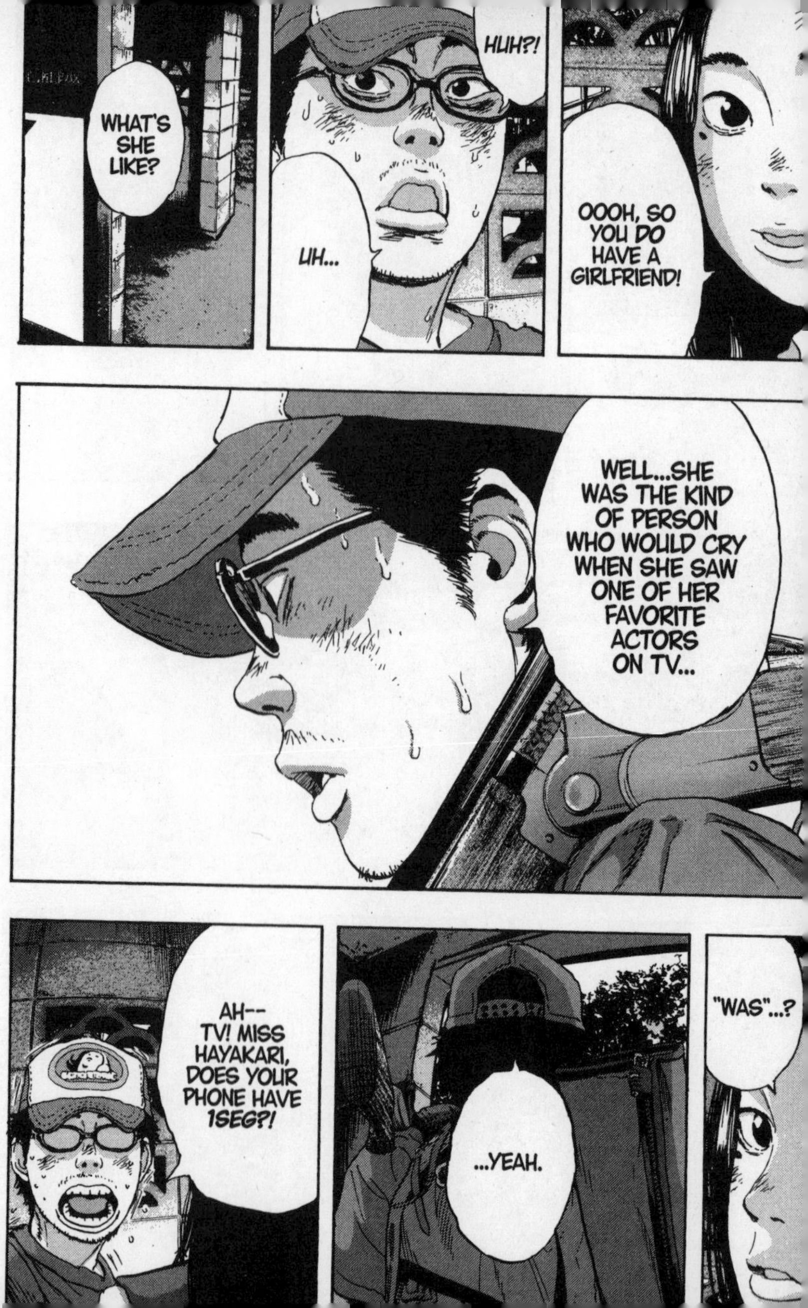
OOOH, SO YOU DO HAVE A GIRLFRIEND!
HUH?!
UH...
WHAT'S SHE LIKE?
WELL...SHE WAS THE KIND OF PERSON WHO WOULD CRY WHEN SHE SAW ONE OF HER FAVORITE ACTORS ON TV...
"WAS"...?
...YEAH.
AH-- TV! MISS HAYAKARI, DOES YOUR PHONE HAVE 1SEG?!

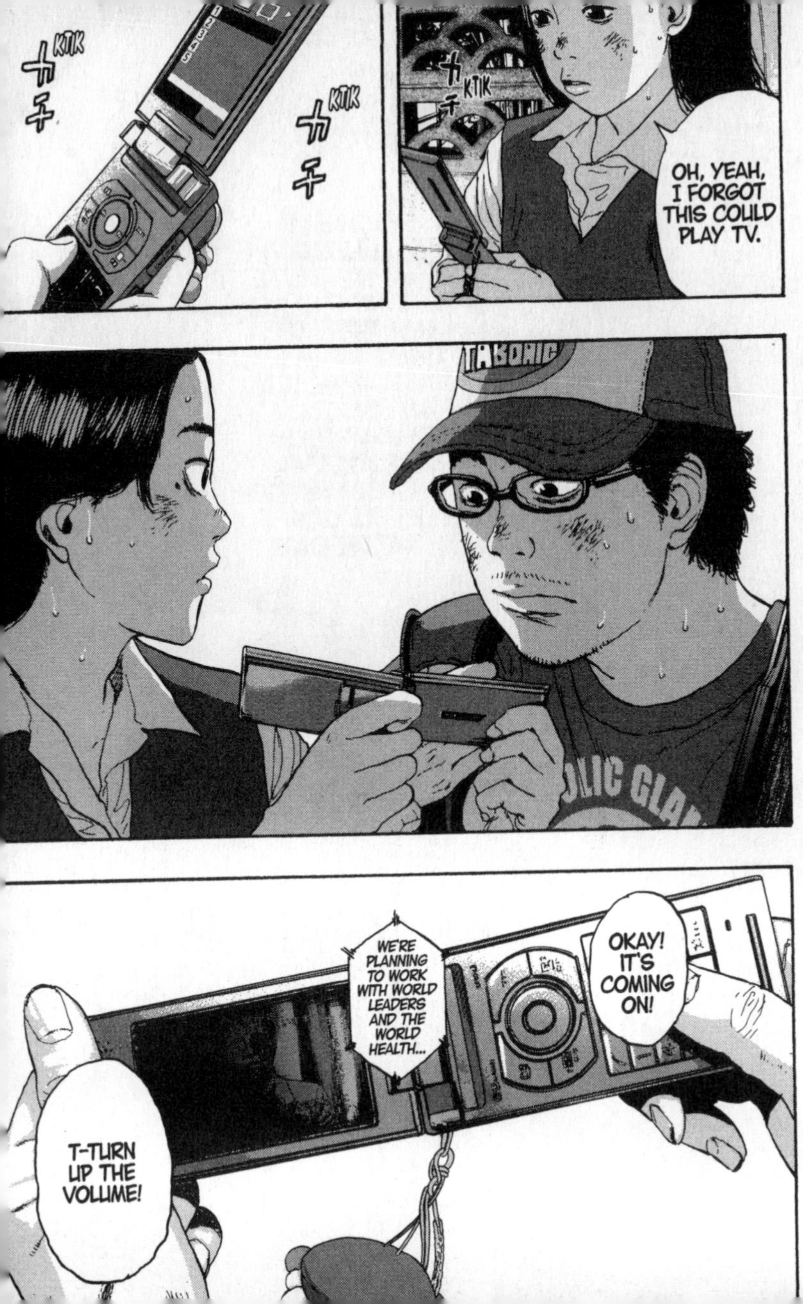
カ KTIK チ
OH, YEAH, I FORGOT THIS COULD PLAY TV.
カ KTIK チ
カ KTIK チ
TABONIC
OKAY! IT'S COMING ON!
WE'RE PLANNING TO WORK WITH WORLD LEADERS AND THE WORLD HEALTH...
T-TURN UP THE VOLUME!

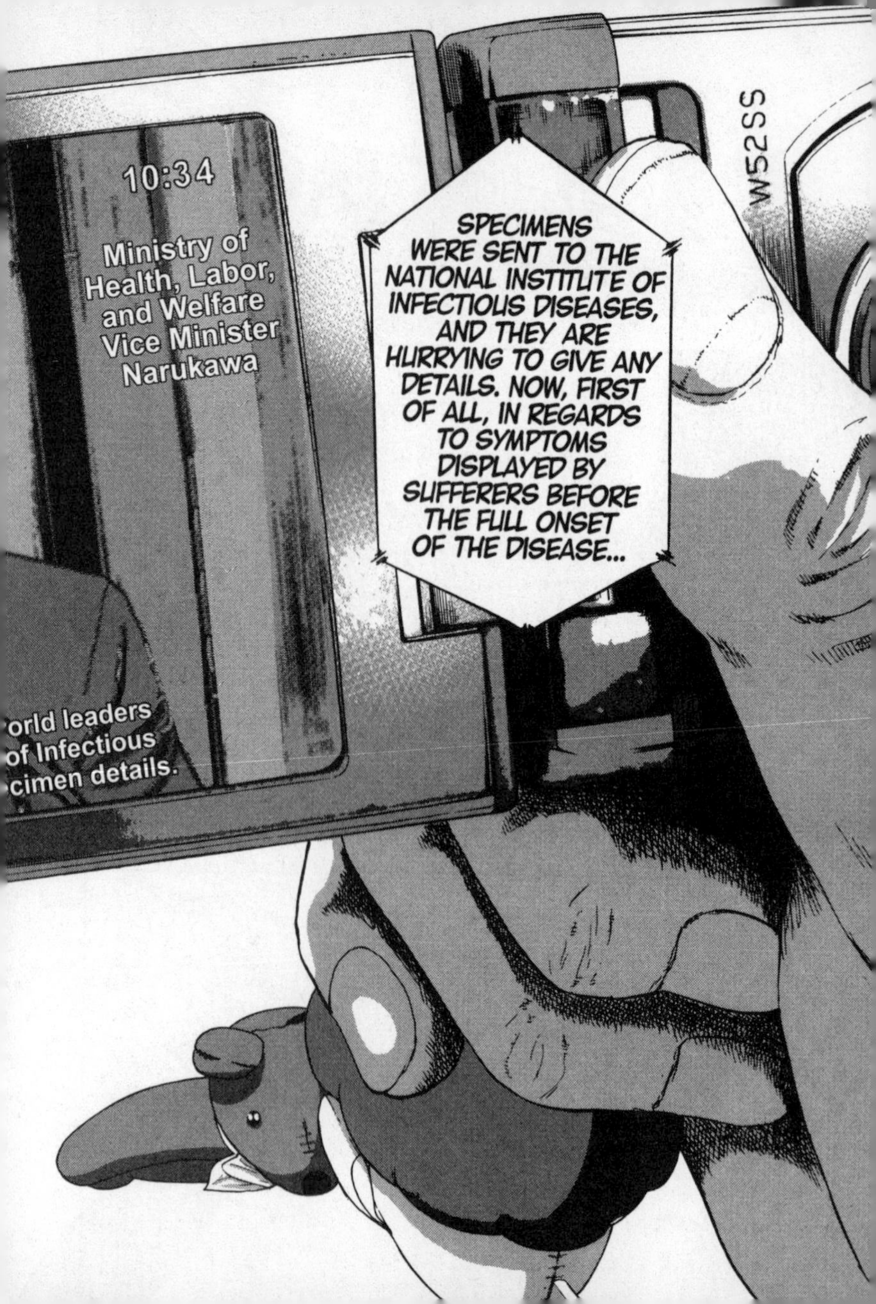

SPECIMENS WERE SENT TO THE NATIONAL INSTITUTE OF INFECTIOUS DISEASES, AND THEY ARE HURRYING TO GIVE ANY DETAILS. NOW, FIRST OF ALL, IN REGARDS TO SYMPTOMS DISPLAYED BY SUFFERERS BEFORE THE FULL ONSET OF THE DISEASE...
10:34
Ministry of Health, Labor, and Welfare Vice Minister Narukawa
orld leaders
of Infectious
cimen details.
W52SS

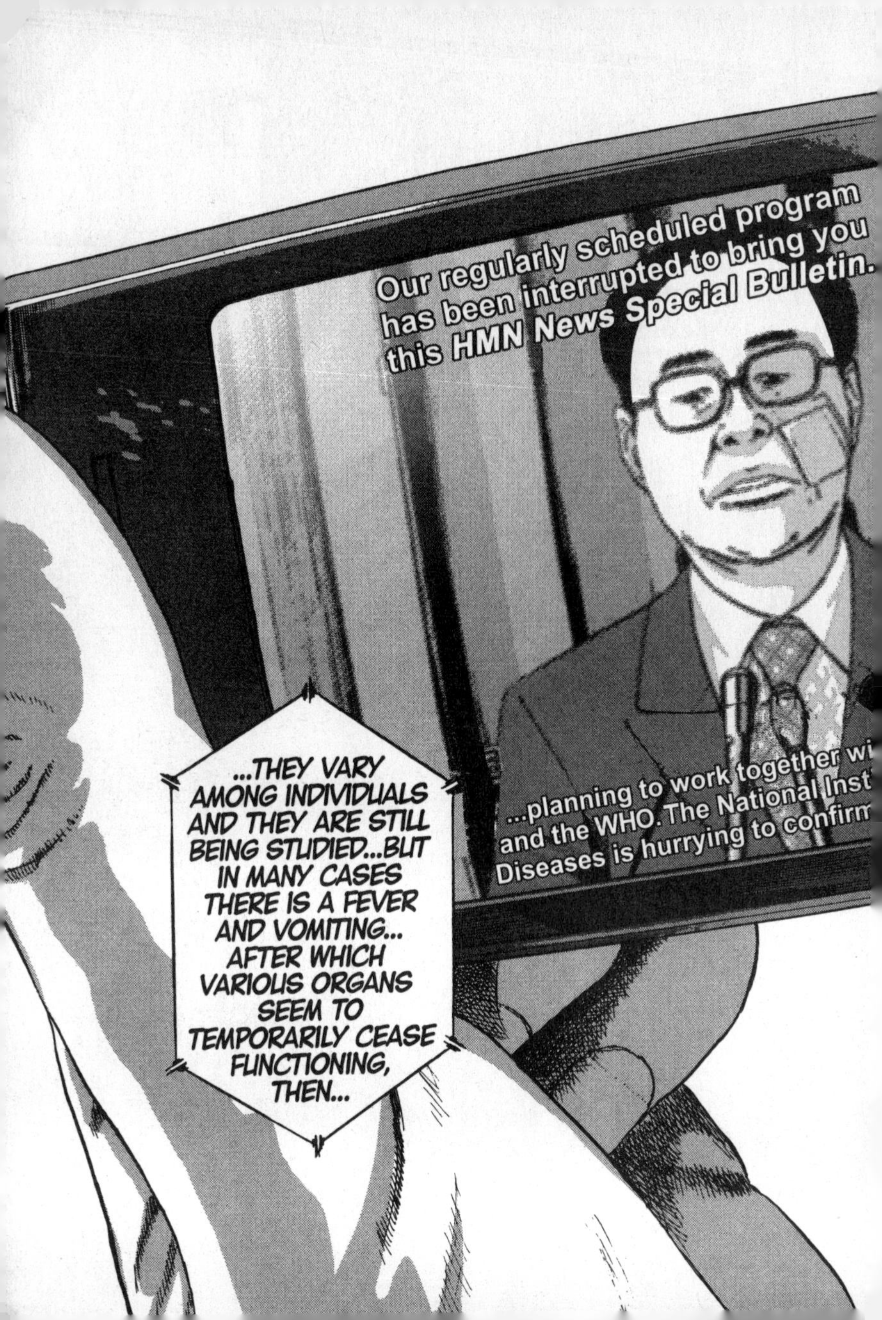
Our regularly scheduled program has been interrupted to bring you this HMN News Special Bulletin.
...planning to work together wi and the WHO. The National Inst Diseases is hurrying to confirm
...THEY VARY AMONG INDIVIDUALS AND THEY ARE STILL BEING STUDIED...BUT IN MANY CASES THERE IS A FEVER AND VOMITING... AFTER WHICH VARIOUS ORGANS SEEM TO TEMPORARILY CEASE FUNCTIONING, THEN...

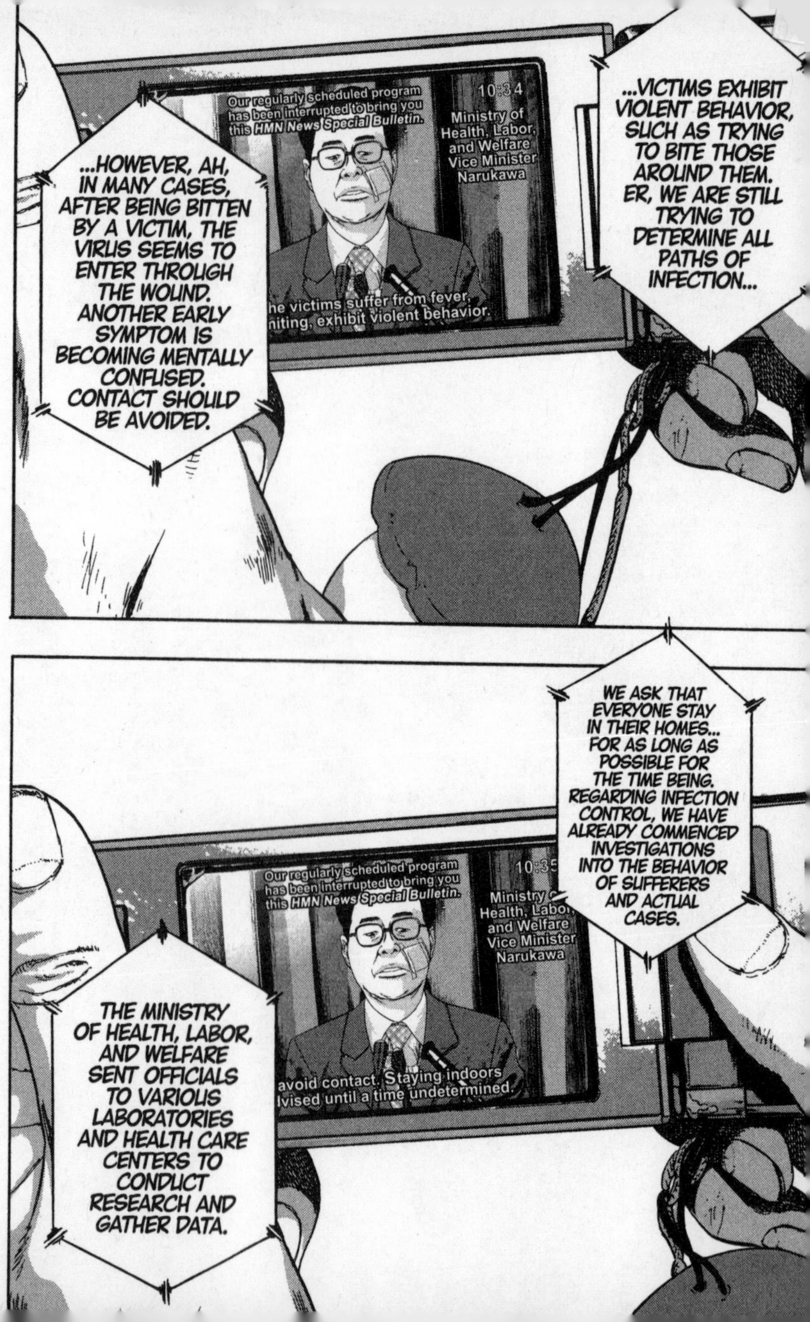
...VICTIMS EXHIBIT VIOLENT BEHAVIOR, SUCH AS TRYING TO BITE THOSE AROUND THEM. ER, WE ARE STILL TRYING TO DETERMINE ALL PATHS OF INFECTION...
10:34
Ministry of Health, Labor, and Welfare Vice Minister Narukawa
Our regularly scheduled program has been interrupted to bring you this HMN News Special Bulletin.
he victims suffer from fever,
niting, exhibit violent behavior.
...HOWEVER, AH, IN MANY CASES, AFTER BEING BITTEN BY A VICTIM, THE VIRUS SEEMS TO ENTER THROUGH THE WOUND. ANOTHER EARLY SYMPTOM IS BECOMING MENTALLY CONFUSED. CONTACT SHOULD BE AVOIDED.
WE ASK THAT EVERYONE STAY IN THEIR HOMES... FOR AS LONG AS POSSIBLE FOR THE TIME BEING. REGARDING INFECTION CONTROL, WE HAVE ALREADY COMMENCED INVESTIGATIONS INTO THE BEHAVIOR OF SUFFERERS AND ACTUAL CASES.
10:35
Ministry o
Health, Labor
and Welfare
Vice Minister
Narukawa
Our regularly scheduled program has been interrupted to bring you this HMN News Special Bulletin.
avoid contact. Staying indoors
lvised until a time undetermined.
THE MINISTRY OF HEALTH, LABOR, AND WELFARE SENT OFFICIALS TO VARIOUS LABORATORIES AND HEALTH CARE CENTERS TO CONDUCT RESEARCH AND GATHER DATA.

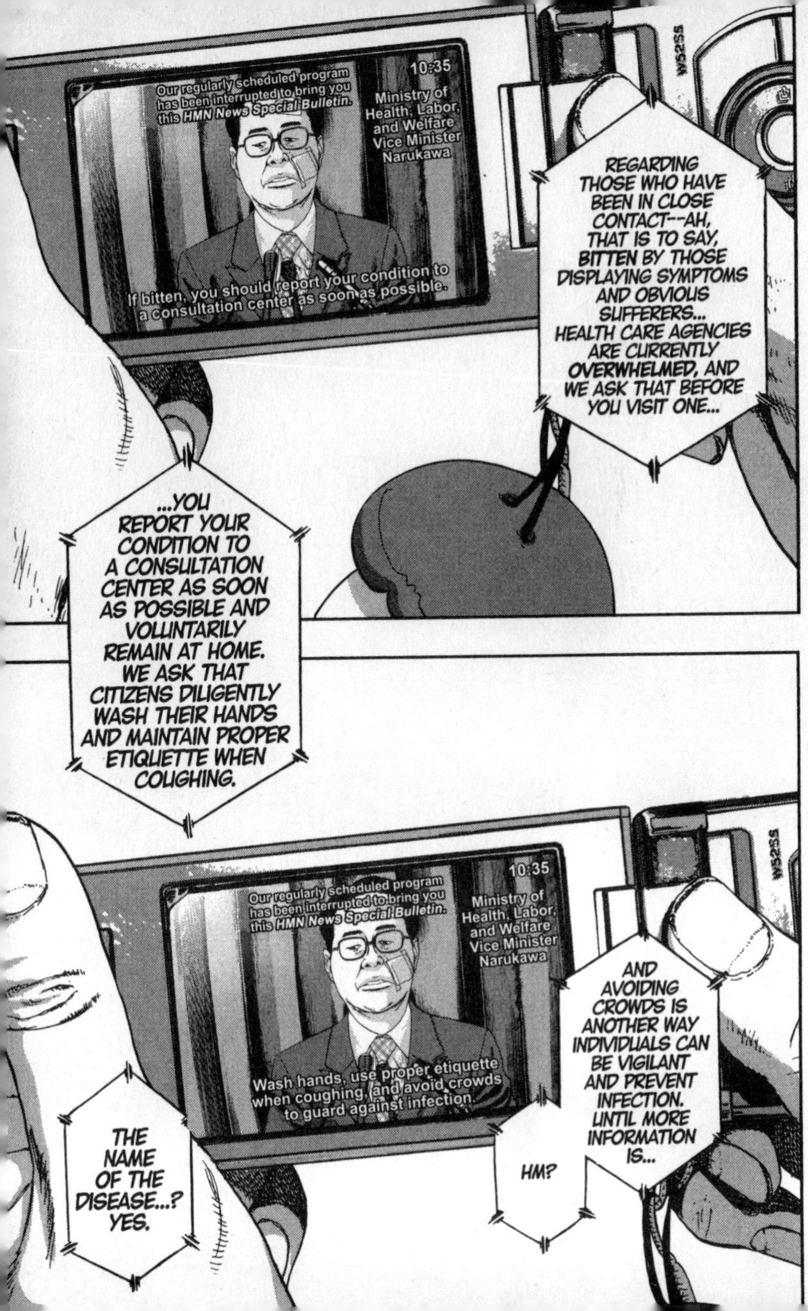
10:35
Our regularly scheduled program has been interrupted to bring you this HMN News Special Bulletin.
Ministry of Health, Labor, and Welfare Vice Minister Narukawa
If bitten, you should report your condition to a consultation center as soon as possible.
REGARDING THOSE WHO HAVE BEEN IN CLOSE CONTACT--AH, THAT IS TO SAY, BITTEN BY THOSE DISPLAYING SYMPTOMS AND OBVIOUS SUFFERERS... HEALTH CARE AGENCIES ARE CURRENTLY OVERWHELMED, AND WE ASK THAT BEFORE YOU VISIT ONE...
...YOU REPORT YOUR CONDITION TO A CONSULTATION CENTER AS SOON AS POSSIBLE AND VOLUNTARILY REMAIN AT HOME. WE ASK THAT CITIZENS DILIGENTLY WASH THEIR HANDS AND MAINTAIN PROPER ETIQUETTE WHEN COUGHING.
10:35
Our regularly scheduled program has been interrupted to bring you this HMN News Special Bulletin.
Ministry of Health, Labor, and Welfare Vice Minister Narukawa
Wash hands, use proper etiquette when coughing, and avoid crowds to guard against infection.
AND AVOIDING CROWDS IS ANOTHER WAY INDIVIDUALS CAN BE VIGILANT AND PREVENT INFECTION. UNTIL MORE INFORMATION IS...
HM?
THE NAME OF THE DISEASE...? YES.

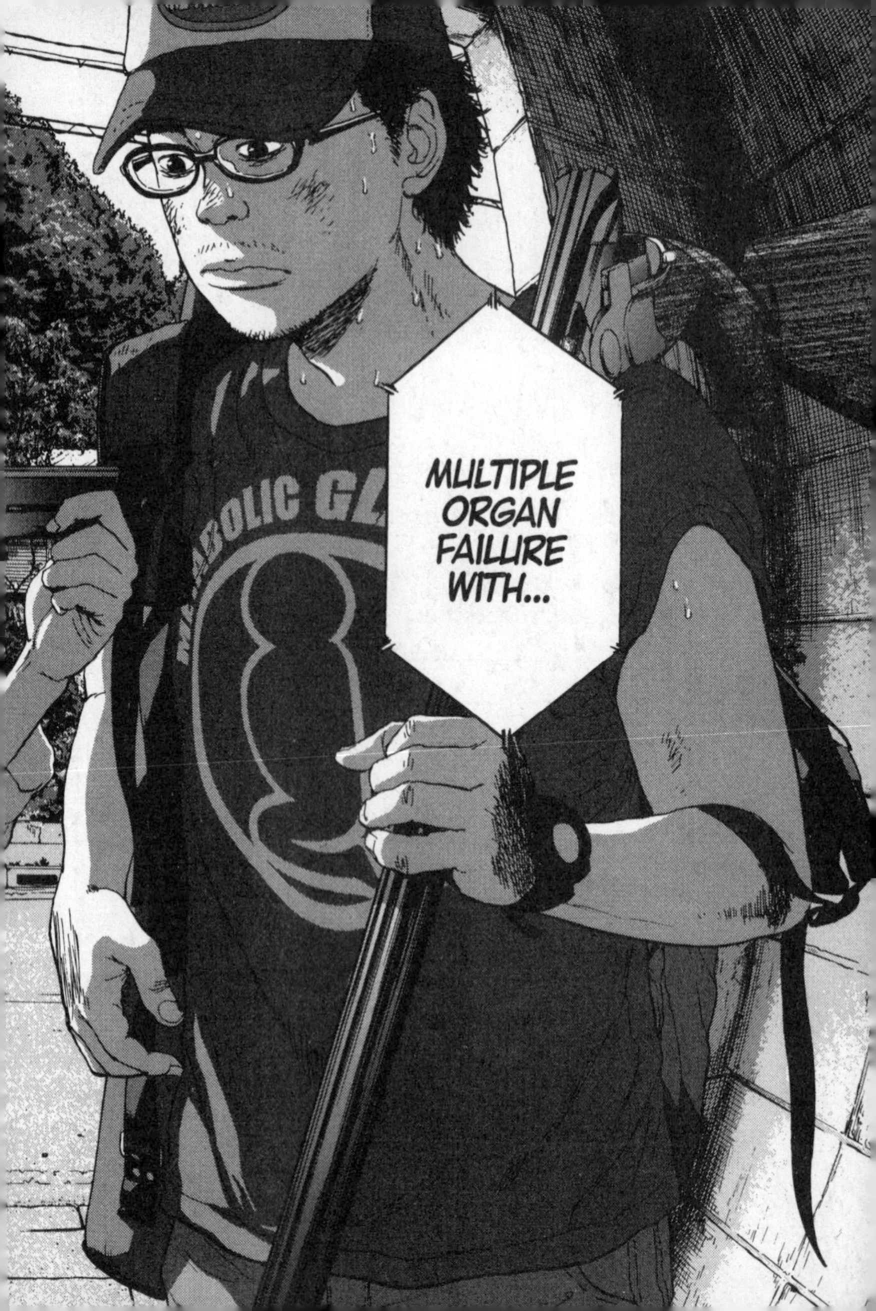
MULTIPLE ORGAN FAILURE WITH...

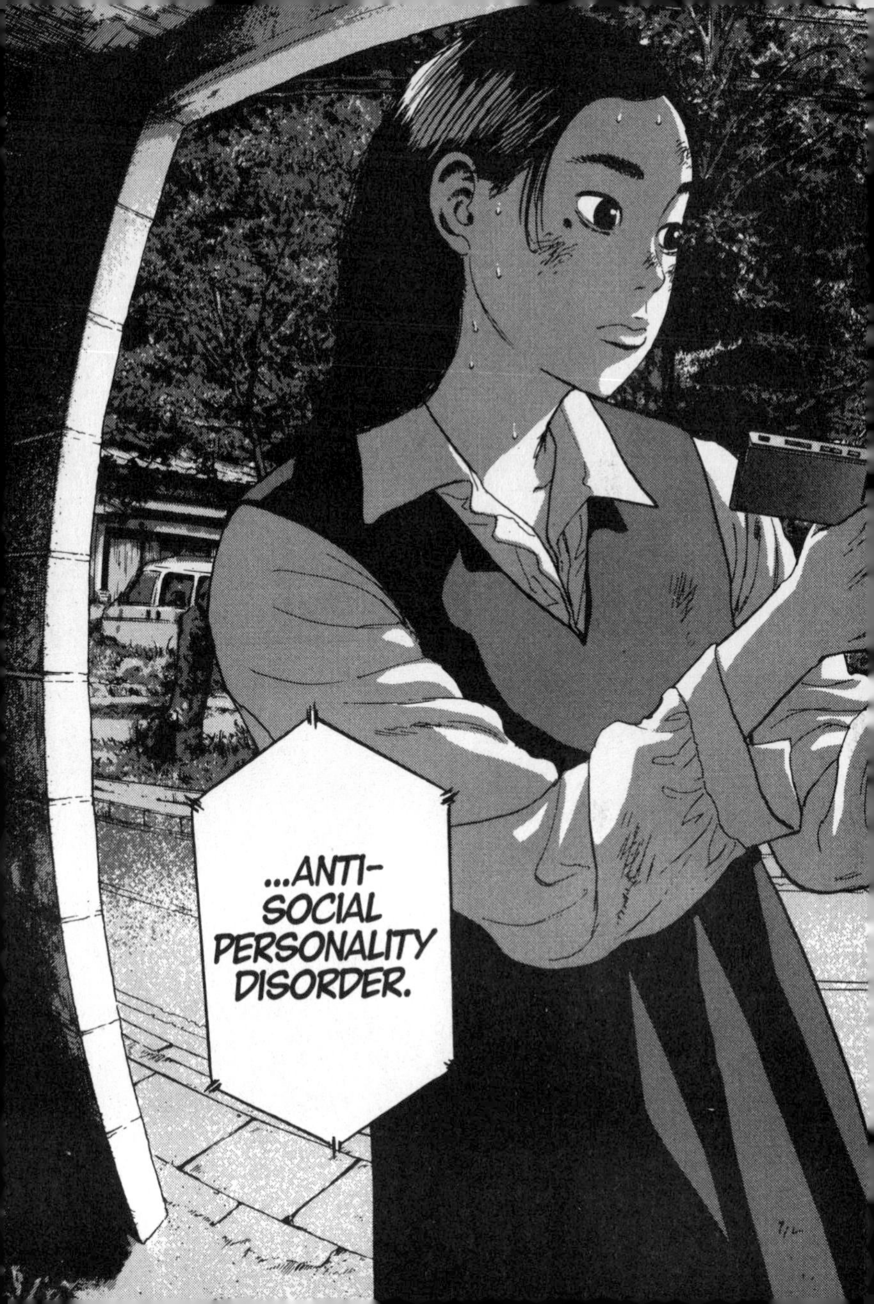
...ANTI-SOCIAL PERSONALITY DISORDER.

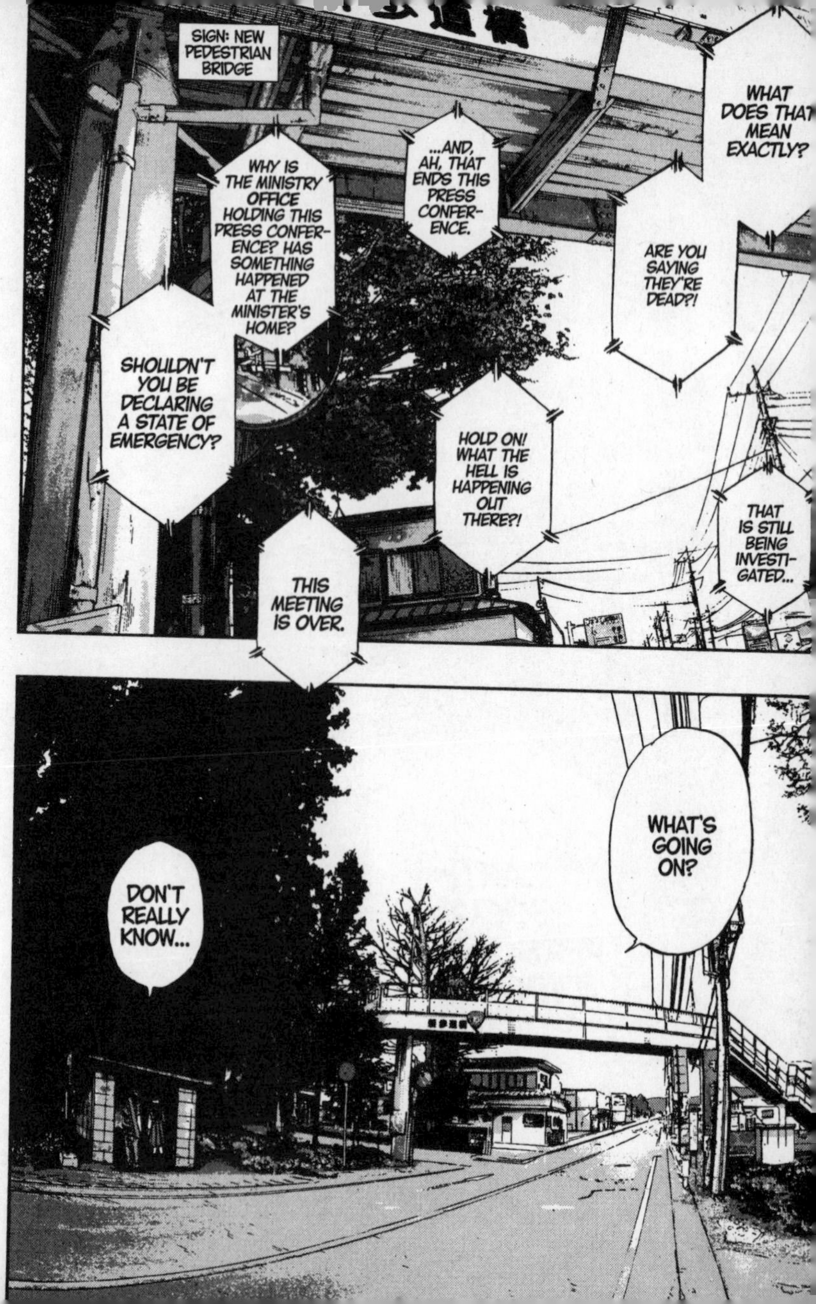
SIGN: NEW PEDESTRIAN BRIDGE
WHAT DOES THAT MEAN EXACTLY?
...AND, AH, THAT ENDS THIS PRESS CONFERENCE.
WHY IS THE MINISTRY OFFICE HOLDING THIS PRESS CONFERENCE? HAS SOMETHING HAPPENED AT THE MINISTER'S HOME?
ARE YOU SAYING THEY'RE DEAD?!
SHOULDN'T YOU BE DECLARING A STATE OF EMERGENCY?
THAT IS STILL BEING INVESTIGATED...
HOLD ON! WHAT THE HELL IS HAPPENING OUT THERE?!
THIS MEETING IS OVER.
WHAT'S GOING ON?
DON'T REALLY KNOW...

I AM
A HERO

URGENT
MINISTRY OF HEALTH, LABOR, AND WELFARE
COUNTERMEASURES AGAINST MULTIPLE ORGAN
FAILURE WITH ANTISOCIAL PERSONALITY DISORDER

At present, we are planning to work together with world leaders and the WHO, and we have sent specimens to the National Institute of Infectious Diseases. They are hurrying to give details.

First of all, in regards to symptoms displayed by sufferers before the full onset of the disease, they vary among individuals, and we are still conducting an epidemiological investigation, but in many cases there is a fever and vomiting, among various other symptoms, following which various organs seem to temporarily cease to function, after which sufferers exhibit violent behavior, such as trying to bite those around them.

They are still being studied

We are also still trying to determine the path of infection; however, in many cases, after being bitten by a sufferer the virus enters through the wound.

Those displaying symptoms become mentally confused and muddled. Contact should be avoided. We ask that people stay in their homes as long as possible.

20%? 30%?
What percentage?

Regarding future infection control, we have already commenced investigations into the behavior of sufferers and actual cases across various localities and healthcare centers. The Ministry of Health, Labor, and Welfare has sent officials to all known affected localities to conduct research and gather data.

Regarding those who have been in close contact with, specifically bitten by, those displaying symptoms and known sufferers, health care agencies are currently very overwhelmed and we ask that before you visit one, you first give a report of your condition to a consultation center as soon as possible and that you voluntarily remain at home.

Until further notice, kindergartens, elementary schools, and junior high schools will be closed, as well as daycare centers and elderly care facilities. High schools and universities are asked to voluntarily do the same. Additionally, new general consultation facilities and infectious disease consultation centers are being established as a further countermeasure. Sufferers should report to these new consultation centers.

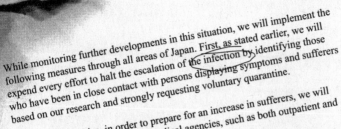

While monitoring further developments in this situation, we will implement the following measures through all areas of Japan. First, as stated earlier, we will expend every effort to halt the escalation of the infection by identifying those who have been in close contact with persons displaying symptoms and sufferers based on our research and strongly requesting voluntary quarantine.

In regional localities, in order to prepare for an increase in sufferers, we will carry out measures to secure all medical agencies, such as both outpatient and inpatient medical treatment facilities.

We ask that citizens diligently wash their hands and mind their etiquette when coughing. Avoiding crowds is another way individuals can be vigilant to avoid infection. Also, until accurate information is made available, we ask that people please remain in their homes for an as-yet-undetermined length of time. In particular, for those who suspect infection, as stated before, before visiting a medical facility, we ask that you be sure to please telephone the consultation centers set up in various health care establishments and also appearing in new locations as we're able to set them up.

Use YouTube?

Information is still being processed and is quite confusing. At present, we believe our top priority is to obtain and process accurate information as soon as possible, so we can use that as the basis for action. Please remain in your homes and do not panic. Action will be determined.

All citizens, please look for further national and local announcements and please continue to respond in a calm manner.

What do we do?
Is it all over?!

I AM A HERO

TRANSLATION NOTES

CHAPTER 23

On the zombie-infested train, Hideo considers taking his shotgun out to defend himself and muses, "If I did anything stupid, they'd amend the laws again. I'd ruin things for everyone." This continues a running gag in this series of Hideo taking Japanese laws and societal mores way too seriously as civilization itself breaks down around him during the zombie apocalypse.

Bitten by the zombie businessman on the train, the infected white-haired man immediately starts singing snippets from popular traditional and children's songs, including "Oborozukiyo" (A hazy moonlit night), "Hato Poppo" (Pigeon Poppo), and "Tan-Tan-Tanuki," a.k.a. "The Tanuki Song."

CHAPTER 24

At the beginning of this chapter, the infected white-haired man sings lines from the 1960s hit "Ue o muite aruko" (I look up when I walk) by Kyu Sakamoto, released in the US and UK as "Sukiyaki." This remains the only Japanese-language song to ever reach the top of the *Billboard Hot 100* record charts.

CHAPTER 25

In the taxicab, Hideo tries the door, but it's locked. This is very common with Japanese taxis. To get in, one will stand by a back door, and the driver opens and closes the door using a lever in the front. It is considered part of the driver's duty to do so, and to open or close a cab door oneself is sometimes considered disrespectful.

In the back seat of the taxi, the infected cheating husband transitions from simply saying "love" to mimicking and repeating the "luv" catch phrase of Japanese comedian Ken Shimura.

CHAPTER 26

Golden Week is mentioned several times in this omnibus volume. This refers to a string of Japanese holidays that run from April 29 to May 5.

CHAPTER 27

After the taxi driver succumbs to his infection and crashes, he sings a line from the popular Japanese children's song "Nanatsu no ko" (Seven baby crows) by Ujo Noguchi and Nagayo Motoori.

The amusement park that Hideo passes is based on the Fuji-Q Highland park—renamed "Lowland" for this story.

CHAPTER 28

Fuji Sugaru Land is a substitute name for the real-world Fuji Subaru Land Doggy Park.

1seg refers to the mobile phone broadcasting service in some countries that carries audio, video, and data signals.

CHAPTER 29

In Hideo's food stall fantasy, his imaginary cook receives three stars, which is a direct reference to the annual Michelin guidebooks that review restaurants and hotels worldwide.

Isolated and panicked, Hideo tries to meditate and calm himself (like he did in *I Am a Hero Omnibus* Volume 1) using the Buddhist *namu amida butsu* and *namu myoho renge kyo* chants.

CHAPTER 30
Still fighting a panic attack, Hideo wonders if he's wandered into the "Suicide Forest." This refers to the Aokigahara Forest that covers Mount Fuji's northwest base, which is known as the Sea of Trees or the Suicide Forest due to its popularity among suicidal visitors.

CHAPTER 32
Outside on a dare to photograph a dead body in the Suicide Forest, Hiromi sings a bit of the theme song to the film *Seeraa fuku to kikanjuu* (*Sailor Suit and Machine Gun*), recorded by actress and singer Hiroko Yakushimaru.

CHAPTER 33
The cruel schoolgirls scheme to get their friend to drink a combination of Dr Pepper and *nigari*, a tofu coagulant derived from seawater.

CHAPTER 37
As Hiromi's infected schoolmates descend on her and Hideo, they begin to fight with each other, possibly because they actually hated each other before the outbreak and possibly because they each want to be the one to infect Hiromi, who they remember sending out into the Suicide Forest.

Walking in the rain, Hiromi and Sae discuss music. Radwimps, Soutaisei Riron (Theory of relativity), 9mm Parabellum Bullet, and Shinsei Kamattechan are Japanese rock bands formed in the 2000s. Andymori and Asian Kung-Fu Generation are alternative rock bands. Happy End is a folk rock band, and Takao Kisugi is a Japanese singer who was born in 1950. Quruli is a popular mainstream band that formed in 1996.

CHAPTER 38
Hideo and Hiromi have names that evoke the word "hero." The exact two kanji that make up the name "Hideo" are the same two used for *eiyuu*, which is the Japanese word for "hero." "Hiromi" sounds like "HERO-me," and people close to her in her life before the outbreak would have called her Hiro or Hiro-*chan* for short.

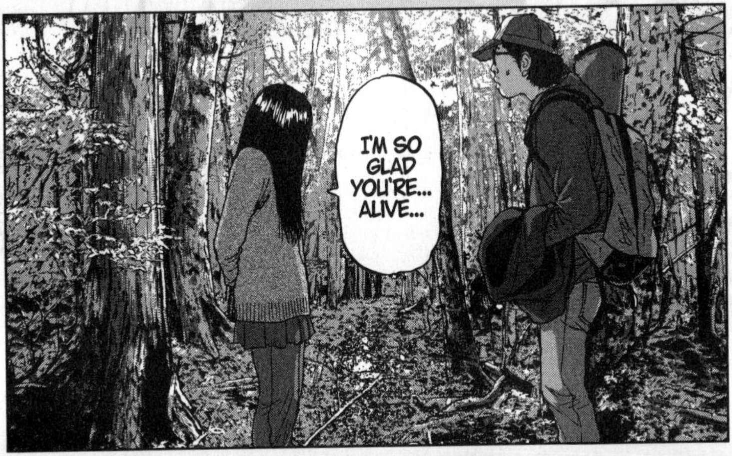
I'M SO GLAD YOU'RE... ALIVE...

NEON GENESIS EVANGELION

Dark Horse Manga is proud to present new original series based on the wildly popular *Neon Genesis Evangelion* manga and anime! Continuing the rich story lines and complex characters, these new visions of *Neon Genesis Evangelion* provide extra dimensions for understanding one of the greatest series ever made!

NEON GENESIS EVANGELION Campus Apocalypse

STORY AND ART BY MINGMING

VOLUME 1
ISBN 978-1-59582-530-8 | $10.99

VOLUME 2
ISBN 978-1-59582-661-9 | $10.99

VOLUME 3
ISBN 978-1-59582-680-0 | $10.99

VOLUME 4
ISBN 978-1-59582-689-3 | $10.99

NEON GENESIS EVANGELION COMIC TRIBUTE

STORY AND ART BY VARIOUS CREATORS

ISBN 978-1-61655-114-8 | $10.99

NEON GENESIS EVANGELION THE Shinji Ikari Detective Diary

STORY AND ART BY TAKUMI YOSHIMURA

VOLUME 1
ISBN 978-1-61655-225-1 | $9.99

VOLUME 2
ISBN 978-1-61655-418-7 | $9.99

TONY TAKEZAKI'S NEON GENESIS EVANGELION

STORY AND ART BY TONY TAKEZAKI

ISBN 978-1-61655-736-2 | $12.99

NEON GENESIS EVANGELION THE SHINJI IKARI RAISING PROJECT

STORY AND ART BY OSAMU TAKAHASHI

VOLUME 1
ISBN 978-1-59582-321-2 | $9.99

VOLUME 2
ISBN 978-1-59582-377-9 | $9.99

VOLUME 3
ISBN 978-1-59582-447-9 | $9.99

VOLUME 4
ISBN 978-1-59582-454-7 | $9.99

VOLUME 5
ISBN 978-1-59582-520-9 | $9.99

VOLUME 6
ISBN 978-1-59582-580-3 | $9.99

VOLUME 7
ISBN 978-1-59582-595-7 | $9.99

VOLUME 8
ISBN 978-1-59582-694-7 | $9.99

VOLUME 9
ISBN 978-1-59582-800-2 | $9.99

VOLUME 10
ISBN 978-1-59582-879-8 | $9.99

VOLUME 11
ISBN 978-1-59582-932-0 | $9.99

VOLUME 12
ISBN 978-1-61655-033-2 | $9.99

VOLUME 13
ISBN 978-1-61655-315-9 | $9.99

VOLUME 14
ISBN 978-1-61655-432-3 | $9.99

VOLUME 15
ISBN 978-1-61655-607-5 | $9.99

Each volume of *Neon Genesis Evangelion* features bonus color pages, your *Evangelion* fan art and letters, and special reader giveaways!

DARK HORSE MANGA

AVAILABLE AT YOUR LOCAL COMICS SHOP OR BOOKSTORE
To find a comics shop in your area, call 1-888-266-4226 • For more information or to order direct: • On the web: darkhorse.com
E-mail: mailorder@darkhorse.com • Phone: 1-800-862-0052 Mon.–Fri. 9 AM to 5 PM Pacific Time.

publisher
MIKE RICHARDSON

editor
PHILIP R. SIMON

collection designer
SANDY TANAKA

digital art technician
CHRISTINA McKENZIE

Special thanks to Michael Gombos, Annie Gullion, and Carl Gustav Horn for editorial assistance and advice. Special thanks to Chitoku Teshima for translation assistance.

Original cover design: Norito INOUE Design Office

This omnibus volume collects the original *I Am a Hero* Volumes 3 and 4, first published in Japan.

Dark Horse Manga
A division of Dark Horse Comics LLC
10956 SE Main Street
Milwaukie, OR 97222

DarkHorse.com

To find a comics shop in your area, visit comicshoplocator.com

First edition: October 2016
ISBN 978-1-50670-019-9
10 9 8 7 6 5 4 3

Printed in the United States of America

STOP

This is the back of the book!

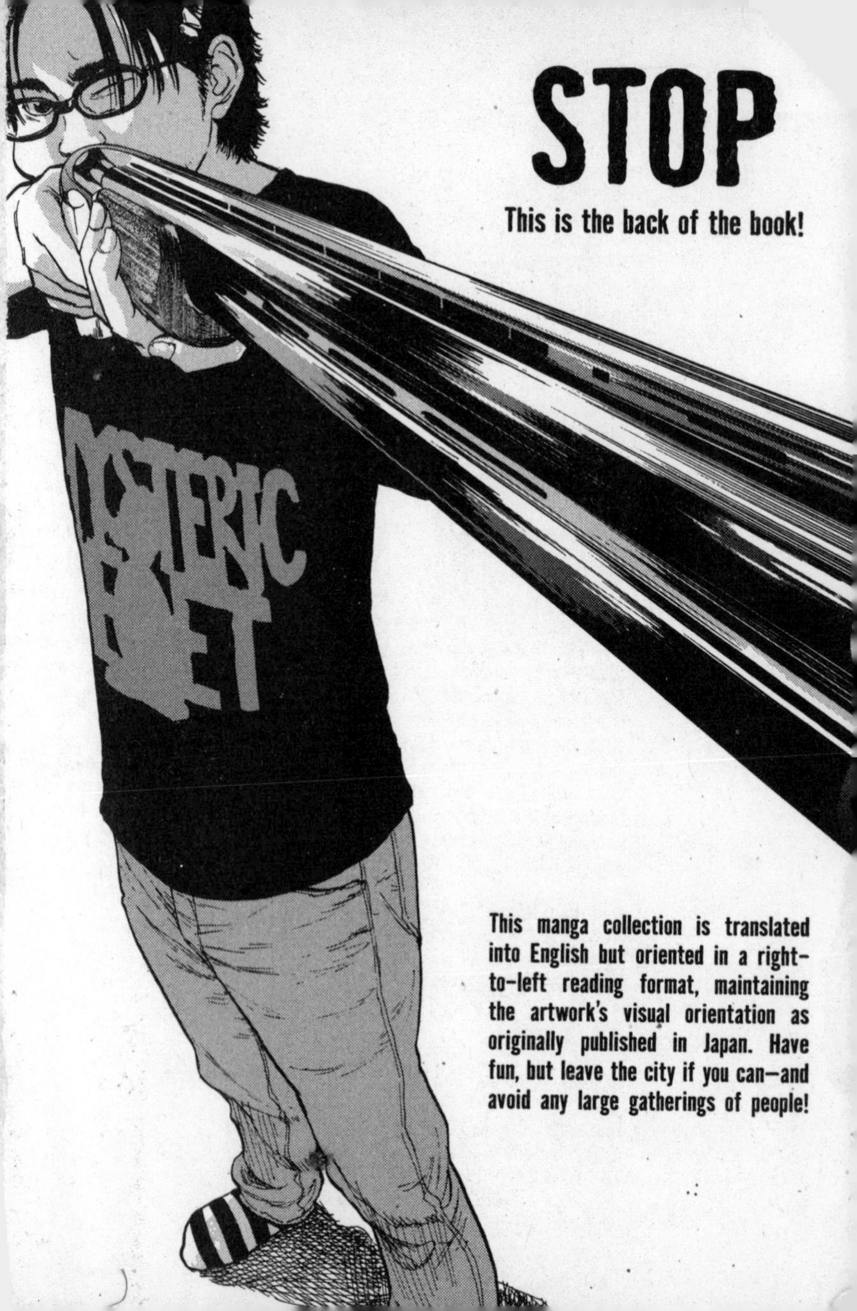

This manga collection is translated into English but oriented in a right-to-left reading format, maintaining the artwork's visual orientation as originally published in Japan. Have fun, but leave the city if you can—and avoid any large gatherings of people!